The Routledge Critical and Cultural Theory Reader

Everything is open to question. Nothing is sacred.

Critical and cultural theory invites a rethinking of some of our most basic assumptions about who we are, how we behave, and how we interpret the world around us.

The Routledge Critical and Cultural Theory Reader brings together 29 key pieces from the last century and a half that have shaped the field. Topics include: subjectivity, language, gender, ethnicity, sexuality, the body, the human, class, culture, everyday life, literature, psychoanalysis, technology, power, and visuality. The choice of texts, together with the editors' introduction and glossary, will allow newcomers to begin from first principles, while the use of unabridged readings will also make the volume suitable for those undertaking more specialized work. Material is arranged chronologically, but the editors have suggested thematic pathways through the selections.

Contributors include key figures in critical theory and cultural studies:

Giorgio Agamben, Gloria Anzaldúa, Roland Barthes, Jean Baudrillard, Walter Benjamin, Lauren Berlant, Judith Butler, Michel de Certeau, Gilles Deleuze, Jacques Derrida, Frantz Fanon, Michel Foucault, Sigmund Freud, Marjorie Garber, Félix Guattari, Stuart Hall, Donna J. Haraway, Julia Kristeva, Jacques Lacan, Henri Lefebvre, Jean-François Lyotard, Karl Marx, Chandra Talpade Mohanty, Laura Mulvey, Joan Riviere, Gayle Rubin, Edward Said, Ferdinand de Saussure, Michael Warner, Hayden White and Raymond Williams.

Neil Badmington is Senior Lecturer in Cultural Criticism and English Literature at Cardiff University. He is the author of *Alien Chic: Posthumanism and the Other Within* (2004) and editor of *Posthumanism* (2000).

Julia Thomas is Senior Lecturer in English Literature at Cardiff University. She is the author of *Victorian Narrative Painting* (2000), *Pictorial Victorians: The Inscription of Values in Word and Image* (2004), and editor of *Reading Images* (2000).

The Routledge Critical and Cultural Theory Reader

Edited by

Neil Badmington
and Julia Thomas

Routledge
Taylor & Francis Group

LONDON AND NEW YORK

First published 2008
by Routledge
2 Park Square, Milton Park, Abingdon, Oxon OX14 4RN

Simultaneously published in the USA and Canada
by Routledge
711 Third Ave, New York, NY 10017

Routledge is an imprint of the Taylor & Francis Group, an informa business

Typeset in Perpetua and Bell Gothic by
RefineCatch Ltd, Bungay, Suffolk
Printed and bound in Great Britain by
CPI Antony Rowe, Chippenham, Wiltshire

British Library Cataloguing in Publication Data
A catalogue record for this book is available from the British Library

Library of Congress Cataloging in Publication Data
The Routledge critical and cultural theory reader / edited by Neil Badmington and Julia Thomas.
   p.cm.
Includes bibliographical references and index.
1. Critical theory.   2. Culture.   I. Badmington, Neil, 1971 – II. Thomas, Julia.
HM480.R682008
301.01–dc22   2008002206

ISBN10: 0–415–43308–8 (hbk)
ISBN10: 0–415–43309–6 (pbk)

ISBN13: 978–0–415–43308–2 (hbk)
ISBN13: 978–0–415–43309–9 (pbk)

Contents

Pathways

The body – Riviere, Lacan, Fanon, Foucault, Mulvey, Kristeva, Rubin, Haraway, Butler, Agamben

Class – Marx, Williams, Lefebvre, Haraway, Mohanty

Culture – Williams, White, Said, Haraway, Anzaldúa

Difference – Saussure, Riviere, Derrida, Fanon, de Certeau, Deleuze and Guattari, Mulvey, Said, Lyotard, Haraway, Anzaldúa, Butler, Mohanty, Berlant and Warner

The everyday – Williams, Lefebvre, de Certeau

Gender – Riviere, Fanon, Mulvey, Rubin, Haraway, Anzaldúa, Butler, Mohanty

Language – Saussure, Lefebvre, Barthes, Derrida, de Certeau, Deleuze and Guattari, Hall, Kristeva, Lyotard, Anzaldúa, Garber

Literature – Williams, White, Barthes, Deleuze and Guattari, Said, Kristeva, Baudrillard, Lyotard, Anzaldúa, Garber

Marxism – Marx, Benjamin, Williams, Lefebvre, Hall, Haraway

Post/colonialism – Fanon, Deleuze and Guattari, Said, Anzaldúa, Mohanty

Power and resistance – Marx, Riviere, Fanon, Williams, Barthes, de Certeau, Deleuze and Guattari, Foucault, Mulvey, Said, Hall, Kristeva, Lyotard, Rubin, Haraway, Anzaldúa, Butler, Mohanty, Agamben, Berlant and Warner

Psychoanalysis – Freud, Riviere, Lacan, Fanon, Derrida, de Certeau, Mulvey, Kristeva, Butler

Race and ethnicity – Fanon, Deleuze and Guattari, Said, Anzaldúa, Mohanty

Sexuality – Riviere, Mulvey, Rubin, Butler, Berlant and Warner

Space – Lefebvre, de Certeau, Foucault

Subjectivity – Marx, Freud, Riviere, Lacan, Fanon, Foucault, Kristeva, Haraway, Anzaldúa, Butler, Agamben, Garber

Technology – Benjamin, Baudrillard, Haraway, Agamben

Visuality – Benjamin, Lacan, Foucault, de Certeau, Mulvey, Hall, Lyotard

Acknowledgements

The following were reproduced with kind permission. Whilst every effort has been made to trace copyright holders and obtain permission, this has not been possible in all cases. Any omissions brought to our attention will be remedied in future editions.

Karl Marx, 'Preface (to a *Contribution to the Critique of Political Economy*)', *Early Writings,* trans. Rodney Livingstone and Gregor Benton (Harmondsworth: Pelican, 1975), pp.424–8. Reproduced by kind permission of *New Left Review.*

Sigmund Freud, 'A note on the unconscious in psychoanalysis', in *Collected Papers,* volume 4, trans. James Strachey, 1959, New York: Basic Books. Reprinted by permission of Basic Books, a member of Perseus Books Group.

Sigmund Freud © Copyrights, The Institute of Psycho-Analysis and The Hogarth Press for permission to quote from THE STANDARD EDITION OF THE COMPLETE PSYCHOLOGICAL WORKS OF SIGMUND FREUD translated and edited by James Strachey. Reprinted by permission of The Random House Group Ltd.

Ferdinand de Saussure, 'Linguistic value', *Course in General Linguistics,* eds. Charles Bally, Albert Sechehaye and Albert Reidlinger, trans. Wade Baskin, Peter Owen Ltd, London, 1974, pp. 111–22. Reproduced with permission.

Joan Riviere, 'Womanliness as a masquerade' , *International Journal of Psychoanalysis* 10 (1929): 303–12. Reproduced by kind permission of the Melanie Klein Trust www.melanie-klein-trust.org.uk.

'The work of art in the age of mechanical reproduction' from ILLUMINATIONS by Walter Benjamin, copyright © 1955 by Suhrkamp Verlag, Frankfurt a.M., English translation by Harry Zohn copyright © 1968 and renewed 1996 by Harcourt, Inc., reprinted by permission of Harcourt, Inc.

'The mirror stage as formative of the function of the I' , from ÉCRITS: A SELECTION by Jacques Lacan, translated by Alan Sheridan. Copyright © 1966 by Editions du Seuil. English translation copyright © 1977 by Tavistock Publications. Used by permission of W. W. Norton & Company, Inc.

'The mirror stage as formative of the function of the I as revealed in psychoanalytic experience', Jacques Lacan, from *Écrits: A Selection*, trans. Alan Sheridan, Copyright © 1977 Tavistock Publications. Reproduced by permission of Taylor & Francis Books UK.

From Frantz Fanon, 'The fact of blackness' , *Black Skin/White Masks*, trans. Charles Lam Markmann. Copyright © 1967 by Grove Press, Inc. Used by permission of Grove/Atlantic, Inc.

Raymond Williams, 'Culture is ordinary', *Resources of Hope: Culture, Democracy, Socialism* (London and New York: Verso, 1989), pp. 3–18. Reproduced by permission of the publisher.

Henri Lefebvre, 'The social text' , *Henri Lefebvre: Key Writings*, eds. Stuart Elden, Elizabeth Lebes and Eleonore Kofman (New York and London: Continuum, 2003). Reproduced by kind permission of Continuum.

White, Hayden 'The burden of history' , *Tropics of Discourse: Essays in Cultural Criticism*, pp. 27–50. © 1978 The Johns Hopkins University Press. Reprinted by permission of The Johns Hopkins University Press.

'The Death of the Author', from *The Rustle of Language* by Roland Barthes, translated by Richard Howard. Translation copyright © 1986 by Farrar, Straus & Giroux, Inc. Reprinted by permission of Hill and Wang, a division of Farrar, Straus and Giroux, LLC.

Jacques Derrida, 'Differance', *'Speech and Phenomena' and Other Essays on Husserl's Theory of Signs*, trans. David B. Allison (Evanston: Northwestern University Press, 1973), pp. 129–60 'Differance' appeared in French under the title '*La Différance*' in the *Bulletin de la société française de philosophie*, Volume LXII (1968) and was reprinted in *Théorie d'ensemble*, a collection of essays published by Editions du Seuil in 1968. Copyright © 1973 by Northwestern University Press. Reproduced by permission of the publisher.

DISCIPLINE AND PUNISH by Michel Foucault. English Translation copyright © 1977 by Alan Sheridan (New York: Pantheon). Originally published in French as *Surveiller et Punir*. Copyright © 1975 by Editions Gallimard. Reprinted by permission of Georges Borchardt, Inc., for Editions Gallimard.

From DISCIPLINE AND PUNISH: The Birth of Prison by Michel Foucault, translated by Alan Sheridan (first published as *Surveiller et Punir: Naissance de la Prison* by Editions Gallimard 1975, Allen Lane 1975). Copyright Alan Sheridan, 1977. Reproduced by permission of Penguin Books Ltd.

Michel de Certeau, 'Walking in the city', *The Practice of Everyday Life*, trans. Steven F. Rendall (Berkeley and Los Angeles: University of California Press, 1984), pp. 91–110. Copyright © 2002, The Regents of the University of California. Reproduced with permission.

Laura Mulvey, 'Visual pleasure and narrative cinema', *Screen* 16.3 (1975): 6–18. Reproduced by kind permission of the author and *Screen*.

From ORIENTALISM by Edward W. Said, copyright © 1978 by Edward W. Said. Used by permission of Pantheon Books, a division of Random House, Inc.

'Encoding/decoding', Stuart Hall from *Culture, Media, Language: Working Papers in Cultural Studies, 1972–79*, ed. Stuart Hall et al., Copyright © 1992 Routledge. Reproduced by permission of Taylor & Francis Books UK and the author.

Julia Kristeva, 'Approaching abjection', *Powers of Horror: An Essay on Abjection*, trans. Leon S. Roudiez (New York: Columbia University Press, 1982), pp. 1–31. Reproduced by permission of the publisher.

Gilles Deleuze and Félix Guattari, 'What is a minor literature?', in *Kafka: Toward a Minor Literature*, trans. Dana Polan (Minneapolis and London: University of Minnesota Press, 1986), pp. 16–27. Copyright 1986 by the University of Minnesota. Originally published as *Kafka: Pour une littérature mineure*. Copyright 1975 by Éditions de Minuit, Paris.

Jean-François Lyotard, 'Answer to the question: what is the postmodern?', *The Postmodern Explained to Children* © 1992 Power Institute of Fine Arts. Originally published in French as *Le Postmoderne expliqué aux enfants* © Éditions Galilée, 1986. Reproduced with permission.

Gayle Rubin, 'Thinking sex: notes towards a radical theory of the Politics of Sexuality', *Pleasure and Danger: Exploring Female Sexuality*, ed. Carole S. Vance (London: Pandora, 1992), pp.267–319. Reproduced by kind permission of Gayle Rubin.

Donna J. Haraway, 'A manifesto for cyborgs: science, technology, and socialist feminism in the 1980s', *Socialist Review* 80 (1985): 65–108. Reproduced by kind permission of the author.

'How to tame a wild tongue' from *Borderlands/La Frontera: The New Mestiza*. Copyright © 1987, 1999 by Gloria Anzaldúa. Reprinted by permission of Aunt Lute Books.

Jean Baudrillard, 'Simulacra and science fiction', in *Simulacra and Simulation*, trans. Sheila Faria Glaser (Ann Arbor: University of Michigan Press, 1994), pp. 121–7. English translation copyright © by The University of Michigan 1994. Originally published in French by Éditions Galilée 1981. All rights reserved. Published in the United States of America by The University of Michigan Press. Reproduced by permission of the publisher.

Chandra Talpade Mohanty, 'Under western eyes: feminist scholarship and colonial discourse,' in *boundary 2*, Volume 12, no. 3, pp. 333–58. Copyright, 1984, Duke University Press. All rights reserved. Used by permission of the publisher.

INSIDE/OUT: LESBIAN THEORIES, GAY THEORIES (PAPER) by JUDITH BUTLER. Copyright 1991 by Routledge Publishing Inc – Books. Reproduced with permission of Routledge Publishing Inc – Books in the format Other book via Copyright Clearance Center.

Reprinted by permission of the Modern Language Association of America from Lauren Berlant and Michael Warner, 'What does queer theory tell us about X?', PMLA 110 (1995): 343–9

Giorgio Agamben, 'Introduction', *Homo Sacer: Sovereign Power and Bare Life*, trans. Daniel Heller-Roazen. Copyright © 1998 by the Board of Trustees of the Leland Stanford Jr. University.

QUOTATION MARKS by MARJORIE GARBER. Copyright 2003 by Routledge Publishing Inc – Books. Reproduced with permission of Routledge Publishing Inc – Books in the format Other book via Copyright Clearance Center.

The editors wish to thank: Carl Distefano, Becky Munford, and Carl Plasa for their advice; Natalie Foster and Charlotte Wood at Routledge; Rosemary Morlin for copy-editing; and Yale University Art Gallery for permission to reproduce Edward Hopper's *Rooms by the Sea* on the cover of the book.

Editors' introduction

YOU ARE HOLDING in front of you a book that contains twenty-nine very different texts, each of which has its own concerns, propositions, style, conclusions, and place in history. The pieces span nearly a century and a half, with Karl Marx's 'Preface (to a *Contribution to the Critique of Political Economy*)' dating from 1859, and Marjorie Garber's 'Who owns "human nature"?' published in 2003. Within this historical sweep, there are also significant disagreements: Chandra Talpade Mohanty's 'Under western eyes: feminist scholarship and colonial discourses', for instance, takes issue with some of the assumptions of Western feminist theory, to which Joan Riviere, Laura Mulvey, Gayle Rubin, and Judith Butler have all made prominent contributions. Although all twenty-nine pieces are presented here in English, over half of them were originally written and published in other languages. In fact, the movement and interaction between languages, cultures, and geographical spaces is the explicit concern of several of the extracts (Ferdinand de Saussure's 'Linguistic value', Raymond Williams' 'Culture is ordinary', Edward Said's introduction to *Orientalism*, Gilles Deleuze and Félix Guattari's 'What is a minor literature?', Gloria Anzaldúa's 'How to tame a wild tongue', and Mohanty's 'Under western eyes'). What we find ourselves attempting to introduce in these pages, therefore, are pieces that do not make a whole. We cannot, it follows, summarize the reader's agenda in the singular. While there are points of connection between some of the extracts (with this in mind, we have suggested pathways through the material on the page following the table of contents), each text should be treated as a distinct entity and on its own terms. This is as much a book *of* differences as it is a book *about* differences.

The very fact that you are holding something called *The Routledge Critical and Cultural Theory Reader* signals the extent to which theory has, within the last few decades, become visible within the English-speaking world. As it has been institutionalized, however, many people have stopped reading the theories themselves, and have preferred instead to acquire what they believe to be an understanding of the issues from the numerous secondary sources now available. They have, that is to say, opted to read other people's descriptions of the ideas apparently embodied in the primary texts without ever consulting those texts or realizing that many of them are actively concerned with rethinking the practice of reading itself. It is for this reason that *The Routledge Critical and Cultural Theory Reader* does not contain editorial summaries alongside the extracts, and any brief description of the material that we offer in this introduction is merely *one* reading. You need to encounter the texts and decide for yourself.

But who are *you*? The very first piece in this collection asks that question in an attempt to offer a new understanding of who we are and why we do what we do. According to common sense, the human subject is prior to language and culture: who I am goes without saying. For Marx, however, the 'I' is neither given nor fixed; it is, rather, a product of everyday societal conditions: 'It is not the consciousness of men that determines their existence', he proposes, 'but their social existence that determines their consciousness.' There is no predetermined, unified subjectivity: who we are, what we do, and what we believe are the effects of varying external conditions. Other extracts in this volume draw similar conclusions, even if the external conditions differ from piece to piece. After theory, you may no longer be the same. Your most basic, everyday assumptions might no longer hold.

Many of the texts, for example, denaturalize the role of language. In a radical challenge to the conventional, idealist model which makes language the instrument of thought, Ferdinand de Saussure's 'Linguistic value' discusses a system of differences *constitutive* of thought. 'Without language', as he puts it, 'thought is a vague, uncharted nebula. There are no pre-existing ideas, and nothing is distinct before the appearance of language.' Signifiers do not come to be meaningful by acting as labels for concepts that already exist; they acquire meaning, rather, through their position in a system of differences. While she does not refer directly to Saussure, and while her work treads a very different path, Gloria Anzaldúa comes to a related conclusion when she proposes: 'Ethnic identity is twin skin to linguistic identity – I am my language.' The problem, however, is that Anzaldúa finds herself caught between different languages – a predicament that her text stages in its mixing of tongues – and that there is a constant, painful power struggle between them for dominance, recognition, and authenticity. Hybrid languages make hybrid humans.

Linguistic tension is also the subject of Gilles Deleuze and Félix Guattari's contribution to the reader, where what 'a minority constructs within a major language' is examined with reference to the work of Franz Kafka, a German-speaking Jew in early-twentieth-century Prague who found himself writing in what Deleuze and Guattari call 'a deterritorialized language'. Major colonial languages and modes of representation are also the concern of Edward Said, who examines how Orientalism has constructed the East as the West's defining other. As he puts it: 'European culture gained in strength and identity by setting itself off against the Orient as a sort of surrogate and even underground self.' If Said's propositions draw implicitly upon Saussure's differential theory of meaning, Jacques Derrida engages with Saussure in a much more explicit manner when he argues that meaning depends not only upon difference but also upon *deferral*. (His neologism 'differance' embodies this duality.)

In the light of Derrida's work, meaning is neither stable nor singular: the moment of closure never comes. It follows that the human subject cannot have control over meaning – an idea explored in different ways elsewhere in this volume by Sigmund Freud (for whom the actions of the subject are driven by unconscious desires and motives to which the conscious mind has no access), Jacques Lacan (for whom the ego is split and in process), and Roland Barthes (who undermines the conventional ability of the author to control textual meaning by suggesting that 'writing is the destruction of every voice, every origin').

If meaning could be fixed, in fact, the kinds of radical interrogations found in this volume (and elsewhere in the field of critical and cultural theory) would not be possible. The discussions of gender, for example, propose that 'man' and 'woman' are not fixed categories given in nature or guaranteed by the body. In Joan Riviere's influential 'Womanliness as a masquerade', the traits of femininity are adopted like masks by women who seek acceptance in a patriarchal society. Riviere's argument is that there is no genuine femininity outside this performance: 'The reader may now ask how I define womanliness or where I draw the line between genuine womanliness and the "masquerade". My suggestion is not, however, that there is any such difference; whether radical or superficial, they are the same thing.' Writing over half a century later, Judith Butler draws upon more recent developments in queer theory and psycho-analysis to argue that gender and sexuality are constituted in culture by repeated performances. (For an account of queer theory and the difference that it makes, see 'What does queer theory teach us about *X*?', Lauren Berlant and Michael Warner's contribution to this volume.) Precisely because these performances must be repeated, there is never a moment at which gender and sexuality are fixed or identical to themselves. 'If', Butler concludes, 'the "I" is the effect of a certain repetition . . . then there is no "I" that precedes the gender that it is said to perform; the repetition and the failure to repeat, produce a string of performances that constitute and contest the coherence of that "I".' Identity is, to use Derrida's terms, always differed and deferred.

One of the implications of feminist theory is that gender and sexuality are sites of constant power struggles. This is made explicit in 'Thinking sex: notes towards a radical theory of the politics of sexuality', where Gayle Rubin proposes that, in addition to having a history, 'sex is always political'. Moreover, for Rubin, it is not enough to rely upon feminism's analysis of gender oppression to address *sexual* injustices; a specific theory is needed that takes account of the fact that sexuality is not reducible to biology, and that the body and its erotic desires are always historically and culturally constituted.

With that constitution comes social regulation. For Michel Foucault, whose theories influence Butler and Rubin, this regulation is often a visual one: how bodies are scrutinized in relations of power changes how they behave. Sometimes, however, bodies do not behave. In Julia Kristeva's chapter on abjection, for instance, the brute materiality of the unruly body subverts stable categories of subjecthood: 'It is thus not lack of cleanliness or health that causes abjection but what disturbs identity, system, order. What does not respect borders, positions, rules. The in-between, the ambiguous, the composite.'

In Foucault's discussion of panopticism, it is possible to see glimpses of a theme that would be developed in more detail in his later work: biopolitics. The effects of the intersection of politics and the living body that he discusses are pursued by Giorgio Agamben and Donna J. Haraway, for whom 'the human' and life itself have been thrown into question by recent social developments. In Haraway's 'A manifesto for cyborgs', the invasion of technology into everyday life is one of the key factors in the unsettling of centuries of humanism. So much so, in fact, that we are longer human; instead, we are cyborgs, 'hybrid[s] of machine and organism'. In Walter Benjamin's 'The work of art in the age of mechanical reproduction', meanwhile, it is not the human that is disrupted with the rise of technology, but aesthetic objects. Benjamin argues that modern techniques of reproduction undermine the 'aura' of an artwork, 'its presence in time and space, its unique existence at the place where it happens to be'. The copy replaces and devalues the original. Jean Baudrillard extends these ideas to propose that the entire Western distinction between the real and the fake has collapsed, opening up the realm of the hyperreal: 'The imaginary was the alibi of the real, in a world dominated by the reality principle. Today, it is the real that has become the alibi of the model, in a world controlled by the principle of simulation.'

Subjectivity, language, meaning, gender, ethnicity, sexuality, the body, the human, life, authenticity: the pieces contained in this reader, as examples of critical and cultural theory, create spaces for the interrogation of what we regularly take for granted or perhaps believe to be obvious. They invite us to rethink our assumptions about ourselves and our world. This is why critical theory is *critical*. Everything is open to question. Nothing is sacred.

How to use this reader

People have different ideas of what critical and cultural theory is (and is not). This reader is not intended to be the definitive account, a canon. (In fact, readers' reports commissioned by Routledge on early outlines of the book led us to revise many of our own ideas about the shape and size of the field. What you hold in your hands is not what was originally in our heads.) We have, rather, merely assembled in these pages a sample of texts which have informed and reformed 'theory', and which will, we hope, suggest ways into a much wider discussion. There are, moreover, many pieces that we have had to omit, sometimes at the insistence of copyright holders.

Because of the scale and diversity of the field, we have departed from what has become something of a convention with books of this kind. Instead of printing the texts under subject headings that indicate themes (sexuality, class, language, and so on) or schools (Marxism or psychoanalysis, for example), we have reproduced them chronologically. While this is, of course, a type of ordering, we feel that it is less restrictive than trying to find a single label for each extract. That no text fits conveniently into a sole category is clear from the 'pathways' through the reader suggested after the main table of contents. These are intended to facilitate further reading and to show multiple connections between the different pieces.

Another way in which we have departed from convention is in reproducing uncut essays and chapters. We have done this because many anthologies, in drastically abridging their contents, represent critical and cultural theory in a fragmentary way. The unedited texts will, we hope, appeal to students and teachers with more advanced requirements. Each piece retains its original referencing system in line with Routledge's publishing conventions.

If you are coming to theory for the first time, you will find some of the more unfamiliar, specialized terms explained in the glossary at the end of this book. And, if you want to follow up the concerns of particular pieces that have caught your attention, you will find a few suggestions for further reading after each text. We have made a conscious decision not to recommend basic introductory material that merely summarizes the extracts, but to focus instead upon complementary pieces or works that take the theory forward in new and provocative ways.

Neil Badmington and Julia Thomas
October 2007, Cardiff

Chapter 1

Karl Marx

'PREFACE (TO A *CONTRIBUTION TO THE CRITIQUE OF POLITICAL ECONOMY*)', 1859

I EXAMINE THE SYSTEM of bourgeois economy in the following order: *capital, landed property, wage-labour; the State, foreign trade, world market*. The economic conditions of existence of the three great classes into which modern bourgeois society is divided are analysed under the first three headings; the interconnection of the other three headings is self-evident. The first part of the first book, dealing with Capital, comprises the following chapters: 1. The commodity; 2. Money or simple circulation; 3. Capital in general. The present part consists of the first two chapters. The entire material lies before me in the form of monographs, which were written not for publication but for self-clarification at widely separated periods; their remoulding into an integrated whole according to the plan I have indicated will depend upon circumstances.

A general introduction,[1] which I had drafted, is omitted, since on further consideration it seems to me confusing to anticipate results which still have to be substantiated, and the reader who really wishes to follow me will have to decide to advance from the particular to the general. A few brief remarks regarding the course of my study of political economy may, however, be appropriate here.

Although I studied jurisprudence, I pursued it as a subject subordinated to philosophy and history. In the year 1842–3, as editor of the *Rheinische Zeitung*, I first found myself in the embarrassing position of having to discuss what is known as material interests. The deliberations of the Rhenish Landtag on forest thefts and the division of landed property; the official polemic started by Herr von Schaper, then Oberpräsident of the Rhine Province, against the *Rheinische Zeitung* about the condition of the Moselle peasantry, and finally the debates on free trade and protective tariffs caused me in the first instance to turn my attention to economic questions. On the other hand, at that time when good intentions 'to push forward' often took the place of factual knowledge, an echo of French socialism and communism, slightly tinged by philosophy, was noticeable in the *Rheinische Zeitung*. I objected to this dilettantism, but at the same time frankly admitted in a controversy with the *Allgemeine Augsburger Zeitung* that my previous studies did not allow me to express any opinion on the content of the French theories. When the publishers of the *Rheinische Zeitung* conceived the illusion that by a more compliant policy on the part of the paper it might be possible to secure the abrogation of the death sentence passed upon it, I eagerly grasped the opportunity to withdraw from the public stage to my study.

The first work which I undertook to dispel the doubts assailing me was a critical re-examination of the Hegelian philosophy of law; the introduction to this work being published in the *Deutsch–Französische Jahrbücher* issued in Paris in 1844. My inquiry led me to the conclusion that neither legal relations nor political forms could be comprehended whether by themselves or on the basis of a so-called general development of the human mind, but that on the contrary they originate in the material conditions of life, the totality of which Hegel, following the example of English and French thinkers of the eighteenth century, embraces within the term 'civil society'; that the anatomy of this civil society, however, has to be sought in political economy. The study of this, which I began in Paris, I continued in Brussels, where I moved owing to an expulsion order issued by M. Guizot. The general conclusion at which I arrived and which, once reached, became the guiding principle of my studies can be summarized as follows. In the social production of their existence, men inevitably enter into definite relations, which are independent of their will, namely relations of production appropriate to a given stage in the development of their material forces of production. The totality of these relations of production constitutes the economic structure of society, the real foundation, on which arises a legal and political superstructure and to which correspond definite forms of social consciousness. The mode of production of material life conditions the general process of social, political and intellectual life. It is not the consciousness of men that determines their existence, but their social existence that determines their consciousness. At a certain stage of development, the material productive forces of society come into conflict with the existing relations of production or – this merely expresses the same thing in legal terms – with the property relations within the framework of which they have operated hitherto. From forms of development of the productive forces these relations turn into their fetters. Then begins an era of social revolution. The changes in the economic foundation lead sooner or later to the transformation of the whole immense superstructure. In studying such transformations it is always necessary to distinguish between the material transformation of the economic conditions of production, which can be determined with the precision of natural science, and the legal, political, religious, artistic or philosophic – in short, ideological forms in which men become conscious of this conflict and fight it out. Just as one does not judge an individual by what he thinks about himself, so one cannot judge such a period of transformation by its consciousness, but, on the contrary, this consciousness must be explained from the contradictions of material life, from the conflict existing between the social forces of production and the relations of production. No social order is ever destroyed before all the productive forces for which it is sufficient have been developed, and new superior relations of production never replace older ones before the material conditions for their existence have matured within the framework of the old society. Mankind thus inevitably sets itself only such tasks as it is able to solve, since closer examination will always show that the problem itself arises only when the material conditions for its solution are already present or at least in the course of formation. In broad outline, the Asiatic, ancient, feudal and modern bourgeois modes of production may be designated as epochs marking progress in the economic development of society. The bourgeois mode of production is the last antagonistic form of the social process of production – antagonistic not in the sense of individual antagonism but of an antagonism that emanates from the individuals' social conditions of existence – but the productive forces developing within bourgeois society create also the material conditions for a solution of this antagonism. The prehistory of human society accordingly closes with this social formation.

Frederick Engels, with whom I maintained a constant exchange of ideas by correspondence since the publication of his brilliant essay on the critique of economic categories[2] (printed in the *Deutsch–Französische Jahrbücher*), arrived by another road (compare his *Lage der arbeitenden Klasse in England*[3]) at the same result as I, and when in the spring of 1845 he too came to live in Brussels, we decided to set forth together our conception as opposed to the ideological one of German philosophy, in fact to settle accounts with our former philosophical conscience. The intention was carried out in the form of a critique of post-Hegelian philosophy.[4] The manuscript, two large octavo volumes, had long ago reached the publishers in Westphalia when we were informed that owing to changed circumstances it could not be printed. We abandoned the manuscript to the gnawing criticism of the mice all the more willingly since we had achieved our main purpose – self-clarification. Of the scattered works in which at that time we presented one or another aspect of our views to the public, I shall mention only the *Manifesto of the Communist Party*, jointly written by Engels and myself, and a *Discours sur le libre échange*, which I myself published. The salient points of our conception were first outlined in an academic, although polemical, form in my *Misère de la philosophie . . .*[5] this book which was aimed at Proudhon appeared in 1847. The publication of an essay on *Wage-Labour*[6] written in German in which I combined the lectures I had held on this subject at the German Workers' Association in Brussels, was interrupted by the February Revolution and my forcible removal from Belgium in consequence.

The publication of the *Neue Rheinische Zeitung* in 1848 and 1849 and subsequent events cut short my economic studies, which I could only resume in London in 1850. The enormous amount of material relating to the history of political economy assembled in the British Museum, the fact that London is a convenient vantage-point for the observation of bourgeois society, and finally the new stage of development which this society seemed to have entered with the discovery of gold in California and Australia, induced me to start again from the very beginning and to work carefully through the new material. These studies led partly of their own accord to apparently quite remote subjects on which I had to spend a certain amount of time. But it was in particular the imperative necessity of earning my living which reduced the time at my disposal. My collaboration, continued now for eight years, with the *New York Tribune*, the leading Anglo-American newspaper, necessitated an excessive fragmentation of my studies, for I wrote only exceptionally newspaper correspondence in the strict sense. Since a considerable part of my contributions consisted of articles dealing with important economic events in Britain and on the Continent, I was compelled to become conversant with practical details which, strictly speaking, lie outside the sphere of political economy.

This sketch of the course of my studies in the domain of political economy is intended merely to show that my views – no matter how they may be judged and how little they conform to the interested prejudices of the ruling classes – are the outcome of conscientious research carried on over many years. At the entrance to science, as at the entrance to hell, the demand must be made:

> *Qui si convien lasciare ogni sospetto*
> *Ogni viltà convien che qui sia morta.* [7]

Karl Marx

London, January 1859

Notes

1   '1857 Introduction', in *Grundrisse*, The Pelican Marx Library, 1973, pp. 81–111.
2   'Outlines of a Critique of Political Economy'. (For this and following footnote references, see 'Chronology of Works by Marx and Engels' (pp. 439–42 below) for details of editions in English.) [See original publication.]
3   'The condition of the working class in England'.
4   *The German Ideology*.
5   *The Poverty of Philosophy*.
6   'Wage-labour and capital'.
7   Dante, *Divina Commedia*, Canto III, lines 14–15. ('Here all distrust must be abandoned; here all cowardice must die.')

Suggestions for further reading

Althusser, Louis, *For Marx*, trans. Ben Brewster, London and New York: Verso, 1996.
Macherey, Pierre, *A Theory of Literary Production*, trans. Geoffrey Wall, London: Routledge and Kegan Paul, 1978.
Marx, Karl and Engels, Friedrich, *The German Ideology: Part One*, ed. C.J. Arthur, London: Lawrence and Wishart, 1970.

Chapter 2

Sigmund Freud

'A NOTE ON THE UNCONSCIOUS IN PSYCHOANALYSIS', 1912

I WISH TO EXPOUND in a few words and as plainly as possible what the term 'unconscious' has come to mean in Psychoanalysis and in Psychoanalysis alone.

A conception – or any other psychical[1] element – which is now *present* to my consciousness may become *absent* the next moment, and may become *present again*, after an interval, unchanged, and, as we say, from memory, not as a result of a fresh perception by our senses. It is this fact which we are accustomed to account for by the supposition that during the interval the conception has been present in our mind, although *latent* in consciousness. In what shape it may have existed while present in the mind and latent in consciousness we have no means of guessing.

At this very point we may be prepared to meet with the philosophical objection that the latent conception did not exist as an object of psychology, but as a physical disposition for the recurrence of the same psychical phenomenon, i.e. of the said conception. But we may reply that this is a theory far overstepping the domain of psychology proper; that it simply begs the question by asserting 'conscious' to be an identical term with 'psychical', and that it is clearly at fault in denying psychology the right to account for its most common facts, such as memory, by its own means.

Now let us call 'conscious' the conception which is present to our consciousness and of which we are aware, and let this be the only meaning of the term 'conscious'. As for latent conceptions, if we have any reason to suppose that they exist in the mind – as we had in the case of memory – let them be denoted by the term 'unconscious'.

Thus an unconscious conception is one of which we are not aware, but the existence of which we are nevertheless ready to admit on account of other proofs or signs.

This might be considered an uninteresting piece of descriptive or classificatory work if no experience appealed to our judgement other than the facts of memory, or the cases of association by unconscious links. The well-known experiment, however, of the 'post-hypnotic suggestion' teaches us to insist upon the importance of the distinction between *conscious* and *unconscious* and seems to increase its value.

In this experiment, as performed by Bernheim, a person is put into a hypnotic state and is subsequently aroused. While he was in the hypnotic state, under the influence of the physician, he was ordered to execute a certain action at a certain fixed moment after his awakening, say half an hour later. He awakes, and seems fully conscious and in his ordinary condition; he has no recollection of his hypnotic state, and yet at the prearranged moment there rushes into his mind the impulse to do such and such a thing, and he does it consciously, though not knowing why. It seems impossible to give any other description of the phenomenon than to say that the order had been present in the mind of the person *in a condition of latency*, or had been present *unconsciously*, until the given moment came, and then had become conscious. But not the whole of it emerged into consciousness: only the conception of the act to be executed. All the other ideas associated with this conception – the order, the influence of the physician, the recollection of the hypnotic state, remained unconscious even then.

But we have more to learn from such an experiment. We are led from the purely descriptive to a *dynamic* view of the phenomenon. The idea of the action ordered in hypnosis not only became an object of consciousness at a certain moment, but the more striking aspect of the fact is that this idea grew *active*: it was translated into action as soon as consciousness became aware of its presence. The real stimulus to the action being the order of the physician, it is hard not to concede that the idea of the physician's order became active too. Yet this last idea did not reveal itself to consciousness, as did its outcome, the idea of the action; it remained unconscious, and so it was *active and unconscious* at the same time.

A post-hypnotic suggestion is a laboratory production, an artificial fact. But if we adopt the theory of hysterical phenomena first put forward by P. Janet and elaborated by Breuer and myself, we shall not be at a loss for plenty of natural facts showing the psychological character of the post-hypnotic suggestion even more clearly and distinctly.

The mind of the hysterical patient is full of active yet unconscious ideas; all her symptoms proceed from such ideas. It is in fact the most striking character of the hysterical mind to be ruled by them. If the hysterical woman vomits, she may do so from the idea of being pregnant. She has, however, no knowledge of this idea, although it can easily be detected in her mind, and made conscious to her, by one of the technical procedures of psychoanalysis. If she is executing the jerks and movements constituting her 'fit', she does not even consciously represent to herself the intended actions, and she may perceive those actions with the detached feelings of an onlooker. Nevertheless analysis will show that she was acting her part in the dramatic reproduction of some incident in her life, the memory of which was unconsciously active during the attack. The same preponderance of active unconscious ideas is revealed by analysis as the essential fact in the psychology of all other forms of neurosis.

We learn therefore by the analysis of neurotic phenomena that a latent or unconscious idea is not necessarily a weak one, and that the presence of such an idea in the mind admits of indirect proofs of the most cogent kind, which are equivalent to the direct proof furnished by consciousness. We feel justified in making our classification agree with this addition to our knowledge by introducing a fundamental distinction between different kinds of latent or unconscious ideas. We were accustomed to think that every latent idea was so because it was weak and that it grew conscious as soon as it became strong. We have now gained the conviction that there are some latent ideas which do not penetrate into consciousness, however strong they may have become. Therefore we may call the latent ideas of the first type *foreconscious*,[2] while we reserve the term *unconscious* (proper) for the latter type which we came to study in the neuroses. The term *unconscious*, which was used in the purely descriptive sense before, now comes to imply something more. It designates not only latent ideas in general, but especially ideas with a certain dynamic character, ideas keeping apart from consciousness in spite of their intensity and activity.

Before continuing my exposition I will refer to two objections which are likely to be raised at this point. The first of these may be stated thus: instead of subscribing to the hypothesis of unconscious ideas of which we know nothing, we had better assume that consciousness can be split up, so that certain ideas or other psychical acts may constitute a consciousness apart, which has become detached and estranged from the bulk of conscious psychical activity. Well-known pathological cases like that of Dr Azam[3] seem to go far to show that the splitting up of consciousness is no fanciful imagination.

I venture to urge against this theory that it is a gratuitous assumption, based on the abuse of the word 'conscious'. We have no right to extend the meaning of this word so far as to make it include a consciousness of which its owner himself is not aware. If philosophers find difficulty in accepting the existence of unconscious ideas, the existence of an unconscious consciousness seems to me even more objectionable. The cases described as splitting of consciousness, like Dr Azam's, might better be denoted as shifting of consciousness, – that function – or whatever it be – oscillating between two different psychical complexes which become conscious and unconscious in alternation.

The other objection that may probably be raised would be that we apply to normal psychology conclusions which are drawn chiefly from the study of pathological conditions. We are enabled to answer it by another fact, the knowledge of which we owe to psychoanalysis. Certain deficiencies of function of most frequent occurrence among healthy people, e.g. *lapsus linguae*, errors in memory and speech, forgetting of names, etc., may easily be shown to depend on the action of strong unconscious ideas in the same way as neurotic symptoms. We shall meet with another still more convincing argument at a later stage of this discussion.

By the differentiation of foreconscious and unconscious ideas, we are led on to leave the field of classification and to form an opinion about functional and dynamical relations in psychical action. We have found a *foreconscious activity* passing into consciousness with no difficulty, and an *unconscious activity* which remains so and seems to be cut off from consciousness.

Now we do not know whether these two modes of psychical activity are identical or essentially divergent from their beginning, but we may ask why they should become different in the course of psychical action. To this last question psychoanalysis gives a clear and unhesitating answer. It is by no means impossible for the product of unconscious activity to pierce into consciousness, but a certain amount of exertion is needed for this task. When we try to do it in ourselves, we become aware of a distinct feeling of *repulsion*[4] which must be overcome, and when we produce it in a patient we get the most unquestionable signs of what we call his *resistance* to it. So we learn that the unconscious idea is excluded from consciousness by living forces which oppose themselves to its reception, while they do not object to other ideas, the foreconscious ones. Psychoanalysis leaves no room for doubt that the repulsion from unconscious ideas is only provoked by the tendencies embodied in their contents. The next and most probable theory which can be formulated at this stage of our knowledge is the following. Unconsciousness is a regular and inevitable phase in the processes constituting our psychical activity; every psychical act begins as an unconscious one, and it may either remain so or go on developing into consciousness, according as it meets with resistance or not. The distinction between foreconscious and unconscious activity is not a primary one, but comes to be established after repulsion has sprung up. Only then the difference between foreconscious ideas, which can appear in consciousness and reappear at any moment, and unconscious ideas which cannot do so gains a theoretical as well as a practical value. A rough but not inadequate analogy to this supposed relation of conscious to unconscious activity might be drawn from the field of ordinary photography. The first stage of the photograph is the 'negative'; every photographic picture has to pass through the 'negative process', and some of these negatives which have held good in examination are admitted to the 'positive process' ending in the picture.

But the distinction between foreconscious and unconscious activity, and the recognition of the barrier which keeps them asunder, is not the last or the most important result of the psychoanalytic investigation of psychical life. There is one psychical product to be met with in the most normal persons, which yet presents a very striking analogy to the wildest productions of insanity, and was no more intelligible to philosophers than insanity itself. I refer to dreams. Psychoanalysis is founded upon the analysis of dreams; the interpretation of dreams is the most complete piece of work the young science has done up to the present. One of the most common types of dream-formation may be described as follows: a train of thoughts has been aroused by the working of the mind in the daytime, and retained some of its activity, escaping from the general inhibition of interests which introduces sleep and constitutes the psychical preparation for sleeping. During the night this train of thoughts succeeds in finding connections with one of the unconscious tendencies present ever since his childhood in the mind of the dreamer, but ordinarily *repressed* and excluded from his conscious life. By the borrowed force of this unconscious help, the thoughts, the residue of the day's work,[5] now become active again, and emerge into consciousness in the shape of the dream. Now three things have happened:

(1)   The thoughts have undergone a change, a disguise and a distortion, which represents the part of the unconscious helpmate.
(2)   The thoughts have occupied consciousness at a time when they ought not.

(3)   Some part of the unconscious, which could not otherwise have
      done so, has emerged into consciousness.

We have learnt the art of finding out the 'residual thoughts', the *latent thoughts
of the dream*,[6] and, by comparing them with the apparent[7] *dream*, we are able to
form a judgement on the changes they underwent and the manner in which these
were brought about.

The latent thoughts of the dream differ in no respect from the products of our
regular conscious activity; they deserve the name of foreconscious thoughts, and
may indeed have been conscious at some moment of waking life. But by entering
into connection with the unconscious tendencies during the night they have
become assimilated to the latter, degraded as it were to the condition of
unconscious thoughts, and subjected to the laws by which unconscious activity is
governed. And here is the opportunity to learn what we could not have guessed
from speculation, or from another source of empirical information – that the laws
of unconscious activity differ widely from those of the conscious. We gather
in detail what the peculiarities of the *Unconscious* are, and we may hope to learn
still more about them by a profounder investigation of the processes of dream-
formation.

This inquiry is not yet half finished, and an exposition of the results obtained
hitherto is scarcely possible without entering into the most intricate problems of
dream-analysis. But I would not break off this discussion without indicating the
change and progress in our comprehension of the Unconscious which are due to
our psychoanalytic study of dreams.

Unconsciousness seemed to us at first only an enigmatical characteristic of a
definite psychical act. Now it means more for us. It is a sign that this act partakes of
the nature of a certain psychical category known to us by other and more important characters[8] and that it belongs to a system of psychical activity which is
deserving of our fullest attention. The index-value of the unconscious has far
outgrown its importance as a property. The system revealed by the sign that the
single acts forming parts of it are unconscious we designate by the name 'The
Unconscious', for want of a better and less ambiguous term. In German, I propose
to denote this system by the letters *Ubw*, an abbreviation of the German word
'Unbewusst'.[9] And this is the third and most significant sense which the term
'unconscious' has acquired in psychoanalysis.

Notes

1   [In the 1925 English version, throughout the paper, 'psychical' was altered to 'mental'.]
2   [In the 1925 English version, throughout the paper, 'foreconscious' was altered to
    'preconscious', which has, of course, become the regular translation of the German
    '*vorbewusst*'.]
3   [The reference is to the case of Félida X., a striking example of alternating or double
    personality and probably the first of its kind to be investigated and recorded in detail.
    The case was first described by E. Azam of Bordeaux. (See Azam, 1876 and 1887.)]
4   [In the German translation the word 'repulsion', here and lower down, is rendered by
    '*Abwehr*', of which the usual English version is 'defence' or 'fending off'.]
5   [In the 1925 English version the word 'mental' was inserted before 'work'.]

6   [In the German translation the last nine words are replaced by: 'the "day's residues", and
     the *latent dream-thoughts*, . . .'.]
7   [This word was altered to 'manifest' in the 1925 English version.]
8   [This was altered to 'features' in the 1925 English version.]
9   [The equivalent English abbreviation is, of course, '*Ucs.*']

Reference

Azam, E. (1876) 'Amnésie périodique ou dédoublement de la vie', *Ann. méd. psychol.*
     (5ᶜ série), **16**, 5. (53)
          (1887) *Hypnotisme, double conscience, et altérations de la personnalité*, Paris. (53)

Suggestions for further reading

Easthope, Antony, *The Unconscious*, London and New York: Routledge, 1999.
Freud, Sigmund, 'The Unconscious', in *On Metapsychology: The Theory of Psycho-
     analysis*, ed. Angela Richards, trans. James Strachey, Harmondsworth: Penguin,
     1991, pp. 159–222.
Mitchell, Juliet, *Psychoanalysis and Feminism*, Harmondsworth: Pelican, 1975.

Chapter 3

Ferdinand de Saussure

'LINGUISTIC VALUE', 1916

1. Language as organized thought coupled with sound

TO PROVE THAT language is only a system of pure values, it is enough to consider the two elements involved in its functioning: ideas and sounds.

Psychologically our thought—apart from its expression in words—is only a shapeless and indistinct mass. Philosophers and linguists have always agreed in recognizing that without the help of signs we would be unable to make a clear-cut, consistent distinction between two ideas. Without language, thought is a vague, uncharted nebula. There are no pre-existing ideas, and nothing is distinct before the appearance of language.

Against the floating realm of thought, would sounds by themselves yield predelimited entities? No more so than ideas. Phonic substance is neither more fixed nor more rigid than thought; it is not a mold into which thought must of necessity fit but a plastic substance divided in turn into distinct parts to furnish the signifiers needed by thought. The linguistic fact can therefore be pictured in its totality—i.e. language—as a series of contiguous subdivisions marked off on both the indefinite plane of jumbled ideas (A) and the equally vague plane of sounds (B). The following diagram gives a rough idea of it:

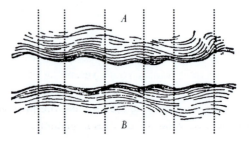

The characteristic role of language with respect to thought is not to create a material phonic means for expressing ideas but to serve as a link between thought and sound, under conditions that of necessity bring about the reciprocal delimitations of units. Thought, chaotic by nature, has to become ordered in the process of its decomposition. Neither are thoughts given material form nor are sounds transformed into mental entities; the somewhat mysterious fact is rather that "thought-sound" implies division, and that language works out its units while taking shape between two shapeless masses. Visualize the air in contact with a sheet of water; if the atmospheric pressure changes, the surface of the water will be broken up into a series of divisions, waves; the waves resemble the union or coupling of thought with phonic substance.

Language might be called the domain of articulations, using the word as it was defined earlier [see original publication]. Each linguistic term is a member, an *articulus* in which an idea is fixed in a sound and a sound becomes the sign of an idea.

Language can also be compared with a sheet of paper: thought is the front and the sound the back; one cannot cut the front without cutting the back at the same time; likewise in language, one can neither divide sound from thought nor thought from sound; the division could be accomplished only abstractedly, and the result would be either pure psychology or pure phonology.

Linguistics then works in the borderland where the elements of sound and thought combine; *their combination produces a form, not a substance.*

These views give a better understanding of what was said before about the arbitrariness of signs. Not only are the two domains that are linked by the linguistic fact shapeless and confused, but the choice of a given slice of sound to name a given idea is completely arbitrary. If this were not true, the notion of value would be compromised, for it would include an externally imposed element. But actually values remain entirely relative, and that is why the bond between the sound and the idea is radically arbitrary.

The arbitrary nature of the sign explains in turn why the social fact alone can create a linguistic system. The community is necessary if values that owe their existence solely to usage and general acceptance are to be set up; by himself the individual is incapable of fixing a single value.

In addition, the idea of value, as defined, shows that to consider a term as simply the union of a certain sound with a certain concept is grossly misleading. To define it in this way would isolate the term from its system; it would mean assuming that one can start from the terms and construct the system by adding them together when, on the contrary, it is from the interdependent whole that one must start and through analysis obtain its elements.

To develop this thesis, we shall study value successively from the viewpoint of the signified or concept (Section 2), the signifier (Section 3), and the complete sign (Section 4).

Being unable to seize the concrete entities or units of language directly, we shall work with words. While the word does not conform exactly to the definition of the linguistic unit, it at least bears a rough resemblance to the unit and has the advantage of being concrete; consequently, we shall use words as specimens equivalent to real terms in a synchronic system, and the principles that we evolve with respect to words will be valid for entities in general.

2. Linguistic value from a conceptual viewpoint

When we speak of the value of a word, we generally think first of its property of standing for an idea, and this is in fact one side of linguistic value. But if this is true, how does *value* differ from *signification*? Might the two words be synonyms? I think not, although it is easy to confuse them, since the confusion results not so much from their similarity as from the subtlety of the distinction that they mark.

From a conceptual viewpoint, value is doubtless one element in signification, and it is difficult to see how signification can be dependent upon value and still be distinct from it. But we must clear up the issue or risk reducing language to a simple naming-process.

Let us first take signification as it is generally understood [. . .]. As the arrows in the drawing show, it is only the counterpart of the sound-image. Everything that occurs concerns only the sound-image and the concept when we look upon the word as independent and self-contained.

But here is the paradox: on the one hand the concept seems to be the counterpart of the sound-image, and on the other hand the sign itself is in turn the counterpart of the other signs of language.

Language is a system of interdependent terms in which the value of each term results solely from the simultaneous presence of the others, as in the diagram:

How, then, can value be confused with signification, i.e. the counterpart of the sound-image? It seems impossible to liken the relations represented here by horizontal arrows to those represented above by vertical arrows. Putting it another way—and again taking up the example of the sheet of paper that is cut in two—it is clear that the observable relation between the different pieces A, B, C, D, etc. is distinct from the relation between the front and back of the same piece as in A/A', B/B', etc.

To resolve the issue, let us observe from the outset that even outside language all values are apparently governed by the same paradoxical principle. They are always composed:

(1)   of a *dissimilar* thing that can be *exchanged* for the thing of which the value is to be determined; and

(2)   of *similar* things that can be *compared* with the thing of which the value is to be determined.

Both factors are necessary for the existence of a value. To determine what a five-franc piece is worth one must therefore know: (1) that it can be exchanged for a fixed quantity of a different thing, e.g. bread; and (2) that it can be compared with a similar value of the same system, e.g. a one-franc piece, or with coins of another system (a dollar, etc.). In the same way a word can be exchanged for something dissimilar, an idea; besides, it can be compared with something of the same nature, another word. Its value is therefore not fixed so long as one simply states that it can be "exchanged" for a given concept, i.e. that it has this or that signification: one must also compare it with similar values, with other words that stand in opposition to it. Its content is really fixed only by the concurrence of everything that exists outside it. Being part of a system, it is endowed not only with a signification but also and especially with a value, and this is something quite different.

A few examples will show clearly that this is true. Modern French *mouton* can have the same signification as English *sheep* but not the same value, and this for several reasons, particularly because in speaking of a piece of meat ready to be served on the table, English uses *mutton* and not *sheep*. The difference in value between *sheep* and *mouton* is due to the fact that *sheep* has beside it a second term while the French word does not.

Within the same language, all words used to express related ideas limit each other reciprocally; synonyms like French *redouter* 'dread,' *craindre* 'fear,' and *avoir peur* 'be afraid' have value only through their opposition: if *redouter* did not exist, all its content would go to its competitors. Conversely, some words are enriched through contact with others: e.g. the new element introduced in *décrépit* (un vieillard *décrépit*) results from the co-existence of *décrépi* (un mur *décrépi*). The value of just any term is accordingly determined by its environment; it is impossible to fix even the value of the word signifying "sun" without first considering its surroundings: in some languages it is not possible to say "sit in the *sun*."

Everything said about words applies to any term of language, e.g. to grammatical entities. The value of a French plural does not coincide with that of a Sanskrit plural even though their signification is usually identical; Sanskrit has three numbers instead of two (*my eyes, my ears, my arms, my legs*, etc. are dual);[1] it would be wrong to attribute the same value to the plural in Sanskrit and in French; its value clearly depends on what is outside and around it.

If words stood for pre-existing concepts, they would all have exact equivalents in meaning from one language to the next; but this is not true. French uses *louer* (une maison) 'let (a house)' indifferently to mean both "pay for" and "receive payment for," whereas German uses two words, *mieten* and *vermieten*; there is obviously no exact correspondence of values. The German verbs *schätzen* and *urteilen* share a number of significations, but that correspondence does not hold at several points.

Inflection offers some particularly striking examples. Distinctions of time, which are so familiar to us, are unknown in certain languages. Hebrew does not recognize even the fundamental distinctions between the past, present, and future. Proto-Germanic has no special form for the future; to say that the future is expressed by the present is wrong, for the value of the present is not the same in Germanic as in languages that have a future along with the present. The Slavic languages regularly single out two aspects of the verb: the perfective represents action as a point, complete in its totality; the imperfective represents it as taking place, and on the line of time. The categories are difficult for a Frenchman to understand, for they are unknown in French; if they were predetermined, this would not be true. Instead of pre-existing ideas then, we find in all the foregoing examples *values* emanating from the system. When they are said to correspond to concepts, it is understood that the concepts are purely differential and defined not by their positive content but negatively by their relations with the other terms of the system. Their most precise characteristic is in being what the others are not.

Now the real interpretation of the diagram of the signal becomes apparent. Thus

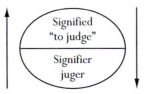

means that in French the concept "to judge" is linked to the sound-image *juger*; in short, it symbolizes signification. But it is quite clear that initially the concept is nothing, that is only a value determined by its relations with other similar values, and that without them the signification would not exist. If I state simply that a word signifies something when I have in mind the associating of a sound-image with a concept, I am making a statement that may suggest what actually happens, but by no means am I expressing the linguistic fact in its essence and fullness.

3. Linguistic value from a material viewpoint

The conceptual side of value is made up solely of relations and differences with respect to the other terms of language, and the same can be said of its material side. The important thing in the word is not the sound alone but the phonic differences that make it possible to distinguish this word from all others, for differences carry signification.

This may seem surprising, but how indeed could the reverse be possible? Since one vocal image is no better suited than the next for what it is commissioned to express, it is evident, even *a priori*, that a segment of language can never in the final analysis be based on anything except its noncoincidence with the rest. *Arbitrary* and *differential* are two correlative qualities.

The alteration of linguistic signs clearly illustrates this. It is precisely because the terms *a* and *b* as such are radically incapable of reaching the level of consciousness—one is always conscious of only the *a/b* difference—that each term is free to change according to laws that are unrelated to its signifying function. No positive sign characterizes the genitive plural in Czech *žen*; still the two forms *žena: žen* function as well as the earlier forms *žena: ženb; žen* has value only because it is different.

Here is another example that shows even more clearly the systematic role of phonic differences: in Greek, *éphēn* is an imperfect and *éstēn* an aorist although both words are formed in the same way; the first belongs to the system of the present indicative of *phēmī* 'I say,' whereas there is no present **stēmi*; now it is precisely the relation *phēmī: éphēn* that corresponds to the relation between the present and the imperfect (cf. *déiknūmi: edéiknūn*, etc.). Signs function, then, not through their intrinsic value but through their relative position.

In addition, it is impossible for sound alone, a material element, to belong to language. It is only a secondary thing, substance to be put to use. All our conventional values have the characteristic of not being confused with the tangible element which supports them. For instance, it is not the metal in a piece of money that fixes its value. A coin nominally worth five francs may contain less than half its worth of silver. Its value will vary according to the amount stamped upon it and according to its use inside or outside a political boundary. This is even more true of the linguistic signifier, which is not phonic but incorporeal—constituted not by its material substance but by the differences that separate its sound-image from all others.

The foregoing principle is so basic that it applies to all the material elements of language, including phonemes. Every language forms its words on the basis of a system of sonorous elements, each element being a clearly delimited unit and one of a fixed number of units. Phonemes are characterized not, as one might think, by their own positive quality but simply by the fact that they are distinct. Phonemes are above all else opposing, relative, and negative entities.

Proof of this is the latitude that speakers have between points of convergence in the pronunciation of distinct sounds. In French, for instance, general use of a dorsal *r* does not prevent many speakers from using a tongue-tip trill; language is not in the least disturbed by it; language requires only that the sound be different and not as one might imagine, that it have an invariable quality. I can even pronounce the French *r* like German *ch* in *Bach, doch*, etc., but in German I could not use *r* instead of *ch*, for German gives recognition to both elements and must keep them apart. Similarly, in Russian there is no latitude for *t* in the direction of *t'* (palatalized *t*), for the result would be the confusing of two sounds differentiated by the language (cf. *govorit'* 'speak' and *goverit* 'he speaks'), but more freedom may be taken with respect to *th* (aspirated *t*) since this sound does not figure in the Russian system of phonemes.

Since an identical state of affairs is observable in writing, another system of signs, we shall use writing to draw some comparisons that will clarify the whole issue. In fact:

(1)   The signs used in writing are arbitrary; there is no connection, for example, between the letter *t* and the sound that it designates.
(2)   The value of letters is purely negative and differential. The same person can write *t*, for instance, in different ways:

The only requirement is that the sign for *t* not be confused in his script with the signs used for *l, d,* etc.

(3)   Values in writing function only through reciprocal opposition within a fixed system that consists of a set number of letters. This third characteristic, though not identical to the second, is closely related to it, for both depend on the first. Since the graphic sign is arbitrary, its form matters little or rather matters only within the limitations imposed by the system.

(4)   The means by which the sign is produced is completely unimportant, for it does not affect the system (this also follows from characteristic 1). Whether I make the letters in white or black, raised or engraved, with pen or chisel—all this is of no importance with respect to their signification.

4. The sign considered in its totality

Everything that has been said up to this point boils down to this: in language there are only differences. Even more important: a difference generally implies positive terms between which the difference is set up; but in language there are only differences *without positive terms*. Whether we take the signified or the signifier, language has neither ideas nor sounds that existed before the linguistic system, but only conceptual and phonic differences that have issued from the system. The idea or phonic substance that a sign contains is of less importance than the other signs that surround it. Proof of this is that the value of a term may be modified without either its meaning or its sound being affected, solely because a neighboring term has been modified.

But the statement that everything in language is negative is true only if the signified and the signifier are considered separately; when we consider the sign in its totality, we have something that is positive in its own class. A linguistic system is a series of differences of sound combined with a series of differences of ideas; but the pairing of a certain number of acoustical signs with as many cuts made from the mass of thought engenders a system of values; and this system serves as the effective link between the phonic and psychological elements within each sign. Although both the signified and the signifier are purely differential and negative when considered separately, their combination is a positive fact; it is even the sole type of facts that language has, for maintaining the parallelism between the two classes of differences is the distinctive function of the linguistic institution.

Certain diachronic facts are typical in this respect. Take the countless instances where alteration of the signifier occasions a conceptual change and where it is obvious that the sum of the ideas distinguished corresponds in principle to the sum of the distinctive signs. When two words are confused through phonetic alteration (e.g. French *décrépit* from *dēcrepitus* and *décrépi* from *crispus*), the ideas that they express will also tend to become confused if only they have something in common. Or a word may have different forms (cf. *chaise* 'chair' and *chaire* 'desk'). Any nascent difference will tend invariably to become significant but without always succeeding or being successful on the first trial. Conversely, any conceptual difference perceived by the mind seeks to find expression through a distinct signifier, and two ideas that are no longer distinct in the mind tend to merge into the same signifier.

When we compare signs—positive terms—with each other, we can no longer speak of difference; the expression would not be fitting, for it applies only to the comparing of two sound-images, e.g. *father* and *mother*, or two ideas, e.g. the idea "father" and the idea "mother"; two signs, each having a signified and signifier, are not different but only distinct. Between them there is only *opposition*. The entire mechanism of language, with which we shall be concerned later, is based on oppositions of this kind and on the phonic and conceptual differences that they imply.

What is true of value is true also of the unit. A unit is a segment of the spoken chain that corresponds to a certain concept; both are by nature purely differential.

Applied to units, the principle of differentiation can be stated in this way: *the characteristics of the unit blend with the unit itself*. In language, as in any semiological system, whatever distinguishes one sign from the others constitutes it. Difference makes character just as it makes value and the unit.

Another rather paradoxical consequence of the same principle is this: in the last analysis what is commonly referred to as a "grammatical fact" fits the definition of the unit, for it always expresses an opposition of terms; it differs only in that the opposition is particularly significant (e.g. the formation of German plurals of the type *Nacht: Nächte*). Each term present in the grammatical fact (the singular without umlaut or final *e* in opposition to the plural with umlaut and -*e*) consists of the interplay of a number of oppositions within the system. When isolated, neither *Nacht* nor *Nächte* is anything: thus everything is opposition. Putting it another way, the *Nacht: Nächte* relation can be expressed by an algebraic formula *a/b* in which *a* and *b* are not simple terms but result from a set of relations. Language, in a manner of speaking, is a type of algebra consisting solely of complex terms. Some of its oppositions are more significant than others; but units and grammatical facts are only different names for designating diverse aspects of the same general fact; the functioning of linguistic oppositions. This statement is so true that we might very well approach the problem of units by starting from grammatical facts. Taking an opposition like *Nacht: Nächte*, we might ask what are the units involved in it. Are they only the two words, the whole series of similar words, *a* and *ä*, or all singulars and plurals, etc.?

Units and grammatical facts would not be confused if linguistic signs were made up of something besides differences. But language being what it is, we shall find nothing simple in it regardless of our approach; everywhere and always there is the same complex equilibrium of terms that mutually condition each other. Putting it another way, *language is a form and not a substance*. This truth could not be overstressed, for all the mistakes in our terminology, all our incorrect ways of naming things that pertain to language, stem from the involuntary supposition that the linguistic phenomenon must have substance.

Note

1   The use of the comparative form for two and the superlative for more than two in English (e.g. *may the* better *boxer win: the* best *boxer in the world*) is probably a remnant of the old distinction between the dual and the plural number. [Tr.]

Suggestions for further reading

Barthes, Roland, *Mythologies*, ed. and trans. Annette Lavers, London: Vintage, 1993.

Benveniste, Emile, *Problems in General Linguistics*, Miami: University of Miami Press, 1971.

Derrida, Jacques, *Of Grammatology*, trans. Gayatri Chakravorty Spivak, Baltimore: Johns Hopkins University Press, 1976. See especially Part I, Chapter 2, 'Linguistics and Grammatology'.

Chapter 4

Joan Riviere

'WOMANLINESS AS A MASQUERADE', 1929

EVERY DIRECTION IN which psycho-analytic research has pointed seems in its turn to have attracted the interest of Ernest Jones, and now that of recent years investigation has slowly spread to the development of the sexual life of women, we find as a matter of course one by him among the most important contributions to the subject. As always, he throws great light on his material, with his peculiar gift both clarifying the knowledge we had already and also adding to it fresh observations of his own.

In his paper on 'The Early Development of Female Sexuality'[1] he sketches out a rough scheme of types of female development, which he first divides into heterosexual and homosexual, subsequently subdividing the latter homosexual group into two types. He acknowledges the roughly schematic nature of his classification and postulates a number of intermediate types. It is with one of these intermediate types that I am to-day concerned. In daily life types of men and women are constantly met with who, while mainly heterosexual in their development, plainly display strong features of the other sex. This has been judged to be an expression of the bisexuality inherent in us all; and analysis has shown that what appears as homosexual or heterosexual character-traits, or sexual manifestations, is the end-result of the interplay of conflicts and not necessarily evidence of a radical or fundamental tendency. The difference between homosexual and heterosexual development results from differences in the degree of anxiety, with the corresponding effect this has on development. Ferenczi pointed out a similar reaction in behaviour,[2] namely, that homosexual men exaggerate their heterosexuality as a 'defence' against their homosexuality. I shall attempt to show that women who wish for masculinity may put on a mask of womanliness to avert anxiety and the retribution feared from men.

It is with a particular type of intellectual woman that I have to deal. Not long ago intellectual pursuits for women were associated almost exclusively with an overtly masculine type of woman, who in pronounced cases made no secret of her wish or claim to be a man. This has now changed. Of all the women engaged in professional work to-day, it would be hard to say whether the greater number are more feminine than masculine in their mode of life and character. In University life, in scientific professions and in business, one constantly meets women who seem to fulfil every criterion of complete feminine development. They are excellent wives and mothers, capable housewives; they maintain social life and assist culture; they have no lack of feminine interests, e.g. in their personal appearance, and when called upon they can still find time to play the part of devoted and disinterested mother-substitutes among a wide circle of relatives and friends. At the same time they fulfil the duties of their profession at least as well as the average man. It is really a puzzle to know how to classify this type psychologically.

Some time ago, in the course of an analysis of a woman of this kind, I came upon some interesting discoveries. She conformed in almost every particular to the description just given; her excellent relations with her husband included a very intimate affectionate attachment between them and full and frequent sexual enjoyment; she prided herself on her proficiency as a housewife. She had followed her profession with marked success all her life. She had a high degree of adaptation to reality, and managed to sustain good and appropriate relations with almost everyone with whom she came in contact.

Certain reactions in her life showed, however, that her stability was not as flawless as it appeared; one of these will illustrate my theme. She was an American woman engaged in work of a propagandist nature, which consisted principally in speaking and writing. All her life a certain degree of anxiety, sometimes very severe, was experienced after every public performance, such as speaking to an audience. In spite of her unquestionable success and ability, both intellectual and practical, and her capacity for managing an audience and dealing with discussions, etc., she would be excited and apprehensive all night after, with misgivings whether she had done anything inappropriate, and obsessed by a need for reassurance. This need for reassurance led her compulsively on any such occasion to seek some attention or complimentary notice from a man or men at the close of the proceedings in which she had taken part or been the principal figure; and it soon became evident that the men chosen for the purpose were always unmistakable father-figures, although often not persons whose judgement on her performance would in reality carry much weight. There were clearly two types of reassurance sought from these father-figures; first, direct reassurance of the nature of compliments about her performance; secondly, and more important, indirect reassurance of the nature of sexual attentions from these men. To speak broadly, analysis of her behaviour after her performance showed that she was attempting to obtain sexual advances from the particular type of men by means of flirting and coquetting with them in a more or less veiled manner. The extraordinary incongruity of this attitude with her highly impersonal and objective attitude during her intellectual performance, which it succeeded so rapidly in time, was a problem.

Analysis showed that the Œdipus situation of rivalry with the mother was extremely acute and had never been satisfactorily solved. I shall come back to this later. But beside the conflict in regard to the mother, the rivalry with the father was also very great. Her intellectual work, which took the form of speaking and writing, was based on an evident identification with her father, who had first been a literary man and later had taken to political life; her adolescence had been characterized by conscious revolt against him, with rivalry and contempt of him. Dreams and phantasies of this nature, castrating the husband, were frequently uncovered by analysis. She had quite conscious feelings of rivalry and claims to superiority over many of the 'father-figures' whose favour she would then woo after her own performances! She bitterly resented any assumption that she was not equal to them, and (in private) would reject the idea of being subject to their judgement or criticism. In this she corresponded clearly to one type Ernest Jones has sketched: his first group of homosexual women who, while taking no interest in other women, wish for 'recognition' of their masculinity from men and claim to be the equals of men, or in other words, to be men themselves. Her resentment, however, was not openly expressed; publicly she acknowledged her condition of womanhood.

Analysis then revealed that the explanation of her compulsive ogling and coquetting—which actually she was herself hardly aware of till analysis made it manifest—was as follows: it was an unconscious attempt to ward off the anxiety which would ensue on account of the reprisals she anticipated from the father-figures after her intellectual performance. The exhibition in public of her intel-lectual proficiency, which was in itself carried through successfully, signified an exhibition of herself in possession of the father's penis, having castrated him. The display once over, she was seized by horrible dread of the retribution the father would then exact. Obviously it was a step towards propitiating the avenger to endeavour to offer herself to him sexually. This phantasy, it then appeared, had been very common in her childhood and youth, which had been spent in the Southern States of America; if a negro came to attack her, she planned to defend herself by making him kiss her and make love to her (ultimately so that she could then deliver him over to justice). But there was a further determinant of the obsessive behaviour. In a dream which had a rather similar content to this child-hood phantasy, she was in terror alone in the house; then a negro came in and found her washing clothes, with her sleeves rolled up and arms exposed. She resisted him, with the secret intention of attracting him sexually, and he began to admire her arms and to caress them and her breasts. The meaning was that she had killed father and mother and obtained everything for herself (alone in the house), became terrified of their retribution (expected shots through the window), and defended herself by taking on a menial rôle (washing clothes) and by *washing off* dirt and sweat, guilt and blood, everything she had obtained by the deed, and 'disguising herself' as merely a castrated woman. In that guise the man found no stolen property on her which he need attack her to recover and, further, found her attractive as an object of love. Thus the aim of the compulsion was not merely to secure reassurance by evoking friendly feelings towards her in the man; it was chiefly to make sure of safety by masquerading as guiltless and innocent. It was a compulsive reversal of her intellectual performance; and the two together formed the 'double-action' of an obsessive act, just as her life as a whole consisted alternately of masculine and feminine activities.

Before this dream she had had dreams of people putting masks on their faces in order to avert disaster. One of these dreams was of a high tower on a hill being pushed over and falling down on the inhabitants of a village below, but the people put on masks and escaped injury!

Womanliness therefore could be assumed and worn as a mask, both to hide the possession of masculinity and to avert the reprisals expected if she was found to possess it—much as a thief will turn out his pockets and ask to be searched to prove that he has not the stolen goods. The reader may now ask how I define womanliness or where I draw the line between genuine womanliness and the 'masquerade'. My suggestion is not, however, that there is any such difference; whether radical or superficial, they are the same thing. The capacity for womanliness was there in this woman—and one might even say it exists in the most completely homosexual woman—but owing to her conflicts it did not represent her main development, and was used far more as a device for avoiding anxiety than as a primary mode of sexual enjoyment.

I will give some brief particulars to illustrate this. She had married late, at twenty-nine; she had had great anxiety about defloration, and had had the hymen stretched or slit before the wedding by a woman doctor. Her attitude to sexual intercourse before marriage was a set determination to obtain and experience the enjoyment and pleasure which she knew some women have in it, and the orgasm. She was afraid of impotence in exactly the same way as a man. This was partly a determination to surpass certain mother-figures who were frigid, but on deeper levels it was a determination not to be beaten by the man.[3] In effect, sexual enjoyment was full and frequent, with complete orgasm; but the fact emerged that the gratification it brought was of the nature of a reassurance and restitution of something lost, and not ultimately pure enjoyment. The man's love gave her back her self-esteem. During analysis, while the hostile castrating impulses towards the husband were in process of coming to light, the desire for intercourse very much abated, and she became for periods relatively frigid. The mask of womanliness was being peeled away, and she was revealed either as castrated (lifeless, incapable of pleasure), or as wishing to castrate (therefore afraid to receive the penis or welcome it by gratification). Once, while for a period her husband had had a love-affair with another woman, she had detected a very intense identification with him in regard to the rival woman. It is striking that she had had no homosexual experiences (since before puberty with a younger sister); but it appeared during analysis that this lack was compensated for by frequent homosexual dreams with intense orgasm.

In every-day life one may observe the mask of femininity taking curious forms. One capable housewife of my acquaintance is a woman of great ability, and can herself attend to typically masculine matters. But when, e.g. any builder or upholsterer is called in, she has a compulsion to hide all her technical knowledge from him and show deference to the workman, making her suggestions in an innocent and artless manner, as if they were 'lucky guesses'. She has confessed to me that even with the butcher and baker, whom she rules in reality with a rod of iron, she cannot openly take up a firm straightforward stand; she feels herself as it were 'acting a part', she puts on the semblance of a rather uneducated, foolish and bewildered woman, yet in the end always making her point. In all other relations in life this woman is a gracious, cultured lady, competent and well-informed, and can manage her affairs by sensible rational behaviour without any subterfuges. This woman is now aged fifty, but she tells me that as a young woman she had great anxiety in dealings with men such as porters, waiters, cabmen, tradesmen, or any other potentially hostile father-figures, such as doctors, builders and lawyers; moreover, she often quarrelled with such men and had altercations with them, accusing them of defrauding her and so forth.

Another case from every-day observation is that of a clever woman, wife and mother, a University lecturer in an abstruse subject which seldom attracts women. When lecturing, not to students but to colleagues, she chooses particularly feminine clothes. Her behaviour on these occasions is also marked by an inappropriate feature: she becomes flippant and joking, so much so that it has caused comment and rebuke. She has to treat the situation of displaying her masculinity to men as a 'game', as something *not real*, as a 'joke'. She cannot treat herself and her subject seriously, cannot seriously contemplate herself as on equal terms with men; moreover, the flippant attitude enables some of her sadism to escape, hence the offence it causes.

Many other instances could be quoted, and I have met with a similar mechanism in the analysis of manifest homosexual men. In one such man with severe inhibition and anxiety, homosexual activities really took second place, the source of greatest sexual gratification being actually masturbation under special conditions, namely, while looking at himself in a mirror dressed in a particular way. The excitation was produced by the sight of himself with hair parted in the centre, wearing a bow tie. These extraordinary 'fetishes' turned out to represent a *disguise of himself* as his sister; the hair and bow were taken from her. His conscious attitude was a desire to *be* a woman, but his manifest relations with men had never been stable. Unconsciously the homosexual relation proved to be entirely sadistic and based on masculine rivalry. Phantasies of sadism and '*possession of a penis*' could be indulged only while reassurance against anxiety was being obtained from the mirror that he was safely 'disguised as a woman'.

To return to the case I first described. Underneath her apparently satisfactory heterosexuality it is clear that this woman displayed well-known manifestations of the castration complex. Horney was the first among others to point out the sources of that complex in the Œdipus situation; my belief is that the fact that womanliness may be assumed as a mask may contribute further in this direction to the analysis of female development. With that in view I will now sketch the early libido-development in this case.

But before this I must give some account of her relations with women. She was conscious of rivalry of almost any woman who had either good looks or intellectual pretensions. She was conscious of flashes of hatred against almost any woman with whom she had much to do, but where permanent or close relations with women were concerned she was none the less able to establish a very satisfactory footing. Unconsciously she did this almost entirely by means of feeling herself superior in some way to them (her relations with her inferiors were uniformly excellent). Her proficiency as a housewife largely had its root in this. By it she surpassed her mother, won her approval and proved her superiority among rival 'feminine' women. Her intellectual attainments undoubtedly had in part the same object. They too proved her superiority to her mother; it seemed probable that since she reached womanhood her rivalry with women had been more acute in regard to intellectual things than in regard to beauty, since she could usually take refuge in her superior brains where beauty was concerned.

The analysis showed that the origin of all these reactions, both to men and to women, lay in the reaction to the parents during the oralbiting sadistic phase. These reactions took the form of the phantasies sketched by Melanie Klein[4] in her Congress paper, 1927. In consequence of disappointment or frustration during sucking or weaning, coupled with experiences during the primal scene which is interpreted in oral terms, extremely intense sadism develops towards both parents.[5] The desire to bite off the nipple shifts, and desires to destroy, penetrate and disembowel the mother and devour her and the contents of her body succeed it. These contents include the father's penis, her fæces and her children—all her possessions and love-objects, imagined as within her body.[6] The desire to bite off the nipple is also shifted, as we know, on to the desire to castrate the father by biting off his penis. Both parents are rivals in this stage, both possess desired objects; the sadism is directed against both and the revenge of both is feared. But, as always with girls, the mother is the more hated, and consequently the more feared. She will execute the punishment that fits the crime—destroy the girl's body, her beauty, her children, her capacity for having children, mutilate her, devour her, torture her and kill her. In this appalling predicament the girl's only safety lies in placating the mother and atoning for her crime. She must retire from rivalry with the mother, and if she can, endeavour to restore to her what she has stolen. As we know, she identifies herself with the father; and then she uses the masculinity she thus obtains by *putting it at the service of the mother*. She becomes the father, and takes his place; so she can 'restore' him to the mother. This position was very clear in many typical situations in my patient's life. She delighted in using her great practical ability to aid or assist weaker and more helpless women, and could maintain this attitude successfully so long as rivalry did not emerge too strongly. But this restitution could be made on one condition only; it must procure her a lavish return in the form of gratitude and 'recognition'. The recognition desired was supposed by her to be owing for her self-sacrifices; more unconsciously what she claimed was recognition of her *supremacy* in *having* the penis to give back. If her supremacy were not acknowledged, then rivalry became at once acute; if gratitude and recognition were withheld, her sadism broke out in full force and she would be subject (in private) to paraoxysms of oral-sadistic fury, exactly like a raging infant.

In regard to the father, resentment against him arose in two ways: (1) during the primal scene he took from the mother the milk, etc., which the child missed; (2) at the same time he gave to the mother the penis or children instead of to her. Therefore all that he had or took should be taken from him by her; he was castrated and reduced to nothingness, like the mother. Fear of him, though never so acute as of the mother, remained; partly, too, because his vengeance for the death and destruction of the mother was expected. So he too must be placated and appeased. This was done by masquerading in a feminine guise for him, thus showing him her 'love' and guiltlessness towards him. It is significant that this woman's mask, though transparent to other women, was successful with men, and served its purpose very well. Many men were attracted in this way, and gave her reassurance by showing her favour. Closer examination showed that these men were of the type who themselves fear the ultra-womanly woman. They prefer a woman who herself has male attributes, for to them her claims on them are less.

At the primal scene the talisman which both parents possess and which she lacks is the father's penis: hence her rage, also her dread and helplessness.[7] By depriving the father of it and possessing it herself she obtains the talisman – the invincible sword, the 'organ of sadism'; he becomes powerless and helpless (her gentle husband), but she still guards herself from attack by wearing towards him the mask of womanly subservience, and under that screen, performing many of his masculine functions herself— 'for him' – (her practical ability and management). Likewise with the mother: having robbed her of the penis, destroyed her and reduced her to pitiful inferiority, she triumphs over her, but again secretly; outwardly she acknowledges and admires the virtues of 'feminine' women. But the task of guarding herself against the woman's retribution is harder than with the man; her efforts to placate and make reparation by restoring and using the penis in the mother's service were never enough; this device was worked to death, and sometimes it almost worked her to death.

It appeared, therefore, that this woman had saved herself from the intolerable anxiety resulting from her sadistic fury against both parents by creating in phantasy a situation in which she became supreme and no harm could be done to her. The essence of the phantasy was her *supremacy* over the parent-objects; by it her sadism was gratified, she triumphed over them. By this same supremacy she also succeeded in averting their revenges; the means she adopted for this were reaction-formations and concealment of her hostility. Thus she could gratify her id-impulses, her narcissistic ego and her super-ego at one and the same time. The phantasy was the main-spring of her whole life and character, and she came within a narrow margin of carrying it through to complete perfection. But its weak point was the megalomanic character, under all the disguises, of the necessity for supremacy. When this supremacy was seriously disturbed during analysis, she fell into an abyss of anxiety, rage and abject depression; before the analysis, into illness.

I should like to say a word about Ernest Jones' type of homosexual woman whose aim is to obtain 'recognition' of her masculinity from men. The question arises whether the need for recognition in this type is connected with the mechanism of the same need, operating differently (recognition for services performed), in the case I have described. In my case direct recognition of the possession of the penis was not claimed openly; it was claimed for the reaction-formations, though only the possession of the penis made them possible. Indirectly, therefore, recognition was none the less claimed for the penis. This indirectness was due to apprehension lest her possession of a penis *should be* 'recognized', in other words 'found out'. One can see that with less anxiety my patient too would have openly claimed recognition from men for her possession of a penis, and in private she did in fact, like Ernest Jones' cases, bitterly resent any lack of this direct recognition. It is clear that in his cases the primary sadism obtains more gratification; the father has been castrated, and shall even acknowledge his defeat. But how then is the anxiety averted by these women? In regard to the mother, this is done of course by denying her existence. To judge from indications in analyses I have carried out, I conclude that, first, as Jones implies, this claim is simply a displacement of the original sadistic claim that the desired object, nipple, milk, penis, should be instantly surrendered; secondarily, the need for recognition is largely a need for absolution. Now the mother has been relegated to limbo; no relations with her are possible. Her existence appears to be denied, though in truth it is only too much feared. So the guilt of having triumphed over both can only be absolved by the father; if he sanctions her possession of the penis by acknowledging it, she is safe. By *giving* her recognition, he *gives* her the penis and to her instead of to the mother; then she has it, and she may have it, and all is well. 'Recognition' is always in part reassurance, sanction, love; further, it renders her supreme again. Little as he may know it, to her the man has admitted his defeat. Thus in its content such a woman's phantasy-relation to the father is similar to the normal Œdipus one; the difference is that it rests on a basis of sadism. The mother she has indeed killed, but she is thereby excluded from enjoying much that the mother had, and what she does obtain from the father she has still in great measure to extort and extract.

These conclusions compel one once more to face the question: what is the essential nature of fully-developed femininity? What is *das ewig Weibliche?* The conception of womanliness as a mask, behind which man suspects some hidden danger, throws a little light on the enigma. Fully-developed heterosexual woman-hood is founded, as Helene Deutsch and Ernest Jones have stated, on the oral-sucking stage. The sole gratification of a primary order in it is that of receiving the (nipple, milk) penis, semen, child from the father. For the rest it depends upon reaction-formations. The acceptance of 'castration', the humility, the admiration of men, come partly from the over-estimation of the object on the oral-sucking plane; but chiefly from the renunciation (lesser intensity) of sadistic castration-wishes deriving from the later oral-biting level. 'I must not take. I must not even ask; it must be *given* me'. The capacity for self-sacrifice, devotion, self-abnegation expresses efforts to restore and make good, whether to mother or to father figures, what has been taken from them. It is also what Radó has called a 'narcis-sistic insurance' of the highest value.

It becomes clear how the attainment of full heterosexuality coincides with that of genitality. And once more we see, as Abraham first stated, that genitality implies attainment of a *post-ambivalent* state. Both the 'normal' woman and the homo-sexual desire the father's penis and rebel against frustration (or castration); but one of the differences between them lies in the difference in the degree of sadism and of the power of dealing both with it and with the anxiety it gives rise to in the two types of women.

Notes

1   This JOURNAL, Vol. VIII. 1927.
2   'The Nosology of Male Homosexuality', *Contributions to Psycho-Analysis* (1916).
3   I have found this attitude in several women analysands and the self-ordained defloration in nearly all of them (five cases). In the light of Freud's 'Taboo of Virginity', this latter symptomatic act is instructive.
4   'Early Stages of the Œdipus Conflict', this JOURNAL, Vol. IX, 1928.
5   Ernest Jones, op cit., p. 469, regards an intensification of the oral sadistic stage as the central feature of homosexual development in women.

6   As it was not essential to my argument, I have omitted all reference to the further development of the relation to children.
7   Cf. M. N. Searl, 'Danger Situations of the Immature Ego', Oxford Congress, 1929.

Suggestions for further reading

Belsey, Catherine, 'Popular Fiction and the Feminine Masquerade', *European Journal of English Studies*, 1998, vol. 2.3, 343–58.

Butler, Judith, *Gender Trouble: Feminism and the Subversion of Identity*, New York and London: Routledge, 1990.

Heath, Stephen, 'Joan Riviere and the Masquerade', in Victor Burgin *et al.* (eds.), *Formations of Fantasy*, London: Methuen, 1986, pp. 45–61.

Chapter 5

Walter Benjamin

'THE WORK OF ART IN THE AGE OF MECHANICAL REPRODUCTION', 1936

'*Our fine arts were developed, their types and uses were established, in times very different from the present, by men whose power of action upon things was insignificant in comparison with ours. But the amazing growth of our techniques, the adaptability and precision they have attained, the ideas and habits they are creating, make it a certainty that profound changes are impending in the ancient craft of the Beautiful. In all the arts there is a physical component which can no longer be considered or treated as it used to be, which cannot remain unaffected by our modern knowledge and power. For the last twenty years neither matter nor space nor time has been what it was from time immemorial. We must expect great innovations to transform the entire technique of the arts, thereby affecting artistic invention itself and perhaps even bring about an amazing change in our very notion of art.*'[1]

> – Paul Valéry, PIÈCES SUR L'ART,
> 'La Conquète de l'ubiquitè,' Paris.

Preface

WHEN MARX UNDERTOOK his critique of the capitalistic mode of production, this mode was in its infancy. Marx directed his efforts in such a way as to give them prognostic value. He went back to the basic conditions underlying capitalistic production and through his presentation showed what could be expected of capitalism in the future. The result was that one could expect it not only to exploit the proletariat with increasing intensity, but ultimately to create conditions which would make it possible to abolish capitalism itself.

The transformation of the superstructure, which takes place far more slowly than that of the substructure, has taken more than half a century to manifest in all areas of culture the change in the conditions of production. Only today can it be indicated what form this has taken. Certain prognostic requirements should be met by these statements. However, theses about the art of the proletariat after its assumption of power or about the art of a classless society would have less bearing on these demands than theses about the developmental tendencies of art under present conditions of production. Their dialectic is no less noticeable in the super-structure than in the economy. It would therefore be wrong to underestimate the value of such theses as a weapon. They brush aside a number of outmoded concepts, such as creativity and genius, eternal value and mystery – concepts whose uncontrolled (and at present almost uncontrollable) application would lead to a processing of data in the Fascist sense. The concepts which are introduced into the theory of art in what follows differ from the more familiar terms in that they are completely useless for the purposes of Fascism. They are, on the other hand, useful for the formulation of revolutionary demands in the politics of art.

I

In principle a work of art has always been reproducible. Man-made artifacts could always be imitated by men. Replicas were made by pupils in practice of their craft, by masters for diffusing their works, and, finally, by third parties in the pursuit of gain. Mechanical reproduction of a work of art, however, represents something new. Historically, it advanced intermittently and in leaps at long intervals, but with accelerated intensity. The Greeks knew only two procedures of technically repro-ducing works of art: founding and stamping. Bronzes, terra cottas, and coins were the only art works which they could produce in quantity. All others were unique and could not be mechanically reproduced. With the woodcut graphic art became mechanically reproducible for the first time, long before script became repro-ducible by print. The enormous changes which printing, the mechanical reproduc-tion of writing, has brought about in literature are a familiar story. However, within the phenomenon which we are here examining from the perspective of world history, print is merely a special, though particularly important, case. During the Middle Ages engraving and etching were added to the woodcut; at the beginning of the nineteenth century lithography made its appearance.

With lithography the technique of reproduction reached an essentially new stage. This much more direct process was distinguished by the tracing of the design on a stone rather than its incision on a block of wood or its etching on a copperplate and permitted graphic art for the first time to put its products on the market, not only in large numbers as hitherto, but also in daily changing forms. Lithography enabled graphic art to illustrate everyday life, and it began to keep pace with printing. But only a few decades after its invention, lithography was surpassed by photography. For the first time in the process of pictorial reproduc-tion, photography freed the hand of the most important artistic functions which henceforth devolved only upon the eye looking into a lens. Since the eye perceives more swiftly than the hand can draw, the process of pictorial reproduction was accelerated so enormously that it could keep pace with speech. A film operator shooting a scene in the studio captures the images at the speed of an actor's speech. Just as lithography virtually implied the illustrated newspaper, so did photography foreshadow the sound film. The technical reproduction of sound was tackled at the end of the last century. These convergent endeavours made predictable a situation which Paul Valéry pointed up in this sentence: 'Just as water, gas, and electricity are brought into our houses from far off to satisfy our needs in response to a minimal effort, so we shall be supplied with visual or auditory images, which will appear and disappear at a simple movement of the hand, hardly more than a sign' (*op. cit.*, p. 226). Around 1900 technical reproduction had reached a standard that not only permitted it to reproduce all transmitted works of art and thus to cause the most profound change in their impact upon the public; it also had captured a place of its own among the artistic processes. For the study of this standard nothing is more revealing than the nature of the repercussions that these two different manifestations – the reproduction of works of art and the art of the film – have had on art in its traditional form.

II

Even the most perfect reproduction of a work of art is lacking in one element: its presence in time and space, its unique existence at the place where it happens to be. This unique existence of the work of art determined the history to which it was subject throughout the time of its existence. This includes the changes which it may have suffered in physical condition over the years as well as the various changes in its ownership.[2] The traces of the first can be revealed only by chemical or physical analyses which it is impossible to perform on a reproduction; changes of ownership are subject to a tradition which must be traced from the situation of the original.

The presence of the original is the prerequisite to the concept of authenticity. Chemical analyses of the patina of a bronze can help to establish this, as does the proof that a given manuscript of the Middle Ages stems from an archive of the fifteenth century. The whole sphere of authenticity is outside technical – and, of course, not only technical – reproducibility.[3] Confronted with its manual reproduction, which was usually branded as a forgery, the original preserved all its authority; not so *vis à vis* technical reproduction. The reason is twofold. First, process reproduction is more independent of the original than manual reproduction. For example, in photography, process reproduction can bring out those aspects of the original that are unattainable to the naked eye yet accessible to the lens, which is adjustable and chooses its angle at will. And photographic reproduction, with the aid of certain processes, such as enlargement or slow motion, can capture images which escape natural vision. Secondly, technical reproduction can put the copy of the original into situations which would be out of reach for the original itself. Above all, it enables the original to meet the beholder halfway, be it in the form of a photograph or a phonograph record. The cathedral leaves its locale to be received in the studio of a lover of art; the choral production, performed in an auditorium or in the open air, resounds in the drawing room.

The situations into which the product of mechanical reproduction can be brought may not touch the actual work of art, yet the quality of its presence is always depreciated. This holds not only for the art work but also, for instance, for a landscape which passes in review before the spectator in a movie. In the case of the art object, a most sensitive nucleus – namely, its authenticity – is interfered with whereas no natural object is vulnerable on that score. The authenticity of a thing is the essence of all that is transmissible from its beginning, ranging from its substantive duration to its testimony to the history which it has experienced. Since the historical testimony rests on the authenticity, the former, too, is jeopardized by reproduction when substantive duration ceases to matter. And what is really jeopardized when the historical testimony is affected is the authority of the object.[4]

One might subsume the eliminated element in the term 'aura' and go on to say: that which withers in the age of mechanical reproduction is the aura of the work of art. This is a symptomatic process whose significance points beyond the realm of art. One might generalize by saying: the technique of reproduction detaches the reproduced object from the domain of tradition. By making many reproductions it substitutes a plurality of copies for a unique existence. And in permitting the reproduction to meet the beholder or listener in his own particular situation, it reactivates the object reproduced. These two processes lead to a tremendous shattering of tradition which is the obverse of the contemporary crisis and renewal of mankind. Both processes are intimately connected with the contemporary mass movements. Their most powerful agent is the film. Its social significance, particularly in its most positive form, is inconceivable without its destructive, cathartic aspect, that is, the liquidation of the traditional value of the cultural heritage. This phenomenon is most palpable in the great historical films. It extends to ever new positions. In 1927 Abel Gance exclaimed enthusiastically: 'Shakespeare, Rembrandt, Beethoven will make films . . . all legends, all mythologies and all myths, all founders of religion, and the very religions . . . await their exposed resurrection, and the heroes crowd each other at the gate.'[5] Presumably without intending it, he issued an invitation to a far-reaching liquidation.

III

During long periods of history, the mode of human sense perception changes with humanity's entire mode of existence. The manner in which human sense perception is organized, the medium in which it is accomplished, is determined not only by nature but by historical circumstances as well. The fifth century, with its great shifts of population, saw the birth of the late Roman art industry and the Vienna Genesis, and there developed not only an art different from that of antiquity but also a new kind of perception. The scholars of the Viennese school, Riegl and Wickhoff, who resisted the weight of classical tradition under which these later art forms had been buried, were the first to draw conclusions from them concerning the organization of perception at the time. However far-reaching their insight, these scholars limited themselves to showing the significant, formal hallmark which characterized perception in late Roman times. They did not attempt – and, perhaps, saw no way – to show the social transformations expressed by these changes of perception. The conditions for an analogous insight are more favourable in the present. And if changes in the medium of contemporary perception can be comprehended as decay of the aura, it is possible to show its social causes.

The concept of aura which was proposed above with reference to historical objects may usefully be illustrated with reference to the aura of natural ones. We define the aura of the latter as the unique phenomenon of a distance, however close it may be. If, while resting on a summer afternoon, you follow with your eyes a mountain range on the horizon or a branch which casts its shadow over you, you experience the aura of those mountains, of that branch. This image makes it easy to comprehend the social bases of the contemporary decay of the aura. It rests on two circumstances, both of which are related to the increasing significance of the masses in contemporary life. Namely, the desire of contemporary masses to bring things 'closer' spatially and humanly, which is just as ardent as their bent toward overcoming the uniqueness of every reality by accepting its reproduction.[6] Every day the urge grows stronger to get hold of an object at very close range by way of its likeness, its reproduction. Unmistakably, reproduction as offered by picture magazines and newsreels differs from the image seen by the unarmed eye. Uniqueness and permanence are as closely linked in the latter as are transitoriness and reproducibility in the former. To pry an object from its shell, to destroy its aura, is the mark of a perception whose 'sense of the universal equality of things' has increased to such a degree that it extracts it even from a unique object by means of reproduction. Thus is manifested in the field of perception what in the theoretical sphere is noticeable in the increasing importance of statistics. The adjustment of reality to the masses and of the masses to reality is a process of unlimited scope, as much for thinking as for perception.

IV

The uniqueness of a work of art is inseparable from its being imbedded in the fabric of tradition. This tradition itself is thoroughly alive and extremely change-able. An ancient statue of Venus, for example, stood in a different traditional context with the Greeks, who made it an object of veneration, than with the clerics of the Middle Ages, who viewed it as an ominous idol. Both of them, however, were equally confronted with its uniqueness, that is, its aura. Originally the contextual integration of art in tradition found its expression in the cult. We know that the earliest art works originated in the service of a ritual – first the magical, then the religious kind. It is significant that the existence of the work of art with reference to its aura is never entirely separated from its ritual function.[7] In other words, the unique value of the 'authentic' work of art has its basis in ritual, the location of its original use value. This ritualistic basis, however remote, is still recognizable as secularized ritual even in the most profane forms of the cult of beauty.[8] The secular cult of beauty, developed during the Renaissance and prevailing for three centuries, clearly showed that ritualistic basis in its decline and the first deep crisis which befell it. With the advent of the first truly revolutionary means of reproduction, photography, simultaneously with the rise of socialism, art sensed the approaching crisis which has become evident a century later. At the time, art reacted with the doctrine of *l'art pour l'art*, that is, with a theology of art. This gave rise to what might be called a negative theology in the form of the idea of 'pure' art, which not only denied any social function of art but also any categorizing by subject matter. (In poetry, Mallarmé was the first to take this position.)

An analysis of art in the age of mechanical reproduction must do justice to these relationships, for they lead us to an all-important insight: for the first time in world history, mechanical reproduction emancipates the work of art from its parasitical dependence on ritual. To an ever greater degree the work of art reproduced becomes the work of art designed for reproducibility.[9] From a photographic negative, for example, one can make any number of prints; to ask for the 'authentic' print makes no sense. But the instant the criterion of authenticity ceases to be applicable to artistic production, the total function of art is reversed. Instead of being based on ritual, it begins to be based on another practice – politics.

V

Works of art are received and valued on different planes. Two polar types stand out: with one, the accent is on the cult value; with the other, on the exhibition value of the work.[10] Artistic production begins with ceremonial objects destined to serve in a cult. One may assume that what mattered was their existence, not their being on view. The elk portrayed by the man of the Stone Age on the walls of his cave was an instrument of magic. He did expose it to his fellow men, but in the main it was meant for the spirits. Today the cult value would seem to demand that the work of art remain hidden. Certain statues of gods are accessible only to the priest in the cella; certain Madonnas remain covered nearly all year round; certain sculptures on medieval cathedrals are invisible to the spectator on ground level. With the emancipation of the various art practices from ritual go increasing opportunities for the exhibition of their products. It is easier to exhibit a portrait bust that can be sent here and there than to exhibit the statue of a divinity that has its fixed place in the interior of a temple. The same holds for the painting as against the mosaic or fresco that preceded it. And even though the public presentability of a mass originally may have been just as great as that of a symphony, the latter originated at the moment when its public presentability promised to surpass that of the mass.

With the different methods of technical reproduction of a work of art, its fitness for exhibition increased to such an extent that the quantitative shift between its two poles turned into a qualitative transformation of its nature. This is comparable to the situation of the work of art in prehistoric times when, by the absolute emphasis on its cult value, it was, first and foremost, an instrument of magic. Only later did it come to be recognized as a work of art. In the same way today, by the absolute emphasis on its exhibition value the work of art becomes a creation with entirely new functions, among which the one we are conscious of, the artistic function, later may be recognized as incidental.[11] This much is certain: today photography and the film are the most serviceable exemplifications of this new function.

VI

In photography, exhibition value begins to displace cult value all along the line. But cult value does not give way without resistance. It retires into an ultimate retrenchment: the human countenance. It is no accident that the portrait was the focal point of early photography. The cult of remembrance of loved ones, absent or dead, offers a last refuge for the cult value of the picture. For the last time the aura emanates from the early photographs in the fleeting expression of a human face. This is what constitutes their melancholy, incomparable beauty. But as man withdraws from the photographic image, the exhibition value for the first time shows its superiority to the ritual value. To have pinpointed this new stage constitutes the incomparable significance of Atget, who, around 1900, took photographs of deserted Paris streets. It has quite justly been said of him that he photographed them like scenes of crime. The scene of a crime, too, is deserted; it is photographed for the purpose of establishing evidence. With Atget, photographs become standard evidence for historical occurrences, and acquire a hidden political significance. They demand a specific kind of approach; free-floating contemplation is not appropriate to them. They stir the viewer; he feels challenged by them in a new way. At the same time picture magazines begin to put up signposts for him, right ones or wrong ones, no matter. For the first time, captions have become obligatory. And it is clear that they have an altogether different character than the title of a painting. The directives which the captions give to those looking at pictures in illustrated magazines soon become even more explicit and more imperative in the film where the meaning of each single picture appears to be prescribed by the sequence of all preceding ones.

VII

The nineteenth-century dispute as to the artistic value of painting versus photography today seems devious and confused. This does not diminish its importance, however; if anything, it underlines it. The dispute was in fact the symptom of a historical transformation the universal impact of which was not realized by either of the rivals. When the age of mechanical reproduction separated art from its basis in cult, the semblance of its autonomy disappeared forever. The resulting change in the function of art transcended the perspective of the century; for a long time it even escaped that of the twentieth century, which experienced the development of the film.

Earlier much futile thought had been devoted to the question of whether photography is an art. The primary question – whether the very invention of photography had not transformed the entire nature of art – was not raised. Soon the film theoreticians asked the same ill-considered question with regard to the film. But the difficulties which photography caused traditional aesthetics were mere child's play as compared to those raised by the film. Whence the insensitive and forced character of early theories of the film. Abel Gance, for instance, compares the film with hieroglyphs: 'Here, by a remarkable regression, we have come back to the level of expression of the Egyptians . . . Pictorial language has not yet matured because our eyes have not yet adjusted to it. There is as yet insufficient respect for, insufficient cult of, what it expresses.'[12] Or, in the words of Séverin-Mars: 'What art has been granted a dream more poetical and more real at the same time! Approached in this fashion the film might represent an incomparable means of expression. Only the most high-minded persons, in the most perfect and mysterious moments of their lives, should be allowed to enter its ambience.'[13] Alexandre Arnoux concludes his fantasy about the silent film with the question: 'Do not all the bold descriptions we have given amount to the definition of prayer?'[14] It is instructive to note how their desire to class the film among the 'arts' forces these theoreticians to read ritual elements into it – with a striking lack of discretion. Yet when these speculations were published, films like *L'Opinion publique* and *The Gold Rush* had already appeared. This, however, did not keep Abel Gance from adducing hieroglyphs for purposes of comparison, nor Séverin-Mars from speaking of the film as one might speak of paintings by Fra Angelico. Characteristically, even today ultrareactionary authors give the film a similar contextual significance – if not an outright sacred one, then at least a supernatural one. Commenting on Max Reinhardt's film version of *A Midsummer Night's Dream*, Werfel states that undoubtedly it was the sterile copying of the exterior world with its streets, interiors, railroad stations, restaurants, motorcars, and beaches which until now had obstructed the elevation of the film to the realm of art. 'The film has not yet realized its true meaning, its real possibilities . . . these consist in its unique faculty to express by natural means and with incomparable persuasiveness all that is fairylike, marvellous, supernatural.'[15]

VIII

The artistic performance of a stage actor is definitely presented to the public by the actor in person; that of the screen actor, however, is presented by a camera, with a twofold consequence. The camera that presents the performance of the film actor to the public need not respect the performance as an integral whole. Guided by the cameraman, the camera continually changes its position with respect to the performance. The sequence of positional views which the editor composes from the material supplied him constitutes the completed film. It comprises certain factors of movement which are in reality those of the camera, not to mention special camera angles, close-ups, etc. Hence, the performance of the actor is subjected to a series of optical tests. This is the first consequence of the fact that the actor's performance is presented by means of a camera. Also, the film actor lacks the opportunity of the stage actor to adjust to the audience during his performance, since he does not present his performance to the audience in person. This permits the audience to take the position of a critic, without experiencing any personal contact with the actor. The audience's identification with the actor is really an identification with the camera. Consequently the audience takes the position of the camera; its approach is that of testing.[16] This is not the approach to which cult values may be exposed.

IX

For the film, what matters primarily is that the actor represents himself to the public before the camera, rather than representing someone else. One of the first to sense the actor's metamorphosis by this form of testing was Pirandello. Though his remarks on the subject in his novel *Si Gira* were limited to the negative aspects of the question and to the silent film only, this hardly impairs their validity. For in this respect, the sound film did not change anything essential. What matters is that the part is acted not for an audience but for a mechanical contrivance – in the case of the sound film, for two of them. 'The film actor,' wrote Pirandello, 'feels as if in exile – exiled not only from the stage but also from himself. With a vague sense of discomfort he feels inexplicable emptiness: his body loses its corporeality, it evaporates, it is deprived of reality, life, voice, and the noises caused by his moving about, in order to be changed into a mute image, flickering an instant on the screen, then vanishing into silence . . . The projector will play with his shadow before the public, and he himself must be content to play before the camera.'[17] This situation might also be characterized as follows: for the first time – and this is the effect of the film – man has to operate with his whole living person, yet forgoing its aura. For aura is tied to his presence; there can be no replica of it. The aura which, on the stage, emanates from Macbeth, cannot be separated for the spectators from that of the actor. However, the singularity of the shot in the studio is that the camera is substituted for the public. Consequently, the aura that envelops the actor vanishes, and with it the aura of the figure he portrays.

It is not surprising that it should be a dramatist such as Pirandello who, in characterizing the film, inadvertently touches on the very crisis in which we see the theatre. Any thorough study proves that there is indeed no greater contrast than that of the stage play to a work of art that is completely subject to or, like the film, founded in mechanical reproduction. Experts have long recognized that in the film 'the greatest effects are almost always obtained by "acting" as little as possible . . .' In 1932 Rudolf Arnheim saw 'the latest trend . . . in treating the actor as a stage prop chosen for its characteristics and . . . inserted at the proper place.'[18] With this idea something else is closely connected. The stage actor identifies himself with the character of his role. The film actor very often is denied this opportunity. His creation is by no means all of a piece; it is composed of many separate performances. Besides certain fortuitous considerations, such as cost of studio, availability of fellow players, décor, etc., there are elementary necessities of equipment that split the actor's work into a series of mountable episodes. In particular, lighting and its installation require the presentation of an event that, on the screen, unfolds as a rapid and unified scene, in a sequence of separate shootings which may take hours at the studio; not to mention more obvious montage. Thus a jump from the window can be shot in the studio as a jump from a scaffold, and the ensuing flight, if need be, can be shot weeks later when outdoor scenes are taken. Far more paradoxical cases can easily be construed. Let us assume that an actor is supposed to be startled by a knock at the door. If his reaction is not satisfactory, the director can resort to an expedient: when the actor happens to be at the studio again he has a shot fired behind him without his being forewarned of it. The frightened reaction can be shot now and be cut into the screen version. Nothing more strikingly shows that art has left the realm of the 'beautiful semblance' which, so far, had been taken to be the only sphere where art could thrive.

X

The feeling of strangeness that overcomes the actor before the camera, as Pirandello describes it, is basically of the same kind as the estrangement felt before one's own image in the mirror. But now the reflected image has become separable, transportable. And where is it transported? Before the public.[19] Never for a moment does the screen actor cease to be conscious of this fact. While facing the camera he knows that ultimately he will face the public, the consumers who constitute the market. This market, where he offers not only his labour but also his whole self, his heart and soul, is beyond his reach. During the shooting he has as little contact with it as any article made in a factory. This may contribute to that oppression, that new anxiety which, according to Pirandello, grips the actor before the camera. The film responds to the shrivelling of the aura with an artificial build-up of the 'personality' outside the studio. The cult of the movie star, fostered by the money of the film industry, preserves not the unique aura of the person but the 'spell of the personality,' the phony spell of a commodity. So long as the movie-makers' capital sets the fashion, as a rule no other revolutionary merit can be accredited to today's film than the promotion of a revolutionary criticism of traditional concepts of art. We do not deny that in some cases today's film can also promote revolutionary criticism of social conditions, even of the distribution of property. However, our present study is no more specifically concerned with this than is the film production of Western Europe.

It is inherent in the technique of the film as well as that of sports that everybody who witnesses its accomplishments is somewhat of an expert. This is obvious to anyone listening to a group of newspaper boys leaning on their bicycles and discussing the outcome of a bicycle race. It is not for nothing that newspaper publishers arrange races for their delivery boys. These arouse great interest among the participants, for the victor has an opportunity to rise from delivery boy to professional racer. Similarly, the newsreel offers everyone the opportunity to rise from passer-by to movie extra. In this way any man might even find himself part of a work of art, as witness Vertoff's *Three Songs About Lenin* or Ivens' *Borinage*. Any man today can lay claim to being filmed. This claim can best be elucidated by a comparative look at the historical situation of contemporary literature.

For centuries a small number of writers were confronted by many thousands of readers. This changed toward the end of the last century. With the increasing extension of the press, which kept placing new political, religious, scientific, professional, and local organs before the readers, an increasing number of readers became writers – at first, occasional ones. It began with the daily press opening to its readers space for 'letters to the editor.' And today there is hardly a gainfully employed European who could not, in principle, find an opportunity to publish somewhere or other comments on his work, grievances, documentary reports, or that sort of thing. Thus, the distinction between author and public is about to lose its basic character. The difference becomes merely functional; it may vary from case to case. At any moment the reader is ready to turn into a writer. As expert, which he had to become willy-nilly in an extremely specialized work process, even if only in some minor respect, the reader gains access to authorship. In the Soviet Union work itself is given a voice. To present it verbally is part of a man's ability to perform the work. Literary licence is now founded on polytechnic rather than specialized training and thus becomes common property.[20]

All this can easily be applied to the film, where transitions that in literature took centuries have come about in a decade. In cinematic practice, particularly in Russia, this change-over has partially become established reality. Some of the players whom we meet in Russian films are not actors in our sense but people who portray *themselves* – and primarily in their own work process. In Western Europe the capitalistic exploitation of the film denies consideration to modern man's legitimate claim to being reproduced. Under these circumstances the film industry is trying hard to spur the interest of the masses through illusion-promoting spectacles and dubious speculations.

XI

The shooting of a film, especially of a sound film, affords a spectacle unimaginable anywhere at any time before this. It presents a process in which it is impossible to assign to a spectator a viewpoint which would exclude from the actual scene such extraneous accessories as camera equipment, lighting machinery, staff assistants, etc. – unless his eye were on a line parallel with the lens. This circumstance, more than any other, renders superficial and insignificant any possible similarity between a scene in the studio and one on the stage. In the theatre one is well aware of the place from which the play cannot immediately be detected as illusionary. There is no such place for the movie scene that is being shot. Its illusionary nature is that of the second degree, the result of cutting. That is to say, in the studio the mechanical equipment has penetrated so deeply into reality that its pure aspect freed from the foreign substance of equipment is the result of a special procedure, namely, the shooting by the specially adjusted camera and the mounting of the shot together with other similar ones. The equipment-free aspect of reality here has become the height of artifice; the sight of immediate reality has become an orchid in the land of technology.

Even more revealing is the comparison of these circumstances, which differ so much from those of the theatre, with the situation in painting. Here the question is: How does the cameraman compare with the painter? To answer this we take recourse to an analogy with a surgical operation. The surgeon represents the polar opposite of the magician. The magician heals a sick person by the laying on of hands; the surgeon cuts into the patient's body. The magician maintains the natural distance between the patient and himself; though he reduces it very slightly by the laying on of hands, he greatly increases it by virtue of his authority. The surgeon does exactly the reverse; he greatly diminishes the distance between himself and the patient by penetrating into the patient's body, and increases it but little by the caution with which his hand moves among the organs. In short, in contrast to the magician – who is still hidden in the medical practitioner – the surgeon at the decisive moment abstains from facing the patient man to man; rather, it is through the operation that he penetrates into him.

Magician and surgeon compare to painter and cameraman. The painter maintains in his work a natural distance from reality, the cameraman penetrates deeply into its web.[21] There is a tremendous difference between the pictures they obtain. That of the painter is a total one, that of the cameraman consists of multiple fragments which are assembled under a new law. Thus, for contemporary man the representation of reality by the film is incomparably more significant than that of the painter, since it offers, precisely because of the thoroughgoing permeation of reality with mechanical equipment, an aspect of reality which is free of all equipment. And that is what one is entitled to ask from a work of art.

XII

Mechanical reproduction of art changes the reaction of the masses toward art. The reactionary attitude toward a Picasso painting changes into the progressive reaction toward a Chaplin movie. The progressive reaction is characterized by the direct, intimate fusion of visual and emotional enjoyment with the orientation of the expert. Such fusion is of great social significance. The greater the decrease in the social significance of an art form, the sharper the distinction between criticism and enjoyment by the public. The conventional is uncritically enjoyed, and the truly new is criticized with aversion. With regard to the screen, the critical and the receptive attitudes of the public coincide. The decisive reason for this is that individual reactions are predetermined by the mass audience response they are about to produce, and this is nowhere more pronounced than in the film. The moment these responses become manifest they control each other. Again, the comparison with painting is fruitful. A painting has always had an excellent chance to be viewed by one person or by a few. The simultaneous contemplation of paintings by a large public, such as developed in the nineteenth century, is an early symptom of the crisis of painting, a crisis which was by no means occasioned exclusively by photography but rather in a relatively independent manner by the appeal of art works to the masses.

Painting simply is in no position to present an object for simultaneous collective experience, as it was possible for architecture at all times, for the epic poem in the past, and for the movie today. Although this circumstance in itself should not lead one to conclusions about the social role of painting, it does constitute a serious threat as soon as painting, under special conditions and, as it were, against its nature, is confronted directly by the masses. In the churches and monasteries of the Middle Ages and at the princely courts up to the end of the eighteenth century, a collective reception of paintings did not occur simultaneously, but by graduated and hierarchized mediation. The change that has come about is an expression of the particular conflict in which painting was implicated by the mechanical reproducibility of paintings. Although paintings began to be publicly exhibited in galleries and salons, there was no way for the masses to organize and control themselves in their reception.[22] Thus the same public which responds in a progressive manner toward a grotesque film is bound to respond in a reactionary manner to surrealism.

XIII

The characteristics of the film lie not only in the manner in which man presents himself to mechanical equipment but also in the manner in which, by means of this apparatus, man can represent his environment. A glance at occupational psychology illustrates the testing capacity of the equipment. Psychoanalysis illustrates it in a different perspective. The film has enriched our field of perception with methods which can be illustrated by those of Freudian theory. Fifty years ago, a slip of the tongue passed more or less unnoticed. Only exceptionally may such a slip have revealed dimensions of depth in a conversation which had seemed to be taking its course on the surface. Since the *Psychopathology of Everyday Life* things have changed. This book isolated and made analyzable things which had heretofore floated along unnoticed in the broad stream of perception. For the entire spectrum of optical, and now also acoustical, perception the film has brought about a similar deepening of apperception. It is only an obverse of this fact that behaviour items shown in a movie can be analyzed much more precisely and from more points of views than those presented on paintings or on the stage. As compared with painting, filmed behaviour lends itself more readily to analysis because of its incomparably more precise statements of the situation. In comparison with the stage scene, the filmed behaviour item lends itself more readily to analysis because it can be isolated more easily. This circumstance derives its chief importance from its tendency to promote the mutual penetration of art and science. Actually, of a screened behaviour item which is neatly brought out in a certain situation, like a muscle of a body, it is difficult to say which is more fascinating, its artistic value or its value for science. To demonstrate the identity of the artistic and scientific uses of photography which heretofore usually were separated will be one of the revolutionary functions of the film.[23]

By close-ups of the things around us, by focusing on hidden details of familiar objects, by exploring commonplace milieus under the ingenious guidance of the camera, the film, on the one hand, extends our comprehension of the necessities which rule our lives; on the other hand, it manages to assure us of an immense and unexpected field of action. Our taverns and our metropolitan streets, our offices and furnished rooms, our railroad stations and our factories appeared to have us locked up hopelessly. Then came the film and burst this prison-world asunder by the dynamite of the tenth of a second, so that now, in the midst of its far-flung ruins and debris, we calmly and adventurously go travelling. With the close-up, space expands; with slow motion, movement is extended. The enlargement of a snapshot does not simply render more precise what in any case was visible, though unclear: it reveals entirely new structural formations of the subject. So, too, slow motion not only presents familiar qualities of movement but reveals in them entirely unknown ones 'which, far from looking like retarded rapid movements, give the effect of singularly gliding, floating, supernatural motions.'[24] Evidently a different nature opens itself to the camera than opens to the naked eye — if only because an unconsciously penetrated space is substituted for a space consciously explored by man. Even if one has a general knowledge of the way people walk, one knows nothing of a person's posture during the fractional second of a stride. The act of reaching for a lighter or a spoon is familiar routine, yet we hardly know what really goes on between hand and metal, not to mention how this fluctuates with our moods. Here the camera intervenes with the resources of its lowerings and liftings, its interruptions and isolations, its extensions and accelerations, its enlargements and reductions. The camera introduces us to unconscious optics as does psychoanalysis to unconscious impulses.

XIV

One of the foremost tasks of art has always been the creation of a demand which could be fully satisfied only later.[25] The history of every art form shows critical epochs in which a certain art form aspires to effects which could be fully obtained only with a changed technical standard, that is to say, in a new art form. The extravagances and crudities of art which thus appear, particularly in the so-called decadent epochs, actually arise from the nucleus of its richest historical energies. In recent years, such barbarisms were abundant in Dadaism. It is only now that its impulse becomes discernible: Dadaism attempted to create by pictorial – and literary – means the effects which the public today seeks in the film.

Every fundamentally new, pioneering creation of demands will carry beyond its goal. Dadaism did so to the extent that it sacrificed the market values which are so characteristic of the film in favor of higher ambitions – though of course it was not conscious of such intentions as here described. The Dadaists attached much less importance to the sales value of their work than to its uselessness for contemplative immersion. The studied degradation of their material was not the least of their means to achieve this uselessness. Their poems are 'word salad' containing obscenities and every imaginable waste product of language. The same is true of their paintings, on which they mounted buttons and tickets. What they intended and achieved was a relentless destruction of the aura of their creations, which they branded as reproductions with the very means of production. Before a painting of Arp's or a poem by August Stramm it is impossible to take time for contemplation and evaluation as one would before a canvas of Derain's or a poem by Rilke. In the decline of middle-class society, contemplation became a school for asocial behaviour; it was countered by distraction as a variant of social conduct.[26] Dadaistic activities actually assured a rather vehement distraction by making works of art the centre of scandal. One requirement was foremost: to outrage the public.

From an alluring appearance or persuasive structure of sound the work of art of the Dadaists became an instrument of ballistics. It hit the spectator like a bullet, it happened to him, thus acquiring a tactile quality. It promoted a demand for the film, the distracting element of which is also primarily tactile, being based on changes of place and focus which periodically assail the spectator. Let us compare the screen on which a film unfolds with the canvas of a painting. The painting invites the spectator to contemplation; before it the spectator can abandon himself to his associations. Before the movie frame he cannot do so. No sooner has his eye grasped a scene than it is already changed. It cannot be arrested. Duhamel, who detests the film and knows nothing of its significance, though something of its structure, notes this circumstance as follows: 'I can no longer think what I want to think. My thoughts have been replaced by moving images.'[27] The spectator's process of association in view of these images is indeed interrupted by their constant, sudden change. This constitutes the shock effect of the film, which, like all shocks, should be cushioned by heightened presence of mind.[28] By means of its technical structure, the film has taken the physical shock effect out of the wrappers in which Dadaism had, as it were, kept it inside the moral shock effect.[29]

XV

The mass is a matrix from which all traditional behaviour toward works of art issues today in a new form. Quantity has been transmuted into quality. The greatly increased mass of participants has produced a change in the mode of participation. The fact that the new mode of participation first appeared in a disreputable form must not confuse the spectator. Yet some people have launched spirited attacks against precisely this superficial aspect. Among these, Duhamel has expressed himself in the most radical manner. What he objects to most is the kind of participation which the movie elicits from the masses. Duhamel calls the movie 'a pastime for helots, a diversion for uneducated, wretched, worn-out creatures who are consumed by their worries . . ., a spectacle which requires no concentration and presupposes no intelligence . . ., which kindles no light in the heart and awakens no hope other than the ridiculous one of someday becoming a "star" in Los Angeles.'[30] Clearly, this is at bottom the same ancient lament that the masses seek distraction whereas art demands concentration from the spectator. That is a commonplace. The question remains whether it provides a platform for the analysis of the film. A closer look is needed here. Distraction and concentration from polar opposites which may be stated as follows: A man who concentrates before a work of art is absorbed by it. He enters into this work of art the way legend tells of the Chinese painter when he viewed his finished painting. In contrast, the distracted mass absorbs the work of art. This is most obvious with regard to buildings. Architecture has always represented the prototype of a work of art the reception of which is consummated by a collectivity in a state of distraction. The laws of its reception are most instructive.

Buildings have been man's companions since primeval times. Many art forms have developed and perished. Tragedy begins with the Greeks, is extinguished with them, and after centuries its 'rules' only are revived. The epic poem, which had its origin in the youth of nations, expires in Europe at the end of the Renaissance. Panel painting is a creation of the Middle Ages, and nothing guarantees its uninterrupted existence. But the human need for shelter is lasting. Architecture has never been idle. Its history is more ancient than that of any other art, and its claim to being a living force has significance in every attempt to comprehend the relationship of the masses to art. Buildings are appropriated in a twofold manner: by use and by perception – or rather, by touch and sight. Such appropriation cannot be understood in terms of the attentive concentration of a

THE WORK OF ART 49

tourist before a famous building. On the tactile side there is no counterpart to contemplation on the optical side. Tactile appropriation is accomplished not so much by attention as by habit. As regards architecture, habit determines to a large extent even optical reception. The latter, too, occurs much less through rapt attention than by noticing the object in incidental fashion. This mode of appropriation, developed with reference to architecture, in certain circumstances acquires canonical value. For the tasks which face the human apparatus of perception at the turning points of history cannot be solved by optical means, that is, by contemplation, alone. They are mastered gradually by habit, under the guidance of tactile appropriation.

The distracted person, too, can form habits. More, the ability to master certain tasks in a state of distraction proves that their solution has become a matter of habit. Distraction as provided by art presents a covert control of the extent to which new tasks have become soluble by apperception. Since, moreover, individuals are tempted to avoid such tasks, art will tackle the most difficult and most important ones where it is able to mobilize the masses. Today it does so in the film. Reception in a state of distraction, which is increasing noticeably in all fields of art and is symptomatic of profound changes in apperception, finds in the film its true means of exercise. The film with its shock effect meets this mode of reception halfway. The film makes the cult value recede into the background not only by putting the public in the position of the critic, but also by the fact that at the movies this position requires no attention. The public is an examiner, but an absent-minded one.

Epilogue

The growing proletarianization of modern man and the increasing formation of masses are two aspects of the same process. Fascism attempts to organize the newly created proletarian masses without affecting the property structure which the masses strive to eliminate. Fascism sees its salvation in giving these masses not their right, but instead a chance to express themselves.[31] The masses have a right to change property relations; Fascism seeks to give them an expression while preserving property. The logical result of Fascism is the introduction of aesthetics into political life. The violation of the masses, whom Fascism, with its *Führer* cult, forces to their knees, has its counterpart in the violation of an apparatus which is pressed into the production of ritual values.

All efforts to render politics aesthetic culminate in one thing: war. War and war only can set a goal for mass movements on the largest scale while respecting the traditional property system. This is the political formula for the situation. The technological formula may be stated as follows: Only war makes it possible to mobilize all of today's technical resources while maintaining the property system. It goes without saying that the Fascist apotheosis of war does not employ such arguments. Still, Marinetti says in his manifesto on the Ethiopian colonial war: 'For twenty-seven years we Futurists have rebelled against the branding of war as antiaesthetic . . . Accordingly we state: . . . War is beautiful because it establishes man's dominion over the subjugated machinery by means of gas masks, terrifying megaphones, flame throwers, and small tanks. War is beautiful because it initiates the dreamt-of metallization of the human body. War is beautiful because it enriches a flowering meadow with the fiery orchids of machine guns. War is beautiful because it combines the gunfire, the cannonades, the cease-fire, the scents, and the stench of putrefaction into a symphony. War is beautiful because it creates new architecture, like that of the big tanks, the geometrical formation flights, the smoke spirals from burning villages, and many others . . . Poets and artists of Futurism! . . . remember these principles of an aesthetics of war so that your struggle for a new literature and a new graphic art . . . may be illumined by them!'

This manifesto has the virtue of clarity. Its formulations deserve to be accepted by dialecticians. To the latter, the aesthetics of today's war appears as follows: If the natural utilization of productive forces is impeded by the property system, the increase in technical devices, in speed, and in the sources of energy will press for an unnatural utilization, and this is found in war. The destructiveness of war furnishes proof that society has not been mature enough to incorporate technology as its organ, that technology has not been sufficiently developed to cope with the elemental forces of society. The horrible features of imperialistic warfare are attributable to the discrepancy between the tremendous means of production and their inadequate utilization in the process of production – in other words, to unemployment and the lack of markets. Imperialistic war is a rebellion of technology which collects, in the form of 'human material,' the claims to which society has denied its natural material. Instead of draining rivers, society directs a human stream into a bed of trenches; instead of dropping seeds from airplanes, it drops incendiary bombs over cities; and through gas warfare the aura is abolished in a new way.

'*Fiat ars – pereat mundus*,' says Fascism, and, as Marinetti admits, expects war to supply the artistic gratification of a sense perception that has been changed by technology. This is evidently the consummation of '*l'art pour l'art*.' Mankind, which in Homer's time was an object of contemplation for the Olympian gods, now is one for itself. Its self-alienation has reached such a degree that it can experience its own destruction as an aesthetic pleasure of the first order. This is the situation of politics which Fascism is rendering aesthetic. Communism responds by politicizing art.

Notes

1   Quoted from Paul Valéry, *Aesthetics*, 'The Conquest of Ubiquity,' translated by Ralph Manheim, p. 225. Pantheon Books, Bollingen Series, New York, 1964.

2   Of course, the history of a work of art encompasses more than this. The history of the 'Mona Lisa,' for instance, encompasses the kind and number of its copies made in the 17th, 18th, and 19th centuries.

3   Precisely because authenticity is not reproducible, the intensive penetration of certain (mechanical) processes of reproduction was instrumental in differentiating and grading authenticity. To develop such differentiations was an important function of the trade in works of art. The invention of the woodcut may be said to have struck at the root of the quality of authenticity even before its late flowering. To be sure, at the time of its origin a medieval picture of the Madonna could not yet be said to be 'authentic.' It became

'authentic' only during the succeeding centuries and perhaps most strikingly so during the last one.

4   The poorest provincial staging of *Faust* is superior to a Faust film in that, ideally, it competes with the first performance at Weimar. Before the screen it is unprofitable to remember traditional contents which might come to mind before the stage – for instance, that Goethe's friend Johann Heinrich Merck is hidden in Mephisto, and the like.

5   Abel Gance, 'Le Temps de l'image est venu,' *L'Art cinématographique*, Vol. 2, pp. 94 f., Paris, 1927.

6   To satisfy the human interest of the masses may mean to have one's social function removed from the field of vision. Nothing guarantees that a portraitist of today, when painting a famous surgeon at the breakfast table in the midst of his family, depicts his social function more precisely than a painter of the 17th century who portrayed his medical doctors as representing this profession, like Rembrandt in his 'Anatomy Lesson.'

7   The definition of the aura as a 'unique phenomenon of a distance however close it may be' represents nothing but the formulation of the cult value of the work of art in categories of space and time perception. Distance is the opposite of closeness. The essentially distant object is the unapproachable one. Unapproachability is indeed a major quality of the cult image. True to its nature, it remains 'distant, however close it may be.' The closeness which one may gain from its subject matter does not impair the distance which it retains in its appearance.

8   To the extent to which the cult value of the painting is secularized the ideas of its fundamental uniqueness lose distinctness. In the imagination of the beholder the uniqueness of the phenomena which hold sway in the cult image is more and more displaced by the empirical uniqueness of the creator or of his creative achievement. To be sure, never completely so; the concept of authenticity always transcends mere genuineness. (This is particularly apparent in the collector who always retains some traces of the fetishist and who, by owning the work of art, shares in its ritual power.) Nevertheless, the function of the concept of authenticity remains determinate in the evaluation of art; with the secularization of art, authenticity displaces the cult value of the work.

9   In the case of films, mechanical reproduction is not, as with literature and painting, an external condition for mass distribution. Mechanical reproduction is inherent in the very technique of film production. This technique not only permits in the most direct way but virtually causes mass distribution. It enforces distribution because the production of a film is so expensive that an individual who, for instance, might afford to buy a painting no longer can afford to buy a film. In 1927 it was calculated that a major film, in order to pay its way, had to reach an audience of nine million. With the sound film, to be sure, a setback in its international distribution occurred at first: audiences became limited by language barriers. This coincided with the Fascist emphasis on national interests. It is more important to focus on this connection with Fascism than on this setback, which was soon minimized by synchronization. The simultaneity of both phenomena is attributable to the depression. The same disturbances which, on a larger scale, led to an attempt to maintain the existing property structure by sheer force led the endangered film capital to speed up the development of the sound film. The introduction of the sound film brought about a temporary relief, not only because it again brought the masses into the theatres but also because it merged new capital from the electrical industry with that of the film industry. Thus, viewed from the outside, the sound film promoted national interests, but seen from the inside it helped to internationalize film production even more than previously.

10   This polarity cannot come into its own in the aesthetics of Idealism. Its idea of beauty comprises these polar opposites without differentiating between them and consequently excludes their polarity. Yet in Hegel this polarity announces itself as clearly as possible within the limits of Idealism. We quote from his *Philosophy of History*:

'Images were known of old. Piety at an early time required them for worship, but it could do without *beautiful* images. These might even be disturbing. In every beautiful painting there is also something nonspiritual, merely external, but its spirit speaks to man through its beauty. Worshipping, conversely, is concerned with the work as an object, for it is but a spiritless stupor of the soul . . . Fine art has arisen . . . in the church . . ., although it has already gone beyond its principle as art.'

Likewise, the following passage from *The Philosophy of Fine Art* indicates that Hegel sensed a problem here.

'We are beyond the stage of reverence for works of art as divine and objects deserving our worship. The impression they produce is one of a more reflective kind, and the emotions they arouse require a higher test . . .'
— G. W.F. Hegel, *The Philosophy of Fine Art*, trans., with notes, by F.P.B. Osmaston, Vol. 1, p. 12, London, 1920

The transition from the first kind of artistic reception to the second characterizes the history of artistic reception in general. Apart from that, a certain oscillation between these two polar modes of reception can be demonstrated for each work of art. Take the Sistine Madonna. Since Hubert Grimme's research it has been known that the Madonna originally was painted for the purpose of exhibition. Grimme's research was inspired by the question: What is the purpose of the moulding in the foreground of the painting which the two cupids lean upon? How, Grimme asked further, did Raphael come to furnish the sky with two draperies? Research proved that the Madonna had been commissioned for the public lying-in-state of Pope Sixtus. The Popes lay in state in a certain side chapel of St Peter's. On that occasion Raphael's picture had been fastened in a nichelike background of the chapel, supported by the coffin. In this picture Raphael portrays the Madonna approaching the papal coffin in clouds from the background of the niche, which was demarcated by green drapes. At the obsequies of Sixtus a preeminent exhibition value of Raphael's picture was taken advantage of. Some time later it was placed on the high altar in the church of the Black Friars at Piacenza. The reason for this exile is to be found in the Roman rites which forbid the use of paintings exhibited at obsequies as cult objects on the high altar. This regulation devalued Raphael's picture to some degree. In order to obtain an adequate price nevertheless, the Papal See resolved to add to the bargain the tacit toleration of the picture above the high altar. To avoid attention the picture was given to the monks of the far-off provincial town.

11   Bertolt Brecht, on a different level, engaged in analogous reflections: 'If the concept of "work of art" can no longer be applied to the thing that emerges once the work is transformed into a commodity, we have to eliminate this concept with cautious care but without fear, lest we liquidate the function of the very thing as well. For it has to go through this phase without mental reservation, and not as noncommittal deviation from the straight path; rather, what happens here with the work of art will change it fundamentally and erase its past to such an extent that should the old concept be taken up again — and it will, why not? — it will no longer stir any memory of the thing it once designated.'

12   Abel Gance, op. cit., pp. 100–1.

13   Séverin-Mars, quoted by Abel Gance, op. cit., p. 100.

14   Alexandre Arnoux, *Cinéma pris*, 1929, p. 28.

15   Franz Werfel, 'Ein Sommernachtstraum, Ein Film von Shakespeare und Reinhardt,' *Neues Wiener Journal*, cited in *Lu* 15, November, 1935.

16   'The film . . . provides — or could provide — useful insight into the details of human actions . . . Character is never used as a source of motivation; the inner life of the persons never supplies the principal cause of the plot and seldom is its main result.'

(Bertolt Brecht, *Versuche*, 'Der Dreigroschenprozess,' p. 268.) The expansion of the field of the testable which mechanical equipment brings about for the actor corresponds to the extraordinary expansion of the field of the testable brought about for the individual through economic conditions. Thus, vocational aptitude tests become constantly more important. What matters in these tests are segmental performances of the individual. The film shot and the vocational aptitude test are taken before a committee of experts. The camera director in the studio occupies a place identical with that of the examiner during aptitude tests.

17   Luigi Pirandello, *Si Gira*, quoted by Léon Pierre-Quint, 'Signification du cinéma,' *L'Art cinématographique*, op. cit., pp. 14–15.

18   Rudolf Arnheim, *Film als Kunst*, Berlin, 1932, pp. 176f. In this context certain seemingly unimportant details in which the film director deviates from stage practices gain in interest. Such is the attempt to let the actor play without make-up, as made among others by Dreyer in his *Jeanne d'Arc*. Dreyer spent months seeking the forty actors who constitute the Inquisitors' tribunal. The search for these actors resembled that for stage properties that are hard to come by. Dreyer made every effort to avoid resemblances of age, build, and physiognomy. If the actor thus becomes a stage property, this latter, on the other hand, frequently functions as actor. At least it is not unusual for the film to assign a role to the stage property. Instead of choosing at random from a great wealth of examples, let us concentrate on a particularly convincing one. A clock that is working will always be a disturbance on the stage. There it cannot be permitted its function of measuring time. Even in a naturalistic play, astronomical time would clash with theatrical time. Under these circumstances it is highly revealing that the film can, whenever appropriate, use time as measured by a clock. From this more than from many other touches it may clearly be recognized that under certain circumstances each and every prop in a film may assume important functions. From here it is but one step to Pudovkin's statement that 'the playing of an actor which is connected with an object and is built around it . . . is always one of the strongest methods of cinematic construction.' (W. Pudovkin, *Filmregie und Filmmanuskript*, Berlin, 1928, p. 126.) The film is the first art form capable of demonstrating how matter plays tricks on man. Hence, films can be an excellent means of materialistic representation.

19   The change noted here in the method of exhibition caused by mechanical reproduction applies to politics as well. The present crisis of the bourgeois democracies comprises a crisis of the conditions which determine the public presentation of the rulers. Democracies exhibit a member of government directly and personally before the nation's representatives. Parliament is his public. Since the innovations of camera and recording equipment make it possible for the orator to become audible and visible to an unlimited number of persons, the presentation of the man of politics before camera and recording equipment becomes paramount. Parliaments, as much as theatres, are deserted. Radio and film not only affect the function of the professional actor but likewise the function of those who also exhibit themselves before this mechanical equipment, those who govern. Though their tasks may be different, the change affects equally the actor and the ruler. The trend is toward establishing controllable and transferable skills under certain social conditions. This results in a new selection, a selection before the equipment from which the star and the dictator emerge victorious.

20   The privileged character of the respective techniques is lost. Aldous Huxley writes:

> 'Advances in technology have led . . . to vulgarity . . . Process reproduction and the rotary press have made possible the indefinite multiplication of writing and pictures. Universal education and relatively high wages have created an enormous public who know how to read and can afford to buy reading and pictorial matter. A great industry has been called into existence in order to supply these commodities. Now, artistic talent is a very rare phenomenon; whence it follows . . . that, at every epoch and in all countries, most art has been bad. But the proportion of trash in this total

artistic output is greater now than at any other period. That it must be so is a matter of simple arithmetic. The population of Western Europe has a little more than doubled during the last century. But the amount of reading – and seeing – matter has increased, I should imagine, at least twenty and possibly fifty or even a hundred times. If there were n men of talent in a population of x millions, there will presumably be 2n men of talent among 2x millions. The situation may be summed up thus. For every page of print and pictures published a century ago, twenty or perhaps even a hundred pages are published today. But for every man of talent then living, there are now only two men of talent. It may be of course that, thanks to universal education, many potential talents which in the past would have been still-born are now enabled to realize themselves. Let us assume, then, that there are now three or even four men of talent to every one of earlier times. It still remains true to say that the consumption of reading – and seeing – matter has far outstripped the natural production of gifted writers and draughtsmen. It is the same with hearing-matter. Prosperity, the gramophone and the radio have created an audience of hearers who consume an amount of hearing-matter that has increased out of all proportion to the increase of population and the consequent natural increase of talented musicians. It follows from all this that in all the arts the output of trash is both absolutely and relatively greater than it was in the past; and that it must remain greater for just so long as the world continues to consume the present inordinate quantities of reading-matter, seeing-matter, and hearing-matter.'

– Aldous Huxley, *Beyond the Mexique Bay. A Traveller's Journal*, London, 1949, pp. 274 ff. First published in 1934.

This mode of observation is obviously not progressive.

21   The boldness of the cameraman is indeed comparable to that of the surgeon. Luc Durtain lists among specific technical sleights of hand those 'which are required in surgery in the case of certain difficult operations. I choose as an example a case of oto-rhinolaryngology; . . . the so-called endonasal perspective procedure; or I refer to the acrobatic tricks of larynx surgery which have to be performed following the reversed picture in the laryngoscope. I might also speak of ear surgery which suggests the precision work of watchmakers. What range of the most subtle muscular acrobatics is required from the man who wants to repair or save the human body! We have only to think of the couching of a cataract where there is virtually a debate of steel with nearly fluid tissue, or of the major abdominal operations (laparotomy).' – Luc Durtain, *op. cit.*

22   This mode of observation may seem crude, but as the great theoretician Leonardo has shown, crude modes of observation may at times be usefully adduced. Leonardo compares painting and music as follows: 'Painting is superior to music because, unlike unfortunate music, it does not have to die as soon as it is born . . . Music which is consumed in the very act of its birth is inferior to painting which the use of varnish has rendered eternal.' (Trattato I, 29.)

23   Renaissance painting offers a revealing analogy to this situation. The incomparable development of this art and its significance rested not least on the integration of a number of new sciences, or at least of new scientific data. Renaissance painting made use of anatomy and perspective, of mathematics, meteorology, and chromatology. Valéry writes: 'What could be further from us than the strange claim of a Leonardo to whom painting was a supreme goal and the ultimate demonstration of knowledge? Leonardo was convinced that painting demanded universal knowledge, and he did not even shrink from a theoretical analysis which to us is stunning because of its very depth and precision . . .' – Paul Valéry, *Pièces sur l'art*, 'Autour de Corot,' Paris, p. 191.

24   Rudolf Arnheim, loc. cit., p. 138.

25   'The work of art,' says André Breton, 'is valuable only in so far as it is vibrated by the

reflexes of the future.' Indeed, every developed art form intersects three lines of development. Technology works toward a certain form of art. Before the advent of the film there were photo booklets with pictures which flitted by the onlooker upon pressure of the thumb, thus portraying a boxing bout or a tennis match. Then there were the slot machines in bazaars; their picture sequences were produced by the turning of a crank.

Secondly, the traditional art forms in certain phases of their development strenuously work toward effects which later are effortlessly attained by the new ones. Before the rise of the movie the Dadaists' performances tried to create an audience reaction which Chaplin later evoked in a more natural way.

Thirdly, unspectacular social changes often promote a change in receptivity which will benefit the new art form. Before the movie had begun to create its public, pictures that were no longer immobile captivated an assembled audience in the so-called *Kaiserpanorama*. Here the public assembled before a screen into which stereoscopes were mounted, one to each beholder. By a mechanical process individual pictures appeared briefly before the stereoscopes, then made way for others. Edison still had to use similar devices in presenting the first movie strip before the film screen and projection were known. This strip was presented to a small public which stared into the apparatus in which the succession of pictures was reeling off. Incidentally, the institution of the *Kaiserpanorama* shows very clearly a dialectic of the development. Shortly before the movie turned the reception of pictures into a collective one, the individual viewing of pictures in these swiftly outmoded establishments came into play once more with an intensity comparable to that of the ancient priest beholding the statue of a divinity in the cella.

26   The theological archetype of this contemplation is the awareness of being alone with one's God. Such awareness, in the heyday of the bourgeoisie, went to strengthen the freedom to shake off clerical tutelage. During the decline of the bourgeoisie this awareness had to take into account the hidden tendency to withdraw from public affairs those forces which the individual draws upon in his communion with God.

27   Georges Duhamel, *Scènes de la vie future*, Paris, 1930, p. 52.

28   The film is the art form that is in keeping with the increased threat to his life which modern man has to face. Man's need to expose himself to shock effects is his adjustment to the dangers threatening him. The film corresponds to profound changes in the apperceptive apparatus – changes that are experienced on an individual scale by the man in the street in big-city traffic, on a historical scale by every present-day citizen.

29   As for Dadaism, insights important for Cubism and Futurism are to be gained from the movie. Both appear as deficient attempts of art to accommodate the pervasion of reality by the apparatus. In contrast to the film, these schools did not try to use the apparatus as such for the artistic presentation of reality, but aimed at some sort of alloy in the joint presentation of reality and apparatus. In Cubism, the premonition that this apparatus will be structurally based on optics plays a dominant part; in Futurism, it is the premonition of the effects of this apparatus which are brought out by the rapid sequence of the film strip.

30   Duhamel, op. cit., p. 58.

31   One technical feature is significant here, especially with regard to newsreels, the propagandist importance of which can hardly be overestimated. Mass reproduction is aided especially by the reproduction of masses. In big parades and monster rallies, in sports events, and in war, all of which nowadays are captured by camera and sound recording, the masses are brought face to face with themselves. This process, whose significance need not be stressed, is intimately connected with the development of the techniques of reproduction and photography. Mass movements are usually discerned more clearly by a camera than by the naked eye. A bird's-eye view best captures gatherings of hundreds of thousands. And even though such a view may be as accessible to the human eye as it is to the camera, the image received by the eye cannot be enlarged the way a negative is enlarged. This means that mass movements, including war, constitute a form of human behaviour which particularly favours mechanical equipment.

Suggestions for further reading

Adorno, Theodor and Horkheimer, Max, *Dialectic of Enlightenment,* trans. John Cumming, London and New York: Verso, 1997.

Berger, John, *Ways of Seeing,* London: BBC/Penguin, 1972.

Smith, Gary (ed.), *Benjamin: Philosophy, Aesthetics, History,* Chicago: University of Chicago Press, 1989.

Chapter 6

Jacques Lacan

'THE MIRROR STAGE AS FORMATIVE OF THE FUNCTION OF THE I AS REVEALED IN PSYCHOANALYTIC EXPERIENCE', 1949

Delivered at the 16th International Congress of Psychoanalysis, Zürich, July 17, 1949

THE CONCEPTION OF the mirror stage that I introduced at our last congress, thirteen years ago, has since become more or less established in the practice of the French group. However, I think it worthwhile to bring it again to your attention, especially today, for the light it sheds on the formation of the *I* as we experience it in psychoanalysis. It is an experience that leads us to oppose any philosophy directly issuing from the *Cogito*.

Some of you may recall that this conception originated in a feature of human behaviour illuminated by a fact of comparative psychology. The child, at an age when he is for a time, however short, outdone by the chimpanzee in instrumental intelligence, can nevertheless already recognize as such his own image in a mirror. This recognition is indicated in the illuminative mimicry of the *Aha-Erlebnis*, which Köhler sees as the expression of situational apperception, an essential stage of the act of intelligence.

This act, far from exhausting itself, as in the case of the monkey, once the image has been mastered and found empty, immediately rebounds in the case of the child in a series of gestures in which he experiences in play the relation between the movements assumed in the image and the reflected environment, and between this virtual complex and the reality it reduplicates – the child's own body, and the persons and things, around him.

This event can take place, as we have known since Baldwin, from the age of six months, and its repetition has often made me reflect upon the startling spectacle of the infant in front of the mirror. Unable as yet to walk, or even to stand up, and held tightly as he is by some support, human or artificial (what, in France, we call a '*trotte-bébé*'), he nevertheless overcomes, in a flutter of jubilant activity, the obstructions of his support and, fixing his attitude in a slightly leaning-forward position, in order to hold it in his gaze, brings back an instantaneous aspect of the image.

For me, this activity retains the meaning I have given it up to the age of eighteen months. This meaning discloses a libidinal dynamism, which has hitherto remained problematic, as well as an ontological structure of the human world that accords with my reflections on paranoiac knowledge.

We have only to understand the mirror stage *as an identification*, in the full sense that analysis gives to the term: namely, the transformation that takes place in the subject when he assumes an image – whose predestination to this phase-effect is sufficiently indicated by the use, in analytic theory, of the ancient term *imago*.

This jubilant assumption of his specular image by the child at the *infans* stage, still sunk in his motor incapacity and nursling dependence, would seem to exhibit in an exemplary situation the symbolic matrix in which the *I* is precipitated in a primordial form, before it is objectified in the dialectic of identification with the other, and before language restores to it, in the universal, its function as subject.

This form would have to be called the Ideal-I,[1] if we wished to incorporate it into our usual register, in the sense that it will also be the source of secondary identifications, under which term I would place the functions of libidinal normalization. But the important point is that this form situates the agency of the ego, before its social determination, in a fictional direction, which will always remain irreducible for the individual alone, or rather, which will only rejoin the coming-into-being (*le devenir*) of the subject asymptotically, whatever the success of the dialectical syntheses by which he must resolve as *I* his discordance with his own reality.

The fact is that the total form of the body by which the subject anticipates in a mirage the maturation of his power is given to him only as *Gestalt*, that is to say, in an exteriority in which this form is certainly more constituent than constituted, but in which it appears to him above all in a contrasting size (*un relief de stature*) that fixes it and in a symmetry that inverts it, in contrast with the turbulent movements that the subject feels are animating him. Thus, this *Gestalt* – whose pregnancy should be regarded as bound up with the species, though its motor style remains scarcely recognizable – by these two aspects of its appearance, symbolizes the mental permanence of the *I*, at the same time as it prefigures its alienating destination; it is still pregnant with the correspondences that unite the *I* with the statue in which man projects himself, with the phantoms that dominate him, or with the automaton in which, in an ambiguous relation, the world of his own making tends to find completion.

Indeed, for the *imagos* – whose veiled faces it is our privilege to see in outline in our daily experience and in the penumbra of symbolic efficacity[2] – the mirror-image would seem to be the threshold of the visible world, if we go by the mirror disposition that the *image of one's own body* presents in hallucinations or dreams, whether it concerns its individual features, or even its infirmities, or its object-projections; or if we observe the role of the mirror apparatus in the appearances of the *double*, in which psychical realities, however heterogeneous, are manifested.

That a *Gestalt* should be capable of formative effects in the organism is attested by a piece of biological experimentation that is itself so alien to the idea of psychical causality that it cannot bring itself to formulate its results in these terms. It nevertheless recognizes that it is a necessary condition for the maturation of the gonad of the female pigeon that it should see another member of its species, of either sex; so sufficient in itself is this condition that the desired effect may be obtained merely by placing the individual within reach of the field of reflection of a mirror. Similarly, in the case of the migratory locust, the transition within a generation from the solitary to the gregarious form can be obtained by exposing the individual, at a certain stage, to the exclusively visual action of a similar image, provided it is animated by movements of a style sufficiently close to that character-istic of the species. Such facts are inscribed in an order of homeomorphic identifi-cation that would itself fall within the larger question of the meaning of beauty as both formative and erogenic.

But the facts of mimicry are no less instructive when conceived as cases of heteromorphic identification, in as much as they raise the problem of the significa-tion of space for the living organism – psychological concepts hardly seem less appropriate for shedding light on these matters than ridiculous attempts to reduce them to the supposedly supreme law of adaptation. We have only to recall how Roger Caillois (who was then very young, and still fresh from his breach with the sociological school in which he was trained) illuminated the subject by using the term '*legendary psychasthenia*' to classify morphological mimicry as an obsession with space in its derealizing effect.

I have myself shown in the social dialectic that structures human knowledge as paranoiac[3] why human knowledge has greater autonomy than animal knowledge in relation to the field of force of desire, but also why human knowledge is determined in that 'little reality' (*ce peu de réalité*), which the Surrealists, in their restless way, saw as its limitation. These reflections lead me to recognize in the spatial captation manifested in the mirror-stage, even before the social dialectic, the effect in man of an organic insufficiency in his natural reality – in so far as any meaning can be given to the word 'nature'.

I am led, therefore, to regard the function of the mirror-stage as a particular case of the function of the *imago*, which is to establish a relation between the organism and its reality – or, as they say, between the *Innenwelt* and the *Umwelt*.

In man, however, this relation to nature is altered by a certain dehiscence at the heart of the organism, a primordial Discord betrayed by the signs of uneasiness and motor unco-ordination of the neo-natal months. The objective notion of the anatomical incompleteness of the pyramidal system and likewise the presence of certain humoral residues of the maternal organism confirm the view I have formulated as the fact of a real *specific prematurity of birth* in man.

It is worth noting, incidentally, that this is a fact recognized as such by embryologists, by the term *foetalization*, which determines the prevalence of the so-called superior apparatus of the neurax, and especially of the cortex, which psycho-surgical operations lead us to regard as the intra-organic mirror.

This development is experienced as a temporal dialectic that decisively pro-jects the formation of the individual into history. The *mirror stage* is a drama whose internal thrust is precipitated from insufficiency to anticipation – and which manufactures for the subject, caught up in the lure of spatial identification, the succession of phantasies that extends from a fragmented body-image to a form of its totality that I shall call orthopaedic — and, lastly, to the assumption of the armour of an alienating identity, which will mark with its rigid structure the subject's entire mental development. Thus, to break out of the circle of the *Innenwelt* into the *Umwelt* generates the inexhaustible quadrature of the ego's verifications.

This fragmented body — which term I have also introduced into our system of theoretical references — usually manifests itself in dreams when the movement of the analysis encounters a certain level of aggressive disintegration in the individual. It then appears in the form of disjointed limbs, or of those organs represented in exoscopy, growing wings and taking up arms for intestinal persecutions — the very same that the visionary Hieronymus Bosch has fixed, for all time, in painting, in their ascent from the fifteenth century to the imaginary zenith of modern man. But this form is even tangibly revealed at the organic level, in the lines of 'fragilization' that define the anatomy of phantasy, as exhibited in the schizoid and spasmodic symptoms of hysteria.

Correlatively, the formation of the *I* is symbolized in dreams by a fortress, or a stadium — its inner arena and enclosure, surrounded by marshes and rubbish-tips, dividing it into two opposed fields of contest where the subject flounders in quest of the lofty, remote inner castle whose form (sometimes juxtaposed in the same scenario) symbolizes the id in a quite startling way. Similarly, on the mental plane, we find realized the structures of fortified works, the metaphor of which arises spontaneously, as if issuing from the symptoms themselves, to designate the mechanisms of obsessional neurosis — inversion, isolation, reduplication, cancellation and displacement.

But if we were to build on these subjective givens alone — however little we free them from the condition of experience that makes us see them as partaking of the nature of a linguistic technique — our theoretical attempts would remain exposed to the charge of projecting themselves into the unthinkable of an absolute subject. This is why I have sought in the present hypothesis, grounded in a conjunction of objective data, the guiding grid for a *method of symbolic reduction*.

It establishes in the *defences of the ego* a genetic order, in accordance with the wish formulated by Miss Anna Freud, in the first part of her great work, and situates (as against a frequently expressed prejudice) hysterical repression and its returns at a more archaic stage than obsessional inversion and its isolating processes, and the latter in turn as preliminary to paranoic alienation, which dates from the deflection of the specular *I* into the social *I*.

This moment in which the mirror-stage comes to an end inaugurates, by the identification with the *image* of the counterpart and the drama of primordial jealousy (so well brought out by the school of Charlotte Bühler in the phenomenon of infantile *transitivism*), the dialectic that will henceforth link the *I* to socially elaborated situations.

It is this moment that decisively tips the whole of human knowledge into mediatization through the desire of the other, constitutes its objects in an abstract equivalence by the co-operation of others, and turns the I into that apparatus for which every instinctual thrust constitutes a danger, even though it should correspond to a natural maturation — the very normalization of this maturation being henceforth dependent, in man, on a cultural mediation as exemplified, in the case of the sexual object, by the Oedipus complex.

In the light of this conception, the term primary narcissism, by which analytic doctrine designates the libidinal investment characteristic of that moment, reveals in those who invented it the most profound awareness of semantic latencies. But it also throws light on the dynamic opposition between this libido and the sexual libido, which the first analysts tried to define when they invoked destructive and, indeed, death instincts, in order to explain the evident connection between the narcissistic libido and the alienating function of the *I*, the aggressivity it releases in any relation to the other, even in a relation involving the most Samaritan of aid.

In fact, they were encountering that existential negativity whose reality is so vigorously proclaimed by the contemporary philosophy of being and nothingness.

But unfortunately that philosophy grasps negativity only within the limits of a self-sufficiency of consciousness, which, as one of its premises, links to the *méconnaissances* that constitute the ego, the illusion of autonomy to which it entrusts itself. This flight of fancy, for all that it draws, to an unusual extent, on borrowings from psychoanalytic experience, culminates in the pretention of providing an existential psychoanalysis.

At the culmination of the historical effort of a society to refuse to recognize that it has any function other than the utilitarian one, and in the anxiety of the individual confronting the 'concentrational'[4] form of the social bond that seems to arise to crown this effort, existentialism must be judged by the explanations it gives of the subjective impasses that have indeed resulted from it; a freedom that is never more authentic than when it is within the walls of a prison; a demand for commitment, expressing the impotence of a pure consciousness to master any situation; a voyeuristic-sadistic idealization of the sexual relation; a personality that realizes itself only in suicide; a consciousness of the other than can be satisfied only by Hegelian murder.

These propositions are opposed by all our experience, in so far as it teaches us not to regard the ego as centred on the *perception-consciousness system*, or as organized by the 'reality principle' – a principle that is the expression of a scientific prejudice most hostile to the dialectic of knowledge. Our experience shows that we should start instead from the *function of méconnaissance* that characterizes the ego in all its structures, so markedly articulated by Miss Anna Freud. For, if the *Verneinung* represents the patent form of that function, its effects will, for the most part, remain latent, so long as they are not illuminated by some light reflected on to the level of fatality, which is where the id manifests itself.

We can thus understand the inertia characteristic of the formations of the *I*, and find there the most extensive definition of neurosis – just as the captation of the subject by the situation gives us the most general formula for madness, not only the madness that lies behind the walls of asylums, but also the madness that deafens the world with its sound and fury.

The sufferings of neurosis and psychosis are for us a schooling in the passions of the soul, just as the beam of the psychoanalytic scales, when we calculate the tilt of its threat to entire communities, provides us with an indication of the deadening of the passions in society.

At this junction of nature and culture, so persistently examined by modern anthropology, psychoanalysis alone recognizes this knot of imaginary servitude that love must always undo again, or sever.

For such a task, we place no trust in altruistic feeling, we who lay bare the aggressivity that underlies the activity of the philanthropist, the idealist, the peda-gogue, and even the reformer.

In the recourse of subject to subject that we preserve, psychoanalysis may accompany the patient to the ecstatic limit of the '*Thou art that*', in which is revealed to him the cipher of his mortal destiny, but it is not in our mere power as practitioners to bring him to that point where the real journey begins.

Notes

1   Throughout this article I leave in its peculiarity the translation I have adopted for Freud's *Ideal-Ich* [i.e., 'je-idéal'], without further comment, other than to say that I have not maintained it since.

2   Cf. Claude Lévi-Strauss, *Structural Anthropology*, Chapter X.

3   Cf. 'Aggressivity in Psychoanalysis', p. 8 and *Écrits*, p. 180.

4   '*Concentrationnaire*', an adjective coined after World War II (this article was written in 1949) to describe the life of the concentration-camp. In the hands of certain writers it became, by extension, applicable to many aspects of 'modern' life [Tr.].

Suggestions for further reading

Lacan, Jacques, 'The Signification of the Phallus', in *Écrits: A Selection*, trans. Alan Sheridan, London: Tavistock, 1977, pp. 281–91.

Rose, Jacqueline, *Sexuality in the Field of Vision*, London: Verso, 1986.

Žižek, Slavoj, *Looking Awry: An Introduction to Jacques Lacan Through Popular Culture*, Cambridge, MA: MIT Press, 1991.

Chapter 7

Frantz Fanon

'THE FACT OF BLACKNESS', 1952

"**D**IRTY NIGGER!" OR simply, "Look, a Negro!"
I came into the world imbued with the will to find a meaning in things, my spirit filled with the desire to attain to the source of the world, and then I found that I was an object in the midst of other objects.

Sealed into that crushing objecthood, I turned beseechingly to others. Their attention was a liberation, running over my body suddenly abraded into nonbeing, endowing me once more with an agility that I had thought lost, and by taking me out of the world, restoring me to it. But just as I reached the other side, I stumbled, and the movements, the attitudes, the glances of the other fixed me there, in the sense in which a chemical solution is fixed by a dye. I was indignant; I demanded an explanation. Nothing happened. I burst apart. Now the fragments have been put together again by another self.

As long as the black man is among his own, he will have no occasion, except in minor internal conflicts, to experience his being through others. There is of course the moment of "being for others," of which Hegel speaks, but every ontology is made unattainable in a colonized and civilized society. It would seem that this fact has not been given sufficient attention by those who have discussed the question. In the *Weltanschauung* of a colonized people there is an impurity, a flaw that outlaws any ontological explanation. Someone may object that this is the case with every individual, but such an objection merely conceals a basic problem. Ontology— once it is finally admitted as leaving existence by the wayside—does not permit us to understand the being of the black man. For not only must the black man be black; he must be black in relation to the white man. Some critics will take it on themselves to remind us that this proposition has a converse. I say that this is false. The black man has no ontological resistance in the eyes of the white man. Over- night the Negro has been given two frames of reference within which he has had to place himself. His metaphysics, or, less pretentiously, his customs and the sources on which they were based, were wiped out because they were in conflict with a civilization that he did not know and that imposed itself on him.

The black man among his own in the twentieth century does not know at what moment his inferiority comes into being through the other. Of course I have talked about the black problem with friends, or, more rarely, with American Negroes. Together we protested, we asserted the equality of all men in the world. In the Antilles there was also that little gulf that exists among the almost-white, the mulatto, and the nigger. But I was satisfied with an intellectual understanding of these differences. It was not really dramatic. And then. . . .

And then the occasion arose when I had to meet the white man's eyes. An unfamiliar weight burdened me. The real world challenged my claims. In the white world the man of color encounters difficulties in the development of his bodily schema. Consciousness of the body is solely a negating activity. It is a third-person consciousness. The body is surrounded by an atmosphere of certain uncertainty. I know that if I want to smoke, I shall have to reach out my right arm and take the pack of cigarettes lying at the other end of the table. The matches, however, are in the drawer on the left, and I shall have to lean back slightly. And all these movements are made not out of habit but out of implicit knowledge. A slow composition of my *self* as a body in the middle of a spatial and temporal world— such seems to be the schema. It does not impose itself on me; it is, rather, a definitive structuring of the self and of the world—definitive because it creates a real dialectic between my body and the world.

For several years certain laboratories have been trying to produce a serum for "denegrification"; with all the earnestness in the world, laboratories have sterilized their test tubes, checked their scales, and embarked on researches that might make it possible for the miserable Negro to whiten himself and thus to throw off the burden of that corporeal malediction. Below the corporeal schema I had sketched a historico-racial schema. The elements that I used had been provided for me not by "residual sensations and perceptions primarily of a tactile, vestibular, kines-thetic, and visual character,"[1] but by the other, the white man, who had woven me out of a thousand details, anecdotes, stories. I thought that what I had in hand was to construct a physiological self, to balance space, to localize sensations, and here I was called on for more.

"Look, a Negro!" It was an external stimulus that flicked over me as I passed by. I made a tight smile.

"Look, a Negro!" It was true. It amused me.

"Look, a Negro!" The circle was drawing a bit tighter. I made no secret of my amusement.

"Mama, see the Negro! I'm frightened!" Frightened! Frightened! Now they were beginning to be afraid of me. I made up my mind to laugh myself to tears, but laughter had become impossible.

I could no longer laugh, because I already knew that there were legends, stories, history, and above all *historicity*, which I had learned about from Jaspers. Then, assailed at various points, the corporeal schema crumbled, its place taken by a racial epidermal schema. In the train it was no longer a question of being aware of my body in the third person but in a triple person. In the train I was given not one but two, three places. I had already stopped being amused. It was not that I was finding febrile coordinates in the world. I existed triply: I occupied space. I moved toward the other . . . and the evanescent other, hostile but not opaque, transparent, not there, disappeared. Nausea. . . .

I was responsible at the same time for my body, for my race, for my ancestors. I subjected myself to an objective examination, I discovered my blackness, my ethnic characteristics; and I was battered down by tom-toms, cannibalism, intellectual deficiency, fetishism, racial defects, slave-ships, and above all else, above all: "Sho' good eatin'."

On that day, completely dislocated, unable to be abroad with the other, the white man, who unmercifully imprisoned me, I took myself far off from my own presence, far indeed, and made myself an object. What else could it be for me but an amputation, an excision, a hemorrhage that spattered my whole body with black blood? But I did not want this revision, this thematization. All I wanted was to be a man among other men. I wanted to come lithe and young into a world that was ours and to help to build it together.

But I rejected all immunization of the emotions. I wanted to be a man, nothing but a man. Some identified me with ancestors of mine who had been enslaved or lynched: I decided to accept this. It was on the universal level of the intellect that I understood this inner kinship—I was the grandson of slaves in exactly the same way in which President Lebrun was the grandson of tax-paying, hard-working peasants. In the main, the panic soon vanished.

In America, Negroes are segregated. In South America, Negroes are whipped in the streets, and Negro strikers are cut down by machine-guns. In West Africa, the Negro is an animal. And there beside me, my neighbor in the university, who was born in Algeria, told me: "As long as the Arab is treated like a man, no solution is possible."

"Understand, my dear boy, color prejudice is something I find utterly foreign. . . . But of course, come in, sir, there is no color prejudice among us. . . . Quite, the Negro is a man like ourselves. . . . It is not because he is black that he is less intelligent than we are. . . . I had a Senegalese buddy in the army who was really clever. . . ."

Where am I to be classified? Or, if you prefer, tucked away?

"A Martinican, a native of 'our' old colonies."

Where shall I hide?

"Look at the nigger! . . . Mama, a Negro! . . . Hell, he's getting mad. . . . Take no notice, sir, he does not know that you are as civilized as we. . . ."

My body was given back to me sprawled out, distorted, recolored, clad in mourning in that white winter day. The Negro is an animal, the Negro is bad, the Negro is mean, the Negro is ugly; look, a nigger, it's cold, the nigger is shivering, the nigger is shivering because he is cold, the little boy is trembling because he is afraid of the nigger, the nigger is shivering with cold, that cold that goes through your bones, the handsome little boy is trembling because he thinks that the nigger is quivering with rage, the little white boy throws himself into his mother's arms: Mama, the nigger's going to eat me up.

All round me the white man, above the sky tears at its navel, the earth rasps under my feet, and there is a white song, a white song. All this whiteness that burns me. . . .

I sit down at the fire and I become aware of my uniform. I had not seen it. It is indeed ugly. I stop there, for who can tell me what beauty is?

Where shall I find shelter from now on? I felt an easily identifiable flood mounting out of the countless facets of my being. I was about to be angry. The fire was long since out, and once more the nigger was trembling.

"Look how handsome that Negro is! . . ."

"Kiss the handsome Negro's ass, madame!"

Shame flooded her face. At last I was set free from my rumination. At the same time I accomplished two things: I identified my enemies and I made a scene. A grand slam. Now one would be able to laugh.

The field of battle having been marked out, I entered the lists.

What? While I was forgetting, forgiving, and wanting only to love, my message was flung back in my face like a slap. The white world, the only honorable one, barred me from all participation. A man was expected to behave like a man. I was expected to behave like a black man—or at least like a nigger. I shouted a greeting to the world and the world slashed away my joy. I was told to stay within bounds, to go back where I belonged.

They would see, then! I had warned them, anyway. Slavery? It was no longer even mentioned, that unpleasant memory. My supposed inferiority? A hoax that it was better to laugh at. I forgot it all, but only on condition that the world not protect itself against me any longer. I had incisors to test. I was sure they were strong. And besides. . . .

What! When it was I who had every reason to hate, to despise, I was rejected? When I should have been begged, implored, I was denied the slightest recognition? I resolved, since it was impossible for me to get away from an *inborn complex*, to assert myself as a BLACK MAN. Since the other hesitated to recognize me, there remained only one solution: to make myself known.

In *Anti-Semite and Jew* (p. 95), Sartre says: "They [the Jews] have allowed themselves to be poisoned by the stereotype that others have of them, and they live in fear that their acts will correspond to this stereotype. . . . We may say that their conduct is perpetually overdetermined from the inside."

All the same, the Jew can be unknown in his Jewishness. He is not wholly what he is. One hopes, one waits. His actions, his behavior are the final determinant. He is a white man, and, apart from some rather debatable characteristics, he can sometimes go unnoticed. He belongs to the race of those who since the beginning of time have never known cannibalism. What an idea, to eat one's father! Simple enough, one has only not to be a nigger. Granted, the Jews are harassed—what am I thinking of? They are hunted down, exterminated, cremated. But these are little family quarrels. The Jew is disliked from the moment he is tracked down. But in my case everything takes on a *new* guise. I am given no chance. I am over-determined from without. I am the slave not of the "idea" that others have of me but of my own appearance.

I move slowly in the world, accustomed now to seek no longer for upheaval. I progress by crawling. And already I am being dissected under white eyes, the only real eyes. I am *fixed*. Having adjusted their microtomes, they objectively cut away slices of my reality. I am laid bare. I feel, I see in those white faces that it is not a new man who has come in, but a new kind of man, a new genus. Why, it's a Negro!

I slip into corners, and my long antennae pick up the catch-phrases strewn over the surface of things—nigger underwear smells of nigger—nigger teeth are white—nigger feet are big—the nigger's barrel chest—I slip into corners, I remain silent, I strive for anonymity, for invisibility. Look, I will accept the lot, as long as no one notices me!

"Oh, I want you to meet my black friend. . . . Aimé Césaire, a black man and a university graduate. . . . Marian Anderson, the finest of Negro singers. . . . Dr. Cobb, who invented white blood, is a Negro. . . . Here, say hello to my friend from Martinique (be careful, he's extremely sensitive) . . ."

Shame. Shame and self-contempt. Nausea. When people like me, they tell me it is in spite of my color. When they dislike me, they point out that it is not because of my color. Either way, I am locked into the infernal circle.

I turn away from these inspectors of the Ark before the Flood and I attach myself to my brothers, Negroes like myself. To my horror, they too reject me. They are almost white. And besides they are about to marry white women. They will have children faintly tinged with brown. Who knows, perhaps little by little. . . .

I had been dreaming.

"I want you to understand, sir, I am one of the best friends the Negro has in Lyon."

The evidence was there, unalterable. My blackness was there, dark and unarguable. And it tormented me, pursued me, disturbed me, angered me.

Negroes are savages, brutes, illiterates. But in my own case I knew that these statements were false. There was a myth of the Negro that had to be destroyed at all costs. The time had long since passed when a Negro priest was an occasion for wonder. We had physicians, professors, statesmen. Yes, but something out of the ordinary still clung to such cases. "We have a Senegalese history teacher. He is quite bright . . . Our doctor is colored. He is very gentle."

It was always the Negro teacher, the Negro doctor; brittle as I was becoming, I shivered at the slightest pretext. I knew, for instance, that if the physician made a mistake it would be the end of him and of all those who came after him. What could one expect, after all, from a Negro physician? As long as everything went well, he was praised to the skies, but look out, no nonsense, under any conditions! The black physician can never be sure how close he is to disgrace. I tell you, I was walled in: No exception was made for my refined manners, or my knowledge of literature, or my understanding of the quantum theory.

I requested, I demanded explanations. Gently, in the tone that one uses with a child, they introduced me to the existence of a certain view that was held by certain people, but, I was always told, "We must hope that it will very soon disappear." What was it? Color prejudice.

It [colour prejudice] is nothing more than the unreasoning hatred of one race for another, the contempt of the stronger and richer peoples for those whom they consider inferior to themselves, and the bitter resentment of those who are kept in subjection and are so frequently insulted. As colour is the most obvious outward manifestation of race it has been made the criterion by which men are judged, irrespective of

their social or educational attainments. The light-skinned races have
come to despise all those of a darker colour, and the dark-skinned
peoples will no longer accept without protest the inferior position to
which they have been relegated.[2]

I had read it rightly. It was hate; I was hated, despised, detested, not by the
neighbor across the street or my cousin on my mother's side, but by an entire race.
I was up against something unreasoned. The psychoanalysts say that nothing is
more traumatizing for the young child than his encounters with what is rational. I
would personally say that for a man whose only weapon is reason there is nothing
more neurotic than contact with unreason.

I felt knife blades open within me. I resolved to defend myself. As a good
tactician, I intended to rationalize the world and to show the white man that he
was mistaken.

In the Jew, Jean-Paul Sartre says, there is

> a sort of impassioned imperialism of reason: for he wishes not only to
> convince others that he is right; his goal is to persuade them that there
> is an absolute and unconditioned value to rationalism. He feels himself
> to be a missionary of the universal; against the universality of the
> Catholic religion, from which he is excluded, he asserts the "cathol-
> icity" of the rational, an instrument by which to attain to the truth and
> establish a spiritual bond among men.[3]

And, the author adds, though there may be Jews who have made intuition the basic
category of their philosophy, their intuition

> has no resemblance to the Pascalian subtlety of spirit, and it is this
> latter—based on a thousand imperceptible perceptions—which to the
> Jew seems his worst enemy. As for Bergson, his philosophy offers
> the curious appearance of an anti-intellectualist doctrine constructed
> entirely by the most rational and most critical of intelligences. It is
> through argument that he establishes the existence of pure duration, of
> philosophic intuition; and that very intuition which discovers duration
> or life, is itself universal, since anyone may practice it, and it leads
> toward the universal, since its objects can be named and conceived.[4]

With enthusiasm I set to cataloguing and probing my surroundings. As times
changed, one had seen the Catholic religion at first justify and then condemn
slavery and prejudices. But by referring everything to the idea of the dignity of
man, one had ripped prejudice to shreds. After much reluctance, the scientists had
conceded that the Negro was a human being; *in vivo* and *in vitro* the Negro had
been proved analogous to the white man: the same morphology, the same hist-
ology. Reason was confident of victory on every level. I put all the parts back
together. But I had to change my tune.

That victory played cat and mouse; it made a fool of me. As the other put it,
when I was present, it was not; when it was there, I was no longer. In the abstract

there was agreement: The Negro is a human being. That is to say, amended the less firmly convinced, that like us he has his heart on the left side. But on certain points the white man remained intractable. Under no conditions did he wish any intimacy between the races, for it is a truism that "crossings between widely different races can lower the physical and mental level. . . . Until we have a more definite know-ledge of the effect of race-crossings we shall certainly do best to avoid crossings between widely different races."[5]

For my own part, I would certainly know how to react. And in one sense, if I were asked for a definition of myself, I would say that I am one who waits; I investigate my surroundings, I interpret everything in terms of what I discover, I become sensitive.

In the first chapter of the history that the others have compiled for me, the foundation of cannibalism has been made eminently plain in order that I may not lose sight of it. My chromosomes were supposed to have a few thicker or thinner genes representing cannibalism. In addition to the *sex-linked*, the scholars had now discovered the *racial-linked*.[6] What a shameful science!

But I understand this "psychological mechanism." For it is a matter of common knowledge that the mechanism is only psychological. Two centuries ago I was lost to humanity, I was a slave forever. And then came men who said that it all had gone on far too long. My tenaciousness did the rest; I was saved from the civilizing deluge. I have gone forward.

Too late. Everything is anticipated, thought out, demonstrated, made the most of. My trembling hands take hold of nothing; the vein has been mined out. Too late! But once again I want to understand.

Since the time when someone first mourned the fact that he had arrived too late and everything had been said, a nostalgia for the past has seemed to persist. Is this that lost original paradise of which Otto Rank speaks? How many such men, apparently rooted to the womb of the world, have devoted their lives to studying the Delphic oracles or exhausted themselves in attempts to plot the wanderings of Ulysses! The pan-spiritualists seek to prove the existence of a soul in animals by using this argument: A dog lies down on the grave of his master and starves to death there. We had to wait for Janet to demonstrate that the aforesaid dog, in contrast to man, simply lacked the capacity to liquidate the past. We speak of the glory of Greece, Artaud says; but, he adds, if modern man can no longer understand the *Choephoroi* of Aeschylus, it is Aeschylus who is to blame. It is tradition to which the anti-Semites turn in order to ground the validity of their "point of view." It is tradition, it is that long historical past, it is that blood relation between Pascal and Descartes, that is invoked when the Jew is told, "There is no possibility of your finding a place in society." Not long ago, one of those good Frenchmen said in a train where I was sitting: "Just let the real French virtues keep going and the race is safe. Now more than ever, national union must be made a reality. Let's have an end of internal strife! Let's face up to the foreigners (here he turned toward my corner) no matter who they are."

It must be said in his defense that he stank of cheap wine; if he had been capable of it, he would have told me that my emancipated-slave blood could not possibly be stirred by the name of Villon or Taine.

An outrage!

The Jew and I: Since I was not satisfied to be racialized, by a lucky turn of fate I was humanized. I joined the Jew, my brother in misery.

An outrage!

At first thought it may seem strange that the anti-Semite's outlook should be related to that of the Negro-phobe. It was my philosophy professor, a native of the Antilles, who recalled the fact to me one day: "Whenever you hear anyone abuse the Jews, pay attention, because he is talking about you." And I found that he was universally right—by which I meant that I was answerable in my body and in my heart for what was done to my brother. Later I realized that he meant, quite simply, an anti-Semite is inevitably anti-Negro.

You come too late, much too late. There will always be a world—a white world—between you and us. . . . The other's total inability to liquidate the past once and for all. In the face of this affective ankylosis of the white man, it is understandable that I could have made up my mind to utter my Negro cry. Little by little, putting out pseudopodia here and there, I secreted a race. And that race staggered under the burden of a basic element. What was it? *Rhythm!* Listen to our singer, Léopold Senghor:

> It is the thing that is most perceptible and least material. It is the archetype of the vital element. It is the first condition and the hallmark of Art, as breath is of life: breath, which accelerates or slows, which becomes even or agitated according to the tension in the individual, the degree and the nature of his emotion. This is rhythm in its primordial purity, this is rhythm in the masterpieces of Negro art, especially sculpture. It is composed of a theme-sculptural form—which is set in opposition to a sister theme, as inhalation is to exhalation, and that is repeated. It is not the kind of symmetry that gives rise to monotony; rhythm is alive, it is free. . . . This is how rhythm affects what is least intellectual in us, tyrannically, to make us penetrate to the spirituality of the object; and that character of abandon which is ours is itself rhythmic.[7]

Had I read that right? I read it again with redoubled attention. From the opposite end of the white world a magical Negro culture was hailing me. Negro sculpture! I began to flush with pride. Was this our salvation?

I had rationalized the world and the world had rejected me on the basis of color prejudice. Since no agreement was possible on the level of reason, I threw myself back toward unreason. It was up to the white man to be more irrational than I. Out of the necessities of my struggle I had chosen the method of regression, but the fact remained that it was an unfamiliar weapon; here I am at home; I am made of the irrational; I wade in the irrational. Up to the neck in the irrational. And now how my voice vibrates!

> Those who invented neither gunpowder nor the compass
> Those who never learned to conquer steam or electricity
> Those who never explored the seas or the skies

But they know the farthest corners of the land of anguish
Those who never knew any journey save that of abduction
Those who learned to kneel in docility
Those who were domesticated and Christianized
Those who were injected with bastardy. . . .

Yes, all those are my brothers—a "bitter brotherhood" imprisons all of us alike. Having stated the minor thesis, I went overboard after something else.

. . . But those without whom the earth would not be the earth
Tumescence all the more fruitful
than
the empty land
still more the land
Storehouse to guard and ripen all
on earth that is most earth
My blackness is no stone, its deafness
hurled against the clamor of the day
My blackness is no drop of lifeless water
on the dead eye of the world
My blackness is neither a tower nor a cathedral
It thrusts into the red flesh of the sun
It thrusts into the burning flesh of the sky
It hollows through the dense dismay of its own pillar of patience.[8]

Eyah! the tom-tom chatters out the cosmic message. Only the Negro has the capacity to convey it, to decipher its meaning, its import. Astride the world, my strong heels spurring into the flanks of the world, I stare into the shoulders of the world as the celebrant stares at the midpoint between the eyes of the sacrificial victim.

But they abandon themselves, possessed, to the essence of all things, knowing nothing of externals but possessed by the movement of all things

uncaring to subdue but playing the play of the world
truly the eldest sons of the world
open to all the breaths of the world
meeting-place of all the winds of the world
undrained bed of all the waters of the world
spark of the sacred fire of the World
flesh of the flesh of the world, throbbing with the very movement
   of the world![9]

Blood! Blood! . . . Birth! Ecstasy of becoming! Three-quarters engulfed in the confusions of the day, I feel myself redden with blood. The arteries of all the world, convulsed, torn away, uprooted, have turned toward me and fed me.

"Blood! Blood! All our blood stirred by the male heart of the sun."[10]

Sacrifice was a middle point between the creation and myself—now I went back no longer to sources but to The Source. Nevertheless, one had to distrust rhythm, earthmother love, this mystic, carnal marriage of the group and the cosmos.

In *La vie sexuelle en Afrique noire*, a work rich in perceptions, De Pédrals implies that always in Africa, no matter what field is studied, it will have a certain magico-social structure. He adds:

> All these are the elements that one finds again on a still greater scale in the domain of secret societies. To the extent, moreover, to which persons of either sex, subjected to circumcision during adolescence, are bound under penalty of death not to reveal to the uninitiated what they have experienced, and to the extent to which initiation into a secret society always excites to acts of *sacred love*, there is good ground to conclude by viewing both male and female circumcision and the rites that they embellish as constitutive of minor secret societies.[11]

I walk on white nails. Sheets of water threaten my soul on fire. Face to face with these rites, I am doubly alert. Black magic! Orgies, witches' sabbaths, heathen ceremonies, amulets. Coitus is an occasion to call on the gods of the clan. It is a sacred act, pure, absolute, bringing invisible forces into action. What is one to think of all these manifestations, all these initiations, all these acts? From every direction I am assaulted by the obscenity of dances and of words. Almost at my ear there is a song:

> First our hearts burned hot
> Now they are cold
> All we think of now is Love
> When we return to the village
> When we see the great phallus
> Ah how then we will make Love
> For our parts will be dry and clean.[12]

The soil, which only a moment ago was still a tamed steed, begins to revel. Are these virgins, these nymphomaniacs? Black Magic, primitive mentality, animism, animal eroticism, it all floods over me. All of it is typical of peoples that have not kept pace with the evolution of the human race. Or, if one prefers, this is humanity at its lowest. Having reached this point, I was long reluctant to commit myself. Aggression was in the stars. I had to choose. What do I mean? I had no choice. . . .

Yes, we are—we Negroes—backward, simple, free in our behavior. That is because for us the body is not something opposed to what you call the mind. We are in the world. And long live the couple, Man and Earth! Besides, our men of letters helped me to convince you; your white civilization overlooks subtle riches and sensitivity. Listen:

> Emotive sensitivity. *Emotion is completely Negro as reason is Greek.*[13] Water rippled by every breeze? Unsheltered soul blown by every wind, whose fruit often drops before it is ripe? Yes, in one way, the Negro today is richer *in gifts than in works.*[14] But the tree thrusts its roots into the earth. The river runs deep, carrying precious seeds. And, the Afro-American poet, Langston Hughes, says:

> > I have known rivers
> > ancient dark rivers
> > my soul has grown deep
> > like the deep rivers.

> The very nature of the Negro's emotion, of his sensitivity, further-more, explains his attitude toward the object perceived with such basic intensity. It is an abandon that becomes need, an active state of com-munion, indeed of identification, however negligible the action—I almost said the personality—of the object. A rhythmic attitude: The adjective should be kept in mind.[15]

So here we have the Negro rehabilitated, "standing before the bar," ruling the world with his intuition, the Negro recognized, set on his feet again, sought after, taken up, and he is a Negro—no, he is not a Negro but the Negro, exciting the fecund antennae of the world, placed in the foreground of the world, raining his poetic power on the world, "open to all the breaths of the world." I embrace the world! I am the world! The white man has never understood this magic substitu-tion. The white man wants the world; he wants it for himself alone. He finds himself predestined master of this world. He enslaves it. An acquisitive relation is established between the world and him. But there exist other values that fit only my forms. Like a magician, I robbed the white man of "a certain world," forever after lost to him and his. When that happened, the white man must have been rocked backward by a force that he could not identify, so little used as he is to such reactions. Somewhere beyond the objective world of farms and banana trees and rubber trees, I had subtly brought the real world into being. The essence of the world was my fortune. Between the world and me a relation of coexistence was established. I had discovered the primeval One. My "speaking hands" tore at the hysterical throat of the world. The white man had the anguished feeling that I was escaping from him and that I was taking something with me. He went through my pockets. He thrust probes into the least circumvolution of my brain. Everywhere he found only the obvious. So it was obvious that I had a secret. I was interrogated; turning away with an air of mystery, I murmured:

> Tokowaly, uncle, do you remember the nights gone by
> When my head weighed heavy on the back of your patience
> > or

Holding my hand your hand led me by shadows and signs
The fields are flowers of glowworms, stars hang on the bushes, on the trees
Silence is everywhere
Only the scents of the jungle hum, swarms of reddish bees that overwhelm
    the crickets' shrill sounds,
And covered tom-tom, breathing in the distance of the night.
You, Tokowaly, you listen to what cannot be heard, and you explain to me
    what the ancestors are saying in the liquid calm of the constellations,
The bull, the scorpion, the leopard, the elephant, and the fish we know,
And the white pomp of the Spirits in the heavenly shell that has no end,
But now comes the radiance of the goddess Moon and the veils of the
    shadows fall.
Night of Africa, my black night, mystical and bright, black and shining.[16]

I made myself the poet of the world. The white man had found a poetry in which there was nothing poetic. The soul of the white man was corrupted, and, as I was told by a friend who was a teacher in the United States, "The presence of the Negroes beside the whites is in a way an insurance policy on humanness. When the whites feel that they have become too mechanized, they turn to the men of color and ask them for a little human sustenance." At last I had been recognized, I was no longer a zero.

I had soon to change my tune. Only momentarily at a loss, the white man explained to me that, genetically, I represented a stage of development: "Your properties have been exhausted by us. We have had earth mystics such as you will never approach. Study our history and you will see how far this fusion has gone." Then I had the feeling that I was repeating a cycle. My originality had been torn out of me. I wept a long time, and then I began to live again. But I was haunted by a galaxy of erosive stereotypes: the Negro's *sui generis* odor . . . the Negro's *sui generis* good nature . . . the Negro's *sui generis* gullibility. . . .

I had tried to flee myself through my kind, but the whites had thrown themselves on me and hamstrung me. I tested the limits of my essence; beyond all doubt there was not much of it left. It was here that I made my most remarkable discovery. Properly speaking, this discovery was a rediscovery.

I rummaged frenetically through all the antiquity of the black man. What I found there took away my breath. In his book *L'abolition de l'esclavage* Schoelcher presented us with compelling arguments. Since then, Frobenius, Westermann, Delafosse—all of them white—had joined the chorus: Ségou, Djenné, cities of more than a hundred thousand people; accounts of learned blacks (doctors of theology who went to Mecca to interpret the Koran). All of that, exhumed from the past, spread with its insides out, made it possible for me to find a valid historic place. The white man was wrong, I was not a primitive, not even a half-man, I belonged to a race that had already been working in gold and silver two thousand years ago. And too there was something else, something else that the white man could not understand. Listen:

What sort of men were these, then, who had been torn away from their families, their countries, their religions, with a savagery unparalleled in history?

Gentle men, polite, considerate, unquestionably superior to those who tortured them—that collection of adventurers who slashed and violated and spat on Africa to make the stripping of her the easier.

The men they took away knew how to build houses, govern empires, erect cities, cultivate fields, mine for metals, weave cotton, forge steel.

Their religion had its own beauty, based on mystical connections with the founder of the city. Their customs were pleasing, built on unity, kindness, respect for age.

No coercion, only mutual assistance, the joy of living, a free acceptance of discipline.

Order—Earnestness—Poetry and Freedom.

From the untroubled private citizen to the almost fabulous leader there was an unbroken chain of understanding and trust. No science? Indeed yes; but also, to protect them from fear, they possessed great myths in which the most subtle observation and the most daring imagination were balanced and blended. No art? They had their magnificent sculpture, in which human feeling erupted so unrestrained yet always followed the obsessive laws of rhythm in its organization of the major elements of a material called upon to capture, in order to redistribute, the most secret forces of the universe. . . . [17]

Monuments in the very heart of Africa? Schools? Hospitals? Not a single good burgher of the twentieth century, no Durand, no Smith, no Brown even suspects that such things existed in Africa before the Europeans came . . .

But Schoelcher reminds us of their presence, discovered by Caillé, Mollien, the Cander brothers. And, though he nowhere reminds us that when the Portuguese landed on the banks of the Congo in 1498, they found a rich and flourishing state there and that the courtiers of Ambas were dressed in robes of silk and brocade, at least he knows that Africa had brought itself up to a juridical concept of the state, and he is aware, living in the very flood of imperialism, that European civilization, after all, is only one more civilization among many—and not the most merciful. [18]

I put the white man back into his place; growing bolder, I jostled him and told him point-blank, "Get used to me, I am not getting used to anyone." I shouted my laughter to the stars. The white man, I could see, was resentful. His reaction time lagged interminably. . . . I had won. I was jubilant.

"Lay aside your history, your investigations of the past, and try to feel yourself into our rhythm. In a society such as ours, industrialized to the highest degree, dominated by scientism, there is no longer room for your sensitivity. One must be though if one is to be allowed to live. What matters now is no longer playing the game of the world but subjugating it with integers and atoms. Oh, certainly, I will be told, now and then when we are worn out by our lives in big buildings, we will turn to you as we do to our children—to the innocent, the ingenuous, the spontaneous. We will turn to you as to the childhood of the world. You are so real in your life—so funny, that is. Let us run away for a little while from our ritualized, polite civilization and let us relax, bend to those heads, those adorably expressive faces. In a way, you reconcile us with ourselves."

Thus my unreason was countered with reason, my reason with "real reason." Every hand was a losing hand for me. I analyzed my heredity. I made a complete audit of my ailment. I wanted to be typically Negro—it was no longer possible. I wanted to be white—that was a joke. And, when I tried, on the level of ideas and intellectual activity, to reclaim my negritude, it was snatched away from me. Proof was presented that my effort was only a term in the dialectic:

> But there is something more important: The Negro, as we have said, creates an anti-racist racism for himself. In no sense does he wish to rule the world: He seeks the abolition of all ethnic privileges, wherever they come from; he asserts his solidarity with the oppressed of all colors. At once the subjective, existential, ethnic idea of *negritude* "passes," as Hegel puts it, into the objective, positive, exact idea of *proletariat*. "For Césaire," Senghor says, "the white man is the symbol of capital as the Negro is that of labor. . . . Beyond the black-skinned men of his race it is the battle of the world proletariat that is his song."
>
> That is easy to say, but less easy to think out. And undoubtedly it is no coincidence that the most ardent poets of negritude are at the same time militant Marxists.
>
> But that does not prevent the idea of race from mingling with that of class: The first is concrete and particular, the second is universal and abstract; the one stems from what Jaspers calls understanding and the other from intellection; the first is the result of a psychobiological syncretism and the second is a methodical construction based on experience. In fact, negritude appears as the minor term of a dialectical progression: The theoretical and practical assertion of the supremacy of the white man is its thesis; the position of negritude as an antithetical value is the moment of negativity. But this negative moment is insufficient by itself, and the Negroes who employ it know this very well; they know that it is intended to prepare the synthesis or realization of the human in a society without races. Thus negritude is the root of its own destruction, it is a transition and not a conclusion, a means and not an ultimate end.[19]

When I read that page, I felt that I had been robbed of my last chance. I said to my friends, "The generation of the younger black poets has just suffered a blow that can never be forgiven." Help had been sought from a friend of the colored peoples, and that friend had found no better response than to point out the relativity of what they were doing. For once, that born Hegelian had forgotten that consciousness has to lose itself in the night of the absolute, the only condition to attain to consciousness of self. In opposition to rationalism, he summoned up the negative side, but he forgot that this negativity draws its worth from an almost substantive absoluteness. A consciousness committed to experience is ignorant, has to be ignorant, of the essences and the determinations of its being.

Orphée Noir is a date in the intellectualization of the *experience* of being black. And Sartre's mistake was not only to seek the source of the source but in a certain sense to block that source:

> Will the source of Poetry be dried up? Or will the great black flood, in spite of everything, color the sea into which it pours itself? It does not matter: Every age has its own poetry; in every age the circumstances of history choose a nation, a race, a class to take up the torch by creating situations that can be expressed or transcended only through Poetry; sometimes the poetic impulse coincides with the revolutionary impulse, and sometimes they take different courses. Today let us hail the turn of history that will make it possible for the black men to utter "the great Negro cry with a force that will shake the pillars of the world" (Césaire).[20]

And so it is not I who make a meaning for myself, but it is the meaning that was already there, pre-existing, waiting for me. It is not out of my bad nigger's misery, my bad nigger's teeth, my bad nigger's hunger that I will shape a torch with which to burn down the world, but it is the torch that was already there, waiting for that turn of history.

In terms of consciousness, the black consciousness is held out as an absolute density, as filled with itself, a stage preceding any invasion, any abolition of the ego by desire. Jean-Paul Sartre, in this work, has destroyed black zeal. In opposition to historical becoming, there had always been the unforeseeable. I needed to lose myself completely in negritude. One day, perhaps, in the depths of that unhappy romanticism. . . .

In any case I *needed* not to know. This struggle, this new decline had to take on an aspect of completeness. Nothing is more unwelcome than the commonplace: "You'll change, my boy; I was like that too when I was young . . . you'll see, it will all pass."

The dialectic that brings necessity into the foundation of my freedom drives me out of myself. It shatters my unreflected position. Still in terms of consciousness, black consciousness is immanent in its own eyes. I am not a potentiality of something, I am wholly what I am. I do not have to look for the universal. No probability has any place inside me. My Negro consciousness does not hold itself out as a lack. It *is*. It is its own follower.

But, I will be told, your statements show a misreading of the processes of history. Listen then:

> Africa I have kept your memory Africa
> you are inside me
> Like the splinter in the wound
> like a guardian fetish in the center of the village
> make me the stone in your sling
> make my mouth the lips of your wound
> make my knees the broken pillars of your abasement
> AND YET

I want to be of your race alone
workers peasants of all lands . . .
. . . white worker in Detroit black peon in Alabama
uncountable nation in capitalist slavery
destiny ranges us shoulder to shoulder
repudiating the ancient maledictions of blood taboos
we roll away the ruins of our solitudes
If the flood is a frontier
we will strip the gully of its endless
covering flow
If the Sierra is a frontier
we will smash the jaws of the volcanoes
upholding the Cordilleras
and the plain will be the parade ground of the dawn
where we regroup our forces sundered
by the deceits of our masters
As the contradiction among the features
creates the harmony of the face
we proclaim the oneness of the suffering
and the revolt
of all the peoples on all the face of the earth and we mix the mortar of the
    age of brotherhood out of the dust of idols.[21]

Exactly, we will reply, Negro experience is not a whole, for there is not merely *one* Negro, there are *Negroes*. What a difference, for instance, in this other poem:

The white man killed my father
Because my father was proud
The white man raped my mother
Because my mother was beautiful
The white man wore out my brother in the hot sun of the roads
Because my brother was strong
Then the white man came to me
His hands red with blood
Spat his contempt into my black face
Out of his tyrant's voice:
"Hey boy, a basin, a towel, water."[22]

Or this other one:

My brother with teeth that glisten at the compliments of hypocrites
My brother with gold-rimmed spectacles
Over eyes that turn blue at the sound of the Master's voice
My poor brother in dinner jacket with its silk lapels
Clucking and whispering and strutting through the drawing rooms of
    Condescension
How pathetic you are

The sun of your native country is nothing more now than a shadow
On your composed civilized face
And your grandmother's hut
Brings blushes into cheeks made white by years of abasement and *Mea culpa*
But when regurgitating the flood of lofty empty words
Like the load that presses on your shoulders
You walk again on the rough red earth of Africa
These words of anguish will state the rhythm of your uneasy gait
I feel so alone, so alone here![23]

From time to time one would like to stop. To state reality is a wearing task. But, when one has taken it into one's head to try to express existence, one runs the risk of finding only the nonexistent. What is certain is that, at the very moment when I was trying to grasp my own being, Sartre, who remained The Other, gave me a name and thus shattered my last illusion. While I was saying to him:

"My negritude is neither a tower nor a cathedral,
   it thrusts into the red flesh of the sun,
   it thrusts into the burning flesh of the sky, it hollows through the
      dense dismay of its own pillar of patience . . ."

while I was shouting that, in the paroxysm of my being and my fury, he was reminding me that my blackness was only a minor term. In all truth, in all truth I tell you, my shoulders slipped out of the framework of the world, my feet could no longer feel the touch of the ground. Without a Negro past, without a Negro future, it was impossible for me to live my Negrohood. Not yet white, no longer wholly black, I was damned. Jean-Paul Sartre had forgotten that the Negro suffers in his body quite differently from the white man.[24] Between the white man and me the connection was irrevocably one of transcendence.[25]

But the constancy of my love had been forgotten. I defined myself as an absolute intensity of beginning. So I took up my negritude, and with tears in my eyes I put its machinery together again. What had been broken to pieces was rebuilt, reconstructed by the intuitive lianas of my hands.

My cry grew more violent: I am a Negro, I am a Negro, I am a Negro . . .

And there was my poor brother—living out his neurosis to the extreme and finding himself paralyzed:

THE NEGRO: I can't, ma'am.
LIZZIE: Why not?
THE NEGRO: I can't shoot white folks.
LIZZIE: Really! That would bother them, wouldn't it?
THE NEGRO: They're white folks, ma'am.
LIZZIE: So what? Maybe they got a right to bleed you like a pig just because
                    they're white?
THE NEGRO: But they're white folks.

A feeling of inferiority? No, a feeling of nonexistence. Sin is Negro as virtue is white. All those white men in a group, guns in their hands, cannot be wrong. I am guilty. I do not know of what, but I know that I am no good.

THE NEGRO: That's how it goes, ma'am. That's how it always goes with white folks.

LIZZIE: You too? You feel guilty?

THE NEGRO: Yes, ma'am.[26]

It is Bigger Thomas—he is afraid, he is terribly afraid. He is afraid, but of what is he afraid? Of himself. No one knows yet who he is, but he knows that fear will fill the world when the world finds out. And when the world knows, the world always expects something of the Negro. He is afraid lest the world know, he is afraid of the fear that the world would feel if the world knew. Like that old woman on her knees who begged me to tie her to her bed:

"I just know, Doctor: Any minute that thing will take hold of me."

"What thing?"

"The wanting to kill myself. Tie me down, I'm afraid."

In the end; Bigger Thomas acts. To put an end to his tension, he acts, he responds to the world's anticipation.[27]

So it is with the character in *If He Hollers Let Him Go*[28]—who does precisely what he did not want to do. That big blonde who was always in his way, weak, sensual, offered, open, fearing (desiring) rape, became his mistress in the end.

The Negro is a toy in the white man's hands; so, in order to shatter the hellish cycle, he explodes. I cannot go to a film without seeing myself. I wait for me. In the interval, just before the film starts, I wait for me. The people in the theater are watching me, examining me, waiting for me. A Negro groom is going to appear. My heart makes my head swim.

The crippled veteran of the Pacific war says to my brother, "Resign yourself to your color the way I got used to my stump; we're both victims."[29]

Nevertheless with all my strength I refuse to accept that amputation. I feel in myself a soul as immense as the world, truly a soul as deep as the deepest of rivers, my chest has the power to expand without limit. I am a master and I am advised to adopt the humility of the cripple. Yesterday, awakening to the world, I saw the sky turn upon itself utterly and wholly. I wanted to rise, but the disemboweled silence fell back upon me, its wings paralyzed. Without responsibility, straddling Nothingness and Infinity, I began to weep.

Notes

1   Jean Lhermitte, *L'Image de notre corps* (Paris, Nouvelle Revue critique, 1939), p. 17.

2   Sir Alan Burns, *Colour Prejudice* (London, Allen and Unwin, 1948), p. 16.

3   *Anti-Semite and Jew* (New York, Grove Press, 1960), pp. 112–113.

4   *Ibid.*, p. 115.

5   Jon Alfred Mjoen, "Harmonic and Disharmonic Race-crossings," The Second International Congress of Eugenics (1921), *Eugenics in Race and State*, vol. II, p. 60, quoted in Sir Alan Burns, *op. cit.*, p. 120.

6   In English in the original. (Translator's note.)

7   "Ce que l'homme noir apporte," in Claude Nordey, *L'Homme de couleur* (Paris, Plon, 1939), pp. 309–310.

8   Aimé Césaire, *Cahier d'un retour au pays natal* (Paris, Présence Africaine, 1958), pp. 77–78.

9   *Ibid.*, p. 78.

10 *Ibid.*, p. 79.

11 De Pédrals, *La vie sexuelle en Afrique noire* (Paris, Payot), p. 83.

12 A. M. Vergiat, *Les rites secrets des primitifs de l'Oubangui* (Paris, Payot, 1951), p. 113.

13 My italics—F.F.

14 My italics—F.F.

15 Léopold Senghor, "Ce que l'homme noir apporte," in Nordey, *op. cit.*, p. 205.

16 Léopold Senghor, *Chants d'ombre* (Paris, Editions du Seuil, 1945).

17 Aimé Césaire, Introduction to Victor Schoelcher, *Esclavage et colonisation* (Paris, Presses Universitaires de France, 1948), p. 7.

18 *Ibid.*, p. 8.

19 Jean-Paul Sartre, *Orphée Noir*, preface to *Anthologie de la nouvelle poésie nègre et malgache* (Paris, Presses Universitaires de France, 1948), pp. xl ff.

20 *Ibid.*, p. xliv.

21 Jacques Roumain, "Bois-d'Ebène," Prelude, in *Anthologie de la nouvelle poésie nègre et malgache*, p. 113.

22 David Diop, "Le temps du martyre," in *ibid.*, p. 174.

23 David Diop, "Le Renégat."

24 Though Sartre's speculations on the existence of The Other may be correct (to the extent, we must remember, to which *Being and Nothingness* describes an alienated consciousness), their application to a black consciousness proves fallacious. That is because the white man is not only The Other but also the master, whether real or imaginary.

25 In the sense in which the word is used by Jean Wahl in *Existence humaine et transcendance* (Neuchâtel, La Baconnière, 1944).

26 Jean-Paul Sartre, *The Respectful Prostitute*, in *Three Plays* (New York, Knopf, 1949), pp. 189, 191. Originally, *La Putain respectueuse* (Paris, Callimard, 1947). See also *Home of the Brave*, a film by Mark Robson.

27 Richard Wright, *Native Son* (New York, Harper, 1940).

28 By Chester Himes (Garden City, Doubleday, 1945).

29 *Home of the Brave.*

Suggestions for further reading

Bhabha, Homi K., *The Location of Culture*, London and New York: Routledge, 1994.

Dyer, Richard, *White*, London and New York: Routledge, 1997.

hooks, bell, *Black Looks: Race and Representation*, Boston: South End Press, 1992.

Chapter 8

Raymond Williams

'CULTURE IS ORDINARY', 1958

THE BUS STOP was outside the cathedral. I had been looking at the Mappa Mundi, with its rivers out of Paradise, and at the chained library, where a party of clergymen had got in easily, but where I had waited an hour and cajoled a verger before I even saw the chains. Now, across the street, a cinema advertised the *Six-Five Special* and a cartoon version of *Gulliver's Travels*. The bus arrived, with a driver and a conductress deeply absorbed in each other. We went out of the city, over the old bridge, and on through the orchards and the green meadows and the fields red under the plough. Ahead were the Black Mountains, and we climbed among them, watching the steep fields end at the grey walls, beyond which the bracken and heather and whin had not yet been driven back. To the east, along the ridge, stood the line of grey Norman castles; to the west, the fortress wall of the mountains. Then, as we still climbed, the rock changed under us. Here, now, was limestone, and the line of the early iron workings along the scarp. The farming valleys, with their scattered white houses, fell away behind. Ahead of us were the narrower valleys: the steel-rolling mill, the gasworks, the grey terraces, the pit-heads. The bus stopped, and the driver and conductress got out, still absorbed. They had done this journey so often, and seen all its stages. It is a journey, in fact, that in one form or another we have all made.

I was born and grew up halfway along that bus journey. Where I lived is still a farming valley, though the road through it is being widened and straightened, to carry the heavy lorries to the north. Not far away, my grandfather, and so back through the generations, worked as a farm labourer until he was turned out of his cottage and, in his fifties, became a roadman. His sons went at thirteen or fourteen on to the farms, his daughters into service. My father, his third son, left the farm at fifteen to be a boy porter on the railway, and later became a signalman, working in a box in this valley until he died. I went up the road to the village school, where a curtain divided the two classes – Second to eight or nine,

First to fourteen. At eleven I went to the local grammar school, and later to Cambridge.

Culture is ordinary: that is where we must start. To grow up in that country was to see the shape of a culture, and its modes of change. I could stand on the mountains and look north to the farms and the cathedral, or south to the smoke and the flare of the blast furnace making a second sunset. To grow up in that family was to see the shaping of minds: the learning of new skills, the shifting of relationships, the emergence of different language and ideas. My grandfather, a big hard labourer, wept while he spoke, finely and excitedly, at the parish meeting, of being turned out of his cottage. My father, not long before he died, spoke quietly and happily of when he had started a trade-union branch and a Labour Party group in the village, and, without bitterness, of the 'kept men' of the new politics. I speak a different idiom, but I think of these same things.

Culture is ordinary: that is the first fact. Every human society has its own shape, its own purposes, its own meanings. Every human society expresses these, in institutions, and in arts and learning. The making of a society is the finding of common meanings and directions, and its growth is an active debate and amendment under the pressure of experience, contact, and discovery, writing themselves into the land. The growing society is there, yet it is also made and remade in every individual mind. The making of a mind is, first, the slow learning of shapes, purposes, and meanings, so that work, observation and communication are possible. Then, second, but equal in importance, is the testing of these in experience, the making of new observations, comparisons, and meanings. A culture has two aspects: the known meanings and directions, which its members are trained to; the new observations and meanings, which are offered and tested. These are the ordinary processes of human societies and human minds, and we see through them the nature of a culture: that it is always both traditional and creative; that it is both the most ordinary common meanings and the finest individual meanings. We use the word culture in these two senses: to mean a whole way of life – the common meanings; to mean the arts and learning – the special processes of discovery and creative effort. Some writers reserve the word for one or other of these senses; I insist on both, and on the significance of their conjunction. The questions I ask about our culture are questions about our general and common purposes, yet also questions about deep personal meanings. Culture is ordinary, in every society and in every mind.

Now there are two senses of culture – two colours attached to it – that I know about but refuse to learn. The first I discovered at Cambridge, in a teashop. I was not, by the way, oppressed by Cambridge. I was not cast down by old buildings, for I had come from a country with twenty centuries of history written visibly into the earth: I liked walking through a Tudor court, but it did not make me feel raw. I was not amazed by the existence of a place of learning; I had always known the cathedral, and the bookcases I now sit to work at in Oxford are of the same design as those in the chained library. Nor was learning, in my family, some strange eccentricity; I was not, on a scholarship in Cambridge, a new kind of animal up a brand-new ladder. Learning was ordinary; we learned where we could. Always, from those scattered white houses, it had made sense to go out and become a scholar or a poet or a teacher. Yet few of us could be spared from the immediate work; a price had been set on this kind of learning, and it was more, much more, than we could individually pay. Now, when we could pay in common, it was a good, ordinary life.

I was not oppressed by the university, but the teashop, acting as if it were one of the older and more respectable departments, was a different matter. Here was culture, not in any sense I knew, but in a special sense: the outward and emphatically visible sign of a special kind of people, cultivated people. They were not, the great majority of them, particularly learned; they practised few arts; but they had it, and they showed you they had it. They are still there, I suppose, still showing it, though even they must be hearing rude noises from outside, from a few scholars and writers they call – how comforting a label is! – angry young men. As a matter of fact there is no need to be rude. It is simply that if that is culture, we don't want it; we have seen other people living.

But of course it is not culture, and those of my colleagues who, hating the teashop, make culture, on its account, a dirty word, are mistaken. If the people in the teashop go on insisting that culture is their trivial differences of behaviour, their trivial variations of speech habit, we cannot stop them, but we can ignore them. They are not that important, to take culture from where it belongs.

Yet, probably also disliking the teashop, there were writers I read then, who went into the same category in my mind. When I now read a book such as Clive Bell's *Civilisation*, I experience not so much disagreement as stupor. What kind of life can it be, I wonder, to produce this extraordinary fussiness, this extraordinary decision to call certain things culture and then separate them, as with a park wall, from ordinary people and ordinary work? At home we met and made music, listened to it, recited and listened to poems, valued fine language. I have heard better music and better poems since; there is the world to draw on. But I know, from the most ordinary experience, that the interest is there, the capacity is there. Of course, farther along that bus journey, the old social organization in which these things had their place has been broken. People have been driven and concentrated into new kinds of work, new kinds of relationship; work, by the way, which built the park walls, and the houses inside them, and which is now at last bringing, to the unanimous disgust of the teashop, clean and decent and furnished living to the people themselves. Culture is ordinary: through every change let us hold fast to that.

The other sense, or colour, that I refuse to learn, is very different. Only two English words rhyme with culture, and these, as it happens, are sepulture and vulture. We don't yet call museums or galleries or even universities culture-sepultures, but I hear a lot, lately, about culture-vultures (man must rhyme), and I hear also, in the same North Atlantic argot, of do-gooders and highbrows and superior prigs. Now I don't like the teashop, but I don't like this drinking-hole either. I know there are people who are humourless about the arts and learning, and I know there is a difference between goodness and sanctimony. But the growing implications of this spreading argot – the true cant of a new kind of rogue – I reject absolutely. For, honestly, how can anyone use a word like 'do-gooder' with this new, offbeat complacency? How can anyone wither himself to a state where he must use these new flip words for any attachment to learning or the arts? It is plain that what may have started as a feeling about hypocrisy, or about pretentiousness (in itself a two-edged word), is becoming a guilt-ridden tic at the mention of any serious standards whatever. And the word 'culture' has been heavily compromised by this conditioning: Goering reached for his gun; many reach for their chequebooks; a growing number, now, reach for the latest bit of argot.

'Good' has been drained of much of its meaning, in these circles, by the exclusion of its ethical content and emphasis on a purely technical standard; to do a good job is better than to be a do-gooder. But do we need reminding that any crook can, in his own terms, do a good job? The smooth reassurance of technical efficiency is no substitute for the whole positive human reference. Yet men who once made this reference, men who were or wanted to be writers or scholars, are now, with every appearance of satisfaction, advertising men, publicity boys, names in the strip newspapers. These men were given skills, given attachments, which are now in the service of the most brazen money-grabbing exploitation of the inexperience of ordinary people. And it is these men – this new, dangerous class – who have invented and disseminated the argot, in an attempt to influence ordinary people – who because they do real work have real standards in the fields they know – against real standards in the fields these men knew and have abandoned. The old cheapjack is still there in the market, with the country boys' half-crowns on his reputed packets of gold rings or watches. He thinks of his victims as a slow, ignorant crowd, but they live, and farm, while he coughs behind his portable stall. The new cheapjack is in offices with contemporary *décor*, using scraps of linguistics, psychology and sociology to influence what he thinks of as the mass mind. He too, however, will have to pick up and move on, and meanwhile we are not to be influenced by his argot; we can simply refuse to learn it. Culture is ordinary. An interest in learning or the arts is simple, pleasant and natural. A desire to know what is best, and to do what is good, is the whole positive nature of man. We are not to be scared from these things by noises. There are many versions of what is wrong with our culture. So far I have tried only to clear away the detritus which makes it difficult for us to think seriously about it at all. When I got to Cambridge I encountered two serious influences which have left a very deep impression on my mind. The first was Marxism, the second the teaching of Leavis. Through all subsequent disagreement I retain my respect for both.

The Marxists said many things, but those that mattered were three. First, they said that a culture must be finally interpreted in relation to its underlying system of production. I have argued this theoretically elsewhere – it is a more difficult idea than it looks – but I still accept its emphasis. Everything I had seen, growing up in that border country, had led me towards such an emphasis: a culture is a whole way of life, and the arts are part of a social organization which economic change clearly radically affects. I did not have to be taught dissatisfaction with the existing economic system, but the subsequent questions about our culture were, in these terms, vague. It was said that it was a class-dominated culture, deliberately restricting a common inheritance to a small class, while leaving the masses ignor-ant. The fact of restriction I accepted – it is still very obvious that only the *deserving* poor get much educational opportunity, and I was in no mood, as I walked about Cambridge, to feel glad that I had been thought deserving; I was no better and no worse than the people I came from. On the other hand, just because of this, I got angry at my friends' talk about the ignorant masses: one kind of Communist has always talked like this, and has got his answer, at Poznan and Budapest, as the imperialists, making the same assumption, were answered in India, in Indo-China, in Africa. There is an English bourgeois culture, with its powerful educational, literary and social institutions, in close contact with the actual centres of power. To say that most working people are excluded from these is self-evident, though the doors, under sustained pressure, are slowly opening. But to go on to say that working people are excluded from English culture is nonsense; they have their own growing institutions, and much of the strictly bourgeois culture they would in any case not want. A great part of the English way of life, and of its arts and learning, is not bourgeois in any discoverable sense. There are institutions, and common meanings, which are in no sense the sole product of the commercial middle class; and there are art and learning, a common English inheritance, produced by many kinds of men, including many who hated the very class and system which now take pride in consuming it. The bourgeoisie has given us much, including a narrow but real system of morality; that is at least better than its court predecessors. The leisure which the bourgeoisie attained has given us much of cultural value. But this is not to say that contemporary culture is bourgeois culture: a mistake that everyone, from Conservatives to Marxists, seems to make. There is a distinct working-class way of life, which I for one value – not only because I was bred in it, for I now, in certain respects, live differently. I think this way of life, with its emphases of neighbourhood, mutual obligation, and common betterment, as expressed in the great working-class political and industrial institutions, is in fact the best basis for any future English society. As for the arts and learning, they are in a real sense a national inheritance, which is, or should be, available to everyone. So when the Marxists say that we live in a dying culture, and that the masses are ignorant, I have to ask them, as I asked them then, where on earth they have lived. A dying culture, and ignorant masses, are not what I have known and see.

What I had got from the Marxists then, so far, was a relationship between culture and production, and the observation that education was restricted. The other things I rejected, as I rejected also their third point, that since culture and production are related, the advocacy of a different system of production is in some way a cultural directive, indicating not only a way of life but new arts and learning. I did some writing while I was, for eighteen months, a member of the Communist Party, and I found out in trivial ways what other writers, here and in Europe, have found out more gravely: the practical consequences of this kind of theoretical error. In this respect, I saw the future, and it didn't work. The Marxist interpretation of culture can never be accepted while it retains, as it need not retain, this directive element, this insistence that if you honestly want socialism you must write, think, learn in certain prescribed ways. A culture is common meanings, the product of a whole people, and offered individual meanings, the product of a man's whole committed personal and social experience. It is stupid and arrogant to suppose that any of these meanings can in any way be prescribed; they are made by living, made and remade, in ways we cannot know in advance. To try to jump the future, to pretend that in some way you *are* the future, is strictly insane. Prediction is another matter, an offered meaning, but the only thing we can say about culture in an England that has socialized its means of production is that all the channels of expression and communication should be cleared and open, so that the whole actual life, that we cannot know in advance, that we can know only in part even while it is being lived, may be brought to consciousness and meaning.

Leavis has never liked Marxists, which is in one way a pity, for they know more than he does about modern English society, and about its immediate history. He, on the other hand, knows more than any Marxist I have met about the real relations between art and experience. We have all learned from him in this, and we have also learned his version of what is wrong with English culture. The diagnosis is radical, and is rapidly becoming orthodox. There was an old, mainly agricultural England, with a traditional culture of great value. This has been replaced by a modern, organized, industrial state, whose characteristic institutions deliberately cheapen our natural human responses, making art and literature into desperate survivors and witnesses, while a new mechanized vulgarity sweeps into the centres of power. The only defence is in education, which will at least keep certain things alive, and which will also, at least in a minority, develop ways of thinking and feeling which are competent to understand what is happening and to maintain the finest individual values. I need not add how widespread this diagnosis has become, though little enough acknowledgement is still made to Leavis himself. For my own part, I was deeply impressed by it; deeply enough for my ultimate rejection of it to be a personal crisis lasting several years.

For obviously, it seemed to fit a good deal of my experience. It did not tell me that my father and grandfather were ignorant wage-slaves; it did not tell me that the smart, busy, commercial culture (which I had come to as a stranger, so much so that for years I had violent headaches whenever I passed through London and saw underground advertisements and evening newspapers) was the thing I had to catch up with. I even made a fool of myself, or was made to think so, when after a lecture in which the usual point was made that 'neighbour' now does not mean what it did to Shakespeare, I said – imagine! – that to me it did. (When my father was dying, this year, one man came in and dug his garden; another loaded and delivered a lorry of sleepers for firewood; another came and chopped the sleepers into blocks; another – I don't know who, it was never said – left a sack of potatoes at the back door; a woman came in and took away a basket of washing.) But even this was explicable; I came from a bit of the old society, but my future was Surbiton (it took me years to find Surbiton, and have a good look at it, but it's served a good many as a symbol – without having lived there I couldn't say whether rightly). So there I was, and it all seemed to fit.

Yet not all. Once I got away, and thought about it, it didn't really fit properly. For one thing I knew this: at home we were glad of the Industrial Revolution, and of its consequent social and political changes. True, we lived in a very beautiful farming valley, and the valleys beyond the limestone we could all see were ugly. But there was one gift that was overriding, one gift which at any price we would take, the gift of power that is everything to men who have worked with their hands. It was slow in coming to us, in all its effects, but steam power, the petrol engine, electricity, these and their host of products in commodities and services, we took as quickly as we could get them, and were glad. I have seen all these things being used, and I have seen the things they replaced. I will not listen with patience to any acid listing of them – you know the sneer you can get into plumbing, baby Austins, aspirin, contraceptives, canned food. But I say to these Pharisees: dirty water, an earth bucket, a four-mile walk each way to work, headaches, broken women, hunger and monotony of diet. The working people, in town and country alike, will not listen (and I support them) to any account of our society which supposes that these things are not progress: not just mechanical, external progress either, but a real service of life. Moreover, in the new conditions, there was more real freedom to dispose of our lives, more real personal grasp where it mattered, more real say. Any account of our culture which explicitly or implicity denies the value of an industrial society is really irrelevant; not in a million years would you make us give up this power.

So then the social basis of the case was unacceptable, but could one, trying to be a writer, a scholar, a teacher, ignore the indictment of the new cultural vulgarity? For the plumbing and the tractors and the medicines could one ignore the strip newspapers, the multiplying cheapjacks, the raucous triviality? As a matter of priorities, yes, if necessary; but was the cheapening of response really a consequence of the cheapening of power? It looks like it, I know, but is this really as much as one can say? I believe the central problem of our society, in the coming half-century, is the use of our new resources to make a good common culture; the means to a good, abundant economy we already understand. I think the good common culture can be made, but before we can be serious about this, we must rid ourselves of a legacy from our most useful critics – a legacy of two false equations, one false analogy, and one false proposition.

The false proposition is easily disposed of. It is a fact that the new power brought ugliness: the coal brought dirt, the factory brought overcrowding, communications brought a mess of wires. But the proposition that ugliness is a price we pay, or refuse to pay, for economic power need no longer be true. New sources of power, new methods of production, improved systems of transport and communication can, quite practically, make England clean and pleasant again, and with much more power, not less. Any new ugliness is the product of stupidity, indifference, or simply incoordination; these things will be easier to deal with than when power was necessarily noisy, dirty, and disfiguring.

The false equations are more difficult. One is the equation between popular education and the new commerical culture: the latter proceeding inevitably from the former. Let the masses in, it is said, and this is what you inevitably get. Now the question is obviously difficult, but I can't accept this equation, for two reasons. The first is a matter of faith: I don't believe that the ordinary people in fact resemble the normal description of the masses, low and trivial in taste and habit. I put it another way; that there are in fact no masses, but only ways of seeing people as masses. With the coming of industrialism, much of the old social organization broke down and it became a matter of difficult personal experience that we were constantly seeing people we did not know, and it was tempting to mass them, as 'the others', in our minds. Again, people were physically massed, in the industrial towns, and a new class structure (the names of our social classes, and the word 'class' itself in this sense, date only from the Industrial Revolution) was practically imposed. The improvement in communications, in particular the development of new forms of multiple transmission of news and entertainment, created unbridgeable divisions between transmitter and audience, which again led to the audience being interpreted as an unknown mass. Masses became a new word for mob: the others, the unknown, the unwashed, the crowd beyond one. As a way of knowing other people, this formula is obviously ridiculous, but, in the new conditions, it seemed an effective formula – the only one possible. Certainly it was the formula that was used by those whose money gave them access to the new communication techniques; the lowness of taste and habit, which human beings assign very easily to other human beings, was assumed, as a bridge. The new culture was built on this formula, and if I reject the formula, if I insist that this lowness is not inherent in ordinary people, you can brush my insistence aside, but I shall go on holding to it. A different formula, I know from experience, gets a radically different response.

My second reason is historical: I deny, and can prove my denial, that popular education and commercial culture are cause and effect. I have shown elsewhere that the myth of 1870 – the Education Act which is said to have produced, as its children grew up, a new cheap and nasty press – is indeed myth. There was more than enough literacy, long before 1870, to support a cheap press, and in fact there were cheap and really bad newspapers selling in great quantities before the 1870 Act was heard of. The bad new commercial culture came out of the social chaos of industrialism, and out of the success, in this chaos, of the 'masses' formula, not out of popular education. Northcliffe did few worse things than start this myth, for while the connection between bad culture and the social chaos of industrialism is significant, the connection between it and popular education is vicious. The Northcliffe Revolution, by the way, was a radical change in the financial structure of the press, basing it on a new kind of revenue – the new mass advertising of the 1890s – rather than the making of a cheap popular press, in which he had been widely and successfully preceded. But I tire of making these points. Everyone prefers to believe Northcliffe. Yet does nobody, even a Royal Commission, read the most ordinarily accessible newspaper history? When people do read the history, the false equation between popular education and commercial culture will disappear for ever. Popular education came out of the other camp, and has had quite opposite effects.

The second false equation is this: that the observable badness of so much widely distributed popular culture is a true guide to the state of mind and feeling, the essential quality of living of its consumers. Too many good men have said this for me to treat it lightly, but I still, on evidence, can't accept it. It is easy to assemble, from print and cinema and television, a terrifying and fantastic congress of cheap feelings and moronic arguments. It is easy to go on from this and assume this deeply degrading version of the actual lives of our contemporaries. Yet do we find this confirmed, when we meet people? This is where 'masses' comes in again, of course: the people *we* meet aren't vulgar, but God, think of Bootle and Surbiton and Aston! I haven't lived in any of those places; have you? But a few weeks ago I was in a house with a commercial traveller, a lorry driver, a bricklayer, a shopgirl, a fitter, a signalman, a nylon operative, a domestic help (perhaps, dear, she is your very own treasure). I hate describing people like this, for in fact they were my family and family friends. Now they read, they watch, this work we are talking about; some of them quite critically, others with a good deal of pleasure. Very well, I read different things, watch different entertainments, and I am quite sure why they are better. But could I sit down in that house and make this equation we are offered? Not, you understand, that shame was stopping me; I've learned, thank you, how to behave. But talking to my family, to my friends, talking, as we were, about our own lives, about people, about feelings, could I in fact find this lack of quality we are discussing? I'll be honest – I looked; my training has done that for me. I can only say that I found as much natural fineness of feeling, as much quick discrimination, as much clear grasp of ideas within the range of experience as I have found anywhere. I don't altogether understand this, though I am not really surprised. Clearly there is something in the psychology of print and image that none of us has yet quite grasped. For the equation looks sensible, yet when you test it, in experience – and there's nowhere else you can test it – it's wrong. I can understand the protection of critical and intelligent reading: my father, for instance, a satisfied reader of the *Daily Herald*, got simply from reading the company reports a clear idea, based on names, of the rapid development of combine and interlocking ownership in British industry, which I had had made easy for me in two or three academic essays; and he had gone on to set these facts against the opinions in a number of articles in the paper on industrial ownership. That I understand; that is simply intelligence, however partly trained. But there is still this other surprising fact: that people whose quality of personal living is high are apparently satisfied by a low quality of printed feeling and opinion. Many of them still live, it is true, in a surprisingly enclosed personal world, much more so than mine, and some of their personal observations are the finer for it. Perhaps this is enough to explain it, but in any case, I submit, we need a new equation, to fit the observable facts.

Now the false analogy, that we must also reject. This is known, in discussions of culture, as a 'kind of Gresham's Law'. Just as bad money will drive out good, so bad culture will drive out good, and this, it is said, has in fact been happening. If you can't see, straight away, the defect of the analogy, your answer, equally effective, will have to be historical. For in fact, of course, it has not been happening. There is more, much more bad culture about; it is easier, now, to distribute it, and there is more leisure to receive it. But test this in any field you like, and see if this has been accompanied by a shrinking consumption of things we can all agree to be good. The editions of good literature are very much larger than they were; the listeners to good music are much more numerous than they were; the number of people who look at good visual art is larger than it has ever been. If bad newspapers drive out good newspapers, by a kind of Gresham's Law, why is it that, allowing for the rise in population, *The Times* sells nearly three times as many copies as in the days of its virtual monopoly of the press, in 1850? It is the law I am questioning, not the seriousness of the facts as a whole. Instead of a kind of Gresham's Law, keeping people awake at nights with the now orthodox putropian nightmare, let us put it another way, to fit the actual facts: we live in an expanding culture, and all the elements in this culture are themselves expanding. If we start from this, we can then ask real questions: about relative rates of expansion; about the social and economic problems raised by these; about the social and economic answers. I am working now on a book to follow my *Culture and Society*, trying to interpret, historically and theoretically, the nature and conditions of an expanding culture of our kind. I could not have begun this work if I had not learned from the Marxists and from Leavis; I cannot complete it unless I radically amend some of the ideas which they and others have left us.

I give myself three wishes, one for each of the swans I have just been watching on the lake. I ask for things that are part of the ethos of our working-class movement. I ask that we may be strong and human enough to realize them. And I ask, naturally, in my own fields of interest.

I wish, first, that we should recognize that education is ordinary: that it is, before everything else, the process of giving to the ordinary members of society its full common meanings, and the skills that will enable them to amend these meanings, in the light of their personal and common experience. If we start from that, we can get rid of the remaining restrictions, and make the necessary changes. I do not mean only money restrictions, though these, of course, are ridiculous and must go. I mean also restrictions in the mind: the insistence, for example, that there is a hard maximum number – a fraction of the population as a whole – capable of really profiting by a university education, or a grammar school education, or by any full course of liberal studies. We are told that this is not a question of what we might personally prefer, but of the hard cold facts of human intelligence, as shown by biology and psychology. But let us be frank about this: are biology and psychology different in the USA and USSR (each committed to expansion, and not to any class rigidities), where much larger numbers, much larger fractions, pass through comparable stages of education? Or were the English merely behind in the queue for intelligence? I believe, myself, that our educational system, with its golden fractions, is too like our social system – a top layer of leaders, a middle layer of supervisors, a large bottom layer of operatives – to be coincidence. I cannot accept that education is a training for jobs, or for making useful citizens (that is, fitting into this system). It is a society's confirmation of its common meanings, and of the human skills for their amendment. Jobs follow from this confirmation: the purpose, and then the working skill. We are moving into an economy where we shall need many more highly trained specialists. For this precise reason, I ask for a common education that will give our society its cohesion, and prevent it disintegrating into a series of specialist departments, the nation become a firm.

But I do not mean only the reorganization of entry into particular kinds of education, though I welcome and watch the experiments in this. I mean also the rethinking of content, which is even more important. I have the honour to work for an organization through which, quite practically, working men amended the English university curriculum. It is now as it was then: the defect is not what is in, but what is out. It will be a test of our cultural seriousness whether we can, in the coming generation, redesign our syllabuses to a point of full human relevance and control. I should like to see a group working on this, and offering its conclusions. For we need not fear change; oldness may or may not be relevant. I come from an old place; if a man tells me that his family came over with the Normans, I say 'Yes, how interesting; and are you liking it here?' Oldness is relative, and many 'immemorial' English traditions were invented, just like that, in the nineteenth century. What that vital century did for its own needs, we can do for ours; we can make, in our turn, a true twentieth-century syllabus. And by this I do not mean simply more technology; I mean a full liberal education for everyone in our society, and then full specialist training to earn our living in terms of what we want to make of our lives. Our specialisms will be finer if they have grown from a common culture, rather than being a distinction from it. And we must at all costs avoid the polarization of our culture, of which there are growing signs. High literacy is expanding, in direct relation to exceptional educational opportunities, and the gap between this and common literacy may widen, to the great damage of both, and with great consequent tension. We must emphasize not the ladder but the common highway, for every man's ignorance diminishes me, and every man's skill is a common gain of breath.

My second wish is complementary: for more and more active public provision for the arts and for adult learning. We now spend £20,000,000 annually on all our libraries, museums, galleries, orchestras, on the Arts Council, and on all forms of adult education. At the same time we spend £365,000,000 annually on advertising. When these figures are reversed, we can claim some sense of proportion and value. And until they are reversed, let there be no sermons from the Establishment about materialism: this is their way of life, let them look at it. (But there is no shame in them: for years, with their own children away at school, they have lectured working-class mothers on the virtues of family life; this is a similar case.)

I ask for increased provision on three conditions. It is not to be a disguised way of keeping up consumption, but a thing done for its own sake. A minister in the last Labour government said that we didn't want any geniuses in the film industry; he wanted, presumably, just to keep the turnstiles clicking. The short answer to this is that we don't want any Wardour Street thinkers in the leadership of the Labour Party. We want leaders of a society, not repair-workers on this kind of cultural economy.

The second condition is that while we must obviously preserve and extend the great national institutions, we must do something to reverse the concentration of this part of our culture. We should welcome, encourage and foster the tendencies to regional recreation that are showing themselves; for culture is ordinary, you should not have to go to London to find it.

The third condition is controversial. We should not seek to extend a ready-made culture to the benighted masses. We should accept, frankly, that if we extend our culture we shall change it: some that is offered will be rejected, other parts will be radically criticized. And this is as it should be, for our arts, now, are in no condition to go down to eternity unchallenged. There is much fine work; there is also shoddy work, and work based on values that will find no acceptance if they ever come out into the full light of England. To take our arts to new audiences is to be quite certain that in many respects those arts will be changed. I, for one, do not fear this. I would not expect the working people of England to support works which, after proper and patient preparation, they could not accept. The real growth will be slow and uneven, but state provision, frankly, should be a growth in this direction, and not a means of diverting public money to the preservation of a fixed and finished partial culture. At the same time, if we understand cultural growth, we shall know that it is a continual offering for common acceptance; that we should not, therefore, try to determine in advance what should be offered, but clear the channels and let all the offerings be made, taking care to give the difficult full space, the original full time, so that it is a real growth, and not just a wider confirmation of old rules.

Now, of course, we shall hear the old cry that things shouldn't be supported at a loss. Once again, this is a nation, not a firm. Parliament itself runs at a loss, because we need it, and if it would be better at a greater loss, I and others would willingly pay. But why, says Sir George Mammon, should *I* support a lot of doubtful artists? Why, says Mrs Mink, should I pay good money to educate, at *my* expense, a lot of irresponsible and ungrateful state scholars? The answer, dear sir, dear madam, is that *you* don't. On your own – learn your size – you could do practically nothing. We are talking about a method of common payment, for common services; we too shall be paying.

My third wish is in a related field: the field now dominated by the institutions of 'mass culture'. Often, it is the people at the head of these institutions who complain of running things at a loss. But the great popular newspapers, as news-papers, run at a loss. The independent television companies are planned to run at a loss. I don't mean temporary subsidies, but the whole basis of financing such institutions. The newspapers run at a heavy loss, which they make up with money from advertising – that is to say a particular use of part of the product of our common industry. To run at a loss, and then cover yourself with this kind of income, is of the essence of this kind of cultural institution, and this is entirely characteristic of our kind of capitalist society. The whole powerful array of mass cultural institutions has one keystone: money from advertising. Let them stop being complacent about other cultural institutions which run at a smaller loss, and meet it out of another part of the common product.

But what is it then that I wish? To pull out this keystone? No, not just like that. I point out merely that the organization of our present mass culture is so closely involved with the organization of capitalist society that the future of one cannot be considered except in terms of the future of the other. I think much of contemporary advertising is necessary only in terms of the kind of economy we now have: a stimulation of consumption in the direction of particular products and firms, often by irrelevant devices, rather than real advertising, which is an ordinary form of public notice. In a socialist economy, which I and others want, the whole of this pseudo-advertising would be irrelevant. But then what? My wish is that we may solve the problems that would then arise, where necessary things like newspapers would be running at something like their real loss, without either pricing them out of ordinary means, or exposing them to the dangers of control and standardization (for we want a more free and more varied press, not one less so). It is going to be very difficult, but I do not believe we are so uninventive as to be left showing each other a pair of grim alternatives: either the continuance of this crazy peddling, in which news and opinion are inextricably involved with the shouts of the market, bringing in their train the new slavery and prostitution of the selling of personalities; or else a dull, monolithic, controlled system, in which news and opinion are in the gift of a ruling party. We should be thinking, now, about ways of paying for our common services which will guarantee proper freedom to those who actu-ally provide the service, while protecting them and us against a domineering minority whether political or financial. I think there are ways, if we really believe in democracy.

But that is the final question: how many of us really believe in it? The capitalists don't; they are consolidating a power which can survive parliamentary changes. Many Labour planners don't; they interpret it as a society run by experts for an abstraction called the public interest. The people in the teashop don't; they are quite sure it is not going to be nice. And the others, the new dissenters? Nothing has done more to sour the democratic idea, among its natural supporters, and to drive them back into an angry self-exile, than the plain, overwhelming cultural issues: the apparent division of our culture into, on the one hand, a remote and self-gracious sophistication, on the other hand, a doped mass. So who then believes in democracy? The answer is really quite simple: the millions in England who still haven't got it, where they work and feel. There, as always, is the transforming energy and the business of the socialist intellectual is what it always was: to attack the clamps on that energy – in industrial relations, public administration, education, for a start; and to work in his own field on ways in which that energy, as released, can be concentrated and fertile. The technical means are difficult enough, but the biggest difficulty is in accepting, deep in our minds, the values on which they depend: that the ordinary people should govern; that culture and education are ordinary; that there are no masses to save, to capture, or to direct, but rather this crowded people in the course of an extraordinarily rapid and confusing expansion of their lives. A writer's job is with individual meanings, and with making these meanings common. I find these meanings in the expansion, there along the journey where the necessary changes are writing themselves into the land, and where the language changes but the voice is the same.

Suggestions for further reading

Geertz, Clifford, *The Interpretation of Cultures*, New York: Basic Books, 1973.
Hoggart, Richard, *The Uses of Literacy: Aspects of Working-class Life with Special Reference to Publications and Entertainments*, London: Chatto & Windus, 1957.
Williams, Raymond, *Culture and Society 1780–1950*, London: Chatto & Windus, 1958.

Chapter 9

Henri Lefebvre

'THE SOCIAL TEXT', 1961

THE SOCIAL TEXT. For the moment, we are going to present this notion, without developing its content. In fact, it will only acquire its full scope within the 'communications model'. Nevertheless, it also has a place in the theory of the semantic field. To tell the truth, the 'social text' is merely one aspect of the semantic field. It is the semantic field as it appears to everyone in daily life, in a non-conceptual or pre-conceptual (affective and perceptive) way.

It is the result of the combination, in infinitely variable proportions, of the formants mentioned above: *signals*, which tell us nothing, issue imperative commands, and repeat themselves in the exactly identical form; *symbols*, hidden and transparent, deep-seated phenomena of the social spectacle that transform it into something other than a spectacle because they have influence, because they demand or refuse participation, because they always bring surprise and the unexpected, even when they are making a reappearance; and lastly, *signs*, which bring only limited surprises and differences that are to some extent predictable.

Each of us is constantly – every day – faced with a social text. We move through it, we read it. Through this text, and through reading it, we communicate with others, with the wider [*globale*] society on the one hand and with nature on the other. At the same time, we are all part of a social text. Not only do we read, we are also read, deciphered, made plain (or not). We are all both subject and object, indivisibly (*first, object*; the social text encompasses us and we have to see ourselves as encompassed; *then, subject*; because we decipher and read the text from within, in that we see ourselves inside it, never entirely outside it).

In relation to information theory, we should say that *signals* represent redundancy of the modern social text: banality and clarity, triviality and intelligibility. *Signs* carry information. *Symbols* may be compared with the 'noise' that jostles out information, pouring forth in a familiar repertoire (codified and conventional) but at the same time enveloping information from all directions (background noise, white noise, etc.).

Still in relation to information theory, we will say that a social text is to some degree readable. Overloaded with symbolism or too full of information, too rich, or disjointed, it loses its legibility. Reduced to signals, it becomes utterly banal; it is clear, intelligible, boring; it repeats itself endlessly; it is swamped by redundancy. A good social text, readable and informative, surprises but does not overstretch its 'subjects'; it teaches them a lot, and constantly, but without overwhelming them; it is easily understood, without being trivial. The richness of a social text is thus measured by its accessible variability: by the wealth of novelty and possibility it offers individuals.

Armed with these concepts, let us analyse some forms of the social text, as we encounter them every day. The everyday reader misunderstands what is revealed upon analysis. But the informed reader realizes that he has before him part of the structures: a level of existence and reality, in which no level, of course, comprises the global reality.

In the *village* everything is symbolic, and reveals the truth of symbolism: ancient and powerful, strongly attached to things, and also to rhythms. Houses, fields, trees, sky, mountains or the sea are not simply or solely themselves. Cosmic and vital rhythms surround them; they contain subtle resonances; every 'thing' is part of a chorus. Space and soil symbolize the community; the church sets the time and symbolizes, in the cemetery, the world, life and death. In this poignantly archaic world, daily life presents itself in all simplicity, both utterly quotidian and inseparable from its resonances.

Every action, connected with some fundamental 'thing' – need, property, object, presence or absence – has symbolic import: taking bread, cutting it, opening or closing the door of the house, crossing the yard, or the garden, going out into the fields. In the village, everything abounds in life, the life of actions made more powerful by the symbols embodied in them. And it is all antiquated, outmoded, distant . . .

The *landscape* also presents us with a social text, usually readable and sometimes wonderfully composed, in which man and nature – the signs of the one, the symbols of the other – meet.

If we look closely at the *city*, we will soon see how hard it is to understand this masterly *oeuvre*, created by social groups and the whole society, an *oeuvre* that bears the traces of struggles that stimulated creativity but which also tends to erase out these traces. In the big cities, symbols have lost the ubiquity they had in the village. They are localized, and condensed. But their role is not less important. Quite the contrary: everything that has, or seeks, prestige and influence, everything that organizes and dominates this enormous mass of humanity, does all it can to retain the old symbols in order to benefit from their ancient authority, or offers new symbols to give itself legitimacy. Symbolism is condensed in the monuments; churches, cathedrals, palaces, great public and private buildings are full of symbols mingled with their decoration and aesthetic style. Monuments are works [*oeuvres*] that give a city its face and its rhythm. They are its memory and the figuration of its past, the active and affective hubs of its present everyday life, prefiguration of its future. We will call them 'supra-functional' or 'trans-functional', which is not to say they have no function, or transcend function, but that they have such diverse functions that no single functionality characterizes them or exhausts their social function. In working-class districts, by contrast, and around factories, inside actual businesses – few monuments or none at all. Symbols have disappeared (which means that in a horrible way everything symbolizes power and oppression). Nature has disappeared and culture is nowhere to be seen. Here, everything is a signal: a signal of work and work-related actions, and actions that sustain the workforce.

Beside its monuments and proletarian neighbourhoods, the city presents its informative text, rich in signs and meanings. Here, analytical description should typify and specify cities: the ancient city, organizing in a majestic fashion movements still close to vital rhythms around certain monuments – the arena, the temple, the agora, the forum or the theatre; the medieval city, with its enormous vitality, where all elements are interconnected: city and country, house and street, artisanal production and forms of exchange. Let us briefly mention the *street*, that characteristic feature of the modern city. It is the street, in the large industrial city, that has the most real, most original life. It is the street that in the big city offers incomparably more choices and possibilities than in the village or hamlet, what we call 'seductions', 'temptations', opportunities, appeals, whether we're talking about objects or people, encounters or solicitations and adventures. As soon as the street loses this attraction, either because it is deserted or because, contrariwise, dense traffic makes it unbearable, the city turns into a lunar desert.

The fact is, that in the society we're looking at – that we're reading – and of which we are a part, intermediaries enjoy extraordinary, sometimes outrageous privileges, to the detriment of those who have, or might have, more reality. This proposition could be based on economic analysis: the role of merchandise and money, intermediaries that become dominant, things that become fetishes, mediating processes that make themselves determinative by disguising and overwhelming the things they connect. Here, in the social text, this proposition should be directly legible. It is situated at the level of common sense and everyday argument; nevertheless, it looks paradoxical. It means that round about us, the place where we come and go, and meet – the street, the café, the station – is more important and genuinely more interesting than our homes, houses, places connected one with another. There lies the living paradox that everyday familiarity makes us accept, and whose absurdity it hides from us. Once, in the ancient or medieval city, this was not so. Circulation, of people, merchandise and vehicles, was not preponderant. The means of communication were subordinate to their ends and to human beings, as were every kind of medium and intermediary. Today, we're tempted to accept this state of affairs, and even to exaggerate it: when the street ceases to be interesting, daily life loses its interest. So, what is becoming of the city, jam-packed with cars, reduced to a system of signals?

The busy, active street, with no relation to nature apart from the sky and the clouds, or a few trees and flowers, represents the everyday in our social life. It is an almost complete representation of it, a 'digest' made interesting by being condensed. And this despite its being outside, or because it is outside, individual and social existences. A site of coming and going, of intrusion, circulation and communication, in an astonishing reversal it turns into the mirror image of the things it connects, more alive than those things. It becomes a microcosm of modern life. It plucks from obscurity all that is hidden. It makes it public. It takes away its private character and drags it across the stage of an informal theatre, where the actors are putting on a play that is also without form. The street publishes what happens elsewhere, in secret. It distorts it, but introduces it into the social text.

Like the everyday, the street changes constantly and always repeats itself. In the ceaseless alteration of times of day, people, objects and light, it tirelessly reiterates itself. The street is spectacle, almost solely spectacle, but not quite, because we are there, we walk, we stand still, we participate. The person in a hurry does not see the spectacle, but is part of it nevertheless. Almost, but not quite, pure spectacle, it is a book, or rather, an open paper, full of news, trivia, sensational stories, advertisements.[1] The street and the newspaper (analogues or homologues) join together in our everyday life, which, at the same time, they make and represent. Changing and constant, the street offers only limited surprises. The (truly) sensational, the outrageous, the absurd, the terrible and the sublime vaguely interrupt the pure, monotonously variable quasi-spectacle. Symbols go unnoticed. Who today takes seriously, or with a sense of tragedy the symbolic language of cathedrals: devils and divine figures? The street brings before our eyes a social text that is generally speaking good – dense and legible. All kinds of people mingle and get mixed up together in the street. Once, when class differences were less clear-cut than in our day, when there were 'estates' and 'castes' rather than classes, these differences were conspicuously expressed. The street was expressive. Today, these conspicuous differences have disappeared; they would make the crowds walking along the Champs Elysées or the boulevards intolerably colourful. But these social differences continue to be visible; they express meaning, through many signs and indicators scarcely visible to the casual observer. That is to say that the spectacle of the street encompasses multiple semiologies. Are faces expressive? A little, not very much. Clothes and manners signify. The spectacle of the street thus trains the eye and stimulates the faculty of observation. Think how many women, getting right inside (without knowing them) subtle systems of signs, are able at first glance to categorize another woman, assessing her shoes, stockings, hairstyle, hands and nails, jewellery and general appearance! A detailed analysis of the social text would pick up these partial systems of signs and significations, which are meshed and intertwined like the columns of a newspaper.[2]

The 'world of objects' as they present themselves in the street forms one of the most important commentaries, one of the subtlest but least well-defined system of signs. Merchandise offers itself in the street, but in so doing hides its commercial essence. It calls itself beauty, transquillity, luxury, sensuousness. The streets of a big modern city postulate and assert the harmony of needs, desires and goods. Paradise lost is parodically regained; at every step, original unity is caricaturally recreated. Goods, things, objects are displayed; they put themselves on view to attract and arouse desire, proclaiming their aim without perceptible irony: 'To every object its desire, to each his desires, to each desire its possession and enjoyment. There are goods and desires for all, democratically, even for children, even for the not-very-well-off, but even more – everything – for the rich'. At one and the same time completely within reach, since they answer to true and false desire, and horribly inaccessible, like women who are superbly dressed and presented, objects lead their sovereign life behind display windows. In the street, the inter-mediary among human lives, merchandise, these exchange-values, achieves auton-omy. Fetishism, taken to its extreme, acquires a sort of splendour; and the thing, the possession, the object, make their way back to symbolism via an amazing detour, by becoming symbols of wealth and pleasure without end or limit. Some streets have the beauty of museums, the same tired, dead beauty. This is where the process that changes the product – the merchandise – into a desirable and desired possession, comes full circle. Here, in this unpremeditated work of art – the street achieves the beauty of its society. Through the play of objects offered and rejected, the street becomes the place of dreams, the place where the imaginary, but also the most unsparingly real, come closest. It is where men and women, but women especially, pay court to things. Things with magical and regal powers, wonders and marvels, have the ability to transform (from the other side of the clear window-glass, in a parody of transparency in human relations) their courtiers and cour-tesans into things. 'Shopping' and 'window-shopping' have their magical practices, their religion, the cult of merchandise, sovereign and paramount. 'Goods', sancti-fied as such, are identical to their spectacle and advertising. Consumption is radiant and becomes holy. In pleasures possible and impossible, in dreams and frustrations, money proclaims more than its royalty – it proclaims its empire, its pontificate.

Far away, in the factories (factories that produce the wonderful objects, or pro-duce the means of producing them), everything is functional, or tries to be; everything is a signal of the repetitive actions of work and its technical organiza-tion. Far away, in the workers' suburbs or on the working-class housing estates, everything is functional, a signal of the repetitive actions that maintain the workforce in its everyday life . . .

Notes

1   [Editors' note: The notion of spectacle was also central to Situationist writings. See, above all, Guy Debord, *The Society of the Spectacle*, tr. Donald Nicolson-Smith (Zone Books: New York, 1994).]

2   Problems of semiology, general semantics, 'semantemes' and partial systems of social signs will be dealt with under 'models of communication'.

Suggestions for further reading

Baudrillard, Jean, *The System of Objects*, trans. James Benedict, London and New York: Verso, 1996.

de Certeau, Michel, *The Practice of Everyday Life*, trans. Steven Rendall, Berkeley and London: University of California Press, 1984.

Lefebvre, Henri, *Everyday Life in the Modern World*, trans. Sacha Rabinovitch, New York: Harper and Row, 1971.

Chapter 10

Hayden White

'THE BURDEN OF HISTORY', 1966

I

FOR BETTER THAN a century many historians have found it useful to employ a Fabian tactic against critics in related fields of intellectual endeavor. The tactic works like this: when criticized by social scientists for the softness of his method, the crudity of his organizing metaphors, or the ambiguity of his socio-logical and psychological presuppositions, the historian responds that history has never claimed the status of a pure science, that it depends as much upon intuitive as upon analytical methods, and that historical judgments should not therefore be evaluated by critical standards properly applied only in the mathematical and experimental disciplines. All of which suggests that history is a kind of art. But when reproached by literary artists for his failure to probe the more arcane strata of human consciousness and his unwillingness to utilize contemporary modes of literary representation, the historian falls back upon the view that history is after all a *semi*-science, that historical data do not lend themselves to "free" artistic manipulation, and that the form of his narratives is not a matter of choice, but is required by the nature of historical materials themselves.

This tactic has a long record of success in disarming critics of history; and it has allowed historians to claim occupancy of an epistemologically neutral middle ground that supposedly exists between art and science. Thus, historians sometimes argue that it is only in history that art and science meet in harmonious synthesis. According to this view, the historian not only mediates between past and present; he also has the special task of joining together two modes of comprehending the world that would normally be unalterably separated.

But there is mounting evidence that this Fabian tactic has outlived its useful-ness, and that the position which it had formerly secured for the historian among the various intellectual disciplines has been placed in serious jeopardy. Among contemporary historians one senses a growing suspicion that the tactic functions primarily to block serious consideration of the more significant advances in literature, social science, and philosophy in the twentieth century. And the opinion seems to be growing among nonhistorians that, far from being the desirable mediator between art and science that he claims to be, the historian is the irredeemable enemy of both. In short, everywhere there is resentment over what appears to be the historian's bad faith in claiming the privileges of both the artist and the scientist while refusing to submit to critical standards currently obtaining in either art or science.

There are two general causes of this resentment. One has to do with the nature of the historical profession itself. History is perhaps the conservative discipline par excellence. Since the middle of the nineteenth century, most historians have affected a kind of willful methodological naiveté. Originally this naiveté served a good purpose: it protected the historian from the tendency to embrace the monistic explanatory systems of a militant idealism in philosophy and an equally militant positivism in science. But this suspicion of system has become a sort of conditioned response among historians which has led to a resistance throughout the entire profession to almost any kind of critical self-analysis. Moreover, as history has become increasingly professionalized and specialized, the ordinary historian, wrapped up in the search for the elusive document that will establish him as an authority in a narrowly defined field, has had little time to inform himself of the latest developments in the more remote fields of art and science. Many historians are not aware, therefore, that the radical disjunction between art and science which their self-arrogated roles as mediators between them presupposes may perhaps be no longer justified.

Here is the second general cause of the current hostility towards history. That supposedly neutral middle ground between art and science which many nineteenth-century historians occupied with such self-confidence and pride of possession has dissolved in the discovery of the common constructivist character of both artistic and scientific statements. Most contemporary thinkers do not concur in the conventional historian's assumption that art and science are essentially different ways of comprehending the world. It now seems fairly clear that the nineteenth-century belief in the radical dissimilarity of art to science was a consequence of a misunderstanding fostered by the romantic artist's fear of science and the positivistic scientist's ignorance of art. No doubt both the romantic artist's fear of positivistic science and the positivistic scientist's disdain for romantic art were justified in the intellectual atmosphere in which they were born. But modern criticism—mostly as a result of advances made by psychologists in the investigation of the human synthesizing faculties—has achieved a clearer understanding of the operations by which the artist expresses his vision of the world and the scientist frames his hypotheses about it. As the implications of this achievement become more fully recognized, the need for a mediating agent between art and science disappears; at least it is no longer obvious that the historian is especially qualified to play the mediating role.

Thus, historians of this generation must be prepared to face the possibility that the prestige which their profession enjoyed among nineteenth-century intellectuals was a consequence of determinable cultural forces. They must be prepared to entertain the notion that history, as currently conceived, is a kind of historical accident, a product of a specific historical situation, and that, with the passing of the misunderstandings that produced that situation, history itself may lose its status as an autonomous and self-authenticating mode of thought. It may well be that the most difficult task which the current generation of historians will be called upon to perform is to expose the historically conditioned character of the historical discipline, to preside over the dissolution of history's claim to autonomy among the disciplines, and to aid in the assimilation of history to a higher kind of intellectual inquiry which, because it is founded on an awareness of the *similarities* between art and science, rather than their differences, can be properly designated as neither.

II

It should not be necessary to trace again the main lines of the quarrel between social science and history which has exercised the philosophically self-conscious practitioners of each during this century. It is an old controversy that goes back to the early nineteenth century. But it may be worthwhile to recall that the quarrel has achieved a kind of resolution which was not possible in the nineteenth century and that, as currently pursued, the quarrel transcends the limits of any mere discussion of method.

In the first place, during the nineteenth century science had not attained to the hegemonic position among the learned disciplines that it enjoys today. Contemporary philosophers of science are clearer about the nature of scientific explanations, and scientists themselves have succeeded in gaining that mastery over the physical world of which they could only dream throughout most of the last century. Thus, in our time, a statement such as that made by the late Ernst Cassirer, that "there is no second power in our modern world which may be compared with scientific thought," can be accepted as simple fact; it cannot be dismissed as mere rhetoric in the dispute for primacy among the learned disciplines, as it might have been in the nineteenth century. Today, science is recognized, as Cassirer went on to say, as "the summit and consummation of all our human activities, the last chapter in the history of mankind, and the most important subject of a philosophy of man. . . . We may dispute concerning the results of science or its first principles, but its general function seems to be unquestionable. It is science that gives us assurance of a common world."

The dazzling triumphs of science in our time have not only spurred investigators of social processes in their efforts to construct a science of society similar to the science of nature; they have also sharpened their hostility toward history. The most striking feature of *current* thought about history by many practitioners of the social sciences is the underlying implication that the conventional historian's conceptions of history are at once a symptom and a cause of a potentially fatal cultural illness. Thus the criticism of history by responsible social scientists takes on a moral dimension. To many of them the destruction of the conventional historian's conception of history is a necessary stage in the construction of a true science of society, and an essential component of the therapy which they will ultimately propose as a way of leading a sick society back to the path of enlightenment and progress.

In their devaluation of the conventional historian's approach to historical problems, contemporary social scientists are sustained by the course taken by the current debate among philosophers over the nature of historical investigation and the epistemological status of historical explanations. Significant contributions to this debate have been made by continental thinkers, but it has been developed with extraordinary intensity in the English-speaking world since 1942, when Carl Hempel published his essay "The Function of General Laws in History."

It would be untrue to suggest that contributors to this debate have arrived at any kind of general agreement about the nature of historical explanation. But it must be admitted that the course of the debate thus far is nothing if not disconcert-ing to anyone who shares Cassirer's evaluation of the hegemonic role of the physical sciences among the learned disciplines, and at the same time values the study of history. For a significant number of philosophers seem to have decided that history is either a third-order form of science, related to the social sciences as natural history was once related to the physical sciences, or that it is a second-order form of art, the epistemological value of which is questionable, the aesthetic worth of which is uncertain. These philosophers seem to have concluded that, if there is any such thing as a hierarchy of the sciences, history falls somewhere between Aristotelian physics and Linnaean biology—which is to say that it may have a certain interest for collectors of exotic world-views and debased mythologies, but not very much to contribute to the establishment of that "common world" spoken of by Cassirer as finding its daily confirmation in science.

III

Now, the expulsion of history from the first rank of the sciences would not be quite so unnerving if a good deal of twentieth-century literature did not manifest a hostility toward the historical consciousness even more marked than anything found in the scientific thought of our time. It could even be argued that one of the distinctive characteristics of contemporary literature is its underlying conviction that the historical consciousness must be obliterated if the writer is to examine with proper seriousness those strata of human experience which it is *modern* art's peculiar purpose to disclose. This conviction is so widespread that the historian's claim to be an artist appears pathetic when it does not appear merely ludicrous.

The modern writer's hostility towards history is evidenced most clearly in the practice of using the historian to represent the extreme example of repressed sensibility in the novel and theatre. Writers who have used historians in this way include Gide, Ibsen, Malraux, Aldous Huxley, Hermann Broch, Wyndham Lewis, Thomas Mann, Jean-Paul Sartre, Camus, Pirandello, Kingsley Amis, Angus Wilson, Elias Canetti, and Edward Albee—to mention only major or currently fashionable writers. The list could be extended considerably if one included the names of authors who have implicitly condemned the historical consciousness by suggesting the essential contemporaneity of all significant human experience. Virginia Woolf, Proust, Robert Musil, Italo Svevo, Gottfried Benn, Ernst Jünger, Valéry, Yeats,

Kafka, and D. H. Lawrence—all reflect the currency of the conviction voiced by Joyce's Stephen Dedalus, that history is the "nightmare" from which Western man must awaken if humanity is to be served and saved.

True, in many modern novels and plays the scientist appears as the antitype to the artist even more often than the historian does. But the writer usually displays some affection and even a certain willingness to forgive that is not extended to the historian characters. Whereas the scientist is most often shown as one who betrays the spirit out of a positive commitment to something else, such as a Faustian desire to control the world, or a need to plumb the secrets of sheer material process, the historian by contrast is usually portrayed as the enemy within the walls, as one who counterfeits pious attitudes of respect for the spirit only the better to subvert the spirit's claims on the creative individual. In short, the charge levelled against the historian by modern writers is also a moral one: but whereas the scientist accuses him only of a failure of method or intellect, the artist indicts him for a failure of sensibility or will.

The specifications of the indictment and the tactics by which it is prosecuted have not changed very much since Nietzsche set the pattern nearly a century ago. In *The Birth of Tragedy* (1872) Nietzsche set art over against all forms of abstractive intelligence as life against death for humanity. He included history among the many possible perversions of the Apollonian faculties of man and specifically charged it with having contributed to the destruction of the mythic fundaments of both individual and communal selfhood. Two years later, in "The Use and Abuse of History" (1874), he sharpened his conception of the opposition between the artistic and historical imaginations and claimed that wherever the "eunuchs" in the "harem of history" flourished, art must necessarily perish. "The unrestrained historical sense," he wrote, "pushed to its logical extreme, uproots the future, because it destroys illusions and robs existing things of the only atmosphere in which they can live."

Nietzsche hated history even more than he hated religion. History promoted a debilitating voyeurism in men, made them feel that they were latecomers to a world in which everything worth doing had already been done, and thereby undermined that impulse to heroic exertion that might give a peculiarly human, if only transient, meaning to an absurd world. The sense of history was the product of a faculty which distinguished man from the animal, namely memory, also the source of conscience. History had to be "seriously 'hated,' " Nietzsche concluded, "as a costly and superfluous luxury of the understanding," if human life itself were not to die in the senseless cultivation of those vices which a false morality, based on memory, induced in men.

Whatever else, for good or evil, the next generation learned from Nietzsche, it took up his hostility towards history as practiced by late-nineteenth-century academic historians with a vengeance. But Nietzsche was not alone responsible for the decline of history's authority among *fin de siècle* artists. Similar indictments, more or less explicit, can be found in writers as different in temperament and purpose as George Eliot, Ibsen, and Gide.

In *Middlemarch*, published in the same year as *The Birth of Tragedy*, Eliot used the encounter between Dorothea Brooke and Mr. Casaubon to provide a suitably

English indictment of the perils of antiquarianism. Miss Brooke, a Victorian virgin of assured income who desires to do just one self-transcending thing in her life, sees in Mr. Casaubon, twenty-five years her senior, "a living Bossuet, whose work would reconcile complete knowledge with devoted piety." And in spite of their difference in age, she resolves to marry him and dedicate her life to the service of his proposed historical study of the religious systems of the world. But during her honeymoon in Rome, her illusions are shattered. There, Casaubon reveals his incapacity to respond to the past which lives about him in the monuments of the city and, moreover, his inability to bring his own intellectual labors to completion in the present. "With his taper stuck before him," the author says of Casaubon, "he forgot the absence of windows, and in bitter manuscript remarks on other men's notions about the solar deities, he had become indifferent to the sunlight." In the end, Dorothea denies her obligations to Casaubon the scholar and marries young Ladislaw the artist, achieving her escape from the incubus of history thereby. George Eliot does not worry over the matter, but the gist of her thought is clear: artistic insight and historical learning are opposed, and the qualities of the responses to life which they respectively evoke are mutually exclusive.

Ibsen, writing in the next decade, is characteristically more concerned and more explicit about the limitations of a culture which values the past more than the present. Hedda Gabler suffers under the same burden as Dorothea Brooke: the incubus of the past, a surfeit of history—compounded by, or reflected in, a pervasive fear of the future. Upon their return from their honeymoon, Hedda and her husband, George Tesman, are welcomed by Tesman's aunt, who hints at the delights which their wedding-tour must have afforded them. To this George responds: "Well, for me it has been a sort of tour of research as well. I have had to do so much grubbing among old records—and to read no end of books too, Auntie."

Tesman, of course, is a historian, a younger Mr. Casaubon, writing the definitive study of domestic industries in Brabant during the Middle Ages. His labors consume his by no means ample supply of human affection; so much, in fact, that much of Hedda's restlessness can be said to have its origin in George's devotion to domestic industries of the past when he might be showing more domestic industry in the present. "You should just try it," Hedda shrieks at one point: "To hear nothing but the history of civilization, morning, noon, and night!"

Not that the cause of Hedda's complex dissatisfactions can be localized within such a limited range as the merely sexual. She is the victim of a whole web of repressions that are endemic to bourgeois society, only one of which is represented by Tesman's use of the past to avoid the problems of the present. Nonetheless. Hedda's growing contempt for her husband centers on his ascetic devotion to history, the realm of the dead and dying, which mirrors and reinforces Hedda's fear of an unknown future, symbolized by the child taking shape within her.

Tesman's rival is Eilert Lövberg, also an historian, but in the grander Hegelian style. He is a philosopher of history, whose book, "dealing with the march of civilization—in broad outline, as it were," inspires in Hedda the hope that his vision may afford a possible release from the narrow world circumscribed by Tesman's fractured imagination. Ibsen means us to see Lövberg as a man of talent and potential creative effort. He is composing a work on civilization that will undermine, rather than sustain, conventional morality, one that will tell a nobler truth than the comfortable half-truth upon which his first book and his youthful reputation are based. But as the play develops, Hedda comes to hate him; she gains possession of his manuscript, destroys it, and causes Lövberg's suicide. The destruction of the manuscript is, on the one hand, an act of personal revenge on Lövberg for his affair with Hedda's rival, Mrs. Elvsted. But on the other it is a symbolic repudiation of that "civilization" of which both Tesman and Lövberg, each in his own way, are thoughtless devotees. In the end, Hedda is threatened with subjection to Judge Brack, another custodian of tradition, which leads finally to her own suicide. And in the last scene, Tesman and Mrs. Elvsted, survivors of the tragedy, dedicate themselves to the lifelong task of editing Lövberg's *Nachlass*, thus indicating that neither has learned anything from the tragic events to which they might have borne choric witness. Tesman composes his own epitaph when he says: "Arranging other people's papers is just the work for me." Ibsen means us to see this as the scholar's equivalent of Judge Brack's philistine comment on Hedda's suicide: "People don't do such things."

In Gide's *Immoralist* (1902) the revolt against historical consciousness is even more explicit, the opposition between art's response to the living present and history's worship of the dead past more brutally drawn. The protagonist of the work, Michel, suffers from a sickness which combines all of the symptoms ascribed by Ibsen to the various characters of *Hedda Gabler*. Michel is at once a philistine, a historian, and increasingly, as the novel progresses, a philosopher of history. But his role as philosopher is earned only after he has suffered through his roles as philistine and as historian. And it is a purely temporary role, since it brings with it the realization that history, like civilization itself, must be transcended if the needs of life are to be served.

Michel's tuberculosis is just one manifestation of a general fear of living, which shows itself psychologically as an obsessive concern with dead cultures and dead forms of life. Thus, after his recovery from his physical illness has begun, Michel discovers that he has lost all interest in the past. He says:

> When . . . I wanted to start my work again and immerse myself once more in a minute study of the past, I discovered that something had, if not destroyed, at any rate modified my pleasure in it . . . and this something was the feeling of the present. The history of the past had now taken on for me the immobility, the terrifying fixity of the nocturnal shadows in the little courtyard of Biskra—the immobility of death. In the old days, I had taken pleasure in this very fixity, which enabled my mind to work with precision; the facts of history all appeared to me like specimens in a museum, or rather like plants in a herbarium, permanently dried, so that it was easy to forget they had once upon a time been juicy with sap and alive with sun. . . . I ended by avoiding ruins . . . I ended by despising the learning that had at first been my pride . . . In as much as I was a specialist, I appeared to myself as senseless; in as much as I was a man, did I know myself at all?

And so, when he returns to Paris to lecture on late Latin culture, Michel turns his awareness of the present against this debilitating sense of the past:

> I depicted artistic culture as welling up in a whole people, like a secretion, which is at first a sign of plethora, of a superabundance of health, but which afterwards stiffens, hardens, forbids the perfect contact of mind with nature, hides under the persistent appearance of life a diminution of life, turns into an outside sheath, in which the cramped mind languishes and pines, in which at last it dies. Finally, pushing my thought to its logical conclusions, I showed culture, born of life, as the destroyer of life.

But soon even this Lövbergian use of the past to destroy the past loses its attraction for Michel, and he gives up his academic career to seek communion with those dark forces which history had obscured and culture had weakened in him. The problematical conclusion of the book suggests that Gide wants us to see Michel as permanently crippled by his early devotion to a historicized culture, a living confirmation of the Nietzschean dictum that history banishes instinct and turns men into "shades and abstractions."

IV

In the decade before the First World War this hostility towards the historical consciousness and the historian gained wide currency among intellectuals in every country of Western Europe. Everywhere there was a growing suspicion that Europe's feverish rummaging among the ruins of its past expressed less a sense of firm control over the present than an unconscious fear of a future too horrible to contemplate. Even before the nineteenth century had ended, a great historian, Jacob Burckhardt, had foreseen the death of European culture and had responded by abandoning history as practiced in the academy, frankly proclaiming the necessity of its transformation into art but refusing to enter the public lists in the defense of his heresy. Schopenhauer had taught him not only the futility of historical inquiry of the conventional sort, but the folly of public exertion as well. Another great Schopenhauerian, Thomas Mann, in his novel *Buddenbrooks* (1901), had located the cause of this sense of imminent degeneration in the hyperconsciousness of an advanced middle-class culture. The aesthetic sensitivity of Hanno Buddenbrooks is at once the finest product of his bourgeois family's history and the sign of its disintegration. Meanwhile, philosophers such as Bergson and Klages argued that the conception of historical time itself, which bound men to antiquated institutions, ideas, and values, was the cause of the sickness.

Among social scientists the hostility towards history was less marked. Sociologists, for example, continued to search for some way of uniting history and science in new disciplines, the so-called "sciences of the spirit," in accordance with the program mapped out by Wilhelm Dilthey and executed by Max Weber in Germany and by Emile Durkheim in France. Neo-Kantians like Wilhelm Windelband, on the other hand, sought to distinguish between history and science, designating history as a kind of art which, even though it could not provide *laws* of social change, still offered valuable insights into the totality of possible human experiences. Croce went further, arguing that history was a form of art but at the same time a master discipline, the sole possible basis for a social wisdom adequate to the needs of contemporary Western man.

The First World War did much to destroy what remained of history's prestige among both artists and social scientists, for the war seemed to confirm what Nietzsche had maintained two generations earlier. History, which was supposed to provide some sort of training for life, which was supposed to be "philosophy teaching by examples," had done little to prepare men for the coming of the war; it had not taught them what would be expected of them during the war; and when the war was over historians seemed incapable of rising above narrow partisan loyalties and making sense of the war in any significant way. When they did not merely parrot the current slogans of the governments regarding the criminal intent of the enemy, historians tended to fall back on the view that no one had really wanted the war at all; it had "just happened."

Such may well have been the case, of course; but it seemed less an explanation than an admission that *no* explanation, at least on historical grounds, was possible. Whether the same could have been said of other disciplines was unimportant. Historical studies, if we include classics under that term, had formed the center of humanistic and social scientific studies before the war; and it was therefore natural that they should become a prime target of those who had lost faith in man's capacity to make sense out of his situation when the war had ended. Paul Valéry expressed the new antihistoricist attitude best when he wrote:

> History is the most dangerous product evolved from the chemistry of the intellect. . . . History will justify anything. It teaches precisely nothing, for it contains everything and furnishes examples of everything. . . . Nothing was more completely ruined by the last war than the pretension to foresight. But it was not from any lack of knowledge of history, surely?

To the more desperate spiritual casualties of the war neither past nor future could provide orientation for specifically human actions in the present. As the German poet Gottfried Benn put it: "A wise man is ignorant/of change and development/his children and his children's children/are not part of his world." And he drew from this radically ahistorical conception of the world its inevitable ethical consequences:

> I am struck by the thought that it might be more revolutionary and worthier of a vigorous and active man to teach his fellow man this simple truth: You are what you are and you will never be different; this is, was, and always will be your life. He who has money, lives long; he who has authority, can do no wrong; he who has might, establishes right. Such is history! *Ecce historia!* Here is the present; take of its body, eat, and die.

In Russia, where the Revolution of 1917 had raised with especial immediacy the problem of the relationship of the new to the old, M. O. Gershenson wrote to the historian V. I. Ivanov of his hope that the violence of the time would usher in a new and more creative interaction between "naked man and the naked earth." "For me," he wrote, "there is a prospect of happiness in a Lethean bath that would erase the memory of all religions and philosophical systems"—in short, relieve him of the burden of history.

This antihistorical attitude underlay both the Nazism and the Existentialism that would constitute the legacy of the thirties to our time. Both Spengler, in so many ways the progenitor of Nazism, and Malraux, the recognized father of French Existentialism, taught that history was valuable only insofar as it destroyed, rather than established, responsibility towards the past. Even that transparent humanist Ortega y Gasset, writing in 1923, shares their belief that the past was *only* a burden. "Our institutions, like our theatres," he wrote in *The Modern Theme* (1923), "are anachronisms. We have neither the courage to break resolutely with such devitalized accretions of the past nor can we in any way adjust to them." And during the mid-thirties, in a work dedicated to a victim of Nazi oppression, he confessed that the only lesson that history had taught him was that "man is an infinitely plastic entity of which one may make what one will, precisely because of itself it is nothing save only the mere potentiality to be 'as you like.' " Hitler's "revolution of nihilism" was based precisely on this sense of the irrelevancy of known past to lived present. "What was true in the nineteenth century," Hitler said on one occasion to Rauschning, "is no longer true in the twentieth." And both Nazi intellectuals (such as Heidegger and Jünger) and Existentialist enemies of Nazism in France (such as Camus and Sartre) agreed with him on this matter. For both, the issue was not *how* the past was to be studied, but *if* it ought to be studied at all.

Meursault, the hero of Camus's first novel, *The Stranger* (1942), is an "inno-cent" murderer. His killing of a man he does not know is a totally meaningless gesture, no different in essence from the thousands of other thoughtless acts which make up his daily life. It is the "historically" wise prosecutor who shows the jury how the atomic events that constitute Meursault's existence can be linked together in such a way as to make him "responsible" for a "crime" and to justify his condem-nation as a murderer. Meursault's life, represented by the author as a perfectly random set of events, is woven into a pattern of conscious intention by those who "know" what both private sensibility and public gesture ought to "mean." It is this ability to cast a web of specious "meaning" over the past which alone, according to Camus, allows society to distinguish between Mersault's "crime" and society's "execution" of him as a murderer. Camus denied that there is any real distinction between different kinds of killing. It is only hypocrisy, sustained by historical consciousness, that allows society to call Meursault's act a "murder" and its own execution of Meursault "justice."

In *The Rebel* (1951) Camus returned to this theme, arguing that both the totalitarianism and the anarchism of the present age had their origins in a nihilistic attitude that derived from Western man's obsessive desire to make sense of his-tory. "Purely historical thought is nihilistic," he wrote; "it wholeheartedly accepts the evil of history," and delivers the earth to naked force. And then, echoing the

Nietzsche he had just decried, he sets art over against history as that which alone can reunite man with a nature from which he has become all but totally estranged. The poet René Char provides Camus with an epitaph for his basic posture on the matter: "Obsession with the harvest and indifference to history are the two extremities of my bow."

Whatever their differences on other subjects, the two leaders of French Existentialism, Camus and Sartre, agreed in their contempt for historical consciousness. The protagonist of Sartre's first novel, Roquentin, in *Nausea* (1938), is a professional historian who, as he himself puts it, has "written lots of articles," but nothing that required any "talent." Roquentin is trying to write a book on an eighteenth-century diplomat, one Marquis de Rollebon. But he is overwhelmed by the documents; there are just "too many" of them. Moreover, they lack all "firmness and consistency." It is not that they contradict each other, Roquentin says it is that "they do not seem to be about the same persons." And yet, Roquentin notes in his diary; "Other historians work from the same sources of information. How do they do it?"

The answer, of course, lies in Roquentin's own sense of the absence of all "firmness and consistency" in himself. Roquentin experiences his own body as "nature without humanity" and his mental life as an illusion: "Nothing happens while you live. The scenery changes, people come in and go out, that's all. There are no beginnings. Days are tacked on to days without rhyme or reason, an interminable, monotonous addition." Roquentin lacks any central consciousness on the basis of which the world, either of past or present, can be ordered. "I hadn't the right to exist," Roquentin writes; "I had appeared by chance, I existed like a stone, a plant, a microbe. My life put out feelers towards small pleasures in every direction. Sometimes it put out vague signals; at other times I felt nothing more than a harmless buzzing." His friend, the Autodidact, who possesses a simple faith in the power of learning to bring salvation, holds up before Roquentin the model of The American Optimist. The Optimist believes, like the old-fashioned humanist, that "life has a meaning if we choose to give it one." But Roquentin's sickness arises precisely from his incapacity to believe in such fatuous slogans. To him, "Everything is born without reason, prolongs itself out of weakness, and dies by chance." Sartre had only to add the "*Ecce historia!*" of Gottfried Benn to telegraph more explicitly the antihistoricist bent of his first philosophical work, *Being and Nothingness* (1943), on which he was working while he was writing *Nausea*. Reviewers of Sartre's *Words* (1964) would have done well to have kept *Nausea* and *Being and Nothingness* in mind. Had they done so they would have been less offended by the opaqueness of Sartre's "confessions." They would have known that he believes that the only important history is what the individual remembers and that the individual remembers only what he *wills* to remember. Sartre rejects the psychoanalytical doctrine of the unconscious and argues that the past is what we decide to remember of it; it enjoys no existence apart from our consciousness of it. We choose our past in the same way that we choose our future. The historical past, therefore, is, like our various personal pasts, at best a myth, justifying our gamble on a specific future, and at worst a lie, a retrospective rationalization of what we have in fact become through our choices.

I could continue to add to these examples of the revolt against history in modern writing. But if I have not made my point by now, I shall probably not succeed in making it at all: the modern artist does not think very much of what used to be called the historical imagination. In fact, to many of them the phrase "historical imagination" not only contains a contradiction in terms; it constitutes the fundamental barrier to any attempt by men in the present to close realistically with their most pressing spiritual problems. The attitude of many modern artists towards history is much like that of N. O. Brown, who sees history as a kind of "fixation" which "alienates the neurotic from the present and commits him to the unconscious quest for the past in the future." For them, as for Brown, history is not only a substantive burden imposed upon the present by the past in the form of outmoded institutions, ideas, and values, but also *the way of looking at the world* which gives to these outmoded forms their specious authority. In short, to a significant segment of the artistic community the historian appears to be the carrier of a disease which was at once the motive force and the nemesis of nineteenth-century civilization. This is why so much of modern fiction turns upon the attempt to liberate Western man from the tyranny of the historical consciousness. It tells us that it is only by disenthralling human intelligence from the sense of history that men will be able to confront creatively the problems of the present. The implications of all this for any historian who values the artistic vision as anything more than mere play are obvious: he must ask himself how he can participate in this liberating activity and whether his participation entails the destruction of history itself.

Historians cannot ignore criticism from the intellectual community at large, nor take refuge in the favor which they enjoy with the literate laity. For an appeal to the esteem in which a learned discipline is held by the common man might be used to justify any kind of activity, harmful as well as beneficial to civilization. Such an appeal can be used to justify the most banal journalism. In fact, taking the case of journalism a bit further, the more banal the journalism, the better its chances of being esteemed by the common man. And far from providing a source of comfort, there might be genuine cause for concern when any learned discipline loses its occult character and begins to deal in truths which *only* the general public finds exciting. Insofar as historians pretended to belong to a community of intellectuals distinguishable from the literate public in general, they have obligations to the former that transcend their obligations to the latter. If, therefore, both artists and scientists—in their capacities as artists and scientists and not in their capacities as members of the Civil War Book Club—find the truths which historians deal in trivial and possibly harmful, then it is time for historians to ask themselves seriously whether such charges may not have some basis in reality.

Nor can historians plead that the judgments of artists and scientists about how the past ought to be studied are irrelevant. After all, historians have conventionally maintained that neither a specific methodology nor a special intellectual equipment is required for the study of history. What is usually called the "training" of the historian consists for the most part of study in a few languages, journeyman work in the archives, and the performance of a few set exercises to acquaint him with standard reference works and journals in his field. For the rest, a general experience of human affairs, reading in peripheral fields, self-discipline, and *Sitzfleisch* are all that are necessary. Anyone can master the requirements fairly easily. How can it be said then that the professional historian is peculiarly qualified to define the questions which one may ask of the historical record and is alone able to determine when adequate answers to the questions thus posed have been given? It is no longer self-evidently true for the intellectual community at large that the disinterested study of the past—"for its own sake," as the cliché has it—is either ennobling or even illuminative of our humanity. In fact, the general consensus in both the arts and the sciences seems to be precisely the opposite. And it follows that *the burden of the historian* in our time is to reestablish the dignity of historical studies on a basis that will make them consonant with the aims and purposes of the intellectual community at large, that is, transform historical studies in such a way as to allow the historian to participate positively in the liberation of the present from *the burden of history*.

V

How can this be done? First of all, historians must admit the justification of the current rebellion against the past. Contemporary Western man has good reason to be obsessed by his sense of the uniqueness of his problems and is justifiably convinced that the historical record as presently provided offers little help in the quest for adequate solutions to those problems. To anyone who is sensitive to the radical dissimilarity of our present to all past situations, the study of the past "as an end in itself" can only appear as thoughtless obstructionism, as willful resistance to the attempt to close with the present world in all its strangeness and mystery. In the world in which we daily live, anyone who studies the past as an end in itself must appear to be either an antiquarian, fleeing from the problems of the present into a purely personal past, or a kind of cultural necrophile, that is, one who finds in the dead and dying a value he can never find in the living. The contemporary historian has to establish the value of the study of the past, not as an end in itself, but as a way of providing perspectives on the present that contribute to the solution of problems peculiar to our own time.

Since the historian claims no way of knowing uniquely his own, this implies a willingness on the part of the contemporary historian to come to terms with the techniques of analysis and representation which *modern* science and *modern* art have offered for understanding the operations of consciousness and social process. In short, the historian can claim a voice in the contemporary cultural dialogue only insofar as he takes seriously the kind of questions that the art and the science *of his own time* demand that he ask of the materials he has chosen to study.

Historians frequently look back upon the early nineteenth century as the classic age of their discipline, not only because history emerged as a distinct way of looking at the world at that time, but also because there was a close working relationship and interchange between history, art, science, and philosophy. Romantic artists went to history for their themes and appealed to "historical consciousness" as a justification for their attempts at cultural palingenesis, their attempts to make the past a living presence to their contemporaries. And certain sciences—geology and biology in particular—availed themselves of ideas and concepts which had been commonly used only in history up to that time. The category of the historical dominated philosophy among the post-Kantian idealists and served as the organizing category among the later Hegelians, of both the Left and the Right. To the modern historian reflecting on the achievements of that age in all fields of thought and expression, the critical importance of the sense of history appears obvious, the function of the historian as mediator between the arts and sciences of the age seems manifest.

It would be more correct, however, to recognize that the early nineteenth century was a time when art, science, philosophy, and history were united in a *common effort* to comprehend the experiences of the French Revolution. What is most impressive about the achievements of that age is not "the sense of history" as such, but the willingness of intellectuals in all fields to cross the boundaries that divided one discipline from another and to open themselves up to the use of illuminating metaphors for organizing reality, whatever their origins in particular disciplines or world-views. Men like Michelet and Tocqueville are properly designated as historians only by their subject matter, not by their methods. Insofar as their method alone is concerned, they are just as easily designated as scientists, artists, or philosophers. The same can be said of "historians" like Ranke and Niebuhr, of "novelists" like Stendhal and Balzac, of "philosophers" like Hegel and Marx, and of "poets" like Heine and Lamartine.

But some time during the nineteenth century all this changed—not because artists, scientists, and philosophers ceased to be interested in historical questions, but because many historians had become wedded to certain early-nineteenth-century conceptions of what art, science, and philosophy *ought to be*. And insofar as historians of the second half of the nineteenth century continued to see their work as a combination of art and science, they saw it as a combination of *romantic* art on the one hand and of *positivistic* science on the other. In sum, by the middle of the nineteenth century, historians, for whatever reason, had become locked into conceptions of art and science which both artists and scientists had progressively to abandon if they were to understand the changing world of internal and external perceptions offered to them by the historical process itself. One of the reasons, then, that the modern artist, unlike his early-nineteenth-century counterpart, refuses to admit a common cause with the modern historian is that he rightly sees the historian as the custodian of an antiquated notion of what art is.

In fact, when many contemporary historians speak of the "art" of history, they seem to have in mind a conception of art that would admit little more than the nineteenth-century novel as a paradigm. And when they say that they are artists, they seem to mean that they are artists in the way that Scott or Thackeray were artists. They certainly do not mean to identify themselves with action painters, kinetic sculptors, existentialist novelists, imagist poets, or *nouvelle vague* cinematographers. While often displaying the works of modern nonobjective artists on their walls and in their bookcases, historians continue to act as if they believed that the major, not to say the sole, purpose of art is to tell a story. Thus, for example, H. Stuart Hughes argues in a recent work on the relation of history to science and art that "the historian's supreme technical virtuosity lies in fusing the new method of social and psychological analysis with his traditional storytelling function." It is of course true that the artist's purpose *may* be served by telling a story, but this is only one of the possible modes of representation offered to him today, and it is a decreasingly important one at that, as the *nouvelle roman* in France has impressively shown.

A similar criticism can be levelled at the historian's claim to a place among the scientists. When historians speak of themselves as scientists, they seem to be invoking a conception of science that was perfectly suitable for the world in which Herbert Spencer lived and worked, but it has very little to do with physical sciences as they have developed *since* Einstein and with the social sciences as they have evolved *since* Weber. Again, when Hughes speaks of "the new method of social and psychological analysis," he seems to have in mind the methods offered by Weber and Freud—methods which some contemporary social scientists regard as being at best the primitive roots, rather than the mature fruit, of their disciplines.

In sum, when historians claim that history is a combination of science and art, they generally mean that it is a combination of *late-nineteenth-century* social science and *mid-nineteenth-century* art. That is to say, they seem to be aspiring to little more than a synthesis of modes of analysis and expression that have their antiquity alone to commend them. If this is the case, then artists and scientists alike are justified in criticizing historians, *not because they study the past*, but because they are studying it with *bad* science and *bad* art.

The "badness" of these hoary conceptions of science and art is contained above all in the outmoded conceptions of objectivity which characterize them. Many historians continue to treat their "facts" as though they were "given" and refuse to recognize, unlike most scientists, that they are not so much found as constructed by the kinds of questions which the investigator asks of the phenomena before him. It is the same notion of objectivity that binds historians to an uncritical use of the chronological framework for their narratives. When historians try to relate their "findings" about the "facts" in what they call an "artistic" manner, they uniformly eschew the techniques of literary representation which Joyce, Yeats, and Ibsen have contributed to modern culture. There have been no significant attempts at surrealistic, expressionistic, or existentialist historiography in this century (except by novelists and poets themselves), for all of the vaunted "artistry" of the historians of modern times. It is almost as if the historians believed that the *sole possible form* of historical narration was that used in the English novel as it had developed by the late nineteenth century. And the result of this has been the progressive antiquation of the "art" of historiography itself.

Burckhardt, for all his Schopenhauerian pessimism (or perhaps because of it), was willing to experiment with the most advanced artistic techniques of *his* time. His *Civilization of the Renaissance* can be regarded as an exercise in impressionistic historiography, constituting, in its own way, as radical a departure from the conventional historiography of the nineteenth century as that of the impressionist painters, or that of Baudelaire in poetry. Beginning students in history—and not a few professionals—have trouble with Burckhardt because he broke with the dogma that an historical account has to "tell a story," at least in the usual, chronologically ordered way. To account for the strangeness of Burckhardt's work, modern historians of historical writing have put him down as a kind of embryonic social scientist who dealt in ideal types and therefore anticipated Weber. The generalization would be true only if it were set within the context of an awareness of the extent to which Burckhardt and Weber both shared a peculiarly aesthetic conception of science. Like his contemporaries in art, Burckhardt cuts into the historical record at different points and suggests different perspectives on it, omitting, ignoring, or distorting as his artistic purpose requires. His intention was not to tell the *whole* truth about the Italian Renaissance but *one* truth about it, in precisely the same way that Cézanne abandoned any attempt to tell the whole truth about a landscape. He had abandoned the dream of telling the truth about the past by means of telling a story because he had long since abandoned the belief that history had any inherent meaning or significance. The only "truth" that Burckhardt recognized was that which he had learned from Schopenhauer—namely, that every attempt to give form to the world, every human affirmation, was tragically doomed in the end, but that individual affirmation attained to a worth of its own insofar as it succeeded in imposing upon the chaos of the world a momentary form.

Thus, in Burckhardt's work the concept of "individualism" serves primarily as a focussing metaphor which, precisely because it filters out certain kinds of information and heightens awareness of others, allows him to see what he wants to see with especial clarity. The usual chronological framework would have hindered this attempt at achieving a *specific* perspective on his problem, and so Burckhardt abandoned it. And once he was freed from the limitations of the "storytelling" technique, he was liberated from the necessity of constructing a "plot" with heroes, villains, and chorus, as the conventional historian is always driven to do. Since he possessed the courage to use a metaphor constructed out of his own immediate experience, Burckhardt was able to see things in the life of the fifteenth century that no one had seen with a similar clarity before him. Even those conventional historians who find him wrong in his facts grant to his work the title of a classic. What most fail to see, however, is that in praising Burckhardt they often condemn their own rigid commitment to conceptions of science and art which Burckhardt himself had transcended.

Many historians today show interest in the latest technical and methodological developments in the social sciences. Some are attempting to utilize econometrics, game theory, theory of conflict resolution, role analysis, and the rest of it whenever they sense that their conventional historiographical purposes can be served in so doing. But very few historians have tried to utilize modern artistic techniques in any significant way. One of the few to have made the effort is Norman O. Brown.

In *Life Against Death*, Brown offers the historiographical equivalent of the antinovel; for he is writing antihistory. Those historians who have even bothered to notice Brown's book have usually labelled him a Freudian and dismissed him. But Brown's true significance lies in his willingness to follow out a line of investigation suggested by Nietzsche and carried forward by Klages, Heidegger, and contemporary existentially oriented phenomenologists. He begins by assuming nothing about the validity of history, either as a mode of existence or as a form of knowing. He uses historical materials, but he uses them in precisely the same way that one might use contemporary experience. He reduces all of the data of consciousness, past as well as present, to the same ontological level, and then, by a series of brilliant and shocking juxtapositions, involutions, reductions, and distortions, forces the reader to see with new clarity materials to which he has become oblivious through sustained association, or which he has repressed in response to social imperatives. In short, in his history Brown achieves the same effects as those sought by a "Pop" artist or by John Cage in one of his "happenings."

Is there anything intrinsic to our approach to the past that allows us to regard Brown as unworthy of consideration as a serious historian? Certainly, we cannot do so if we maintain the myth that historians are as much artists as scientists. For in Brown's book we are forced to confront the problem of the style he has chosen for his work as a historian before we can go on to the further question of whether his history constitutes an "adequate" portrayal of the past or not.

But where are we to find the criterion to determine when, on the one hand, the "account" is adequate to the "facts" and if, on the other, the "style" chosen by the historian is appropriate or inappropriate to the "account"? Those historians who credit the belief that history is a combination of art and science ought to address themselves to the further "internal" problem of the equation, that is to say, the problem of the choice of *one* artistic style among the many offered for consideration by the literary heritage in which the historian works. For it is no longer obvious that we can use the terms *artist* and *storyteller* synonymously. If we are going to call into question the right of a historian to use a nineteenth-century notion of social science, we must also be prepared to call into question his use of a nineteenth-century conception of art.

VI

There is a sense in which the notion that history is a combination of science and art is merely a further indication of the antiquated views of both which obtain among historians. For nearly three decades now, philosophers of science and aestheticians have been working toward a better understanding of the similarities between scientific statements on the one hand and artistic statements on the other. Inquiries such as those of Karl Popper into the logic of scientific explanation and the impact of probability theory on considerations of the nature of scientific laws have undermined the naive positivist's notion of the absolute character of scientific propositions. Contemporary British and American philosophers have modulated the harsh distinctions originally drawn by positivists between scientific statements and metaphysical statements, removing the stigma of "meaninglessness" from the latter. Within the atmosphere of exchange between the "two cultures" thus generated, a better understanding of the nature of artistic statements has been achieved—and with it a better possibility of resolving the old problem of the relation of the scientific to the artistic components in historical explanations.

It now seems possible to hold that an explanation need not be assigned unilaterally to the category of the literally truthful on the one hand or the purely imaginary on the other, but can be judged solely in terms of the richness of the metaphors which govern its sequence of articulation. Thus envisaged, the governing metaphor of an historical account could be treated as a *heuristic rule which self-consciously eliminates certain kinds of data from consideration as evidence*. The historian operating under such a conception could thus be viewed as one who, like the modern artist and scientist, seeks to exploit a certain perspective on the world that does not pretend to exhaust description or analysis of all of the data in the entire phenomenal field but rather offers itself as *one way among many* of disclosing certain aspects of the field. As Gombrich points out in *Art and Illusion*, we do not expect that Constable and Cézanne will have looked for the same thing in a given landscape, and when we confront their respective representations of a landscape, we do not expect to have to choose between them and determine which is the "more correct" one. The result of this attitude is not relativism but the recognition that the style chosen by the artist to represent either an inner or an outer experience carries with it, on the one hand, specific criteria for determining when a given representation is internally consistent and, on the other, provides a system of translation which allows the viewer to link the image with the thing represented on specific levels of objectification. Style thus functions as what Gombrich calls a "system of notation," as a provisional protocol or an etiquette. When we view the work of an artist—or, for that matter, of a scientist—we do not ask if he sees what we would see in the same general phenomenal field, but whether or not he has introduced into his representation of it anything that could be considered false information *for anyone who is capable of understanding the system of notation used*.

If applied to historical writing, the methodological and stylistic cosmopolitanism which this conception of representation promotes would force historians to abandon the attempt to portray "one particular portion of life, *right side up* and in *true* perspective," as a famous historian put it some years ago, and to recognize that there is no such thing as a *single* correct view of any object under study but that there are *many* correct views, each requiring its own style of representation. This would allow us to entertain seriously those creative distortions offered by minds capable of looking at the past with the same seriousness as ourselves but with different affective and intellectual orientations. Then we should no longer naively expect that statements about a given epoch or complex of events in the past "correspond" to some preexistent body of "raw facts." For we should recognize that *what constitutes the facts themselves* is the problem that the historian, like the artist, has tried to solve in the choice of the metaphor by which he orders his world, past, present, and future. We should ask only that the historian show some tact in the use of his governing metaphors: that he neither overburden them with data nor fail to use them to their limit; that he respect the logic implicit in the mode of discourse he has decided upon; and that, when his metaphor begins to show itself unable to accommodate certain kinds of data, he abandon that metaphor and seek another, richer, and more inclusive metaphor than that with which he began—in the same way that a scientist abandons a hypothesis when its use is exhausted.

Such a conception of historical inquiry and representation would open up the possibility of using contemporary scientific *and* artistic insights in history without leading to radical relativism and the assimilation of history to propaganda, or to that fatal monism which has always heretofore resulted from attempts to wed history and science. It would permit the plunder of psychoanalysis, cybernetics, game theory, and the rest without forcing the historian to treat the metaphors thus confiscated from them as inherent in the data under analysis, as he is forced to do when he works under the demand for an impossibly comprehensive objectivity. And it would permit historians to conceive of the possibility of using impressionistic, expressionistic, surrealistic, and (perhaps) even actionist modes of representation for dramatizing the significance of data which they have uncovered but which, all too frequently, they are prohibited from seriously contemplating as evidence. If historians of our generation were willing to participate actively in the general intellectual and artistic life of our time, the worth of history would not have to be defended in the timid and ambivalent ways that are now used. The methodological ambiguity of history offers opportunities for creative comment on past and present that no other discipline enjoys. If historians were to seize the opportunities thus offered, they might in time convince their colleagues in other fields of intellectual and expressive endeavor of the falsity of Nietzsche's claim that history is "a costly and superflous luxury of the understanding."

But to what purpose ultimately? Merely to exploit the human capacity for play or mind's ability to frolic in images? There are worse activities for a morally responsible man, of course, but merely to demand the exercise of our image-making abilities does not necessarily lead to the conclusion that we should exercise them on the historical past. Here it would be well to bear in mind the line of argument which descends from Schopenhauer to Sartre and which suggests that the historical record can never become the occasion of either significant aesthetic or scientific experience. The documentary record, this tradition maintains, first invites the exercise of the speculative imagination by its incompleteness, and then discourages it by requiring that the historian remain bound to the consideration of those few facts which it does provide. To both Schopenhauer and Sartre, therefore, the artist is well advised to ignore the historical record and limit himself to the consideration of the phenomenal world as presented to him in his everyday experience. It is worth asking, then, why the past ought to be studied at all and what function can be served by a contemplation of things under the aspect of history. Put another way: is there any reason why we ought to study things under the aspect of their past-ness rather than under the aspect of their present-ness, which is the aspect under which everything offers itself for contemplation immediately?

In my view, the most suggestive answer to this question was provided by thinkers who flourished during history's golden age—the period between 1800 and 1850. Thinkers of that age recognized that the function of history, as distinguished from both the art and the science *of that time*, was to provide a specific temporal dimension to man's awareness of himself. Whereas both before and after this time students of human affairs tended to reduce human phenomena to manifestations of hypostatized natural or mental processes (as in idealism, naturalism, vitalism, and the like), the best representatives of historical thought between 1800 and 1850 saw the historical imagination as a faculty which, beginning in man's impulse to clothe the chaos of the phenomenal world in stable images—that is, in an aesthetic impulse—discharged itself in a tragic reaffirmation of the fundamental fact of change and process, providing thereby a ground for the celebration of man's responsibility for his own fate.

The exponents of realistic historicism—Hegel, Balzac, and Tocqueville, to take representatives from philosophy, the novel, and historiography, respectively

—agreed that the task of the historian was less to remind men of their obligation to the past than to force upon them an awareness of how the past could be used to effect an ethically responsible transition from present to future. All three saw history as educating men to the fact that their own present world had once existed in the minds of men as an unknown and frightening future, but how, as a consequence of specific human decisions, this future had been transformed into a present, that familiar world in which the historian himself lived and worked. All three saw history as informed by a tragic sense of the absurdity of individual human aspiration and, at the same time, a sense of the necessity of such aspiration if the human residuum were to be saved from the potentially destructive awareness of the movement of time. Thus, for all three, history was less an end in itself than a preparation for a more perfect understanding and acceptance of the individual's responsibility in the fashioning of the common humanity of the future. Hegel, for example, writes that in historical reflection Spirit is "engulfed in the night of its own self-consciousness; its vanished existence is, however, conserved therein; and this superseded existence—the previous state, but born anew from the womb of knowledge—is the new stage of existence, a new world, and a new embodiment or mode of Spirit." Balzac presents his *Human Comedy* as a "history of the human heart" which advances the novel beyond the point where Scott had left it by virtue of the "system" that links the various pieces of the whole together in a "complete history of which each chapter is a novel and each novel the picture of a period," the whole promoting a more realistic awareness of the uniqueness of the present age. And, finally, Tocqueville offers his *Ancien Régime* as an effort to "make clear in what respects [the present social system] resembles and in what it differs from the social system that preceded it; and to determine what was gained by that upheaval." And he goes on to point out: "When I have found in our forefathers any of those virtues so vital to a nation but now well-nigh extinct—a spirit of healthy independence, high ambitions, faith in oneself and in a cause—I have thrown them into relief. Similarly, whenever I found traces of any of those vices which after destroying the old order still affect the body politic, I have emphasized them; for it is in the light of evils to which they formerly gave rise that we can gauge the harm they yet may do." In short, all three interpreted the burden of the historian as a moral charge to free men from the burden of history. They did not see the historian as prescribing a specific ethical system valid for all times and places, but they did see him as charged with the special task of inducing in men an awareness that their present condition was always in part a product of specifically human choices, which could therefore be changed or altered by further human action in precisely that degree. History thus sensitized men to the *dynamic* elements in every achieved present, taught the inevitability of change, and thereby contributed to the release of that present to the past without ire or resentment. It was only after historians lost sight of these dynamic elements in their own lived present, and began to relegate all significant change to a mythic past—thereby implicitly contributing only to the justification of the *status quo*—that critics such as Nietzsche could rightly accuse them of being servants of the present triviality, whatever it might be.

History today has an opportunity to avail itself of the new perspectives on the world which a dynamic science and an equally dynamic art offer. Both science and art have transcended the older, stable conceptions of the world which required that they render a literal copy of a presumably static reality. And both have discovered the essentially *provisional* character of the metaphorical constructions which they use to comprehend a dynamic universe. Thus they affirm implicitly the truth arrived at by Camus when he wrote: "It was previously a question of finding out whether or not life had to have a meaning to be lived. It now becomes clear, on the contrary, that it will be lived all the better if it has no meaning." We might amend the statement to read: it will be lived all the better if it has no single meaning but many different ones.

Since the second half of the nineteenth century, history has become increasingly the refuge of all of those "sane" men who excel at finding the simple in the complex and the familiar in the strange. This was all very well for an earlier age, but if the present generation needs anything at all it is a willingness to confront heroically the dynamic and disruptive forces in contemporary life. The historian serves no one well by constructing a specious continuity between the present world and that which preceded it. On the contrary, we require a history that will educate us to discontinuity more than ever before; for discontinuity, disruption, and chaos is our lot. If, as Nietzsche said, "we have art in order not to die of the truth," we also have truth in order to escape the seduction of a world which is nothing but the creation of our longings. History can provide a ground upon which we can seek that "impossible transparency" demanded by Camus for the distracted humanity of our time. Only a chaste historical consciousness can truly challenge the world anew every second, for only history mediates between what is and what men think ought to be with truly humanizing effect. But history can serve to humanize experience only if it remains sensitive to the more general world of thought *and* action from which it proceeds and to which it returns. And as long as it refuses to use the eyes which *both* modern art and modern science can give it, it must remain blind—citizen of a world in which "the pallid shades of memory struggle in vain with the life and freedom of the present."

Suggestions for further reading

Belsey, Catherine, 'Towards Cultural History – In Theory and Practice', *Textual Practice*, 1989, vol. 3.2, 159–172.

de Certeau, Michel, *The Writing of History*, trans. Tom Conley, New York: Columbia University Press, 1988.

Young, Robert, *White Mythologies: Writing History and the West*, London and New York: Routledge, 1990.

Chapter 11

Roland Barthes

'THE DEATH OF THE AUTHOR', 1968

I N H I S T A L E *Sarrasine*, Balzac, speaking of a castrato disguised as a woman, writes this sentence: "She was Woman, with her sudden fears, her inexplicable whims, her instinctive fears, her meaningless bravado, her defiance, and her delicious delicacy of feeling." Who speaks in this way? Is it the hero of the tale, who would prefer not to recognize the castrato hidden beneath the "woman"? Is it Balzac the man, whose personal experience has provided him with a philosophy of Woman? Is it Balzac the author, professing certain "literary" ideas about femininity? Is it universal wisdom? Romantic psychology? We can never know, for the good reason that writing is the destruction of every voice, every origin. Writing is that neuter, that composite, that obliquity into which our subject flees, the black-and-white where all identity is lost, beginning with the very identity of the body that writes.

No doubt it has always been so: once a fact is *recounted*—for intransitive purposes, and no longer to act directly upon reality, i.e., exclusive of any function except that exercise of the symbol itself—this gap appears, the voice loses its origin, the author enters into his own death, writing begins. However, the affect of this phenomenon has been variable; in ethnographic societies, narrative is never assumed by a person but by a mediator, shaman, or reciter, whose "performance" (i.e., his mastery of the narrative code) can be admired, but never his "genius." The *author* is a modern character, no doubt produced by our society as it emerged from the Middle Ages, inflected by English empiricism, French rationalism, and the personal faith of the Reformation, thereby discovering the prestige of the individual, or, as we say more nobly, of the "human person." Hence, it is logical that in literary matters it should be positivism, crown and conclusion of capitalist ideology, which has granted the greatest importance to the author's "person." The *author* still reigns in manuals of literary history, in biographies of writers, magazine interviews, and in the very consciousness of litterateurs eager to unite, by means of private journals, their person and their work; the image of literature to be found in contemporary culture is tyrannically centered on the author, his person, his history, his tastes, his passions; criticism still largely consists in saying that Baudelaire's oeuvre is the failure of the man Baudelaire, Van Gogh's is his madness, Tchaikovsky's his vice: *explanation* of the work is still sought in the person of its producer, as if, through the more or less transparent allegory of fiction, it was always, ultimately, the voice of one and the same person, the *author*, which was transmitting his "confidences."

Though the Author's empire is still very powerful (the new criticism has quite often merely consolidated it), we know that certain writers have already tried to subvert it. In France, Mallarmé, no doubt the first, saw and foresaw in all its scope the necessity to substitute language itself for the subject hitherto supposed to be its owner; for Mallarmé, as for us, it is language which speaks, not the author; to write is to reach, through a preliminary impersonality—which we can at no moment identify with the realistic novelist's castrating "objectivity"—that point where not "I" but only language functions, "performs": Mallarmé's whole poetics consists in suppressing the author in favor of writing (and thereby restoring, as we shall see, the reader's place). Valéry, entangled in a psychology of the ego, greatly edulcorated Mallarmean theory, but led by a preference for classicism to conform to the lessons of Rhetoric, he continued to cast the Author into doubt and derision, emphasized the linguistic and "accidental" nature of his activity, and throughout his prose works championed the essentially verbal condition of literature, as opposed to which any resort to the writer's interiority seemed to him pure superstition. Proust himself, despite the apparently psychological character of what is called his *analyses*, visibly undertook to blur by an extreme subtilization the relation of the writer and his characters: by making the narrator not the one who has seen or felt, or even the one who writes, but the one who *is going to write* (the young man of the novel—but, as a matter of fact, how old is he and *who* is he?—wants to write but cannot, and the novel ends when writing finally becomes possible), Proust has given modern writing its epic: by a radical reversal, instead of putting his life into his novel, as is so often said, he made his life itself a work of which his own book was the model, so that it is quite clear to us that it is not Charlus who imitates Montesquiou, but Montesquiou, in his anecdotal, historical reality, who is only a secondary, derived fragment of Charlus. Finally Surrealism, to keep to this prehistory of modernity, could doubtless not attribute a sovereign place to language, since language is system, and what this movement sought was, romantically, a direct subversion of the codes—an illusory subversion, moreover, for a code cannot be destroyed, only "flouted"; yet, by constantly striving to disappoint expected meanings (this was the famous surrealist "shock"), by urging the hand to write as fast as possible what the head was unaware of (this was automatic writing), by accepting the principle and the experiment of collective writing, Surrealism helped desacralize the image of the Author. Last, outside literature itself (in fact, such distinctions are becoming quite dated), linguistics furnishes the destruction of the Author with a precious analytic instrument, showing that the speech-act in its entirety is an "empty" process, which functions perfectly without its being necessary to "fill" it with the person of the interlocutors: linguistically, the author is nothing but the one who writes, just as *I* is nothing but the one who says *I*: language knows a "subject," not a "person," and this subject, empty outside of the very speech-act which defines it, suffices to "hold" language, i.e., to exhaust it.

The removal of the Author (with Brecht, we might speak here of a veritable *distancing*, the Author diminishing like a figure at the far end of the literary stage) is not only a historical fact or an act of writing: it utterly transforms the modern text (or—which is the same thing—the text is henceforth produced and read so that the author absents himself from it at every level). Time, first of all, is no longer the same. The Author, when we believe in him, is always conceived as the past of his own book: book and author are voluntarily placed on one and the same line, distributed as a *before* and an *after*: the Author is supposed to *feed* the book, i.e., he lives before it, thinks, suffers, lives for it; he has the same relation of antecedence with his work that a father sustains with his child. Quite the contrary, the modern *scriptor* is born *at the same time* as his text; he is not furnished with a being which precedes or exceeds his writing, he is not the subject of which his book would be the predicate; there is no time other than that of the speech-act, and every text is written eternally *here* and *now*. This is because (or it follows that) *writing* can no longer designate an operation of recording, of observation, of representation, of "painting" (as the Classics used to say), but instead what the linguists, following Oxfordian philosophy, call a performative, a rare verbal form (exclusively found in the first person and in the present), in which the speech-act has no other content (no other statement) than the act by which it is uttered: something like the *I declare* of kings or the *I sing* of the earliest poets; the modern *scriptor*, having buried the Author, can therefore no longer believe, according to the pathos of his predecessors, that his hand is slower than his passion and that in consequence, making a law of necessity, he must emphasize this delay and endlessly "elaborate" his form; for him, on the contrary, his hand, detached from any voice, borne by a pure gesture of inscription (and not of expression), traces a field without origin—or at least with no origin but language itself, i.e., the very thing which ceaselessly calls any origin into question.

We know now that a text consists not of a line of words, releasing a single "theological" meaning (the "message" of the Author-God), but of a multi-dimensional space in which are married and contested several writings, none of which is original: the text is a fabric of quotations, resulting from a thousand sources of culture. Like Bouvard and Pécuchet, those eternal copyists, at once sublime and comical, whose profound absurdity *precisely* designates the truth of writing, the writer can only imitate an ever anterior, never original gesture; his sole power is to mingle writings, to counter some by others, so as never to rely on just one; if he seeks to *express himself*, at least he knows that the interior "thing" he claims to "translate" is itself no more than a ready-made lexicon, whose words can be explained only through other words, and this ad infinitum: an adventure which exemplarily befell young Thomas De Quincey, so versed in his Greek that in order to translate certain absolutely modern ideas and images into this dead language, Baudelaire tells us, "he had a dictionary made for himself, one much more complex and extensive than the kind produced by the vulgar patience of purely literary themes" (*Les Paradis artificiels*); succeeding the Author, the *scriptor* no longer contains passions, moods, sentiments, impressions, but that immense dictionary from which he draws a writing which will be incessant: life merely imitates the book, and this book itself is but a tissue of signs, endless imitation, infinitely postponed.

Once the Author is distanced, the claim to "decipher" a text becomes entirely futile. To assign an Author to a text is to impose a brake on it, to furnish it with a final signified, to close writing. This conception is quite suited to criticism, which then undertakes the important task of discovering the Author (or his hypostases: society, history, the psyche, freedom) beneath the work: once the Author is found, the text is "explained," the critic has won; hence it is hardly surprising that historically the Author's empire has been the Critic's as well, and also that (even new) criticism is today unsettled at the same time as the Author. In multiple writing, in effect, everything is to be *disentangled*, but nothing *deciphered*, structure can be followed, "threaded" (as we say of a run in a stocking) in all its reprises, all its stages, but there is no end to it, no bottom; the space of writing is to be traversed, not pierced; writing constantly posits meaning, but always in order to evaporate it: writing seeks a systematic exemption of meaning. Thereby, literature (it would be better, from now on, to say *writing*), by refusing to assign to the text (and to the world-as-text) a "secret," i.e., an ultimate meaning, liberates an activity we may call countertheological, properly revolutionary, for to refuse to halt meaning is finally to refuse God and his hypostases, reason, science, the law.

To return to Balzac's sentence. No one (i.e., no "person") says it: its source, its voice is not the true site of writing, it is reading. Another very specific example will help us here: recent investigations (J.-P. Vernant) have shed some light on the constitutively ambiguous nature of Greek tragedy, whose text is "woven" of words with double meanings, words which each character understands unilaterally (this perpetual misunderstanding is precisely what we call the "tragic"); there is, however, someone who understands each word in its duplicity, and further understands, one may say, the very deafness of the characters speaking in his presence: this "someone" is precisely the reader (or here the listener). Here we discern the total being of writing: a text consists of multiple writings, proceeding from several cultures and entering into dialogue, into parody, into contestation; but there is a site where this multiplicity is collected, and this site is not the author, as has hitherto been claimed, but the reader: the reader is the very space in which are inscribed, without any of them being lost, all the citations out of which a writing is made; the unity of a text is not in its origin but in its destination, but this destination can no longer be personal: the reader is a man without history, without biography, without psychology; he is only that *someone* who holds collected into one and the same field all of the traces from which writing is constituted. That is why it is absurd to hear the new writing condemned in the name of a humanism which hypocritically claims to champion the reader's rights. Classical criticism has never been concerned with the reader; for that criticism, there is no other man in literature than the one who writes. We are no longer so willing to be the dupes of such antiphrases, by which a society proudly recriminates in favor of precisely what it discards, ignores, muffles, or destroys; we know that in order to restore writing to its future, we must reverse the myth: the birth of the reader must be requited by the death of the Author.

Manteia, 1968

Suggestions for further reading

Barthes, Roland, *S/Z*, trans. Richard Miller, London: Cape, 1975.

Caughie, John (ed.), *Theories of Authorship: A Reader*, London: Routledge and Kegan Paul, 1981.

Foucault, Michel, 'What is an Author?', trans. Donald F. Bouchard, *Screen*, 1979, vol. 20.1, 13–29.

Chapter 12

Jacques Derrida

'DIFFERANCE', 1968

T HE VERB "TO DIFFER" [*différer*] seems to differ from itself. On the one hand, it indicates difference as distinction, inequality, or discernibility; on the other, it expresses the interposition of delay, the interval of a *spacing* and *temporalizing* that puts off until "later" what is presently denied, the possible that is presently impossible. Sometimes the *different* and sometimes the *deferred* correspond [in French] to the verb "to differ." This correlation, however, is not simply one between act and object, cause and effect, or primordial and derived.

In the one case "to differ" signifies nonidentity; in the other case it signifies the order of the *same*. Yet there must be a common, although entirely differant[1] [*différante*], root within the sphere that relates the two movements of differing to one another. We provisionally give the name *differance* to this *sameness* which is not *identical*: by the silent writing of its *a*, it has the desired advantage of referring to differing, *both* as spacing/temporalizing and as the movement that structures every dissociation.

As distinct from difference, differance thus points out the irreducibility of temporalizing (which is also temporalization—in transcendental language which is no longer adequate here, this would be called the constitution of primordial temporality—just as the term "spacing" also includes the constitution of primordial spatiality). Differance is not simply active (any more than it is a subjective accomplishment); it rather indicates the middle voice, it precedes and sets up the opposition between passivity and activity. With its *a*, differance more properly refers to what in classical language would be called the origin or production of differences and the differences between differences, the *play* [*jeu*] of differences. Its locus and operation will therefore be seen wherever speech appeals to difference.

Differance is neither a *word* nor a *concept*. In it, however, we shall see the juncture—rather than the summation—of what has been most decisively inscribed in the thought of what is conveniently called our "epoch": the difference of forces in

Nietzsche, Saussure's principle of semiological difference, differing as the possibility of [neurone] facilitation,[2] impression and delayed effect in Freud, difference as the irreducibility of the trace of the other in Levinas, and the ontic-ontological difference in Heidegger.

Reflection on this last determination of difference will lead us to consider differance as the *strategic* note or connection—relatively or provisionally *privileged*—which indicates the closure of presence, together with the closure of the conceptual order and denomination, a closure that is effected in the functioning of traces.

I SHALL SPEAK, THEN, OF A LETTER—the first one, if we are to believe the alphabet and most of the speculations that have concerned themselves with it.

I shall speak then of the letter *a*, this first letter which it seemed necessary to introduce now and then in writing the word "difference." This seemed necessary in the course of writing about writing, and of writing within a writing whose different strokes all pass, in certain respects, through a gross spelling mistake, through a violation of the rules governing writing, violating the law that governs writing and regulates its conventions of propriety. In fact or theory we can always erase or lessen this spelling mistake, and, in each case, while these are analytically different from one another but for practical purposes the same, find it grave, unseemly, or, indeed, supposing the greatest ingenuousness, amusing. Whether or not we care to quietly overlook this infraction, the attention we give it beforehand will allow us to recognize, as though prescribed by some mute irony, the inaudible but displaced character of this literal permutation. We can always act as though this makes no difference. I must say from the start that my account serves less to justify this silent spelling mistake, or still less to excuse it, than to aggravate its obtrusive character.

On the other hand, I must be excused if I refer, at least implicitly, to one or another of the texts that I have ventured to publish. Precisely what I would like to attempt to some extent (although this is in principle and in its highest degree impossible, due to essential *de jure* reasons) is to bring together an *assemblage* of the different ways I have been able to utilize—or, rather, have allowed to be imposed on me—what I will provisionally call the word or concept of differance in its new spelling. It is literally neither a word nor a concept, as we shall see. I insist on the word "assemblage" here for two reasons: on the one hand, it is not a matter of describing a history, of recounting the steps, text by text, context by context, each time showing which scheme has been able to impose this graphic disorder, although this could have been done as well; rather, we are concerned with the *general system of all these schemata*. On the other hand, the word "assemblage" seems more apt for suggesting that the kind of bringing-together proposed here has the structure of an interlacing, a weaving, or a web, which would allow the different threads and different lines of sense or force to separate again, as well as being ready to bind others together.

In a quite preliminary way, we now recall that this particular graphic intervention was conceived in the writing-up of a question about writing; it was not made simply to shock the reader or grammarian. Now, in point of fact, it happens that this graphic difference (the *a* instead of the *e*), this marked difference between two apparently vocalic notations, between vowels, remains purely graphic: it is written or read, but it is not heard. It cannot be heard, and we shall see in what respects it is also beyond the order of understanding. It is put forward by a silent mark, by a tacit monument, or, one might even say, by a pyramid—keeping in mind not only the capital form of the printed letter but also that passage from Hegel's *Encyclopaedia* where he compares the body of the sign to an Egyptian pyramid. The *a* of differance, therefore, is not heard; it remains silent, secret, and discreet, like a tomb.[3]

It is a tomb that (provided one knows how to decipher its legend) is not far from signaling the death of the king.

It is a tomb that cannot even be made to resonate. For I cannot even let you know, by my talk, now being spoken before the Société Française de Philosophie, which difference I am talking about at the very moment I speak of it. I can only talk about this graphic difference by keeping to a very indirect speech about writing, and on the condition that I specify each time that I am referring to difference with an *e* or differance with an *a*. All of which is not going to simplify matters today, and will give us all a great deal of trouble when we want to understand one another. In any event, when I do specify which difference I mean —when I say "with an *e*" or "with an *a*"—this will refer irreducibly to a *written text*, a text governing my talk, a text that I keep in front of me, that I will read, and toward which I shall have to try to lead your hands and eyes. We cannot refrain here from going by way of a written text, from ordering ourselves by the disorder that is produced therein—and this is what matters to me first of all.

Doubtless this pyramidal silence of the graphic difference between the *e* and the *a* can function only within the system of phonetic writing and within a language or grammar historically tied to phonetic writing and to the whole culture which is inseparable from it. But I will say that it is just this—this silence that functions only within what is called phonetic writing—that points out or reminds us in a very opportune way that, contrary to an enormous prejudice, there is no phonetic writing. There is no purely and strictly phonetic writing. What is called phonetic writing can only function—in principle and *de jure*, and not due to some factual and technical inadequacy—by incorporating nonphonetic "signs" (punctuation, spacing, etc.); but when we examine their structure and necessity, we will quickly see that they are ill described by the concept of signs. Saussure had only to remind us that the play of difference was the functional condition, the condition of possibility, for every sign; and it is itself silent. The difference between two phonemes, which enables them to exist and to operate, is inaudible. The inaudible opens the two present phonemes to hearing, as they present themselves. If, then, there is no purely phonetic writing, it is because there is no purely phonetic phone. The difference that brings out phonemes and lets them be heard and understood [*entendre*] itself remains inaudible.

It will perhaps be objected that, for the same reasons, the graphic difference itself sinks into darkness, that it never constitutes the fullness of a sensible term, but draws out an invisible connection, the mark of an inapparent relation between two spectacles. That is no doubt true. Indeed, since from this point of view the difference between the *e* and the *a* marked in "differance" eludes vision and hearing, this happily suggests that we must here let ourselves be referred to an order that no longer refers to sensibility. But we are not referred to intelligibility either, to an ideality not fortuitously associated with the objectivity of *theōrein* or understanding. We must be referred to an order, then, that resists philosophy's founding opposition between the sensible and the intelligible. The order that resists this opposition, that resists it because it sustains it, is designated in a movement of differance (with an *a*) between two differences or between two letters. This differance belongs neither to the voice nor to writing in the ordinary sense, and it takes place, like the strange space that will assemble us here for the course of an hour, *between* speech and writing and beyond the tranquil familiarity that binds us to one and to the other, reassuring us sometimes in the illusion that they are two separate things.

Now, HOW AM I TO SPEAK OF the *a* of differance? It is clear that it cannot be *exposed*. We can expose only what, at a certain moment, can become *present*, manifest; what can be shown, presented as a present, a being-present in its truth, the truth of a present or the presence of a present. However, if differance is (I also cross out the "is") what makes the presentation of being-present possible, it never presents itself as such. It is never given in the present or to anyone. Holding back and not exposing itself, it goes beyond the order of truth on this specific point and in this determined way, yet is not itself concealed, as if it were some-thing, a mysterious being, in the occult zone of a nonknowing. Any exposition would expose it to disappearing as a disappearance. It would risk appearing, thus disappearing.

Thus, the detours, phrases, and syntax that I shall often have to resort to will resemble—will sometimes be practically indiscernible from—those of negative theology. Already we had to note *that* differance *is not*, does not exist, and is not any sort of being-present (*on*). And we will have to point out everything *that it is not*, and, consequently, that it has neither existence nor essence. It belongs to no category of being, present or absent. And yet what is thus denoted as differance is not theological, not even in the most negative order of negative theology. The latter, as we know, is always occupied with letting a supraessential reality go beyond the finite categories of essence and existence, that is, of presence, and always hastens to remind us that, if we deny the predicate of existence to God, it is in order to recognize him as a superior, inconceivable, and ineffable mode of being. Here there is no question of such a move, as will be confirmed as we go along. Not only is differance irreducible to every ontological or theological—onto-theological—reappropriation, but it opens up the very space in which onto-theology—philosophy—produces its system and its history. It thus encompasses and irrevocably surpasses onto-theology or philosophy.

For the same reason, I do not know where *to begin* to mark out this assem-blage, this graph, of differance. Precisely what is in question here is the require-ment that there be a *de jure* commencement, an absolute point of departure, a responsibility arising from a principle. The problem of writing opens by question-ing the *archē*. Thus what I put forth here will not be developed simply as a philosophical discourse that operates on the basis of a principle, of postulates, axioms, and definitions and that moves according to the discursive line of a rational order. In marking out differance, everything is a matter of strategy and risk. It is a question of strategy because no transcendent truth present outside the sphere of writing can theologically command the totality of this field. It is hazardous because this strategy is not simply one in the sense that we say that strategy orients the tactics according to a final aim, a *telos* or the theme of a domination, a mastery or an ultimate reappropriation of movement and field. In the end, it is a strategy without finality. We might call it blind tactics or empirical errance, if the value of empiricism did not itself derive all its meaning from its opposition to philosophical responsibility. If there is a certain errance in the tracing-out of differance, it no longer follows the line of logico-philosophical speech or that of its integral and symmetrical opposite, logico-empirical speech. The concept of *play* [*jeu*] remains beyond this opposition; on the eve and aftermath of philosophy, it designates the unity of chance and necessity in an endless calculus.

By decision and, as it were, by the rules of the game, then, turning this thought around, let us introduce ourselves to the thought of differance by way of the theme of strategy or strategem. By this merely strategic justification, I want to emphasize that the efficacy of this thematics of differance very well may, and even one day must, be sublated, i.e., lend itself, if not to its own replacement, at least to its involvement in a series of events which in fact it never commanded. This also means that it is not a theological thematics.

I will say, first of all, that differance, which is neither a word nor a concept, seemed to me to be strategically the theme most proper to think out, if not master (thought being here, perhaps, held in a certain necessary relation with the structional limits of mastery), in what is most characteristic of our "epoch." I start off, then, strategically, from the place and time in which "we" are, even though my opening is not justifiable in the final account, and though it is always on the basis of differance and its "history" that we can claim to know who and where "we" are and what the limits of an "epoch" can be.

Although "differance" is neither a word nor a concept, let us nonetheless attempt a simple and approximative semantic analysis which will bring us in view of what is at stake [*en vue de l'enjeu*].

We do know that the verb "to differ" [*différer*] (the Latin verb *differre*) has two seemingly quite distinct meanings; in the *Littré* dictionary, for example, they are the subject of two separate articles. In this sense, the Latin *differre* is not the simple translation of the Greek *diapherein*; this fact will not be without consequence for us in tying our discussion to a particular language, one that passes for being less philosophical, less primordially philosophical, than the other, For the distribution of sense in the Greek *diapherein* does not carry one of the two themes of the Latin *differre*, namely, the action of postponing until later, of taking into account, the taking-account of time and forces in an operation that implies an economic reckoning, a detour, a respite, a delay, a reserve, a representation—all the concepts that I will sum up here in a word I have never used but which could be added to this series: *temporalizing*. "To differ" in this sense is to temporalize, to resort, consciously or unconsciously, to the temporal and temporalizing mediation of a detour that suspends the accomplishment or fulfillment of "desire" or "will," or carries desire or will out in a way that annuls or tempers their effect. We shall see, later, in what respects this temporalizing is also a temporalization and spacing, is space's becoming-temporal and time's becoming-spatial, is "primordial constitution" of space and time, as metaphysics or transcendental phenomenology would call it in the language that is here criticized and displaced.

The other sense of "to differ" [*différer*] is the most common and most identifiable, the sense of not being identical, of being other, of being discernible, etc. And in "differents," whether referring to the alterity of dissimilarity or the alterity of allergy or of polemics, it is necessary that interval, distance, *spacing* occur among the different elements and occur actively, dynamically, and with a certain perseverence in repetition.

But the word "difference" (with an *e*) could never refer to differing as temporalizing or to difference as *polemos*. It is this loss of sense that the word differance (with an *a*) will have to schematically compensate for. Differance can refer to the whole complex of its meanings at once, for it is immediately and irreducibly multivalent, something which will be important for the discourse I am trying to develop. It refers to this whole complex of meanings not only when it is supported by a language or interpretive context (like any signification), but it already does so somehow of itself. Or at least it does so more easily by itself than does any other word: here the *a* comes more immediately from the present participle [*différant*] and brings us closer to the action of "differing" that is in progress, even before it has produced the effect that is constituted as different or resulted in difference (with an *e*). Within a conceptual system and in terms of classical requirements, differance could be said to designate the productive and primordial constituting causality, the process of scission and division whose differings and differences would be the constituted products or effects. But while bringing us closer to the infinitive and active core of differing, "difference" with an *a* neutralizes what the infinitive denotes as simply active, in the same way that "parlance" does not signify the simple fact of speaking, of speaking to or being spoken to. Nor is resonance the act of resonating. Here in the usage of our language we must consider that the ending *-ance* is undecided between active and passive. And we shall see why what is designated by "difference" is neither simply active nor simply passive, that it announces or rather recalls something like the middle voice, that it speaks of an operation which is not an operation, which cannot be thought of either as a passion or as an action of a subject upon an object, as starting from an agent or from a patient, or on the basis of, or in view of, any of these *terms*. But philosophy has perhaps commenced by distributing the middle voice, expressing a certain intransitiveness, into the active and the passive voice, and has itself been constituted in this repression.

How are differance as temporalizing and differance as spacing conjoined?

Let us begin with the problem of signs and writing—since we are already in the midst of it. We ordinarily say that a sign is put in place of the thing itself, the present thing—"thing" holding here for the sense as well as the referent. Signs represent the present in its absence; they take the place of the present. When we cannot take hold of or show the thing, let us say the present, the being-present, when the present does not present itself, then we signify, we go through the detour of signs. We take up or give signs; we make signs. The sign would thus be a deferred presence. Whether it is a question of verbal or written signs, monetary signs, electoral delegates, or political representatives, the movement of signs defers the moment of encountering the thing itself, the moment at which we could lay hold of it, consume or expend it, touch it, see it, have a present intuition of it. What I am describing here is the structure of signs as classically determined, in order to define—through a commonplace characterization of its traits— signification as the difference of temporalizing. Now this classical determination presupposes that the sign (which defers presence) is conceivable only *on the basis of* the presence that it defers and *in view of* the deferred presence one intends to reappropriate. Following this classical semiology, the substitution of the sign for the thing itself is both *secondary* and *provisional*: it is second in order after an original and lost presence, a presence from which the sign would be derived. It is provisional with respect to this final and missing presence, in view of which the sign would serve as a movement of mediation.

In attempting to examine these secondary and provisional aspects of the substitute, we shall no doubt catch sight of something like a primordial difference. Yet we could no longer even call it primordial or final, inasmuch as the character-istics of origin, beginning, *telos, eschaton*, etc., have always denoted presence— *ousia, parousia*, etc. To question the secondary and provisional character of the sign, to oppose it to a "primordial" difference, would thus have the following consequences:

1   Difference can no longer be understood according to the concept of "sign," which has always been taken to mean the representation of a presence and has been constituted in a system (of thought or language) determined on the basis of and in view of presence.
2   In this way we question the authority of presence or its simple symmetrical contrary, absence or lack. We thus interrogate the limit that has always constrained us, that always constrains us—we who inhabit a language and a system of thought—to form the sense of being in general as presence or absence, in the categories of being or beingness (*ousia*). It already appears that the kind of questioning we are thus led back to is, let us say, the Heideggerian kind, and that difference *seems* to lead us back to the ontic-ontological difference. But permit me to postpone this reference. I shall only note that between difference as temporalizing-temporalization (which we can no longer conceive within the horizon of the present) and what Heidegger says about temporalization in *Sein und Zeit* (namely, that as the transcendental horizon of the question of being it must be freed from the traditional and metaphysical domination by the present or the now) —between these two there is a close, if not exhaustive and irreducibly necessary, interconnection.

But first of all, let us remain with the semiological aspects of the problem to see how difference as temporalizing is conjoined with difference as spacing. Most of the semiological or linguistic research currently dominating the field of thought (whether due to the results of its own investigations or due to its role as a generally recognized regulative model) traces its genealogy, rightly or wrongly, to Saussure as its common founder. It was Saussure who first of all set forth the *arbitrariness of signs* and the *differential character* of signs as principles of general semiology and particularly of linguistics. And, as we know, these two themes—the arbitrary and the differential—are in his view inseparable. Arbitrariness can occur only because the system of signs is constituted by the differences between the terms, and not by their fullness. The elements of signification function not by virtue of the compact force of their cores but by the network of oppositions that distinguish them and relate them to one another. "Arbitrary and differential" says Saussure "are two correlative qualities."

As the condition for signification, this principle of difference affects the *whole sign*, that is, both the signified and the signifying aspects. The signified aspect is the concept, the ideal sense. The signifying aspect is what Saussure calls the material or physical (e.g., acoustical) "image." We do not here have to enter into all the problems these definitions pose. Let us only cite Saussure where it interests us:

> The conceptual side of value is made up solely of relations and differ-
> ences with respect to the other terms of language, and the same can be
> said of its material side. . . . Everything that has been said up to this
> point boils down to this: in language there are only differences. Even
> more important: a difference generally implies positive terms bet-
> ween which the difference is set up; but in language there are only
> differences *without positive terms*. Whether we take the signified or the
> signifier, language has neither ideas nor sounds that existed before the
> linguistic system, but only conceptual and phonic differences that
> have issued from the system. The idea or phonic substance that a sign
> contains is of less importance than the other signs that surround it.[4]

The first consequence to be drawn from this is that the signified concept is never present in itself, in an adequate presence that would refer only to itself. Every concept is necessarily and essentially inscribed in a chain or a system, within which it refers to another and to other concepts, by the systematic play of differ-ences. Such a play, then—differance—is no longer simply a concept, but the possibility of conceptuality, of the conceptual system and process in general. For the same reason, differance, which is not a concept, is not a mere word; that is, it is not what we represent to ourselves as the calm and present self-referential unity of a concept and sound [*phonie*]. We shall later discuss the consequences of this for the notion of a word.

The difference that Saussure speaks about, therefore, is neither itself a concept nor one word among others. We can say this *a fortiori* for differance. Thus we are brought to make the relation between the one and the other explicit.

Within a language, within the *system* of language, there are only differences. A taxonomic operation can accordingly undertake its systematic, statistical, and clas-sificatory inventory. But, on the one hand, these differences *play a role* in language, in speech as well, and in the exchange between language and speech. On the other hand, these differences are themselves *effects*. They have not fallen from the sky ready made; they are no more inscribed in a *topos noëtos* than they are prescribed in the wax of the brain. If the word "history" did not carry with it the theme of a final repression of differance, we could say that differences alone could be "historical" through and through and from the start.

What we note as *differance* will thus be the movement of play that "produces" (and not by something that is simply an activity) these differences, these effects of difference. This does not mean that the differance which produces differences is before them in a simple and in itself unmodified and indifferent present. Differance is the nonfull, nonsimple "origin"; it is the structured and differing origin of differences.

Since language (which Saussure says is a classification) has not fallen from the sky, it is clear that the differences have been produced; they are the effects produced, but effects that do not have as their cause a subject or substance, a thing in general, or a being that is somewhere present and itself escapes the play of difference. If such a presence were implied (quite classically) in the general concept of cause, we would therefore have to talk about an effect without a cause, something that would very quickly lead to no longer talking about effects. I have tried to indicate a way out of the closure imposed by this system, namely, by means of the "trace." No more an effect than a cause, the "trace" cannot of itself, taken outside its context, suffice to bring about the required transgression.

As there is no presence before the semiological difference or outside it, we can extend what Saussure writes about language to signs in general: "Language is necessary in order for speech to be intelligible and to produce all of its effects; but the latter is necessary in order for language to be established; historically, the fact of speech always comes first."[5]

Retaining at least the schema, if not the content, of the demand formulated by Saussure, we shall designate by the term *differance* the movement by which language, or any code, any system of reference in general, becomes "historically" constituted as a fabric of differences. Here, the terms "constituted," "produced," "created," "movement," "historically" etc., with all they imply, are not to be understood only in terms of the language of metaphysics, from which they are taken. It would have to be shown why the concepts of production, like those of constitution and history, remain accessories in this respect to what is here being questioned; this, however, would draw us too far away today, toward the theory of the representation of the "circle" in which we seem to be enclosed. I only use these terms here, like many other concepts, out of strategic convenience and in order to prepare the deconstruction of the system they form at the point which is now most decisive. In any event, we will have understood, by virtue of the very circle we appear to be caught up in, that differance, as it is written here, is no more static than genetic, no more structural than historical. Nor is it any less so. And it is completely to miss the point of this orthographical impropriety to want to object to it on the basis of the oldest of metaphysical oppositions—for example, by opposing some generative point of view to a structuralist-taxonomic point of view, or conversely. These oppositions do not pertain in the least to differance; and this, no doubt, is what makes thinking about it difficult and uncomfortable.

If we now consider the chain to which "differance" gets subjected, according to the context, to a certain number of nonsynonymic substitutions, one will ask why we resorted to such concepts as "reserve," "protowriting," "prototrace," "spacing," indeed to "supplement" or "*pharmakon*," and, before long, to "hymen," etc.[6]

Let us begin again. Differance is what makes the movement of signification possible only if each element that is said to be "present," appearing on the stage of presence, is related to something other than itself but retains the mark of a past element and already lets itself be hollowed out by the mark of its relation to a future element. This trace relates no less to what is called the future than to what is called the past, and it constitutes what is called the present by this very relation to what it is not, to what it absolutely is not; that is, not even to a past or future considered as a modified present. In order for it to be, an interval must separate it from what it is not; but the interval that constitutes it in the present must also, and by the same token, divide the present in itself, thus dividing, along with the present, everything that can be conceived on its basis, that is, every being—in particular, for our metaphysical language, the substance or subject. Constituting itself, dynamically dividing itself, this interval is what could be called *spacing*; time's becoming-spatial or space's becoming-temporal (*temporalizing*). And it is this constitution of the present as a "primordial" and irreducibly nonsimple, and, therefore, in the strict sense nonprimordial, synthesis of traces, retentions, and protentions (to reproduce here, analogically and provisionally, a phenomeno-logical and transcendental language that will presently be revealed as inadequate) that I propose to call protowriting, prototrace, or differance. The latter (is) (both) spacing (and) temporalizing.[7]

Given this (active) movement of the (production of) differance without origin, could we not, quite simply and without any neographism, call it *differentiation*? Among other confusions, such a word would suggest some organic unity, some primordial and homogeneous unity, that would eventually come to be divided up and take on difference as an event. Above all, formed on the verb "to differenti-ate," this word would annul the economic signification of detour, temporalizing delay, "deferring." I owe a remark in passing to a recent reading of one of Koyré's texts entitled "Hegel at Jena."[8] In that text, Koyré cites long passages from the Jena *Logic* in German and gives his own translation. On two occasions in Hegel's text he encounters the expression "*differente Beziehung.*" This word (*different*), whose root is Latin, is extremely rare in German and also, I believe, in Hegel, who instead uses *verschieden* or *ungleich*, calling difference *Unterschied* and qualitative variety *Verschiedenheit*. In the Jena *Logic*, he uses the word *different* precisely at the point where he deals with time and the present. Before coming to Koyré's valuable remark, here are some passages from Hegel, as rendered by Koyré:

> The infinite, in this simplicity is—as a moment opposed to the self-identical—the negative. In its moments, while the infinite presents the totality to (itself) and in itself, (it is) excluding in general, the point or limit; but in this, its own (action of) negating, it relates itself immediately to the other and negates itself. The limit or moment of the present (*der Gegen-wart*), the absolute "this" of time or the now, is an absolutely negative simplicity, absolutely excluding all multiplicity from itself, and by this very fact is absolutely determined; it is not an extended whole or *quantum* within itself (and) which would in itself also have an undetermined aspect or qualitative variety, which of itself would be related, indifferently (*gleichgültig*) or externally to another, but on the contrary, this is an absolutely different relation of the simple.[9]

And Koyré specifies in a striking note: "Different relation: *differente Beziehung*. We could say: differentiating relation." And on the following page, from another text of Hegel, we can read: "*Diese Beziehung ist Gegenwart, als eine differente Beziehung*" (This relation is [the] present, as a different relation). There is another note by Koyré: "The term '*different*' is taken here in an active sense."

Writing "differing" or "differance" (with an *a*) would have had the utility of making it possible to translate Hegel on precisely this point with no further qualifi-cations—and it is a quite decisive point in his text. The translation would be, as it always should be, the transformation of one language by another. Naturally, I maintain that the word "differance" can be used in other ways, too; first of all, because it denotes not only the activity of primordial difference but also the temporalizing detour of deferring. It has, however, an even more important usage. Despite the very profound affinities that differance thus written has with Hegelian speech (as it should be read), it can, at a certain point, not exactly break with it, but rather work a sort of displacement with regard to it. A definite rupture with Hegelian language would make no sense, nor would it be at all likely; but this displacement is both infinitesimal and radical. I have tried to indicate the extent of this displacement elsewhere; it would be difficult to talk about it with any brevity at this point.

Differences are thus "produced"—differed—by differance. But *what* differs, or *who* differs? In other words, *what is* differance? With this question we attain another stage and another source of the problem.

What differs? Who differs? What is differance?

If we answered these questions even before examining them as questions, even before going back over them and questioning their form (even what seems to be most natural and necessary about them), we would fall below the level we have now reached. For if we accepted the form of the question in its own sense and syntax ("What?," "What is?," "Who is?"), we would have to admit that differance is derived, supervenient, controlled, and ordered from the starting point of a being-present, one capable of being something, a force, a state, or power in the world, to which we could give all kinds of names: a *what*, or being-present as a *subject*, a *who*. In the latter case, notably, we would implicitly admit that the being-present (for example, as a self-present being or consciousness) would eventually result in differing: in delaying or in diverting the fulfillment of a "need" or "desire," or in differing from itself. But in none of these cases would such a being-present be "constituted" by this differance.

Now if we once again refer to the semiological difference, what was it that Saussure in particular reminded us of? That "language [which consists only of differences] is not a function of the speaking subject." This implies that the subject (self-identical or even conscious of self-identity, self-conscious) is inscribed in the language, that he is a "function" of the language. He becomes a *speaking* subject only by conforming his speech—even in the aforesaid "creation," even in the aforesaid "transgression"—to the system of linguistic prescriptions taken as the system of differences, or at least to the general law of differance, by conforming to that law of language which Saussure calls "language without speech." "Language is necessary for the spoken word to be intelligible and so that it can produce all of its effects."[10]

If, by hypothesis, we maintain the strict opposition between speech and language, then difference will be not only the play of differences within the language but the relation of speech to language, the detour by which I must also pass in order to speak, the silent token I must give, which holds just as well for linguistics in the strict sense as it does for general semiology; it dictates all the relations between usage and the formal schema, between the message and the particular code, etc. Elsewhere I have tried to suggest that this difference within language, and in the relation between speech and language, forbids the essential dissociation between speech and writing that Saussure, in keeping with tradition, wanted to draw at another level of his presentation. The use of language or the employment of any code which implies a play of forms—with no determined or invariable substratum—also presupposes a retention and protention of differences, a spacing and temporalizing, a play of traces. This play must be a sort of inscription prior to writing, a protowriting without a present origin, without an *archē*. From this comes the systematic crossing-out of the *archē* and the transformation of general semiology into a grammatology, the latter performing a critical work upon everything within semiology—right down to its matrical concept of signs—that retains any metaphysical presuppositions incompatible with the theme of difference.

We might be tempted by an objection: to be sure, the subject becomes a *speaking* subject only by dealing with the system of linguistic differences; or again, he becomes a *signifying* subject (generally by speech or other signs) only by entering into the system of differences. In this sense, certainly, the speaking or signifying subject would not be self-present, insofar as he speaks or signifies, except for the play of linguistic or semiological difference. But can we not conceive of a presence and self-presence of the subject before speech or its signs, a subject's self-presence in a silent and intuitive consciousness?

Such a question therefore supposes that prior to signs and outside them, and excluding every trace and difference, something such as consciousness is possible. It supposes, moreover, that, even before the distribution of its signs in space and in the world, consciousness can gather itself up in its own presence. What then is consciousness? What does "consciousness" mean? Most often in the very form of "meaning" ["*vouloir-dire*"], consciousness in all its modifications is conceivable only as self-presence, a self-perception of presence. And what holds for consciousness also holds here for what is called subjective existence in general. Just as the category of subject is not and never has been conceivable without reference to presence as *hypokeimenon* or *ousia*, etc., so the subject as consciousness has never been able to be evinced otherwise than as self-presence. The privilege accorded to consciousness thus means a privilege accorded to the present; and even if the transcendental temporality of consciousness is described in depth, as Husserl described it, the power of synthesis and of the incessant gathering-up of traces is always accorded to the "living present."

This privilege is the ether of metaphysics, the very element of our thought insofar as it is caught up in the language of metaphysics. We can only de-limit such a closure today by evoking this import of presence, which Heidegger has shown to be the onto-theological determination of being. Therefore, in evoking this import of presence, by an examination which would have to be of a quite peculiar nature, we question the absolute privilege of this form or epoch of presence in general, that is, consciousness as meaning [*vouloir-dire*] in self-presence.

We thus come to posit presence—and, in particular, consciousness, the being-next-to-itself of consciousness—no longer as the absolutely matrical form of being but as a "determination" and an "effect." Presence is a determination and effect within a system which is no longer that of presence but that of differance; it no more allows the opposition between activity and passivity than that between cause and effect or in-determination and determination, etc. This system is of such a kind that even to designate consciousness as an effect or determination—for strategic reasons, reasons that can be more or less clearly considered and system-atically ascertained—is to continue to operate according to the vocabulary of that very thing to be de-limited.

Before being so radically and expressly Heideggerian, this was also Nietzsche's and Freud's move, both of whom, as we know, and often in a very similar way, questioned the self-assured certitude of consciousness. And is it not remarkable that both of them did this by starting out with the theme of differance?

This theme appears almost literally in their work, at the most crucial places. I shall not expand on this here; I shall only recall that for Nietzsche "the important main activity is unconscious" and that consciousness is the effect of forces whose essence, ways, and modalities are not peculiar to it. Now force itself is never present; it is only a play of differences and quantities. There would be no force in general without the difference between forces; and here the difference in quantity counts more than the content of quantity, more than the absolute magnitude itself.

> Quantity itself therefore is not separable from the difference in quan-tity. The difference in quantity is the essence of force, the relation of force with force. To fancy two equal forces, even if we grant them opposing directions, is an approximate and crude illusion, a statistical dream in which life is immersed, but which chemistry dispels.[11]

Is not the whole thought of Nietzsche a critique of philosophy as active indiffer-ence to difference, as a system of reduction or adiaphoristic repression? Following the same logic—logic itself—this does not exclude the fact that philosophy lives *in* and *from* differance, that it thereby blinds itself to the *same*, which is not the identical. The same is precisely differance (with an *a*), as the diverted and equivo-cal passage from one difference to another, from one term of the opposition to the other. We could thus take up all the coupled oppositions on which philosophy is constructed, and from which our language lives, not in order to see opposition vanish but to see the emergence of a necessity such that one of the terms appears as the differance of the other, the other as "differed" within the systematic ordering of the same (e.g., the intelligible as differing from the sensible, as sensible differed; the concept as differed-differing intuition, life as differing-differed matter; mind as differed-differing life; culture as differed-differing nature; and all the terms desig-nating what is other than *physis*—*technē, nomos*, society, freedom, history, spirit, etc.—as *physis* differed or *physis* differing: *physis in differance*). It is out of the unfolding of this "same" as differance that the sameness of difference and of repetition is presented in the eternal return.

In Nietzsche, these are so many themes that can be related with the kind of symptomatology that always serves to diagnose the evasions and ruses of anything disguised in its differance. Or again, these terms can be related with the entire thematics of active interpretation, which substitutes an incessant deciphering for the disclosure of truth as a presentation of the thing itself in its presence, etc. What results is a cipher without truth, or at least a system of ciphers that is not dominated by truth value, which only then becomes a function that is understood, inscribed, and circumscribed.

We shall therefore call differance this "active" (in movement) discord of the different forces and of the differences between forces which Nietzsche opposes to the entire system of metaphysical grammar, wherever that system controls culture, philosophy, and science.

It is historically significant that this diaphoristics, understood as an energetics or an economy of forces, set up to question the primacy of presence qua consciousness, is also the major theme of Freud's thought; in his work we find another diaphoristics, both in the form of a theory of ciphers or traces and an energetics. The questioning of the authority of consciousness is first and always differential.

The two apparently different meanings of differance are tied together in Freudian theory: differing [le différer] as discernibility, distinction, deviation, diastem, *spacing*; and deferring [le différer] as detour, delay, relay, reserve, *temporalizing*. I shall recall only that:

1   The concept of trace (*Spur*), of facilitation (*Bahnung*), of forces of facilitation are, as early as the composition of the *Entwurf*, inseparable from the concept of difference. The origin of memory and of the psyche as a memory in general (conscious or unconscious) can only be described by taking into account the difference between the facilitation thresholds, as Freud says explicitly. There is no facilitation [*Bahnung*] without difference and no difference without a trace.

2   All the differences involved in the production of unconscious traces and in the process of inscription (*Niederschrift*) can also be interpreted as moments of differance, in the sense of "placing on reserve." Following a schema that continually guides Freud's thinking, the movement of the trace is described as an effort of life to protect itself *by deferring* the dangerous investment, by constituting a reserve (*Vorrat*). And all the conceptual oppositions that furrow Freudian thought relate each concept to the other like movements of a detour, within the economy of differance. The one is only the other deferred, the one differing from the other. The one is the other in differance, the one is the differance from the other. Every apparently rigorous and irreducible opposition (for example, that between the secondary and primary) is thus said to be, at one time or another, a "theoretical fiction." In this way again, for example (but such an example covers everything or communicates with everything), the difference between the pleasure principle and the reality principle is only differance as detour (*Aufschieben, Aufschub*). In *Beyond the Pleasure Principle*, Freud writes:

Under the influence of the ego's instincts of self-preservation, the

> pleasure principle is replaced by the reality principle. This latter prin-
> ciple does not abandon the intention of ultimately obtaining pleasure,
> but it nevertheless demands and carries into effect the postponement
> of satisfaction, the abandonment of a number of possibilities of gaining
> satisfaction and the temporary toleration of unpleasure as a step on the
> long indirect road (*Aufschub*) to pleasure.[12]

Here we touch on the point of greatest obscurity, on the very enigma of differance, on how the concept we have of it is divided by a strange separation. We must not hasten to make a decision too quickly. How can we conceive of differance as a systematic detour which, within the element of the same, always aims at either finding again the pleasure or the presence that had been deferred by (conscious or unconscious) calculation, and, *at the same time*, how can we, on the other hand, conceive of differance as the relation to an impossible presence, as an expenditure without reserve, as an irreparable loss of presence, an irreversible wearing-down of energy, or indeed as a death instinct and a relation to the absolutely other that apparently breaks up any economy? It is evident—it is evidence itself—that system and nonsystem, the same and the absolutely other, etc., cannot be conceived *together*.

If differance is this inconceivable factor, must we not perhaps hasten to make it evident, to bring it into the philosophical element of evidence, and thus quickly dissipate its mirage character and illogicality, dissipate it with the infallibility of the calculus we know well—since we have recognized its place, necessity, and function within the structure of differance? What would be accounted for philosophically here has already been taken into account in the system of differance as it is here being calculated. I have tried elsewhere, in a reading of Bataille,[13] to indicate what might be the establishment of a rigorous, and in a new sense "scientific," *relating* of a "restricted economy"—one having nothing to do with an unreserved expenditure, with death, with being exposed to nonsense, etc.—to a "general economy" or system that, so to speak, *takes account of* what is unreserved. It is a relation between a differance that is accounted for and a differance that fails to be accounted for, where the establishment of a pure presence, without loss, is one with the occurrence of absolute loss, with death. By establishing this relation between a restricted and a general system, we shift and recommence the very project of philosophy under the privileged heading of Hegelianism.

The economic character of difference in no way implies that the deferred presence can always be recovered, that it simply amounts to an investment that only temporarily and without loss delays the presentation of presence, that is, the perception of gain or the gain of perception. Contrary to the metaphysical, dialectical, and "Hegelian" interpretation of the economic movement of differance, we must admit a game where whoever loses wins and where one wins and loses each time. If the diverted presentation continues to be somehow definitively and irreducibly withheld, this is not because a particular present remains hidden or absent, but because differance holds us in a relation with what exceeds (though we necessarily fail to recognize this) the alternative of presence or absence. A certain alterity—Freud gives it a metaphysical name, the unconscious—is definitively taken away from every process of presentation in which we would demand for it to be shown forth in person. In this context and under this heading, the unconscious is not, as we know, a hidden, virtual, and potential self-presence. It is differed— which no doubt means that it is woven out of differences, but also that it sends out, that it delegates, representatives or proxies; but there is no chance that the mandating subject "exists" somewhere, that it is present or is "itself," and still less chance that it will become conscious. In this sense, contrary to the terms of an old debate, strongly symptomatic of the metaphysical investments it has always assumed, the "unconscious" can no more be classed as a "thing" than as anything else; it is no more of a thing than an implicit or masked consciousness. This radical alterity, removed from every possible mode of presence, is characterized by irreducible aftereffects, by delayed effects. In order to describe them, in order to read the traces of the "unconscious" traces (there are no "conscious" traces), the language of presence or absence, the metaphysical speech of phenomenology, is in principle inadequate.

The structure of delay (*retardement: Nachträglichkeit*) that Freud talks about indeed prohibits our taking temporalization (temporalizing) to be a simple dialectical complication of the present; rather, this is the style of transcendental phenomenology. It describes the living present as a primordial and incessant synthesis that is constantly led back upon itself, back upon its assembled and assembling self, by retentional traces and protentional openings. With the alterity of the "unconscious," we have to deal not with the horizons of modified presents—past or future—but with a "past" that has never been nor will ever be present, whose "future" will never be produced or reproduced in the form of presence. The concept of trace is therefore incommensurate with that of retention, that of the becoming-past of what had been present. The trace cannot be conceived—nor, therefore, can differance—on the basis of either the present or the presence of the present.

A past that has never been present: with this formula Emmanuel Levinas designates (in ways that are, to be sure, not those of psychoanalysis) the trace and the enigma of absolute alterity, that is, the Other [*autrui*]. At least within these limits, and from this point of view, the thought of differance implies the whole critique of classical ontology undertaken by Levinas. And the concept of trace, like that of differance, forms—across these different traces and through these differences between traces, as understood by Nietzsche, Freud, and Levinas (these "authors' names" serve only as indications)—the network that sums up and permeates our "epoch" as the de-limitation of ontology (of presence).

The ontology of presence is the ontology of beings and beingness. Everywhere, the dominance of beings is solicited by differance—in the sense that *sollicitare* means, in old Latin, to shake all over, to make the whole tremble. What is questioned by the thought of differance, therefore, is the determination of being in presence, or in beingness. Such a question could not arise and be understood without the difference between Being and begins opening up somewhere. The first consequence of this is that differance is not. It is not a being-present, however excellent, unique, principal, or transcendent one makes it. It commands nothing, rules over nothing, and nowhere does it exercise any authority. It is not marked by a capital letter. Not only is there no realm of differance, but differance is even the subversion of every realm. This is obviously what makes it threatening and necessarily dreaded by everything in us that desires a realm, the past or future presence of a realm. And it is always in the name of a realm that, believing one sees it ascend to the capital letter, one can reproach it for wanting to rule.

Does this mean, then, that differance finds its place within the spread of the ontic-ontological difference, as it is conceived, as the "epoch" conceives itself within it, and particularly "across" the Heideggerian meditation, which cannot be gotten around?

There is no simple answer to such a question.

In one particular respect, differance is, to be sure, but the historical and epochal *deployment* of Being or of the ontological difference. The *a* of differance marks the *movement* of this deployment.

And yet, is not the thought that conceives the *sense* or *truth* of Being, the determination of differance as ontic-ontological difference—difference conceived within the horizon of the question of *Being*—still an intrametaphysical effect of differance? Perhaps the deployment of differance is not only the truth or the epochality of Being. Perhaps we must try to think this *unheard-of* thought, this silent tracing, namely, that the history of Being (the thought of which is committed to the Greco-Western logos), as it is itself produced across the ontological differ-ence, is only one epoch of the *diapherein*. Then we could no longer even call it an "epoch," for the concept of epochality belongs within history understood as the history of Being. Being has always made "sense," has always been conceived or spoken of as such, only by dissimulating itself in beings; thus, in a particular and very strange way, differance (is) "older" than the ontological difference or the truth of Being. In this age it can be called the play of traces. It is a trace that no longer belongs to the horizon of Being but one whose sense of Being is borne and bound by this play; it is a play of traces or differance that has no sense and is not, a play that does not belong. There is no support to be found and no depth to be had for this bottomless chessboard where being is set in play.

It is perhaps in this way that the Heraclitean play of the *hen diapheron heautōi*, of the one differing from itself, of what is in difference with itself, already becomes lost as a trace in determining the *diapherein* as ontological difference.

To think through the ontological difference doubtless remains a difficult task, a task whose statement has remained nearly inaudible. And to prepare ourselves for venturing beyond our own logos, that is, for a differance so violent that it refuses to be stopped and examined as the epochality of Being and ontological difference, is neither to give up this passage through the truth of Being, nor is it in any way to "criticize," "contest," or fail to recognize the incessant necessity for it. On the contrary, we must stay within the difficulty of this passage; we must repeat this passage in a rigorous reading of metaphysics, wherever metaphysics serves as the norm of Western speech, and not only in the texts of "the history of philosophy." Here we must allow the trace of whatever goes beyond the truth of Being to appear/disappear in its fully rigorous way. It is a trace of something that can never present itself; it is itself a trace that can never be presented, that is, can never appear and manifest itself as such in its phenomenon. It is a trace that lies beyond what profoundly ties fundamental ontology to phenomenology. Like differance, the trace is never presented as such. In presenting itself it becomes effaced; in being sounded it dies away, like the writing of the *a*, inscribing its pyramid in differance.

We can always reveal the precursive and secretive traces of this movement in metaphysical speech, especially in the contemporary talk about the closure of ontology, i.e., through the various attempts we have looked at (Nietzsche, Freud, Levinas)—and particularly in Heidegger's work.

The latter provokes us to question the essence of the present, the presence of the present.

What is the present? What is it to conceive the present in its presence?

Let us consider, for example, the 1946 text entitled "Der Spruch des Anaximander." Heidegger there recalls that the forgetting of Being forgets about the difference between Being and beings:

> But the point of Being (*die Sache des Seins*) is to be the Being of beings. The linguistic form of this enigmatic and multivalent genitive desig- nates a genesis (*Genesis*), a provenance (*Herkunft*) of the present from presence (*des Anwesenden aus dem Anwesen*). But with the unfolding of these two, the essence (*Wesen*) of this provenance remains hidden (*ver- borgen*). Not only is the essence of this provenance not thought out, but neither is the simple relation between presence and present (*Anwesen und Anwesenden*). Since the dawn, it seems that presence and being-present are each separately something. Imperceptibly, presence becomes itself a present. . . . The essence of presence (*Das Wesen des Anwesens*), and thus the difference between presence and present, is forgotten. *The forgetting of Being is the forgetting of the difference between Being and beings.*[14]

In recalling the difference between Being and beings (the ontological differ- ence) as the difference between presence and present, Heidegger puts forward a proposition, indeed, a group of propositions; it is not our intention here to idly or hastily "criticize" them but rather to convey them with all their provocative force.

Let us then proceed slowly. What Heidegger wants to point out is that the difference between Being and beings, forgotten by metaphysics, has disappeared without leaving a trace. The very trace of difference has sunk from sight. If we admit that differance (is) (itself) something other than presence and absence, if it *traces*, then we are dealing with the forgetting of the difference (between Being and beings), and we now have to talk about a disappearance of the trace's trace. This is certainly what this passage from "Der Spruch des Anaximander" seems to imply:

> The forgetting of Being is a part of the very essence of Being, and is concealed by it. The forgetting belongs so essentially to the destination of Being that the dawn of this destination begins precisely as an uncon- cealment of the present in its presence. This means: the history of Being begins by the forgetting of Being, in that Being retains its essence, its difference from beings. Difference is wanting; it remains forgotten. Only what is differentiated—the present and presence (*das Anwesende und das Anwesen*)—becomes uncovered, but not *insofar as* it is differenti- ated. On the contrary, the matinal trace (*die frühe Spur*) of difference effaces itself from the moment that presence appears as a being-present

(*das Anwesen wie ein Anwesendes erscheint*) and finds its provenance in a supreme (being)-present (*in einem höchsten Anwesenden*).[15]

The trace is not a presence but is rather the simulacrum of a presence that dislocates, displaces, and refers beyond itself. The trace has, properly speaking, no place, for effacement belongs to the very structure of the trace. Effacement must always be able to overtake the trace; otherwise it would not be a trace but an indestructible and monumental substance. In addition, and from the start, efface-ment constitutes it as a trace—effacement establishes the trace in a change of place and makes it disappear in its appearing, makes it issue forth from itself in its very position. The effacing of this early trace (*die frühe Spur*) of difference is therefore "the same" as its tracing within the text of metaphysics. This metaphysical text must have retained a mark of what it lost or put in reserve, set aside. In the language of metaphysics the paradox of such a structure is the inversion of the metaphysical concept which produces the following effect: the present becomes the sign of signs, the trace of traces. It is no longer what every reference refers to in the last instance; it becomes a function in a generalized referential structure. It is a trace, and a trace of the effacement of a trace.

In this way the metaphysical text is *understood;* it is still readable, and remains to be read. It proposes *both* the monument and the mirage of the trace, the trace as simultaneously traced and effaced, simultaneously alive and dead, alive as always to simulate even life in its preserved inscription; it is a pyramid.

Thus we think through, without contradiction, or at least without granting any pertinence to such contradiction, what is perceptible and imperceptible about the trace. The "matinal trace" of difference is lost in an irretrievable invisibility, and yet even its loss is covered, preserved, regarded, and retarded. This happens in a text, in the form of presence.

Having spoken about the effacement of the matinal trace, Heidegger can thus, in this contradiction without contradiction, consign or countersign the sealing of the trace. We read on a little further:

> The difference between Being and beings, however, can in turn be experienced as something forgotten only if it is already discovered with the presence of the present (*mit dem Anwesen des Anwesenden*) and if it is thus sealed in a trace (*so eine Spur geprägt hat*) that remains preserved (*gewahrt bleibt*) in the language which Being appropriates.[16]

Further on still, while meditating upon Anaximander's τὸ χρεών, translated as *Brauch* (sustaining use), Heidegger writes the following:

> Dispensing accord and deference (*Fug und Ruch verfügend*), our sustain-ing use frees the pre*sent* (*das Anwesende*) in its sojourn and sets it free every time for its sojourn. But by the same token the present is equally seen to be exposed to the constant danger of hardening in the insist-ence (*in das blosse Beharren verhärtet*) out of its sojourning duration. In this way sustaining use (*Brauch*) remains itself and at the same time an abandonment (*Aushändigung:* handing-over) of presence (*des Anwesens*)

in den Un-fug, to discord (disjointedness). Sustaining use joins together the dis- (*Der Brauch fügt das Un-*).[17]

And it is at the point where Heidegger determines *sustaining use* as *trace* that the question must be asked: can we, and how far can we, think of this trace and the *dis-* of difference as *Wesen des Seins*? Doesn't the *dis* of differance refer us beyond the history of Being, beyond our language as well, and beyond everything that can be named by it? Doesn't it call for—in the language of being—the necessarily violent transformation of this language by an entirely different language?

Let us be more precise here. In order to dislodge the "trace" from its cover (and whoever believes that one tracks down some *thing?*—one tracks down tracks), let us continue reading this passage:

> The translation of τὸ χρεών by "sustaining use" (*Brauch*) does not derive from cogitations of an etymologico-lexical nature. The choice of the word "sustaining use" derives from an antecedent *trans*lation (*Über*setzen) of the thought that attempts to conceive difference in the deployment of Being (*im Wesen des Seins*) toward the historical begin-ning of the forgetting of Being. The word "sustaining use" is dictated to thought in the apprehension (*Erfahrung*) of the forgetting of Being. Tò χρεών properly names a trace (*Spur*) of what remains to be conceived in the word "sustaining use," a trace that quickly disappears (*alsbald verschwindet*) into the history of Being, in its world-historical unfolding as Western metaphysics.[18]

How do we conceive of the outside of a text? How, for example, do we conceive of what stands opposed to the text of Western metaphysics? To be sure, the "trace that quickly disappears into the history of Being, . . . as Western meta-physics," escapes all the determinations, all the names it might receive in the metaphysical text. The trace is sheltered and thus dissimulated in these names; it does not appear in the text as the trace "itself." But this is because the trace itself could never itself appear as such. Heidegger also says that difference can never appear *as such*: "Lichtung des Unterschiedes kann deshalb auch nicht bedeuten, dass der Unterschied als der Unterschied erscheint." There is no essence of difference; not only can it not allow itself to be taken up into the *as such* of its name or its appearing, but it threatens the authority of the *as such* in general, the thing's presence in its essence. That there is no essence of differance at this point also implies that there is neither Being nor truth to the play of writing, *insofar* as it involves differance.

For us, differance remains a metaphysical name; and all the names that it receives from our language are still, so far as they are names, metaphysical. This is particularly so when they speak of determining difference as the difference between presence and present (*Anwesen/Anwesend*), but already and especially so when, in the most general way, they speak of determining difference as the difference between Being and beings.

"Older" than Being itself, our language has no name for such a differance. But we "already know" that if it is unnamable, this is not simply provisional; it is not because our language has still not found or received this *name*, or because we would have to look for it in another language, outside the finite system of our language. It is because there is no *name* for this, not even essence or Being—not even the name "differance," which is not a name, which is not a pure nominal unity, and continually breaks up in a chain of different substitutions.

"There is no name for this": we read this as a truism. What is unnamable here is not some ineffable being that cannot be approached by a name; like God, for example. What is unnamable is the play that brings about the nominal effects, the relatively unitary or atomic structures we call names, or chains of substitutions for names. In these, for example, the nominal effect of "differance" is itself involved, carried off, and reinscribed, just as the false beginning or end of a game is still part of the game, a function of the system.

What we do know, what we could know if it were simply a question of knowing, is that there never has been and never will be a unique word, a master name. This is why thinking about the letter *a* of differance is not the primary prescription, nor is it the prophetic announcement of some imminent and still unheard-of designation. There is nothing kerygmatic about this "word" so long as we can perceive its reduction to a lower-case letter.

There will be no unique name, not even the name of Being. It must be conceived without *nostalgia*; that is, it must be conceived outside the myth of the purely maternal or paternal language belonging to the lost fatherland of thought. On the contrary, we must *affirm* it—in the sense that Nietzsche brings affirmation into play—with a certain laughter and with a certain dance.

After this laughter and dance, after this affirmation that is foreign to any dialectic, the question arises as to the other side of nostalgia, which I will call Heideggerian *hope*. I am not unaware that this term may be somewhat shocking. I venture it all the same, without excluding any of its implications, and shall relate it to what seems to me to be retained of metaphysics in "Der Spruch des Anaximander," namely, the quest for the proper word and the unique name. In talking about the "first word of Being" (*das frühe Wort des Seins:* τὸ χρεών), Heidegger writes,

> The relation to the pre*sent*, unfolding its order in the very essence of pre*sence*, is unique (*ist eine einzige*). It is pre-eminently incomparable to any other relation; it belongs to the uniqueness of Being itself (*Sie gehört zur Einzigkeit des Seins selbst*). Thus, in order to name what is deployed in Being (*das Wesende des Seins*), language will have to find a single word, the unique word (*ein einziges, das einzige Wort*). There we see how hazardous is every word of thought (every thoughtful word: *denkende Wort*) that addresses itself to Being (*das dem Sein zugesprochen wird*). What is haz-arded here, however, is not something impossible, because Being speaks through every language; everywhere and always.[19]

Such is the question: the marriage between speech and Being in the unique word, in the finally proper name. Such is the question that enters into the affirmation put into play by differance. The question bears (upon) each of the words in this sentence: "Being / speaks / through every language; / everywhere and always /."

This essay appeared originally in the *Bulletin de la Société française de philosophie*, LXII, No. 3 (July–September, 1968), 73–101. Derrida's remarks were delivered as a lecture at a meeting of the Société at the Sorbonne, in the Amphithéâtre Michelet, on January 27, 1968, with Jean Wahl presiding. Professor Wahl's introductory and closing remarks have not been translated. The essay was reprinted in *Théorie d'ensemble*, a collection of essays by Derrida and others, published by Editions Seuil in 1968. It is reproduced here by permission of Editions Seuil.

Notes

1   [The reader should bear in mind that "differance," or difference with an *a*, incorporates two significations: "to differ" and "to defer." See also above, footnote 8, p. 82.—Translator.] [See original text.]

2   [For the term "facilitation" (*frayage*) in Freud, cf. "Project for a Scientific Psychology I" in *The Complete Psychological Works of Sigmund Freud*, 24 vols. (New York and London: Macmillan, 1964), I, 300, note 4 by the translator, James Strachey: "The word 'facilitation' as a rendering of the German '*Bahnung*' seems to have been introduced by Sherrington a few years after the *Project* was written. The German word, however, was already in use." The sense that Derrida draws upon here is stronger in the French or German; that is, the opening-up or clearing-out of a pathway. In the context of the "Project for a Scientific Psychology I," facilitation denotes the conduction capability that results from a difference in resistance levels in the memory and perception circuits of the nervous system. Thus, lowering the resistance threshold of a contact barrier serves to "open up" a nerve pathway and "facilitates" the excitatory process for the circuit. Cf. also J. Derrida, *L'Ecriture et la différence*, Chap. VII, "Freud et la scène de l'écriture" (Paris: Seuil, 1967), esp. pp. 297–305.—Translator.]

3   [On "pyramid" and "tomb" see J. Derrida, "Le Puits et la pyramide" in *Hegel et la pensée moderne* (Paris: Presses Universitaires de France, 1970), esp. pp. 44–45.—Translator.]

4   Ferdinand de Saussure, *Cours de linguistique générale*, ed. C. Bally and A. Sechehaye (Paris: Payot, 1916); English translation by Wade Baskin, *Course in General Linguistics* (New York: Philosophical Library, 1959), pp. 117–18, 120.

5   *Course in General Linguistics*, p. 18.

6   [On "supplement" see above, *Speech and Phenomena*, Chap. 7, pp. 88–104. Cf. also Derrida, *De la grammatologie* (Paris: Editions de Minuit, 1967). On "*pharmakon*" see Derrida, "La Pharmacie de Platon," *Tel Quel*, No. 32 (Winter, 1967), pp. 17–59; No. 33 (Spring, 1968), pp. 4–48. On "hymen" see Derrida, "La Double séance," *Tel Quel*, No. 41 (Spring, 1970), pp. 3–43; No. 42 (Summer, 1970), pp. 3–45. "La Pharmacie de Platon" and "La Double séance" have been reprinted in a recent text of Derrida, *La Dissémination* (Paris: Editions du Seuil, 1972).—Translator.]

7   [Derrida often brackets or "crosses out" certain key terms taken from metaphysics and logic, and in doing this, he follows Heidegger's usage in *Zur Seinsfrage*. The terms in question no longer have their full meaning, they no longer have the status of a purely signified content of expression—no longer, that is, after the deconstruction of metaphysics. Generated out of the play of differance, they still retain a vestigial trace of sense, however, a trace that cannot simply be gotten around (*incontournable*). An extensive discussion of all this is to be found in *De la grammatologie*, pp. 31–40.—Translator.]

8   Alexandre Koyré, "Hegel à Iéna," *Revue d'histoire et de philosophie religieuse*, XIV (1934), 420–58; reprinted in Koyré, *Etudes d'histoire de la pensée philosophique* (Paris: Armand Colin, 1961), pp. 135–73.

9   Koyré, *Etudes d'histoire*, pp. 153–54. [The quotation from Hegel (my translation) comes from "Jenenser Logik, Metaphysik, und Naturphilosophie," *Sämtliche Werke* (Leipzig: F. Meiner, 1925), XVIII, 202. Koyré reproduces the original German text on pp. 153–54, note 2.—Translator.]

10   De Saussure, *Course in General Linguistics*, p. 37.
11   G. Deleuze, *Nietzsche et la philosophie* (Paris: Presses Universitaires de France, 1970), p. 49.
12   Freud, *Complete Psychological Works*, XVIII, 10.
13   Derrida, *L'Ecriture et la différence*, pp. 369–407.
14   Martin Heidegger, *Holzwege* (Frankfurt: V. Klostermann, 1957), pp. 335–36. [All translations of quotations from *Holzwege* are mine.—Translator.]
15   *Ibid.*, p. 336.
16   *Ibid.*
17   *Ibid.*, pp. 339–40.
18   *Ibid.*, p. 340.
19   *Ibid.*, pp. 337–38.

Suggestions for further reading

Belsey, Catherine, *Critical Practice*, 2nd edn., London and New York: Routledge, 2002. See especially Chapter 7, 'Deconstruction and the Differance it Makes'.

Derrida, Jacques, *Of Grammatology*, trans. Gayatri Chakravorty Spivak, Baltimore: Johns Hopkins University Press, 1976.

Wood, David and Bernasconi, Robert (eds.), *Derrida and Différance*, Evanston, IL: Northwestern University Press, 1988.

Chapter 13

Michel de Certeau

'WALKING IN THE CITY', 1974

S EEING MANHATTAN FROM the 110th floor of the World Trade Center. Beneath the haze stirred up by the winds, the urban island, a sea in the middle of the sea, lifts up the skyscrapers over Wall Street, sinks down at Greenwich, then rises again to the crests of Midtown, quietly passes over Central Park and finally undulates off into the distance beyond Harlem. A wave of verticals. Its agitation is momentarily arrested by vision. The gigantic mass is immobilized before the eyes. It is transformed into a texturology in which extremes coincide—extremes of ambition and degradation, brutal oppositions of races and styles, contrasts between yesterday's buildings, already transformed into trash cans, and today's urban irruptions that block out its space. Unlike Rome, New York has never learned the art of growing old by playing on all its pasts. Its present invents itself, from hour to hour, in the act of throwing away its previous accomplishments and challenging the future. A city composed of paroxysmal places in monumental reliefs. The spectator can read in it a universe that is constantly exploding. In it are inscribed the architectural figures of the *coincidatio oppositorum* formerly drawn in miniatures and mystical textures. On this stage of concrete, steel and glass, cut out between two oceans (the Atlantic and the American) by a frigid body of water, the tallest letters in the world compose a gigantic rhetoric of excess in both expenditure and production.[1]

Voyeurs or walkers

To what erotics of knowledge does the ecstasy of reading such a cosmos belong? Having taken a voluptuous pleasure in it, I wonder what is the source of this pleasure of "seeing the whole," of looking down on, totalizing the most immoderate of human texts.

To be lifted to the summit of the World Trade Center is to be lifted out of the city's grasp. One's body is no longer clasped by the streets that turn and return it according to an anonymous law; nor is it possessed, whether as player or played, by the rumble of so many differences and by the nervousness of New York traffic. When one goes up there, he leaves behind the mass that carries off and mixes up in itself any identity of authors or spectators. An Icarus flying above these waters, he can ignore the devices of Daedalus in mobile and endless labyrinths far below. His elevation transfigures him into a voyeur. It puts him at a distance. It transforms the bewitching world by which one was "possessed" into a text that lies before one's eyes. It allows one to read it, to be a solar Eye, looking down like a god. The exaltation of a scopic and gnostic drive: the fiction of knowledge is related to this lust to be a viewpoint and nothing more.

Must one finally fall back into the dark space where crowds move back and forth, crowds that, though visible from on high, are themselves unable to see down below? An Icarian fall. On the 110th floor, a poster, sphinx-like, addresses an enigmatic message to the pedestrian who is for an instant transformed into a visionary: *It's hard to be down when you're up.*

The desire to see the city preceded the means of satisfying it. Medieval or Renaissance painters represented the city as seen in a perspective that no eye had yet enjoyed.[2] This fiction already made the medieval spectator into a celestial eye. It created gods. Have things changed since technical procedures have organized an "all-seeing power"?[3] The totalizing eye imagined by the painters of earlier times lives on in our achievements. The same scopic drive haunts users of architectural productions by materializing today the utopia that yesterday was only painted. The 1370 foot high tower that serves as a prow for Manhattan continues to construct the fiction that creates readers, makes the complexity of the city readable, and immobilizes its opaque mobility in a transparent text.

Is the immense texturology spread out before one's eyes anything more than a representation, an optical artifact? It is the analogue of the facsimile produced, through a projection that is a way of keeping aloof, by the space planner urbanist, city planner or cartographer. The panorama-city is a "theoretical" (that is, visual) simulacrum, in short a picture, whose condition of possibility is an oblivion and a misunderstanding of practices. The voyeur-god created by this fiction, who, like Schreber's God, knows only cadavers,[4] must disentangle himself from the murky intertwining daily behaviors and make himself alien to them.

The ordinary practitioners of the city live "down below," below the thresholds at which visibility begins. They walk—an elementary form of this experience of the city; they are walkers, *Wandersmänner*, whose bodies follow the thicks and thins of an urban "text" they write without being able to read it. These practitioners make use of spaces that cannot be seen; their knowledge of them is as blind as that of lovers in each other's arms. The paths that correspond in this intertwining, unrecognized poems in which each body is an element signed by many others, elude legibility. It is as though the practices organizing a bustling city were characterized by their blindness.[5] The networks of these moving, intersecting writings compose a manifold story that has neither author nor spectator, shaped out of fragments of trajectories and alterations of spaces: in relation to representations, it remains daily and indefinitely other.

Escaping the imaginary totalizations produced by the eye, the everyday has a certain strangeness that does not surface, or whose surface is only its upper limit, outlining itself against the visible. Within this ensemble, I shall try to locate the practices that are foreign to the "geometrical" or "geographical" space of visual, panoptic, or theoretical constructions. These practices of space refer to a specific form of *operations* ("ways of operating"), to "another spatiality"[6] (an "anthropo-logical," poetic and mythic experience of space), and to an *opaque and blind* mobil-ity characteristic of the bustling city. A *migrational*, or metaphorical, city thus slips into the clear text of the planned and readable city.

From the concept of the city to urban practices

The World Trade Center is only the most monumental figure of Western urban development. The atopia-utopia of optical knowledge has long had the ambition of surmounting and articulating the contradictions arising from urban agglomeration. It is a question of managing a growth of human agglomeration or accumulation. "The city is a huge monastery," said Erasmus. Perspective vision and prospective vision constitute the twofold projection of an opaque past and an uncertain future onto a surface that can be dealt with. They inaugurate (in the sixteenth century?) the transformation of the urban *fact* into the *concept* of a city. Long before the concept itself gives rise to a particular figure of history, it assumes that this fact can be dealt with as a unity determined by an urbanistic *ratio*. Linking the city to the concept never makes them identical, but it plays on their progressive sym-biosis: to plan a city is both to *think the very plurality* of the real and to make that way of thinking the plural *effective*; it is to know how to articulate it and be able to do it.

An operational concept?

The "city" founded by utopian and urbanistic discourse[7] is defined by the possibil-ity of a threefold operation:

1   The production of its *own* space (*un espace propre*): rational organization must thus repress all the physical, mental and political pollutions that would compromise it;
2   the substitution of a nowhen or of a synchronic system, for the indetermin-able and stubborn resistances offered by traditions; univocal scientific strat-egies, made possible by the flattening out of all the data in a plane projection, must replace the tactics of users who take advantage of "opportunities" and who, through these trap-events, these lapses in visibility, reproduce the opacities of history everywhere;
3   finally, the creation of a *universal* and anonymous *subject* which is the city itself: it gradually becomes possible to attribute to it, as to its political model, Hobbes' State, all the functions and predicates that were previously scattered and assigned to many different real subjects—groups, associations, or indi-viduals. "The city," like a proper name, thus provides a way of conceiving and

constructing space on the basis of a finite number of stable, isolatable, and interconnected properties.

Administration is combined with a process of elimination in this place organized by "speculative" and classificatory operations.[8] On the one hand, there is a differentiation and redistribution of the parts and functions of the city, as a result of inversions, displacements, accumulations, etc.; on the other there is a rejection of everything that is not capable of being dealt with in this way and so constitutes the "waste products" of a functionalist administration (abnormality, deviance, illness, death, etc.) To be sure, progress allows an increasing number of these waste products to be reintroduced into administrative circuits and transforms even deficiencies (in health, security, etc.) into ways of making the networks of order denser. But in reality, it repeatedly produces effects contrary to those at which it aims: the profit system generates a loss which, in the multiple forms of wretchedness and poverty outside the system and of waste inside it, constantly turns production into "expenditure." Moreover, the rationalization of the city leads to its mythification in strategic discourses, which are calculations based on the hypothesis or the necessity of its destruction in order to arrive at a final decision.[9] Finally, the functionalist organization, by privileging progress (i.e., time), causes the condition of its own possibility—space itself—to be forgotten; space thus becomes the blind spot in a scientific and political technology. This is the way in which the Concept-city functions; a place of transformations and appropriations, the object of various kinds of interference but also a subject that is constantly enriched by new attributes, it is simultaneously the machinery and the hero of modernity.

Today, whatever the avatars of this concept may have been, we have to acknowledge that if in discourse the city serves as a totalizing and almost mythical landmark for socioeconomic and political strategies, urban life increasingly permits the re-emergence of the element that the urbanistic project excluded. The language of power is in itself "urbanizing," but the city is left prey to contradictory movements that counter-balance and combine themselves outside the reach of panoptic power. The city becomes the dominant theme in political legends, but it is no longer a field of programmed and regulated operations. Beneath the discourses that ideologize the city, the ruses and combinations of powers that have no readable identity proliferate; without points where one can take hold of them, without rational transparency, they are impossible to administer.

The return of practices

The Concept-city is decaying. Does that mean that the illness afflicting both the rationality that founded it and its professionals afflicts the urban populations as well? Perhaps cities are deteriorating along with the procedures that organized them. But we must be careful here. The ministers of knowledge have always assumed that the whole universe was threatened by the very changes that affected their ideologies and their positions. They transmute the misfortune of their theories into theories of misfortune. When they transform their bewilderment into "catastrophes," when they seek to enclose the people in the "panic" of their discourses, are they once more necessarily right?

Rather than remaining within the field of a discourse that upholds its privilege by inverting its content (speaking of catastrophe and no longer of progress), one can try another path: one can analyze the microbe-like, singular and plural practices which an urbanistic system was supposed to administer or suppress, but which have outlived its decay; one can follow the swarming activity of these procedures that, far from being regulated or eliminated by panoptic administration, have reinforced themselves in a proliferating illegitimacy, developed and insinuated themselves into the networks of surveillance, and combined in accord with unreadable but stable tactics to the point of constituting everyday regulations and surreptitious creativities that are merely concealed by the frantic mechanisms and discourses of the observational organization.

This pathway could be inscribed as a consequence, but also as the reciprocal, of Foucault's analysis of the structures of power. He moved it in the direction of mechanisms and technical procedures, "minor instrumentalities" capable, merely by their organization of "details," of transforming a human multiplicity into a "disciplinary" society and of managing, differentiating, classifying, and hierarchizing all deviances concerning apprenticeship, health, justice, the army, or work.[10] "These often miniscule ruses of discipline," these "minor but flawless" mechanisms, draw their efficacy from a relationship between procedures and the space that they redistribute in order to make an "operator" out of it. But what *spatial practices* correspond, in the area where discipline is manipulated, to these apparatuses that produce a disciplinary space? In the present conjuncture, which is marked by a contradiction between the collective mode of administration and an individual mode of reappropriation, this question is no less important, if one admits that spatial practices in fact secretly structure the determining conditions of social life. I would like to follow out a few of these multiform, resistance, tricky and stubborn procedures that elude discipline without being outside the field in which it is exercised, and which should lead us to a theory of everyday practices, of lived space, of the disquieting familiarity of the city.

The chorus of idle footsteps

"The goddess can be recognized by her step"
Virgil, Aeneid, I, 405

Their story begins on ground level, with footsteps. They are myriad, but do not compose a series. They cannot be counted because each unit has a qualitative character: a style of tactile apprehension and kinesthetic appropriation. Their swarming mass is an innumerable collection of singularities. Their intertwined paths give their shape to spaces. They weave places together. In that respect, pedestrian movements form one of these "real systems whose existence in fact makes up the city."[11] They are not localized; it is rather they that spatialize. They are no more inserted within a container than those Chinese characters speakers sketch out on their hands with their fingertips.

It is true that the operations of walking on can be traced on city maps in such a way as to transcribe their paths (here well-trodden, there very faint) and their trajectories (going this way and not that). But these thick or thin curves only refer, like words, to the absence of what has passed by. Surveys of routes miss what was: the act itself of passing by. The operation of walking, wandering, or "window shopping," that is, the activity of passers-by, is transformed into points that draw a totalizing and reversible line on the map. They allow us to grasp only a relic set in the nowhen of a surface of projection. Itself visible, it has the effect of making invisible the operation that made it possible. These fixations constitute procedures for forgetting. The trace left behind is substituted for the practice. It exhibits the (voracious) property that the geographical system has of being able to transform action into legibility, but in doing so it causes a way of being in the world to be forgotten.

Pedestrian speech acts

A comparison with the speech act will allow us to go further[12] and not limit ourselves to the critique of graphic representations alone, looking from the shores of legibility toward an inaccessible beyond. The act of walking is to the urban system what the speech act is to language or to the statements uttered.[13] At the most elementary level, it has a triple "enunciative" function: it is a process of *appropriation* of the topographical system on the part of the pedestrian (just as the speaker appropriates and takes on the language); it is a spatial acting-out of the place (just as the speech act is an acoustic acting-out of language); and it implies *relations* among differentiated positions, that is, among pragmatic "contracts" in the form of movements (just as verbal enunciation is an "allocution," "posits another opposite" the speaker and puts contracts between interlocutors into action).[14] It thus seems possible to give a preliminary definition of walking as a space of enunciation.

We could moreover extend this problematic to the relations between the act of writing and the written text, and even transpose it to the relationships between the "hand" (the touch and the tale of the paint-brush [*le et la geste du pinceau*]) and the finished painting (forms, colors, etc.). At first isolated in the area of verbal communication, the speech act turns out to find only one of its applications there, and its linguistic modality is merely the first determination of a much more general distinction between the *forms used* in a system and the *ways of using* this system (i.e., *rules*), that is, between two "different worlds," since "the same things" are considered from two opposite formal viewpoints.

Considered from this angle, the pedestrian speech act has three characteristics which distinguish it at the outset from the spatial system: the present, the discrete, the "phatic."

First, if it is true that a spatial order organizes an ensemble of possibilities (e.g., by a place in which one can move) and interdictions (e.g.; by a wall that prevents one from going further), then the walker actualizes some of these possibilities. In that way, he makes them exist as well as emerge. But he also moves them about and he invents others, since the crossing, drifting away, or improvisation of walking privilege, transform or abandon spatial elements. Thus Charlie Chaplin multiplies the possibilities of his cane: he does other things with the same thing and he goes beyond the limits that the determinants of the object set on its utilization.

In the same way, the walker transforms each spatial signifier into something else. And if on the one hand he actualizes only a few of the possibilities fixed by the constructed order (he goes only here and not there), on the other he increases the number of possibilities (for example, by creating shortcuts and detours) and prohibitions (for example, he forbids himself to take paths generally considered accessible or even obligatory). He thus makes a selection. "The user of a city picks out certain fragments of the statement in order to actualize them in secret."[15]

He thus creates a discreteness, whether by making choices among the signifiers of the spatial "language" or by displacing them through the use he makes of them. He condemns certain places to inertia or disappearance and composes with others spatial "turns of phrase" that are "rare," "accidental" or illegitimate. But that already leads into a rhetoric of walking.

In the framework of enunciation, the walker constitutes, in relation to his position, both a near and a far, a *here* and a *there*. To the fact that the adverbs *here* and *there* are the indicators of the locutionary seat in verbal communication[16]—a coincidence that reinforces the parallelism between linguistic and pedestrian enunciation—we must add that this location (*here—there*) (necessarily implied by walking and indicative of a present appropriation of space by an "I") also has the function of introducing an other in relation to this "I" and of thus establishing a conjunctive and disjunctive articulation of places. I would stress particularly the "phatic" aspect, by which I mean the function, isolated by Malinowski and Jakobson, of terms that initiate, maintain, or interrupt contact, such as "hello," "well, well," etc.[17] Walking, which alternately follows a path and has followers, creates a mobile organicity in the environment, a sequence of phatic *topoi*. And if it is true that the phatic function, which is an effort to ensure communication, is already characteristic of the language of talking birds, just as it constitutes the "first verbal function acquired by children," it is not surprising that it also gambols, goes on all fours, dances, and walks about, with a light or heavy step, like a series of "hellos" in an echoing labyrinth, anterior or parallel to informative speech.

The modalities of pedestrian enunciation which a plane representation on a map brings out could be analyzed. They include the kinds of relationship this enunciation entertains with particular paths (or "statements") by according them a truth value ("alethic" modalities of the necessary, the impossible, the possible, or the contingent), an epistemological value ("epistemic" modalities of the certain, the excluded, the plausible, or the questionable) or finally an ethical or legal value ("deontic" modalities of the obligatory, the forbidden, the permitted, or the optional).[18] Walking affirms, suspects, tries out, transgresses, respects, etc., the trajectories it "speaks." All the modalities sing a part in this chorus, changing from step to step, stepping in through proportions, sequences, and intensities which vary according to the time, the path taken and the walker. These enunciatory operations are of an unlimited diversity. They therefore cannot be reduced to their graphic trail.

Walking rhetorics

The walking of passers-by offers a series of turns (*tours*) and detours that can be compared to "turns of phrase" or "stylistic figures." There is a rhetoric of walking.

The art of "turning" phrases finds an equivalent in an art of composing a path (*tourner un parcours*). Like ordinary language,[19] this art implies and combines styles and uses. *Style* specifies "a linguistic structure that manifests on the symbolic level . . . an individual's fundamental way of being in the world";[20] it connotes a singular. Use defines the social phenomenon through which a system of communication manifests itself in actual fact; it refers to a norm. Style and use both have to do with a "way of operating" (of speaking, walking, etc.), but style involves a peculiar processing of the symbolic, while use refers to elements of a code. They intersect to form a style of use, a way of being and a way of operating.[21]

In introducing the notion of a "residing rhetoric" ("*rhétorique habitante*"), the fertile pathway opened up by A. Médam[22] and systematized by S. Ostrowetsky[23] and J.-F. Augoyard,[24] we assume that the "tropes" catalogued by rhetoric furnish models and hypotheses for the analysis of ways of appropriating places. Two postulates seem to me to underlie the validity of this application: 1) it is assumed that practices of space also correspond to manipulations of the basic elements of a constructed order; 2) it is assumed that they are, like the tropes in rhetoric, deviations relative to a sort of "literal meaning" defined by the urbanistic system. There would thus be a homology between verbal figures and the figures of walking (a stylized selection among the latter is already found in the figures of dancing) insofar as both consist in "treatments" or operations bearing on isolatable units,[25] and in "ambiguous dispositions" that divert and displace meaning in the direction of equivocalness[26] in the way a tremulous image confuses and multiplies the photographed object. In these two modes, the analogy can be accepted. I would add that the geometrical space of urbanists and architects seems to have the status of the "proper meaning" constructed by grammarians and linguists in order to have a normal and normative level to which they can compare the drifting of "figurative" language. In reality, this faceless "proper" meaning (*ce "propre" sans figure*) cannot be found in current use, whether verbal or pedestrian; it is merely the fiction produced by a use that is also particular, the metalinguistic use of science that distinguishes itself by that very distinction.[27]

The long poem of walking manipulates spatial organizations, no matter how panoptic they may be: it is neither foreign to them (it can take place only within them) nor in conformity with them (it does not receive its identity from them). It creates shadows and ambiguities within them. It inserts its multitudinous references and citations into them (social models, cultural mores, personal factors). Within them it is itself the effect of successive encounters and occasions that constantly alter it and make it the other's blazon: in other words, it is like a peddler, carrying something surprising, transverse or attractive compared with the usual choice. These diverse aspects provide the basis of a rhetoric. They can even be said to define it.

By analyzing this "modern art of everyday expression" as it appears in accounts of spatial practices,[28] J.-F. Augoyard discerns in it two especially fundamental stylistic figures: synecdoche and asyndeton. The predominance of these two figures seems to me to indicate, in relation to two complementary poles, a formal structure of these practices. *Synecdoche* consists in "using a word in a sense which is part of another meaning of the same word."[29] In essence, it names a part instead of the whole which includes it. Thus "sail" is taken for "ship" in the expression "a fleet of fifty sails"; in the same way, a brick shelter or a hill is taken for the park in the narration of a trajectory. *Asyndeton* is the suppression of linking words such as conjunctions and adverbs, either within a sentence or between sentences. In the same way, in walking it selects and fragments the space traversed; it skips over links and whole parts that it omits. From this point of view, every walk constantly leaps, or skips like a child, hopping on one foot. It practices the ellipsis of conjunctive *loci*.

In reality, these two pedestrian figures are related. Synecdoche expands a spatial element in order to make it play the role of a "more" (a totality) and take its place (the bicycle or the piece of furniture in a store window stands for a whole street or neighborhood). Asyndeton, by elision, creates a "less," opens gaps in the spatial continuum, and retains only selected parts of it that amount almost to relics. Synecdoche replaces totalities by fragments (a *less* in the place of a *more*); asyndeton disconnects them by eliminating the conjunctive or the consecutive (nothing in place of something). Synecdoche makes more dense: it amplifies the detail and miniaturizes the whole. Asyndeton cuts out: it undoes continuity and undercuts its plausibility. A space treated in this way and shaped by practices is transformed into enlarged singularities and separate islands.[30] Through these swell-ings, shrinkings, and fragmentations, that is, through these rhetorical operations a spatial phrasing of an analogical (composed of juxtaposed citations) and elliptical (made of gaps, lapses, and allusions) type is created. For the technological system of a coherent and totalizing space that is "linked" and simultaneous, the figures of pedestrian rhetoric substitute trajectories that have a mythical structure, at least if one understands by "myth" a discourse relative to the place/nowhere (or origin) of concrete existence, a story jerry-built out of elements taken from common say-ings, an allusive and fragmentary story whose gaps mesh with the social practices it symbolizes.

Figures are the acts of this stylistic metamorphosis of space. Or rather, as Rilke puts it, they are moving "trees of gestures." They move even the rigid and contrived territories of the medico-pedagogical institute in which retarded children find a place to play and dance their "spatial stories."[31] These "trees of gestures" are in movement everywhere. Their forests walk through the streets. They transform the scene, but they cannot be fixed in a certain place by images. If in spite of that an illustration were required, we could mention the fleeting images, yellowish-green and metallic blue calligraphies that howl without raising their voices and emblazon themselves on the subterranean passages of the city, "embroideries" composed of letters and numbers, perfect gestures of violence painted with a pistol, Shivas made of written characters, dancing graphics whose fleeting apparitions are accompanied by the rumble of subway trains: New York graffiti.

If it is true that *forests of gestures* are manifest in the streets, their movement cannot be captured in a picture, nor can the meaning of their movements be circumscribed in a text. Their rhetorical transplantation carries away and displaces the analytical, coherent proper meanings of urbanism; it constitutes a "wandering of the semantic"[32] produced by masses that make some parts of the city disappear and exaggerate others, distorting it, fragmenting it, and diverting it from its immobile order.

Myths: what "makes things go"

The figures of these movements (synecdoches, ellipses, etc.) characterize both a "symbolic order of the unconscious" and "certain typical processes of subjectivity manifested in discourse."[33] The similarity between "discourse"[34] and dreams[35] has to do with their use of the same "stylistic procedures"; it therefore includes pedestrian practices as well. The "ancient catalog of tropes" that from Freud to Benveniste has furnished an appropriate inventory for the rhetoric of the first two registers of expression is equally valid for the third. If there is a parallelism, it is not only because enunciation is dominant in these three areas, but also because its discursive (verbalized, dreamed, or walked) development is organized as a relation between the *place* from which it proceeds (an origin) and the nowhere it produces (a way of "going by").

From this point of view, after having compared pedestrian processes to linguistic formations, we can bring them back down in the direction of oneiric figuration, or at least discover on that other side what, in a spatial practice, is inseparable from the dreamed place. To walk is to lack a place. It is the indefinite process of being absent and in search of a proper. The moving about that the city multiplies and concentrates makes the city itself an immense social experience of lacking a place—an experience that is, to be sure, broken up into countless tiny deportations (displacements and walks), compensated for by the relationships and intersections of these exoduses that intertwine and create an urban fabric, and placed under the sign of what ought to be, ultimately, the place but is only a name, the City. The identity furnished by this place is all the more symbolic (named) because, in spite of the inequality of its citizens' positions and profits, there is only a pullulation of passer-by, a network of residences temporarily appropriated by pedestrian traffic, a shuffling among pretenses of the proper, a universe of rented spaces haunted by a nowhere or by dreamed-of places.

Names and symbols

An indication of the relationship that spatial practices entertain with that absence is furnished precisely by their manipulations of and with "proper" names. The relationships between the direction of a walk (*le sens de la marche*) and the meaning of words (*le sens des mots*) situate two sorts of apparently contrary movements, one extrovert (to walk is to go outside), the other introvert (a mobility under the stability of the signifier). Walking is in fact determined by semantic tropisms; it is attracted and repelled by nominations whose meaning is not clear, whereas the city, for its part, is transformed for many people into a "desert" in which the meaningless, indeed the terrifying, no longer takes the form of shadows but becomes, as in Genet's plays, an implacable light that produces this urban text without obscurities, which is created by a technocratic power everywhere and which puts the city-dweller under control (under the control of what? No one knows): "The city keeps us under its gaze, which one cannot bear without feeling dizzy," says a resident of Rouen.[36] In the spaces brutally lit by an alien reason, proper names carve out pockets of hidden and familiar meanings. They "make sense"; in other words, they are the impetus of movements, like vocations and calls that turn or divert an itinerary by giving it a meaning (or a direction) (*sens*) that was previously unforeseen. These names create a nowhere in places; they change them into passages.

A friend who lives in the city of Sèvres drifts, when he is in Paris, toward the rue des Saints-*Pères* and the rue de *Sèvres*, even though he is going to see his mother in another part of town: these names articulate a sentence that his steps compose without his knowing it. Numbered streets and street numbers (112th St., or 9 rue Saint-Charles) orient the magnetic field of trajectories just as they can haunt dreams. Another friend unconsciously represses the streets which have names and by this fact, transmit her—orders or identities in the same way as summonses and classifications; she goes instead along paths that have no name or signature. But her walking is thus still controlled negatively by proper names.

What is it then that they spell out? Disposed in constellations that hierarchize and semantically order the surface of the city, operating chronological arrangements and historical justifications, these words (*Borrégo, Botzaris, Bougainville . . .*) slowly lose, like worn coins, the value engraved on them, but their ability to signify outlives its first definition. *Saints-Pères, Corentin Celton, Red Square . . .* these names make themselves available to the diverse meanings given them by passers-by; they detach themselves from the places they were supposed to define and serve as imaginary meeting-points on itineraries which, as metaphors, they determine for reasons that are foreign to their original value but may be recognized or not by passers-by. A strange toponymy that is detached from actual places and flies high over the city like a foggy geography of "meanings" held in suspension, directing the physical deambulations below: *Place de l'Étoile, Concorde, Poissonnière . . .* These constellations of names provide traffic patterns: they are stars directing itineraries. "The Place de la Concorde does not exist," Malaparte said, "it is an idea."[37] It is much more than an "idea." A whole series of comparisons would be necessary to account for the magical powers proper names enjoy. They seem to be carried as emblems by the travellers they direct and simultaneously decorate.

Linking acts and footsteps, opening meanings and directions, these words operate in the name of an emptying-out and wearing-away of their primary role. They become liberated spaces that can be occupied. A rich indetermination gives them, by means of a semantic rarefaction, the function of articulating a second, poetic geography on top of the geography of the literal, forbidden or permitted meaning. They insinuate other routes into the functionalist and historical order of movement. Walking follows them: "I fill this great empty space with a beautiful name."[38] People are put in motion by the remaining relics of meaning, and sometimes by their waste products, the inverted remainders of great ambitions.[39] Things that amount to nothing, or almost nothing, symbolize and orient walkers' steps: names that have ceased precisely to be "proper."

In these symbolizing kernels three distinct (but connected) functions of the relations between spatial and signifying practices are indicated (and perhaps founded): the *believable*, the *memorable*, and the *primitive*. They designate what "authorizes" (or makes possible or credible) spatial appropriations, what is repeated in them (or is recalled in them) from a silent and withdrawn memory, and what is structured in them and continues to be signed by an infantile (*in-fans*) origin. These three symbolic mechanisms organize the topoi of a discourse on/of

the city (legend, memory, and dream) in a way that also eludes urbanistic systema-
ticity. They can already be recognized in the functions of proper names: they make
habitable or believable the place that they clothe with a word (by emptying
themselves of their classifying power, they acquire that of "permitting" something
else); they recall or suggest phantoms (the dead who are supposed to have disappeared) that still move about, concealed in gestures and in bodies in motion; and,
by naming, that is, by imposing an injunction proceeding from the other (a story)
and by altering functionalist identity by detaching themselves from it, they create
in the place itself that erosion or nowhere that the law of the other carves out
within it.

Credible things and memorable things: habitability

By a paradox that is only apparent, the discourse that makes people believe is the
one that takes away what it urges them to believe in, or never delivers what it
promises. Far from expressing a void or describing a lack, it creates such. It makes
room for a void. In that way, it opens up clearings; it "allows" a certain play within
a system of defined places. It "authorizes" the production of an area of free play
(*Spielraum*) on a checkerboard that analyzes and classifies identities. It makes places
habitable. On these grounds, I call such discourse a "local authority." It is a crack
in the system that saturates places with signification and indeed so reduces them to
this signification that it is "impossible to breathe in them." It is a symptomatic
tendency of functionalist totalitarianism (including its programming of games and
celebrations) that it seeks precisely to eliminate these local authorities, because
they compromise the univocity of the system. Totalitarianism attacks what it quite
correctly calls *superstitions*: supererogatory semantic overlays that insert themselves
"over and above" and "in excess,"[40] and annex to a past or poetic realm a part of the
land the promoters of technical rationalities and financial profitabilities had
reserved for themselves.

   Ultimately, since proper names are already "local authorities" or "superstitions," they are replaced by numbers: on the telephone, one no longer dials *Opera*,
but 073. The same is true of the stories and legends that haunt urban space like
superfluous or additional inhabitants. They are the object of a witch-hunt, by the
very logic of the techno-structure. But their extermination (like the extermination
of trees, forests, and hidden places in which such legends live)[41] makes the city a
"suspended symbolic order."[42] The habitable city is thereby annulled. Thus, as a
woman from Rouen put it, no, here "there isn't any place special, except for my
own home, that's all . . . There isn't anything." Nothing "special": nothing that is
marked, opened up by a memory or a story, signed by something or someone else.
Only the cave of the home remains believable, still open for a certain time to
legends, still full of shadows. Except for that, according to another city-dweller,
there are only "places in which one can no longer believe in anything."[43]

   It is through the opportunity they offer to store up rich silences and wordless
stories, or rather through their capacity to create cellars and garrets everywhere,
that local legends (*legenda*: what is *to be read*, but also what *can be read*) permit exits,
ways of going out and coming back in, and thus habitable spaces. Certainly walking
about and traveling substitute for exits, for going away and coming back, which

were formerly made available by a body of legends that places nowadays lack. Physical moving about has the itinerant function of yesterday's or today's "superstitions." Travel (like walking) is a substitute for the legends that used to open up space to something different. What does travel ultimately produce if it is not, by a sort of reversal, "an exploration of the deserted places of my memory," the return to nearby exoticism by way of a detour through distant places, and the "discovery" of relics and legends: "fleeting visions of the French countryside," "fragments of music and poetry,"[44] in short, something like an "uprooting in one's origins" (Heidegger?) What this walking exile produces is precisely the body of legends that is currently lacking in one's own vicinity; it is a fiction, which moreover has the double characteristic, like dreams or pedestrian rhetoric, of being the effect of displacements and condensations.[45] As a corollary, one can measure the importance of these signifying practices (to tell oneself legends) as practices that invent spaces.

From this point of view, their contents remain revelatory, and still more so is the principle that organizes them. Stories about places are makeshift things. They are composed with the world's debris. Even if the literary form and the actantial schema of "superstitions" correspond to stable models whose structures and combinations have often been analyzed over the past thirty years, the materials (all the rhetorical details of their "manifestation") are furnished by the leftovers from nominations, taxonomies, heroic or comic predicates, etc., that is, by fragments of scattered semantic places. These heterogeneous and even contrary elements fill the homogeneous form of the story. Things *extra* and *other* (details and excesses coming from elsewhere) insert themselves into the accepted framework, the imposed order. One thus has the very relationship between spatial practices and the constructed order. The surface of this order is everywhere punched and torn open by ellipses, drifts, and leaks of meaning: it is a sieve-order.

The verbal relics of which the story is composed, being tied to lost stories and opaque acts, are juxtaposed in a collage where their relations are not thought, and for this reason they form a symbolic whole.[46] They are articulated by lacunae. Within the structured space of the text, they thus produce anti-texts, effects of dissimulation and escape, possibilities of moving into other landscapes, like cellars and bushes: "*ô massifs, ô pluriels*."[47] Because of the process of dissemination that they open up, stories differ from *rumors* in that the latter are always injunctions, initiators and results of a levelling of space, creators of common movements that reinforce an order by adding an activity of making people believe things to that of making people do things. Stories diversify, rumors totalize. If there is still a certain oscillation between them, it seems that today there is rather a stratification: stories are becoming private and sink into the secluded places in neighborhoods, families, or individuals, while the rumors propagated by the media cover everything and, gathered under the figure of the City, the masterword of an anonymous law, the substitute for all proper names, they wipe out or combat any superstitions guilty of still resisting the figure.

The dispersion of stories points to the dispersion of the memorable as well. And in fact memory is a sort of anti-museum: it is not localizable. Fragments of it come out in legends. Objects and words also have hollow places in which a past sleeps, as in the everyday acts of walking, eating, going to bed, in which ancient revolutions slumber. A memory is only a Prince Charming who stays just long enough to awaken the Sleeping Beauties of our wordless stories. "*Here*, there used to be a bakery." "*That's* where old lady Dupuis used to live." It is striking here that the places people live in are like the presences of diverse absences. What can be seen designates what is no longer there: "you *see*, here there used to be . . .," but it can no longer be seen. Demonstratives indicate the invisible identities of the visible: it is the very definition of a place, in fact, that it is composed by these series of displacements and effects among the fragmented strata that form it and that it plays on these moving layers.

"Memories tie us to that place. . . . It's personal, not interesting to anyone else, but after all that's what gives a neighborhood its character."[48] There is no place that is not haunted by many different spirits hidden there in silence, spirits one can "invoke" or not. Haunted places are the only ones people can live in—and this inverts the schema of the *Panopticon*. But like the gothic sculptures of kings and queens that once adorned Notre-Dame and have been buried for two centuries in the basement of a building in the rue de la Chaussée-d'Antin,[49] these "spirits," themselves broken into pieces in like manner, do not *speak* any more than they *see*. This is a sort of knowledge that remains silent. Only hints of what is known but unrevealed are passed on "just between you and me."

Places are fragmentary and inward-turning histories, pasts that others are not allowed to read, accumulated times that can be unfolded but like stories held in reserve, remaining in an enigmatic state, symbolizations encysted in the pain or pleasure of the body. "I feel good here"[50] the well-being under-expressed in the language it appears in like a fleeting glimmer is a spatial practice.

Childhood and metaphors of places

> Metaphor consists in giving the thing a name that belongs to something else.
>
> Aristotle, Poetics 1457b

The memorable is that which can be dreamed about a place. In this place that is a palimpsest, subjectivity is already linked to the absence that structures it as existence and makes it "be there," *Dasein*. But as we have seen, this being-there acts only in spatial practices, that is, in *ways of moving into something different* (*manières de passer à l'autre*). It must ultimately be seen as the repetition, in diverse metaphors, of a decisive and originary experience, that of the child's differentiation from the mother's body. It is through that experience that the possibility of space and of a localization (a "not everything") of the subject is inaugurated. We need not return to the famous analysis Freud made of this matrix-experience by following the game played by his eighteen-month-old grandson, who threw a reel away from himself, crying *oh-oh-oh* in pleasure, *fort*! (i.e., "over there," "gone," or "no more") and then pulled it back with the piece of string attached to it with a delighted *da*! (i.e., "here," "back again");[51] it suffices here to remember this (perilous and satisfied) process of detachment from indifferentiation in the mother's body, whose substitute is the spool: this departure of the mother (sometimes she disappears by herself, sometimes the child makes her disappear) constitutes localization and exteriority against the background of an absence. There is a joyful manipulation that can make the maternal object "go away" and make *oneself* disappear (insofar as one considers oneself identical with that object), making it possible to be *there* (because) *without* the other but in a necessary relation to what has disappeared; this manipulation is an "original spatial structure."

No doubt one could trace this differentiation further back, as far as the naming that separates the foetus identified as masculine from his mother—but how about the female foetus, who is from this very moment introduced into another relationship to space? In the initiatory game, just as in the "joyful activity" of the child who, standing before a mirror, sees itself as *one* (it is *she* or *he*, seen as a whole) but *another* (*that*, an image with which the child identifies itself),[52] what counts is the process of this "spatial captation" that inscribes the passage toward the other as the law of being and the law of place. To practice space is thus to repeat the joyful and silent experience of childhood; it is, in a place, *to be other and to move toward the other*.

Thus begins the walk that Freud compares to the trampling underfoot of the mother-land.[53] This relationship of oneself to oneself governs the internal alterations of the place (the relations among its strata) or the pedestrian unfolding of the stories accumulated in a place (moving about the city and travelling). The childhood experience that determines spatial practices later develops its effects, proliferates, floods private and public spaces, undoes their readable surfaces, and creates within the planned city a "metaphorical" or mobile city, like the one Kandinsky dreamed of: "a great city built according to all the rules of architecture and then suddenly shaken by a force that defies all calculation."[54]

Notes

1   See Alain Médam's admirable "New York City," *Les Temps modernes*, August–September 1976, 15–33; and the same author's *New York Terminal* (Paris: Galilée, 1977).

2   See H. Lavedan, *Les Représentations des villes dans l'art du Moyen Age* (Paris: Van Oest, 1942); R. Wittkower, *Architectural Principles in the Age of Humanism* (New York: Norton, 1962); L. Marin, *Utopiques: Jeux d'espaces* (Paris: Minuit, 1973); etc.

3   M. Foucault, "L'Oeil du pouvoir," in J. Bentham, *Le Panoptique* (Paris: Belfond, 1977), 16.

4   D. P. Schreber, *Mémoires d'un névropathe* (Paris: Seuil, 1975), 41, 60, etc.

5   Descartes, in his *Regulae*, had already made the blind man the guarantor of the knowledge of things and places against the illusions and deceptions of vision.

6   M. Merleau-Ponty, *Phénoménologie de la perception* (Paris: Gallimard Tel, 1976), 332–333.

7   See F. Choay, "Figures d'un discours inconnu," *Critique*, April 1973, 293–317.

8   Urbanistic techniques, which classify things spatially, can be related to the tradition of the "art of memory": see Frances A. Yates, *The Art of Memory* (London: Routledge and Kegan Paul, 1966). The ability to produce a spatial organization of knowledge (with "places" assigned to each type of "figure" or "function") develops its procedures on the basis of this "art." It determines utopias and can be recognized even in Bentham's *Panopticon*. Such a form remains stable in spite of the diversity of its contents (past, future, present) and its projects (conserving or creating) relative to changes in the status of knowledge.

9   See André Glucksmann, "Le Totalitarisme en effet," *Traverses*, No. 9, 1977, 34–40.

10 M. Foucault, *Surveiller et punir* (Paris: Gallimard, 1975); *Discipline and Punish*, trans. A. Sheridan (New York: Pantheon, 1977).

11 Ch. Alexander, "La Cité semi-treillis, mais non arbre," *Architecture, Mouvement, Continuité*, 1967.

12 See R. Barthes's remarks in *Architecture d'aujourd'hui*, No. 153, December 1970—

January 1971, 11–13: "We speak our city . . . merely by inhabiting it, walking through it, looking at it." Cf. C. Soucy, *L'Image du centre dans quatre romans contemporains* (Paris: CSU, 1971), 6–15.

13   See the numerous studies devoted to the subject since J. Searle's "What is a Speech Act?" in *Philosophy in America*, ed. Max Black (London: Allen & Unwin; Ithaca, N.Y.: Cornell University Press, 1965), 221–239.

14   E. Benveniste, *Problèmes de linguistique générale* (Paris: Gallimard, 1974), II, 79–88, etc.

15   R. Barthes, quoted in C. Soucy, *L'Image du centre*, 10.

16   "*Here* and *now* delimit the spatial and temporal instance coextensive and contemporary with the present instance of discourse containing I": E. Benveniste, *Problèmes de linguistique générale* (Paris: Gallimard, 1966), I, p. 253.

17   R. Jakobson, *Essais de linguistique générale* (Paris: Seuil Points, 1970), p. 217.

18   On modalities, see H. Parret, *La Pragmatique des modalités* (Urbino: Centro di Semiotica, 1975); A. R. White, *Modal Thinking* (Ithaca, N.Y.: Cornell University Press, 1975).

19   See Paul Lemaire's analyses, *Les Signes sauvages. Une Philosophie du langage ordinaire* (Ottawa: Université d'Ottawa et Université Saint-Paul, 1981), in particular the introduction.

20   A. J. Greimas, "Linguistique statistique et linguistique structurale," *Le Français moderne*, October 1962, 245.

21   In a neighboring field, rhetoric and poetics in the gestural language of mute people, I am grateful to E. S. Klima of the University of California, San Diego and U. Bellugi, "Poetry and Song in a Language without Sound," an unpublished paper; see also Klima, "The Linguistic Symbol with and without Sound," in *The Role of Speech in Language*, ed. J. Kavanagh and J. E. Cuttings (Cambridge, Mass.: MIT, 1975).

22   *Conscience de la ville* (Paris: Anthropos, 1977).

23   See Ostrowetsky, "Logiques du lieu," in *Sémiotique de l'espace* (Paris: Denoël-Gonthier Médiations, 1979), 155–173.

24   *Pas à pas. Essai sur le cheminement quotidien en milieu urbain* (Paris: Seuil, 1979).

25   In his analysis of culinary practices, P. Bourdieu regards as decisive not the ingredients but the way in which they are prepared and used: "Le Sens pratique," *Actes de la recherche en sciences sociales*, February 1976, 77.

26   J. Sumpf, *Introduction à la stylistique du français* (Paris: Larousse, 1971), 87.

27   On the "theory of the proper," see J. Derrida, *Marges de la philosophie* (Paris: Minuit, 1972), 247–324; *Margins of Philosophy*, trans. A. Bass (Chicago: University of Chicago Press, 1982).

28   Augoyard, *Pas à pas*.

29   T. Todorov, "Synecdoques," *Communications*, No. 16 (1970), 30. See also P. Fontanier, *Les Figures du discours* (Paris: Flammarion, 1968), 87–97; J. Dubois et al., *Rhétorique générale* (Paris: Larousse, 1970), 102–112.

30   On this space that practices organize into "islands," see P. Bourdieu, *Esquisse d'une théorie de la pratique* (Genève: Droz, 1972), 215, etc.; "Le Sens pratique," 51–52.

31   See Anne Baldassari and Michel Joubert, *Pratiques relationnelles des enfants à l'espace et institution* (Paris: CRECELE-CORDES, 1976); and by the same authors, "Ce qui se trame," *Parallèles*, No. 1, June 1976.

32   Derrida, *Marges*, 287, on metaphor.

33   Benveniste, *Problèmes*, I, 86–87.

34   For Benveniste, "discourse is language considered as assumed by the person who is speaking and in the condition of intersubjectivity" (ibid., 266).

35   See for example S. Freud, *The Interpretation of Dreams*, trans. J. Strachey (New York: Basic Books, 1955), Chapter VI, § 1–4, on condensation and displacement, "processes of figuration" that are proper to "dreamwork."

36   Ph. Dard, F. Desbons et al., *La Ville, symbolique en souffrance* (Paris: CEP, 1975), 200.

37   See also, for example, the epigraph in Patrick Modiano, *Place de l'Étoile* (Paris: Gallimard, 1968).

38   Joachim du Bellay, *Regrets*, 189.

39   For example, *Sarcelles*, the name of a great urbanistic ambition (near Paris), has taken on a symbolic value for the inhabitants of the town by becoming in the eyes of France as a whole the example of a total failure. This extreme avatar provides its citizens with the "prestige" of an exceptional identity.

40   *Superstare*: "to be above," as something in addition or superfluous.

41   See F. Lugassy, *Contribution à une psychosociologie de l'espace urbain. L'Habitat et la forêt* (Paris: Recherche urbaine, 1970).

42   Dard, Desbons et al., *La Ville, symbolique en souffrance.*

43   Ibid., 174, 206.

44   C. Lévi-Strauss, *Tristes tropiques* (Paris: Plon, 1955), 434–436; *Tristes tropiques*, trans. J. Russell (New York: Criterion, 1962).

45   One could say the same about the photos brought back from trips, substituted for and turned into legends about the starting place.

46   Terms whose relationships are not thought but postulated as necessary can be said to be symbolic. On this definition of symbolism as a cognitive mechanism characterized by a "deficit" of thinking, see Dan Sperber, *Le Symbolisme en général* (Paris: Hermann, 1974); *Rethinking Symbolism*, trans. A. L. Morton (Cambridge: Cambridge University Press, 1975).

47   F. Ponge, *La Promenade dans nos serres* (Paris: Gallimard, 1967).

48   A woman living in the Croix-Rousse quarter in Lyon (interview by Pierre Mayol): see *L'Invention du quotidien*, II, *Habiter, cuisiner* (Paris: UGE 10/18, 1980).

49   See *Le Monde* for May 4, 1977.

50   See note 48.

51   See the two analyses provided by Freud in *The Interpretation of Dreams* and *Beyond the Pleasure Principle*, trans. J. Strachey (New York: Liveright, 1980); and also Sami-Ali, *L'Espace imaginaire* (Paris: Gallimard, 1974), 42–64.

52   J. Lacan, "Le Stade du miroir," *Écrits* (Paris: Seuil, 1966), 93–100; "The Mirror Stage," in *Écrits: A Selection*, trans. A. Sheridan (New York: Norton, 1977).

53   S. Freud, *Inhibitions, Symptoms and Anxiety* (New York: Norton, 1977).

54   V. Kandinsky, *Du spirituel dans l'art* (Paris: Denoël, 1969), 57.

Suggestions for further reading

Barthes, Roland, 'The Eiffel Tower', in *The Eiffel Tower and Other Mythologies*, trans. Richard Howard, Berkeley and Los Angeles: University of California Press, 1997, pp. 3–17.

Benjamin, Walter, *Charles Baudelaire: A Lyric Poet in the Era of High Capitalism*, trans. Harry Zohn, London: Verso, 1997.

Thrift, Nigel, '*Driving* in the City', *Theory, Culture & Society*, 2004, vol. 21.4/5, 41–59.

Chapter 14

Gilles Deleuze and Félix Guattari

'WHAT IS A MINOR LITERATURE?', 1975

S O FAR WE have dealt with little more than contents and their forms: bent head – straightened head, triangles – lines of escape. And it is true that in the realm of expression, the bent head connects to the photo, and the erect head to sound. But as long as the form and the deformation or expression are not considered for themselves, there can be no real way out, even at the level of contents. Only expression gives us the *method*. The problem of expression is staked out by Kafka not in an abstract and universal fashion but in relation to those literatures that are considered minor, for example, the Jewish literature of Warsaw and Prague. A minor literature doesn't come from a minor language; it is rather that which a minority constructs within a major language. But the first characteristic of minor literature in any case is that in it language is affected with a high coefficient of deterritorialization. In this sense, Kafka marks the impasse that bars access to writing for the Jews of Prague and turns their literature into something impossible—the impossibility of not writing, the impossibility of writing in German, the impossibility of writing otherwise.[1] The impossibility of not writing because national consciousness, uncertain or oppressed, necessarily exists by means of literature ("The literary struggle has its real justification at the highest possible levels"). The impossibility of writing other than in German is for the Prague Jews the feeling of an irreducible distance from their primitive Czech territoriality. And the impossibility of writing in German is the deterritoralization of the German population itself, an oppressive minority that speaks a language cut off from the masses, like a "paper language" or an artificial language; this is all the more true for the Jews who are simultaneously a part of this minority and excluded from it, like "gypsies who have stolen a German child from its crib." In short, Prague German is a deterritorialized language, appropriate for strange and minor uses. (This can be compared in another context to what blacks in America today are able to do with the English language.)

The second characteristic of minor literatures is that everything in them is political. In major literatures, in contrast, the individual concern (familial, marital, and so on) joins with other no less individual concerns, the social milieu serving as a mere environment or a background; this is so much the case that none of these Oedipal intrigues are specifically indispensable or absolutely necessary but all become as one in a large space. Minor literature is completely different; its cramped space forces each individual intrigue to connect immediately to politics. The individual concern thus becomes all the more necessary, indispensable, magnified, because a whole other story is vibrating within it. In this way, the family triangle connects to other triangles – commercial, economic, bureaucratic, juridical – that determine its values. When Kafka indicates that one of the goals of a minor literature is the "purification of the conflict that opposes father and son and the possibility of discussing that conflict," it isn't a question of an Oedipal phantasm but of a political program. "Even though something is often thought through calmly, one still does not reach the boundary where it connects up with similar things, one reaches the boundary soonest in politics, indeed, one even strives to see it before it is there, and often sees this limiting boundary everywhere. . . . What in great literature goes on down below, constituting a not indispensable cellar of the structure, here takes place in the full light of day, what is there a matter of passing interest for a few, here absorbs everyone no less than as a matter of life and death."[2]

The third characteristic of minor literature is that in it everything takes on a collective value. Indeed, precisely because talent isn't abundant in a minor literature, there are no possibilities for an individuated enunciation that would belong to this or that "master" and that could be separated from a collective enunciation. Indeed, scarcity of talent is in fact beneficial and allows the conception of something other than a literature of masters; what each author says individually already constitutes a common action, and what he or she says or does is necessarily political, even if others aren't in agreement. The political domain has contaminated every statement (énoncé). But above all else, because collective or national consciousness is "often inactive in external life and always in the process of breakdown," literature finds itself positively charged with the role and function of collective, and even revolutionary, enunciation. It is literature that produces an active solidarity in spite of skepticism; and if the writer is in the margins or completely outside his or her fragile community, this situation allows the writer all the more the possibility to express another possible community and to forge the means for another consciousness and another sensibility; just as the dog of "Investigations" calls out in his solitude to *another science*. The literary machine thus becomes the relay for a revolutionary machine-to-come, not at all for ideological reasons but because the literary machine alone is determined to fill the conditions of a collective enunciation that is lacking elsewhere in this milieu: *literature is the people's concern.*[3] It is certainly in these terms that Kafka sees the problem. The message doesn't refer back to an enunciating subject who would be its cause, no more than to a subject of the statement (*sujet d'énoncé*) who would be its effect. Undoubtedly, for a while, Kafka thought according to these traditional categories of the two subjects, the author and the hero, the narrator and the character, the dreamer and the one dreamed of.[4] But he will quickly reject the role of the narrator, just as he will refuse an author's or master's literature, despite his admiration for Goethe. Josephine the mouse renounces the individual act of sing-ing in order to melt into the collective enunciation of "the immense crowd of the heros of [her] people." A movement from the individuated animal to the pack or to a collective multiplicity – seven canine musicians. In "The Investigations of a Dog," the expressions of the solitary researcher tend toward the assemblage (*agencement*) of a collective enunciation of the canine species even if this collectivity is no longer or not yet given. There isn't a subject; *there are only collective assemblages of enunci-ation*, and literature expresses these acts insofar as they're not imposed from without and insofar as they exist only as diabolical powers to come or revolution-ary forces to be constructed. Kafka's solitude opens him up to everything going on in history today. The letter K no longer designates a narrator or a character but an assemblage that becomes all the more machine-like, an agent that becomes all the more collective because an individual is locked into it in his or her solitude (it is only in connection to a subject that something individual would be separable from the collective and would lead its own life).

The three characteristics of minor literature are the deterritorialization of language, the connection of the individual to a political immediacy, and the col-lective assemblage of enunciation. We might as well say that minor no longer designates specific literatures but the revolutionary conditions for every literature within the heart of what is called great (or established) literature. Even he who has the misfortune of being born in the country of a great literature must write in its language, just as a Czech Jew writes in German, or an Ouzbekian writes in Russian. Writing like a dog digging a hole, a rat digging its burrow. And to do that, finding his own point of underdevelopment, his own *patois*, his own third world, his own desert. There has been much discussion of the questions "What is a marginal literature?" and "What is a popular literature, a proletarian literature?" The criteria are obviously difficult to establish if one doesn't start with a more objective concept – that of minor literature. Only the possibility of setting up a minor practice of major language from within allows one to define popular litera-ture, marginal literature, and so on.[5] Only in this way can literature really become a collective machine of expression and really be able to treat and develop its contents. Kafka emphatically declares that a minor literature is much more able to work over its material.[6] Why this machine of expression, and what is it? We know that it is in a relation of multiple deterritorializations with language; it is the situation of the Jews who have dropped the Czech language at the same time as the rural environment, but it is also the situation of the German language as a "paper language." Well, one can go even farther; one can push this movement of deter-ritorialization of expression even farther. But there are only two ways to do this. One way is to artificially enrich this German, to swell it up through all the resources of symbolism, of oneirism, of esoteric sense, of a hidden signifier. This is the approach of the Prague school, Gustav Meyrink and many others, including Max Brod.[7] But this attempt implies a desperate attempt at symbolic reter-ritorialization, based in archetypes, Kabbala, and alchemy, that accentuates its break from the people and will find its political result only in Zionism and such things as the "dream of Zion." Kafka will quickly choose the other way, or, rather, he will invent another way. He will opt for the German language of Prague as it is and in its very poverty. Go always farther in the direction of deterritorialization, to the point of sobriety. Since the language is arid, make it vibrate with a new intensity. Oppose a purely intensive usage of language to all symbolic or even significant or simply signifying usages of it. Arrive at a perfect and unformed expression, a materially intense expression. (For these two possible paths, couldn't we find the same alternatives, under other conditions, in Joyce and Beckett? As Irishmen, both of them live within the genial conditions of a minor literature. That is the glory of this sort of minor literature – to be the revolutionary force for all literature. The utilization of English and of every language in Joyce. The utilization of English and French in Beckett. But the former never stops operating by exhilaration and overdetermination and brings about all sorts of worldwide reterritorializations. The other proceeds by dryness and sobriety, a willed poverty, pushing deterritorialization to such an extreme that nothing remains but intensities.)

How many people today live in a language that is not their own? Or no longer, or not yet, even know their own and know poorly the major language that they are forced to serve? This is the problem of immigrants, and especially of their children, the problem of minorities, the problem of a minor literature, but also a problem for all of us: how to tear a minor literature away from its own language, allowing it to challenge the language and making it follow a sober revolutionary path? How to become a nomad and an immigrant and a gypsy in relation to one's own language? Kafka answers: steal the baby from its crib, walk the tightrope.

Rich or poor, each language always implies a deterritorialization of the mouth, the tongue, and the teeth. The mouth, tongue, and teeth find their primitive territoriality in food. In giving themselves over to the articulation of sounds, the mouth, tongue, and teeth deterritorialize. Thus, there is a certain disjunction between eating and speaking, and even more, despite all appearances, between eating and writing. Undoubtedly, one can write while eating more easily than one can speak while eating, but writing goes further in transforming words into things capable of competing with food. Disjunction between content and expression. To speak, and above all to write, is to fast. Kafka manifests a permanent obsession with food, and with that form of food *par excellence*, in other words, the animal or meat – an obsession with the mouth and with teeth and with large, unhealthy, or gold-capped teeth.[8] This is one of Kafka's main problems with Felice. Fasting is also a constant theme in Kafka's writings. His writings are a long history of fasts. The Hunger Artist, surveyed by butchers, ends his career next to beasts who eat their meat raw, placing the visitors before an irritating alternative. The dogs try to take over the mouth of the investigating hound by filling it with food so that he'll stop asking questions, and there too there is an irritating alternative: "[T]hey would have done better to drive me away and refuse to listen to my questions. No, they did not want to do that; they did not indeed want to listen to my questions, but it was because I asked these questions that they did not want to drive me away." The investigating hound oscillates between two sciences, that of food – a science of the Earth and of the bent head ("Whence does the Earth procure this food?") – and that of music which is a science of the air and of the straightened head, as the seven musical dogs of the beginning and the singing dog of the end well demonstrate. But between the two there is something in common, since food can come from high up and the science of food can only develop through fasting, just as the music is strangely silent.

Ordinarily, in fact, language compensates for its deterritorialization by a reterritorialization in sense. Ceasing to be the organ of one of the senses, it becomes an instrument of Sense. And it is sense, as a correct sense, that presides over the designation of sounds (the thing or the state of things that the word designates) and, as figurative sense, over the affectation of images and metaphors (those other things that words designate under certain situations or conditions). Thus, there is not only a spiritual reterritorialization of sense, but also a physical one. Similarly, language exists only through the distinction and the complementarity of a subject of enunciation, who is in connection with sense, and a subject of the statement, who is in connection, directly or metaphorically, with the designated thing. This sort of ordinary use of language can be called extensive or representative – the reterritorializing function of language (thus, the singing dog at the end of the "Investigations" forces the hero to abandon his fast, a sort of re-Oedipalization).

Now something happens: the situation of the German language in Czechoslovakia, as a fluid language intermixed with Czech and Yiddish, will allow Kafka the possibility of invention. Since things are as they are ("it is as it is, it is as it is," a formula dear to Kafka, marker of a state of facts), he will abandon sense, render it no more than implicit; he will retain only the skeleton of sense, or a paper cutout.

Since articulated sound was a deterritorialized noise but one that will be reterritorialized in sense, it is now sound itself that will be deterritorialized irrevocably, absolutely. The sound or the word that traverses this new deterritorialization no longer belongs to a language of sense, even though it derives from it, nor is it an organized music or song, even though it might appear to be. We noted Gregor's warbling and the ways it blurred words, the whistling of the mouse, the cough of the ape, the pianist who doesn't play, the singer who doesn't sing and gives birth to her song out of her nonsinging, the musical dogs who are musicians in the very depths of their bodies since they don't emit any music. Everywhere, organized music is traversed by a line of abolition—just as a language of sense is traversed by a line of escape—in order to liberate a living and expressive material that speaks for itself and has no need of being put into a form.[9] This language torn from sense, conquering sense, bringing about an active neutralization of sense, no longer finds its value in anything but an accenting of the word, an inflection: "I live only here or there in a small word in whose vowel. . . . I lose my useless head for a moment. The first and last letters are the beginning and end of my fishlike emotion."[10] Children are well skilled in the exercise of repeating a word, the sense of which is only vaguely felt, in order to make it vibrate around itself (at the beginning of The Castle, the schoolchildren are speaking so fast that one cannot understand what they are saying). Kafka tells how, as a child, he repeated one of his father's expressions in order to make it take flight on a line of non-sense: "end of the month, end of the month"[11] The proper name, which has no sense in itself, is particularly propitious for this sort of exercise. Milena, with an accent on the i, begins by evoking "a Greek or a Roman gone astray in Bohemia, violated by Czech, cheated of its accent," and then, by a more delicate approximation, it evokes "a woman whom one carries in one's arms out of the world, out of the fire," the accent marking here an always possible fall or, on the contrary, "the lucky leap which you yourself make with your burden."[12]

It seems to us that there is a certain difference, even if relative and highly nuanced, between the two evocations of the name Milena: one still attaches itself to an extensive, figurative scene of the fantasmatic sort; the second is already much more intensive, marking a fall or a leap as a threshold of intensity contained within the name itself. In fact, we have here what happens when sense is actively neutralized. As Wagenbach says, "The word is master; it directly gives birth to the image." But how can we define this procedure? Of sense there remains only enough to direct the lines of escape. There is no longer a designation of something by means of a proper name, nor an assignation of metaphors by means of a figurative sense. But *like* images, the thing no longer forms anything but a sequence of intensive states, a ladder or a circuit for intensities that one can make race around in one sense or another, from high to low, or from low to high. The image is this very race itself; it has become becoming – the becoming-dog of the man and the becoming-man of the dog, the becoming-ape or the becoming-beetle of the man and vice versa. We are no longer in the situation of an ordinary, rich language where the word dog, for example, would directly designate an animal and would apply metaphorically to other things (so that one could say "like a dog").[13] *Diaries*, 1921: "Metaphors are one of the things that makes me despair of literature." Kafka deliberately kills all metaphor, all symbolism, all signification, no less than all designation. Metamorphosis is the contrary of metaphor. There is no longer any proper sense or figurative sense, but only a distribution of states that is part of the range of the word. The thing and other things are no longer anything but intensities overrun by deterritorialized sound or words that are following their line of escape. It is no longer a question of a resemblance between the comportment of an animal and that of a man; it is even less a question of a simple wordplay. There is no longer man or animal, since each deterritorializes the other, in a conjunction of flux, in a continuum of reversible intensities. Instead, it is now a question of a becoming that includes the maximum of difference as a difference of intensity, the crossing of a barrier, a rising or a falling, a bending or an erecting, an accent on the word. The animal does not speak "like" a man but pulls from the language tonalities lacking in signification; the words themselves are not "like" the animals but in their own way climb about, bark and roam around, being properly linguistic dogs, insects, or mice.[14] To make the sequences vibrate, to open the word onto unexpected internal intensities – in short, an asignifying *intensive utilization* of language. Furthermore, there is no longer a subject of the enunciation, nor a subject of the statement. It is no longer the subject of the statement who is a dog, with the subject of the enunciation remaining "like" a man; it is no longer the subject of enunciation who is "like" a beetle, the subject of the statement remaining a man. Rather, there is a circuit of states that forms a mutual becoming, in the heart of a necessarily multiple or collective assemblage.

How does the situation of the German language in Prague – a withered vocabulary, an incorrect syntax – contribute to such a utilization? Generally, we might call the linguistic elements, however varied they may be, that express the "internal tensions of a language" *intensives* or *tensors*. It is in this sense that the linguist Vidal Sephiha terms intensive "any linguistic tool that allows a move toward the limit of a notion or a surpassing of it," marking a movement of language toward its extremes, toward a reversible beyond or before.[15] Sephiha well shows the variety of such elements which can be all sorts of master-words, verbs, or prepositions that assume all sorts of senses; prenominal or purely intensive verbs as in Hebrew; conjunctions, exclamations, adverbs; and *terms that connote pain*.[16] One could equally cite the accents that are interior to words, their discordant function. And it would seem that the language of a minor literature particularly develops these tensors or these intensives. In the lovely pages where he analyzes the Prague German that was influenced by Czech, Wagenbach cites as the characteristics of this form of German the incorrect use of prepositions; the abuse of the pronominal; the employment of malleable verbs (such as *Giben*, which is used for the series "put, sit, place, take away" and which thereby becomes intensive); the multiplication and succession of adverbs; the use of pain-filled connotations; the importance of the accent as a tension internal to the word; and the distribution of consonants and vowels as part of an internal discordance. Wagenbach insists on this point: all these marks of the poverty of a language show up in Kafka but have been taken over by a creative utilization for the purposes of a new sobriety, a new expressivity, a new flexibility, a new intensity.[17] "Almost every word I write jars up against the next, I hear the consonants rub leadenly against each other and the vowels sing an accompaniment like Negroes in a minstrel show."[18] *Language stops being representative in order to now move toward its extremities or its limits.* The connotation of pain accompanies this metamorphosis, as in the words that become a painful warbling with Gregor, or in Franz's cry "single and irrevocable." Think about the utilization of French as a spoken language in the films of Godard. There too is an accumulation of stereotypical adverbs and conjunctions that form the base of all the phrases – a strange poverty that makes French a minor language within French; a creative process that directly links the word to the image; a technique that surges up at the end of sequences in connection with the intensity of the limit "that's enough, enough, he's had enough," and a generalized intensification, coinciding with a panning shot where the camera pivots and sweeps around without leaving the spot, making the image vibrate.

Perhaps the comparative study of images would be less interesting than the study of the functions of language that can work in the same group across different languages – bilingualism or even multilingualism. Because the study of the functions in distinct languages alone can account for social factors, relations of force, diverse centers of power, it escapes from the "informational" myth in order to evaluate the hierarchic and imperative system of language as a transmission of orders, an exercise of power or of resistance to this exercise. Using the research of Ferguson and Gumperz, Henri Gobard has proposed a tetralinguistic model: vernacular, maternal, or territorial language, used in rural communities or rural in its origins; a vehicular, urban, governmental, even worldwide language, a language of businesses, commercial exchange, bureaucratic transmission, and so on, a language of the first sort of deterritorialization; referential language, language of sense and of culture, entailing a cultural reterritorialization; mythic language, on the horizon of cultures, caught up in a spiritual or religious reterritorialization. The spatiotemporal categories of these languages differ sharply: vernacular language is *here*; vehicular language is *everywhere*; referential language is *over there*; mythic language is *beyond*. But above all else, the distribution of these languages varies from one group to the next and, in a single group, from one epoch to the next (for a long time in Europe, Latin was a vehicular language before becoming referential, then mythic; English has become the worldwide vehicular language for today's world).[19] What can be said in one language cannot be said in another, and the totality of what can and can't be said varies necessarily with each language and with the connections between these languages.[20] Moreover, all these factors can have ambiguous edges, changing borders, that differ for this or that material. One language can fill a certain function for one material and another function for another material. Each function of a language divides up in turn and carries with it multiple centers of power. A blur of languages, and not at all a system of languages. We can understand the indignation of integrationists who cry when Mass is said in French, since Latin is being robbed of its mythic function. But the classicists are even more behind the times and cry because Latin has even been robbed of its referential cultural function. They express regret in this way for the religious or educational forms of powers that this language exercised and that have now been replaced by other forms. There are even more serious examples that cross over between groups. The revival of regionalisms, with a reterritorialization through dialect or patois, a vernacular language – how does that serve a worldwide or transnational technocracy? How can that contribute to revolutionary movements, since they are also filled with archaisms that they are trying to impart a contemporary sense to? From Servan-Schreiber to the Breton bard to the Canadian singer. And that's not really how the borders divide up, since the Canadian singer can also bring about the most reactionary, the most Oedipal of reterritorializations, oh mama, oh my native land, my cabin, olé, olé. We would call this a blur, a mixed-up history, a political situation, but linguists don't know about this, don't want to know about this, since, as linguists, they are "apolitical," pure scientists. Even Chomsky compensated for his scientific apoliticism only by his courageous struggle against the war in Vietnam.

Let's return to the situation in the Hapsburg empire. The breakdown and fall of the empire increases the crisis, accentuates everywhere movements of deterritorialization, and invites all sorts of complex reterritorializations – archaic, mythic, or symbolist. At random, we can cite the following among Kafka's contemporaries: Einstein and his deterritorialization of the representation of the universe (Einstein teaches in Prague, and the physicist Philipp Frank gives conferences there with Kafka in attendance); the Austrian dodecaphonists and their deterritorialization of musical representation (the cry that is Marie's death in *Wozzeck*, or Lulu's, or the echoed *si* that seems to us to follow a musical path similar in certain ways to what Kafka is doing); the expressionist cinema and its double movement of deterritorialization and reterritorialization of the image (Robert Wiene, who has Czech background; Fritz Lang, born in Vienna; Paul Wegener and his utilization of Prague themes). Of course, we should mention Viennese psychoanalysis and Prague school linguistics.[21] What is the specific situation of the Prague Jews in relation to the "four languages?" The vernacular language for these Jews who have come from a rural milieu is Czech, but the Czech language tends to be forgotten and repressed; as for Yiddish, it is often disdained or viewed with suspicion – it *frightens*, as Kafka tells us. German is the vehicular language of the towns, a bureaucratic language of the state, a commercial language of exchange (but English has already started to become indispensable for this purpose). The German language – but this time, Goethe's German – has a cultural and referential function (as does French to a lesser degree). As a mythic language, Hebrew is connected with the start of Zionism and still possesses the quality of an active dream. For each of these languages, we need to evaluate the degrees of territoriality, deterritorialization, and reterritorialization. Kafka's own situation: he is one of the few Jewish writers in Prague to understand and speak Czech (and this language will have a great importance in his relationship with Milena). German plays precisely the double role of vehicular and cultural language, with Goethe always on the horizon (Kafka also knows French, Italian, and probably a bit of English). He will not learn Hebrew until later. What is complicated is Kafka's relation to Yiddish; he sees it less as a sort of linguistic territoriality for the Jews than as a nomadic movement of deterritorialization that reworks German language. What fascinates him in Yiddish is less a language of a religious community than that of a popular theater (he will become patron and impresario for the travelling theater of Isak Lowy).[22] The manner in which Kafka, in a public meeting, presented Yiddish to a rather hostile Jewish bourgeois audience is completely remarkable: Yiddish is a language that frightens more than it invites disdain, "dread mingled with a certain fundamental distaste"; it is a language that is lacking a grammar and that is filled with vocables that are fleeting, mobilized, emigrating, and turned into nomads that interiorize "relations of force." It is a language that is grafted onto Middle-High German and that so reworks the German language from within that one cannot translate it into German without destroying it; one can understand Yiddish only by feeling it in the heart. In short, it is a language where minor utilizations will carry you away: "Then you will come to feel the true unity of Yiddish and so strongly that it will frighten you, yet it will no longer be fear of Yiddish but of yourselves. Enjoy this self-confidence as much as you can!"[23]

Kafka does not opt for a reterritorialization through the Czech language. Nor toward a hypercultural usage of German with all sorts of oneiric or symbolic or mythic flights (even Hebrew-ifying ones), as was the case with the Prague school. Nor toward an oral, popular Yiddish. Instead, using the path that Yiddish opens up to him, he takes it in such a way as to convert it into a unique and solitary form of writing. Since Prague German is deterritorialized to several degrees, he will always take it farther, to a greater degree of intensity, but in the direction of a new sobriety, a new and unexpected modification, a pitiless rectification, a straightening of the head. Schizo politeness, a drunkenness caused by water.[24] He will make the German language take flight on a line of escape. He will feed himself on abstinence; he will tear out of Prague German all the qualities of underdevelopment that it has tried to hide; he will make it cry with an extremely sober and rigorous cry. He will pull from it the barking of the dog, the cough of the ape, and the bustling of the beetle. He will turn syntax into a cry that will embrace the rigid syntax of this dried-up German. He will push it toward a deterritorialization that will no longer be saved by culture or by myth, that will be an absolute deterritorialization, even if it is slow, sticky, coagulated. To bring language slowly and progressively to the desert. To use syntax in order to cry, to give a syntax to the cry.

There is nothing that is major or revolutionary except the minor. To hate all languages of masters. Kafka's fascination for servants and employees (the same thing in Proust in relation to servants, to their language). What interests him even more is the possibility of making of his own language – assuming that it is unique, that it is a major language or has been – a minor utilization. To be a sort of stranger *within* his own language; this is the situation of Kafka's Great Swimmer.[25] Even when it is unique, a language remains a mixture, a schizophrenic mélange, a Harlequin costume in which very different functions of language and distinct centers of power are played out, blurring what can be said and what can't be said; one function will be played off against the other, all the degrees of territoriality and relative deterritorialization will be played out. Even when major, a language is open to an intensive utilization that makes it take flight along creative lines of escape which, no matter how slowly, no matter how cautiously, can now form an absolute deterritorialization. All this inventiveness, not only lexically, since the lexical matters little, but sober syntactical invention, simply to write like a dog (but a dog can't write – exactly, exactly). It's what Artaud did with French – cries, gasps; what Céline did with French, following another line, one that was exclamatory to the highest degree. Céline's syntactic evolution went from *Voyage* to *Death on the Credit Plan*, then from *Death on the Credit Plan* to *Guignol's Band*. (After that, Céline had nothing more to talk about except his own misfortunes; in other words, he had no longer any desire to write, only the need to make money. And it always ends like that, language's lines of escape: silence, the interrupted, the interminable, or even worse. But until that point, what a crazy creation, what a writing machine! Céline was so applauded for *Voyage* that he went even further in *Death on the Credit Plan* and then in the prodigious *Guignol's Band* where language is nothing more than intensities. He spoke with a kind of "minor music." Kafka, too, is a minor music, a different one, but always made up of deterritorialized sounds, a language that moves head over heels and away.) These are the true minor authors. An escape for language, for music, for writing. What we call pop – pop music, pop philosophy, pop writing – Worterflucht. To make use of the polylingualism of one's own language, to make a minor or intensive use of it, to oppose the oppressed quality of this language to its oppressive quality, to find points of nonculture or under-development, linguistic Third World zones by which a language can escape, an animal enters into things, an assemblage comes into play. How many styles or genres or literary movements, even very small ones, have only one single dream: to assume a major function in language, to offer themselves as a sort of state language, an official language (for example, psychoanalysis today, which would like to be a master of the signifier, of metaphor, of wordplay). Create the opposite dream: know how to create a becoming-minor. (Is there a hope for philosophy, which for a long time has been an official, referential genre? Let us profit from this moment in which antiphilosophy is trying to be a language of power.)

Notes

1   See letter to Brod, Kafka, *Letters*, June 1921, 289, and commentaries in Wagenbach, *Franz Kafka*, 84.

2   Kafka, *Diaries*, 25 December 1911, 194.

3   Ibid., 193: "[L]iterature is less a concern of literary history, than of the people."

4   See "Wedding Preparations in the Country", in Kafka, *Complete Stories*: "And so long as you say 'one' instead of 'I,' there's nothing in it" (p. 53). And the two subjects appear several pages later: "I don't even need to go to the country myself, it isn't necessary. I'll send my clothed body," while the narrator stays in bed like a bug or a beetle (p. 55). No doubt, this is one of the origins of Gregor's becoming-beetle in "The Metamorphosis" (in the same way, Kafka will give up going to meet Felice and will prefer to stay in bed). But in "The Metamorphosis," the animal takes on all the value of a true becoming and no longer has any of the stagnancy of a subject of enunciation.

5   See Michel Ragon, *Historie de la littérature prolétarienne en France* (Paris: Albin Michel, 1974) on the difficulty of criteria and on the need to use a concept of a "secondary zone literature."

6   Kafka, *Diaries*, 25 December 1911, 193: "A small nation's memory is not smaller than the memory of a large one and so can digest the existing material more thoroughly."

7   See the excellent chapter "Prague at the turn of the century," in Wagenbach, *Franz Kafka*, on the situation of the German language in Czechoslovakia and on the Prague school.

8   Constancy of the theme of teeth in Kafka. A grandfather-butcher; a streetwise education at the butcher-shop; Felice's jaws; the refusal to eat meat except when he sleeps with Felice in Marienbad. See: Michel Cournot's article, "Toi qui as de si grandes dents," *Nouvel Observateur*, April 17, 1972. This is one of the most beautiful texts on Kafka. One can find a similar opposition between eating and speaking in Lewis Carroll, and a comparable escape into non-sense.

9   Franz Kafka, *The Trial*, trans. Willa and Edwin Muir (New York: Schocken Books, 1956): "[H]e noticed that they were talking to him, but he could not make out what they were saying, he heard nothing but the din that filled the whole place, through which a shrill unchanging note like that of a siren seemed to sing."

10   Kafka, *Diaries* 20 August 1911, 61–62.

11   Kafka, *Diaries*: "Without gaining a sense, the phrase 'end of the month' held a terrible secret for me" especially since it was repeated every month – Kafka himself suggests that if this expression remained shorn of sense, this was due to laziness and "weakened curiosity." A negative explication invoking lack or powerlessness, as taken by Wagenbach. It is well-known that Kafka makes this sort of negative suggestion to present or to hide the objects of his passion.

12   Kafka, *Letters to Milena*, 58. Kafka's fascination with proper names, beginning with those that he invented: see Kafka, *Diaries*, 11 February 1913 (à propos of the names in *The Verdict*).

13   Kafka commentators are at their worst in their interpretations in this respect when they regulate everything through metaphors: thus, Marthe Robert reminds us that the Jews are *like* dogs or, to take another example, that "since the artist is treated as someone starving to death Kafka makes him into a hunger artist; or since he is treated as a parasite, Kafka makes him into an enormous insect" (*Oeuvres complètes*, Cercle du livre precieux, 5:311). It seems to us that this is a simplistic conception of the literary machine – Robbe-Grillet has insisted on the destruction of all metaphors in Kafka.

14   See, for example, the letter to Pollak in Kafka, *Letters*, 4 February 1902, 1–2.

15   See H. Vidal Sephiha, "Introduction à l'étude de l'intensif," in *Langages* 18 (June 1970): 104–20. We take the term *tensor* from J.-F. Lyotard who uses it to indicate the connection of intensity and libido.

16   Sephiha, "Introduction," 107 ("We can imagine that any phrase conveying a negative notion of pain, evil, fear, violence can cast off the notion in order to retain no more than its limit-value – that is, its intensive value": for example, the German word *sehr*, which comes from the Middle High German word, *Ser* meaning "painful").

17   Wagenbach, *Franz Kafka*, 78–88 (especially 78, 81, 88).

18   Kafka, *Diaries*, 15 December 1910, 33.

19   Henri Gobard, "De la vehicularité de la langue anglaise," *Langues modernes* (January 1972) (and *L'Alienation linguistique: analyse tetraglossique*, [Paris: Flammarion, 1976]).

20   Michel Foucault insists on the importance of the distribution between what can be said in a language at a certain moment and what cannot be said (even if it can be *done*). Georges Devereux (cited by H. Gobard) analyzes the case of the young Mohave Indians who speak about sexuality with great ease in their vernacular language but who are incapable of doing so in that vehicular language that English constitutes for them; and this is so not only because the English instructor exercises a repressive function, but also because there is a problem of languages (see *Essais d'ethnopsychiatrie générale* [Paris: Gallimard, 1970], 125–26).

21   On the Prague Circle and its role in linguistics, see *Change*, No. 3 (1969) and 10 (1972). (It is true that the Prague circle was only formed in 1925. But in 1920, Jakobson came to Prague where there was already a Czech movement directed by Mathesius and connected with Anton Marty who had taught in the German university system. From 1902 to 1905, Kafka followed the courses given by Marty, a disciple of Brentano, and participated in Brentanoist meetings.)

22   On Kafka's connections to Lowy and Yiddish theater, see Brod, *Franz Kafka*, 110–16; and Wagenbach, *Franz Kafka*, 163–67. In this mime theater, there must have been many bent heads and straightened heads.

23   "An Introductory Talk on the Yiddish Language," trans. Ernst Kaiser and Eithne Wilkins in Franz Kafka, *Dearest Father* (New York: Schocken Books, 1954), 381–86.

24   A magazine editor will declare that Kafka's prose has "the air of the cleanliness of a child who takes care of himself" (see Wagenbach, *Franz Kafka*, 82).

25   "The Great Swimmer" is undoubtedly one of the most Beckett-like of Kafka's texts: "I have to well admit that I am in my own country and that, in spite of all my efforts, I don't understand a word of the language that you are speaking."

Suggestions for further reading

Bogue, Ronald, *Deleuze on Literature*, London and New York: Routledge, 2003.

Deleuze, Gilles, and Guattari, Félix, 'He Stuttered', in *Essays Critical and Clinical*, trans. Daniel A. Smith and Michael W. Greco, London and New York: Verso, 1998, pp. 107–14.

Lecercle, Jean-Jacques, *Deleuze and Language*, Basingstoke and New York: Palgrave, 2002.

Chapter 15

Michel Foucault

'PANOPTICISM', 1975

T HE FOLLOWING, ACCORDING to an order published at the end of the seventeenth century, were the measures to be taken when the plague appeared in a town.[1]

First, a strict spatial partitioning: the closing of the town and its outlying districts, a prohibition to leave the town on pain of death, the killing of all stray animals; the division of the town into distinct quarters, each governed by an intendant. Each street is placed under the authority of a syndic, who keeps it under surveillance; if he leaves the street, he will be condemned to death. On the appointed day, everyone is ordered to stay indoors: it is forbidden to leave on pain of death. The syndic himself comes to lock the door of each house from the outside; he takes the key with him and hands it over to the intendant of the quarter; the intendant keeps it until the end of the quarantine. Each family will have made its own provisions; but, for bread and wine, small wooden canals are set up between the street and the interior of the houses, thus allowing each person to receive his ration without communicating with the suppliers and other residents; meat, fish and herbs will be hoisted up into the houses with pulleys and baskets. If it is absolutely necessary to leave the house, it will be done in turn, avoiding any meeting. Only the intendants, syndics and guards will move about the streets and also, between the infected houses, from one corpse to another, the 'crows', who can be left to die: these are 'people of little substance who carry the sick, bury the dead, clean and do many vile and abject offices'. It is a segmented, immobile, frozen space. Each individual is fixed in his place. And, if he moves, he does so at the risk of his life, contagion or punishment.

Inspection functions ceaselessly. The gaze is alert everywhere: 'A considerable body of militia, commanded by good officers and men of substance', guards at the gates, at the town hall and in every quarter to ensure the prompt obedience of the people and the most absolute authority of the magistrates, 'as also to observe all disorder, theft and extortion'. At each of the town gates there will be an observation post; at the end of each street sentinels. Every day, the intendant visits the quarter in his charge, inquires whether the syndics have carried out their tasks, whether the inhabitants have anything to complain of; they 'observe their actions'. Every day, too, the syndic goes into the street for which he is responsible; stops before each house: gets all the inhabitants to appear at the windows (those who live overlooking the courtyard will be allocated a window looking onto the street at which no one but they may show themselves); he calls each of them by name; informs himself as to the state of each and every one of them – 'in which respect the inhabitants will be compelled to speak the truth under pain of death'; if someone does not appear at the window, the syndic must ask why: 'In this way he will find out easily enough whether dead or sick are being concealed.' Everyone locked up in his cage, everyone at his window, answering to his name and showing himself when asked – it is the great review of the living and the dead.

This surveillance is based on a system of permanent registration: reports from the syndics to the intendants, from the intendants to the magistrates or mayor. At the beginning of the 'lock up', the role of each of the inhabitants present in the town is laid down, one by one; this document bears 'the name, age, sex of everyone, notwithstanding his condition': a copy is sent to the intendant of the quarter, another to the office of the town hall, another to enable the syndic to make his daily roll call. Everything that may be observed during the course of the visits – deaths, illnesses, complaints, irregularities – is noted down and transmitted to the intendants and magistrates. The magistrates have complete control over medical treatment; they have appointed a physician in charge; no other practitioner may treat, no apothecary prepare medicine, no confessor visit a sick person without having received from him a written note 'to prevent anyone from concealing and dealing with those sick of the contagion, unknown to the magistrates'. The registration of the pathological must be constantly centralized. The relation of each individual to his disease and to his death passes through the representatives of power, the registration they make of it, the decisions they take on it.

Five or six days after the beginning of the quarantine, the process of purifying the houses one by one is begun. All the inhabitants are made to leave; in each room 'the furniture and goods' are raised from the ground or suspended from the air; perfume is poured around the room; after carefully sealing the windows, doors and even the keyholes with wax, the perfume is set alight. Finally, the entire house is closed while the perfume is consumed; those who have carried out the work are searched, as they were on entry, 'in the presence of the residents of the house, to see that they did not have something on their persons as they left that they did not have on entering'. Four hours later, the residents are allowed to re-enter their homes.

This enclosed, segmented space, observed at every point, in which the individuals are inserted in a fixed place, in which the slightest movements are supervised, in which all events are recorded, in which an uninterrupted work of writing links the centre and periphery, in which power is exercised without division, according to a continuous hierarchical figure, in which each individual is constantly located, examined and distributed among the living beings, the sick and the dead

– all this constitutes a compact model of the disciplinary mechanism. The plague is met by order; its function is to sort out every possible confusion: that of the disease, which is transmitted when bodies are mixed together; that of the evil, which is increased when fear and death overcome prohibitions. It lays down for each individual his place, his body, his disease and his death, his well-being, by means of an omnipresent and omniscient power that subdivides itself in a regular, uninterrupted way even to the ultimate determination of the individual, of what characterizes him, of what belongs to him, of what happens to him. Against the plague, which is a mixture, discipline brings into play its power, which is one of analysis. A whole literary fiction of the festival grew up around the plague: suspended laws, lifted prohibitions, the frenzy of passing time, bodies mingling together without respect, individuals unmasked, abandoning their statutory identity and the figure under which they had been recognized, allowing a quite different truth to appear. But there was also a political dream of the plague, which was exactly its reverse: not the collective festival, but strict divisions; not laws transgressed, but the penetration of regulation into even the smallest details of everyday life through the mediation of the complete hierarchy that assured the capillary functioning of power; not masks that were put on and taken off, but the assignment to each individual of his 'true' name, his 'true' place, his 'true' body, his 'true' disease. The plague as a form, at once real and imaginary, of disorder had as its medical and political correlative discipline. Behind the disciplinary mechanisms can be read the haunting memory of 'contagions', of the plague, of rebellions, crimes, vagabondage, desertions, people who appear and disappear, live and die in disorder.

If it is true that the leper gave rise to rituals of exclusion, which to a certain extent provided the model for and general form of the great Confinement, then the plague gave rise to disciplinary projects. Rather than the massive, binary division between one set of people and another, it called for multiple separations, individualizing distributions, an organization in depth of surveillance and control, an intensification and a ramification of power. The leper was caught up in a practice of rejection, of exile-enclosure; he was left to his doom in a mass among which it was useless to differentiate; those sick of the plague were caught up in a meticulous tactical partitioning in which individual differentiations were the constricting effects of a power that multiplied, articulated and subdivided itself; the great confinement on the one hand; the correct training on the other. The leper and his separation; the plague and its segmentations. The first is marked; the second analysed and distributed. The exile of the leper and the arrest of the plague do not bring with them the same political dream. The first is that of a pure community, the second that of a disciplined society. Two ways of exercising power over men, of controlling their relations, of separating out their dangerous mixtures. The plague-stricken town, traversed throughout with hierarchy, surveillance, observation, writing; the town immobilized by the functioning of an extensive power that bears in a distinct way over all individual bodies – this is the utopia of the perfectly governed city. The plague (envisaged as a possibility at least) is the trial in the course of which one may define ideally the exercise of disciplinary power. In order to make rights and laws function according to pure theory, the jurists place themselves in imagination in the state of nature; in order to see perfect disciplines functioning, rulers dreamt of the state of plague. Underlying disciplinary projects the image of the plague stands for all forms of confusion and disorder; just as the image of the leper, cut off from all human contact, underlies projects of exclusion.

They are different projects, then, but not incompatible ones. We see them coming slowly together, and it is the peculiarity of the nineteenth century that it applied to the space of exclusion of which the leper was the symbolic inhabitant (beggars, vagabonds, madmen and the disorderly formed the real population) the technique of power proper to disciplinary partitioning. Treat 'lepers' as 'plague victims', project the subtle segmentations of discipline onto the confused space of internment, combine it with the methods of analytical distribution proper to power, individualize the excluded, but use procedures of individualization to mark exclusion – this is what was operated regularly by disciplinary power from the beginning of the nineteenth century in the psychiatric asylum, the penitentiary, the reformatory, the approved school and, to some extent, the hospital. Generally speaking, all the authorities exercising individual control function according to a double mode; that of binary division and branding (mad/sane; dangerous/harmless; normal/abnormal); and that of coercive assignment, of differential distribution (who he is; where he must be; how he is to be characterized; how he is to be recognized; how a constant surveillance is to be exercised over him in an individual way, etc.). On the one hand, the lepers are treated as plague victims; the tactics of individualizing disciplines are imposed on the excluded; and, on the other hand, the universality of disciplinary controls makes it possible to brand the 'leper' and to bring into play against him the dualistic mechanisms of exclusion. The constant division between the normal and the abnormal, to which every individual is subjected, brings us back to our own time, by applying the binary branding and exile of the leper to quite different objects; the existence of a whole set of techniques and institutions for measuring, supervising and correcting the abnormal brings into play the disciplinary mechanisms to which the fear of the plague gave rise. All the mechanisms of power which, even today, are disposed around the abnormal individual, to brand him and to alter him, are composed of those two forms from which they distantly derive.

Bentham's *Panopticon* is the architectural figure of this composition. We know the principle on which it was based: at the periphery, an annular building; at the centre, a tower; this tower is pierced with wide windows that open onto the inner side of the ring; the peripheric building is divided into cells, each of which extends the whole width of the building; they have two windows, one on the inside, corresponding to the windows of the tower; the other, on the outside, allows the light to cross the cell from one end to the other. All that is needed, then, is to place a supervisor in a central tower and to shut up in each cell a madman, a patient, a condemned man, a worker or a schoolboy. By the effect of backlighting, one can observe from the tower, standing out precisely against the light, the small captive shadows in the cells of the periphery. They are like so many cages, so many small theatres, in which each actor is alone, perfectly individualized and constantly visible. The panoptic mechanism arranges spatial unities that make it possible to see constantly and to recognize immediately. In short, it reverses the principle of the dungeon; or rather of its three functions – to enclose, to deprive of light and to hide – it preserves only the first and eliminates the other two. Full lighting and the eye of a supervisor capture better than darkness, which ultimately protected. Visibility is a trap.

To begin with, this made it possible – as a negative effect – to avoid those compact, swarming, howling masses that were to be found in places of confinement, those painted by Goya or described by Howard. Each individual, in his place, is securely confined to a cell from which he is seen from the front by the supervisor; but the side walls prevent him from coming into contact with his companions. He is seen, but he does not see; he is the object of information, never a subject in communication. The arrangement of his room, opposite the central tower, imposes on him an axial visibility; but the divisions of the ring, those separated cells, imply a lateral invisibility. And this invisibility is a guarantee of order. If the inmates are convicts, there is no danger of a plot, an attempt at collective escape, the planning of new crimes for the future, bad reciprocal influences; if they are patients, there is no danger of contagion; if they are madmen there is no risk of their committing violence upon one another; if they are school-children, there is no copying, no noise, no chatter, no waste of time; if they are workers, there are no disorders, no theft, no coalitions, none of those distractions that slow down the rate of work, make it less perfect or cause accidents. The crowd, a compact mass, a locus of multiple exchanges, individualities merging together, a collective effect, is abolished and replaced by a collection of separated individualities. From the point of view of the guardian, it is replaced by a multiplicity that can be numbered and supervised; from the point of view of the inmates, by a sequestered and observed solitude (Bentham, 60–64).

Hence the major effect of the Panopticon: to induce in the inmate a state of conscious and permanent visibility that assures the automatic functioning of power. So to arrange things that the surveillance is permanent in its effects, even if it is discontinuous in its action; that the perfection of power should tend to render its actual exercise unnecessary; that this architectural apparatus should be a machine for creating and sustaining a power relation independent of the person who exercises it; in short, that the inmates should be caught up in a power situation of which they are themselves the bearers. To achieve this, it is at once too much and too little that the prisoner should be constantly observed by an inspector: too little, for what matters is that he knows himself to be observed; too much, because he has no need in fact of being so. In view of this, Bentham laid down the principle that power should be visible and unverifiable. Visible: the inmate will constantly have before his eyes the tall outline of the central tower from which he is spied upon. Unverifiable: the inmate must never know whether he is being looked at at any one moment; but he must be sure that he may always be so. In order to make the presence or absence of the inspector unverifiable, so that the prisoners, in their cells, cannot even see a shadow, Bentham envisaged not only venetian blinds on the windows of the central observation hall, but, on the inside, partitions that intersected the hall at right angles and, in order to pass from one quarter to the other, not doors but zig-zag openings; for the slightest noise, a gleam of light, a brightness in a half-opened door would betray the presence of the guardian.[2] The Panopticon is a machine for dissociating the see/being seen dyad:

in the peripheric ring, one is totally seen, without ever seeing; in the central tower, one sees everything without ever being seen.[3]

It is an important mechanism, for it automatizes and disindividualizes power. Power has its principle not so much in a person as in a certain concerted distribution of bodies, surfaces, lights, gazes; in an arrangement whose internal mechanisms produce the relation in which individuals are caught up. The ceremonies, the rituals, the marks by which the sovereign's surplus power was manifested are useless. There is a machinery that assures dissymmetry, disequilibrium, difference. Consequently, it does not matter who exercises power. Any individual, taken almost at random, can operate the machine: in the absence of the director, his family, his friends, his visitors, even his servants (Bentham, 45). Similarly, it does not matter what motive animates him: the curiosity of the indiscreet, the malice of a child, the thirst for knowledge of a philosopher who wishes to visit this museum of human nature, or the perversity of those who take pleasure in spying and punishing. The more numerous those anonymous and temporary observers are, the greater the risk for the inmate of being surprised and the greater his anxious awareness of being observed. The Panopticon is a marvellous machine which, whatever use one may wish to put it to, produces homogeneous effects of power.

A real subjection is born mechanically from a fictitious relation. So it is not necessary to use force to constrain the convict to good behaviour, the madman to calm, the worker to work, the schoolboy to application, the patient to the observation of the regulations. Bentham was surprised that panoptic institutions could be so light: there were no more bars, no more chains, no more heavy locks; all that was needed was that the separations should be clear and the openings well arranged. The heaviness of the old 'houses of security', with their fortress-like architecture, could be replaced by the simple, economic geometry of a 'house of certainty'. The efficiency of power, its constraining force have, in a sense, passed over to the other side – to the side of its surface of application. He who is subjected to a field of visibility, and who knows it, assumes responsibility for the constraints of power; he makes them play spontaneously upon himself; he inscribes in himself the power relation in which he simultaneously plays both roles; he becomes the principle of his own subjection. By this very fact, the external power may throw off its physical weight; it tends to the non-corporal; and, the more it approaches this limit, the more constant, profound and permanent are its effects: it is a perpetual victory that avoids any physical confrontation and which is always decided in advance.

Bentham does not say whether he was inspired, in his project, by Le Vaux's menagerie at Versailles: the first menagerie in which the different elements are not, as they traditionally were, distributed in a park (Loisel, 104–7). At the centre was an octagonal pavilion which, on the first floor, consisted of only a single room, the king's *salon*; on every side large windows looked out onto seven cages (the eighth side was reserved for the entrance), containing different species of animals. By Bentham's time, this menagerie had disappeared. But one finds in the programme of the Panopticon a similar concern with individualizing observation, with characterization and classification, with the analytical arrangement of space. The Panopticon is a royal menagerie; the animal is replaced by man, individual distribution by specific grouping and the king by the machinery of a furtive power.

With this exception, the Panopticon also does the work of a naturalist. It makes it possible to draw up differences: among patients, to observe the symptoms of each individual, without the proximity of beds, the circulation of miasmas, the effects of contagion confusing the clinical tables; among school-children, it makes it possible to observe performances (without there being any imitation or copying), to map aptitudes, to assess characters, to draw up rigorous classifications and, in relation to normal development, to distinguish 'laziness and stubbornness' from 'incurable imbecility'; among workers, it makes it possible to note the aptitudes of each worker, compare the time he takes to perform a task, and if they are paid by the day, to calculate their wages (Bentham, 60–64).

So much for the question of observation. But the Panopticon was also a laboratory; it could be used as a machine to carry out experiments, to alter behaviour, to train or correct individuals. To experiment with medicines and monitor their effects. To try out different punishments on prisoners, according to their crimes and character, and to seek the most effective ones. To teach different techniques simultaneously to the workers, to decide which is the best. To try out pedagogical experiments – and in particular to take up once again the well-debated problem of secluded education, by using orphans. One would see what would happen when, in their sixteenth or eighteenth year, they were presented with other boys or girls; one could verify whether, as Helvetius thought, anyone could learn anything; one would follow 'the genealogy of every observable idea'; one could bring up different children according to different systems of thought, making certain children believe that two and two do not make four or that the moon is a cheese, then put them together when they are twenty or twenty-five years old; one would then have discussions that would be worth a great deal more than the sermons or lectures on which so much money is spent; one would have at least an opportunity of making discoveries in the domain of metaphysics. The Panopticon is a privileged place for experiments on men, and for analysing with complete certainty the transformations that may be obtained from them. The Panopticon may even provide an apparatus for supervising its own mechanisms. In this central tower, the director may spy on all the employees that he has under his orders: nurses, doctors, foremen, teachers, warders; he will be able to judge them continuously, alter their behaviour, impose upon them the methods he thinks best; and it will even be possible to observe the director himself. An inspector arriving unexpectedly at the centre of the Panopticon will be able to judge at a glance, without anything being concealed from him, how the entire establishment is functioning. And, in any case, enclosed as he is in the middle of this architectural mechanism, is not the director's own fate entirely bound up with it? The incompetent physician who has allowed contagion to spread, the incompetent prison governor or workshop manager will be the first victims of an epidemic or a revolt. ' "By every tie I could devise", said the master of the Panopticon, "my own fate had been bound up by me with theirs" ' (Bentham, 177). The Panopticon functions as a kind of laboratory of power. Thanks to its mechanisms of observation, it gains in efficiency and in the ability to penetrate into men's behaviour; knowledge follows the advances of power, discovering new objects of knowledge over all the surfaces on which power is exercised.

The plague-stricken town, the panoptic establishment – the differences are important. They mark, at a distance of a century and a half, the transformations of the disciplinary programme. In the first case, there is an exceptional situation: against an extraordinary evil, power is mobilized; it makes itself everywhere present and visible; it invents new mechanisms; it separates, it immobilizes, it partitions; it constructs for a time what is both a counter-city and the perfect society; it imposes an ideal functioning, but one that is reduced, in the final analysis, like the evil that it combats, to a simple dualism of life and death: that which moves brings death, and one kills that which moves. The Panopticon, on the other hand, must be understood as a generalizable model of functioning; a way of defining power relations in terms of the everyday life of men. No doubt Bentham presents it as a particular institution, closed in upon itself. Utopias, perfectly closed in upon themselves, are common enough. As opposed to the ruined prisons, littered with mechanisms of torture, to be seen in Piranesi's engravings, the Panopticon presents a cruel, ingenious cage. The fact that it should have given rise, even in our own time, to so many variations, projected or realized, is evidence of the imaginary intensity that it has possessed for almost two hundred years. But the Panopticon must not be understood as a dream building: it is the diagram of a mechanism of power reduced to its ideal form; its functioning, abstracted from any obstacle, resistance or friction, must be represented as a pure architectural and optical system: it is in fact a figure of political technology that may and must be detached from any specific use.

It is polyvalent in its applications; it serves to reform prisoners, but also to treat patients, to instruct schoolchildren, to confine the insane, to supervise workers, to put beggars and idlers to work. It is a type of location of bodies in space, of distribution of individuals in relation to one another, of hierarchical organization, of disposition of centres and channels of power, of definition of the instruments and modes of intervention of power, which can be implemented in hospitals, workshops, schools, prisons. Whenever one is dealing with a multiplicity of individuals on whom a task or a particular form of behaviour must be imposed, the panoptic schema may be used. It is – necessary modifications apart – applicable 'to all establishments whatsoever, in which, within a space not too large to be covered or commanded by buildings, a number of persons are meant to be kept under inspection' (Bentham, 40; although Bentham takes the penitentiary house as his prime example, it is because it has many different functions to fulfil – safe custody, confinement, solitude, forced labour and instruction).

In each of its applications, it makes it possible to perfect the exercise of power. It does this in several ways: because it can reduce the number of those who exercise it, while increasing the number of those on whom it is exercised. Because it is possible to intervene at any moment and because the constant pressure acts even before the offences, mistakes or crimes have been committed. Because, in these conditions, its strength is that it never intervenes, it is exercised spontaneously and without noise, it constitutes a mechanism whose effects follow from one another. Because, without any physical instrument other than architecture and geometry, it acts directly on individuals; it gives 'power of mind over mind'. The panoptic schema makes any apparatus of power more intense: it assures its economy (in material, in personnel, in time); it assures its efficacity by its preventative character, its continuous functioning and its automatic mechanisms. It is a way of obtaining from power 'in hitherto unexampled quantity', 'a great and new instrument of government . . .; its great excellence consists in the great strength it is capable of giving to *any* institution it may he thought proper to apply it to' (Bentham, 66).

It's a case of 'it's easy once you've thought of it' in the political sphere. It can in fact be integrated into any function (education, medical treatment, production, punishment); it can increase the effect of this function, by being linked closely with it; it can constitute a mixed mechanism in which relations of power (and of knowledge) may be precisely adjusted, in the smallest detail, to the processes that are to be supervised; it can establish a direct proportion between 'surplus power' and 'surplus production'. In short, it arranges things in such a way that the exercise of power is not added on from the outside, like a rigid, heavy constraint, to the functions it invests, but is so subtly present in them as to increase their efficiency by itself increasing its own points of contact. The panoptic mechanism is not simply a hinge, a point of exchange between a mechanism of power and a function; it is a way of making power relations function in a function, and of making a function function through these power relations. Bentham's Preface to *Panopticon* opens with a list of the benefits to be obtained from his 'inspection-house': '*Morals reformed – health preserved – industry invigorated – instruction diffused – public burthens lightened –* Economy seated, as it were, upon a rock – the gordian knot of the Poor-Laws not cut, but untied – all by a simple idea in architecture!' (Bentham, 39).

Furthermore, the arrangement of this machine is such that its enclosed nature does not preclude a permanent presence from the outside: we have seen that anyone may come and exercise in the central tower the functions of surveillance, and that, this being the case, he can gain a clear idea of the way in which the surveillance is practised. In fact, any panoptic institution, even if it is as rigorously closed as a penitentiary, may without difficulty be subjected to such irregular and constant inspections: and not only by the appointed inspectors, but also by the public; any member of society will have the right to come and see with his own eyes how the schools, hospitals, factories, prisons function. There is no risk, therefore, that the increase of power created by the panoptic machine may degenerate into tyranny; the disciplinary mechanism will be democratically controlled, since it will be constantly accessible 'to the great tribunal committee of the world'.[4] This Panopticon, subtly arranged so that an observer may observe, at a glance, so many different individuals, also enables everyone to come and observe any of the observers. The seeing machine was once a sort of dark room into which individuals spied; it has become a transparent building in which the exercise of power may be supervised by society as a whole.

The panoptic schema, without disappearing as such or losing any of its properties, was destined to spread throughout the social body; its vocation was to become a generalized function. The plague-stricken town provided an exceptional disciplinary model: perfect, but absolutely violent; to the disease that brought death, power opposed its perpetual threat of death; life inside it was reduced to its simplest expression; it was, against the power of death, the meticulous exercise of the right of the sword. The Panopticon, on the other hand, has a role of amplification; although it arranges power, although it is intended to make it more economic and more effective, it does so not for power itself, nor for the immediate salvation of a threatened society: its aim is to strengthen the social forces – to increase production, to develop the economy, spread education, raise the level of public morality; to increase and multiply.

How is power to be strengthened in such a way that, far from impeding progress, far from weighing upon it with its rules and regulations, it actually facilitates such progress? What intensificator of power will be able at the same time to be a multiplicator of production? How will power, by increasing its forces, be able to increase those of society instead of confiscating them or impeding them? The Panopticon's solution to this problem is that the productive increase of power can be assured only if, on the one hand, it can be exercised continuously in the very foundations of society, in the subtlest possible way, and if, on the other hand, it functions outside these sudden, violent, discontinuous forms that are bound up with the exercise of sovereignty. The body of the king, with its strange material and physical presence, with the force that he himself deploys or transmits to some few others, is at the opposite extreme of this new physics of power represented by panopticism; the domain of panopticism is, on the contrary, that whole lower region, that region of irregular bodies, with their details, their multiple movements, their heterogeneous forces, their spatial relations; what are required are mechanisms that analyse distributions, gaps, series, combinations, and which use instruments that render visible, record, differentiate and compare: a physics of a relational and multiple power, which has its maximum intensity not in the person of the king, but in the bodies that can be individualized by these relations. At the theoretical level, Bentham defines another way of analysing the social body and the power relations that traverse it; in terms of practice, he defines a procedure of subordination of bodies and forces that must increase the utility of power while dispensing with the need for the prince. Panopticism is the general principle of a new 'political anatomy' whose object and end are not the relations of sovereignty but the relations of discipline.

The celebrated, transparent, circular cage, with its high tower, powerful and knowing, may have been for Bentham a project of a perfect disciplinary institution; but he also set out to show how one may 'unlock' the disciplines and get them to function in a diffused, multiple, polyvalent way throughout the whole social body. These disciplines, which the classical age had elaborated in specific, relatively enclosed places – barracks, schools, workshops – and whose total implementation had been imagined only at the limited and temporary scale of a plague-stricken town, Bentham dreamt of transforming into a network of mechanisms that would be everywhere and always alert, running through society without interruption in space or in time. The panoptic arrangement provides the formula for this generalization. It programmes, at the level of an elementary and easily transferable mechanism, the basic functioning of a society penetrated through and through with disciplinary mechanisms.

There are two images, then, of discipline. At one extreme, the discipline-blockade, the enclosed institution, established on the edges of society, turned inwards towards negative functions: arresting evil, breaking communications, suspending time. At the other extreme, with panopticism, is the discipline-mechanism: a functional mechanism that must improve the exercise of power by making it lighter, more rapid, more effective, a design of subtle coercion for a society to come. The movement from one project to the other, from a schema of exceptional discipline to one of a generalized surveillance, rests on a historical transformation: the gradual extension of the mechanisms of discipline throughout the seventeenth and eighteenth centuries, their spread throughout the whole social body, the formation of what might be called in general the disciplinary society.

A whole disciplinary generalization – the Benthamite physics of power represents an acknowledgement of this – had operated throughout the classical age. The spread of disciplinary institutions, whose network was beginning to cover an ever larger surface and occupying above all a less and less marginal position, testifies to this: what was an islet, a privileged place, a circumstantial measure, or a singular model, became a general formula; the regulations characteristic of the Protestant and pious armies of William of Orange or of Gustavus Adolphus were transformed into regulations for all the armies of Europe; the model colleges of the Jesuits, or the schools of Batencour or Demia, following the example set by Sturm, provided the outlines for the general forms of educational discipline; the ordering of the naval and military hospitals provided the model for the entire reorganization of hospitals in the eighteenth century.

But this extension of the disciplinary institutions was no doubt only the most visible aspect of various, more profound processes.

1. *The functional inversion of the disciplines*. At first, they were expected to neutralize dangers, to fix useless or disturbed populations, to avoid the inconveniences of over-large assemblies; now they were being asked to play a positive role, for they were becoming able to do so, to increase the possible utility of individuals. Military discipline is no longer a mere means of preventing looting, desertion or failure to obey orders among the troops; it has become a basic technique to enable the army to exist, not as an assembled crowd, but as a unity that derives from this very unity an increase in its forces; discipline increases the skill of each individual, coordinates these skills, accelerates movements, increases fire power, broadens the fronts of attack without reducing their vigour, increases the capacity for resistance, etc. The discipline of the workshop, while remaining a way of enforcing respect for the regulations and authorities, of preventing thefts or losses, tends to increase aptitudes, speeds, output and therefore profits; it still exerts a moral influence over behaviour, but more and more it treats actions in terms of their results, introduces bodies into a machinery, forces into an economy. When, in the seventeenth century, the provincial schools or the Christian elementary schools were founded, the justifications given for them were above all negative: those poor who were unable to bring up their children left them 'in ignorance of their obligations: given the difficulties they have in earning a living, and themselves having been badly brought up, they are unable to communicate a sound upbringing that they themselves never had'; this involves three major inconveniences: ignorance of God, idleness (with its consequent drunkenness, impurity, larceny, brigandage); and the formation of those gangs of beggars, always ready to stir up public disorder and 'virtually to exhaust the funds of the Hôtel-Dieu' (Demia, 60–61). Now, at the beginning of the Revolution, the end laid down for primary education was to be, among other things, to 'fortify', to 'develop the body', to prepare the child 'for

a future in some mechanical work', to give him 'an observant eye, a sure hand and prompt habits' (Talleyrand's Report to the Constituent Assembly, 10 September 1791, quoted by Léon, 106). The disciplines function increasingly as techniques for making useful individuals. Hence their emergence from a marginal position on the confines of society, and detachment from the forms of exclusion or expiation, confinement or retreat. Hence the slow loosening of their kinship with religious regularities and enclosures. Hence also their rooting in the most important, most central and most productive sectors of society. They become attached to some of the great essential functions: factory production, the transmission of knowledge, the diffusion of aptitudes and skills, the war-machine. Hence, too, the double tendency one sees developing throughout the eighteenth century to increase the number of disciplinary institutions and to discipline the existing apparatuses.

   2. *The swarming of disciplinary mechanisms.* While, on the one hand, the discip-linary establishments increase, their mechanisms have a certain tendency to become 'de-institutionalized', to emerge from the closed fortresses in which they once functioned and to circulate in a 'free' state; the massive, compact disciplines are broken down into flexible methods of control, which may be transferred and adapted. Sometimes the closed apparatuses add to their internal and specific func-tion a role of external surveillance, developing around themselves a whole margin of lateral controls. Thus the Christian School must not simply train docile children; it must also make it possible to supervise the parents, to gain information as to their way of life, their resources, their piety, their morals. The school tends to constitute minute social observatories that penetrate even to the adults and exercise regular supervision over them: the bad behaviour of the child, or his absence, is a legiti-mate pretext, according to Demia, for one to go and question the neighbours, especially if there is any reason to believe that the family will not tell the truth; one can then go and question the parents themselves, to find out whether they know their catechism and the prayers, whether they are determined to root out the vices of their children, how many beds there are in the house and what the sleeping arrangements are; the visit may end with the giving of alms, the present of a religious picture, or the provision of additional beds (Demia, 39–40). Similarly, the hospital is increasingly conceived of as a base for the medical observation of the population outside; after the burning down of the Hôtel-Dieu in 1772, there were several demands that the large buildings, so heavy and so disordered, should be replaced by a series of smaller hospitals; their function would be to take in the sick of the quarter, but also to gather information, to be alert to any endemic or epidemic phenomena, to open dispensaries, to give advice to the inhabitants and to keep the authorities informed of the sanitary state of the region.[5]

   One also sees the spread of disciplinary procedures, not in the form of enclosed institutions, but as centres of observation disseminated throughout soci-ety. Religious groups and charity organizations had long played this role of 'discip-lining' the population. From the Counter-Reformation to the philanthropy of the July monarchy, initiatives of this type continued to increase; their aims were religious (conversion and moralization), economic (aid and encouragement to work) or political (the struggle against discontent or agitation). One has only to cite by way of example the regulations for the charity associations in the Paris parishes. The territory to be covered was divided into quarters and cantons and the members of the associations divided themselves up along the same lines. These members had to visit their respective areas regularly. 'They will strive to eradicate places of ill-repute, tobacco shops, life-classes, gaming house, public scandals, blasphemy, impiety, and any other disorders that may come to their knowledge.' They will also have to make individual visits to the poor; and the information to be obtained is laid down in regulations: the stability of the lodging, knowledge of prayers, attendance at the sacraments, knowledge of a trade, morality (and 'whether they have not fallen into poverty through their own fault'); lastly, 'one must learn by skilful questioning in what way they behave at home. Whether there is peace between them and their neighbours, whether they are careful to bring up their children in the fear of God . . . whether they do not have their older children of different sexes sleeping together and with them, whether they do not allow licentiousness and cajolery in their families, especially in their older daughters. If one has any doubts as to whether they are married, one must ask to see their marriage certificate'.[6]

3. *The state-control of the mechanisms of discipline*. In England, it was private religious groups that carried out, for a long time, the functions of social discipline (cf. Radzinovitz, 203–14); in France, although a part of this role remained in the hands of parish guilds or charity associations, another – and no doubt the most important part – was very soon taken over by the police apparatus.

The organization of a centralized police had long been regarded, even by contemporaries, as the most direct expression of royal absolutism; the sovereign had wished to have 'his own magistrate to whom he might directly entrust his orders, his commissions, intentions, and who was entrusted with the execution of orders and orders under the King's private seal' (a note by Duval, first secretary at the police magistrature, quoted in Funck-Brentano, 1). In effect, in taking over a number of pre-existing functions – the search for criminals, urban surveillance, economic and political supervision – the police magistratures and the magistrature-general that presided over them in Paris transposed them into a single, strict, administrative machine: 'All the radiations of force and information that spread from the circumference culminate in the magistrate-general. . . . It is he who operates all the wheels that together produce order and harmony. The effects of his administration cannot be better compared than to the movement of the celestial bodies' (Des Essarts, 344 and 528).

But, although the police as an institution were certainly organized in the form of a state apparatus, and although this was certainly linked directly to the centre of political sovereignty, the type of power that it exercises, the mechanisms it oper-ates and the elements to which it applies them are specific. It is an apparatus that must be coextensive with the entire social body and not only by the extreme limits that it embraces, but by the minuteness of the details it is concerned with. Police power must bear 'over everything': it is not however the totality of the state nor of the kingdom as visible and invisible body of the monarch; it is the dust of events, actions, behaviour, opinions – 'everything that happens';[7] the police are concerned with 'those things of every moment', those 'unimportant things', of which Catherine II spoke in her Great Instruction (Supplement to the *Instruction for the drawing up of a new code*, 1769, article 535). With the police, one is in the indefinite world of a supervision that seeks ideally to reach the most elementary particle, the most passing phenomenon of the social body: 'The ministry of the magistrates and police officers is of the greatest importance; the objects that it embraces are in a sense definite, one may perceive them only by a sufficiently detailed examination' (Delamare, unnumbered Preface): the infinitely small of political power.

And, in order to be exercised, this power had to be given the instrument of permanent, exhaustive, omnipresent surveillance, capable of making all visible, as long as it could itself remain invisible. It had to be like a faceless gaze that transformed the whole social body into a field of perception: thousands of eyes posted everywhere, mobile attentions ever on the alert, a long, hierarchized network which, according to Le Maire, comprised for Paris the forty-eight *commissaires*, the twenty *inspecteurs*, then the 'observers', who were paid regularly, the '*basses mouches*', or secret agents, who were paid by the day, then the informers, paid according to the job done, and finally the prostitutes. And this unceasing observation had to be accumulated in a series of reports and registers; throughout the eighteenth century, an immense police text increasingly covered society by means of a complex documentary organization (on the police registers in the eighteenth century, cf. Chassaigne). And, unlike the methods of judicial or administrative writing, what was registered in this way were forms of behaviour, attitudes, possibilities, suspicions – a permanent account of individuals' behaviour.

Now, it should be noted that, although this police supervision was entirely 'in the hands of the king', it did not function in a single direction. It was in fact a double-entry system: it had to correspond, by manipulating the machinery of justice, to the immediate wishes of the king, but it was also capable of responding to solicitations from below; the celebrated *lettres de cachet*, or orders under the king's private seal, which were long the symbol of arbitrary royal rule and which brought detention into disrepute on political grounds, were in fact demanded by families, masters, local notables, neighbours, parish priests; and their function was to punish by confinement a whole infra-penality, that of disorder, agitation, disobedience, bad conduct; those things that Ledoux wanted to exclude from his architecturally perfect city and which he called 'offences of non-surveillance'. In short, the eighteenth-century police added a disciplinary function to its role as the auxiliary of justice in the pursuit of criminals and as an instrument for the political supervision of plots, opposition movements or revolts. It was a complex function since it linked the absolute power of the monarch to the lowest levels of power disseminated in society; since, between these different, enclosed institutions of discipline (workshops, armies, schools), it extended an intermediary network, acting where they could not intervene, disciplining the non-disciplinary spaces; but it filled in the gaps, linked them together, guaranteed with its armed force an interstitial discipline and a meta-discipline. 'By means of a wise police, the sovereign accustoms the people to order and obedience' (Vattel, 162).

The organization of the police apparatus in the eighteenth century sanctioned a generalization of the disciplines that became co-extensive with the state itself. Although it was linked in the most explicit way with everything in the royal power that exceeded the exercise of regular justice, it is understandable why the police offered such slight resistance to the rearrangement of the judicial power; and why it has not ceased to impose its prerogatives upon it, with ever-increasing weight, right up to the present day; this is no doubt because it is the secular arm of the judiciary; but it is also because, to a far greater degree than the judicial institution, it is identified, by reason of its extent and mechanisms, with a society of the disciplinary type. Yet it would be wrong to believe that the disciplinary functions were confiscated and absorbed once and for all by a state apparatus.

'Discipline' may be identified neither with an institution nor with an apparatus; it is a type of power, a modality for its exercise, comprising a whole set of instruments, techniques, procedures, levels of application, targets; it is a 'physics' or an 'anatomy' of power, a technology. And it may be taken over either by 'specialized' institutions (the penitentiaries or 'houses of correction' of the nineteenth century), or by institutions that use it as an essential instrument for a particular end (schools, hospitals), or by pre-existing authorities that find in it a means of reinforcing or reorganizing their internal mechanisms of power (one day we should show how intra-familial relations, essentially in the parents–children cell, have become 'disciplined', absorbing since the classical age external schemata, first educational and military, then medical, psychiatric, psychological, which have made the family the privileged locus of emergence for the disciplinary question of the normal and the abnormal); or by apparatuses that have made discipline their principle of internal functioning (the disciplinarization of the administrative apparatus from the Napoleonic period), or finally by state apparatuses whose major, if not exclusive, function is to assure that discipline reigns over society as a whole (the police).

On the whole, therefore, one can speak of the formation of a disciplinary society in this movement that stretches from the enclosed disciplines, a sort of social 'quarantine', to an indefinitely generalizable mechanism of 'panopticism'. Not because the disciplinary modality of power has replaced all the others; but because it has infiltrated the others, sometimes undermining them, but serving as an intermediary between them, linking them together, extending them and above all making it possible to bring the effects of power to the most minute and distant elements. It assures an infinitesimal distribution of the power relations.

A few years after Bentham, Julius gave this society its birth certificate (Julius, 384–6). Speaking of the panoptic principle, he said that there was much more there than architectural ingenuity: it was an event in the 'history of the human mind'. In appearance, it is merely the solution of a technical problem; but, through it, a whole type of society emerges. Antiquity had been a civilization of spectacle. 'To render accessible to a multitude of men the inspection of a small number of objects': this was the problem to which the architecture of temples, theatres and circuses responded. With spectacle, there was a predominance of public life, the intensity of festivals, sensual proximity. In these rituals in which blood flowed, society found new vigour and formed for a moment a single great body. The modern age poses the opposite problem: 'To procure for a small number, or even for a single individual, the instantaneous view of a great multitude.' In a society in which the principal elements are no longer the community and public life, but, on the one hand, private individuals and, on the other, the state, relations can be regulated only in a form that is the exact reverse of the spectacle: 'It was to the modern age, to the ever-growing influence of the state, to its ever more profound intervention in all the details and all the relations of social life, that was reserved the task of increasing and perfecting its guarantees, by using and directing towards that great aim the building and distribution of buildings intended to observe a great multitude of men at the same time.'

Julius saw as a fulfilled historical process that which Bentham had described as a technical programme. Our society is one not of spectacle, but of surveillance; under the surface of images, one invests bodies in depth; behind the great abstraction of exchange, there continues the meticulous, concrete training of useful forces; the circuits of communication are the supports of an accumulation and a centralization of knowledge; the play of signs defines the anchorages of power; it is not that the beautiful totality of the individual is amputated, repressed, altered by our social order, it is rather that the individual is carefully fabricated in it, according to a whole technique of forces and bodies. We are much less Greeks than we believe. We are neither in the amphitheatre, nor on the stage, but in the panoptic machine, invested by its effects of power, which we bring to ourselves since we are part of its mechanism. The importance, in historical mythology, of the Napoleonic character probably derives from the fact that it is at the point of junction of the monarchical, ritual exercise of sovereignty and the hierarchical, permanent exercise of indefinite discipline. He is the individual who looms over everything with a single gaze which no detail, however minute, can escape: 'You may consider that no part of the Empire is without surveillance, no crime, no offence, no contravention that remains unpunished, and that the eye of the genius who can enlighten all embraces the whole of this vast machine, without, however, the slightest detail escaping his attention' (Treilhard, 14). At the moment of its full blossoming, the disciplinary society still assumes with the Emperor the old aspect of the power of spectacle. As a monarch who is at one and the same time a usurper of the ancient throne and the organizer of the new state, he combined into a single symbolic, ultimate figure the whole of the long process by which the pomp of sovereignty, the necessarily spectacular manifestations of power, were extinguished one by one in the daily exercise of surveillance, in a panopticism in which the vigilance of intersecting gazes was soon to render useless both the eagle and the sun.

The formation of the disciplinary society is connected with a number of broad historical processes – economic, juridico-political and, lastly, scientific – of which it forms part.

1. Generally speaking, it might be said that the disciplines are techniques for assuring the ordering of human multiplicities. It is true that there is nothing exceptional or even characteristic in this: every system of power is presented with the same problem. But the peculiarity of the disciplines is that they try to define in relation to the multiplicities a tactics of power that fulfils three criteria: firstly, to obtain the exercise of power at the lowest possible cost (economically, by the low expenditure it involves; politically, by its discretion, its low exteriorization, its relative invisibility, the little resistance it arouses); secondly, to bring the effects of this social power to their maximum intensity and to extend them as far as possible, without either failure or interval; thirdly, to link this 'economic' growth of power with the output of the apparatuses (educational, military, industrial or medical) within which it is exercised; in short, to increase both the docility and the utility of all the elements of the system. This triple objective of the disciplines corresponds to a well-known historical conjuncture. One aspect of this conjuncture was the large demographic thrust of the eighteenth century; an increase in the floating

population (one of the primary objects of discipline is to fix; it is an anti-nomadic technique); a change of quantitative scale in the groups to be supervised or manipulated (from the beginning of the seventeenth century to the eve of the French Revolution, the school population had been increasing rapidly, as had no doubt the hospital population; by the end of the eighteenth century, the peace-time army exceeded 200,000 men). The other aspect of the conjuncture was the growth in the apparatus of production, which was becoming more and more extended and complex; it was also becoming more costly and its profitability had to be increased. The development of the disciplinary methods corresponded to these two processes, or rather, no doubt, to the new need to adjust their correl-ation. Neither the residual forms of feudal power nor the structures of the administrative monarchy, nor the local mechanisms of supervision, nor the unstable, tangled mass they all formed together could carry out this role: they were hindered from doing so by the irregular and inadequate extension of their network, by their often conflicting functioning, but above all by the 'costly' nature of the power that was exercised in them. It was costly in several senses: because directly it cost a great deal to the Treasury; because the system of corrupt offices and farmed-out taxes weighed indirectly, but very heavily, on the population; because the resistance it encountered forced it into a cycle of perpetual reinforce-ment; because it proceeded essentially by levying (levying on money or products by royal, seigniorial, ecclesiastical taxation; levying on men or time by *corvées* of press-ganging, by locking up or banishing vagabonds). The development of the disciplines marks the appearance of elementary techniques belonging to a quite different economy: mechanisms of power which, instead of proceeding by deduc-tion, are integrated into the productive efficiency of the apparatuses from within, into the growth of this efficiency and into the use of what it produces. For the old principle of 'levying-violence', which governed the economy of power, the discip-lines substitute the principle of 'mildness-production-profit'. These are the tech-niques that make it possible to adjust the multiplicity of men and the multiplication of the apparatuses of production (and this means not only 'production' in the strict sense, but also the production of knowledge and skills in the school, the production of health in the hospitals, the production of destructive force in the army).

In this task of adjustment, discipline had to solve a number of problems for which the old economy of power was not sufficiently equipped. It could reduce the inefficiency of mass phenomena: reduce what, in a multiplicity, makes it much less manageable than a unity; reduce what is opposed to the use of each of its elements and of their sum; reduce everything that may counter the advantages of number. That is why discipline fixes; it arrests or regulates movements; it clears up confu-sion; it dissipates compact groupings of individuals wandering about the country in unpredictable ways; it establishes calculated distributions. It must also master all the forces that are formed from the very constitution of an organized multiplicity; it must neutralize the effects of counter-power that spring from them and which form a resistance to the power that wishes to dominate it: agitations, revolts, spontaneous organizations, coalitions – anything that may establish horizontal con-junctions. Hence the fact that the disciplines use procedures of partitioning and verticality, that they introduce, between the different elements at the same level, as solid separations as possible, that they define compact hierarchical networks, in short, that they oppose to the intrinsic, adverse force of multiplicity the technique of the continuous, individualizing pyramid. They must also increase the particular utility of each element of the multiplicity, but by means that are the most rapid and the least costly, that is to say, by using the multiplicity itself as an instrument of this growth. Hence, in order to extract from bodies the maximum time and force, the use of those overall methods known as time-tables, collective training, exercises, total and detailed surveillance. Furthermore, the disciplines must increase the effect of utility proper to the multiplicities, so that each is made more useful than the simple sum of its elements: it is in order to increase the utilizable effects of the multiple that the disciplines define tactics of distribution, reciprocal adjustment of bodies, gestures and rhythms, differentiation of capacities, recipro-cal coordination in relation to apparatuses or tasks. Lastly, the disciplines have to bring into play the power relations, not above but inside the very texture of the multiplicity, as discreetly as possible, as well articulated on the other functions of these multiplicities and also in the least expensive way possible: to this correspond anonymous instruments of power, coextensive with the multiplicity that they regiment, such as hierarchical surveillance, continuous registration, perpetual assessment and classification. In short, to substitute for a power that is manifested through the brilliance of those who exercise it, a power that insidiously objectifies those on whom it is applied; to form a body of knowledge about these individuals, rather than to deploy the ostentatious signs of sovereignty. In a word, the discip-lines are the ensemble of minute technical inventions that made it possible to increase the useful size of multiplicities by decreasing the inconveniences of the power which, in order to make them useful, must control them. A multiplicity, whether in a workshop or a nation, an army or a school, reaches the threshold of a discipline when the relation of the one to the other becomes favourable.

If the economic take-off of the West began with the techniques that made possible the accumulation of capital, it might perhaps be said that the methods for administering the accumulation of men made possible a political take-off in rela-tion to the traditional, ritual, costly, violent forms of power, which soon fell into disuse and were superseded by a subtle, calculated technology of subjection. In fact, the two processes – the accumulation of men and the accumulation of capital – cannot be separated; it would not have been possible to solve the problem of the accumulation of men without the growth of an apparatus of production capable of both sustaining them and using them; conversely, the techniques that made the cumulative multiplicity of men useful accelerated the accumulation of capital. At a less general level, the technological mutations of the apparatus of production, the division of labour and the elaboration of the disciplinary techniques sustained an ensemble of very close relations (cf. Marx, *Capital*, vol. I, chapter XIII and the very interesting analysis in Guerry and Deleule). Each makes the other possible and necessary; each provides a model for the other. The disciplinary pyramid consti-tuted the small cell of power within which the separation, coordination and supervision of tasks was imposed and made efficient; and analytical partitioning of time, gestures and bodily forces constituted an operational schema that could easily be transferred from the groups to be subjected to the mechanisms of production; the massive projection of military methods onto industrial organiza-tion was an example of this modelling of the division of labour following the model laid down by the schemata of power. But, on the other hand, the technical analysis of the process of production, its 'mechanical' breaking-down, were projected onto the labour force whose task it was to implement it: the constitution of those disciplinary machines in which the individual forces that they bring together are composed into a whole and therefore increased is the effect of this projection. Let us say that discipline is the unitary technique by which the body is reduced as a 'political' force at the least cost and maximized as a useful force. The growth of a capitalist economy gave rise to the specific modality of disciplinary power, whose general formulas, techniques of submitting forces and bodies, in short, 'political anatomy', could be operated in the most diverse political régimes, apparatuses or institutions.

2. The panoptic modality of power – at the elementary, technical, merely physical level at which it is situated – is not under the immediate dependence or a direct extension of the great juridico-political structures of a society; it is nonetheless not absolutely independent. Historically, the process by which the bourgeoisie became in the course of the eighteenth century the politically dominant class was masked by the establishment of an explicit, coded and formally egalitarian juridical framework, made possible by the organization of a parliamentary, representative régime. But the development and generalization of disciplinary mechanisms constituted the other, dark side of these processes. The general juridical form that guaranteed a system of rights that were egalitarian in principle was supported by these tiny, everyday, physical mechanisms, by all those systems of micro-power that are essentially non-egalitarian and asymmetrical that we call the disciplines. And although, in a formal way, the representative régime makes it possible, directly or indirectly, with or without relays, for the will of all to form the fundamental authority of sovereignty, the disciplines provide, at the base, a guarantee of the submission of forces and bodies. The real, corporal disciplines constituted the foundation of the formal, juridical liberties. The contract may have been regarded as the ideal foundation of law and political power; panopticism constituted the technique, universally widespread, of coercion. It continued to work in depth on the juridical structures of society, in order to make the effective mechanisms of power function in opposition to the formal framework that it had acquired. The 'Enlightenment', which discovered the liberties, also invented the disciplines.

In appearance, the disciplines constitute nothing more than an infra-law. They seem to extend the general forms defined by law to the infinitesimal level of individual lives; or they appear as methods of training that enable individuals to become integrated into these general demands. They seem to constitute the same type of law on a different scale, thereby making it more meticulous and more indulgent. The disciplines should be regarded as a sort of counter-law. They have the precise role of introducing insuperable asymmetries and excluding reciprocities. First, because discipline creates between individuals a 'private' link, which is a relation of constraints entirely different from contractual obligation; the acceptance of a discipline may be underwritten by contract; the way in which it is imposed, the mechanisms it brings into play, the non-reversible subordination of one group of people by another, the 'surplus' power that is always fixed on the same side, the inequality of position of the different 'partners' in relation to the common regulation, all these distinguish the disciplinary link from the contractual link, and make it possible to distort the contractual link systematically from the moment it has as its content a mechanism of discipline. We know, for example, how many real procedures undermine the legal fiction of the work contract: workshop discipline is not the least important. Moreover, whereas the juridical systems define juridical subjects according to universal norms, the disciplines characterize, classify, specialize; they distribute along a scale, around a norm, hierarchize individuals in relation to one another and, if necessary, disqualify and invalidate. In any case, in the space and during the time in which they exercise their control and bring into play the asymmetries of their power, they effect a suspension of the law that is never total, but is never annulled either. Regular and institutional as it may be, the discipline, in its mechanism, is a 'counter-law'. And, although the universal juridicism of modern society seems to fix limits on the exercise of power, its universally widespread panopticism enables it to operate, on the underside of the law, a machinery that is both immense and minute, which supports, reinforces, multiplies the asymmetry of power and undermines the limits that are traced around the law. The minute disciplines, the panopticisms of every day may well be below the level of emergence of the great apparatuses and the great political struggles. But, in the genealogy of modern society, they have been, with the class domination that traverses it, the political counterpart of the juridical norms according to which power was redistributed. Hence, no doubt, the importance that has been given for so long to the small techniques of discipline, to those apparently insignificant tricks that it has invented, and even to those 'sciences' that give it a respectable face; hence the fear of abandoning them if one cannot find any substitute; hence the affirmation that they are at the very founda-tion of society, and an element in its equilibrium, whereas they are a series of mechanisms for unbalancing power relations definitively and everywhere; hence the persistence in regarding them as the humble, but concrete form of every morality, whereas they are a set of physico-political techniques.

To return to the problem of legal punishments, the prison with all the correct-ive technology at its disposal is to be resituated at the point where the codified power to punish turns into a disciplinary power to observe; at the point where the universal punishments of the law are applied selectively to certain individuals and always the same ones; at the point where the redefinition of the juridical subject by the penalty becomes a useful training of the criminal; at the point where the law is inverted and passes outside itself, and where the counter-law becomes the effect-ive and institutionalized content of the juridical forms. What generalizes the power to punish, then, is not the universal consciousness of the law in each juridical subject; it is the regular extension, the infinitely minute web of panoptic techniques.

3. Taken one by one, most of these techniques have a long history behind them. But what was new, in the eighteenth century, was that, by being combined and generalized, they attained a level at which the formation of knowledge and the increase of power regularly reinforce one another in a circular process. At this point, the disciplines crossed the 'technological' threshold. First the hospital, then the school, then, later, the workshop were not simply 'reordered' by the discip-lines; they became, thanks to them, apparatuses such that any mechanism of

objectification could be used in them as an instrument of subjection, and any growth of power could give rise in them to possible branches of knowledge; it was this link, proper to the technological systems, that made possible within the disciplinary element the formation of clinical medicine, psychiatry, child psychology, educational psychology, the rationalization of labour. It is a double process, then: an epistemological 'thaw' through a refinement of power relations; a multiplication of the effects of power through the formation and accumulation of new forms of knowledge.

The extension of the disciplinary methods is inscribed in a broad historical process: the development at about the same time of many other technologies – agronomical, industrial, economic. But it must be recognized that, compared with the mining industries, the emerging chemical industries or methods of national accountancy, compared with the blast furnaces or the steam engine, panopticism has received little attention. It is regarded as not much more than a bizarre little utopia, a perverse dream – rather as though Bentham had been the Fourier of a police society, and the Phalanstery had taken on the form of the Panopticon. And yet this represented the abstract formula of a very real technology, that of individuals. There were many reasons why it received little praise; the most obvious is that the discourses to which it gave rise rarely acquired, except in the academic classifications, the status of sciences; but the real reason is no doubt that the power that it operates and which it augments is a direct, physical power that men exercise upon one another. An inglorious culmination had an origin that could be only grudgingly acknowledged. But it would be unjust to compare the disciplinary techniques with such inventions as the steam engine or Amici's microscope. They are much less; and yet, in a way, they are much more. If a historical equivalent or at least a point of comparison had to be found for them, it would be rather in the 'inquisitorial' technique.

The eighteenth century invented the techniques of discipline and the examination, rather as the Middle Ages invented the judicial investigation. But it did so by quite different means. The investigation procedure, an old fiscal and administrative technique, had developed above all with the reorganization of the Church and the increase of the princely states in the twelfth and thirteenth centuries. At this time it permeated to a very large degree the jurisprudence first of the ecclesiastical courts, then of the lay courts. The investigation as an authoritarian search for a truth observed or attested was thus opposed to the old procedures of the oath, the ordeal, the judicial duel, the judgement of God or even of the transaction between private individuals. The investigation was the sovereign power arrogating to itself the right to establish the truth by a number of regulated techniques. Now, although the investigation has since then been an integral part of western justice (even up to our own day), one must not forget either its political origin, its link with the birth of the states and of monarchical sovereignty, or its later extension and its role in the formation of knowledge. In fact, the investigation has been the no doubt crude, but fundamental element in the constitution of the empirical sciences; it has been the juridico-political matrix of this experimental knowledge, which, as we know, was very rapidly released at the end of the Middle Ages. It is perhaps true to say that, in Greece, mathematics were born from techniques of measurement; the sciences of nature, in any case, were born, to some extent, at the end of the Middle Ages, from the practices of investigation. The great empirical knowledge that covered the things of the world and transcribed them into the ordering of an indefinite discourse that observes, describes and establishes the 'facts' (at a time when the western world was beginning the economic and political conquest of this same world) had its operating model no doubt in the Inquisition – that immense invention that our recent mildness has placed in the dark recesses of our memory. But what this politico-juridical, administrative and criminal, religious and lay, investigation was to the sciences of nature, disciplinary analysis has been to the sciences of man. These sciences, which have so delighted our 'humanity' for over a century, have their technical matrix in the petty, malicious minutiae of the disciplines and their investigations. These investigations are perhaps to psychology, psychiatry, pedagogy, criminology, and so many other strange sciences, what the terrible power of investigation was to the calm knowledge of the animals, the plants or the earth. Another power, another knowledge. On the threshold of the classical age, Bacon, lawyer and statesman, tried to develop a methodology of investigation for the empirical sciences. What Great Observer will produce the methodology of examination for the human sciences? Unless, of course, such a thing is not possible. For, although it is true that, in becoming a technique for the empirical sciences, the investigation has detached itself from the inquisitorial procedure, in which it was historically rooted, the examination has remained extremely close to the disciplinary power that shaped it. It has always been and still is an intrinsic element of the disciplines. Of course it seems to have undergone a speculative purification by integrating itself with such sciences as psychology and psychiatry. And, in effect, its appearance in the form of tests, interviews, interrogations and consultations is apparently in order to rectify the mechanisms of discipline: educational psychology is supposed to correct the rigours of the school, just as the medical or psychiatric interview is supposed to rectify the effects of the discipline of work. But we must not be misled; these techniques merely refer individuals from one disciplinary authority to another, and they reproduce, in a concentrated or formalized form, the schema of power-knowledge proper to each discipline (on this subject, cf. Tort). The great investigation that gave rise to the sciences of nature has become detached from its politico-juridical model; the examination, on the other hand, is still caught up in disciplinary technology.

In the Middle Ages, the procedure of investigation gradually superseded the old accusatory justice, by a process initiated from above; the disciplinary technique, on the other hand, insidiously and as if from below, has invaded a penal justice that is still, in principle, inquisitorial. All the great movements of extension that characterize modern penality – the problematization of the criminal behind his crime, the concern with a punishment that is a correction, a therapy, a normalization, the division of the act of judgement between various authorities that are supposed to measure, assess, diagnose, cure, transform individuals – all this betrays the penetration of the disciplinary examination into the judicial inquisition.

What is now imposed on penal justice as its point of application, its 'useful' object, will no longer be the body of the guilty man set up against the body of the king; nor will it be the juridical subject of an ideal contract; it will be the disciplinary individual. The extreme point of penal justice under the Ancien Régime was the infinite segmentation of the body of the regicide: a manifestation of the strongest power over the body of the greatest criminal, whose total destruction made the crime explode into its truth. The ideal point of penality today would be an indefinite discipline: an interrogation without end, an investigation that would be extended without limit to a meticulous and ever more analytical observation, a judgement that would at the same time be the constitution of a file that was never closed, the calculated leniency of a penalty that would be interlaced with the ruthless curiosity of an examination, a procedure that would be at the same time the permanent measure of a gap in relation to an inaccessible norm and the asymptotic movement that strives to meet in infinity. The public execution was the logical culmination of a procedure governed by the Inquisition. The practice of placing individuals under 'observation' is a natural extension of a justice imbued with disciplinary methods and examination procedures. Is it surprising that the cellular prison, with its regular chronologies, forced labour, its authorities of surveillance and registration, its experts in normality, who continue and multiply the functions of the judge, should have become the modern instrument of penality? Is it surprising that prisons resemble factories, schools, barracks, hospitals, which all resemble prisons?

Notes

1   Archives militaires de Vincennes, A 1,516 91 sc. Pièce. This regulation is broadly similar to a whole series of others that date from the same period and earlier.
2   In the *Postscript to the Panopticon*, 1791, Bentham adds dark inspection galleries painted in black around the inspector's lodge, each making it possible to observe two storeys of cells.
3   In his first version of the *Panopticon*, Bentham had also imagined an acoustic surveillance, operated by means of pipes leading from the cells to the central tower. In the *Postscript* he abandoned the idea, perhaps because he could not introduce into it the principle of dissymmetry and prevent the prisoners from hearing the inspector as well as the inspector hearing them. Julius tried to develop a system of dissymmetrical listening (Julius, 18).
4   Imagining this continuous flow of visitors entering the central tower by an underground passage and then observing the circular landscape of the Panopticon, was Bentham aware of the Panoramas that Barker was constructing at exactly the same period (the first seems to have dated from 1787) and in which the visitors, occupying the central place, saw unfolding around them a landscape, a city or a battle? The visitors occupied exactly the place of the sovereign gaze.
5   In the second half of the eighteenth century, it was often suggested that the army should be used for the surveillance and general partitioning of the population. The army, as yet to undergo discipline in the seventeenth century, was regarded as a force capable of instilling it. Cf., for example, Servan, *Le Soldat citoyen*, 1780.
6   Arsenal, MS. 2565. Under this number, one also finds regulations for charity associations of the seventeenth and eighteenth centuries.
7   Le Maire in a memorandum written at the request of Sartine, in answer to sixteen questions posed by Joseph II on the Parisian police. This memorandum was published by Gazier in 1879.

Bibliography

Bentham, J., *Works*, ed. Bowring, IV, 1843.

Chassaigne, M., *La Lieutenance générale de police*, 1906.

Delamore, N., *Traité de police*, 1705.

Demia, C., *Règlement pour les écoles de la ville de Lyon*, 1716.

Des Essarts, T. N., *Dictionnaire universel de police*, 1787.

Funck-Brentano, F., *Catalogue des manuscrits de la bibliothèque de l'Arsenal*, IX.

Guerry, F. and Deleule, D., *Le Corps productif*, 1973.

Julius, N. H. *Leçons sur les prisons*, I, 1831 (Fr. trans.).

Léon, A., *La Révolution française et l'éducation technique*, 1968.

Loisel, G., *Histoire des ménageries*, II, 1912.

Marx, Karl, *Capital*, vol. I, ed. 1970.

Radzinovitz, L., *The English Criminal Law*, II, 1956.

Tort, Michel, *Q.I.*, 1974.

Treilhard, J. B., *Motifs de code d'instruction criminelle*, 1808.

Vattel, E. de, *Le Droit des gens*, 1768.

Suggestions for further reading

Bentham, Jeremy, *The Panopticon Writings*, ed. Miran Božovič, London and New York: Verso, 1995.

Davis, Mike, *City of Quartz: Excavating the Future in Los Angeles*, London: Verso, 1990.

Debord, Guy, *The Society of the Spectacle*, trans. Donald Nicholson-Smith, New York: Zone, 1995.

Chapter 16

Laura Mulvey

'VISUAL PLEASURE AND NARRATIVE CINEMA', 1975

I. Introduction

A. A political use of psychoanalysis

THIS PAPER INTENDS to use psychoanalysis to discover where and how the fascination of film is reinforced by pre-existing patterns of fascination already at work within the individual subject and the social formations that have moulded him. It takes as its starting point the way film reflects, reveals and even plays on the straight, socially established interpretation of sexual difference which controls images, erotic ways of looking and spectacle. It is helpful to understand what the cinema has been, how its magic has worked in the past, while attempting a theory and a practice which will challenge this cinema of the past. Psychoanalytic theory is thus appropriated here as a political weapon, demonstrating the way the unconscious of patriarchal society has structured film form.

The paradox of phallocentrism in all its manifestations is that it depends on the image of the castrated woman to give order and meaning to its world. An idea of woman stands as lynch pin to the system: it is her lack that produces the phallus as a symbolic presence, it is her desire to make good the lack that the phallus signifies. Recent writing in *Screen* about psychoanalysis and the cinema has not sufficiently brought out the importance of the representation of the female form in a symbolic order in which, in the last resort, it speaks castration and nothing else. To summarise briefly: the function of woman in forming the patriarchal unconscious is two-fold, she first symbolises the castration threat by her real absence of a penis and second thereby raises her child into the symbolic. Once this has been achieved, her meaning in the process is at an end, it does not last into the world of law and language except as a memory which oscillates between memory of maternal plenitude and memory of lack. Both are posited on nature (or on anatomy in

Freud's famous phrase). Woman's desire is subjected to her image as bearer of the bleeding wound, she can exist only in relation to castration and cannot transcend it. She turns her child into the signifier of her own desire to possess a penis (the condition, she imagines, of entry into the symbolic). Either she must gracefully give way to the word, the Name of the Father and the Law, or else struggle to keep her child down with her in the half-light of the imaginary. Woman then stands in patriarchal culture as signifier for the male other, bound by a symbolic order in which man can live out his phantasies and obsessions through linguistic command by imposing them on the silent image of woman still tied to her place as bearer of meaning, not maker of meaning.

There is an obvious interest in this analysis for feminists, a beauty in its exact rendering of the frustration experienced under the phallocentric order. It gets us nearer to the roots of our oppression, it brings an articulation of the problem closer, it faces us with the ultimate challenge: how to fight the unconscious structured like a language (formed critically at the moment of arrival of language) while still caught within the language of the patriarchy. There is no way in which we can produce an alternative out of the blue, but we can begin to make a break by examining patriarchy with the tools it provides, of which psychoanalysis is not the only but an important one. We are still separated by a great gap from important issues for the female unconscious which are scarcely relevant to phallocentric theory: the sexing of the female infant and her relationship to the symbolic, the sexually mature woman as non-mother, maternity outside the signification of the phallus, the vagina. . . . But, at this point, psychoanalytic theory as it now stands can at least advance our understanding of the status quo, of the patriarchal order in which we are caught.

B. Destruction of pleasure as a radical weapon

As an advanced representation system, the cinema poses questions of the ways the unconscious (formed by the dominant order) structures ways of seeing and pleasure in looking. Cinema has changed over the last few decades. It is no longer the monolithic system based on large capital investment exemplified at its best by Hollywood in the 1930's, 1940's and 1950's. Technological advances (16mm, etc) have changed the economic conditions of cinematic production, which can now be artisanal as well as capitalist. Thus it has been possible for an alternative cinema to develop. However self-conscious and ironic Hollywood managed to be, it always restricted itself to a formal mise-en-scène reflecting the dominant ideological concept of the cinema. The alternative cinema provides a space for a cinema to be born which is radical in both a political and an aesthetic sense and challenges the basic assumptions of the mainstream film. This is not to reject the latter moralistically, but to highlight the ways in which its formal preoccupations reflect the psychical obsessions of the society which produced it, and, further, to stress that the alternative cinema must start specifically by reacting against these obsessions and assumptions. A politically and aesthetically avant-garde cinema is now possible, but it can still only exist as a counterpoint.

The magic of the Hollywood style at its best (and of all the cinema which fell within its sphere of influence) arose, not exclusively, but in one important aspect, from its skilled and satisfying manipulation of visual pleasure. Unchallenged, main-stream film coded the erotic into the language of the dominant patriarchal order. In the highly developed Hollywood cinema it was only through these codes that the alienated subject, torn in his imaginary memory by a sense of loss, by the terror of potential lack in phantasy, came near to finding a glimpse of satisfaction: through its formal beauty and its play on his own formative obsessions. This article will discuss the interweaving of that erotic pleasure in film, its meaning, and in particular the central place of the image of woman. It is said that analysing pleasure, or beauty, destroys it. That is the intention of this article. The satisfaction and reinforcement of the ego that represent the high point of film history hitherto must be attacked. Not in favour of a reconstructed new pleasure, which cannot exist in the abstract, nor of intellectualised unpleasure, but to make way for a total negation of the ease and plenitude of the narrative fiction film. The alternative is the thrill that comes from leaving the past behind without rejecting it, transcending outworn or oppressive forms, or daring to break with normal pleasurable expectations in order to conceive a new language of desire.

II Pleasure in looking/fascination with the human form

A. The cinema offers a number of possible pleasures. One is scopophilia. There are circumstances in which looking itself is a source of pleasure, just as, in the reverse formation, there is pleasure in being looked at. Originally, in his *Three Essays on Sexuality*, Freud isolated scopophilia as one of the component instincts of sexuality which exist as drives quite independently of the erotogenic zones. At this point he associated scopophilia with taking other people as objects, subjecting them to a controlling and curious gaze. His particular examples centre around the voyeuristic activities of children, their desire to see and make sure of the private and the forbidden (curiosity about other people's genital and bodily functions, about the presence or absence of the penis and, retrospectively, about the primal scene). In this analysis scopophilia is essentially active. (Later, in *Instincts and their Vicissitudes*, Freud developed his theory of scopophilia further, attaching it initially to pre-genital auto-eroticism, after which the pleasure of the look is transferred to others by analogy. There is a close working here of the relationship between the active instinct and its further development in a narcissistic form.) Although the instinct is modified by other factors, in particular the constitution of the ego, it continues to exist as the erotic basis for pleasure in looking at another person as object. At the extreme, it can become fixated into a perversion, producing obsessive voyeurs and Peeping Toms, whose only sexual satisfaction can come from watching, in an active controlling sense, an objectified other.

At first glance, the cinema would seem to be remote from the undercover world of the surreptitious observation of an unknowing and unwilling victim. What is seen of the screen is so manifestly shown. But the mass of mainstream film, and the conventions within which it has consciously evolved, portray a hermetically sealed world which unwinds magically, indifferent to the presence of the audience, producing for them a sense of separation and playing on their voyeuristic phantasy. Moreover, the extreme contrast between the darkness in the auditorium (which also isolates the spectators from one another) and the brilliance of the shifting patterns of light and shade on the screen helps to promote the illusion of voyeuristic separation. Although the film is really being shown, is there to be seen, conditions of screening and narrative conventions give the spectator an illusion of looking in on a private world. Among other things, the position of the spectators in the cinema is blatantly one of repression of their exhibitionism and projection of the repressed desire on to the performer.

B. The cinema satisfies a primordial wish for pleasurable looking, but it also goes further, developing scopophilia in its narcissistic aspect. The conventions of mainstream film focus attention on the human form. Scale, space, stories are all anthropomorphic. Here, curiosity and the wish to look intermingle with a fascination with likeness and recognition: the human face, the human body, the relationship between the human form and its surroundings, the visible presence of the person in the world. Jacques Lacan has described how the moment when a child recognises its own image in the mirror is crucial for the constitution of the ego. Several aspects of this analysis are relevant here. The mirror phase occurs at a time when the child's physical ambitions outstrip his motor capacity, with the result that his recognition of himself is joyous in that he imagines his mirror image to be more complete, more perfect than he experiences his own body. Recognition is thus overlaid with mis-recognition: the image recognised is conceived as the reflected body of the self, but its misrecognition as superior projects this body outside itself as an ideal ego, the alienated subject, which, re-introjected as an ego ideal, gives rise to the future generation of identification with others. This mirror-moment predates language for the child.

Important for this article is the fact that it is an image that constitutes the matrix of the imaginary, of recognition/misrecognition and identification, and hence of the first articulation of the 'I', of subjectivity. This is a moment when an older fascination with looking (at the mother's face, for an obvious example) collides with the initial inklings of self-awareness. Hence it is the birth of the long love affair/despair between image and self-image which has found such intensity of expression in film and such joyous recognition in the cinema audience. Quite apart from the extraneous similarities between screen and mirror (the framing of the human form in its surroundings, for instance), the cinema has structures of fascination strong enough to allow temporary loss of ego while simultaneously reinforcing the ego. The sense of forgetting the world as the ego has subsequently come to perceive it (I forgot who I am and where I was) is nostalgically reminiscent of that pre-subjective moment of image recognition. At the same time the cinema has distinguished itself in the production of ego ideals as expressed in particular in the star system, the stars centring both screen presence and screen story as they act out a complex process of likeness and difference (the glamorous impersonates the ordinary).

C. Sections II. A and B have set out two contradictory aspects of the pleasurable structures of looking in the conventional cinematic situation. The first, scopophilic, arises from pleasure in using another person as an object of sexual stimulation through sight. The second, developed through narcissism and the constitution of the ego, comes from identification with the image seen. Thus, in film terms, one implies a separation of the erotic identity of the subject from the object on the screen (active scopophilia), the other demands identification of the ego with the object on the screen through the spectator's fascination with and recognition of his like. The first is a function of the sexual instincts, the second of ego libido. This dichotomy was crucial for Freud. Although he saw the two as interacting and overlaying each other, the tension between instinctual drives and self-preservation continues to be a dramatic polarisation in terms of pleasure. Both are formative structures, mechanisms not meaning. In themselves they have no signification, they have to be attached to an idealisation. Both pursue aims in indifference to perceptual reality, creating the imagised, eroticised concept of the world that forms the perception of the subject and makes a mockery of empirical objectivity.

During its history, the cinema seems to have evolved a particular illusion of reality in which this contradiction between libido and ego has found a beautifully complementary phantasy world. In *reality* the phantasy world of the screen is subject to the law which produces it. Sexual instincts and identification processes have a meaning within the symbolic order which articulates desire. Desire, born with language, allows the possibility of transcending the instinctual and the imaginary, but its point of reference continually returns to the traumatic moment of its birth: the castration complex. Hence the look, pleasurable in form, can be threatening in content, and it is woman as representation/image that crystallises this paradox.

III Woman as image, man as bearer of the look

A. In a world ordered by sexual imbalance, pleasure in looking has been split between active/male and passive/female. The determining male gaze projects its phantasy on to the female figure which is styled accordingly. In their traditional exhibitionist role women are simultaneously looked at and displayed, with their appearance coded for strong visual and erotic impact so that they can be said to connote *to-be-looked-at-ness*. Woman displayed as sexual object is the leit-motif of erotic spectacle: from pin-ups to strip-tease, from Ziegfeld to Busby Berkeley, she holds the look, plays to and signifies male desire. Mainstream film neatly combined spectacle and narrative. (Note, however, how in the musical song-and-dance numbers break the flow of the diegesis.) The presence of woman is an indispensable element of spectacle in normal narrative film, yet her visual presence tends to work against the development of a story line, to freeze the flow of action in moments of erotic contemplation. This alien presence then has to be integrated into cohesion with the narrative. As Budd Boetticher has put it:

> 'What counts is what the heroine provokes, or rather what she represents. She is the one, or rather the love or fear she inspires in the hero, or else the concern he feels for her, who makes him act the way he does. In herself the woman has not the slightest importance.'

(A recent tendency in narrative film has been to dispense with this problem altogether; hence the development of what Molly Haskell has called the 'buddy movie', in which the active homosexual eroticism of the central male figures can carry the story without distraction.) Traditionally, the woman displayed has functioned on two levels: as erotic object for the characters within the screen story, and as erotic object for the spectator within the auditorium, with a shifting tension between the looks on either side of the screen. For instance, the device of the show-girl allows the two looks to be unified technically without any apparent break in the diegesis. A woman performs within the narrative, the gaze of the spectator and that of the male characters in the film are neatly combined without breaking narrative verisimilitude. For a moment the sexual impact of the performing woman takes the film into a no-man's-land outside its own time and space. Thus Marilyn Monroe's first appearance in *The River of No Return* and Lauren Bacall's songs in *To Have or Have Not*. Similarly, conventional close-ups of legs (Dietrich, for instance) or a face (Garbo) integrate into the narrative a different mode of eroticism. One part of a fragmented body destroys the Renaissance space, the illusion of depth demanded by the narrative, it gives flatness, the quality of a cut-out or icon rather than verisimilitude to the screen.

B. An active/passive heterosexual division of labour has similarly controlled narrative structure. According to the principles of the ruling ideology and the psychical structures that back it up, the male figure cannot bear the burden of sexual objectification. Man is reluctant to gaze at his exhibitionist like. Hence the split between spectacle and narrative supports the man's role as the active one of forwarding the story, making things happen. The man controls the film phantasy and also emerges as the representative of power in a further sense: as the bearer of the look of the spectator, transferring it behind the screen to neutralise the extradiegetic tendencies represented by woman as spectacle. This is made possible through the processes set in motion by structuring the film around a main controlling figure with whom the spectator can identify. As the spectator identifies with the main male[1] protagonist, he projects his look on to that of his like, his screen surrogate, so that the power of the male protagonist as he controls events coincides with the active power of the erotic look, both giving a satisfying sense of omnipotence. A male movie star's glamorous characteristics are thus not those of the erotic object of the gaze, but those of the more perfect, more complete, more powerful ideal ego conceived in the original moment of recognition in front of the mirror. The character in the story can make things happen and control events better than the subject/spectator, just as the image in the mirror was more in control of motor coordination. In contrast to woman as icon, the active male figure (the ego ideal of the identification process) demands a three-dimensional space corresponding to that of the mirror-recognition in which the alienated subject internalised his own representation of this imaginary existence. He is a figure in a landscape. Here the function of film is to reproduce as accurately as possible the so-called natural conditions of human perception. Camera technology (as exemplified by deep focus in particular) and camera movements (determined by the action of the protagonist), combined with invisible editing (demanded by realism) all tend to blur the limits of screen space. The male protagonist is free to command the stage, a stage of spatial illusion in which he articulates the look and creates the action.

C.1 Sections III. A and B have set out a tension between a mode of representation of woman in film and conventions surrounding the diegesis. Each is associated with a look: that of the spectator in direct scopophilic contact with the female form displayed for his enjoyment (connoting male phantasy) and that of the spectator fascinated with the image of his like set in an illusion of natural space, and through him gaining control and possession of the woman within the diegesis. (This tension and the shift from one pole to the other can structure a single text. Thus both in *Only Angels Have Wings* and in *To Have and Have Not*, the film opens with the woman as object of the combined gaze of spectator and all the male protagonists in the film. She is isolated, glamorous, on display, sexualised. But as the narrative progresses she falls in love with the main male protagonist and becomes his property, losing her outward glamorous characteristics, her generalised sexuality, her show-girl connotations; her eroticism is subjected to the male star alone. By means of identification with him, through participation in his power, the spectator can indirectly possess her too.)

But in psychoanalytic terms, the female figure poses a deeper problem. She also connotes something that the look continually circles around but disavows: her lack of a penis, implying a threat of castration and hence unpleasure. Ultimately, the meaning of woman is sexual difference, the absence of the penis as visually ascertainable, the material evidence on which is based the castration complex essential for the organisation of entrance to the symbolic order and the law of the father. Thus the woman as icon, displayed for the gaze and enjoyment of men, the active controllers of the look, always threatens to evoke the anxiety it originally signified. The male unconscious has two avenues of escape from this castration anxiety: preoccupation with the re-enactment of the original trauma (investigating the woman, demystifying her mystery), counterbalanced by the devaluation, punishment or saving of the guilty object (an avenue typified by the concerns of the *film noir*); or else complete disavowal of castration by the substitution of a fetish object or turning the represented figure itself into a fetish so that it becomes reassuring rather than dangerous (hence over-valuation, the cult of the female star). This second avenue, fetishistic scopophilia, builds up the physical beauty of the object, transforming it into something satisfying in itself. The first avenue, voyeurism, on the contrary, has associations with sadism: pleasure lies in ascertaining guilt (immediately associated with castration), asserting control and subjecting the guilty person through punishment or forgiveness. This sadistic side fits in well with narrative. Sadism demands a story, depends on making something happen, forcing a change in another person, a battle of will and strength, victory/defeat, all occuring in a linear time with a beginning and an end. Fetishistic scopophilia, on the other hand, can exist outside linear time as the erotic instinct is focussed on the look alone. These contradictions and ambiguities can be illustrated more simply by using works by Hitchcock and Sternberg, both of whom take the look almost as the content or subject matter of many of their films. Hitchcock is the more complex, as he uses both mechanisms. Sternberg's work, on the other hand, provides many pure examples of fetishistic scopophilia.

C.2 It is well known that Sternberg once said he would welcome his films being projected upside down so that story and character involvement would not interfere with the spectator's undiluted appreciation of the screen image. This statement is revealing but ingenuous. Ingenuous in that his films do demand that the figure of the woman (Dietrich, in the cycle of films with her, as the ultimate example) should be identifiable. But revealing in that it emphasises the fact that for him the pictorial space enclosed by the frame is paramount rather than narrative or identification processes. While Hitchcock goes into the investigative side of voyeurism, Sternberg produces the ultimate fetish, taking it to the point where the powerful look of the male protagonist (characteristic of traditional narrative film) is broken in favour of the image in direct erotic rapport with the spectator. The beauty of the woman as object and the screen space coalesce; she is no longer the bearer of guilt but a perfect product, whose body, stylised and fragmented by close-ups, is the content of the film and the direct recipient of the spectator's look. Sternberg plays down the illusion of screen depth; his screen tends to be one-dimensional, as light and shade, lace, steam, foliage, net, streamers, etc, reduce the visual field. There is little or no mediation of the look through the eyes of the main male protagonist. On the contrary, shadowy presences like La Bessière in *Morocco* act as surrogates for the director, detached as they are from audience identification. Despite Sternberg's insistence that his stories are irrelevant, it is significant that they are concerned with situation, not suspense, and cyclical rather than linear time, while plot complications revolve around misunderstanding rather than conflict. The most important absence is that of the controlling male gaze within the screen scene. The high point of emotional drama in the most typical Dietrich films, her supreme moments of erotic meaning, take place in the absence of the man she loves in the fiction. There are other witnesses, other spectators watching her on the screen, their gaze is one with, not standing in for, that of the audience. At the end of *Morocco*, Tom Brown has already disappeared into the desert when Amy Jolly kicks off her gold sandals and walks after him. At the end of *Dishonoured*, Kranau is indifferent to the fate of Magda. In both cases, the erotic impact, sanctified by death, is displayed as a spectacle for the audience. The male hero misunderstands and, above all, does not see.

In Hitchcock, by contrast, the male hero does see precisely what the audience sees. However, in the films I shall discuss here, he takes fascination with an image through scopophilic eroticism as the subject of the film. Moreover, in these cases the hero portrays the contradictions and tensions experienced by the spectator. In *Vertigo* in particular, but also in *Marnie* and *Rear Window*, the look is central to the plot, oscillating between voyeurism and fetishistic fascination. As a twist, a further manipulation of the normal viewing process which in some sense reveals it, Hitchcock uses the process of identification normally associated with ideological correctness and the recognition of established morality and shows up its perverted side. Hitchcock has never concealed his interest in voyeurism, cinematic and non-cinematic. His heroes are exemplary of the symbolic order and the law – a policeman (*Vertigo*), a dominant male possessing money and power (*Marnie*) – but their erotic drives lead them into compromised situations. The power to subject another person to the will sadistically or to the gaze voyeuristically is turned on to the woman as the object of both. Power is backed by a certainty of legal right and the established guilt of the woman (evoking castration, psychoanalytically speaking). True perversion is barely concealed under a shallow mask of ideological correctness – the man is on the right side of the law, the woman on the wrong. Hitchcock's skilful use of identification processes and liberal use of subjective camera from the point of view of the male protagonist draw the spectators deeply into his position, making them share his uneasy gaze. The audience is absorbed into a voyeuristic situation within the screen scene and diegesis which parodies his own in the cinema. In his analysis of *Rear Window*, Douchet takes the film as a metaphor for the cinema. Jeffries is the audience, the events in the apartment block opposite correspond to the screen. As he watches, an erotic dimension is added to his look, a central image to the drama. His girlfriend Lisa had been of little sexual interest to him, more or less a drag, so long as she remained on the spectator side. When she crosses the barrier between his room and the block opposite, their relationship is re-born erotically. He does not merely watch her through his lens, as a distant meaningful image, he also sees her as a guilty intruder exposed by a dangerous man threatening her with punishment, and thus finally saves her. Lisa's exhibition-ism has already been established by her obsessive interest in dress and style, in being a passive image of visual perfection; Jeffries' voyeurism and activity have also been established through his work as a photo-journalist, a maker of stories and captor of images. However, his enforced inactivity, binding him to his seat as a spectator, puts him squarely in the phantasy position of the cinema audience.

In *Vertigo*, subjective camera predominates. Apart from one flash-back from Judy's point of view, the narrative is woven around what Scottie sees or fails to see. The audience follows the growth of his erotic obsession and subsequent despair precisely from his point of view. Scottie's voyeurism is blatant: he falls in love with a woman he follows and spies on without speaking to. Its sadistic side is equally blatant: he has chosen (and freely chosen, for he had been a successful lawyer) to be a policeman, with all the attendant possibilities of pursuit and investigation. As a result, he follows, watches and falls in love with a perfect image of female beauty and mystery. Once he actually confronts her, his erotic drive is to break her down and force her to tell by persistent cross-questioning. Then, in the second part of the film, he re-enacts his obsessive involvement with the image he loved to watch secretly. He reconstructs Judy as Madeleine, forces her to conform in every detail to the actual physical appearance of his fetish. Her exhibitionism, her masochism, make her an ideal passive counterpart to Scottie's active sadistic voyeurism. She knows her part is to perform, and only by playing it through and then replaying it can she keep Scottie's erotic interest. But in the repetition he does break her down and succeeds in exposing her guilt. His curiosity wins through and she is punished. In *Vertigo*, erotic involvement with the look is disorientating: the spectator's fascin-ation is turned against him as the narrative carries him through and entwines him with the processes that he is himself exercising. The Hitchcock hero here is firmly placed within the symbolic order, in narrative terms. He has all the attributes of the partriachal super-ego. Hence the spectator, lulled into a false sense of security by the apparent legality of his surrogate, sees through his look and finds himself exposed as complicit, caught in the moral ambiguity of looking. Far from being simply an aside on the perversion of the police, *Vertigo* focuses on the implications of the active/looking, passive/looked-at split in terms of sexual difference and the power of the male symbolic encapsulated in the hero. Marnie, too, performs for Mark Rutland's gaze and masquerades as the perfect to-be-looked-at image. He, too, is on the side of the law until, drawn in by obsession with her guilt, her secret, he longs to see her in the act of committing a crime, make her confess and thus save her. So he, too, becomes complicit as he acts out the implications of his power. He controls money and words, he can have his cake and eat it.

IV Summary

The psychoanalytic background that has been discussed in this article is relevant to the pleasure and unpleasure offered by traditional narrative film. The scopophilic instinct (pleasure in looking at another person as an erotic object), and, in contra-distinction, ego libido (forming identification processes) act as formations, mech-anisms, which this cinema has played on. The image of woman as (passive) raw material for the (active) gaze of man takes the argument a step further into the structure of representation, adding a further layer demanded by the ideology of the patriarchal order as it is worked out in its favourite cinematic form – illusion-istic narrative film. The argument returns again to the psychoanalytic background in that woman as representation signifies castration, inducing voyeuristic or fetish-istic mechanisms to circumvent her threat. None of these interacting layers is intrinsic to film, but it is only in the film form that they can reach a perfect and beautiful contradiction, thanks to the possibility in the cinema of shifting the emphasis of the look. It is the place of the look that defines cinema, the possibility of varying it and exposing it. This is what makes cinema quite different in its voyeuristic potential from, say, striptease, theatre, shows, etc. Going far beyond highlighting a woman's to-be-looked-at-ness, cinema builds the way she is to be looked at into the spectacle itself. Playing on the tension between film as control-ling the dimension of time (editing, narrative) and film as controlling the dimen-sion of space (changes in distance, editing), cinematic codes create a gaze, a world, and an object, thereby producing an illusion cut to the measure of desire. It is these cinematic codes and their relationship to formative external structures that must be broken down before mainstream film and the pleasure it provides can be challenged.

To begin with (as an ending), the voyeuristic-scopophilic look that is a crucial part of traditional filmic pleasure can itself be broken down. There are three different looks associated with cinema: that of the camera as it records the pro-filmic event, that of the audience as it watches the final product, and that of the characters at each other within the screen illusion. The conventions of narrative film deny the first two and subordinate them to the third, the conscious aim being always to eliminate intrusive camera presence and prevent a distancing awareness in the audience. Without these two absences (the material existence of the record-ing process, the critical reading of the spectator), fictional drama cannot achieve reality, obviousness and truth. Nevertheless, as this article has argued, the struc-ture of looking in narrative fiction film contains a contradiction in its own prem-ises: the female image as a castration threat constantly endangers the unity of the diegesis and bursts through the world of illusion as an intrusive, static, one-dimensional fetish. Thus the two looks materially present in time and space are obsessively subordinated to the neurotic needs of the male ego. The camera becomes the mechanism for producing an illusion of Renaissance space, flowing movements compatible with the human eye, an ideology of representation that revolves around the perception of the subject; the camera's look is disavowed in order to create a convincing world in which the spectator's surrogate can perform with verisimilitude. Simultaneously, the look of the audience is denied an intrinsic force: as soon as fetishistic representation of the female image threatens to break the spell of illusion, and the erotic image on the screen appears directly (without mediation) to the spectator, the fact of fetishisation, concealing as it does castration fear, freezes the look, fixates the spectator and prevents him from achieving any distance from the image in front of him.

This complex interaction of looks is specific to film. The first blow against the monolithic accumulation of traditional film conventions (already undertaken by radical film-makers) is to free the look of the camera into its materiality in time and space and the look of the audience into dialectics, passionate detachment. There is no doubt that this destroys the satisfaction, pleasure and privilege of the 'invisible guest', and highlights how film has depended on voyeuristic active/ passive mechanisms. Women, whose image has continually been stolen and used for this end, cannot view the decline of the traditional film form with anything much more than sentimental regret.[2]

Notes

1   There are films with a woman as main protagonist, of course. To analyse this phenomenon seriously here would take me too far afield. Pam Cook and Claire Johnston's study of *The Revolt of Mamie Stover* in Phil Hardy, ed: *Raoul Walsh*, Edinburgh 1974, shows in a striking case how the strength of this female protagonist is more apparent than real.
2   This article is a reworked version of a paper given in the French Department of the University of Wisconsin, Madison, in the Spring of 1973.

Suggestions for further reading

Lacan, Jacques, *The Four Fundamental Concepts of Psycho-analysis*, ed. Jacques-Alain Miller, trans. Alan Sheridan, Harmondsworth: Penguin, 1994.

Mulvey, Laura, 'Afterthoughts on "Visual Pleasure and Narrative Cinema" . . . Inspired by "Duel in the Sun" ', *Framework*, 1981, vols. 15–17, 12–15.

Stacey, Jackie, 'Desperately Seeking Difference', *Screen*, 1987, vol. 28.1, 48–61.

Chapter 17

Edward Said

INTRODUCTION TO *ORIENTALISM*, 1978

Introduction

I

ON A VISIT to Beirut during the terrible civil war of 1975–1976 a French journalist wrote regretfully of the gutted downtown area that "it had once seemed to belong to . . . the Orient of Chateaubriand and Nerval."[1] He was right about the place, of course, especially so far as a European was concerned. The Orient was almost a European invention, and had been since antiquity a place of romance, exotic beings, haunting memories and landscapes, remarkable experiences. Now it was disappearing; in a sense it had happened, its time was over. Perhaps it seemed irrelevant that Orientals themselves had something at stake in the process, that even in the time of Chateaubriand and Nerval Orientals had lived there, and that now it was they who were suffering; the main thing for the European visitor was a European representation of the Orient and its contemporary fate, both of which had a privileged communal significance for the journalist and his French readers.

Americans will not feel quite the same about the Orient, which for them is much more likely to be associated very differently with the Far East (China and Japan, mainly). Unlike the Americans, the French and the British—less so the Germans, Russians, Spanish, Portuguese, Italians, and Swiss—have had a long tradition of what I shall be calling *Orientalism*, a way of coming to terms with the Orient that is based on the Orient's special place in European Western experience. The Orient is not only adjacent to Europe; it is also the place of Europe's greatest and richest and oldest colonies, the source of its civilizations and languages, its cultural contestant, and one of its deepest and most recurring images of the Other. In addition, the Orient has helped to define Europe (or the West) as its contrasting image, idea, personality, experience. Yet none of this Orient is merely imaginative. The Orient is an integral part of European *material* civilization and culture. Orientalism expresses and represents that part culturally and even ideologically as a mode of discourse with supporting institutions, vocabulary, scholarship, imagery, doctrines, even colonial bureaucracies and colonial styles. In contrast, the American understanding of the Orient will seem considerably less dense, although our recent Japanese, Korean, and Indochinese adventures ought now to be creating a more sober, more realistic "Oriental" awareness. Moreover, the vastly expanded American political and economic role in the Near East (the Middle East) makes great claims on our understanding of that Orient.

It will be clear to the reader (and will become clearer still throughout the many pages that follow) that by Orientalism I mean several things, all of them, in my opinion, interdependent. The most readily accepted designation for Orientalism is an academic one, and indeed the label still serves in a number of academic institutions. Anyone who teaches, writes about, or researches the Orient—and this applies whether the person is an anthropologist, sociologist, historian, or philologist—either in its specific or its general aspects, is an Orientalist, and what he or she does is Orientalism. Compared with *Oriental studies* or *area studies*, it is true that the term *Orientalism* is less preferred by specialists today, both because it is too vague and general and because it connotes the high-handed executive attitude of nineteenth-century and early-twentieth-century European colonialism. Nevertheless, books are written and congresses held with "the Orient" as their main focus, with the Orientalist in his new or old guise as their main authority. The point is that even if it does not survive as it once did, Orientalism lives on academically through its doctrines and theses about the Orient and the Oriental.

Related to this academic tradition, whose fortunes, transmigrations, specializations, and transmissions are in part the subject of this study, is a more general meaning for Orientalism. Orientalism is a style of thought based upon an ontological and epistemological distinction made between "the Orient" and (most of the time) "the Occident." Thus a very large mass of writers, among whom are poets, novelists, philosophers, political theorists, economists, and imperial administrators, have accepted the basic distinction between East and West as the starting point for elaborate theories, epics, novels, social descriptions, and political accounts concerning the Orient, its people, customs, "mind," destiny, and so on. *This* Orientalism can accommodate Aeschylus, say, and Victor Hugo, Dante and Karl Marx. A little later in this introduction I shall deal with the methodological problems one encounters in so broadly construed a "field" as this.

The interchange between the academic and the more or less imaginative meanings of Orientalism is a constant one, and since the late eighteenth century there has been a considerable, quite disciplined—perhaps even regulated—traffic between the two. Here I come to the third meaning of Orientalism, which is something more historically and materially defined than either of the other two. Taking the late eighteenth century as a very roughly defined starting point Orientalism can be discussed and analyzed as the corporate institution for dealing with the Orient—dealing with it by making statements about it, authorizing views of it, describing it, by teaching it, settling it, ruling over it: in short, Orientalism as a Western style for dominating, restructuring, and having authority over the Orient.

I have found it useful here to employ Michel Foucault's notion of a discourse, as described by him in *The Archaeology of Knowledge* and in *Discipline and Punish*, to identify Orientalism. My contention is that without examining Orientalism as a discourse one cannot possibly understand the enormously systematic discipline by which European culture was able to manage—and even produce—the Orient politically, sociologically, militarily, ideologically, scientifically, and imaginatively during the post-Enlightenment period. Moreover, so authoritative a position did Orientalism have that I believe no one writing, thinking, or acting on the Orient could do so without taking account of the limitations on thought and action imposed by Orientalism. In brief, because of Orientalism the Orient was not (and is not) a free subject of thought or action. This is not to say that Orientalism unilaterally determines what can be said about the Orient, but that it is the whole network of interests inevitably brought to bear on (and therefore always involved in) any occasion when that peculiar entity "the Orient" is in question. How this happens is what this book tries to demonstrate. It also tries to show that European culture gained in strength and identity by setting itself off against the Orient as a sort of surrogate and even underground self.

Historically and culturally there is a quantitative as well as a qualitative difference between the Franco-British involvement in the Orient and—until the period of American ascendancy after World War II—the involvement of every other European and Atlantic power. To speak of Orientalism therefore is to speak mainly, although not exclusively, of a British and French cultural enterprise, a project whose dimensions take in such disparate realms as the imagination itself, the whole of India and the Levant, the Biblical texts and the Biblical lands, the spice trade, colonial armies and a long tradition of colonial administrators, a formidable scholarly corpus, innumerable Oriental "experts" and "hands," an Oriental professorate, a complex array of "Oriental" ideas (Oriental despotism, Oriental splendor, cruelty, sensuality), many Eastern sects, philosophies, and wisdoms domesticated for local European use—the list can be extended more or less indefinitely. My point is that Orientalism derives from a particular closeness experienced between Britain and France and the Orient, which until the early nineteenth century had really meant only India and the Bible lands. From the beginning of the nineteenth century until the end of World War II France and Britain dominated the Orient and Orientalism; since World War II America has dominated the Orient, and approaches it as France and Britain once did. Out of that closeness, whose dynamic is enormously productive even if it always demonstrates the comparatively greater strength of the Occident (British, French, or American), comes the large body of texts I call Orientalist.

It should be said at once that even with the generous number of books and authors that I examine, there is a much larger number that I simply have had to leave out. My argument, however, depends neither upon an exhaustive catalogue of texts dealing with the Orient nor upon a clearly delimited set of texts, authors, and ideas that together make up the Orientalist canon. I have depended instead upon a different methodological alternative—whose backbone in a sense is the set of historical generalizations I have so far been making in this Introduction—and it is these I want now to discuss in more analytical detail.

II

I have begun with the assumption that the Orient is not an inert fact of nature. It is not merely *there*, just as the Occident itself is not just *there* either. We must take seriously Vico's great observation that men make their own history, that what they can know is what they have made, and extend it to geography: as both geographical and cultural entities—to say nothing of historical entities—such locales, regions, geographical sectors as "Orient" and "Occident" are man-made. Therefore as much as the West itself, the Orient is an idea that has a history and a tradition of thought, imagery, and vocabulary that have given it reality and presence in and for the West. The two geographical entities thus support and to an extent reflect each other.

Having said that, one must go on to state a number of reasonable qualifications. In the first place, it would be wrong to conclude that the Orient was *essentially* an idea, or a creation with no corresponding reality. When Disraeli said in his novel *Tancred* that the East was a career, he meant that to be interested in the East was something bright young Westerners would find to be an all-consuming passion; he should not be interpreted as saying that the East was *only* a career for Westerners. There were—and are—cultures and nations whose location is in the East, and their lives, histories, and customs have a brute reality obviously greater than anything that could be said about them in the West. About that fact this study of Orientalism has very little to contribute, except to acknowledge it tacitly. But the phenomenon of Orientalism as I study it here deals principally, not with a correspondence between Orientalism and Orient, but with the internal consistency of Orientalism and its ideas about the Orient (the East as career) despite or beyond any correspondence, or lack thereof, with a "real" Orient. My point is that Disraeli's statement about the East refers mainly to that created consistency, that regular constellation of ideas as the pre-eminent thing about the Orient, and not to its mere being, as Wallace Stevens's phrase has it.

A second qualification is that ideas, cultures, and histories cannot seriously be understood or studied without their force, or more precisely their configurations of power, also being studied. To believe that the Orient was created—or, as I call it, "Orientalized"—and to believe that such things happen simply as a necessity of the imagination, is to be disingenuous. The relationship between Occident and Orient is a relationship of power, of domination, of varying degrees of a complex hegemony, and is quite accurately indicated in the title of K. M. Panikkar's classic *Asia and Western Dominance*.[2] The Orient was Orientalized not only because it was discovered to be "Oriental" in all those ways considered commonplace by an average nineteenth-century European, but also because it *could be*—that is, submitted to being—*made* Oriental. There is very little consent to be found, for example, in the fact that Flaubert's encounter with an Egyptian courtesan produced a widely influential model of the Oriental woman; she never spoke of herself, she never represented her emotions, presence, or history. *He* spoke for and represented her. He was foreign, comparatively wealthy, male, and these were historical facts of domination that allowed him not only to possess Kuchuk Hanem physically but to speak for her and tell his readers in what way she was "typically Oriental." My argument is that Flaubert's situation of strength in relation to Kuchuk Hanem was not an isolated instance. It fairly stands for the pattern of relative strength between East and West, and the discourse about the Orient that it enabled.

This brings us to a third qualification. One ought never to assume that the structure of Orientalism is nothing more than a structure of lies or of myths which, were the truth about them to be told, would simply blow away. I myself believe that Orientalism is more particularly valuable as a sign of European-Atlantic power over the Orient than it is as a veridic discourse about the Orient (which is what, in its academic or scholarly form, it claims to be). Nevertheless, what we must respect and try to grasp is the sheer knitted-together strength of Orientalist discourse, its very close ties to the enabling socio-economic and political institutions, and its redoubtable durability. After all, any system of ideas that can remain unchanged as teachable wisdom (in academies, books, congresses, universities, foreign-service institutes) from the period of Ernest Renan in the late 1840s until the present in the United States must be something more formidable than a mere collection of lies. Orientalism, therefore, is not an airy European fantasy about the Orient, but a created body of theory and practice in which, for many generations, there has been a considerable material investment. Continued investment made Orientalism, as a system of knowledge about the Orient, an accepted grid for filtering through the Orient into Western consciousness, just as that same investment multiplied—indeed, made truly productive—the statements proliferating out from Orientalism into the general culture.

Gramsci has made the useful analytic distinction between civil and political society in which the former is made up of voluntary (or at least rational and noncoercive) affiliations like schools, families, and unions, the latter of state institutions (the army, the police, the central bureaucracy) whose role in the polity is direct domination. Culture, of course, is to be found operating within civil society, where the influence of ideas, of institutions, and of other persons works not through domination but by what Gramsci calls consent. In any society not totalitarian, then, certain cultural forms predominate over others, just as certain ideas are more influential than others; the form of this cultural leadership is what Gramsci has identified as *hegemony*, an indispensable concept for any understanding of cultural life in the industrial West. It is hegemony, or rather the result of cultural hegemony at work, that gives Orientalism the durability and the strength I have been speaking about so far. Orientalism is never far from what Denys Hay has called the idea of Europe,[3] a collective notion identifying "us" Europeans as against all "those" non-Europeans, and indeed it can be argued that the major component in European culture is precisely what made that culture hegemonic both in and outside Europe: the idea of European identity as a superior one in comparison with all the non-European peoples and cultures. There is in addition the hegemony of European ideas about the Orient, themselves reiterating European superiority over Oriental backwardness, usually overriding the possibility that a more independent, or more skeptical, thinker might have had different views on the matter.

In a quite constant way, Orientalism depends for its strategy on this flexible *positional* superiority, which puts the Westerner in a whole series of possible relationships with the Orient without ever losing him the relative upper hand. And why should it have been otherwise, especially during the period of extraordinary European ascendancy from the late Renaissance to the present? The scientist, the scholar, the missionary, the trader, or the soldier was in, or thought about, the Orient because he *could be there*, or could think about it, with very little resistance on the Orient's part. Under the general heading of knowledge of the Orient, and within the umbrella of Western hegemony over the Orient during the period from the end of the eighteenth century, there emerged a complex Orient suitable for study in the academy, for display in the museum, for reconstruction in the colonial office, for theoretical illustration in anthropological, biological, linguistic, racial, and historical theses about mankind and the universe, for instances of economic and sociological theories of development, revolution, cultural personality, national or religious character. Additionally, the imaginative examination of things Oriental was based more or less exclusively upon a sovereign Western consciousness out of whose unchallenged centrality an Oriental world emerged, first according to general ideas about who or what was an Oriental, then according to a detailed logic governed not simply by empirical reality but by a battery of desires, repressions, investments, and projections. If we can point to great Orientalist works of genuine scholarship like Silvestre de Sacy's *Chrestomathie arabe* or Edward William Lane's *Account of the Manners and Customs of the Modern Egyptians*, we need also to note that Renan's and Gobineau's racial ideas came out of the same impulse, as did a great many Victorian pornographic novels (see the analysis by Steven Marcus of "The Lustful Turk"[4]).

And yet, one must repeatedly ask oneself whether what matters in Orientalism is the general group of ideas overriding the mass of material—about which who could deny that they were shot through with doctrines of European superiority, various kinds of racism, imperialism, and the like, dogmatic views of "the Oriental" as a kind of ideal and unchanging abstraction?—or the much more varied work produced by almost uncountable individual writers, whom one would take up as individual instances of authors dealing with the Orient. In a sense the two alternatives, general and particular, are really two perspectives on the same material: in both instances one would have to deal with pioneers in the field like William Jones, with great artists like Nerval or Flaubert. And why would it not be possible to employ both perspectives together, or one after the other? Isn't there an obvious danger of distortion (of precisely the kind that academic Orientalism has always been prone to) if either too general or too specific a level of description is maintained systematically?

My two fears are distortion and inaccuracy, or rather the kind of inaccuracy produced by too dogmatic a generality and too positivistic a localized focus. In trying to deal with these problems I have tried to deal with three main aspects of my own contemporary reality that seem to me to point the way out of the methodological or perspectival difficulties I have been discussing, difficulties that might force one, in the first instance, into writing a coarse polemic on so unacceptably general a level of description as not to be worth the effort, or in the second instance, into writing so detailed and atomistic a series of analyses as to lose all track of the general lines of force informing the field, giving it its special cogency. How then to recognize individuality and to reconcile it with its intelligent, and by no means passive or merely dictatorial, general and hegemonic context?

III

I mentioned three aspects of my contemporary reality: I must explain and briefly discuss them now, so that it can be seen how I was led to a particular course of research and writing.

1. *The distinction between pure and political knowledge*. It is very easy to argue that knowledge about Shakespeare or Wordsworth is not political whereas knowledge about contemporary China or the Soviet Union is. My own formal and professional designation is that of "humanist," a title which indicates the humanities as my field and therefore the unlikely eventuality that there might be anything political about what I do in that field. Of course, all these labels and terms are quite unnuanced as I use them here, but the general truth of what I am pointing to is, I think, widely held. One reason for saying that a humanist who writes about Wordsworth, or an editor whose speciality is Keats, is not involved in anything political is that what he does seems to have no direct political effect upon reality in the everyday sense. A scholar whose field is Soviet economics works in a highly charged area where there is much government interest, and what he might produce in the way of studies or proposals will be taken up by policymakers, government officials, institutional economists, intelligence experts. The distinction between "humanists" and persons whose work has policy implications, or political significance, can be broadened further by saying that the former's ideological color is a matter of incidental importance to politics (although possibly of great moment to his colleagues in the field, who may object to his Stalinism or fascism or too easy liberalism), whereas the ideology of the latter is woven directly into his material—indeed, economics, politics, and sociology in the modern academy are ideological sciences—and therefore taken for granted as being "political."

Nevertheless the determining impingement on most knowledge produced in the contemporary West (and here I speak mainly about the United States) is that it be nonpolitical, that is, scholarly, academic, impartial, above partisan or small-minded doctrinal belief. One can have no quarrel with such an ambition in theory, perhaps, but in practice the reality is much more problematic. No one has ever devised a method for detaching the scholar from the circumstances of life, from the fact of his involvement (conscious or unconscious) with a class, a set of beliefs, a social position, or from the mere activity of being a member of a society. These continue to bear on what he does professionally, even though naturally enough his research and its fruits do attempt to reach a level of relative freedom from the inhibitions and the restrictions of brute, everyday reality. For there is such a thing as knowledge that is less, rather than more, partial than the individual (with his entangling and distracting life circumstances) who produces it. Yet this knowledge is not therefore automatically nonpolitical.

Whether discussions of literature or of classical philology are fraught with—or have unmediated—political significance is a very large question that I have tried to treat in some detail elsewhere.[5] What I am interested in doing now is suggesting how the general liberal consensus that "true" knowledge is fundamentally nonpolitical (and conversely, that overtly political knowledge is not "true" knowledge) obscures the highly if obscurely organized political circumstances obtaining when knowledge is produced. No one is helped in understanding this today when the adjective "political" is used as a label to discredit any work for daring to violate the protocol of pretended suprapolitical objectivity. We may say, first, that civil society recognizes a gradation of political importance in the various fields of knowledge. To some extent the political importance given a field comes from the possibility of its direct translation into economic terms; but to a greater extent political importance comes from the closeness of a field to ascertainable sources of power in political society. Thus an economic study of long-term Soviet energy potential and its effect on military capability is likely to be commissioned by the Defense Department, and thereafter to acquire a kind of political status impossible for a study of Tolstoi's early fiction financed in part by a foundation. Yet both works belong in what civil society acknowledges to be a similar field, Russian studies, even though one work may be done by a very conservative economist, the other by a radical literary historian. My point here is that "Russia" as a general subject matter has political priority over nicer distinctions such as "economics" and "literary history," because political society in Gramsci's sense reaches into such realms of civil society as the academy and saturates them with significance of direct concern to it.

I do not want to press all this any further on general theoretical grounds: it seems to me that the value and credibility of my case can be demonstrated by being much more specific, in the way, for example, Noam Chomsky has studied the instrumental connection between the Vietnam War and the notion of objective scholarship as it was applied to cover state-sponsored military research.[6] Now because Britain, France, and recently the United States are imperial powers, their political societies impart to their civil societies a sense of urgency, a direct political infusion as it were, where and whenever matters pertaining to their imperial interests abroad are concerned. I doubt that it is controversial, for example, to say that an Englishman in India or Egypt in the later nineteenth century took an interest in those countries that was never far from their status in his mind as British colonies. To say this may seem quite different from saying that all academic know-ledge about India and Egypt is somehow tinged and impressed with, violated by, the gross political fact—and yet *that is what I am saying* in this study of Orientalism. For if it is true that no production of knowledge in the human sciences can ever ignore or disclaim its author's involvement as a human subject in his own circum-stances, then it must also be true that for a European or American studying the Orient there can be no disclaiming the main circumstances of *his* actuality: that he comes up against the Orient as a European or American first, as an individual second. And to be a European or an American in such a situation is by no means an inert fact. It meant and means being aware, however dimly, that one belongs to a power with definite interests in the Orient, and more important, that one belongs to a part of the earth with a definite history of involvement in the Orient almost since the time of Homer.

Put in this way, these political actualities are still too undefined and general to be really interesting. Anyone would agree to them without necessarily agreeing also that they mattered very much, for instance, to Flaubert as he wrote *Salammbô*, or to H. A. R. Gibb as he wrote *Modern Trends in Islam*. The trouble is that there is too great a distance between the big dominating fact, as I have described it, and the details of everyday life that govern the minute discipline of a novel or a scholarly text as each is being written. Yet if we eliminate from the start any notion that "big" facts like imperial domination can be applied mechanically and deterministic-ally to such complex matters as culture and ideas, then we will begin to approach an interesting kind of study. My idea is that European and then American interest in the Orient was political according to some of the obvious historical accounts of it that I have given here, but that it was the culture that created that interest, that acted dynamically along with brute political, economic, and military rationales to make the Orient the varied and complicated place that it obviously was in the field I call Orientalism.

Therefore, Orientalism is not a mere political subject matter or field that is reflected passively by culture, scholarship, or institutions; nor is it a large and diffuse collection of texts about the Orient; nor is it representative and expressive of some nefarious "Western" imperialist plot to hold down the "Oriental" world. It is rather a *distribution* of geopolitical awareness into aesthetic, scholarly, eco-nomic, sociological, historical, and philological texts; it is an *elaboration* not only of a basic geographical distinction (the world is made up of two unequal halves, Orient and Occident) but also of a whole series of "interests" which, by such means as scholarly discovery, philological reconstruction, psychological analysis, landscape and sociological description, it not only creates but also maintains; it *is*, rather than expresses, a certain *will* or *intention* to understand, in some cases to control, manipulate, even to incorporate, what is a manifestly different (or alterna-tive and novel) world; it is, above all, a discourse that is by no means in direct, corresponding relationship with political power in the raw, but rather is produced and exists in an uneven exchange with various kinds of power, shaped to a degree by the exchange with power political (as with a colonial or imperial establish-ment), power intellectual (as with reigning sciences like comparative linguistics or anatomy, or any of the modern policy sciences), power cultural (as with ortho-doxies and canons of taste, texts, values), power moral (as with ideas about what "we" do and what "they" cannot do or understand as "we" do). Indeed, my real argument is that Orientalism is—and does not simply represent—a considerable dimension of modern political-intellectual culture, and as such has less to do with the Orient than it does with "our" world.

Because Orientalism is a cultural and a political fact, then, it does not exist in some archival vacuum; quite the contrary, I think it can be shown that what is thought, said, or even done about the Orient follows (perhaps occurs within) certain distinct and intellectually knowable lines. Here too a considerable degree of nuance and elaboration can be seen working as between the broad superstructural pressures and the details of composition, the facts of textuality. Most humanistic scholars are, I think, perfectly happy with the notion that texts exist in contexts, that there is such a thing as intertextuality, that the pressures of conventions, predecessors, and rhetorical styles limit what Walter Benjamin once called the "overtaxing of the productive person in the name of . . . the principle of 'creativ-ity,'" in which the poet is believed on his own, and out of his pure mind, to have brought forth his work.[7] Yet there is a reluctance to allow that political, insti-tutional, and ideological constraints act in the same manner on the individual author. A humanist will believe it to be an interesting fact to any interpreter of Balzac that he was influenced in the *Comédie humaine* by the conflict between

Geoffroy Saint-Hilaire and Cuvier, but the same sort of pressure on Balzac of deeply reactionary monarchism is felt in some vague way to demean his literary "genius" and therefore to be less worth serious study. Similarly—as Harry Bracken has been tirelessly showing—philosophers will conduct their discussions of Locke, Hume, and empiricism without ever taking into account that there is an explicit connection in these classic writers between their "philosophic" doctrines and racial theory, justifications of slavery, or arguments for colonial exploitation.[8] These are common enough ways by which contemporary scholarship keeps itself pure.

Perhaps it is true that most attempts to rub culture's nose in the mud of politics have been crudely iconoclastic; perhaps also the social interpretation of literature in my own field has simply not kept up with the enormous technical advances in detailed textual analysis. But there is no getting away from the fact that literary studies in general, and American Marxist theorists in particular, have avoided the effort of seriously bridging the gap between the superstructural and the base levels in textual, historical scholarship; on another occasion I have gone so far as to say that the literary-cultural establishment as a whole has declared the serious study of imperialism and culture off limits.[9] For Orientalism brings one up directly against that question—that is, to realizing that political imperialism governs an entire field of study, imagination, and scholarly institutions—in such a way as to make its avoidance an intellectual and historical impossibility. Yet there will always remain the perennial escape mechanism of saying that a literary scholar and a philosopher, for example, are trained in literature and philosophy respectively, not in politics or ideological analysis. In other words, the specialist argument can work quite effectively to block the larger and, in my opinion, the more intellectually serious perspective.

Here it seems to me there is a simple two-part answer to be given, at least so far as the study of imperialism and culture (or Orientalism) is concerned. In the first place, nearly every nineteenth-century writer (and the same is true enough of writers in earlier periods) was extraordinarily well aware of the fact of empire: this is a subject not very well studied, but it will not take a modern Victorian specialist long to admit that liberal cultural heroes like John Stuart Mill, Arnold, Carlyle, Newman, Macaulay, Ruskin, George Eliot, and even Dickens had definite views on race and imperialism, which are quite easily to be found at work in their writing. So even a specialist must deal with the knowledge that Mill, for example, made it clear in *On Liberty* and *Representative Government* that his views there could not be applied to India (he was an India Office functionary for a good deal of his life, after all) because the Indians were civilizationally, if not racially, inferior. The same kind of paradox is to be found in Marx, as I try to show in this book. In the second place, to believe that politics in the form of imperialism bears upon the production of literature, scholarship, social theory, and history writing is by no means equivalent to saying that culture is therefore a demeaned or denigrated thing. Quite the contrary: my whole point is to say that we can better understand the persistence and the durability of saturating hegemonic systems like culture when we realize that their internal constraints upon writers and thinkers were *productive*, not unilaterally inhibiting. It is this idea that Gramsci, certainly, and Foucault and Raymond Williams in their very different ways have been trying to illustrate. Even one or two pages by Williams on "the uses of the Empire" in *The*

Long Revolution tell us more about nineteenth-century cultural richness than many volumes of hermetic textual analyses.[10]

Therefore I study Orientalism as a dynamic exchange between individual authors and the large political concerns shaped by the three great empires—British, French, American—in whose intellectual and imaginative territory the writing was produced. What interests me most as a scholar is not the gross political verity but the detail, as indeed what interests us in someone like Lane or Flaubert or Renan is not the (to him) indisputable truth that Occidentals are superior to Orientals, but the profoundly worked over and modulated evidence of his detailed work within the very wide space opened up by that truth. One need only remember that Lane's *Manners and Customs of the Modern Egyptians* is a classic of historical and anthropological observation because of its style, its enormously intelligent and brilliant details, not because of its simple reflection of racial superiority, to understand what I am saying here.

The kind of political questions raised by Orientalism, then, are as follows: What other sorts of intellectual, aesthetic, scholarly, and cultural energies went into the making of an imperialist tradition like the Orientalist one? How did philology, lexicography, history, biology, political and economic theory, novel-writing, and lyric poetry come to the service of Orientalism's broadly imperialist view of the world? What changes, modulations, refinements, even revolutions take place within Orientalism? What is the meaning of originality, of continuity, of individuality, in this context? How does Orientalism transmit or reproduce itself from one epoch to another? In fine, how can we treat the cultural, historical phenomenon of Orientalism as a kind of *willed human work*—not of mere unconditioned ratiocination—in all its historical complexity, detail, and worth without at the same time losing sight of the alliance between cultural work, political tendencies, the state, and the specific realities of domination? Governed by such concerns a humanistic study can responsibly address itself to politics *and* culture. But this is not to say that such a study establishes a hard-and-fast rule about the relationship between knowledge and politics. My argument is that each humanistic investigation must formulate the nature of that connection in the specific context of the study, the subject matter, and its historical circumstances.

2. *The methodological question.* In a previous book I gave a good deal of thought and analysis to the methodological importance for work in the human sciences of finding and formulating a first step, a point of departure, a beginning principle.[11] A major lesson I learned and tried to present was that there is no such thing as a merely given, or simply available, starting point: beginnings have to be made for each project in such a way as to *enable* what follows from them. Nowhere in my experience has the difficulty of this lesson been more consciously lived (with what success—or failure—I cannot really say) than in this study of Orientalism. The idea of beginning, indeed the act of beginning, necessarily involves an act of delimitation by which something is cut out of a great mass of material, separated from the mass, and made to stand for, as well as be, a starting point, a beginning; for the student of texts one such notion of inaugural delimitation is Louis Althusser's idea of the *problematic*, a specific determinate unity of a text, or group of texts, which is something given rise to by analysis.[12] Yet in the case of Orientalism (as opposed to the case of Marx's texts, which is what Althusser studies) there is

not simply the problem of finding a point of departure, or problematic, but also the question of designating which texts, authors, and periods are the ones best suited for study.

It has seemed to me foolish to attempt an encyclopedic narrative history of Orientalism, first of all because if my guiding principle was to be "the European idea of the Orient" there would be virtually no limit to the material I would have had to deal with; second, because the narrative model itself did not suit my descriptive and political interests; third, because in such books as Raymond Schwab's *La Renaissance orientale*, Johann Fück's *Die Arabischen Studien in Europa bis in den Anfang des 20. Jahrhunderts*, and more recently, Dorothee Metlitzki's *The Matter of Araby in Medieval England*[13] there already exist encyclopedic works on certain aspects of the European-Oriental encounter such as make the critic's job, in the general political and intellectual context I sketched above, a different one.

There still remained the problem of cutting down a very fat archive to manageable dimensions, and more important, outlining something in the nature of an intellectual order within that group of texts without at the same time following a mindlessly chronological order. My starting point therefore has been the British, French, and American experience of the Orient taken as a unit, what made that experience possible by way of historical and intellectual background, what the quality and character of the experience has been. For reasons I shall discuss presently I limited that already limited (but still inordinately large) set of questions to the Anglo-French-American experience of the Arabs and Islam, which for almost a thousand years together stood for the Orient. Immediately upon doing that, a large part of the Orient seemed to have been eliminated—India, Japan, China, and other sections of the Far East—not because these regions were not important (they obviously have been) but because one could discuss Europe's experience of the Near Orient, or of Islam, apart from its experience of the Far Orient. Yet at certain moments of that general European history of interest in the East, particular parts of the Orient like Egypt, Syria, and Arabia cannot be discussed without also studying Europe's involvement in the more distant parts, of which Persia and India are the most important; a notable case in point is the connection between Egypt and India so far as eighteenth- and nineteenth-century Britain was concerned. Similarly the French role in deciphering the Zend-Avesta, the pre-eminence of Paris as a center of Sanskrit studies during the first decade of the nineteenth century, the fact that Napoleon's interest in the Orient was contingent upon his sense of the British role in India: all these Far Eastern interests directly influenced French interest in the Near East, Islam, and the Arabs.

Britain and France dominated the Eastern Mediterranean from about the end of the seventeenth century on. Yet my discussion of that domination and systematic interest does not do justice to (*a*) the important contributions to Orientalism of Germany, Italy, Russia, Spain, and Portugal and (*b*) the fact that one of the important impulses toward the study of the Orient in the eighteenth century was the revolution in Biblical studies stimulated by such variously interesting pioneers as Bishop Lowth, Eichhorn, Herder, and Michaelis. In the first place, I had to focus rigorously upon the British-French and later the American material because it seemed inescapably true not only that Britain and France were the pioneer nations in the Orient and in Oriental studies, but that these vanguard positions were held by virtue of the two greatest colonial networks in pre-twentieth-century history; the American Oriental position since World War II has fit—I think, quite self-consciously—in the places excavated by the two earlier European powers. Then too, I believe that the sheer quality, consistency, and mass of British, French, and American writing on the Orient lifts it above the doubtless crucial work done in Germany, Italy, Russia, and elsewhere. But I think it is also true that the major steps in Oriental scholarship were first taken in either Britain or France, then elaborated upon by Germans. Silvestre de Sacy, for example, was not only the first modern and institutional European Orientalist, who worked on Islam, Arabic literature, the Druze religion, and Sassanid Persia; he was also the teacher of Champollion and of Franz Bopp, the founder of German comparative linguistics. A similar claim of priority and subsequent pre-eminence can be made for William Jones and Edward William Lane.

In the second place—and here the failings of my study of Orientalism are amply made up for—there has been some important recent work on the background in Biblical scholarship to the rise of what I have called modern Orientalism. The best and the most illuminatingly relevant is E. S. Shaffer's impressive *"Kubla Khan" and The Fall of Jerusalem*,[14] an indispensable study of the origins of Romanticism, and of the intellectual activity underpinning a great deal of what goes on in Coleridge, Browning, and George Eliot. To some degree Shaffer's work refines upon the outlines provided in Schwab, by articulating the material of relevance to be found in the German Biblical scholars and using that material to read, in an intelligent and always interesting way, the work of three major British writers. Yet what is missing in the book is some sense of the political as well as ideological edge given the Oriental material by the British and French writers I am principally concerned with; in addition, unlike Shaffer I attempt to elucidate subsequent developments in academic as well as literary Orientalism that bear on the connection between British and French Orientalism on the one hand and the rise of an explicitly colonial-minded imperialism on the other. Then too, I wish to show how all these earlier matters are reproduced more or less in American Orientalism after the Second World War.

Nevertheless there is a possibly misleading aspect to my study, where, aside from an occasional reference, I do not exhaustively discuss the German developments after the inaugural period dominated by Sacy. Any work that seeks to provide an understanding of academic Orientalism and pays little attention to scholars like Steinthal, Müller, Becker, Goldziher, Brockelmann, Nöldeke—to mention only a handful—needs to be reproached, and I freely reproach myself. I particularly regret not taking more account of the great scientific prestige that accrued to German scholarship by the middle of the nineteenth century, whose neglect was made into a denunciation of insular British scholars by George Eliot. I have in mind Eliot's unforgettable portrait of Mr. Casaubon in *Middlemarch*. One reason Casaubon cannot finish his Key to All Mythologies is, according to his young cousin Will Ladislaw, that he is unacquainted with German scholarship. For not only has Casaubon chosen a subject "as changing as chemistry: new discoveries are constantly making new points of view": he is undertaking a job similar to a refutation of Paracelsus because "he is not an Orientalist, you know."[15]

Eliot was not wrong in implying that by about 1830, which is when

Middlemarch is set, German scholarship had fully attained its European pre-eminence. Yet at no time in German scholarship during the first two-thirds of the nineteenth century could a close partnership have developed between Orientalists and a protracted, sustained *national* interest in the Orient. There was nothing in Germany to correspond to the Anglo-French presence in India, the Levant, North Africa. Moreover, the German Orient was almost exclusively a scholarly, or at least a classical, Orient: it was made the subject of lyrics, fantasies, and even novels, but it was never actual, the way Egypt and Syria were actual for Chateaubriand, Lane, Lamartine, Burton, Disraeli, or Nerval. There is some significance in the fact that the two most renowned German works on the Orient, Goethe's *Westöstlicher Diwan* and Friedrich Schlegel's *Über die Sprache und Weisheit der Indier*, were based respectively on a Rhine journey and on hours spent in Paris libraries. What German Oriental scholarship did was to refine and elaborate techniques whose application was to texts, myths, ideas, and languages almost literally gathered from the Orient by imperial Britain and France.

Yet what German Orientalism had in common with Anglo-French and later American Orientalism was a kind of intellectual *authority* over the Orient within Western culture. This authority must in large part be the subject of any description of Orientalism, and it is so in this study. Even the name *Orientalism* suggests a serious, perhaps ponderous style of expertise; when I apply it to modern American social scientists (since they do not call themselves Orientalists, my use of the word is anomalous), it is to draw attention to the way Middle East experts can still draw on the vestiges of Orientalism's intellectual position in nineteenth-century Europe.

There is nothing mysterious or natural about authority. It is formed, irradiated, disseminated; it is instrumental, it is persuasive; it has status, it establishes canons of taste and value; it is virtually indistinguishable from certain ideas it dignifies as true, and from traditions, perceptions, and judgments it forms, transmits, reproduces. Above all, authority can, indeed must, be analyzed. All these attributes of authority apply to Orientalism, and much of what I do in this study is to describe both the historical authority in and the personal authorities of Orientalism.

My principal methodological devices for studying authority here are what can be called *strategic location*, which is a way of describing the author's position in a text with regard to the Oriental material he writes about, and *strategic formation*, which is a way of analyzing the relationship between texts and the way in which groups of texts, types of texts, even textual genres, acquire mass, density, and referential power among themselves and thereafter in the culture at large. I use the notion of strategy simply to identify the problem every writer on the Orient has faced: how to get hold of it, how to approach it, how not to be defeated or overwhelmed by its sublimity, its scope, its awful dimensions. Everyone who writes about the Orient must locate himself vis-à-vis the Orient; translated into his text, this location includes the kind of narrative voice he adopts, the type of structure he builds, the kinds of images, themes, motifs that circulate in his text—all of which add up to deliberate ways of addressing the reader, containing the Orient, and finally, representing it or speaking in its behalf. None of this takes place in the abstract, however. Every writer on the Orient (and this is true even of

Homer) assumes some Oriental precedent, some previous knowledge of the Orient, to which he refers and on which he relies. Additionally, each work on the Orient *affiliates* itself with other works, with audiences, with institutions, with the Orient itself. The ensemble of relationships between works, audiences, and some particular aspects of the Orient therefore constitutes an analyzable formation—for example, that of philological studies, of anthologies of extracts from Oriental literature, of travel books, of Oriental fantasies—whose presence in time, in discourse, in institutions (schools, libraries, foreign services) gives it strength and authority.

It is clear, I hope, that my concern with authority does not entail analysis of what lies hidden in the Orientalist text, but analysis rather of the text's surface, its exteriority to what it describes. I do not think that this idea can be over-emphasized. Orientalism is premised upon exteriority, that is, on the fact that the Orientalist, poet or scholar, makes the Orient speak, describes the Orient, renders its mysteries plain for and to the West. He is never concerned with the Orient except as the first cause of what he says. What he says and writes, by virtue of the fact that it is said or written, is meant to indicate that the Orientalist is outside the Orient, both as an existential and as a moral fact. The principal product of this exteriority is of course representation: as early as Aeschylus's play *The Persians* the Orient is transformed from a very far distant and often threatening Otherness into figures that are relatively familiar (in Aeschylus's case, grieving Asiatic women). The dramatic immediacy of representation in *The Persians* obscures the fact that the audience is watching a highly artificial enactment of what a non-Oriental has made into a symbol for the whole Orient. My analysis of the Orientalist text therefore places emphasis on the evidence, which is by no means invisible, for such representations *as representations*, not as "natural" depictions of the Orient. This evidence is found just as prominently in the so-called truthful text (histories, philological analyses, political treatises) as in the avowedly artistic (i.e., openly imaginative) text. The things to look at are style, figures of speech, setting, narrative devices, historical and social circumstances, *not* the correctness of the representation nor its fidelity to some great original. The exteriority of the representation is always governed by some version of the truism that if the Orient could represent itself, it would; since it cannot, the representation does the job, for the West, and *faute de mieux*, for the poor Orient. "Sie können sich nicht vertreten, sie müssen vertreten werden," as Marx wrote in *The Eighteenth Brumaire of Louis Bonaparte*.

Another reason for insisting upon exteriority is that I believe it needs to be made clear about cultural discourse and exchange within a culture that what is commonly circulated by it is not "truth" but representations. It hardly needs to be demonstrated again that language itself is a highly organized and encoded system, which employs many devices to express, indicate, exchange messages and information, represent, and so forth. In any instance of at least written language, there is no such thing as a delivered presence, but a *re-presence*, or a representation. The value, efficacy, strength, apparent veracity of a written statement about the Orient therefore relies very little, and cannot instrumentally depend, on the Orient as such. On the contrary, the written statement is a presence to the reader by virtue of its having excluded, displaced, made supererogatory any such *real thing* as "the Orient." Thus all of Orientalism stands forth and away from the Orient: that

Orientalism makes sense at all depends more on the West than on the Orient, and this sense is directly indebted to various Western techniques of representation that make the Orient visible, clear, "there" in discourse about it. And these representations rely upon institutions, traditions, conventions, agreed-upon codes of understanding for their effects, not upon a distant and amorphous Orient.

The difference between representations of the Orient before the last third of the eighteenth century and those after it (that is, those belonging to what I call modern Orientalism) is that the range of representation expanded enormously in the later period. It is true that after William Jones and Anquetil-Duperron, and after Napoleon's Egyptian expedition, Europe came to know the Orient more scientifically, to live in it with greater authority and discipline than ever before. But what mattered to Europe was the expanded scope and the much greater refinement given its techniques for receiving the Orient. When around the turn of the eighteenth century the Orient definitively revealed the age of its languages—thus outdating Hebrew's divine pedigree—it was a group of Europeans who made the discovery, passed it on to other scholars, and preserved the discovery in the new science of Indo-European philology. A new powerful science for viewing the linguistic Orient was born, and with it, as Foucault has shown in *The Order of Things*, a whole web of related scientific interests. Similarly William Beckford, Byron, Goethe, and Hugo restructured the Orient by their art and made its colors, lights, and people visible through their images, rhythms, and motifs. At most, the "real" Orient provoked a writer to his vision; it very rarely guided it.

Orientalism responded more to the culture that produced it than to its putative object, which was also produced by the West. Thus the history of Orientalism has both an internal consistency and a highly articulated set of relationships to the dominant culture surrounding it. My analyses consequently try to show the field's shape and internal organization, its pioneers, patriarchal authorities, canonical texts, doxological ideas, exemplary figures, its followers, elaborators, and new authorities; I try also to explain how Orientalism borrowed and was frequently informed by "strong" ideas, doctrines, and trends ruling the culture. Thus there was (and is) a linguistic Orient, a Freudian Orient, a Spenglerian Orient, a Darwinian Orient, a racist Orient—and so on. Yet never has there been such a thing as a pure, or unconditional, Orient; similarly, never has there been a nonmaterial form of Orientalism, much less something so innocent as an "idea" of the Orient. In this underlying conviction and in its ensuing methodological consequences do I differ from scholars who study the history of ideas. For the emphases and the executive form, above all the material effectiveness, of statements made by Orientalist discourse are possible in ways that any hermetic history of ideas tends completely to scant. Without those emphases and that material effectiveness Orientalism would be just another idea, whereas it is and was much more than that. Therefore I set out to examine not only scholarly works but also works of literature, political tracts, journalistic texts, travel books, religious and philological studies. In other words, my hybrid perspective is broadly historical and "anthropological," given that I believe all texts to be worldly and circumstantial in (of course) ways that vary from genre to genre, and from historical period to historical period.

Yet unlike Michel Foucault, to whose work I am greatly indebted, I do believe in the determining imprint of individual writers upon the otherwise anonymous collective body of texts constituting a discursive formation like Orientalism. The unity of the large ensemble of texts I analyze is due in part to the fact that they frequently refer to each other: Orientalism is after all a system for citing works and authors. Edward William Lane's *Manners and Customs of the Modern Egyptians* was read and cited by such diverse figures as Nerval, Flaubert, and Richard Burton. He was an authority whose use was an imperative for anyone writing or thinking about the Orient, not just about Egypt: when Nerval borrows passages verbatim from *Modern Egyptians* it is to use Lane's authority to assist him in describing village scenes in Syria, not Egypt. Lane's authority and the opportunities provided for citing him discriminately as well as indiscriminately were there because Orientalism could give his text the kind of distributive currency that he acquired. There is no way, however, of understanding Lane's currency without also understanding the peculiar features of *his* text; this is equally true of Renan, Sacy, Lamartine, Schlegel, and a group of other influential writers. Foucault believes that in general the individual text or author counts for very little; empirically, in the case of Orientalism (and perhaps nowhere else) I find this not to be so. Accordingly my analyses employ close textual readings whose goal is to reveal the dialectic between individual text or writer and the complex collective formation to which his work is a contribution.

Yet even though it includes an ample selection of writers, this book is still far from a complete history or general account of Orientalism. Of this failing I am very conscious. The fabric of as thick a discourse as Orientalism has survived and functioned in Western society because of its richness: all I have done is to describe parts of that fabric at certain moments, and merely to suggest the existence of a larger whole, detailed, interesting, dotted with fascinating figures, texts, and events. I have consoled myself with believing that this book is one installment of several, and hope there are scholars and critics who might want to write others. There is still a general essay to be written on imperialism and culture; other studies would go more deeply into the connection between Orientalism and pedagogy, or into Italian, Dutch, German, and Swiss Orientalism, or into the dynamic between scholarship and imaginative writing, or into the relationship between administrative ideas and intellectual discipline. Perhaps the most important task of all would be to undertake studies in contemporary alternatives to Orientalism, to ask how one can study other cultures and peoples from a libertarian, or a nonrepressive and nonmanipulative, perspective. But then one would have to rethink the whole complex problem of knowledge and power. These are all tasks left embarrassingly incomplete in this study.

The last, perhaps self-flattering, observation on method that I want to make here is that I have written this study with several audiences in mind. For students of literature and criticism, Orientalism offers a marvelous instance of the interrelations between society, history, and textuality; moreover, the cultural role played by the Orient in the West connects Orientalism with ideology, politics, and the logic of power, matters of relevance, I think, to the literary community. For contemporary students of the Orient, from university scholars to policymakers, I have written with two ends in mind: one, to present their intellectual genealogy to them in a way that has not been done; two, to criticize—with the hope of stirring discussion—the often unquestioned assumptions on which their work for the most part depends. For the general reader, this study deals with matters that always compel attention, all of them connected not only with Western conceptions and treatments of the Other but also with the singularly important role played by Western culture in what Vico called the world of nations. Lastly, for readers in the so-called Third World, this study proposes itself as a step towards an understanding not so much of Western politics and of the non-Western world in those politics as of the *strength* of Western cultural discourse, a strength too often mistaken as merely decorative or "superstructural." My hope is to illustrate the formidable structure of cultural domination and, specifically for formerly colonized peoples, the dangers and temptations of employing this structure upon themselves or upon others.

The three long chapters and twelve shorter units into which this book is divided are intended to facilitate exposition as much as possible. Chapter One, "The Scope of Orientalism," draws a large circle around all the dimensions of the subject, both in terms of historical time and experiences and in terms of philosophical and political themes. Chapter Two, "Orientalist Structures and Restructures," attempts to trace the development of modern Orientalism by a broadly chronological description, and also by the description of a set of devices common to the work of important poets, artists, and scholars. Chapter Three, "Orientalism Now," begins where its predecessor left off, at around 1870. This is the period of great colonial expansion into the Orient, and it culminates in World War II. The very last section of Chapter Three characterizes the shift from British and French to American hegemony; I attempt there finally to sketch the present intellectual and social realities of Orientalism in the United States.

3. *The personal dimension.* In the *Prison Notebooks* Gramsci says: "The starting-point of critical elaboration is the consciousness of what one really is, and is 'knowing thyself' as a product of the historical process to date, which has deposited in you an infinity of traces, without leaving an inventory." The only available English translation inexplicably leaves Gramsci's comment at that, whereas in fact Gramsci's Italian text concludes by adding, "therefore it is imperative at the outset to compile such an inventory."[16]

Much of the personal investment in this study derives from my awareness of being an "Oriental" as a child growing up in two British colonies. All of my education, in those colonies (Palestine and Egypt) and in the United States, has been Western, and yet that deep early awareness has persisted. In many ways my study of Orientalism has been an attempt to inventory the traces upon me, the Oriental subject, of the culture whose domination has been so powerful a factor in the life of all Orientals. This is why for me the Islamic Orient has had to be the center of attention. Whether what I have achieved is the inventory prescribed by Gramsci is not for me to judge, although I have felt it important to be conscious of trying to produce one. Along the way, as severely and as rationally as I have been able, I have tried to maintain a critical consciousness, as well as employing those instruments of historical, humanistic, and cultural research of which my education has made me the fortunate beneficiary. In none of that, however, have I ever lost hold of the cultural reality of, the personal involvement in having been constituted as, "an Oriental."

The historical circumstances making such a study possible are fairly complex, and I can only list them schematically here. Anyone resident in the West since the 1950s, particularly in the United States, will have lived through an era of extraordinary turbulence in the relations of East and West. No one will have failed to note how "East" has always signified danger and threat during this period, even as it has meant the traditional Orient as well as Russia. In the universities a growing establishment of area-studies programs and institutes has made the scholarly study of the Orient a branch of national policy. Public affairs in this country include a healthy interest in the Orient, as much for its strategic and economic importance as for its traditional exoticism. If the world has become immediately accessible to a Western citizen living in the electronic age, the Orient too has drawn nearer to him, and is now less a myth perhaps than a place crisscrossed by Western, especially American, interests.

One aspect of the electronic, postmodern world is that there has been a reinforcement of the stereotypes by which the Orient is viewed. Television, the films, and all the media's resources have forced information into more and more standardized molds. So far as the Orient is concerned, standardization and cultural stereotyping have intensified the hold of the nineteenth-century academic and imaginative demonology of "the mysterious Orient." This is nowhere more true than in the ways by which the Near East is grasped. Three things have contributed to making even the simplest perception of the Arabs and Islam into a highly politicized, almost raucous matter: one, the history of popular anti-Arab and anti-Islamic prejudice in the West, which is immediately reflected in the history of Orientalism; two, the struggle between the Arabs and Israeli Zionism, and its effects upon American Jews as well as upon both the liberal culture and the population at large; three, the almost total absence of any cultural position making it possible either to identify with or dispassionately to discuss the Arabs or Islam. Furthermore, it hardly needs saying that because the Middle East is now so identified with Great Power politics, oil economics, and the simple-minded dichotomy of freedom-loving, democratic Israel and evil, totalitarian, and terroristic Arabs, the chances of anything like a clear view of what one talks about in talking about the Near East are depressingly small.

My own experiences of these matters are in part what made me write this book. The life of an Arab Palestinian in the West, particularly in America, is disheartening. There exists here an almost unanimous consensus that politically he does not exist, and when it is allowed that he does, it is either as a nuisance or as an Oriental. The web of racism, cultural stereotypes, political imperialism, dehumanizing ideology holding in the Arab or the Muslim is very strong indeed, and it is this web which every Palestinian has come to feel as his uniquely punishing destiny. It has made matters worse for him to remark that no person academically involved with the Near East—no Orientalist, that is—has ever in the United States culturally and politically identified himself wholeheartedly with the Arabs; certainly there have been identifications on some level, but they have never taken an "acceptable" form as has liberal American identification with Zionism, and all too frequently they have been radically flawed by their association either with discredited political and economic interests (oil-company and State Department Arabists, for example) or with religion.

The nexus of knowledge and power creating "the Oriental" and in a sense obliterating him as a human being is therefore not for me an exclusively academic matter. Yet it is an *intellectual* matter of some very obvious importance. I have been able to put to use my humanistic and political concerns for the analysis and description of a very worldly matter, the rise, development, and consolidation of Orientalism. Too often literature and culture are presumed to be politically, even historically innocent; it has regularly seemed otherwise to me, and certainly my study of Orientalism has convinced me (and I hope will convince my literary colleagues) that society and literary culture can only be understood and studied together. In addition, and by an almost inescapable logic, I have found myself writing the history of a strange, secret sharer of Western anti-Semitism. That anti-Semitism and, as I have discussed it in its Islamic branch, Orientalism resemble each other very closely is a historical, cultural, and political truth that needs only to be mentioned to an Arab Palestinian for its irony to be perfectly understood. But what I should like also to have contributed here is a better understanding of the way cultural domination has operated. If this stimulates a new kind of dealing with the Orient, indeed if it eliminates the "Orient" and "Occident" altogether, then we shall have advanced a little in the process of what Raymond Williams has called the "unlearning" of "the inherent dominative mode."[17]

Notes

1   Thierry Desjardins, *Le Martyre du Liban* (Paris: Plon, 1976), p. 14.
2   K. M. Panikkar, *Asia and Western Dominance* (London: George Allen & Unwin, 1959).
3   Denys Hay, *Europe: The Emergence of an Idea*, 2nd ed. (Edinburgh: Edinburgh University Press, 1968).
4   Steven Marcus, *The Other Victorians: A Study of Sexuality and Pornography in Mid-Nineteenth Century England* (1966; reprint ed., New York: Bantam Books, 1967), pp. 200–19.
5   See my *Criticism Between Culture and System* (Cambridge, Mass.: Harvard University Press, forthcoming).
6   Principally in his *American Power and the New Mandarins: Historical and Political Essays* (New York: Pantheon Books, 1969) and *For Reasons of State* (New York: Pantheon Books, 1973).
7   Walter Benjamin, *Charles Baudelaire: A Lyric Poet in the Era of High Capitalism*, trans. Harry Zohn (London: New Left Books, 1973), p. 71.
8   Harry Bracken, "Essence, Accident and Race," *Hermathena* 116 (Winter 1973): 81–96.
9   In an interview published in *Diacritics* 6, no. 3 (Fall 1976): 38.
10   Raymond Williams, *The Long Revolution* (London: Chatto & Windus, 1961), pp. 66–7.
11   In my *Beginnings: Intention and Method* (New York: Basic Books, 1975).
12   Louis Althusser, *For Marx*, trans. Ben Brewster (New York: Pantheon Books, 1969), pp. 65–7.
13   Raymond Schwab, *La Renaissance orientale* (Paris: Payot, 1950); Johann W. Fück, *Die Arabischen Studien in Europa bis in den Anjang des 20. Jahrhunderts* (Leipzig: Otto Harrassowitz, 1955); Dorothee Metlitzki, *The Matter of Araby in Medieval England* (New Haven, Conn.: Yale University Press, 1977).
14   E. S. Shaffer, *"Kubla Khan" and The Fall of Jerusalem: The Mythological School in Biblical Criticism and Secular Literature, 1770–1880* (Cambridge: Cambridge University Press, 1975).
15   George Eliot, *Middlemarch: A Study of Provincial Life* (1872; reprint ed., Boston: Houghton Mifflin Co., 1956), p. 164.

16   Antonio Gramsci, *The Prison Notebooks: Selections*, trans. and ed. Quintin Hoare and
      Geoffrey Nowell Smith (New York: International Publishers, 1971), p. 324. The full
      passage, unavailable in the Hoare and Smith translation, is to be found in Gramsci,
      Quaderni del Carcere, ed. Valentino Gerratana (Turin: Einaudi Editore, 1975), 2: 1363.
17   Raymond Williams, *Culture and Society, 1780–1950* (London: Chatto & Windus, 1958),
      p. 376.

Suggestions for further reading

Kabbani, Rana, *Imperial Fictions: Europe's Myths of Orient*, rev. ed., London: Pandora,
      1994.
Said, Edward, 'Orientalism Reconsidered', *Cultural Critique*, 1985, vol. 1, 89–107.
Young, Robert, *White Mythologies: Writing History and the West*, London and New
      York: Routledge, 1990.

Chapter 18

Stuart Hall

'ENCODING/DECODING', 1980

TRADITIONALLY, MASS-COMMUNICATIONS research has conceptualized the process of communication in terms of a circulation circuit or loop. This model has been criticized for its linearity – sender/message/receiver – for its concentration on the level of message exchange and for the absence of a structured conception of the different moments as a complex structure of relations. But it is also possible (and useful) to think of this process in terms of a structure produced and sustained through the articulation of linked but distinctive moments – production, circulation, distribution/consumption, reproduction. This would be to think of the process as a 'complex structure in dominance', sustained through the articulation of connected practices, each of which, however, retains its distinctiveness and has its own specific modality, its own forms and conditions of existence. This second approach, homologous to that which forms the skeleton of commodity production offered in Marx's *Grundrisse* and in *Capital*, has the added advantage of bringing out more sharply how a continuous circuit – production-distribution-production – can be sustained through a 'passage of forms'.[1] It also highlights the specificity of the forms in which the product of the process 'appears' in each moment, and thus what distinguishes discursive 'production' from other types of production in our society and in modern media systems.

The 'object' of these practices is meanings and messages in the form of sign-vehicles of a specific kind organized, like any form of communication or language, through the operation of codes within the syntagmatic chain of a discourse. The apparatuses, relations and practices of production thus issue, at a certain moment (the moment of 'production/circulation') in the form of symbolic vehicles constituted within the rules of 'language'. It is in this discursive form that the circulation of the 'product' takes place. The process thus requires, at the production end, its material instruments – its 'means' – as well as its own sets of social (production) relations – the organization and combination of practices within media apparatuses.

But it is in the *discursive* form that the circulation of the product takes place, as well as its distribution to different audiences. Once accomplished, the discourse must then be translated – transformed, again – into social practices if the circuit is to be both completed and effective. If no 'meaning' is taken, there can be no 'consumption'. If the meaning is not articulated in practice, it has no effect. The value of this approach is that while each of the moments, in articulation, is necessary to the circuit as a whole, no one moment can fully guarantee the next moment with which it is articulated. Since each has its specific modality and conditions of existence, each can constitute its own break or interruption of the 'passage of forms' on whose continuity the flow of effective production (that is, 'reproduction') depends.

Thus while in no way wanting to limit research to 'following only those leads which emerge from content analysis',[2] we must recognize that the discursive form of the message has a privileged position in the communicative exchange (from the viewpoint of circulation), and that the moments of 'encoding' and 'decoding', though only 'relatively autonomous' in relation to the communicative process as a whole, are *determinate* moments. A 'raw' historical event cannot, *in that form*, be transmitted by, say, a television newscast. Events can only be signified within the aural-visual forms of the televisual discourse. In the moment when a historical event passes under the sign of discourse, it is subject to all the complex formal 'rules' by which language signifies. To put it paradoxically, the event must become a 'story' before it can become a *communicative event*. In that moment the formal sub-rules of discourse are 'in dominance', without, of course, subordinating out of existence the historical event so signified, the social relations in which the rules are set to work or the social and political consequences of the event having been signified in this way. The 'message form' is the necessary 'form of appearance' of the event in its passage from source to receiver. Thus the transposition into and out of the 'message form' (or the mode of symbolic exchange) is not a random 'moment', which we can take up or ignore at our convenience. The 'message form' is a determinate moment; though, at another level, it comprises the surface movements of the communications system only and requires, at another stage, to be integrated into the social relations of the communication process as a whole, of which it forms only a part.

From this general perspective, we may crudely characterize the television communicative process as follows. The institutional structures of broadcasting, with their practices and networks of production, their organized relations and technical infrastructures, are required to produce a programme. Using the analogy of *Capital*, this is the 'labour process' in the discursive mode. Production, here, constructs the message. In one sense, then, the circuit begins here. Of course, the production process is not without its 'discursive' aspect: it, too, is framed throughout by meanings and ideas: knowledge-in-use concerning the routines of production, historically defined technical skills, professional ideologies, institutional knowledge, definitions and assumptions, assumptions about the audience and so on frame the constitution of the programme through this production structure. Further, though the production structures of television originate the television discourse, they do not constitute a closed system. They draw topics, treatments, agendas, events, personnel, images of the audience, 'definitions of the situation' from other sources and other discursive formations within the wider socio-cultural and political structure of which they are a differentiated part. Philip Elliott has expressed this point succinctly, within a more traditional framework, in his discussion of the way in which the audience is both the 'source' and the 'receiver' of the television message. Thus – to borrow Marx's terms – circulation and reception are, indeed, 'moments' of the production process in television and are reincorporated, via a number of skewed and structured 'feedbacks', into the production process itself. The consumption or reception of the television message is thus also itself a 'moment' of the production process in its larger sense, though the latter is 'predominant' because it is the 'point of departure for the realization' of the message. Production and reception of the television message are not, therefore, indentical, but they are related: they are differentiated moments within the totality formed by the social relations of the communicative process as a whole.

At a certain point, however, the broadcasting structures must yield encoded messages in the form of a meaningful discourse. The institution-societal relations of production must pass under the discursive rules of language for its product to be 'realized'. This initiates a further differentiated moment, in which the formal rules of discourse and language are in dominance. Before this message can have an 'effect' (however defined), satisfy a 'need' or be put to a 'use', it must first be appropriated as a meaningful discourse and be meaningfully decoded. It is this set of decoded meanings which 'have an effect', influence, entertain, instruct or persuade, with very complex perceptual, cognitive, emotional, ideological or behavioural consequences. In a 'determinate' moment the structure employs a code and yields a 'message': at another determinate moment the 'message', via its decodings, issues into the structure of social practices. We are now fully aware that this re-entry into the practices of audience reception and 'use' cannot be understood in simple behavioural terms. The typical processes identified in positivistic research on isolated elements – effects, uses, 'gratifications' – are themselves framed by structures of understanding, as well as being produced by social and economic relations, which shape their 'realization' at the reception end of the chain and which permit the meanings signified in the discourse to be transposed into practice or consciousness (to acquire social use value or political effectivity).

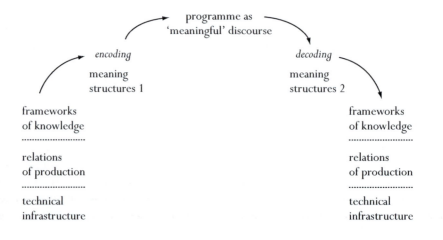

Clearly, what we have labelled in the diagram 'meaning structures 1' and 'meaning structures 2' may not be the same. They do not constitute an 'immediate identity'. The codes of encoding and decoding may not be perfectly symmetrical. The degrees of symmetry – that is, the degrees of 'understanding' and 'misunderstanding' in the communicative exchange – depend on the degrees of symmetry/ asymmetry (relations of equivalence) established between the positions of the 'personifications', encoder-producer and decoder-receiver. But this in turn depends on the degrees of identity/non-identity between the codes which perfectly or imperfectly transmit, interrupt or systematically distort what has been transmitted. The lack of fit between the codes has a great deal to do with the structural differences of relation and position between broadcasters and audiences, but it also has something to do with the asymmetry between the codes of 'source' and 'receiver' at the moment of transformation into and out of the discursive form. What are called 'distortions' or 'misunderstandings' arise precisely from the *lack of equivalence* between the two sides in the communicative exchange. Once again, this defines the 'relative autonomy', but 'determinateness', of the entry and exit of the message in its discursive moments.

The application of this rudimentary paradigm has already begun to transform our understanding of the older term, television 'content'. We are just beginning to see how it might also transform our understanding of audience reception, 'reading' and response as well. Beginnings and endings have been announced in communications research before, so we must be cautious. But there seems some ground for thinking that a new and exciting phase in so-called audience research, of a quite new kind, may be opening up. At either end of the communicative chain the use of the semiotic paradigm promises to dispel the lingering behaviourism which has dogged mass-media research for so long, especially in its approach to content. Though we know the television programme is not a behavioural input, like a tap on the knee cap, it seems to have been almost impossible for traditional researchers to conceptualize the communicative process without lapsing into one or other variant of low-flying behaviourism. We know, as Gerbner has remarked, that representations of violence on the TV screen 'are not violence but messages about violence':[3] but we have continued to research the question of violence, for example, as if we were unable to comprehend this epistemological distinction.

The televisual sign is a complex one. It is itself constituted by the combination of two types of discourse, visual and aural. Moreover, it is an iconic sign, in Peirce's terminology, because 'it possesses some of the properties of the thing represented'.[4] This is a point which has led to a great deal of confusion and has provided the site of intense controversy in the study of visual language. Since the visual discourse translates a three-dimensional world into two-dimensional planes, it cannot, of course, *be* the referent or concept it signifies. The dog in the film can bark but it cannot bite! Reality exists outside language, but it is constantly mediated by and through language: and what we can know and say has to be produced in and through discourse. Discursive 'knowledge' is the product not of the transparent representation of the 'real' in language but of the articulation of language on real relations and conditions. Thus there is no intelligible discourse without the operation of a code. Iconic signs are therefore coded signs too – even if the codes here work differently from those of other signs. There is no degree zero in language. Naturalism and 'realism' – the apparent fidelity of the representation to the thing or concept represented – is the result, the effect, of a certain specific articulation of language on the 'real'. It is the result of a discursive practice.

Certain codes may, of course, be so widely distributed in a specific language community or culture, and be learned at so early an age, that they appear not to be constructed – the effect of an articulation between sign and referent – but to be 'naturally' given. Simple visual signs appear to have achieved a 'near-universality' in this sense: though evidence remains that even apparently 'natural' visual codes are culture-specific. However, this does not mean that no codes have intervened; rather, that the codes have been profoundly *naturalized*. The operation of natural- ized codes reveals not the transparency and 'naturalness' of language but the depth, the habituation and the near-universality of the codes in use. They produce apparently 'natural' recognitions. This has the (ideological) effect of concealing the practices of coding which are present. But we must not be fooled by appearances. Actually, what naturalized codes demonstrate is the degree of habituation pro- duced when there is a fundamental alignment and reciprocity – an achieved equivalence – between the encoding and decoding sides of an exchange of mean- ings. The functioning of the codes on the decoding side will frequently assume the status of naturalized perceptions. This leads us to think that the visual sign for 'cow' actually *is* (rather than *represents*) the animal, cow. But if we think of the visual representation of a cow in a manual on animal husbandry – and, even more, of the linguistic sign 'cow' – we can see that both, in different degrees, are *arbitrary* with respect to the concept of the animal they represent. The articulation of an arbitrary sign – whether visual or verbal – with the concept of a referent is the product not of nature but of convention, and the conventionalism of discourses requires the intervention, the support, of codes. Thus Eco has argued that iconic signs 'look like objects in the real world because they reproduce the conditions (that is, the codes) of perception in the viewer'.[5] These 'conditions of perception' are, however, the result of a highly coded, even if virtually unconscious, set of operations – decodings. This is as true of the photographic or televisual image as it is of any other sign. Iconic signs are, however, particularly vulnerable to being 'read' as natural because visual codes of perception are very widely distributed and because this type of sign is less arbitrary than a linguistic sign: the linguistic sign, 'cow' possesses *none* of the properties of the thing represented, whereas the visual sign appears to possess *some* of those properties.

This may help us to clarify a confusion in current linguistic theory and to define precisely how some key terms are being used in this article. Linguistic theory frequently employs the distinction 'denotation' and 'connotation'. The term 'denotation' is widely equated with the literal meaning of a sign: because this literal meaning is almost universally recognized, especially when visual discourse is being employed, 'denotation' has often been confused with a literal transcription of 'reality' in language – and thus with a 'natural sign', one produced without the intervention of a code. 'Connotation', on the other hand, is employed simply to refer to less fixed and therefore more conventionalized and changeable, associative meanings, which clearly vary from instance to instance and therefore must depend on the intervention of codes.

We do *not* use the distinction – denotation/connotation – in this way. From our point of view, the distinction is an *analytic* one only. It is useful, in analysis, to be able to apply a rough rule of thumb which distinguishes those aspects of a sign which appear to be taken, in any language community at any point in time, as its 'literal' meaning (denotation) from the more associative meanings for the sign which it is possible to generate (connotation). But analytic distinctions must not be confused with distinctions in the real world. There will be very few instances in which signs organized in a discourse signify *only* their 'literal' (that is, near-universally consensualized) meaning. In actual discourse most signs will combine both the denotative and the connotative *aspects* (as redefined above). It may, then, be asked why we retain the distinction at all. It is largely a matter of analytic value. It is because signs appear to acquire their full ideological value – appear to be open to articulation with wider ideological discourses and meanings – at the level of their 'associative' meanings (that is, at the connotative level) – for here 'meanings' are *not* apparently fixed in natural perception (that is, they are not fully naturalized), and their fluidity of meaning and association can be more fully exploited and transformed.[6] So it is at the connotative *level* of the sign that situational ideologies alter and transform signification. At this level we can see more clearly the active intervention of ideologies in and on discourse: here, the sign is open to new accentuations and, in Vološinov's terms, enters fully into the struggle over meanings – the class struggle in language.[7] This does not mean that the denotative or 'literal' meaning is outside ideology. Indeed, we could say that its ideological value is strongly *fixed* – because it has become so fully universal and 'natural'. The terms 'denotation' and 'connotation', then, are merely useful analytic tools for distinguishing, in particular contexts, between not the presence/absence of ideology in language but the different levels at which ideologies and discourses intersect.[8]

The level of connotation of the visual sign, of its contextual reference and positioning in different discursive fields of meaning and association, is the point where *already coded* signs intersect with the deep semantic codes of a culture and take on additional, more active ideological dimensions. We might take an example from advertising discourse. Here, too, there is no 'purely denotative', and certainly no 'natural', representation. Every visual sign in advertising connotes a quality, situation, value or inference, which is present as an implication or implied meaning, depending on the connotational positioning. In Barthes's example, the sweater always signifies a 'warm garment' (denotation) and thus the activity/value of 'keeping warm'. But it is also possible, at its more connotative levels, to signify 'the coming of winter' or 'a cold day'. And, in the specialized sub-codes of fashion, sweater may also connote a fashionable style of *haute couture* or, alternatively, an informal style of dress. But set against the right visual background and positioned by the romantic sub-code, it may connote 'long autumn walk in the woods'.[9] Codes of this order clearly contract relations for the sign with the wider universe of ideologies in a society. These codes are the means by which power and ideology are made to signify in particular discourses. They refer signs to the 'maps of meaning' into which any culture is classified; and those 'maps of social reality' have the whole range of social meanings, practices, and usages, power and interest 'written in' to them. The connotative levels of signifiers, Barthes remarked, 'have a close communication with culture, knowledge, history, and it is through them, so to speak, that the environmental world invades the linguistic and semantic system. They are, if you like, the fragments of ideology'.[10]

The so-called denotative *level* of the televisual sign is fixed by certain, very complex (but limited or 'closed') codes. But its connotative *level*, though also bounded, is more open, subject to more active *transformations*, which exploit its polysemic values. Any such already constituted sign is potentially transformable into more than one connotative configuration. Polysemy must not, however, be confused with pluralism. Connotative codes are *not* equal among themselves. Any society/culture tends, with varying degrees of closure, to impose its classifications of the social and cultural and political world. These constitute a *dominant cultural order*, though it is neither univocal nor uncontested. This question of the 'structure of discourses in dominance' is a crucial point. The different areas of social life appear to be mapped out into discursive domains, hierarchically organized into *dominant or preferred meanings*. New, problematic or troubling events, which breach our expectancies and run counter to our 'common-sense constructs', to our 'taken-for-granted' knowledge of social structures, must be assigned to their discursive domains before they can be said to 'make sense'. The most common way of 'mapping' them is to assign the new to some domain or other of the existing 'maps of problematic social reality'. We say *dominant*, not 'determined', because it is always possible to order, classify, assign and decode an event within more than one 'mapping'. But we say 'dominant' because there exists a pattern of 'preferred readings'; and these both have the institutional/political/ideological order imprinted in them and have themselves become institutionalized.[11] The domains of 'preferred meanings' have the whole social order embedded in them as a set of meanings, practices and beliefs: the everyday knowledge of social structures, of 'how things work for all practical purposes in this culture', the rank order of power and interest and the structure of legitimations, limits and sanctions. Thus to clarify a 'misunderstanding' at the connotative level, we must refer, *through* the codes, to the orders of social life, of economic and political power and of ideology. Further, since these mappings are 'structured in dominance' but not closed, the communicative process consists not in the unproblematic assignment of every visual item to its given position within a set of prearranged codes, but of *performative rules* – rules of competence and use, of logics-in-use – which seek actively to *enforce* or *pre-fer* one semantic domain over another and rule items into and out of their appropriate meaning-sets. Formal semiology has too often neglected this practice of *interpretative work*, though this constitutes, in fact, the real relations of broadcast practices in television.

In speaking of *dominant meanings*, then, we are not talking about a one-sided process which governs how all events will be signified. It consists of the 'work' required to enforce, win plausibility for and command as legitimate a *decoding* of the event within the limit of dominant definitions in which it has been connotatively signified. Terni has remarked:

> By the word *reading* we mean not only the capacity to identify and
> decode a certain number of signs, but also the subjective capacity to put
> them into a creative relation between themselves and with other signs:
> a capacity which is, by itself, the condition for a complete awareness of
> one's total environment.[12]

Our quarrel here is with the notion of 'subjective capacity', as if the referent of a televisional discourse were an objective fact but the interpretative level were an individualized and private matter. Quite the opposite seems to be the case. The televisual practice takes 'objective' (that is, systemic) responsibility precisely for the relations which disparate signs contract with one another in any discursive instance, and thus continually rearranges, delimits and prescribes into what 'awareness of one's total environment' these items are arranged.

This brings us to the question of misunderstandings. Television producers who find their message 'failing to get across' are frequently concerned to straighten out the kinks in the communication chain, thus facilitating the 'effectiveness' of their communication. Much research which claims the objectivity of 'policy-oriented analysis' reproduces this administrative goal by attempting to discover how much of a message the audience recalls and to improve the extent of understanding. No doubt misunderstandings of a literal kind do exist. The viewer does not know the terms employed, cannot follow the complex logic of argument or exposition, is unfamiliar with the language, finds the concepts too alien or difficult or is foxed by the expository narrative. But more often broadcasters are concerned that the audience has failed to take the meaning as they – the broadcasters – intended. What they really mean to say is that viewers are not operating within the 'domin-ant' or 'preferred' code. Their ideal is 'perfectly transparent communication'. Instead, what they have to confront is 'systematically distorted communication'.[13]

In recent years discrepancies of this kind have usually been explained by reference to 'selective perception'. This is the door via which a residual pluralism evades the compulsions of a highly structured, asymmetrical and non-equivalent process. Of course, there will always be private, individual, variant readings. But 'selective perception' is almost never as selective, random or privatized as the concept suggests. The patterns exhibit, across individual variants, significant clus-terings. Any new approach to audience studies will therefore have to begin with a critique of 'selective perception' theory.

It was argued earlier that since there is no necessary correspondence between encoding and decoding, the former can attempt to 'pre-fer' but cannot prescribe or guarantee the latter, which has its own conditions of existence. Unless they are wildly aberrant, encoding will have the effect of constructing some of the limits and parameters within which decodings will operate. If there were no limits, audiences could simply read whatever they liked into any message. No doubt some total misunderstandings of this kind do exist. But the vast range must contain *some* degree of reciprocity between encoding and decoding moments, otherwise we could not speak of an effective communicative exchange at all. Nevertheless, this 'correspondence' is not given but constructed. It is not 'natural' but the product of an articulation between two distinct moments. And the former cannot determine or guarantee, in a simple sense, which decoding codes will be employed. Otherwise communication would be a perfectly equivalent circuit, and every message would be an instance of 'perfectly transparent communication'. We must think, then, of the variant articulations in which encoding/decoding can be combined. To elaborate on this, we offer a hypothetical analysis of some possible decoding positions, in order to reinforce the point of 'no necessary correspondence'.[14]

We identify *three* hypothetical positions from which decodings of a televisual discourse may be constructed. These need to be empirically tested and refined. But the argument that decodings do not follow inevitably from encodings, that they are not identical, reinforces the argument of 'no necessary correspondence'. It also helps to deconstruct the common-sense meaning of 'misunderstanding' in terms of a theory of 'systematically distorted communication'.

The first hypothetical position is that of the *dominant-hegemonic position*. When the viewer takes the connoted meaning from, say, a television newscast or current affairs programme full and straight, and decodes the message in terms of the reference code in which it has been encoded, we might say that the viewer *is operating inside the dominant code*. This is the ideal-typical case of 'perfectly transparent communication' – or as close as we are likely to come to it 'for all practical purposes'. Within this we can distinguish the positions produced by the *professional code*. This is the position (produced by what we perhaps ought to identify as the operation of a 'metacode') which the professional broadcasters assume when encoding a message which has *already* been signified in a hegemonic manner. The professional code is 'relatively independent' of the dominant code, in that it applies criteria and transformational operations of its own, especially those of a technico-practical nature. The professional code, however, operates *within* the 'hegemony' of the dominant code. Indeed, it serves to reproduce the dominant definitions precisely by bracketing their hegemonic quality and operating instead with displaced professional codings which foreground such apparently neutral-technical questions as visual quality, news and presentational values, televisual quality, 'professionalism' and so on. The hegemonic interpretations of, say, the politics of Northern Ireland, or the Chilean *coup* or the Industrial Relations Bill are principally generated by political and military elites: the particular choice of presentational occasions and formats, the selection of personnel, the choice of images, the staging of debates are selected and combined through the operation of the professional code. How the broadcasting professionals are able *both* to operate with 'relatively autonomous' codes of their own *and* to act in such a way as to reproduce (not without contradiction) the hegemonic signification of events is a complex matter which cannot be further spelled out here. It must suffice to say that the professionals are linked with the defining elites not only by the institutional position of broadcasting itself as an 'ideological apparatus',[15] but also by the structure of *access* (that is, the systematic 'over-accessing' of selective elite personnel and their 'definition of the situation' in television). It may even be said that the professional codes serve to reproduce hegemonic definitions specifically by *not overtly* biasing their operations in a dominant direction: ideological reproduction therefore takes place here inadvertently, unconsciously, 'behind men's backs'.[16] Of course, conflicts, contradictions and even misunderstandings regularly arise between the dominant and the professional significations and their signifying agencies.

The second position we would identify is that of the *negotiated code* or position. Majority audiences probably understand quite adequately what has been dominantly defined and professionally signified. The dominant definitions, however, are hegemonic precisely because they represent definitions of situations and events which are 'in dominance', (*global*). Dominant definitions connect events, implicitly or explicitly, to grand totalizations, to the great syntagmatic views-of-the-world: they take 'large views' of issues: they relate events to the 'national interest' or to the level of geo-politics, even if they make these connections in truncated, inverted or mystified ways. The definition of a hegemonic viewpoint is (a) that it defines within its terms the mental horizon, the universe, of possible meanings, of a whole sector of relations in a society or culture; and (b) that it carries with it the stamp of legitimacy – it appears coterminous with what is 'natural', 'inevitable', 'taken for granted' about the social order. Decoding within the *negotiated version* contains a mixture of adaptive and oppositional elements: it acknowledges the legitimacy of the hegemonic definitions to make the grand significations (abstract), while, at a more restricted, situational (situated) level, it makes its own ground rules – it operates with exceptions to the rule. It accords the privileged position to the dominant definitions of events while reserving the right to make a more negotiated application to 'local conditions', to its own more *corporate* positions. This negotiated version of the dominant ideology is thus shot through with contradictions, though these are only on certain occasions brought to full visibility. Negotiated codes operate through what we might call particular or situated logics: and these logics are sustained by their differential and unequal relation to the discourses and logics of power. The simplest example of a negotiated code is that which governs the response of a worker to the notion of an Industrial Relations Bill limiting the right to strike or to arguments for a wages freeze. At the level of the 'national interest' economic debate the decoder may adopt the hegemonic defin-ition, agreeing that 'we must all pay ourselves less in order to combat inflation'. This, however, may have little or no relation to his/her willingness to go on strike for better pay and conditions or to oppose the Industrial Relations Bill at the level of shop-floor or union organization. We suspect that the great majority of so-called 'misunderstandings' arise from the contradictions and disjunctures between hegemonic-dominant encodings and negotiated-corporate decodings. It is just these mismatches in the levels which most provoke defining elites and professionals to identify a 'failure in communications'.

Finally, it is possible for a viewer perfectly to understand both the literal and the connotative inflection given by a discourse but to decode the message in a *globally* contrary way. He/she detotalizes the message in the preferred code in order to retotalize the message within some alternative framework of reference. This is the case of the viewer who listens to a debate on the need to limit wages but 'reads' every mention of the 'national interest' as 'class interest'. He/she is operating with what we must call an *oppositional code*. One of the most significant political moments (they also coincide with crisis points within the broadcasting organizations themselves, for obvious reasons) is the point when events which are normally signified and decoded in a negotiated way begin to be given an oppos-itional reading. Here the 'politics of signification' – the struggle in discourse – is joined.

Notes

* This article is an edited extract from 'Encoding and Decoding in Television Discourse', CCCS Stencilled Paper no. 7.

1 For an explication and commentary on the methodological implications of Marx's argument, see S. Hall, 'A reading of Marx's 1857 *Introduction to the Grundrisse*', in *WPCS* 6 (1974).

2 J.D. Halloran, 'Understanding television', Paper for the Council of Europe Colloquy on 'Understanding Television' (University of Leicester 1973).

3 G. Gerbner *et al., Violence in TV Drama: A Study of Trends and Symbolic Functions* (The Annenberg School, University of Pennsylvania 1970).

4 Charles Peirce, *Speculative Grammar*, in *Collected Papers* (Cambridge, Mass.: Harvard University Press 1931–58).

5 Umberto Eco, 'Articulations of the cinematic code', in *Cinemantics*, no. 1.

6 See the argument in S. Hall, 'Determinations of news photographs', in *WPCS* 3 (1972).

7 Vološinov, *Marxism And The Philosophy of Language* (The Seminar Press 1973).

8 For a similar clarification, see Marina Camargo Heck, 'Ideological dimensions of media messages', pages 122–7 above.

9 Roland Barthes, 'Rhetoric of the image', in *WPCS* 1 (1971).

10 Roland Barthes, *Elements of Semiology* (Cape 1967).

11 For an extended critique of 'preferred reading', see Alan O'Shea, 'Preferred reading' (unpublished paper, CCCS, University of Birmingham).

12 P. Terni, 'Memorandum', Council of Europe Colloquy on 'Understanding Television' (University of Leicester 1973).

13 The phrase is Habermas's, in 'Systematically distorted communications', in P. Dretzel (ed.), *Recent Sociology 2* (Collier-Macmillan 1970). It is used here, however, in a different way.

14 For a sociological formulation which is close, in some ways, to the positions outlined here but which does not parallel the argument about the theory of discourse, see Frank Parkin, *Class Inequality and Political Order* (Macgibbon and Kee 1971).

15 See Louis Althusser, 'Ideology and ideological state apparatuses', in *Lenin and Philosophy and Other Essays* (New Left Books 1971).

16 For an expansion of this argument, see Stuart Hall, 'The external/internal dialectic in broadcasting', *4th Symposium on Broadcasting* (University of Manchester 1972), and 'Broadcasting and the state: the independence/impartiality couplet', AMCR Symposium, University of Leicester 1976 (CCCS unpublished paper).

Suggestions for further reading

Althusser, Louis, 'Ideology and Ideological State Apparatuses (Notes Towards an Investigation)', in *Lenin and Philosophy and Other Essays,* trans. Ben Brewster, New York: Monthly Review Press, 1971, pp. 127–86.

Barthes, Roland, 'Rhetoric of the Image', in *The Responsibility of Forms: Critical Essays on Music, Art, and Representation,* trans. Richard Howard, Berkeley and Los Angeles: University of California Press, 1991, pp. 21–40.

Jenkins, Henry, *Textual Poachers: Television Fans and Participatory Culture,* New York and London: Routledge, 1992.

Chapter 19

Julia Kristeva

'APPROACHING ABJECTION', 1980

No Beast is there without glimmer of infinity,
No eye so vile nor abject that brushes not
Against lightning from on high, now tender, now fierce.
                    Victor Hugo, *La Légende des siècles*

Neither subject nor object

THERE LOOMS, WITHIN abjection, one of those violent, dark revolts of being, directed against a threat that seems to emanate from an exorbitant outside or inside, ejected beyond the scope of the possible, the tolerable, the thinkable. It lies there, quite close, but it cannot be assimilated. It beseeches, worries, and fascinates desire, which, nevertheless, does not let itself be seduced. Apprehensive, desire turns aside; sickened, it rejects. A certainty protects it from the shameful—a certainty of which it is proud holds on to it. But simultaneously, just the same, that impetus, that spasm, that leap is drawn toward an elsewhere as tempting as it is condemned. Unflaggingly, like an inescapable boomerang, a vortex of summons and repulsion places the one haunted by it literally beside himself.

When I am beset by abjection, the twisted braid of affects and thoughts I call by such a name does not have, properly speaking, a definable *object*. The object is not an ob-ject facing me, which I name or imagine. Nor is it an ob-jest, an otherness ceaselessly fleeing in a systematic quest of desire. What is abject is not my correlative, which, providing me with someone or something else as support, would allow me to be more or less detached and autonomous. The abject has only one quality of the object—that of being opposed to *I*. If the object, however, through its opposition, settles me within the fragile texture of a desire for meaning, which, as a matter of fact, makes me ceaselessly and infinitely homologous to it, what is *abject*, on the contrary, the jettisoned object, is radically excluded and draws me toward the place where meaning collapses. A certain "ego" that merged with its master, a superego, has flatly driven it away. It lies outside, beyond the set, and does not seem to agree to the latter's rules of the game. And yet, from its place of banishment, the abject does not cease challenging its master. Without a sign (for him), it beseeches a discharge, a convulsion, a crying out. To each ego its object, to each superego its abject. It is not the white expanse or slack boredom of repression, not the translations and transformations of desire that wrench bodies, nights, and discourse; rather it is a brutish suffering that "I" puts up with, sublime and devastated, for "I" deposits it to the father's account [*verse au père—père-version*]: I endure it, for I imagine that such is the desire of the other. A massive and sudden emergence of uncanniness, which, familiar as it might have been in an opaque and forgotten life, now harries me as radically separate, loathsome. Not me. Not that. But not nothing, either. A "something" that I do not recognize as a thing. A weight of meaninglessness, about which there is nothing insignificant, and which crushes me. On the edge of nonexistence and hallucination, of a reality that, if I acknowledge it, annihilates me. There, abject and abjection are my safeguards. The primers of my culture.

The improper/unclean

Loathing an item of food, a piece of filth, waste, or dung. The spasms and vomiting that protect me. The repugnance, the retching that thrusts me to the side and turns me away from defilement, sewage, and muck. The shame of compromise, of being in the middle of treachery. The fascinated start that leads me toward and separates me from them.

Food loathing is perhaps the most elementary and most archaic form of abjection. When the eyes see or the lips touch that skin on the surface of milk—harmless, thin as a sheet of cigarette paper, pitiful as a nail paring—I experience a gagging sensation and, still farther down, spasms in the stomach, the belly; and all the organs shrivel up the body, provoke tears and bile, increase heartbeat, cause forehead and hands to perspire. Along with sight-clouding dizziness, *nausea* makes me balk at that milk cream, separates me from the mother and father who proffer it. "I" want none of that element, sign of their desire; "I" do not want to listen, "I" do not assimilate it, "I" expel it. But since the food is not an "other" for "me," who am only in their desire, I expel *myself*, I spit *myself* out, I abject *myself* within the same motion through which "I" claim to establish *myself*. That detail, perhaps an insignificant one, but one that they ferret out, emphasize, evaluate, that trifle turns me inside out, guts sprawling; it is thus that *they* see that "I" am in the process of becoming an other at the expense of my own death. During that course in which "I" become, I give birth to myself amid the violence of sobs, of vomit. Mute protest of the symptom, shattering violence of a convulsion that, to be sure, is inscribed in a symbolic system, but in which, without either wanting or being able to become integrated in order to answer to it, it reacts, it abreacts. It abjects.

The corpse (or cadaver: *cadere*, to fall), that which has irremediably come a cropper, is cesspool, and death; it upsets even more violently the one who confronts it as fragile and fallacious chance. A wound with blood and pus, or the sickly, acrid smell of sweat, of decay, does not *signify* death. In the presence of signified death—a flat encephalograph, for instance—I would understand, react, or accept. No, as in true theater, without makeup or masks, refuse and corpses *show me* what I permanently thrust aside in order to live. These body fluids, this defilement, this shit are what life withstands, hardly and with difficulty, on the part of death. There, I am at the border of my condition as a living being. My body extricates itself, as being alive, from that border. Such wastes drop so that I might live, until, from loss to loss, nothing remains in me and my entire body falls beyond the limit—*cadere*, cadaver. If dung signifies the other side of the border, the place where I am not and which permits me to be, the corpse, the most sickening of wastes, is a border that has encroached upon everything. It is no longer I who expel, "I" is expelled. The border has become an object. How can I be without border? That elsewhere that I imagine beyond the present, or that I hallucinate so that I might, in a present time, speak to you, conceive of you—it is now here, jetted, abjected, into "my" world. Deprived of world, therefore, I *fall in a faint*. In that compelling, raw, insolent thing in the morgue's full sunlight, in that thing that no longer matches and therefore no longer signifies anything, I behold the breaking down of a world that has erased its borders: fainting away. The corpse, seen without God and outside of science, is the utmost of abjection. It is death infecting life. Abject. It is something rejected from which one does not part, from which one does not protect oneself as from an object. Imaginary uncanniness and real threat, it beckons to us and ends up engulfing us.

It is thus not lack of cleanliness or health that causes abjection but what disturbs identity, system, order. What does not respect borders, positions, rules. The in-between, the ambiguous, the composite. The traitor, the liar, the criminal with a good conscience, the shameless rapist, the killer who claims he is a savior. . . . Any crime, because it draws attention to the fragility of the law, is abject, but premeditated crime, cunning murder, hypocritical revenge are even more so because they heighten the display of such fragility. He who denies morality is not abject; there can be grandeur in amorality and even in crime that flaunts its disrespect for the law—rebellious, liberating, and suicidal crime. Abjection, on the other hand, is immoral, sinister, scheming, and shady: a terror that dissembles, a hatred that smiles, a passion that uses the body for barter instead of inflaming it, a debtor who sells you up, a friend who stabs you. . . .

In the dark halls of the museum that is now what remains of Auschwitz, I see a heap of children's shoes, or something like that, something I have already seen elsewhere, under a Christmas tree, for instance, dolls I believe. The abjection of Nazi crime reaches its apex when death, which, in any case, kills me, interferes with what, in my living universe, is supposed to save me from death: childhood, science, among other things.

The abjection of self

If it be true that the abject simultaneously beseeches and pulverizes the subject, one can understand that it is experienced at the peak of its strength when that subject, weary of fruitless attempts to identify with something on the outside, finds the impossible within; when it finds that the impossible constitutes its very *being*, that it *is* none other than abject. The abjection of self would be the culminating form of that experience of the subject to which it is revealed that all its objects are based merely on the inaugural *loss* that laid the foundations of its own being. There is nothing like the abjection of self to show that all abjection is in fact recognition of the *want* on which any being, meaning, language, or desire is founded. One always passes too quickly over this word, "want," and today psychoanalysts are finally taking into account only its more or less fetishized product, the "object of want." But if one imagines (and imagine one must, for it is the working of imagination whose foundations are being laid here) the experience of *want* itself as logically preliminary to being and object—to the being of the object—then one understands that abjection, and even more so abjection of self, is its only signified. Its signifier, then, is none but literature. Mystical Christendom turned this abjection of self into the ultimate proof of humility before God, witness Elizabeth of Hungary who "though a great princess, delighted in nothing so much as in abasing herself."[1]

The question remains as to the ordeal, a secular one this time, that abjection can constitute for someone who, in what is termed knowledge of castration, turning away from perverse dodges, presents himself with his own body and ego as the most precious non-objects; they are no longer seen in their own right but forfeited, abject. The termination of analysis can lead us there, as we shall see. Such are the pangs and delights of masochism.

Essentially different from "uncanniness," more violent, too, abjection is elaborated through a failure to recognize its kin; nothing is familiar, not even the shadow of a memory. I imagine a child who has swallowed up his parents too soon, who frightens himself on that account, "all by himself," and, to save himself, rejects and throws up everything that is given to him—all gifts, all objects. He has, he could have, a sense of the abject. Even before things for him *are*—hence before they are signifiable—he drives them out, dominated by drive as he is, and constitutes his own territory, edged by the abject. A sacred configuration. Fear cements his compound, conjoined to another world, thrown up, driven out, forfeited. What he has swallowed up instead of maternal love is an emptiness, or rather a maternal hatred without a word for the words of the father; that is what he tries to cleanse himself of, tirelessly. What solace does he come upon within such loathing? Perhaps a father, existing but unsettled, loving but unsteady, merely an apparition but an apparition that remains. Without him the holy brat would probably have no sense of the sacred; a blank subject, he would remain, discomfited, at the dump for non-objects that are always forfeited, from which, on the contrary, fortified by abjection, he tries to extricate himself. For he is not mad, he through whom the abject exists. Out of the daze that has petrified him before the untouchable, impossible, absent body of the mother, a daze that has cut off his impulses from their objects, that is, from their representations, out of such daze he causes, along with loathing, one word to crop up—fear. The phobic has no other object than the abject. But that word, "fear"—a fluid haze, an elusive clamminess—no sooner has it cropped up than it shades off like a mirage and permeates all words of the language with nonexistence, with a hallucinatory, ghostly glimmer. Thus, fear having been bracketed, discourse will seem tenable only if it ceaselessly confronts that otherness, a burden both repellent and repelled, a deep well of memory that is unapproachable and intimate: the abject.

Beyond the unconscious

Put another way, it means that there are lives not sustained by *desire*, as desire is always for objects. Such lives are based on *exclusion*. They are clearly distinguishable from those understood as neurotic or psychotic, articulated by *negation* and its modalities, *transgression, denial*, and *repudiation*. Their dynamics challenges the theory of the unconscious, seeing that the latter is dependent upon a dialectic of negativity.

The theory of the unconscious, as is well known, presupposes a repression of contents (affects and presentations) that, thereby, do not have access to consciousness but effect within the subject modifications, either of speech (parapraxes, etc.), or of the body (symptoms), or both (hallucinations, etc.). As correlative to the notion of *repression*, Freud put forward that of *denial* as a means of figuring out neurosis, that of *rejection (repudiation)* as a means of situating psychosis. The asymmetry of the two repressions becomes more marked owing to denial's bearing on the object whereas repudiation affects desire itself (Lacan, in perfect keeping with Freud's thought, interprets that as "repudiation of the Name of the Father").

Yet, facing the ab-ject and more specifically phobia and the splitting of the ego (a point I shall return to), one might ask if those articulations of negativity germane to the unconscious (inherited by Freud from philosophy and psychology) have not become inoperative. The "unconscious" contents remain here *excluded* but in strange fashion: not radically enough to allow for a secure differentiation between subject and object, and yet clearly enough for a defensive *position* to be established—one that implies a refusal but also a sublimating elaboration. As if the fundamental opposition were between I and Other or, in more archaic fashion, between Inside and Outside. As if such an opposition subsumed the one between Conscious and Unconscious, elaborated on the basis of neuroses.

Owing to the ambiguous opposition I/Other, Inside/Outside—an opposition that is vigorous but pervious, violent but uncertain—there are contents, "normally" unconscious in neurotics, that become explicit if not conscious in "borderline" patients' speeches and behavior. Such contents are often openly manifested through symbolic practices, without by the same token being integrated into the judging consciousness of those particular subjects. Since they make the conscious/unconscious distinction irrelevant, borderline subjects and their speech constitute propitious ground for a sublimating discourse ("aesthetic" or "mystical," etc.), rather than a scientific or rationalist one.

An exile who asks, "where?"

The one by whom the abject exists is thus a *deject* who places (himself), *separates* (himself), situates (himself), and therefore *strays* instead of getting his bearings, desiring, belonging, or refusing. Situationist in a sense, and not without laughter—since laughing is a way of placing or displacing abjection. Necessarily dichotomous, somewhat Manichaean, he divides, excludes, and without, properly speaking, wishing to know his abjections is not at all unaware of them. Often, moreover, he includes himself among them, thus casting within himself the scalpel that carries out his separations.

Instead of sounding himself as to his "being," he does so concerning his place: "*Where* am I?" instead of "*Who* am I?" For the space that engrosses the deject, the excluded, is never *one*, nor *homogeneous*, nor *totalizable*, but essentially divisible, foldable, and catastrophic. A deviser of territories, languages, works, the *deject* never stops demarcating his universe whose fluid confines—for they are constituted of a non-object, the abject—constantly question his solidity and impel him to start afresh. A tireless builder, the deject is in short a *stray*. He is on a journey, during the night, the end of which keeps receding. He has a sense of the danger, of the loss that the pseudo-object attracting him represents for him, but he cannot help taking the risk at the very moment he sets himself apart. And the more he strays, the more he is saved.

Time: forgetfulness and thunder

For it is out of such straying on excluded ground that he draws his jouissance. The abject from which he does not cease separating is for him, in short, a *land of oblivion* that is constantly remembered. Once upon blotted-out time, the abject must have been a magnetized pole of covetousness. But the ashes of oblivion now serve as a screen and reflect aversion, repugnance. The clean and proper (in the sense of incorporated and incorporable) becomes filthy, the sought-after turns into the banished, fascination into shame. Then, forgotten time crops up suddenly and condenses into a flash of lightning an operation that, if it were thought out, would involve bringing together the two opposite terms but, on account of that flash, is discharged like thunder. The time of abjection is double: a time of oblivion and thunder, of veiled infinity and the moment when revelation bursts forth.

Jouissance and affect

Jouissance, in short. For the stray considers himself as equivalent to a Third Party. He secures the latter's judgment, he acts on the strength of its power in order to condemn, he grounds himself on its law to tear the veil of oblivion but also to set up its object as inoperative. As jettisoned. Parachuted by the Other. A ternary structure, if you wish, held in keystone position by the Other, but a "structure" that is skewed, a topology of catastrophe. For, having provided itself with an *alter ego*, the Other no longer has a grip on the three apices of the triangle where subjective homogeneity resides; and so, it jettisons the object into an abominable real, inaccessible except through jouissance. It follows that jouissance alone causes the abject to exist as such. One does not know it, one does not desire it, one joys in it [*on en jouit*]. Violently and painfully. A passion. And, as in jouissance where the object of desire, known as object *a* [in Lacan's terminology], bursts with the shattered mirror where the ego gives up its image in order to contemplate itself in the Other, there is nothing either objective or objectal to the abject. It is simply a frontier, a repulsive gift that the Other, having become *alter ego*, drops so that "I" does not disappear in it but finds, in that sublime alienation, a forfeited existence. Hence a jouissance in which the subject is swallowed up but in which the Other, in return, keeps the subject from foundering by making it repugnant. One thus understands why so many victims of the abject are its fascinated victims—if not its submissive and willing ones.

We may call it a border; abjection is above all ambiguity. Because, while releasing a hold, it does not radically cut off the subject from what threatens it—on the contrary, abjection acknowledges it to be in perpetual danger. But also because abjection itself is a composite of judgment and affect, of condemnation and yearning, of signs and drives. Abjection preserves what existed in the archaism of pre-objectal relationship, in the immemorial violence with which a body becomes separated from another body in order to be—maintaining that night in which the outline of the signified thing vanishes and where only the imponderable affect is carried out. To be sure, if I am affected by what does not yet appear to me as a thing, it is because laws, connections, and even structures of meaning govern and condition me. That order, that glance, that voice, that gesture, which enact the law for my frightened body, constitute and bring about an effect and not yet a sign. I speak to it in vain in order to exclude it from what will no longer be, for myself, a world that can be assimilated. Obviously, *I am* only *like* someone else: mimetic logic of the advent of the ego, objects, and signs. But when I *seek* (myself), *lose* (myself), or experience *jouissance*—then "I" is *heterogeneous*. Discomfort, unease, dizziness stemming from an ambiguity that, through the violence of a revolt *against*, demarcates a space out of which signs and objects arise. Thus braided, woven, ambivalent, a heterogeneous flux marks out a territory that I can call my own because the Other, having dwelt in me as *alter ego*, points it out to me through loathing.

This means once more that the heterogeneous flow, which portions the abject and sends back abjection, already dwells in a human animal that has been highly altered. I experience abjection only if an Other has settled in place and stead of what will be "me." Not at all an other with whom I identify and incorporate, but an Other who precedes and possesses me, and through such possession causes me to be. A possession previous to my advent: a being-there of the symbolic that a father might or might not embody. Significance is indeed inherent in the human body.

At the limit of primal repression

If, on account of that Other, a space becomes demarcated, separating the abject from what will be a subject and its objects, it is because a repression that one might call "primal" has been effected prior to the springing forth of the ego, of its objects and representations. The latter, in turn, as they depend on another repression, the "secondary" one, arrive only *a posteriori* on an enigmatic foundation that has already been marked off; its return, in a phobic, obsessional, psychotic guise, or more generally and in more imaginary fashion in the shape of *abjection*, notifies us of the limits of the human universe.

On such limits and at the limit one could say that there is no unconscious, which is elaborated when representations and affects (whether or not tied to representations) shape a logic. Here, on the contrary, consciousness has not assumed its rights and transformed into signifiers those fluid demarcations of yet unstable territories where an "I" that is taking shape is ceaselessly straying. We are no longer within the sphere of the unconscious but at the limit of primal repression that, nevertheless, has discovered an intrinsically corporeal and already signifying brand, symptom, and sign: repugnance, disgust, abjection. There is an effervescence of object and sign—not of desire but of intolerable significance; they tumble over into non-sense or the impossible real, but they appear even so in spite of "myself" (which is not) as abjection.

Premises of the sign, linings of the sublime

Let us pause a while at this juncture. If the abject is already a wellspring of sign for a non-object, on the edges of primal repression, one can understand its skirting the somatic symptom on the one hand and sublimation on the other. The *symptom*: a language that gives up, a structure within the body, a non-assimilable alien, a monster, a tumor, a cancer that the listening devices of the unconscious do not hear, for its strayed subject is huddled outside the paths of desire. *Sublimation*, on the contrary, is nothing else than the possibility of naming the pre-nominal, the pre-objectal, which are in fact only a trans-nominal, a trans-objectal. In the symptom, the abject permeates me, I become abject. Through sublimation, I keep it under control. The abject is edged with the sublime. It is not the same moment on the journey, but the same subject and speech bring them into being.

For the sublime has no object either. When the starry sky, a vista of open seas or a stained glass window shedding purple beams fascinate me, there is a cluster of meaning, of colors, of words, of caresses, there are light touches, scents, sighs, cadences that arise, shroud me, carry me away, and sweep me beyond the things that I see, hear, or think. The "sublime" object dissolves in the raptures of a bottomless memory. It is such a memory, which, from stopping point to stopping point, remembrance to remembrance, love to love, transfers that object to the refulgent point of the dazzlement in which I stray in order to be. As soon as I perceive it, as soon as I name it, the sublime triggers—it has always already triggered—a spree of perceptions and words that expands memory boundlessly. I then forget the point of departure and find myself removed to a secondary universe, set off from the one where "I" am—delight and loss. Not at all short of but always with and through perception and words, the sublime is a *something added* that expands us, overstrains us, and causes us to be both *here*, as dejects, and *there*, as others and sparkling. A divergence, an impossible bounding. Everything missed, joy—fascination.

Before the beginning: separation

The abject might then appear as the most *fragile* (from a synchronic point of view), the most *archaic* (from a diachronic one) sublimation of an "object" still inseparable from drives. The abject is that pseudo-object that is made up *before* but appears only *within* the gaps of secondary repression. *The abject would thus be the "object" of primal repression.*

But what is primal repression? Let us call it the ability of the speaking being, always already haunted by the Other, to divide, reject, repeat. Without *one* division, *one* separation, *one* subject/object having been constituted (not yet, or no longer yet). Why? Perhaps because of maternal anguish, unable to be satiated within the encompassing symbolic.

The abject confronts us, on the one hand, with those fragile states where man strays on the territories of *animal*. Thus, by way of abjection, primitive societies have marked out a precise area of their culture in order to remove it from the threatening world of animals or animalism, which were imagined as representatives of sex and murder.

The abject confronts us, on the other hand, and this time within our personal archeology, with our earliest attempts to release the hold of *maternal* entity even before ex-isting outside of her, thanks to the autonomy of language. It is a violent, clumsy breaking away, with the constant risk of falling back under the sway of a power as securing as it is stifling. The difficulty a mother has in acknowledging (or being acknowledged by) the symbolic realm—in other words, the problem she has with the phallus that her father or her husband stands for—is not such as to help the future subject leave the natural mansion. The child can serve its mother as token of her own authentication; there is, however, hardly any reason for her to serve as go-between for it to become autonomous and authentic in its turn. In such close combat, the symbolic light that a third party, eventually the father, can contribute helps the future subject, the more so if it happens to be endowed with a robust supply of drive energy, in pursuing a reluctant struggle against what, having been the mother, will turn into an abject. Repelling, rejecting; repelling itself, rejecting itself. Ab-jecting.

In this struggle, which fashions the human being, the *mimesis*, by means of which he becomes homologous to another in order to become himself, is in short logically and chronologically secondary. Even before being *like*, "I" am not but do *separate, reject, ab-ject*. Abjection, with a meaning broadened to take in subjective diachrony, *is a precondition of narcissism*. It is coexistent with it and causes it to be permanently brittle. The more or less beautiful image in which I behold or recognize myself rests upon an abjection that sunders it as soon as repression, the constant watchman, is relaxed.

The "chora," receptacle of narcissism

Let us enter, for a moment, into that Freudian aporia called primal repression. Curious primacy, where what is repressed cannot really be held down, and where what represses always already borrows its strength and authority from what is apparently very secondary: language. Let us therefore not speak of primacy but of the instability of the symbolic function in its most significant aspect—the prohibition placed on the maternal body (as a defense against autoeroticism and incest taboo). Here, drives hold sway and constitute a strange space that I shall name, after Plato (*Timeus*, 48–53), a *chora*, a receptacle.

For the benefit of the ego or its detriment, drives, whether life drives or death drives, serve to correlate that "not yet" ego with an "object" in order to establish both of them. Such a process, while dichotomous (inside/outside, ego/not ego) and repetitive, has nevertheless something centripetal about it: it aims to settle the ego as center of a solar system of objects. If, by dint of coming back towards the center, the drive's motion should eventually become centrifugal, hence fasten on the Other and come into being as sign so as to produce meaning—that is, literally speaking, exorbitant.

But from that moment on, while I recognize my image as sign and change in order to signify, another economy is instituted. The sign represses the *chora* and its eternal return. Desire alone will henceforth be witness to that "primal" pulsation. But desire ex-patriates the *ego* toward an *other* subject and accepts the exactness of the ego only as narcissistic. Narcissism then appears as a regression to a position set back from the other, a return to a self-contemplative, conservative, self-sufficient haven. Actually, such narcissism never is the wrinkleless image of the Greek youth in a quiet fountain. The conflicts of drives muddle its bed, cloud its water, and bring forth everything that, by not becoming integrated with a given system of signs, is abjection for it.

Abjection is therefore a kind of *narcissistic crisis*: it is witness to the ephemeral aspect of the state called "narcissism" with reproachful jealousy, heaven knows why; what is more, abjection gives narcissism (the thing and the concept) its classification as "seeming."

Nevertheless, it is enough that a prohibition, which can be a superego, block the desire craving an other—or that this other, as its role demands, not fulfill it—for desire and its signifiers to turn back toward the "same," thus clouding the waters of Narcissus. It is precisely at the moment of narcissistic perturbation (all things considered, the permanent state of the speaking being, if he would only hear himself speak) that secondary repression, with its reserve of symbolic means, attempts to transfer to its own account, which has thus been overdrawn, the resources of primal repression. The archaic economy is brought into full light of day, signified, verbalized. Its strategies (rejecting, separating, repeating/abjecting) hence find a symbolic existence, and the very logic of the symbolic—arguments, demonstrations, proofs, etc.—must conform to it. It is then that the object ceases to be circumscribed, reasoned with, thrust aside: it appears as abject.

Two seemingly contradictory causes bring about the narcissistic crisis that provides, along with its truth, a view of the abject. *Too much strictness on the part of the Other*, confused with the One and the Law. The *lapse of the Other*, which shows through the breakdown of objects of desire. In both instances, the abject appears in order to uphold "I" within the Other. The abject is the violence of mourning for an "object" that has always already been lost. The abject shatters the wall of repression and its judgments. It takes the ego back to its source on the abominable limits from which, in order to be, the ego has broken away—it assigns it a source in the non-ego, drive, and death. Abjection is a resurrection that has gone through death (of the ego). It is an alchemy that transforms death drive into a start of life, of new signifiance.

Perverse or artistic

The abject is related to perversion. The sense of abjection that I experience is anchored in the superego. The abject is perverse because it neither gives up nor assumes a prohibition, a rule, or a law; but turns them aside, misleads, corrupts; uses them, takes advantage of them, the better to deny them. It kills in the name of life—a progressive despot; it lives at the behest of death—an operator in genetic experimentations; it curbs the other's suffering for its own profit—a cynic (and a psychoanalyst); it establishes narcissistic power while pretending to reveal the abyss—an artist who practices his art as a "business." Corruption is its most common, most obvious appearance. That is the socialized appearance of the abject.

An unshakable adherence to Prohibition and Law is necessary if that perverse interspace of abjection is to be hemmed in and thrust aside. Religion, Morality, Law. Obviously always arbitrary, more or less; unfailingly oppressive, rather more than less; laboriously prevailing, more and more so.

Contemporary literature does not take their place. Rather, it seems to be written out of the untenable aspects of perverse or superego positions. It acknowledges the impossibility of Religion, Morality, and Law—their power play, their necessary and absurd seeming. Like perversion, it takes advantage of them, gets round them, and makes sport of them. Nevertheless, it maintains a distance where the abject is concerned. The writer, fascinated by the abject, imagines its logic, projects himself into it, introjects it, and as a consequence perverts language—style and content. But on the other hand, as the sense of abjection is both the abject's judge and accomplice, this is also true of the literature that confronts it. One might thus say that with such a literature there takes place a crossing over of the dichotomous categories of Pure and Impure, Prohibition and Sin, Morality and Immorality.

For the subject firmly settled in its superego, a writing of this sort is necessarily implicated in the interspace that characterizes perversion; and for that reason, it gives rise in turn to abjection. And yet, such texts call for a softening of the superego. Writing them implies an ability to imagine the abject, that is, to see oneself in its place and to thrust it aside only by means of the displacements of verbal play. It is only after his death, eventually, that the writer of abjection will escape his condition of waste, reject, abject. Then, he will either sink into oblivion or attain the rank of incommensurate ideal. Death would thus be the chief curator of our imaginary museum; it would protect us in the last resort from the abjection that contemporary literature claims to expend while uttering it. Such a protection, which gives its quietus to abjection, but also perhaps to the bothersome, incandescent stake of the literary phenomenon itself, which, raised to the status of the sacred, is severed from its specificity. Death thus keeps house in our contemporary universe. By purifying (us from) literature, it establishes our secular religion.

As abjection—so the sacred

Abjection accompanies all religious structurings and reappears, to be worked out in a new guise, at the time of their collapse. Several structurations of abjection should be distinguished, each one determining a specific form of the sacred.

Abjection appears as a rite of defilement and pollution in the paganism that accompanies societies with a dominant or surviving matrilinear character. It takes on the form of the *exclusion* of a substance (nutritive or linked to sexuality), the execution of which coincides with the sacred since it sets it up.

Abjection persists as *exclusion* or taboo (dietary or other) in monotheistic religions, Judaism in particular, but drifts over to more "secondary" forms such as *transgression* (of the Law) within the same monotheistic economy. It finally encounters, with Christian sin, a dialectic elaboration, as it becomes integrated in the Christian Word as a threatening otherness—but always nameable, always totalizeable.

The various means of *purifying* the abject—the various catharses—make up the history of religions, and end up with that catharsis par excellence called art, both on the far and near side of religion. Seen from that standpoint, the artistic experience, which is rooted in the abject it utters and by the same token purifies, appears as the essential component of religiosity. That is perhaps why it is destined to survive the collapse of the historical forms of religions.

Outside of the sacred, the abject is written

In the contemporary practice of the West and owing to the crisis in Christianity, abjection elicits more archaic resonances that are culturally prior to sin; through them it again assumes its biblical status, and beyond it that of defilement in primitive societies. In a world in which the Other has collapsed, the aesthetic task—a descent into the foundations of the symbolic construct—amounts to retracing the fragile limits of the speaking being, closest to its dawn, to the bottomless "primacy" constituted by primal repression. Through that experience, which is nevertheless managed by the Other, "subject" and "object" push each other away, confront each other, collapse, and start again—inseparable, contaminated, condemned, at the boundary of what is assimilable, thinkable: abject. Great modern literature unfolds over that terrain: Dostoyevsky, Lautréamont, Proust, Artaud, Kafka, Céline.

Dostoyevsky

The abject is, for Dostoyevsky, the "object" of *The Possessed*: it is the aim and motive of an existence whose meaning is lost in absolute degradation because it absolutely rejected the moral *limit* (a social, religious, familial, and individual one) as absolute—God. Abjection then wavers between the *fading away* of all meaning and all humanity, burnt as by the flames of a conflagration, and the *ecstasy* of an ego that, having lost its Other and its objects, reaches, at the precise moment of this suicide, the height of harmony with the promised land. Equally abject are Verkhovensky and Kirilov, murder and suicide.

> A big fire at night always produces an exciting and exhilarating effect; this explains the attraction of fireworks; but in the case of fireworks, the graceful and regular shape of the flames and the complete immunity from danger produce a light and playful effect comparable to the effect of a glass of champagne. A real fire is quite another matter: there the horror and a certain sense of personal danger, combined with the well-known exhilarating effect of a fire at night, produce in the spectator (not, of course, in one whose house has burnt down) a certain shock to the brain and, as it were, a challenge to his own destructive instincts, which, alas, lie buried in the soul of even the meekest and most domesticated official of the lowest grade. This grim sensation is almost always delightful. "I really don't know if it is possible to watch a fire without some enjoyment."[2]

> There are seconds—they come five or six at a time—when you suddenly feel the presence of eternal harmony in all its fullness. It is nothing earthly. I don't mean that it is heavenly, but a man in his earthly semblance can't endure it. He has to undergo a physical change or die. This feeling is clear and unmistakable. It is as though you suddenly apprehended all nature and suddenly said: "Yes, it is true—it is good." [. . .] What is so terrifying about it is that it is so terribly clear and such gladness. If it went on for more than five seconds, the soul could not endure it and must perish. In those five seconds I live through a lifetime, and I am ready to give my life for them, for it's worth it. To be able to endure it for ten seconds, you would have to undergo a physical change. I think man ought to stop begetting children. What do you want children for, what do you want mental development, if your goal has been attained? It is said in the gospel that in the resurrection they neither marry nor are given in marriage, but are the angels of God in heaven. It's a hint. Is your wife giving birth to a baby?[3]

Verkhovensky is abject because of his clammy, cunning appeal to ideals that no longer exist, from the moment when Prohibition (call it God) is lacking. Stavrogin is perhaps less so, for his immoralism admits of laughter and refusal, something artistic, a cynical and gratuitous expenditure that obviously becomes capitalized for the benefit of private narcissism but does not serve an arbitrary, exterminating power. It is possible to be cynical without being irremediably abject; abjection, on the other hand, is always brought about by that which attempts to get along with trampled-down law.

> He's got everything perfect in his note-book, Verkhovensky went on. Spying. Every member of the society spies on the others, and he is obliged to inform against them. Everyone belongs to all the others, and all belong to everyone. All are slaves and equals in slavery. In extreme

cases slander and murder, but, above all, equality. To begin with, the level of education, science, and accomplishment is lowered. A high level of scientific thought and accomplishment is open only to men of the highest abilities! Men of the highest ability have always seized the power and become autocrats. Such men cannot help being autocrats, and they've always done more harm than good; they are either banished or executed. A Cicero will have his tongue cut out, Copernicus will have his eyes gouged out, a Shakespeare will be stoned—there you have Shigalyov's doctrine! Slaves must be equal: without despotism there never has been any freedom or equality, but in a herd there is bound to be equality—there's the Shigalyov doctrine for you! Ha, ha, ha! You think it strange? I am for the Shigalyov doctrine![4]

Dostoyevsky has X-rayed sexual, moral, and religious abjection, displaying it as collapse of paternal laws. Is not the world of *The Possessed* a world of fathers, who are either repudiated, bogus, or dead, where matriarchs lusting for power hold sway—ferocious fetishes but nonetheless phantomlike? And by symbolizing the abject, through a masterful delivery of the jouissance produced by uttering it, Dostoyevsky delivered himself of that ruthless maternal burden.

But it is with Proust that we find the most immediately erotic, sexual, and desiring mainspring of abjection; and it is with Joyce that we shall discover that the feminine body, the maternal body, in its most un-signifiable, un-symbolizable aspect, shores up, in the individual, the fantasy of the loss in which he is engulfed or becomes inebriated, for want of the ability to name an object of desire.

Proust

Abjection, recognized as inherent in the mellow and impossible alteration of the ego, hence recognized as welded to narcissism, has, in Proust, something domesticated about it; without belonging to the realm of "one's own clean and proper" or of the "self evident," it constitutes a scandal of which one has to acknowledge if not the banality at least the secrets of a telltale snob. Abjection, with Proust, is fashionable, if not social; it is the foul lining of society. That may be why he furnishes the only modern example, certified by dictionaries, of the use of the word "abject" with the weak meaning it has (in French) at the end of the eighteenth century:

In those regions that were almost slums, what a modest existence, abject, if you please, but delightful, nourished by tranquillity and happiness, he would have consented to lead indefinitely.[5]

Proust writes that if the object of desire is real it can only rest upon the abject, which is impossible to fulfill. The object of love then becomes unmentionable, a double of the subject, similar to it, but improper, because inseparable from an impossible identity. Loving desire is thus felt as an inner fold within that impossible identity, as an accident of narcissism, ob-ject, painful alteration, delightfully and dramatically condemned to find the other in the same sex only.

As if one acceded to the truth, to the abject truth of sexuality, only through homosexuality—Sodom and Gomorrah, the *Cities of the Plain*.

> I had not even cause to regret my not having arrived in the shop until several minutes had elapsed. For from what I heard first at Jupien's shop, which was only a series of inarticulate sounds, I imagine that few words had been exchanged. It is true that these sounds were so violent that, if one set had not always been taken up an octave higher by a parallel plaint, I might have thought that one person was strangling another within a few feet of me, and that subsequently the murderer and his resuscitated victim were taking a bath to wash away the traces of the crime. I concluded from this later on that there is another thing as vociferous as pain, namely pleasure, especially when there is added to it—failing the fear of an eventual parturition, which could not be present in this case, despite the hardly convincing example in the *Golden Legend*—an immediate afterthought of cleanliness.[6]

Compared to this one, the orgy in Sade, meshing with a gigantic philosophy, be it that of the boudoir, had nothing abject about it. Methodical, rhetorical, and, from that point of view, regular, it broadens Meaning, Body, and Universe but is not at all exorbitant: everything is nameable for it, the whole is nameable. Sade's scene integrates: it allows for no other, no unthinkable, nothing heterogeneous. Rational and optimistic, it does not exclude. That means that it does not recognize a sacred, and in that sense it is the anthropological and rhetorical acme of atheism. Proustian writing, to the contrary, never gives up a judging prerogative, perhaps a biblical one, which splits, banishes, shares out, or condemns; and it is in relation to it, with it and against it, that the web of Proust's sentence, memory, sexuality, and morality is elaborated—infinitely spinning together differences (sexes, classes, races) into a homogeneity that consists only in signs, a fragile net stretched out over an abyss of incompatibilities, rejections, and abjections. Desire and signs, with Proust, weave the infinite cloth that does not hide but causes the subdued foulness to appear. As lapse, discomfort, shame, or blunder. As permanent threat, in short, to the homogenizing rhetoric that the writer composes against and with the abject.

Joyce

How dazzling, unending, eternal—and so weak, so insignificant, so sickly—is the rhetoric of Joycean language. Far from preserving us from the abject, Joyce causes it to break out in what he sees as prototype of literary utterance: Molly's monologue. If that monologue spreads out the abject, it is not because there is a woman speaking. But because, *from afar*, the writer approaches the hysterical body so that it might speak, so that he might speak, using it as springboard, of what eludes speech and turns out to be the hand to hand struggle of one woman with another, her mother of course, the absolute because primeval seat of the impossible—of the excluded, the outside-of-meaning, the abject. Atopia.

the woman hides it not to give all the trouble they do yes he came
somewhere Im sure by his appetite anyway love its not or hed be off his
feed thinking of her so either it was one of those night women if it was
down there he was really and the hotel story he made up a pack of lies
to hide it planning it Hynes kept me who did I meet ah yes I met do
you remember Menton and who else who let me see that big babbyface
I saw him and he not long married flirting with a young girl at Pooles
Myriorama and turned my back on him when he slinked out looking
quite conscious what harm but he had the impudence to make up to me
one time well done to him mouth almighty and his boiled eyes of all the
big stupoes I ever met and thats called a solicitor only for I hate having
a long wrangle in bed or else if its not that its some little bitch or other
he got in with somewhere or picked up on the sly if they only knew
him as well as I do yes because the day before yesterday he was scrib-
bling something a letter when I came into the front room for the
matches to show him Dignam's death[7]

The abject here does not reside in the thematic of masculine sexuality as Molly
might see it. Not even in the fascinated horror that the other women, sketched out
in back of the men, imbue the speaker with. The abject lies, beyond the themes,
and for Joyce generally, in the way one speaks; it is verbal communication, it is the
Word that discloses the abject. But at the same time, the Word alone purifies from
the abject, and that is what Joyce seems to say when he gives back to the masterly
rhetoric that his *Work in progress* constitutes full powers against abjection. A single
catharsis: the rhetoric of the pure signifier, of music in letters—*Finnegans Wake*.

Céline's journey, to the end of his night, will also encounter rhythm and
music as being the only way out, the ultimate sublimation of the unsignifiable.
Contrary to Joyce, however, Céline will not find salvation in it. Again carrying out
a rejection, without redemption, himself forfeited, Céline will become, body and
tongue, the apogee of that moral, political, and stylistic revulsion that brands our
time. A time that seems to have, for a century now, gone into unending labor
pains. The enchantment will have to wait for some other time, always and forever.

Borges

According to Borges the "object" of literature is in any case vertiginous and
hallucinatory. It is the Aleph, which appears, in its transfinite truth, at the time of a
descent, worthy of Mallarmé's *Igitur*, into the cellar of the native house, condemned
to destruction—by definition. A literature that dares to relate the dizzying pangs
of such a descent is no more than mediocre mockery of an archaic memory that
language lays out as much as it betrays it. The Aleph is exorbitant to the extent
that, within the narrative, nothing could tap its power other than the narration of
infamy. That is, of rampancy, boundlessness, the unthinkable, the untenable, the
unsymbolizable. But what is it? Unless it be the untiring repetition of a drive,
which, propelled by an initial loss, does not cease wandering, unsated, deceived,
warped, until it finds its only stable object—death. Handling that repetition,

staging it, cultivating it until it releases, beyond its eternal return, its sublime destiny of being a struggle with death—is it not that which characterizes writing? And yet, dealing with death in that manner, making sport of it, is that not infamy itself? The literary narrative that utters the workings of repetition must necessarily become, beyond fantastic tales, detective stories, and murder mysteries, a narrative of the infamous (*A Universal History of Infamy*). And the writer cannot but recognize himself, derisive and forfeited, in that abject character, Lazarus Morell, the frightful redeemer, who raises his slaves from the dead only to have them die more fully, but not until they have been circulated—and have brought in a return—like currency. Does that mean that literary objects, our fictional objects, like the slaves of Lazarus Morell, are merely ephemeral resurrections of that elusive Aleph? Does this Aleph, this impossible "object," this impossible imagination, sustain the work of writing, even though the latter is merely a temporary halt in the Borgesian race toward death, which is contained in the chasm of the maternal cave?

> The stealing of horses in one state and selling them in another were barely more than a digression in Morell's criminal career, but they foreshadowed the method that now assures him his rightful place in a Universal History of Infamy. This method is unique not only for the popular circumstances that distinguished it but also for the sordidness it required, for its deadly manipulation of hope, and for its step by step development, so like the hideous unfolding of a nightmare. [. . .]
>
> Flashing rings on their fingers to inspire respect, they traveled up and down the vast plantations of the South. They would pick out a wretched black and offer him freedom. They would tell him that if he ran away from his master and allowed them to sell him, he would receive a portion of the money paid for him, and they would then help him escape again, this second time sending him to a free state. Money and freedom, the jingle of silver dollars together with his liberty—what greater temptation could they offer him? The slave became emboldened for his first escape.
>
> The river provided the natural route. A canoe; the hold of a steamboat; a scow; a great raft as big as the sky, with a cabin at the point or three or four wigwams—the means mattered little, what counted was feeling the movement and the safety of the unceasing river. The black would be sold on some other plantation, then run away again to the canebrakes or the morasses. There his terrible benefactors (about whom he now began to have serious misgivings) cited obscure expenses and told him they had to sell him one final time. On his return, they said, they would give him his part of both sales and his freedom. The man let himself be sold, worked for a while, and on his final escape defied the hounds and the whip. He then made his way back bloodied, sweaty, desperate, and sleepy. [. . .]
>
> The runaway expected his freedom. Lazarus Morell's shadowy mulattoes would give out an order among themselves that was sometimes barely more than a nod of the head, and the slave would be freed

from sight, hearing, touch, day, infamy, time, his benefactors, pity, the air, the hound packs, the world, hope, sweat, and himself. A bullet, a knife, or a blow, and the Mississippi turtles and catfish would receive the last evidence.[8]

Just imagine that imaginary machine transformed into a social institution—and what you get is the infamy of fascism.

Artaud

An "I" overcome by the corpse—such is often the abject in Artaud's text. For it is death that most violently represents the strange state in which a non-subject, a stray, having lost its non-objects, imagines nothingness through the ordeal of abjection. The death that "I" am provokes horror, there is a choking sensation that does not separate inside from outside but draws them the one into the other, indefinitely. Artaud is the inescapable witness of that torture—of that truth.

> The dead little girl says, I am the one who guffaws in horror inside the lungs of the live one. Get me out of there at once.[9]

> Once dead, however, my corpse was thrown out on the dunghill, and I remember having been macerated I don't know how many days or how many hours while waiting to awaken. For I did not know at first that I was dead: I had to make up my mind to understand that before I could succeed in raising myself. A few friends, then, who had completely forsaken me at first, decided to come and embalm my corpse and were joylessly surprised at seeing me again, alive.[10]

> I have no business going to bed with you, things, for I stink more than you do, god, and going to bed does not mean getting soiled but, to the contrary, clearing myself, from you.[11]

At that level of downfall in subject and object, the abject is the equivalent of death. And writing, which allows one to recover, is equal to a resurrection. The writer, then, finds himself marked out for identification with Christ, if only in order for him, too, to be rejected, ab-jected:

> For, as ball-breaking as this may seem, I am that Artaud crucified on Golgotha, not as christ but as Artaud, in other words as complete atheist. I am that body persecuted by erotic golosity, the obscene sexual erotic golosity of mankind, for which pain is a humus, the liquid from a fertile mucus, a serum worth sipping by one who has never on his own gained by being a man while knowing that he was becoming one.[12]

These different literary texts name types of abjects that are answerable to, this goes without saying, different psychic structures. The types of articulation (narrative and syntactic structures, prosodic processes, etc. in the different texts) also vary. Thus the abject, depending on the writer, turns out to be named differently when it is not merely suggested by linguistic modifications that are always some-what elliptic. In the final part of this essay I shall examine in detail a specific articulation of the abject—that of Céline. Let me just say at this point, as an introduction, that contemporary literature, in its multiple variants, and when it is written as the language, possible at last, of that impossible constituted either by a-subjectivity or, by non-objectivity, propounds, as a matter of fact, a sublimation of abjection. Thus it becomes a substitute for the role formerly played by the sacred, at the limits of social and subjective identity. But we are dealing here with a sublimation without consecration. Forfeited.

Catharsis and analysis

That *abjection*, which modernity has learned to repress, dodge, or fake, appears fundamental once the analytic point of view is assumed. Lacan says so when he links that word to the *saintliness* of the analyst, a linkage in which the only aspect of humor that remains is blackness.[13]

One must keep open the wound where he or she who enters into the analytic adventure is located—a wound that the professional establishment, along with the cynicism of the times and of institutions, will soon manage to close up. There is nothing initiatory in that rite, if one understands by "initiation" the accession to a purity that the posture of *death* guaranteed (as in Plato's *Phaedo*) or the unadulter-ated treasure of the "pure signifier" (as is the gold of truth in *The Republic*, or the pure separatism of the statesman in the *Statesman*). It is rather a heterogeneous, corporeal, and verbal ordeal of fundamental incompleteness: a "gaping," "less One." For the unstabilized subject who comes out of that—like a crucified person opening up the stigmata of its desiring body to a speech that structures only on condition that it let go—any signifying or human phenomenon, insofar as it *is*, appears in its being as abjection. For what impossible *catharsis?* Freud, early in his career, used the same word to refer to a therapeutics, the rigor of which was to come out later.

With Plato and Aristotle

The analyst is thus and forever sent back to the question that already haunted Plato when he wanted to take over where Apollonian or Dionysiac religion left off.[14] Purification is something only the Logos is capable of. But is that to be done in the manner of the *Phaedo*, stoically separating oneself from a body whose substance and passions are sources of impurity? Or rather, as in the *Sophist*, after having sorted out the worst from the best; or after the fashion of the *Philebus* by leaving the doors wide open to impurity, provided the eyes of the mind remain focused on truth? In such a case, pleasure, having become pure and true through the harmony of color and form as in the case of accurate and beautiful geometric form, has nothing in common, as the philosopher says, with "the pleasures of scratching" (*Philebus* 51).

Catharsis seems to be a concern that is intrinsic to philosophy, insofar as the latter is an ethics and unable to forget Plato. Even if the *mixture* seems inevitable towards the end of the Platonic course, it is the mind alone, as harmonious wisdom, that insures purity: catharsis has been transformed, where transcendental idealism is concerned, into philosophy. Of the cathartic incantation peculiar to mysteries, Plato has kept only, as we all know, the very uncertain role of poets whose frenzy would be useful to the state only after having been evaluated, sorted out, and purified in its turn by wise men.

Aristotelian catharsis is closer to sacred incantation. It is the one that has bequeathed its name to the common, esthetic concept of catharsis. Through the mimesis of passions—ranging from enthusiasm to suffering—in "language with pleasurable accessories," the most important of which being *rhythm* and *song* (see the *Poetics*), the soul reaches *orgy* and *purity* at the same time. What is involved is a purification of body and soul by means of a heterogeneous and complex circuit, going from "bile" to "fire," from "manly warmth" to the "enthusiasm" of the "mind." Rhythm and song hence arouse the impure, the other of mind, the passionate-corporeal-sexual-virile, but they harmonize it, arrange it differently than the wise man's knowledge does. They thus soothe frenzied outbursts (Plato, in the *Laws*, allowed such use of rhythm and meter only to the mother rocking her child), by contributing an *external* rule, a poetic one, which fills the gap, inherited from Plato, between body and soul. To Platonic *death*, which owned, so to speak, the state of purity, Aristotle opposed the act of *poetic purification*—in itself an impure process that protects from the abject only by dint of being immersed in it. The abject, mimed through sound and meaning, is *repeated*. Getting rid of it is out of the question—the final Platonic lesson has been understood, one does not get rid of the impure; one can, however, bring it into being a second time, and differently from the original impurity. It is a repetition through rhythm and song, therefore through what is not yet, or no longer is "meaning," but arranges, defers, differentiates and organizes, harmonizes pathos, bile, warmth, and enthusiasm. Benveniste translates "rhythm" by "trace" and "concatenation" [*enchaînement*]. Prometheus is "rhythmical," and we call him "bound" [*enchaîné*]. An attachment on the near and far side of language. Aristotle seems to say that there is a discourse of sex and that is not the discourse of knowledge—it is the only possible catharsis. That discourse is audible, and through the speech that it mimics it repeats on another register what the latter does not say.

Philosophical sadness and the spoken disaster of the analyst

Poetic catharsis, which for more than two thousand years behaved as an underage sister of philosophy, face to face and incompatible with it, takes us away from purity, hence from Kantian ethics, which has long governed modern codes and remains more faithful to a certain Platonic stoicism. By means of the "universal-izing of maxims," as is well known, the Kant of the *Foundations of the Metaphysics of Ethics* or of the *Metaphysical Principles of Virtue* advocated an "ethical gymnastics" in order to give us, by means of consciousness, control over our defilements and, through that very consciousness, making us free and joyous.

More skeptical and, from a certain point of view, more Aristotelian, Hegel, on the contrary, rejects a "calculation" that claims to eliminate defilement, for the latter seems *fundamental* to him. Probably echoing the Greek polis, he conceives of no other ethics than that of the *act*. Also distrustful, however, of those fine aestheticizing souls who find purity in the elaboration of empty forms, he obviously does not hold to the mimetic and orgiastic catharsis of Aristotle. It is in the *historical* act that Hegel sees fundamental impurity being expended; as a matter of fact, the latter is a sexual impurity whose historical achievement consists in marriage. But—and this is where transcendental idealism, too, sadly comes to an end—here it is that desire (*Lust*), thus normalized in order to escape abject concupiscence (*Begierde*), sinks into a banality that is sadness and silence. How come? Hegel does not condemn impurity because it is exterior to ideal consciousness; more profoundly—but also more craftily—he thinks that it can and should get rid of itself through the historico-social act. If he thereby differs from Kant, he nevertheless shares his condemnation of (sexual) impurity. He agrees with his aim to keep consciousness apart from defilement, which, nevertheless, dialectically constitutes it. Reabsorbed into the trajectory of the Idea, what can defilement become if not the negative side of consciousness—that is, lack of communication and speech? In other words, defilement as reabsorbed in marriage becomes sadness. In so doing, it has not strayed too far from its logic, according to which it is a border of discourse—a silence.[15]

It is obvious that the analyst, from the abyss of his silence, brushes against the ghost of the sadness Hegel saw in sexual normalization. Such sadness is the more obvious to him as his ethics is rigorous—founded, as it must be in the West, on the remains of transcendental idealism. But one can also argue that the Freudian stance, which is dualistic and dissolving, unsettles those foundations. In that sense, it causes the sad, analytic silence to hover above a strange, foreign discourse, which, strictly speaking, shatters verbal communication (made up of a knowledge and a truth that are nevertheless heard) by means of a device that mimics terror, enthusiasm, or orgy, and is more closely related to rhythm and song than it is to the World. There is mimesis (some say identification) in the analytic passage through castration. And yet it is necessary that the analyst's interpretative speech (and not only his literary or theoretical bilingualism) be affected by it in order to be analytical. As counterpoise to a purity that found its bearings in disillusioned sadness, it is the "poetic" unsettlement of analytic utterance that testifies to its closeness to, cohabitation with, and "knowledge" of abjection.

I am thinking, in short, of the completely mimetic *identification* (transference and countertransference) of the analyst with respect to analysands. That identification allows for securing in their place what, when parcelled out, makes them suffering and barren. It allows one to regress back to the affects that can be heard in the breaks in discourse, to provide rhythm, too, to concatenate (is that what "to become conscious" means?) the gaps of a speech saddened because it turned its back on its abject meaning. If there is analytic jouissance it is there, in the thoroughly poetic mimesis that runs through the architecture of speech and extends from coenesthetic image to logical and phantasmatic articulations. Without for that matter biologizing language, and while breaking away from identification by means of interpretation, analytic speech is one that becomes "incarnate" in the full sense of the term. On that condition only, it is "cathartic"—meaning thereby that it is the equivalent, for the analyst as well as for the analysand, not of purification but of rebirth with and against abjection.

This preliminary survey of abjection, phenomenological on the whole, will now lead me to a more straightforward consideration of analytic theory on the one hand, of the history of religions on the other, and finally of contemporary literary experience.

Notes

1   Francis de Sales, *Introduction to a Devout Life*, Thomas S. Kepler, tr. (New York: World, 1952), p. 125. [Modified to conform to the French text, which reads, "l'abjection de soy-mesme."]

2   Fyodor Dostoyevsky, *The Devils*, David Magarshack, tr. (London: Penguin Books, 1953), p. 512.

3   Dostoyevsky, pp. 586–587.

4   Dostoyevsky, pp. 418–419.

5   Marcel Proust, *Swann's Way*, C. K. Scott-Moncrieff, tr. (New York: Random House, 1922), 2:141.

6   Proust, *Cities of the Plain*, Frederick A. Blossom, tr. (New York: Random House, 1934), p. 9.

7   James Joyce, *Ulysses* (New York: Vintage Books, 1961), pp. 738–739.

8   Jorge Luis Borges, *A Universal History of Infamy*, Norman Thomas Di Giovanni, tr. (New York: Dutton, 1979), pp. 23–25.

9   Antonin Artaud, "Suppôts et supplications," in *Œuvres Complètes* (Paris: Gallimard, 1978), 14:14.

10   Artaud, p. 72.

11   Artaud, p. 203.

12   Artaud, p. 155.

13   Jacques Lacan, *Télévision* (Paris: Seuil, 1974), p. 28.

14   In connection with catharsis in the Greek world, see Louis Molinier, *Le Pur et l'impur dans la pensée des Grecs* (Paris: Klincksieck, 1952).

15   See A. Philonenko, "Note sur les concepts de souillure et de pureté dans l'idéalisme allemand," *Les Etudes Philosophiques* (1972), 4:481–493.

Suggestions for further reading

Douglas, Mary, *Purity and Danger: An Analysis of Concepts of Pollution and Taboo,* London and New York: Routledge, 2002.

Fletcher, John, and Benjamin, Andrew (eds.), *Abjection, Melancholia and Love: The Work of Julia Kristeva,* London: Routledge, 1990.

Kristeva, Julia, *Desire in Language: A Semiotic Approach to Literature and Art,* ed. Leon S. Roudiez, trans. Thomas Gora *et al.,* New York: Columbia University Press, 1980.

Chapter 20

Jean Baudrillard

'SIMULACRA AND SCIENCE FICTION', 1981

THREE ORDERS OF SIMULACRA:

> simulacra that are natural, naturalist, founded on the image, on imitation and counterfeit, that are harmonious, optimistic, and that aim for the restitution or the ideal institution of nature made in God's image;
>
> simulacra that are productive, productivist, founded on energy, force, its materialization by the machine and in the whole system of production—a Promethean aim of a continuous globalization and expansion, of an indefinite liberation of energy (desire belongs to the utopias related to this order of simulacra);
>
> simulacra of simulation, founded on information, the model, the cybernetic game—total operationality, hyperreality, aim of total control.

To the first category belongs the imaginary of the *utopia*. To the second corresponds science fiction, strictly speaking. To the third corresponds—is there an imaginary that might correspond to this order? The most likely answer is that the good old imaginary of science fiction is dead and that something else is in the process of emerging (not only in fiction but in theory as well). The same wavering and indeterminate fate puts an end to science fiction—but also to theory, as specific genres.

There is no real, there is no imaginary except at a certain distance. What happens when this distance, including that between the real and the imaginary, tends to abolish itself, to be reabsorbed on behalf of the model? Well, from one order of simulacra to another, the tendency is certainly toward the reabsorption of this distance, of this gap that leaves room for an ideal or critical projection.

This projection is maximized in the utopian, in which a transcendent sphere, a radically different universe takes form (the romantic dream is still the individualized form of utopia, in which transcendence is outlined in depth, even in unconscious structures, but in any case the dissociation from the real world is maximized, the island of utopia stands opposed to the continent of the real).

This projection is greatly reduced in science fiction: it is most often nothing other than an unbounded projection of the real world of production, but it is not qualitatively different from it. Mechanical or energetic extensions, speed, and power increase to the nth power, but the schemas and the scenarios are those of mechanics, metallurgy, etc. Projected hypostasis of the robot. (To the limited universe of the preindustrial era, utopia *opposed* an ideal, alternative universe. To the potentially infinite universe of production, science fiction *adds* the multiplication of its own possibilities.)

This projection is totally reabsorbed in the implosive era of models. The models no longer constitute either transcendence or projection, they no longer constitute the imaginary in relation to the real, they are themselves an anticipation of the real, and thus leave no room for any sort of fictional anticipation—they are immanent, and thus leave no room for any kind of imaginary transcendence. The field opened is that of simulation in the cybernetic sense, that is, of the manipulation of these models at every level (scenarios, the setting up of simulated situations, etc.) but then *nothing distinguishes this operation from the operation itself and the gestation of the real: there is no more fiction.*

Reality could go beyond fiction: that was the surest sign of the possibility of an ever-increasing imaginary. But the real cannot surpass the model—it is nothing but its alibi.

The imaginary was the alibi of the real, in a world dominated by the reality principle. Today, it is the real that has become the alibi of the model, in a world controlled by the principle of simulation. And, paradoxically, it is the real that has become our true utopia—but a utopia that is no longer in the realm of the possible, that can only be dreamt of as one would dream of a lost object.

Perhaps science fiction from the cybernetic and hyperreal era can only exhaust itself, in its artificial resurrection of "historical" worlds, can only try to reconstruct in vitro, down to the smallest details, the perimeters of a prior world, the events, the people, the ideologies of the past, emptied of meaning, of their original process, but hallucinatory with retrospective truth. Thus in *Simulacra* by Philip K. Dick, the war of Secession. Gigantic hologram in three dimensions, in which fiction will never again be a mirror held toward the future, but a desperate rehallucination of the past.

We can no longer imagine any other universe: the grace of transcendence was taken away from us in that respect too. Classical science fiction was that of an expanding universe, besides, it forged its path in the narratives of spatial exploration, counterparts to the more terrestrial forms of exploration and colonization of the nineteenth and twentieth centuries. There is no relationship of cause and effect there: it is not because terrestrial space today is virtually coded, mapped, registered, saturated, has thus in a sense closed up again in universalizing itself—a universal market, not only of merchandise, but of values, signs, models, leaving no room for the imaginary—it is not exactly because of this that the exploratory universe (technical, mental, cosmic) of science fiction has also ceased to function. But the two are narrowly linked, and they are two versions of the same general process of implosion that follows the gigantic process of explosion and expansion characteristic of past centuries. When a system reaches its own limits and becomes saturated, a reversal is produced—something else takes place, in the imaginary as well.

Until now we have always had a reserve of the imaginary—now the coefficient of reality is proportional to the reserve of the imaginary that gives it its specific weight. This is also true of geographic and spatial exploration: when there is no longer any virgin territory, and thus one available to the imaginary, *when the map covers the whole territory, something like the principle of reality disappears.* In this way, the conquest of space constitutes an irreversible crossing toward the loss of the terrestrial referential. There is a hemorrhaging of reality as an internal coherence of a limited universe, once the limits of this universe recede into infinity. The conquest of space that follows that of the planet is equal to derealizing (dematerializing) human space, or to transferring it into a hyperreal of simulation. Witness this two-bedroom/kitchen/shower put into orbit, raised to a spatial power (one could say) with the most recent lunar module. The everydayness of the terrestrial habitat itself elevated to the rank of cosmic value, hypostatized in space—the satellization of the real in the transcendence of space—it is the end of metaphysics, the end of the phantasm, the end of science fiction—the era of hyperreality begins.

From then onward, something must change: the projection, the extrapolation, the sort of pantographic excess that constituted the charm of science fiction are all impossible. It is no longer possible to fabricate the unreal from the real, the imaginary from the givens of the real. The process will, rather, be the opposite: it will be to put decentered situations, models of simulation in place and to contrive to give them the feeling of the real, of the banal, of lived experience, to reinvent the real as fiction, precisely because it has disappeared from our life. Hallucination of the real, of lived experience, of the quotidian, but reconstituted, sometimes down to disquietingly strange details, reconstituted as an animal or vegetal reserve, brought to light with a transparent precision, but without substance, derealized in advance, hyperrealized.

In this way, science fiction would no longer be a romantic expansion with all the freedom and naïveté that the charm of discovery gave it, but, quite the contrary, it would evolve implosively, in the very image of our current conception of the universe, attempting to revitalize, reactualize, requotidianize fragments of simulation, fragments of this universal simulation that have become for us the so-called real world.

Where would the works be that would meet, here and now, this situational inversion, this situational reversion? Obviously the short stories of Philip K. Dick "gravitate" in this space, if one can use that word (but that is precisely what one can't really do any more, because this new universe is "antigravitational," or if it still gravitates, it is around the *hole* of the real, around the *hole* of the imaginary).

One does not see an alternative cosmos, a cosmic folklore or exoticism, or a galactic prowess there—one is from the start in a total simulation, without origin, immanent, without a past, without a future, a diffusion of all coordinates (mental, temporal, spatial, signaletic)—it is not about a parallel universe, a double universe, or even a possible universe—neither possible, impossible, neither real nor unreal: *hyperreal*—it is a universe of simulation, which is something else altogether. And not because Dick speaks specifically of simulacra—science fiction has always done so, but it played on the double, on doubling or redoubling, either artificial or imaginary, whereas here the double has disappeared, there is no longer a double, one is always already in the other world, which is no longer an other, without a mirror, a projection, or a utopia that can reflect it—simulation is insuperable, unsurpassable, dull and flat, without exteriority—we will no longer even pass through to "the other side of mirror," that was still the golden age of transcendence.

Perhaps a still more convincing example would be that of Ballard and of his evolution from the first very "phantasmagoric" short stories, poetic, dreamlike, disorienting, up to *Crash*, which is without a doubt (more than *IGH* or *Concrete Island*) the current model of this science fiction that is no longer one. *Crash* is *our* world, nothing in it is "invented": everything in it is hyperfunctional, both the circulation and the accident, technique and death, sex and photographic lens, everything in it is like a giant, synchronous, simulated machine: that is to say the acceleration of our own models, of all models that surround us, blended and hyperoperational in the void. This is what distinguishes *Crash* from almost all science fiction, which mostly still revolves around the old (mechanical and mechanistic) couple function/dysfunction, which it projects into the future along the same lines of force and the same finalities that are those of the "normal" universe. Fiction in that universe might surpass reality (or the opposite: that is more subtle) but it still plays by the same rules. In *Crash*, there is neither fiction nor reality anymore—hyperreality abolishes both. It is there that our contemporary science fiction, if there is one, exists. *Jack Barron or Eternity*, some passages from *Everyone to Zanzibar*.

In fact, science fiction in this sense is no longer anywhere, and it is everywhere, in the circulation of models, here and now, in the very principle of the surrounding simulation. It can emerge in its crude state, from the inertia itself of the operational world. What writer of science fiction would have "imagined" (but precisely it can no longer be "imagined") this "reality" of East German factories-simulacra, factories that reemploy all the unemployed to fill all the roles and all the posts of the traditional production process but that don't produce anything, whose activity is consumed in a game of orders, of competition, of writing, of book-keeping, between one factory and another, inside a vast network? All material production is redoubled in the void (one of these simulacra factories even "really" failed, putting its own unemployed out of work a second time). That is simulation: not that the factories are fake, but precisely that they are real, hyperreal, and that because of this they return all "real" production, that of "serious" factories, to the same hyperreality. What is fascinating here is not the opposition between real factories and fake factories, but on the contrary the lack of distinction between the two, the fact that all the rest of production has no greater referent or deeper finality than this "simulacral" business. It is this hyperreal indifference that constitutes the real "science-fictional" quality of this episode. And one can see that it is not necessary to invent it: it is there, emerging from a world without secrets, without depth.

Without a doubt, the most difficult thing today, in the complex universe of science fiction, is to unravel what still complies (and a large part still does) with the imaginary of the second order, of the productive/projective order, and what already comes from this vagueness of the imaginary, of this uncertainty proper to the third order of simulation. Thus one can clearly mark the difference between the mechanical robot machines, characteristic of the second order, and the cybernetic machines, computers, etc., that, in their governing principle, depend on the third order. But one order can certainly contaminate another, and the computer can certainly function as a mechanical supermachine, a superrobot, a superpower machine, exposing the productive genie of the simulacra of the second order: the computer does not come into play as a process of simulation, and it still bears witness to the reflexes of a finalized universe (including ambivalence and revolt, like the computer from *2001* or Shalmanezer in *Everyone to Zanzibar*).

Between the *operatic* (the theatrical status of theatrical and fantastical machinery, the "grand opera" of technique) that corresponds to the first order, the *operative* (the industrial, productive status, productive of power and energy) that corresponds to the second order, and the *operational* (the cybernetic, aleatory, uncertain status of "metatechnique") that corresponds to the third order, all interference can still be produced today at the level of science fiction. But only the last order can still truly interest us.

Suggestions for further reading

Baudrillard, Jean, *The Gulf War Did Not Take Place*, trans. Paul Patton, Bloomington and Indianapolis: Indiana University Press, 1995.

Derrida, Jacques, "The Deconstruction of Actuality: An Interview with Jacques Derrida", *Radical Philosophy*, 1994, vol. 68, 369–418.

Eco, Umberto, *Travels in Hyperreality: Essays*, trans. William Weaver, New York: Harcourt Brace Jovanovich, 1990.

Chapter 21

Jean-François Lyotard

'ANSWER TO THE QUESTION: WHAT IS THE POSTMODERN?', 1982

To Thomas E. Carroll
Milan, May 15, 1982

A demand

WE ARE IN a moment of relaxation – I am speaking of the tenor of the times. Everywhere we are being urged to give up experimentation, in the arts and elsewhere. I have read an art historian who preaches realism and agitates for the advent of a new subjectivity. I have read an art critic who broadcasts and sells "Transavantgardism" in the marketplace of art. I have read that in the name of postmodernism architects are ridding themselves of the Bauhaus project, throwing out the baby – which is still experimentation – with the bath water of functionalism. I have read that a new philosopher has invented something he quaintly calls Judeo-Christianism, with which he intends to put an end to the current impiety for which we are supposedly responsible. I have read in a French weekly that people are unhappy with *Mille Plateaux* because, especially in a book of philosophy, they expect to be rewarded with a bit of sense. I have read from the pen of an eminent historian that avant-garde writers and thinkers of the sixties and seventies introduced a reign of terror into the use of language, and that the imposition of a common mode of speech on intellectuals (that of historians) is necessary to re-establish the conditions for fruitful debate. I have read a young Belgian philosopher of language complaining that continental thought, when faced with the challenge of talking machines, left them to look after reality; that it replaced the paradigm of referentiality with one of adlinguisticity (speaking about speech, writing about writing, intertextuality); he thinks it is time that language recovered a firm anchorage in the referent. I have read a talented theatrologist who says that the tricks and caprices of postmodernism count for little next to authority, especially when a mood of anxiety encourages that authority to adopt a politics of totalitarian vigilance in the face of the threat of nuclear war.

I have read a reputable thinker who defends modernity against those he calls neoconservatives. Under the banner of postmodernism they would like, he believes, to extricate themselves from the still incomplete project of modernity, the project of Englightenment. By his account, even the last partisans of the *Aufklärung*, like Popper or Adorno, were able to defend that project only in particular spheres of life – politics for the author of *The Open Society*, art for the author of *Aesthetic Theory*. Jürgen Habermas (you will have recognised him) thinks that if modernity has foundered, it is because the totality of life has been left to fragment into independent specialties given over to the narrow competence of experts, while the concrete individual experiences "desublimated meaning" and "destructured form", not as a liberation, but in the manner of that immense ennui Baudelaire described over a century ago.

Following Albrecht Wellmer's lead, the philosopher believes that the remedy for this parcelling of culture and its separation from life will only come from a "change in the status of aesthetic experience when it is no longer primarily expressed in judgments of taste", when instead "it is used to illuminate a life-historical situation", that is to say, when "it is related to the problems of existence". For this experience "then enters into a language game which is no longer just that of the aesthetic critic"; it intervenes "in cognitive procedures and normative expectations"; it "changes the way these different moments *refer* to one another". In short, the demand Habermas makes of the arts and the experience they provide is that they should form a bridge over the gap separating the discourses of know-ledge, ethics, and politics, thus opening the way for a unity of experience.

My problem is knowing what sort of unity Habermas has in mind. What is the end envisaged by the project of modernity? Is it the constitution of a sociocultural unity at the heart of which all elements of daily life and thought would have a place, as though within an organic whole? Or is the path to be cut between heterogeneous language games – knowledge, ethics, and politics – of a different order to them? And if so, how would it be capable of realising their effective synthesis?

The first hypothesis, Hegelian in inspiration, does not call into question the notion of a dialectically totalising *experience*. The second is closer in spirit to the *Critique of Judgment*; but, like the *Critique*, it must be submitted to the severe re-examination postmodernity addresses to the thought of the Enlightenment, to the idea of a uniform end of history and the idea of the subject. This critique was started not only by Wittgenstein and Adorno but also by other thinkers, French or otherwise, who have not had the honour of being read by Professor Habermas – at least this spares them getting bad marks for neoconservatism.

Realism

The demands I cited to you at the beginning are not all equivalent. They may even be contradictory. Some are made in the name of postmodernism, some in opposition to it. It is not necessarily the same thing to demand the provision of a referent (and objective reality), or a meaning (and credible transcendence), or an addressee (and a public), or an addressor (and expressive subjectivity), or a communicative consensus (and a general code of exchange, the genre of historical discourse, for example). But in these various invitations to suspend artistic experimentation, there is the same call to order, a desire for unity, identity, security, and popularity (in the sense of *Öffentlichkeit*, "finding a public"). Artists and writers must be made to return to the fold of the community; or at least, if the community is deemed to be ailing, they must be given the responsibility of healing it.

There exists an irrefutable sign of this common disposition: for all these authors, nothing is as urgent as liquidating the legacy of the avant-gardes. The impatience of so-called trans-avantgardism is a case in point. The replies an Italian critic recently gave to French critics leave no doubt on the matter. The procedure of mixing avant-gardes together means that artists and critics can feel more confident of suppressing them than if they were to attack them head on. They can then pass off the most cynical eclecticism as an advance on the no doubt partial nature of earlier explorations. If they turned their backs on such explorations overtly, they would expose themselves to ridicule for neoacademicism. At the time the bourgeoisie was establishing itself in history, the Salons and Academies assumed a purgative function – awarding prizes for good conduct in the plastic and literary arts under the guise of realism. But capitalism in itself has such a capacity to derealise familiar objects, social roles and institutions that so called "realist" representations can no longer evoke reality except through nostalgia or derision – as an occasion for suffering rather than satisfaction. Classicism seems out of the question in a world where reality is so destabilised that it has no material to offer to experience, but only for analysis and experimentation.

This theme is familiar to readers of Walter Benjamin. Still, its precise implications need to be grasped. Photography did not pose an external challenge to painting any more than did industrial cinema to narrative literature. The former refined certain aspects of the program of ordering the visible elaborated by the Quattrocento, and the latter was able to perfect the containment of diachronies within organic totalities – the ideal of exemplary educative novels since the eighteenth century. The substitution of mechanical and industrial production for manual and craft production was not a catastrophe in itself, unless the essence of art is thought to be the expression of individual genius aided by the skills of an artisanal élite.

The greatest challenge lay in the fact that photographic and cinematic processes could accomplish better and faster – and with a diffusion a hundred thousand times greater than was possible for pictorial and narrative realism – the task that academicism had assigned to realism: protecting consciousness from doubt. Industrial photography and cinema always have the edge over painting and the novel when it is a matter of stabilising the referent, of ordering it from a point of view that would give it recognisable meaning, of repeating a syntax and lexicon that would allow addressees to decode images and sequences rapidly, and make it easy for them to become conscious both of their own identities and of the approval they thereby receive from others – since the structures in these images and sequences form a code of communication between them all. So effects of reality – or the fantasms of realism, if you prefer – are multiplied.

If the painter and novelist do not want to be, in their turn, apologists of what exists (and minor ones at that), they have to renounce such therapeutic occupations. They must question the rules of the art of painting and narration as learnt and received from their predecessors. They soon find that such rules are so many methods of deception, seduction and reassurance which make it impossible to be "truthful". An unprecedented split occurs in both painting and literature. Those who refuse to reexamine the rules of art will make careers in mass conformism, using "correct rules" to bring the endemic desire for reality into communication with objects and situations capable of satisfying it. Pornography is the use of photographs and film to this end. It becomes a general model for those pictorial and narrative arts which have not risen to the challenge of the mass media.

As for artists and writers who agree to question the rules of the plastic and narrative arts and perhaps share their suspicions by distributing their work – they are destined to lack credibility in the eyes of the devoted adherents of reality and identity, to find themselves without a guaranteed audience. In this sense, we can impute the dialectic of the avant-gardes to the challenge posed by the realisms of industry and the mass media to the arts of painting and literature. The Duchampian readymade does no more than signify, actively and parodically, this continual process of the dispossession of the painter's craft, and even the artist's. As Thierry de Duve astutely observes, the question of modern aesthetics is not "What is beautiful?" but "What is art to be (and what is literature to be)?"

Realism – which can be defined only by its intention of avoiding the question of reality implied in the question of art – always finds itself somewhere between academicism and kitsch. When authority takes the name of the party, realism and its complement, neoclassicism, triumph over the experimental avant-garde by slandering and censoring it. Even then, "correct" images, "correct" narratives – the correct forms that the party solicits, selects and distributes – must procure a public which will desire them as the appropriate medicine for the depression and anxiety it feels. The demand for reality, that is, for unity, simplicity, communicability, etc., did not have the same intensity or continuity for the German public between the wars as it had for the Russian public after the revolution: here one can draw a distinction between Nazi and Stalinist realism.

All the same, any attack on artistic experimentation mounted by political authority is inherently reactionary: aesthetic judgment would only have to reach a verdict on whether a particular work conforms to the established rules of the beautiful. Instead of the work having to bother with what makes it an art object and whether it will find an appreciative audience, political academicism understands and imposes a priori criteria of the "beautiful", criteria which can, in one move and once and for all, select works and their public. So the use of categories in an aesthetic judgment would be similar to their use in a cognitive judgment. In Kant's terms, both would be determinant judgments: an expression is first "well formed" in the understanding, then only those "cases" which can be subsumed within this expression are retained in experience.

When authority does not take the name of the party but that of capital, the "transavantgardist" solution (postmodernist in Jencks' sense) turns out to be more

appropriate than the anti-modern one. Eclecticism is the degree zero of contemporary general culture: you listen to reggae, you watch a western, you eat
McDonald's at midday and local cuisine at night, you wear Paris perfume in Tokyo
and dress retro in Hong Kong, knowledge is the stuff of TV game shows. It is easy
to find a public for eclectic works. When art makes itself kitsch, it panders to the
disorder which reigns in the "taste" of the patron. Together, artist, gallery owner,
critic and public indulge one another in the Anything Goes – it's time to relax. But
this realism of Anything Goes is the realism of money: in the absence of aesthetic
criteria it is still possible and useful to measure the value of works of art by the
profits they realise. This realism accommodates every tendency just as capitalism
accommodates every "need" – so long as these tendencies and needs have buying
power. As for taste, there is no need to be choosy when you are speculating or
amusing yourself. Artistic and literary investigation is doubly threatened: by "cultural politics" on one side, by the art and book market on the other. The advice it
receives, from one or other of these channels, is to provide works of art which,
first, relate to subjects already existing in the eyes of the public to which they are
addressed and which, second, are made ("well formed") in such a way that this
public will recognise what they are about, understand what they mean, and then be
able to grant or withhold its approval with confidence, possibly even drawing some
solace from those it accepts.

The sublime and the avant-garde

This interpretation of the contact of the mechanical and industrial arts with
the fine arts and literature is acceptable as an outline, but you would have to
agree it is narrowly sociologistic and historicising, in other words, one-sided.
Notwithstanding the reservations of Benjamin and Adorno, it should be remembered that science and industry are just as open to suspicion with regard to reality
as art and writing. To think otherwise would be to subscribe to an excessively
humanist idea of the Mephistophelian functionalism of science and technology.
One cannot deny the predominance of technoscience as it exists today, that is, the
massive subordination of cognitive statements to the finality of the best possible
performance – which is a technical criterion. Yet the mechanical and the industrial, particularly when they enter fields traditionally reserved for the artist, are
bearers of something more than effects of power. The objects and thoughts issuing
from scientific knowledge and the capitalist economy bring with them one of
the rules underwriting their possibility: the rule that there is no reality unless it
is confirmed by a consensus between partners on questions of knowledge and
commitment.

This rule is of no small consequence. It is the stamp left on the politics of both
the scientist and the manager of capital by a sort of flight of reality from the
metaphysical, religious and political assurances which the mind once believed it
possessed. This retreat is indispensable to the birth of science and capitalism.
There would be no physics had doubt not been cast on the Aristotelian theory of
movement. No industry without the refutation of corporatism, mercantilism and
physiocracy. Modernity, whenever it appears, does not occur without a shattering

of belief, without a discovery of the *lack of reality* in reality – a discovery linked to the invention of other realities.

What would this "lack of reality" mean if we were to free it from a purely historicising interpretation? The phrase is clearly related to what Nietzsche calls nihilism. Yet I see a modulation of it well before Nietzschean perspectivism, in the Kantian theme of the sublime. In particular, I think the aesthetic of the sublime is where modern art (including literature) finds its impetus and where the logic of the avantgarde finds its axioms.

The sublime feeling, which is also the feeling of the sublime, is, according to Kant, a powerful and equivocal emotion: it brings both pleasure and pain. Or rather, in it pleasure proceeds from pain. In the tradition of the philosophy of the subject coming from Augustine and Descartes – which Kant does not radically question – this contradiction (which others might call neurosis or masochism) develops as a conflict between all of the faculties of the subject, between the faculty to conceive of something and the faculty to "present" something. There is knowledge first if a statement is intelligible, and then if "cases" which "correspond" to it can be drawn from experience. There is beauty if a particular "case" (a work of art), given first by the sensibility and with no conceptual determination, arouses a feeling of pleasure that is independent of any interest and appeals to a principle of universal consensus (which may never be realised).

Taste in this way demonstrates that an accord between the capacity to conceive and the capacity to present an object corresponding to the concept – an accord that is undetermined, without rule, giving rise to what Kant calls a reflective judgment – may be felt in the form of pleasure. The sublime is a different feeling. It occurs when the imagination in fact fails to present any object which could accord with a concept, even if only in principle. We have the Idea of the world (the totality of what is) but not the capacity to show an example of it. We have the Idea of the simple (the non-decomposable), but we cannot illustrate it by a sensible object which would be a case of it. We can conceive of the absolutely great, the absolutely powerful; but any presentation of an object – which would be intended to "display" that absolute greatness or absolute power – appears sadly lacking to us. These Ideas, for which there is no possible presentation and which therefore provide no knowledge of reality (experience), also prohibit the free accord of the faculties that produces the feeling of the beautiful. They obstruct the formation and stabilisation of taste. One could call them unpresentable.

I shall call modern the art which devotes its "trivial technique", as Diderot called it, to presenting the existence of something unpresentable. Showing that there is something we can conceive of which we can neither see nor show: this is the stake of modern painting. But how do we show something that cannot be seen? Kant himself suggests the direction to follow when he calls *formlessness*, the *absence of form*, a possible index to the unpresentable. And, speaking of the empty *abstraction* felt by the imagination as it searches for a presentation of the infinite (another unpresentable), he says that it is itself like a presentation of the infinite, its *negative presentation*. He cites the passage "Thou shalt not make unto Thee any graven image, etc." (*Exodus 2,4*) as the most sublime in the Bible, in that it forbids any presentation of the absolute. For an outline of an aesthetic of sublime painting, there is little we need to add to these remarks: as painting, it will evidently "present" something, but negatively: it will therefore avoid figuration or representation; it will be "blank" [*blanche*] like one of Malevich's squares; it will make one see only by prohibiting one from seeing; it will give pleasure only by giving pain. In these formulations we can recognise the axioms of the avant-gardes in painting to the extent that they dedicate themselves to allusions to the unpresentable through visible presentations. The systems of reasoning in whose name or with which this task could support and justify itself warrant a good deal of attention; but such systems cannot take shape except by setting out from the vocation of the sublime with the aim of legitimating this vocation, in other words, of disguising it. They remain inexplicable without the incommensurability between reality and concept implied by the Kantian philosophy of the sublime.

I do not intend to analyse in detail here the way the various avant-gardes have, as it were, humiliated and disqualified reality by their scrutiny of the pictorial techniques used to instill a belief in it. Local tone, drawing, the blending of colours, linear perspective, the nature of the support and of tools, "execution", the hanging of the work, the museum: the avant-gardes continually expose the artifices of presentation that allow thought to be enslaved by the gaze and diverted from the unpresentable. If Habermas, like Marcuse, takes this work of derealisation as an aspect of the (repressive) "desublimation" characterising the avant-garde, it is because he confuses the Kantian sublime with Freudian sublimation, and because for him aesthetics is still an aesthetics of the beautiful.

The postmodern

What then is the postmodern? What place, if any, does it occupy in that vertiginous work of questioning the rules that govern images and narratives? It is undoubtedly part of the modern. Everything that is received must be suspected, even if it is only a day old (*modo, modo*, wrote Petronius). What space does Cézanne challenge? The Impressionists'. What object do Picasso and Braque challenge? Cézanne's. What presupposition does Duchamp break with in 1912? The idea that one has to make a painting – even a cubist painting. And Buren examines another presupposition that he believes emerged intact from Duchamp's work: the place of the work's presentation. The "generations" flash by at an astonishing rate. A work can become modern only if it is first postmodern. Thus understood, postmodernism is not modernism at its end, but in a nascent state, and this state is recurrent.

But I would not wish to be held to this somewhat mechanistic use of the word. If it is true that modernity unfolds in the retreat of the real and according to the sublime relationship of the presentable with the conceivable, we can (to use a musical idiom) distinguish two essential modes in this relationship. The accent can fall on the inadequacy of the faculty of presentation, on the nostalgia for presence experienced by the human subject and the obscure and futile will which animates it in spite of everything. Or else the accent can fall on the power of the faculty to conceive, on what one might call its "inhumanity" (a quality Apollinaire insists upon in modern artists) – since it is of no concern to the understanding whether or not the human sensibility or imagination accords with what it conceives – and on the extension of being and jubilation which come from inventing new rules of

the game, whether pictorial, artistic, or something else. A caricatured arrangement of several names on the chessboard of avantgardist history will show you
what I mean: on the side of *melancholy*, the German Expressionists, on the side of
novatio, Braque and Picasso; on the one hand, Malevich, on the other, El Lissitsky;
on one side, de Chirico, on the other, Duchamp. What distinguishes these two
modes may only be the merest nuance: they often coexist almost indiscernibly in
the same piece, and yet they attest to a *différend* [an incommensurable difference of
opinion] within which the fate of thought has, for a long time, been played out and
will continue to be played out – a differend between regret and experimentation.

The works of Proust and Joyce both allude to something that does not let itself
be made present. Allusion (to which Paulo Fabbri has recently drawn my attention) is, perhaps, an indispensable mode of expression for works which belong to
the aesthetic of the sublime. In Proust the thing that is eluded as the price of this
allusion is the identity of consciousness, falling prey to an excess of time. But in
Joyce it is the identity of writing which falls prey to an excess of the book or
literature. Proust invokes the unpresentable by means of a language which keeps its
syntax and lexicon intact, and a writing which, in terms of most of its operators, is
still part of the genre of the narrative novel. The literary institution as Proust
inherits it from Balzac or Flaubert is undoubtedly subverted since the hero is not a
character but the inner consciousness of time, and also because the diachrony of
the diegesis, already shaken by Flaubert, is further challenged by the choice of
narrative voice. But the unity of the book as the odyssey of this consciousness is not
disturbed, even if it is put off from chapter to chapter: the identity of the writing
with itself within the labyrinth of its interminable narration is enough to connote
this unity, which some have compared to that of the *Phenomenology of Spirit*. Joyce
makes us discern the unpresentable in the writing itself, in the signifier. A whole
range of accepted narrative and even stylistic operators is brought into play with
no concern for the unity of the whole, and experiments are conducted with new
operators. The grammar and vocabulary of literary language are no longer taken
for granted; instead they appear as academicisms, rituals born of a piety (as
Nietzsche might call it) that does not allow the invocation of the unpresentable.

So this is the differend: the modern aesthetic is an aesthetic of the sublime, but
it is nostalgic; it allows the unpresentable to be invoked only as absent content,
while form, thanks to its recognisable consistency, continues to offer the reader or
spectator material for consolation and pleasure. But such feelings do not amount
to the true sublime feeling, which is intrinsically a combination of pleasure and
pain: pleasure in reason exceeding all presentation, pain in the imagination or
sensibility proving inadequate to the concept.

The postmodern would be that which in the modern invokes the unpresentable in presentation itself, which refuses the consolation of correct forms, refuses
the consensus of taste permitting a common experience of nostalgia for the impossible, and inquires into new presentations – not to take pleasure in them but to
better produce the feeling that there is something unpresentable. The postmodern
artist or writer is in the position of a philosopher: the text he writes or the work
he creates is not in principle governed by pre-established rules and cannot be
judged according to a determinant judgment, by the application of given categories to this text or work. Such rules and categories are what the work or text is

investigating. The artist and the writer therefore work without rules, and in order to establish the rules for what *will have been made*. This is why the work and the text can take on the properties of an event; it is also why they would arrive too late for their author or, in what amounts to the same thing, why their creation would always begin too soon. *Postmodern* would be understanding according to the paradox of the future (*post*) anterior (*modo*).

It seems to me that the essay (Montaigne) is postmodern, and the fragment (the *Athenaeum*) is modern.

Finally, it should be made clear that it is not up to us to *provide reality* but to invent allusions to what is conceivable but not presentable. And this task should not lead us to expect the slightest reconciliation between "language games" – Kant, naming them the faculties, knew that they are separated by an abyss and that only a transcendental illusion (Hegel's) can hope to totalise them into a real unity. But he also knew that the price of this illusion is terror. The 19th and 20th centuries have given us our fill of terror. We have paid dearly for our nostalgia for the all and the one, for a reconciliation of the concept and the sensible, for a transparent and communicable experience. Beneath the general demand for relaxation and appeasement, we hear murmurings of the desire to reinstitute terror and fulfil the fantasm of taking possession of reality. The answer is: war on totality. Let us attest to the unpresentable, let us activate the differends and save the honour of the name.

Suggestions for further reading

Jameson, Fredric, *Postmodernism, or, the Cultural Logic of Late Capitalism*, Durham, NC: Duke University Press, 1991.

Lyotard, Jean-François, *The Postmodern Condition: A Report on Knowledge,* trans. Geoff Bennington and Brian Massumi, Manchester: Manchester University Press, 1984.

Readings, Bill, *The University in Ruins,* Cambridge, MA and London: Harvard University Press, 1996.

Chapter 22

Gayle Rubin

'THINKING SEX: NOTES TOWARDS A RADICAL THEORY OF THE POLITICS OF SEXUALITY', 1984

The sex wars

> Asked his advice, Dr. J. Guerin affirmed that, after all other treatments had failed, he had succeeded in curing young girls affected by the vice of onanism by burning the clitoris with a hot iron. . . . I apply the hot point three times to each of the large labia and another on the clitoris. . . . After the first operation, from forty to fifty times a day, the number of voluptuous spasms was reduced to three or four. . . . We believe, then, that in cases similar to those submitted to your consideration, one should not hesitate to resort to the hot iron, and at an early hour, in order to combat clitoral and vaginal onanism in little girls.
>
> Demetrius Zambaco[1]

THE TIME HAS come to think about sex. To some, sexuality may seem to be an unimportant topic, a frivolous diversion from the more critical problems of poverty, war, disease, racism, famine, or nuclear annihilation. But it is precisely at times such as these, when we live with the possibility of unthinkable destruction, that people are likely to become dangerously crazy about sexuality. Contemporary conflicts over sexual values and erotic conduct have much in common with the religious disputes of earlier centuries. They acquire immense symbolic weight. Disputes over sexual behavior often become the vehicles for displacing social anxieties, and discharging their attendant emotional intensity. Consequently, sexuality should be treated with special respect in times of great social stress.

The realm of sexuality also has its own internal politics, inequities, and modes of oppression. As with other aspects of human behavior, the concrete institutional forms of sexuality at any given time and place are products of human activity. They are imbued with conflicts of interest and political maneuvering, both deliberate and incidental. In that sense, sex is always political. But there are also historical periods in which sexuality is more sharply contested and more overtly politicized. In such periods, the domain of erotic life is, in effect, renegotiated.

In England and the United States, the late nineteenth century was one such era. During that time, powerful social movements focused on "vices" of all sorts. There were educational and political campaigns to encourage chastity, to eliminate prostitution, and to discourage masturbation, especially among the young. Morality crusaders attacked obscene literature, nude paintings, music halls, abortion, birth control information, and public dancing.[2] The consolidation of Victorian morality, and its apparatus of social, medical, and legal enforcement, was the outcome of a long period of struggle whose results have been bitterly contested ever since.

The consequences of these great nineteenth-century moral paroxysms are still with us. They have left a deep imprint on attitudes about sex, medical practice, child-rearing, parental anxieties, police conduct, and sex law.

The idea that masturbation is an unhealthy practice is part of that heritage. During the nineteenth century, it was commonly thought that "premature" interest in sex, sexual excitement, and, above all, sexual release, would impair the health and maturation of a child. Theorists differed on the actual consequences of sexual precocity. Some thought it led to insanity, while others merely predicted stunted growth. To protect the young from premature arousal, parents tied children down at night so they would not touch themselves; doctors excised the clitorises of onanistic little girls.[3] Although the more gruesome techniques have been abandoned, the attitudes that produced them persist. The notion that sex *per se* is harmful to the young has been chiseled into extensive social and legal structures designed to insulate minors from sexual knowledge and experience.

Much of the sex law currently on the books also dates from the nineteenth-century morality crusades. The first federal anti-obscenity law in the United States was passed in 1873. The Comstock Act – named for Anthony Comstock, an ancestral antiporn activist and the founder of the New York Society for the Suppression of Vice – made it a federal crime to make, advertise, sell, possess, send through the mails, or import books or pictures deemed obscene. The law also banned contraceptive or abortifacient drugs and devices and information about them.[4] In the wake of the federal statute, most states passed their own anti-obscenity laws.

The Supreme Court began to whittle down both federal and state Comstock laws during the 1950s. By 1975, the prohibition of materials used for, and information about, contraception and abortion had been ruled unconstitutional. However, although the obscenity provisions have been modified, their fundamental constitutionality has been upheld. Thus it remains a crime to make, sell, mail, or import material which has no purpose other than sexual arousal.[5]

Although sodomy statutes date from older strata of the law, when elements of canon law were adopted into civil codes, most of the laws used to arrest homosexuals and prostitutes come out of the Victorian campaigns against "white slavery." These campaigns produced myriad prohibitions against solicitation, lewd behavior, loitering for immoral purposes, age offenses, and brothels and bawdy houses.

In her discusssion of the British "white slave" scare, historian Judith Walkowitz observes that: "Recent research delineates the vast discrepancy between lurid journalistic accounts and the reality of prostitution. Evidence of widespread entrapment of British girls in London and abroad is slim."[6] However, public furor over this ostensible problem

> forced the passage of the Criminal Law Amendment Act of 1885, a particularly nasty and pernicious piece of omnibus legislation. The 1885 Act raised the age of consent for girls from 13 to 16, but it also gave police far greater summary jurisdiction over poor working-class women and children . . . it contained a clause making indecent acts between consenting male adults a crime, thus forming the basis of legal prosecution of male homosexuals in Britain until 1967 . . . the clauses of the new bill were mainly enforced against working-class women, and regulated adult rather than youthful sexual behaviour.[7]

In the United States, the Mann Act, also known as the White Slave Traffic Act, was passed in 1910. Subsequently, every state in the union passed anti-prostitution legislation.[8]

In the 1950s, in the United States, major shifts in the organization of sexuality took place. Instead of focusing on prostitution or masturbation, the anxieties of the 1950s condensed most specifically around the image of the "homosexual menace" and the dubious specter of the "sex offender." Just before and after World War II, the "sex offender" became an object of public fear and scrutiny. Many states and cities, including Massachusetts, New Hampshire, New Jersey, New York State, New York City and Michigan, launched investigations to gather information about this menace to public safety.[9] The term "sex offender" sometimes applied to rapists, sometimes to "child molesters," and eventually functioned as a code for homosexuals. In its bureaucratic, medical, and popular versions, the sex offender discourse tended to blur distinctions between violent sexual assault and illegal but consensual acts such as sodomy. The criminal justice system incorporated these concepts when an epidemic of sexual psychopath laws swept through state legislatures.[10] These laws gave the psychological professions increased police powers over homosexuals and other sexual "deviants."

From the late 1940s until the early 1960s, erotic communities whose activities did not fit the postwar American dream drew intense persecution. Homosexuals were, along with communists, the objects of federal witch hunts and purges. Congressional investigations, executive orders, and sensational exposés in the media aimed to root out homosexuals employed by the government. Thousands lost their jobs, and restrictions on federal employment of homosexuals persist to this day.[11] The FBI began systematic surveillance and harassment of homosexuals which lasted at least into the 1970s.[12]

Many states and large cities conducted their own investigations, and the federal witch-hunts were reflected in a variety of local crackdowns. In Boise, Idaho, in 1955, a schoolteacher sat down to breakfast with his morning paper and read that the vice-president of the Idaho First National Bank had been arrested on felony sodomy charges; the local prosecutor said that he intended to eliminate all homosexuality from the community. The teacher never finished his breakfast. "He jumped up from his seat, pulled out his suitcases, packed as fast as he could, got into his car, and drove straight to San Francisco. . . . The cold eggs, coffee, and toast remained on his table for two days before someone from his school came by to see what had happened."[13]

In San Francisco, police and media waged war on homosexuals throughout the 1950s. Police raided bars, patrolled cruising areas, conducted street sweeps, and trumpeted their intention of driving the queers out of San Francisco.[14] Crackdowns against gay individuals, bars, and social areas occurred throughout the country. Although anti-homosexual crusades are the best-documented examples of erotic repression in the 1950s, future research should reveal similar patterns of increased harassment against pornographic materials, prostitutes, and erotic deviants of all sorts. Research is needed to determine the full scope of both police persecution and regulatory reform.[15]

The current period bears some uncomfortable similarities to the 1880s and the 1950s. The 1977 campaign to repeal the Dade County, Florida, gay rights ordinance inaugurated a new wave of violence, state persecution, and legal initiatives directed against minority sexual populations and the commercial sex industry. For the last six years, the United States and Canada have undergone an extensive sexual repression in the political, not the psychological, sense. In the spring of 1977, a few weeks before the Dade County vote, the news media were suddenly full of reports of raids on gay cruising areas, arrests for prostitution, and investigations into the manufacture and distribution of pornographic materials. Since then, police activity against the gay community has increased exponentially. The gay press has documented hundreds of arrests, from the libraries of Boston to the streets of Houston and the beaches of San Francisco. Even the large, organized, and relatively powerful urban gay communities have been unable to stop these depredations. Gay bars and bath houses have been busted with alarming frequency, and police have gotten bolder. In one especially dramatic incident, police, in Toronto raided all four of the city's gay baths. They broke into cubicles with crowbars and hauled almost 300 men out into the winter streets, clad in their bath towels. Even "liberated" San Francisco has not been immune. There have been proceedings against several bars, countless arrests in the parks, and, in the fall of 1981, police arrested over 400 people in a series of sweeps of Polk Street, one of the thoroughfares of local gay nightlife. Queerbashing has become a significant recreational activity for young urban males. They come into gay neighborhoods armed with baseball bats and looking for trouble, knowing that the adults in their lives either secretly approve or will look the other way.

The police crackdown has not been limited to homosexuals. Since 1977, enforcement of existing laws against prostitution and obscenity has been stepped up. Moreover, states and municipalities have been passing new and tighter regulations on commercial sex. Restrictive ordinances have been passed, zoning laws altered, licensing and safety codes amended, sentences increased, and evidentiary requirements relaxed. This subtle legal codification of more stringent controls over adult sexual behavior has gone largely unnoticed outside of the gay press.

For over a century, no tactic for stirring up erotic hysteria has been as reliable as the appeal to protect children. The current wave of erotic terror has reached deepest into those areas bordered in some way, if only symbolically, by the sexuality of the young. The motto of the Dade County repeal campaign was "Save Our Children" from alleged homosexual recruitment. In February 1977, shortly before the Dade County vote, a sudden concern with "child pornography" swept the national media. In May, the *Chicago Tribune* ran a lurid four-day series with three-inch headlines, which claimed to expose a national vice ring organized to lure young boys into prostitution and pornography.[16] Newspapers across the country ran similar stories, most of them worthy of the *National Enquirer*. By the end of May, a congressional investigation was underway. Within weeks, the federal government had enacted a sweeping bill against "child pornography" and many of the states followed with bills of their own. These laws have reestablished restrictions on sexual materials that had been relaxed by some of the important Supreme Court decisions. For instance, the Court ruled that neither nudity nor sexual activity *per se* were obscene. But the child pornography laws define as obscene any depiction of minors who are nude or engaged in sexual activity. This means that photographs of naked children in anthropology textbooks and many of the ethnographic movies shown in college classes are technically illegal in several states. In fact, the instructors are liable to an additional felony charge for showing such images to each student under the age of 18. Although the Supreme Court has also ruled that it is a constitutional right to possess obscene material for private use, the child pornography laws prohibit even the private possession of any sexual material involving minors.

The laws produced by the child porn panic are ill-conceived and misdirected. They represent far-reaching alterations in the regulation of sexual behavior and abrogate important sexual civil liberties. But hardly anyone noticed as they swept through Congress and state legislatures. With the exception of the North American Man/Boy Love Association and the American Civil Liberties Union, no one raised a peep of protest.[17]

A new and even tougher federal child pornography bill has just reached House-Senate conference. It removes any requirement that prosecutors must prove that alleged child pornography was distributed for commercial sale. Once this bill becomes law, a person merely possessing a nude snapshot of a 17-year-old lover or friend may go to jail for fifteen years, and be fined $100,000. This bill passed the House 400 to 1.[18]

The experiences of art photographer Jacqueline Livingston exemplify the climate created by the child porn panic. An assistant professor of photography at Cornell University, Livingston was fired in 1978 after exhibiting pictures of male nudes which included photographs of her seven-year-old son masturbating. *Ms. Magazine*, *Chrysalis*, and *Art News* all refused to run ads for Livingston's posters of male nudes. At one point, Kodak confiscated some of her film, and for several months, Livingston lived with the threat of prosecution under the child pornography laws. The Tompkins County Department of Social Services investigated her fitness as a parent. Livingston's posters have been collected by the Museum of Modern Art, the Metropolitan, and other major museums. But she has paid a high cost in harassment and anxiety for her efforts to capture on film the uncensored male body at different ages.[19]

It is easy to see someone like Livingston as a victim of the child porn wars. It is harder for most people to sympathize with actual boy-lovers. Like communists and homosexuals in the 1950s, boy-lovers are so stigmatized that it is difficult to find defenders for their civil liberties, let alone for their erotic orientation. Consequently, the police have feasted on them. Local police, the FBI, and watch-dog postal inspectors have joined to build a huge apparatus whose sole aim is to wipe out the community of men who love underaged youth. In twenty years or so, when some of the smoke has cleared, it will be much easier to show that these men have been the victims of a savage and undeserved witch-hunt. A lot of people will be embarrassed by their collaboration with this persecution, but it will be too late to do much good for those men who have spent their lives in prison.

While the misery of the boy-lovers affects very few, the other long-term legacy of the Dade County repeal affects almost everyone. The success of the anti-gay campaign ignited long-simmering passions of the American right, and sparked an extensive movement to compress the boundaries of acceptable sexual behavior.

Right-wing ideology linking non-familial sex with communism and political weakness is nothing new. During the McCarthy period, Alfred Kinsey and his Institute for Sex Research were attacked for weakening the moral fiber of Americans and rendering them more vulnerable to communist influence. After congressional investigations and bad publicity, Kinsey's Rockefeller grant was terminated in 1954.[20]

Around 1969, the extreme right discovered the Sex Information and Education Council of the United States (SIECUS). In books and pamphlets, such as *The Sex Education Racket: Pornography in the Schools* and *SIECUS: Corrupter of Youth*, the right attacked SIECUS and sex education as communist plots to destroy the family and sap the national will.[21] Another pamphlet, *Pavlov's Children (They May Be Yours)*, claims that the United Nations Educational, Scientific and Cultural Organization (UNESCO) is in cahoots with SIECUS to undermine religious taboos, to promote the acceptance of abnormal sexual relations, to downgrade absolute moral stand-ards, and to "destroy racial cohesion," by exposing white people (especially white women) to the alleged "lower" sexual standards of black people.[22]

New Right and neo-conservative ideology has updated these themes, and leans heavily on linking "immoral" sexual behavior to putative declines in American power. In 1977, Norman Podhoretz wrote an essay blaming homosexuals for the alleged inability of the United States to stand up to the Russians.[23] He thus neatly linked "the anti-gay fight in the domestic arena and the anti-communist battles in foreign policy."[24]

Right-wing opposition to sex education, homosexuality, pornography, abor-tion, and pre-marital sex moved from the extreme fringes to the political center stage after 1977, when right-wing strategists and fundamentalist religious cru-saders discovered that these issues had mass appeal. Sexual reaction played a significant role in the right's electoral success in 1980.[25] Organizations like the Moral Majority and Citizens for Decency have acquired mass followings, immense financial resources, and unanticipated clout. The Equal Rights Amendment has been defeated, legislation has been passed that mandates new restrictions on abortion, and funding for programs like Planned Parenthood and sex education has been slashed. Laws and regulations making it more difficult for teenage girls to obtain contraceptives or abortions have been promulgated. Sexual backlash was exploited in successful attacks on the Women's Studies Program at California State University at Long Beach.

The most ambitious right-wing legislative initiative has been the Family Protection Act (FPA), introduced in Congress in 1979. The Family Protection Act is a broad assault on feminism, homosexuals, non-traditional families, and teenage sexual privacy.[26] The Family Protection Act has not and probably will not pass, but conservative members of Congress continue to pursue its agenda in a more piecemeal fashion. Perhaps the most glaring sign of the times is the Adolescent Family Life Program. Also known as the Teen Chastity Program, it gets some 15 million federal dollars to encourage teenagers to refrain from sexual inter- course, and to discourage them from using contraceptives if they do have sex, and from having abortions if they get pregnant. In the last few years, there have been countless local confrontations over gay rights, sex education, abortion rights, adult bookstores, and public school curricula. It is unlikely that the anti-sex backlash is over, or that it has even peaked. Unless something changes dramatically, it is likely that the next few years will bring more of the same.

Periods such as the 1880s in England, and the 1950s in the United States, recodify the relations of sexuality. The struggles that were fought leave a residue in the form of laws, social practices, and ideologies which then affect the way in which sexuality is experienced long after the immediate conflicts have faded. All the signs indicate that the present era is another of those watersheds in the politics of sex. The settlements that emerge from the 1980s will have an impact far into the future. It is therefore imperative to understand what is going on and what is at stake in order to make informed decisions about what policies to support and oppose.

It is difficult to make such decisions in the absence of a coherent and intelli- gent body of radical thought about sex. Unfortunately, progressive political analysis of sexuality is relatively underdeveloped. Much of what is available from the feminist movement has simply added to the mystification that shrouds the subject. There is an urgent need to develop radical perspectives on sexuality.

Paradoxically, an explosion of exciting scholarship and political writing about sex has been generated in these bleak years. In the 1950s, the early gay rights movement began and prospered while the bars were being raided and anti-gay laws were being passed. In the last six years, new erotic communities, political alli- ances, and analyses have been developed in the midst of the repression. In this essay, I will propose elements of a descriptive and conceptual framework for thinking about sex and its politics. I hope to contribute to the pressing task of creating an accurate, humane, and genuinely liberatory body of thought about sexuality.

Sexual thoughts

"You see, Tim," Phillip said suddenly, "your argument isn't reasonable. Suppose I granted your first point that homosexuality is justifiable in certain instances and under certain controls. Then there is the catch: where does justification end and degeneracy begin? Society must condemn to protect. Permit even the intellectual homosexual a place of respect and the first bar is down. Then comes the next and the next until the sadist, the flagellist, the criminally insane demand their places, and society ceases to exist. So I ask again: where is the line drawn? Where does degeneracy begin if not at the beginning of individual freedom in such matters?"

Fragment from a discussion between two gay men trying to decide if they may love each other, from a novel published in 1950. [27]

A radical theory of sex must identify, describe, explain, and denounce erotic injustice and sexual oppression. Such a theory needs refined conceptual tools which can grasp the subject and hold it in view. It must build rich descriptions of sexuality as it exists in society and history. It requires a convincing critical language that can convey the barbarity of sexual persecution.

Several persistent features of thought about sex inhibit the development of such a theory. These assumptions are so pervasive in Western culture that they are rarely questioned. Thus, they tend to reappear in different political contexts, acquiring new rhetorical expressions but reproducing fundamental axioms.

One such axiom is sexual essentialism – the idea that sex is a natural force that exists prior to social life and shapes institutions. Sexual essentialism is embedded in the folk wisdoms of Western societies, which consider sex to be eternally unchanging, asocial, and transhistorical. Dominated for over a century by medicine, psychiatry, and psychology, the academic study of sex has reproduced essentialism. These fields classify sex as a property of individuals. It may reside in their hormones or their psyches. It may be construed as physiological or psychological. But within these ethnoscientific categories, sexuality has no history and no significant social determinants.

During the last five years, a sophisticated historical and theoretical scholarship has challenged sexual essentialism both explicitly and implicitly. Gay history, particularly the work of Jeffrey Weeks, has led this assault by showing that homosexuality as we know it is a relatively modern institutional complex. [28] Many historians have come to see the contemporary institutional forms of heterosexuality as an even more recent development. [29] An important contributor to the new scholarship is Judith Walkowitz, whose research has demonstrated the extent to which prostitution was transformed around the turn of the century. She provides meticulous descriptions of how the interplay of social forces such as ideology, fear, political agitation, legal reform, and medical practice can change the structure of sexual behavior and alter its consequences. [30]

Michel Foucault's *The History of Sexuality* has been the most influential and emblematic text of the new scholarship on sex. Foucault criticizes the traditional understanding of sexuality as a natural libido yearning to break free of social constraint. He argues that desires are not preexisting biological entities, but rather, that they are constituted in the course of historically specific social practices. He emphasizes the generative aspects of the social organization of sex rather than its repressive elements by pointing out that new sexualities are constantly produced. And he points to a major discontinuity between kinship-based systems of sexuality and more modern forms. [31]

The new scholarship on sexual behavior has given sex a history and created a constructivist alternative to sexual essentialism. Underlying this body of work is an assumption that sexuality is constituted in society and history, not biologically ordained.[32] This does not mean the biological capacities are not prerequisites for human sexuality. It does mean that human sexuality is not comprehensible in purely biological terms. Human organisms with human brains are necessary for human cultures, but no examination of the body or its parts can explain the nature and variety of human social systems. The belly's hunger gives no clues as to the complexities of cuisine. The body, the brain, the genitalia, and the capacity for language are all necessary for human sexuality. But they do not determine its content, its experiences, or its institutional forms. Moreover, we never encounter the body unmediated by the meanings that cultures give to it. To paraphrase Lévi-Strauss, my position on the relationship between biology and sexuality is a "Kantianism without a transcendental libido."[33]

It is impossible to think with any clarity about the politics of race or gender as long as these are thought of as biological entities rather than as social constructs. Similarly, sexuality is impervious to political analysis as long as it is primarily conceived as a biological phenomenon or an aspect of individual psychology. Sexuality is as much a human product as are diets, methods of transportation, systems of etiquette, forms of labor, types of entertainment, processes of production, and modes of oppression. Once sex is understood in terms of social analysis and historical understanding, a more realistic politics of sex becomes possible. One may then think of sexual politics in terms of such phenomena as populations, neighborhoods, settlement patterns, migration, urban conflict, epidemiology, and police technology. These are more fruitful categories of thought than the more traditional ones of sin, disease, neurosis, pathology, decadence, pollution, or the decline and fall of empires.

By detailing the relationships between stigmatized erotic populations and the social forces which regulate them, work such as that of Allan Bérubé, John D'Emilio, Jeffrey Weeks, and Judith Walkowitz contains implicit categories of political analysis and criticism. Nevertheless, the constructivist perspective has displayed some political weaknesses. This has been most evident in misconstructions of Foucault's position.

Because of his emphasis on the ways that sexuality is produced, Foucault has been vulnerable to interpretations that deny or minimize the reality of sexual repression in the more political sense. Foucault makes it abundantly clear that he is not denying the existence of sexual repression so much as inscribing it within a large dynamic.[34] Sexuality in Western societies has been structured within an extremely punitive social framework, and has been subjected to very real formal and informal controls. It is necessary to recognize repressive phenomena without resorting to the essentialist assumptions of the language of libido. It is important to hold repressive sexual practices in focus, even while situating them within a different totality and a more refined terminology.[35]

Most radical thought about sex has been embedded within a model of the instincts and their restraints. Concepts of sexual oppression have been lodged within that more biological understanding of sexuality. It is often easier to fall back on the notion of a natural libido subjected to inhumane repression than to reformulate concepts of sexual injustice within a more constructivist framework. But it is essential that we do so. We need a radical critique of sexual arrangements that has the conceptual elegance of Foucault and the evocative passion of Reich.

The new scholarship on sex has brought a welcome insistence that sexual terms be restricted to their proper historical and social contexts, and a cautionary scepticism towards sweeping generalizations. But it is important to be able to indicate groupings of erotic behavior and general trends within erotic discourse. In addition to sexual essentialism, there are at least five other ideological formations whose grip on sexual thought is so strong that to fail to discuss them is to remain enmeshed within them. These are sex negativity, the fallacy of misplaced scale, the hierarchical valuation of sex acts, the domino theory of sexual peril, and the lack of a concept of benign sexual variation.

Of these five, the most important is sex negativity. Western cultures generally consider sex to be a dangerous, destructive, negative force.[36] Most Christian tradition, following Paul, holds that sex is inherently sinful. It may be redeemed if performed within marriage for procreative purposes and if the pleasurable aspects are not enjoyed too much. In turn, this idea rests on the assumption that the genitalia are an intrinsically inferior part of the body, much lower and less holy than the mind, the "soul," the "heart," or even the upper part of the digestive system (the status of the excretory organs is close to that of the genitalia).[37] Such notions have by now acquired a life of their own and no longer depend solely on religion for their perseverance.

This culture always treats sex with suspicion. It construes and judges almost any sexual practice in terms of its worst possible expression. Sex is presumed guilty until proven innocent. Virtually all erotic behavior is considered bad unless a specific reason to exempt it has been established. The most acceptable excuses are marriage, reproduction, and love. Sometimes scientific curiosity, aesthetic experience, or a long-term intimate relationship may serve. But the exercise of erotic capacity, intelligence, curiosity, or creativity all require pretexts that are unnecessary for other pleasures, such as the enjoyment of food, fiction, or astronomy.

What I call the fallacy of misplaced scale is a corollary of sex negativity. Susan Sontag once commented that since Christianity focused "on sexual behavior as the root of virtue, everything pertaining to sex has been a 'special case' in our culture."[38] Sex law has incorporated the religious attitude that heretical sex is an especially heinous sin that deserves the harshest punishments. Throughout much of European and American history, a single act of consensual anal penetration was grounds for execution. In some states, sodomy still carries twenty-year prison sentences. Outside the law, sex is also a marked category. Small differences in value or behavior are often experienced as cosmic threats. Although people can be intolerant, silly, or pushy about what constitutes proper diet, differences in menu rarely provoke the kinds of rage, anxiety, and sheer terror that routinely accompany differences in erotic taste. Sexual acts are burdened with an excess of significance.

Modern Western societies appraise sex acts according to a hierarchical system of sexual value. Marital, reproductive heterosexuals are alone at the top of the erotic pyramid. Clamoring below are unmarried monogamous heterosexuals in couples, followed by most other heterosexuals. Solitary sex floats ambiguously.

The powerful nineteenth-century stigma on masturbation lingers in less potent, modified forms, such as the idea that masturbation is an inferior substitute for partnered encounters. Stable, long-term lesbian and gay male couples are verging on respectability, but bar dykes and promiscuous gay men are hovering just above the groups at the very bottom of the pyramid. The most despised sexual castes currently include transsexuals, transvestites, fetishists, sadomasochists, sex workers such as prostitutes and porn models, and the lowliest of all, those whose eroticism transgresses generational boundaries.

Individuals whose behavior stands high in this hierarchy are rewarded with certified mental health, respectability, legality, social and physical mobility, institutional support, and material benefits. As sexual behaviors or occupations fall lower on the scale, the individuals who practice them are subjected to a presumption of mental illness, disreputability, criminality, restricted social and physical mobility, loss of institutional support, and economic sanctions.

Extreme and punitive stigma maintains some sexual behaviors as low status and is an effective sanction against those who engage in them. The intensity of this stigma is rooted in Western religious traditions. But most of its contemporary content derives from medical and psychiatric opprobrium.

The old religious taboos were primarily based on kinship forms of social organization. They were meant to deter inappropriate unions and to provide proper kin. Sex laws derived from Biblical pronouncements were aimed at preventing the acquisition of the wrong kinds of affinal partners: consanguineous kin (incest), the same gender (homosexuality), or the wrong species (bestiality). When medicine and psychiatry acquired extensive powers over sexuality, they were less concerned with unsuitable mates than with unfit forms of desire. If taboos against incest best characterized kinship systems of sexual organization, then the shift to an emphasis on taboos against masturbation was more apposite to the newer systems organized around qualities of erotic experience.[39]

Medicine and psychiatry multiplied the categories of sexual misconduct. The section on psychosexual disorders in the *Diagnostic and Statistical Manual of Mental Disorders (DSM)* of the American Psychiatric Association (APA) is a fairly reliable map of the current moral hierarchy of sexual activities. The APA list is much more elaborate than the traditional condemnations of whoring, sodomy, and adultery. The most recent edition, *DSM-III*, removed homosexuality from the roster of mental disorders after a long political struggle. But fetishism, sadism, masochism, transsexuality, transvestism, exhibitionism, voyeurism, and pedophilia are quite firmly entrenched as psychological malfunctions.[40] Books are still being written about the genesis, etiology, treatment, and cure of these assorted "pathologies."

Psychiatric condemnation of sexual behaviors invokes concepts of mental and emotional inferiority rather than categories of sexual sin. Low status sex practices are vilified as mental diseases or symptoms of defective personality integration. In addition, psychological terms conflate difficulties of psychodynamic functioning with modes of erotic conduct. They equate sexual masochism with self-destructive personality patterns, sexual sadism with emotional aggression, and homoeroticism with immaturity. These terminological muddles have become powerful stereotypes that are indiscriminately applied to individuals on the basis of their sexual orientations.

Popular culture is permeated with ideas that erotic variety is dangerous, unhealthy, depraved, and a menace to everything from small children to national security. Popular sexual ideology is a noxious stew made up of ideas of sexual sin, concepts of psychological inferiority, anti-communism, mob hysteria, accusations of witchcraft, and xenophobia. The mass media nourish these attitudes with relentless propaganda. I would call this system of erotic stigma the last socially respectable form of prejudice if the old forms did not show such obstinate vitality, and new ones did not continually become apparent.

All these hierarchies of sexual value – religious, psychiatric, and popular – function in much the same ways as do ideological systems of racism, ethnocentrism, and religious chauvinism. They rationalize the well-being of the sexually privileged and the adversity of the sexual rabble.

Figure 1 diagrams a general version of the sexual value system. According to this system, sexuality that is "good," "normal" and "natural" should ideally be heterosexual, marital, monogamous, reproductive, and non-commercial. It should be coupled, relational, within the same generation, and occur at home. It should not involve pornography, fetish objects, sex toys of any sort, or roles other than male and female. Any sex that violates these rules is "bad," "abnormal," or "unnatural." Bad sex may be homosexual, unmarried, promiscuous, non-procreative, or commercial. It may be masturbatory or take place at orgies, may be casual, may cross generational lines, and may take place in "public," or at least in the bushes or the baths. It may involve the use of pornography, fetish objects, sex toys, or unusual roles (see Figure 1).

Figure 2 diagrams another aspect of the sexual hierarchy: the need to draw and maintain an imaginary line between good and bad sex. Most of the discourses on sex, be they religious, psychiatric, popular, or political, delimit a very small portion of human sexual capacity as sanctifiable, safe, healthy, mature, legal, or politically correct. The "line" distinguishes these from all other erotic behaviors, which are understood to be the work of the devil, dangerous, psychopathological, infantile, or politically reprehensible. Arguments are then conducted over "where to draw the line," and to determine what other activities, if any, may be permitted to cross over into acceptability.

All these models assume a domino theory of sexual peril. The line appears to stand between sexual order and chaos. It expresses the fear that if anything is permitted to cross this erotic DMZ, the barrier against scary sex will crumble and something unspeakable will skitter across.

Most systems of sexual judgment – religious, psychological, feminist, or socialist – attempt to determine on which side of the line a particular act falls. Only sex acts on the good side of the line are accorded moral complexity. For instance, heterosexual encounters may be sublime or disgusting, free or forced, healing or destructive, romantic or mercenary. As long as it does not violate other rules, heterosexuality is acknowledged to exhibit the full range of human experience. In contrast, all sex acts on the bad side of the line are considered utterly repulsive and devoid of all emotional nuance. The further from the line a sex act is, the more it is depicted as a uniformly bad experience.

As a result of the sex conflicts of the last decade, some behavior near the border is inching across it. Unmarried couples living together, masturbation, and

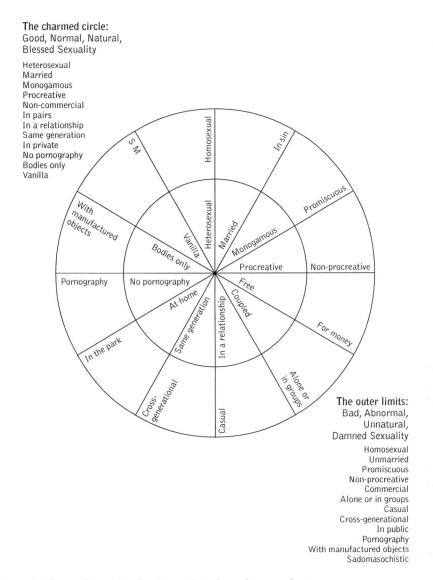

The charmed circle:
Good, Normal, Natural,
Blessed Sexuality

Heterosexual
Married
Monogamous
Procreative
Non-commercial
In pairs
In a relationship
Same generation
In private
No pornography
Bodies only
Vanilla

The outer limits:
Bad, Abnormal,
Unnatural,
Damned Sexuality

Homosexual
Unmarried
Promiscuous
Non-procreative
Commercial
Alone or in groups
Casual
Cross-generational
In public
Pornography
With manufactured objects
Sadomasochistic

Figure 1 The sex hierarchy: the charmed circle vs the outer limits

some forms of homosexuality are moving in the direction of respectability (see Figure 2). Most homosexuality is still on the bad side of the line. But if it is coupled and monogamous, the society is beginning to recognize that it includes the full range of human interaction. Promiscuous homosexuality, sadomasochism, fetishism, transsexuality, and cross-generational encounters are still viewed as unmodulated horrors incapable of involving affection, love, free choice, kindness, or transcendence.

This kind of sexual morality has more in common with ideologies of racism than with true ethics. It grants virtue to the dominant groups, and relegates vice to the underprivileged. A democratic morality should judge sexual acts by the way partners treat one another, the level of mutual consideration, the presence or absence of coercion, and the quantity and quality of the pleasures they provide.

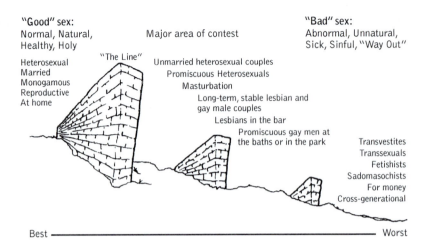

"Good" sex:
Normal, Natural,   Major area of contest
Healthy, Holy

"Bad" sex:
Abnormal, Unnatural,
Sick, Sinful, "Way Out"

"The Line"

Heterosexual   Unmarried heterosexual couples
Married   Promiscuous Heterosexuals
Monogamous   Masturbation
Reproductive   Long-term, stable lesbian and
At home   gay male couples
                        Lesbians in the bar
                        Promiscuous gay men at
                        the baths or in the park   Transvestites
                                                          Transsexuals
                                                          Fetishists
                                                          Sadomasochists
                                                          For money
                                                          Cross-generational

Best ——————————————————————————————————— Worst

Figure 2 The sex hierarchy: the struggle over where to draw the line

Whether sex acts are gay or straight, coupled or in groups, naked or in underwear, commercial or free, with or without video, should not be ethical concerns.

It is difficult to develop a pluralistic sexual ethics without a concept of benign sexual variation. Variation is a fundamental property of all life, from the simplest biological organisms to the most complex human social formations. Yet sexuality is supposed to conform to a single standard. One of the most tenacious ideas about sex is that there is one best way to do it, and that everyone should do it that way.

Most people find it difficult to grasp that whatever they like to do sexually will be thoroughly repulsive to someone else, and that whatever repels them sexually will be the most treasured delight of someone, somewhere. One need not like or perform a particular sex act in order to recognize that someone else will, and that this difference does not indicate a lack of good taste, mental health, or intelligence in either party. Most people mistake their sexual preferences for a universal system that will or should work for everyone.

This notion of a single ideal sexuality characterizes most systems of thought about sex. For religion, the ideal is procreative marriage. For psychology, it is mature heterosexuality. Although its content varies, the format of a single sexual standard is continually reconstituted within other rhetorical frameworks, including feminism and socialism. It is just as objectionable to insist that everyone should be lesbian, non-monogamous, or kinky, as to believe that everyone should be heterosexual, married, or vanilla – though the latter set of opinions are backed by considerably more coercive power than the former.

Progressives who would be ashamed to display cultural chauvinism in other areas routinely exhibit it towards sexual differences. We have learned to cherish different cultures as unique expressions of human inventiveness rather than as the inferior or disgusting habits of savages. We need a similarly anthropological understanding of different sexual cultures.

Empirical sex research is the one field that does incorporate a positive concept of sexual variation. Alfred Kinsey approached the study of sex with the same uninhibited curiosity he had previously applied to examining a species of wasp. His scientific detachment gave his work a refreshing neutrality that enraged moralists and caused immense controversy.[41] Among Kinsey's successors, John Gagnon and William Simon have pioneered the application of sociological understandings to erotic variety.[42] Even some of the older sexology is useful. Although his work is imbued with unappetizing eugenic beliefs, Havelock Ellis was an acute and sympathetic observer. His monumental *Studies in the Psychology of Sex* is resplendent with detail.[43]

Much political writing on sexuality reveals complete ignorance of both classical sexology and modern sex research. Perhaps this is because so few colleges and universities bother to teach human sexuality, and because so much stigma adheres even to scholarly investigation of sex. Neither sexology nor sex research has been immune to the prevailing sexual value system. Both contain assumptions and information which should not be accepted uncritically. But sexology and sex research provide abundant detail, a welcome posture of calm, and a well developed ability to treat sexual variety as something that exists rather than as something to be exterminated. These fields can provide an empirical grounding for a radical theory of sexuality more useful than the combination of psychoanalysis and feminist first principles to which so many texts resort.

Sexual transformation

> As defined by the ancient civil or canonical codes, sodomy was a category of forbidden acts; their perpetrator was nothing more than the juridical subject of them. The nineteenth-century homosexual became a personage, a past, a case history, and a childhood, in addition to being a type of life, a life form, and a morphology, with an indiscreet anatomy and possibly a mysterious physiology. . . . The sodomite had been a temporary aberration; the homosexual was now a species.
>
> Michel Foucault[44]

In spite of many continuities with ancestral forms, modern sexual arrangements have a distinctive character which sets them apart from preexisting systems. In Western Europe and the United States, industrialization and urbanization reshaped the traditional rural and peasant populations into a new urban industrial and service workforce. It generated new forms of state apparatus, reorganized family relations, altered gender roles, made possible new forms of identity, produced new varieties of social inequality, and created new formats for political and ideological conflict. It also gave rise to a new sexual system characterized by distinct types of sexual persons, populations, stratification, and political conflict.

The writings of nineteenth-century sexology suggest the appearance of a kind of erotic speciation. However outlandish their explanations, the early sexologists were witnessing the emergence of new kinds of erotic individuals and their aggregation into rudimentary communities. The modern sexual system contains sets of these sexual populations, stratified by the operation of an ideological and social hierarchy. Differences in social value create friction among these groups, who engage in political contests to alter or maintain their place in the ranking. Contemporary sexual politics should be reconceptualized in terms of the emergence and on-going development of this system, its social relations, the ideologies which interpret it, and its characteristic modes of conflict.

Homosexuality is the best example of this process of erotic speciation. Homosexual behavior is always present among humans. But in different societies and epochs it may be rewarded or punished, required or forbidden, a temporary experience or a life-long vocation. In some New Guinea societies, for example, homosexual activities are obligatory for all males. Homosexual acts are considered utterly masculine, roles are based on age, and partners are determined by kinship status.[45] Although these men engage in extensive homosexual and pedophile behavior, they are neither homosexuals nor pederasts.

Nor was the sixteenth-century sodomite a homosexual. In 1631, Mervyn Touchet, Earl of Castlehaven, was tried and executed for sodomy. It is clear from the proceedings that the earl was not understood by himself or anyone else to be a particular kind of sexual individual. "While from the twentieth-century viewpoint Lord Castlehaven obviously suffered from psychosexual problems requiring the services of an analyst, from the seventeenth century viewpoint he had deliberately broken the Law of God and the Laws of England, and required the simpler services of an executioner."[46] The earl did not slip into his tightest doublet and waltz down to the nearest gay tavern to mingle with his fellow sodomists. He stayed in his manor house and buggered his servants. Gay self-awareness, gay pubs, the sense of group commonality, and even the term homosexual were not part of the earl's universe.

The New Guinea bachelor and the sodomite nobleman are only tangentially related to a modern gay man, who may migrate from rural Colorado to San Francisco in order to live in a gay neighborhood, work in a gay business, and participate in an elaborate experience that includes a self-conscious identity, group solidarity, a literature, a press and a high level of political activity. In modern, Western, industrial societies, homosexuality has acquired much of the institutional structure of an ethnic group.[47]

The relocation of homoeroticism into these quasi-ethnic, nucleated, sexually constituted communities is to some extent a consequence of the transfers of population brought about by industrialization. As laborers migrated to work in cities, there were increased opportunities for voluntary communities to form. Homosexually inclined women and men, who would have been vulnerable and isolated in most pre-industrial villages, began to congregate in small corners of the big cities. Most large nineteenth-century cities in Western Europe and North America had areas where men could cruise for other men. Lesbian communities seem to have coalesced more slowly and on a smaller scale. Nevertheless, by the 1890s, there were several cafes in Paris near the Place Pigalle which catered to a lesbian clientele, and it is likely that there were similar places in the other major capitals of Western Europe.

Areas like these acquired bad reputations, which alerted other interested individuals of their existence and location. In the United States, lesbian and gay male territories were well established in New York, Chicago, San Francisco, and Los Angeles in the 1950s. Sexually motivated migration to places such as Greenwich Village had become a sizable sociological phenomenon. By the late 1970s, sexual migration was occurring on a scale so significant that it began to have a recognizable impact on urban politics in the United States, with San Francisco being the most notable and notorious example.[48]

Prostitution has undergone a similar metamorphosis. Prostitution began to change from a temporary job to a more permanent occupation as a result of nineteenth-century agitation, legal reform, and police persecution. Prostitutes, who had been part of the general working-class population, became increasingly isolated as members of an outcast group.[49] Prostitutes and other sex workers differ from homosexuals and other sexual minorities. Sex work is an occupation, while sexual deviation is an erotic preference. Nevertheless, they share some common features of social organization. Like homosexuals, prostitutes are a criminal sexual population stigmatized on the basis of sexual activity. Prostitutes and male homosexuals are the primary prey of vice police everywhere.[50] Like gay men, prostitutes occupy well demarcated urban territories and battle with police to defend and maintain those territories. The legal persecution of both populations is justified by an elaborate ideology which classifies them as dangerous and inferior undesirables who are not entitled to be left in peace.

Besides organizing homosexuals and prostitutes into localized populations, the "modernization of sex" has generated a system of continual sexual ethnogenesis. Other populations of erotic dissidents – commonly known as the "perversions" or the "paraphilias" – also began to coalesce. Sexualities keep marching out of the *Diagnostic and Statistical Manual* and on to the pages of social history. At present, several other groups are trying to emulate the successes of homosexuals. Bisexuals, sadomasochists, individuals who prefer cross-generational encounters, transsexuals, and transvestites are all in various states of community formation and identity acquisition. The perversions are not proliferating as much as they are attempting to acquire social space, small businesses, political resources, and a measure of relief from the penalties for sexual heresy.

Sexual stratification

> An entire sub-race was born, different – despite certain kinship ties – from the libertines of the past. From the end of the eighteenth century to our own, they circulated through the pores of society; they were always bounded, but not always by laws; were often locked up, but not always in prisons; were sick perhaps, but scandalous, dangerous victims, prey to a strange evil that also bore the name of vice and sometimes crime. They were children wise beyond their years, precocious little girls, ambiguous schoolboys, dubious servants and educators, cruel or maniacal husbands, solitary collectors, ramblers with bizarre impulses; they haunted the houses of correction, the penal colonies, the tribunals, and the asylums; they carried their infamy to the doctors and their sickness to the judges. This was the numberless family of perverts who were on friendly terms with delinquents and akin to madmen.
>
> Michel Foucault[51]

The industrial transformation of Western Europe and North America brought about new forms of social stratification. The resultant inequalities of class are well known and have been explored in detail by a century of scholarship. The construction of modern systems of racism and ethnic injustice has been well documented and critically assessed. Feminist thought has analyzed the prevailing organization of gender oppression. But although specific erotic groups, such as militant homosexuals and sex workers, have agitated against their own mistreatment, there has been no equivalent attempt to locate particular varieties of sexual persecution within a more general system of sexual stratification. Nevertheless, such a system exists, and in its contemporary form it is a consequence of Western industrialization.

Sex law is the most adamantine instrument of sexual stratification and erotic persecution. The state routinely intervenes in sexual behavior at a level that would not be tolerated in other areas of social life. Most people are unaware of the extent of sex law, the quantity and qualities of illegal sexual behavior, and the punitive character of legal sanctions. Although federal agencies may be involved in obscenity and prostitution cases, most sex laws are enacted at the state and municipal level, and enforcement is largely in the hands of local police. Thus, there is a tremendous amount of variation in the laws applicable to any given locale. Moreover, enforcement of sex laws varies dramatically with the local political climate. In spite of this legal thicket, one can make some tentative and qualified generalizations. My discussion of sex law does not apply to laws against sexual coercion, sexual assault, or rape. It does pertain to the myriad prohibitions on consensual sex and the "status" offenses such as statutory rape.

Sex law is harsh. The penalties for violating sex statutes are universally out of proportion to any social or individual harm. A single act of consensual but illicit sex, such as placing one's lips upon the genitalia of an enthusiastic partner, is punished in most states with more severity than rape, battery, or murder. Each such genital kiss, each lewd caress, is a separate crime. It is therefore painfully easy to commit multiple felonies in the course of a single evening of illegal passion. Once someone is convicted of a sex violation, a second performance of the same act is grounds for prosecution as a repeat offender, in which case penalties will be even more severe. In some states, individuals have become repeat felons for having engaged in homosexual love-making on two separate occasions. Once an erotic activity has been proscribed by sex law, the full power of the state enforces conformity to the values embodied in those laws. Sex laws are notoriously easy to pass, as legislators are loath to be soft on vice. Once on the books, they are extremely difficult to dislodge.

Sex law is not a perfect reflection of the prevailing moral evaluations of sexual conduct. Sexual variation *per se* is more specifically policed by the mental-health professions, popular ideology, and extra-legal social practice. Some of the most detested erotic behaviors, such as fetishism and sadomasochism, are not as closely or completely regulated by the criminal justice system as somewhat less stigmatized practices, such as homosexuality. Areas of sexual behavior come under the purview of the law when they become objects of social concern and political uproar. Each sex scare or morality campaign deposits new regulations as a kind of fossil record of its passage. The legal sediment is thickest – and sex law has its greatest potency – in areas involving obscenity, money, minors, and homosexuality.

Obscenity laws enforce a powerful taboo against direct representation of erotic activities. Current emphasis on the ways in which sexuality has become a focus of social attention should not be misused to undermine a critique of this prohibition. It is one thing to create sexual discourse in the form of psychoanalysis, or in the course of a morality crusade. It is quite another to graphically depict sex acts or genitalia. The first is socially permissible in a way the second is not. Sexual speech is forced into reticence, euphemism, and indirection. Freedom of speech about sex is a glaring exception to the protections of the First Amendment, which is not even considered applicable to purely sexual statements.

The anti-obscenity laws also form part of a group of statutes that make almost all sexual commerce illegal. Sex law incorporates a very strong prohibition against mixing sex and money, except via marriage. In addition to the obscenity statutes, other laws impinging on sexual commerce include anti-prostitution laws, alcoholic beverage regulations, and ordinances governing the location and operation of "adult" businesses. The sex industry and the gay economy have both managed to circumvent some of this legislation, but that process has not been easy or simple. The underlying criminality of sex-oriented business keeps it marginal, under-developed, and distorted. Sex business can only operate in legal loopholes. This tends to keep investment down and to divert commercial activity towards the goal of staying out of jail rather than the delivery of goods and services. It also renders sex workers more vulnerable to exploitation and bad working conditions. If sex commerce were legal, sex workers would be more able to organize and agitate for higher pay, better conditions, greater control, and less stigma.

Whatever one thinks of the limitations of capitalist commerce, such an extreme exclusion from the market process would hardly be socially acceptable in other areas of activity. Imagine, for example, that the exchange of money for medical care, pharmacological advice, or psychological counseling were illegal. Medical practice would take place in a much less satisfactory fashion if doctors, nurses, druggists, and therapists could be hauled off to jail at the whim of the local "health squad." But that is essentially the situation of prostitutes, sex workers, and sex entrepreneurs.

Marx himself considered the capitalist market a revolutionary, if limited, force. He argued that capitalism was progressive in its dissolution of pre-capitalist superstition, prejudice, and the bonds of traditional modes of life. "Hence the great civilizing influence of capital, its production of a state of society compared with which all earlier stages appear to be merely local progress and idolatry of nature."[52] Keeping sex from realizing the positive effects of the market economy hardly makes it socialist.

The law is especially ferocious in maintaining the boundary between child-hood "innocence" and "adult" sexuality. Rather than recognizing the sexuality of the young, and attempting to provide for it in a caring and responsible manner, our culture denies and punishes erotic interest and activity by anyone under the local age of consent. The amount of law devoted to protecting young people from premature exposure to sexuality is breathtaking.

The primary mechanism for insuring the separation of sexual generations is age of consent laws. These laws make no distinction between the most brutal rape and the most gentle romance. A 20-year-old convicted of sexual contact with a

17-year-old will face a severe sentence in virtually every state, regardless of the nature of the relationship.[53] Nor are minors permitted access to "adult" sexuality in other forms. They are forbidden to see books, movies, or television in which sexuality is "too" graphically portrayed. It is legal for young people to see hideous depictions of violence, but not to see explicit pictures of genitalia. Sexually active young people are frequently incarcerated in juvenile homes, or otherwise punished for their "precocity."

Adults who deviate too much from conventional standards of sexual conduct are often denied contact with the young, even their own. Custody laws permit the state to steal the children of anyone whose erotic activities appear questionable to a judge presiding over family court matters. Countless lesbians, gay men, prostitutes, swingers, sex workers, and "promiscuous" women have been declared unfit parents under such provisions. Members of the teaching professions are closely monitored for signs of sexual misconduct. In most states, certification laws require that teachers arrested for sex offenses lose their jobs and credentials. In some cases, a teacher may be fired merely because an unconventional lifestyle becomes known to school officials. Moral turpitude is one of the few legal grounds for revoking academic tenure.[54] The more influence one has over the next generation, the less latitude one is permitted in behavior and opinion. The coercive power of the law ensures the transmission of conservative sexual values with these kinds of controls over parenting and teaching.

The only adult sexual behavior that is legal in every state is the placement of the penis in the vagina in wedlock. Consenting adults statutes ameliorate this situation in fewer than half the states. Most states impose severe criminal penalties on consensual sodomy, homosexual contact short of sodomy, adultery, seduction, and adult incest. Sodomy laws vary a great deal. In some states, they apply equally to homosexual and heterosexual partners and regardless of marital status. Some state courts have ruled that married couples have the right to commit sodomy in private. Only homosexual sodomy is illegal in some states. Some sodomy statutes prohibit both anal sex and oral-genital contact. In other states, sodomy applies only to anal penetration, and oral sex is covered under separate statutes.[55]

Laws like these criminalize sexual behavior that is freely chosen and avidly sought. The ideology embodied in them reflects the value hierarchies discussed above. That is, some sex acts are considered to be so intrinsically vile that no one should be allowed under any circumstance to perform them. The fact that individuals consent to or even prefer them is taken to be additional evidence of depravity. This system of sex law is similar to legalized racism. State prohibition of same sex contact, anal penetration, and oral sex make homosexuals a criminal group denied the privileges of full citizenship. With such laws, prosecution is persecution. Even when they are not strictly enforced, as is usually the case, the members of criminalized sexual communities remain vulnerable to the possibility of arbitrary arrest, or to periods in which they become the objects of social panic. When those occur, the laws are in place and police action is swift. Even sporadic enforcement serves to remind individuals that they are members of a subject population. The occasional arrest for sodomy, lewd behavior, solicitation, or oral sex keeps everyone else afraid, nervous, and circumspect.

The state also upholds the sexual hierarchy through bureaucratic regulation.

Immigration policy still prohibits the admission of homosexuals (and other sexual "deviates") into the United States. Military regulations bar homosexuals from serving in the armed forces. The fact that gay people cannot legally marry means that they cannot enjoy the same legal rights as heterosexuals in many matters, including inheritance, taxation, protection from testimony in court, and the acquisition of citizenship for foreign partners. These are but a few of the ways that the state reflects and maintains the social relations of sexuality. The law buttresses structures of power, codes of behavior, and forms of prejudice. At their worst, sex law and sex regulation are simply sexual apartheid.

Although the legal apparatus of sex is staggering, most everyday social control is extra-legal. Less formal, but very effective social sanctions are imposed on members of "inferior" sexual populations.

In her marvelous ethnographic study of gay life in the 1960s, Esther Newton observed that the homosexual population was divided into what she called the "overts" and the "coverts." "The overts live their *entire* working lives within the context of the [gay] community; the coverts live their entire *nonworking* lives within it."[56] At the time of Newton's study, the gay community provided far fewer jobs than it does now, and the non-gay work world was almost completely intolerant of homosexuality. There were some fortunate individuals who could be openly gay and earn decent salaries. But the vast majority of homosexuals had to choose between honest poverty and the strain of maintaining a false identity.

Though this situation has changed a great deal, discrimination against gay people is still rampant. For the bulk of the gay population, being out on the job is still impossible. Generally, the more important and higher paid the job, the less the society will tolerate overt erotic deviance. If it is difficult for gay people to find employment where they do not have to pretend, it is doubly and triply so for more exotically sexed individuals. Sadomasochists leave their fetish clothes at home, and know that they must be especially careful to conceal their real identities. An exposed pedophile would probably be stoned out of the office. Having to maintain such absolute secrecy is a considerable burden. Even those who are content to be secretive may be exposed by some accidental event. Individuals who are erotically unconventional risk being unemployable or unable to pursue their chosen careers.

Public officials and anyone who occupies a position of social consequence are especially vulnerable. A sex scandal is the surest method for hounding someone out of office or destroying a political career. The fact that important people are expected to conform to the strictest standards of erotic conduct discourages sex perverts of all kinds from seeking such positions. Instead, erotic dissidents are channeled into positions that have less impact on the mainstream of social activity and opinion.

The expansion of the gay economy in the last decade has provided some employment alternatives and some relief from job discrimination against homosexuals. But most of the jobs provided by the gay economy are low-status and low-paying. Bartenders, bathhouse attendants, and disc jockeys are not bank officers or corporate executives. Many of the sexual migrants who flock to places like San Francisco are downwardly mobile. They face intense competition for choice positions. The influx of sexual migrants provides a pool of cheap and exploitable labor for many of the city's businesses, both gay and straight.

Families play a crucial role in enforcing sexual conformity. Much social pressure is brought to bear to deny erotic dissidents the comforts and resources that families provide. Popular ideology holds that families are not supposed to produce or harbor erotic non-conformity. Many families respond by trying to reform, punish, or exile sexually offending members. Many sexual migrants have been thrown out by their families, and many others are fleeing from the threat of institutionalization. Any random collection of homosexuals, sex workers, or miscellaneous perverts can provide heart-stopping stories of rejection and mistreatment by horrified families. Christmas is the great family holiday in the United States and consequently it is a time of considerable tension in the gay community. Half the inhabitants go off to their families of origin; many of those who remain in the gay ghettoes cannot do so, and relive their anger and grief.

In addition to economic penalties and strain on family relations, the stigma of erotic dissidence creates friction at all other levels of everyday life. The general public helps to penalize erotic non-conformity when, according to the values they have been taught, landlords refuse housing, neighbors call in the police, and hoodlums commit sanctioned battery. The ideologies of erotic inferiority and sexual danger decrease the power of sex perverts and sex workers in social encounters of all kinds. They have less protection from unscrupulous or criminal behavior, less access to police protection, and less recourse to the courts. Dealings with institutions and bureaucracies – hospitals, police, coroners, banks, public officials – are more difficult.

Sex is a vector of oppression. The system of sexual oppression cuts across other modes of social inequality, sorting out individuals and groups according to its own intrinsic dynamics. It is not reducible to, or understandable in terms of, class, race, ethnicity, or gender. Wealth, white skin, male gender, and ethnic privileges can mitigate the effects of sexual stratification. A rich, white male pervert will generally be less affected than a poor, black, female pervert. But even the most privileged are not immune to sexual oppression. Some of the consequences of the system of sexual hierarchy are mere nuisances. Others are quite grave. In its most serious manifestations, the sexual system is a Kafkaesque nightmare in which unlucky victims become herds of human cattle whose identification, surveillance, apprehension, treatment, incarceration, and punishment produce jobs and self-satisfaction for thousands of vice police, prison officials, psychiatrists, and social workers.[57]

Sexual conflicts

The moral panic crystallizes widespread fears and anxieties, and often deals with them not by seeking the real causes of the problems and conditions which they demonstrate but by displacing them on to 'Folk Devils' in an identified social group (often the 'immoral' or 'degenerate'). Sexuality has had a peculiar centrality in such panics, and sexual 'deviants' have been omnipresent scapegoats.

Jeffrey Weeks[58]

The sexual system is not a monolithic, omnipotent structure. There are continuous battles over the definitions, evaluations, arrangements, privileges, and costs of sexual behavior. Political struggle over sex assumes characteristic forms.

Sexual ideology plays a crucial role in sexual experience. Consequently, definitions and evaluations of sexual conduct are objects of bitter contest. The confrontations between early gay liberation and the psychiatric establishment are the best example of this kind of fight, but there are constant skirmishes. Recurrent battles take place between the primary producers of sexual ideology – the churches, the family, the shrinks, and the media – and the groups whose experience they name, distort, and endanger.

The legal regulation of sexual conduct is another battleground. Lysander Spooner dissected the system of state sanctioned moral coercion over a century ago in a text inspired primarily by the temperance campaigns. In *Vices Are Not Crimes: A Vindication of Moral Liberty*, Spooner argued that government should protect its citizens against crime, but that it is foolish, unjust, and tyrannical to legislate against vice. He discusses rationalizations still heard today in defense of legalized moralism – that "vices" (Spooner is referring to drink, but homosexuality, prostitution, or recreational drug use may be substituted) lead to crimes, and should therefore be prevented; that those who practice "vice" are *non compos mentis* and should therefore be protected from their self-destruction by state-accomplished ruin; and that children must be protected from supposedly harmful knowledge.[59] The discourse on victimless crimes has not changed much. Legal struggle over sex law will continue until basic freedoms of sexual action and expression are guaranteed. This requires the repeal of all sex laws except those few that deal with actual, not statutory, coercion; and it entails the abolition of vice squads, whose job it is to enforce legislated morality.

In addition to the definitional and legal wars, there are less obvious forms of sexual political conflict which I call the territorial and border wars. The processes by which erotic minorities form communities and the forces that seek to inhibit them lead to struggle over the nature and boundaries of sexual zones.

Dissident sexuality is rarer and more closely monitored in small towns and rural areas. Consequently, metropolitan life continually beckons to young perverts. Sexual migration creates concentrated pools of potential partners, friends, and associates. It enables individuals to create adult, kin-like networks in which to live. But there are many barriers which sexual migrants have to overcome.

According to the mainstream media and popular prejudice, the marginal sexual worlds are bleak and dangerous. They are portrayed as impoverished, ugly, and inhabited by psychopaths and criminals. New migrants must be sufficiently motivated to resist the impact of such discouraging images. Attempts to counter negative propaganda with more realistic information generally meet with censorship, and there are continuous ideological struggles over which representations of sexual communities make it into the popular media.

Information on how to find, occupy, and live in the marginal sexual worlds is also suppressed. Navigational guides are scarce and inaccurate. In the past, fragments of rumor, distorted gossip, and bad publicity were the most available clues to the location of underground erotic communities. During the late 1960s and early 1970s, better information became available. Now groups like the Moral

Majority want to rebuild the ideological walls around the sexual undergrounds and make transit in and out of them as difficult as possible.

Migration is expensive. Transportation costs, moving expenses, and the necessity of finding new jobs and housing are economic difficulties that sexual migrants must overcome. These are especially imposing barriers to the young, who are often the most desperate to move. There are, however, routes into the erotic communities which mark trails through the propaganda thicket and provide some economic shelter along the way. Higher education can be a route for young people from affluent backgrounds. In spite of serious limitations, the information on sexual behavior at most colleges and universities is better than elsewhere, and most colleges and universities shelter small erotic networks of all sorts.

For poorer kids, the military is often the easiest way to get the hell out of wherever they are. Military prohibitions against homosexuality make this a perilous route. Although young queers continually attempt to use the armed forces to get out of intolerable hometown situations and closer to functional gay communities, they face the hazards of exposure, court martial, and dishonorable discharge.

Once in the cities, erotic populations tend to nucleate and to occupy some regular, visible territory. Churches and other anti-vice forces constantly put pressure on local authorities to contain such areas, reduce their visibility, or to drive their inhabitants out of town. There are periodic crackdowns in which local vice squads are unleashed on the populations they control. Gay men, prostitutes, and sometimes transvestites are sufficiently territorial and numerous to engage in intense battles with the cops over particular streets, parks, and alleys. Such border wars are usually inconclusive, but they result in many casualties.

For most of this century, the sexual underworlds have been marginal and impoverished, their residents subjected to stress and exploitation. The spectacular success of gay entrepreneurs in creating a variegated gay economy has altered the quality of life within the gay ghetto. The level of material comfort and social elaboration achieved by the gay community in the last fifteen years is unprecedented. But it is important to recall what happened to similar miracles. The growth of the black population in New York in the early part of the twentieth century led to the Harlem Renaissance, but that period of creativity was doused by the Depression. The relative prosperity and cultural florescence of the gay ghetto may be equally fragile. Like blacks who fled the South for the metropolitan North, homosexuals may have merely traded rural problems for urban ones.

Gay pioneers occupied neighborhoods that were centrally located but run down. Consequently, they border poor neighborhoods. Gays, especially low-income gays, end up competing with other low-income groups for the limited supply of cheap and moderate housing. In San Francisco, competition for low-cost housing has exacerbated both racism and homophobia, and is one source of the epidemic of street violence against homosexuals. Instead of being isolated and invisible in rural settings, city gays are now numerous and obvious targets for urban frustrations.

In San Francisco, unbridled construction of downtown skyscrapers and high-cost condominiums is causing affordable housing to evaporate. Megabuck construction is creating pressure on all city residents. Poor gay renters are visible in low-income neighborhoods; multimillionaire contracters are not. The specter of the "homosexual invasion" is a convenient scapegoat which deflects attention from the banks, the planning commission, the political establishment, and the big developers. In San Francisco, the well-being of the gay community has become embroiled in the high-stakes politics of urban real estate.

Downtown expansion affects all the territorial erotic underworlds. In both San Francisco and New York, high investment construction and urban renewal have intruded on the main areas of prostitution, pornography, and leather bars. Developers are salivating over Times Square, the Tenderloin, what is left of North Beach, and South of Market. Anti-sex ideology, obscenity law, prostitution regulations, and the alcoholic beverage codes are all being used to dislodge seedy adult businesses, sex workers, and leathermen. Within ten years, most of these areas will have been bulldozed and made safe for convention centers, international hotels, corporate headquarters, and housing for the rich.

The most important and consequential kind of sex conflict is what Jeffrey Weeks has termed the "moral panic." Moral panics are the "political moment" of sex, in which diffuse attitudes are channeled into political action and from there into social change.[60] The white slavery hysteria of the 1880s, the anti-homosexual campaigns of the 1950s, and the child pornography panic of the late 1970s were typical moral panics.

Because sexuality in Western societies is so mystified, the wars over it are often fought at oblique angles, aimed at phony targets, conducted with misplaced passions, and are highly, intensely symbolic. Sexual activities often function as signifiers for personal and social apprehensions to which they have no intrinsic connection. During a moral panic, such fears attach to some unfortunate sexual activity or population. The media become ablaze with indignation, the public behaves like a rabid mob, the police are activated, and the state enacts new laws and regulations. When the furor has passed, some innocent erotic group has been decimated, and the state has extended its power into new areas of erotic behavior.

The system of sexual stratification provides easy victims who lack the power to defend themselves, and a preexisting apparatus for controlling their movements and curtailing their freedoms. The stigma against sexual dissidents renders them morally defenseless. Every moral panic has consequences on two levels. The target population suffers most, but everyone is affected by the social and legal changes.

Moral panics rarely alleviate any real problem, because they are aimed at chimeras and signifiers. They draw on the pre-existing discursive structure which invents victims in order to justify treating "vices" as crimes. The criminalization of innocuous behaviors such as homosexuality, prostitution, obscenity, or recreational drug use, is rationalized by portraying them as menaces to health and safety, women and children, national security, the family, or civilization itself. Even when activity is acknowledged to be harmless, it may be banned because it is alleged to "lead" to something ostensibly worse (another manifestation of the domino theory).[61] Great and mighty edifices have been built on the basis of such phantasms. Generally, the outbreak of a moral panic is preceded by an intensification of such scapegoating.

It is always risky to prophesy. But it does not take much prescience to detect potential moral panics in two current developments: the attacks on sadomasochists by a segment of the feminist movement, and the right's increasing use of AIDS to incite virulent homophobia.

Feminist anti-pornography ideology has always contained an implied, and sometimes overt, indictment of sadomasochism. The pictures of sucking and fucking that comprise the bulk of pornography may be unnerving to those who are not familiar with them. But it is hard to make a convincing case that such images are violent. All of the early anti-porn slide shows used a highly selective sample of S/M imagery to sell a very flimsy analysis. Taken out of context, such images are often shocking. This shock value was mercilessly exploited to scare audiences into accepting the anti-porn perspective.

A great deal of anti-porn propaganda implies that sadomasochism is the underlying and essential "truth" towards which all pornography tends. Porn is thought to lead to S/M porn which in turn is alleged to lead to rape. This is a just-so story that revitalizes the notion that sex perverts commit sex crimes, not normal people. There is no evidence that the readers of S/M erotica or practicing sadomasochists commit a disproportionate number of sex crimes. Anti-porn literature scapegoats an unpopular sexual minority and its reading material for social problems they do not create.

The use of S/M imagery in anti-porn discourse is inflammatory. It implies that the way to make the world safe for women is to get rid of sadomasochism. The use of S/M images in the movie *Not a Love Story* was on a moral par with the use of depictions of black men raping white women, or of drooling old Jews pawing young Aryan girls, to incite racist or anti-Semitic frenzy.

Feminist rhetoric has a distressing tendency to reappear in reactionary contexts. For example, in 1980 and 1981, Pope John Paul II delivered a series of pronouncements reaffirming his commitment to the most conservative and Pauline understandings of human sexuality. In condemning divorce, abortion, trial marriage, pornography, prostitution, birth control, unbridled hedonism, and lust, the pope employed a great deal of feminist rhetoric about sexual objectification. Sounding like lesbian feminist polemicist Julia Penelope, His Holiness explained that "considering anyone in a lustful way makes that person a sexual object rather than a human being worthy of dignity."[62]

The right wing opposes pornography and has already adopted elements of feminist anti-porn rhetoric. The anti-S/M discourse developed in the women's movement could easily become a vehicle for a moral witch hunt. It provides a ready-made defenseless target population. It provides a rationale for the recriminalization of sexual materials which have escaped the reach of current obscenity laws. It would be especially easy to pass laws against S/M erotica resembling the child pornography laws. The ostensible purpose of such laws would be to reduce violence by banning so-called violent porn. A focused campaign against the leather menace might also result in the passage of laws to criminalize S/M behavior that is not currently illegal. The ultimate result of such a moral panic would be the legalized violation of a community of harmless perverts. It is dubious that such a sexual witch-hunt would make any appreciable contribution towards reducing violence against women.

An AIDS panic is even more probable. When fears of incurable disease mingle with sexual terror, the resulting brew is extremely volatile. A century ago, attempts to control syphilis led to the passage of the Contagious Diseases Acts in England. The Acts were based on erroneous medical theories and did nothing to halt the spread of the disease. But they did make life miserable for the hundreds of women who were incarcerated, subjected to forcible vaginal examination, and stigmatized for life as prostitutes.[63]

Whatever happens, AIDS will have far-reaching consequences on sex in general, and on homosexuality in particular. The disease will have a significant impact on the choices gay people make. Fewer will migrate to the gay meccas out of fear of the disease. Those who already reside in the ghettos will avoid situations they fear will expose them. The gay economy, and the political apparatus it supports, may prove to be evanescent. Fear of AIDS has already affected sexual ideology. Just when homosexuals have had some success in throwing off the taint of mental disease, gay people find themselves metaphorically welded to an image of lethal physical deterioration. The syndrome, its peculiar qualities, and its transmissibility are being used to reinforce old fears that sexual activity, homosexuality, and promiscuity led to disease and death.

AIDS is both a personal tragedy for those who contract the syndrome and a calamity for the gay community. Homophobes have gleefully hastened to turn this tragedy against its victims. One columnist has suggested that AIDS has always existed, that the Biblical prohibitions on sodomy were designed to protect people from AIDS, and that AIDS is therefore an appropriate punishment for violating the Levitical codes. Using fear of infection as a rationale, local right-wingers attempted to ban the gay rodeo from Reno, Nevada. A recent issue of the *Moral Majority Report* featured a picture of a "typical" white family of four wearing surgical masks. The headline read: "AIDS: HOMOSEXUAL DISEASES THREATEN AMERICAN FAMILIES."[64] Phyllis Schlafly has recently issued a pamphlet arguing that passage of the Equal Rights Amendment would make it impossible to "legally protect ourselves against AIDS and other diseases carried by homosexuals."[65] Current right-wing literature calls for shutting down the gay baths, for a legal ban on homosexual employment in food-handling occupations, and for state-mandated prohibitions on blood donations by gay people. Such policies would require the government to identify all homosexuals and impose easily recognizable legal and social markers on them.

It is bad enough that the gay community must deal with the medical misfortune of having been the population in which a deadly disease first became widespread and visible. It is worse to have to deal with the social consequences as well. Even before the AIDS scare, Greece passed a law that enabled police to arrest suspected homosexuals and force them to submit to an examination for venereal disease. It is likely that until AIDS and its methods of transmission are understood, there will be all sorts of proposals to control it by punishing the gay community and by attacking its institutions. When the cause of Legionnaires' Disease was unknown, there were no calls to quarantine members of the American Legion or to shut down their meeting halls. The Contagious Diseases Acts in England did little to control syphilis, but they caused a great deal of suffering for the women who came under their purview. The history of panic that has accompanied new epidemics, and of the casualties incurred by their scapegoats, should make everyone pause and consider with extreme scepticism any attempts to justify anti-gay policy initiatives on the basis of AIDS.

The limits of feminism

> We know that in an overwhelmingly large number of cases, sex crime is associated with pornography. We know that sex criminals read it, are clearly influenced by it. I believe that, if we can eliminate the distribution of such items among impressionable children, we shall greatly reduce our frightening sex-crime rate.
>
> J. Edgar Hoover[66]

In the absence of a more articulated radical theory of sex, most progressives have turned to feminism for guidance. But the relationship between feminism and sex is complex. Because sexuality is a nexus of the relationships between genders, much of the oppression of women is borne by, mediated through, and constituted within, sexuality. Feminism has always been vitally interested in sex. But there have been two strains of feminist thought on the subject. One tendency has criticized the restrictions on women's sexual behavior and denounced the high costs imposed on women for being sexually active. This tradition of feminist sexual thought has called for a sexual liberation that would work for women as well as for men. The second tendency has considered sexual liberalization to be inherently a mere extension of male privilege. This tradition resonates with conservative, anti-sexual discourse. With the advent of the anti-pornography movement, it achieved temporary hegemony over feminist analysis.

The anti-pornography movement and its texts have been the most extensive expression of this discourse.[67] In addition, proponents of this viewpoint have condemned virtually every variant of sexual expression as anti-feminist. Within this framework, monogamous lesbianism that occurs within long-term, intimate relationships and which does not involve playing with polarized roles, has replaced married, procreative heterosexuality at the top of the value hierarchy. Heterosexuality has been demoted to somewhere in the middle. Apart from this change, everything else looks more or less familiar. The lower depths are occupied by the usual groups and behaviors: prostitution, transsexuality, sadomasochism, and cross-generational activities.[68] Most gay male conduct, all casual sex, promiscuity, and lesbian behavior that does involve roles or kink or non-monogamy are also censured.[69] Even sexual fantasy during masturbation is denounced as a phallocentric holdover.[70]

This discourse on sexuality is less a sexology than a demonology. It presents most sexual behavior in the worst possible light. Its descriptions of erotic conduct always use the worst available example as if it were representative. It presents the most disgusting pornography, the most exploited forms of prostitution, and the least palatable or most shocking manifestations of sexual variation. This rhetorical tactic consistently misrepresents human sexuality in all its forms. The picture of human sexuality that emerges from this literature is unremittingly ugly.

In addition, this anti-porn rhetoric is a massive exercise in scapegoating. It criticizes non-routine acts of love rather than routine acts of oppression, exploitation, or violence. This demon sexology directs legitimate anger at women's lack of personal safety against innocent individuals, practices, and communities. Anti-porn propaganda often implies that sexism originates within the commercial sex industry and subsequently infects the rest of society. This is sociologically nonsensical. The sex industry is hardly a feminist utopia. It reflects the sexism that exists in the society as a whole. We need to analyze and oppose the manifestations of gender inequality specific to the sex industry. But this is not the same as attempting to wipe out commercial sex.

Similarly, erotic minorities such as sadomasochists and transsexuals are as likely to exhibit sexist attitudes or behavior as any other politically random social grouping. But to claim that they are inherently anti-feminist is sheer fantasy. A good deal of current feminist literature attributes the oppression of women to graphic representations of sex, prostitution, sex education, sadomasochism, male homosexuality, and transsexualism. Whatever happened to the family, religion, education, child-rearing practices, the media, the state, psychiatry, job discrimination, and unequal pay?

Finally, this so-called feminist discourse recreates a very conservative sexual morality. For over a century, battles have been waged over just how much shame, distress, and punishment should be incurred by sexual activity. The conservative tradition has promoted opposition to pornography, prostitution, homosexuality, all erotic variation, sex education, sex research, abortion, and contraception. The opposing, pro-sex tradition has included individuals like Havelock Ellis, Magnus Hirshfeld, Alfred Kinsey, and Victoria Woodhull, as well as the sex education movement, organizations of militant prostitutes and homosexuals, the reproductive rights movement, and organizations such as the Sexual Reform League of the 1960s. This motley collection of sex reformers, sex educators, and sexual militants has mixed records on both sexual and feminist issues. But surely they are closer to the spirit of modern feminism than are moral crusaders, the social purity movement, and anti-vice organizations. Nevertheless, the current feminist sexual demonology generally elevates the anti-vice crusaders to positions of ancestral honor, while condemning the more liberatory tradition as anti-feminist. In an essay that exemplifies some of these trends, Sheila Jeffreys blames Havelock Ellis, Edward Carpenter, Alexandra Kollantai, "believers in the joy of sex of every possible political persuasion," and the 1929 congress of the World League for Sex Reform for making "a great contribution to the defeat of militant feminism."[71]

The anti-pornography movement and its avatars have claimed to speak for all feminism. Fortunately, they do not. Sexual liberation has been and continues to be a feminist goal. The women's movement may have produced some of the most retrogressive sexual thinking this side of the Vatican. But it has also produced an exciting, innovative, and articulate defense of sexual pleasure and erotic justice. This "pro-sex" feminism has been spearheaded by lesbians whose sexuality does not conform to movement standards of purity (primarily lesbian sadomasochists and butch/femme dykes), by unapologetic heterosexuals, and by women who adhere to classic radical feminism rather than to the revisionist celebrations of femininity which have become so common.[72] Although the anti-porn forces have attempted to weed anyone who disgrees with them out of the movement, the fact remains that feminist thought about sex is profoundly polarized.[73]

Whenever there is polarization, there is an unhappy tendency to think the truth lies somewhere in between. Ellen Willis has commented sarcastically that "the feminist bias is that women are equal to men and the male chauvinist bias is that women are inferior. The unbiased view is that the truth lies somewhere in between."[74] The most recent development in the feminist sex wars is the emergence of a "middle" that seeks to evade the dangers of anti-porn fascism, on the one hand, and a supposed "anything goes" libertarianism, on the other.[75] Although it is hard to criticize a position that is not yet fully formed, I want to draw attention to some incipient problems.

The emergent middle is based on a false characterization of the poles of the debate, construing both sides as equally extremist. According to B. Ruby Rich, "the desire for a language of sexuality has led feminists into locations (pornography, sadomasochism) too narrow or overdetermined for a fruitful discussion. Debate has collapsed into a rumble."[76] True, the fights between Women Against Pornography (WAP) and lesbian sadomasochists have resembled gang warfare. But the responsibility for this lies primarily with the anti-porn movement, and its refusal to engage in principled discussion. S/M lesbians have been forced into a struggle to maintain their membership in the movement, and to defend themselves against slander. No major spokeswoman for lesbian S/M has argued for any kind of S/M supremacy, or advocated that everyone should be a sadomasochist. In addition to self-defense, S/M lesbians have called for appreciation for erotic diversity and more open discussion of sexuality.[77] Trying to find a middle course between WAP and Samois is a bit like saying that the truth about homosexuality lies somewhere between the positions of the Moral Majority and those of the gay movement.

In political life, it is all too easy to marginalize radicals, and to attempt to buy acceptance for a moderate position by portraying others as extremists. Liberals have done this for years to communists. Sexual radicals have opened up the sex debates. It is shameful to deny their contribution, misrepresent their positions, and further their stigmatization.

In contrast to cultural feminists, who simply want to purge sexual dissidents, the sexual moderates are willing to defend the rights of erotic non-conformists to political participation. Yet this defense of political rights is linked to an implicit system of ideological condescension. The argument has two major parts. The first is an accusation that sexual dissidents have not paid close enough attention to the meaning, sources, or historical construction of their sexuality. This emphasis on meaning appears to function in much the same way that the question of etiology has functioned in discussions of homosexuality. That is, homosexuality, sadomasochism, prostitution, or boy-love are taken to be mysterious and problematic in some way that more respectable sexualities are not. The search for a cause is a search for something that could change so that these "problematic" eroticisms would simply not occur. Sexual militants have replied to such exercises that although the question of etiology or cause is of intellectual interest, it is not high on the political agenda and that, moreover, the privileging of such questions is itself a regressive political choice.

The second part of the "moderate" position focuses on questions of consent. Sexual radicals of all varieties have demanded the legal and social legitimation of consenting sexual behavior. Feminists have criticized them for ostensibly finessing questions about "the limits of consent" and "structural constraints" on consent.[78] Although there are deep problems with the political discourse of consent, and although there are certainly structural constraints on sexual choice, this criticism has been consistently misapplied in the sex debates. It does not take into account the very specific semantic content that consent has in sex law and sex practice.

As I mentioned earlier, a great deal of sex law does not distinguish between consensual and coercive behavior. Only rape law contains such a distinction. Rape law is based on the assumption, correct in my view, that heterosexual activity may be freely chosen or forcibly coerced. One has the legal right to engage in hetero-sexual behavior as long as it does not fall under the purview of other statutes and as long as it is agreeable to both parties.

This is not the case for most other sexual acts. Sodomy laws, as I mentioned above, are based on the assumption that the forbidden acts are an "abominable and detestable crime against nature." Criminality is intrinsic to the acts themselves, no matter what the desires of the participants. "Unlike rape, sodomy or an unnatural or perverted sexual act may be committed between two persons both of whom consent, and, regardless of which is the aggressor, both may be prosecuted."[79] Before the consenting adults statute was passed in California in 1976, lesbian lovers could have been prosecuted for committing oral copulation. If both partici-pants were capable of consent, both were equally guilty.[80]

Adult incest statutes operate in a similar fashion. Contrary to popular myth-ology, the incest statutes have little to do with protecting children from rape by close relatives. The incest statutes themselves prohibit marriage or sexual inter-course between adults who are closely related. Prosecutions are rare, but two were reported recently. In 1979, a 19-year-old Marine met his 42-year-old mother, from whom he had been separated at birth. The two fell in love and got married. They were charged and found guilty of incest, which under Virginia law carries a maximum ten-year sentence. During their trial, the Marine testified, "I love her very much. I feel that two people who love each other should be able to live together."[81] In another case, a brother and sister who had been raised separ-ately met and decided to get married. They were arrested and pleaded guilty to felony incest in return for probation. A condition of probation was that they not live together as husband and wife. Had they not accepted, they would have faced twenty years in prison.[82]

In a famous S/M case, a man was convicted of aggravated assault for a whip-ping administered in an S/M scene. There was no complaining victim. The session had been filmed and he was prosecuted on the basis of the film. The man appealed his conviction by arguing that he had been involved in a consensual sexual encounter and had assaulted no one. In rejecting his appeal, the court ruled that one may not consent to an assault or battery "except in a situation involving ordinary physical contact or blows incident to sports such as football, boxing, or wrestling."[83] The court went on to note that the "consent of a person without legal capacity to give consent, such as a child or insane person, is ineffective," and that "It is a matter of common knowledge that a normal person in full possession of his mental faculties does not freely consent to the use, upon himself, of force likely to produce great bodily injury."[84] Therefore, anyone who would consent to a whipping would be presumed *non compos mentis* and legally incapable of consenting. S/M sex generally involves a much lower level of force than the average football game, and results in far fewer injuries than most sports. But the court ruled that football players are sane, whereas masochists are not.

Sodomy laws, adult incest laws, and legal interpretations such as the one above clearly interfere with consensual behavior and impose criminal penalties on it. Within the law, consent is a privilege enjoyed only by those who engage in the highest-status sexual behavior. Those who enjoy low-status sexual behavior do not have the legal right to engage in it. In addition, economic sanctions, family pressures, erotic stigma, social discrimination, negative ideology, and the paucity of information about erotic behavior, all serve to make it difficult for people to make unconventional sexual choices. There certainly are structural constraints that impede free sexual choice, but they hardly operate to coerce anyone into being a pervert. On the contrary, they operate to coerce everyone toward normality.

The "brainwash theory" explains erotic diversity by assuming that some sexual acts are so disgusting that no one would willingly perform them. Therefore, the reasoning goes, anyone who does so must have been forced or fooled. Even constructivist sexual theory has been pressed into the service of explaining away why otherwise rational individuals might engage in variant sexual behavior. Another position that is not yet fully formed uses the ideas of Foucault and Weeks to imply that the "perversions" are an especially unsavory or problematic aspect of the construction of modern sexuality.[85] This is yet another version of the notion that sexual dissidents are victims of the subtle machinations of the social system. Weeks and Foucault would not accept such an interpretation, since they consider all sexuality to be constructed, the conventional no less than the deviant.

Psychology is the last resort of those who refuse to acknowledge that sexual dissidents are as conscious and free as any other group of sexual actors. If deviants are not responding to the manipulations of the social system, then perhaps the source of their incomprehensible choices can be found in a bad childhood, unsuccessful socialization, or inadequate identity formation. In her essay on erotic domination, Jessica Benjamin draws upon psychoanalysis and philosophy to explain why what she calls "sadomasochism" is alienated, distorted, unsatisfactory, numb, purposeless, and an attempt to "relieve an original effort at differentiation that failed."[86] This essay substitutes a psycho-philosophical inferiority for the more usual means of devaluing dissident eroticism. One reviewer has already construed Benjamin's argument as showing that sadomasochism is merely an "obsessive replay of the infant power struggle."[87]

The position which defends the political rights of perverts but which seeks to understand their "alienated" sexuality is certainly preferable to the WAP-style bloodbaths. But for the most part, the sexual moderates have not confronted their discomfort with erotic choices that differ from their own. Erotic chauvinism cannot be redeemed by tarting it up in Marxist drag, sophisticated constructivist theory, or retro-psychobabble.

Whichever feminist position on sexuality – right, left, or center – eventually attains dominance, the existence of such a rich discussion is evidence that the feminist movement will always be a source of interesting thought about sex. Nevertheless, I want to challenge the assumption that feminism is or should be the privileged site of a theory of sexuality. Feminism is the theory of gender oppression. To automatically assume that this makes it the theory of sexual oppression is to fail to distinguish between gender, on the one hand, and erotic desire, on the other.

In the English language, the word "sex" has two very different meanings. It means gender and gender identity, as in "the female sex" or "the male sex." But sex also refers to sexual activity, lust, intercourse, and arousal, as in "to have sex." This semantic merging reflects a cultural assumption that sexuality is reducible to sexual intercourse and that it is a function of the relations between women and men. The cultural fusion of gender with sexuality has given rise to the idea that a theory of sexuality may be derived directly out of a theory of gender.

In an earlier essay, "The Traffic in Women," I used the concept of a sex/gender system, defined as a "set of arrangements by which a society transforms biological sexuality into products of human activity."[88] I went on to argue that "Sex as we know it – gender identity, sexual desire and fantasy, concepts of childhood – is itself a social product."[89] In that essay, I did not distinguish between lust and gender, treating both as modalities of the same underlying social process.

"The Traffic in Women" was inspired by the literature on kinbased systems of social organization. It appeared to me at the time that gender and desire were systemically intertwined in such social formations. This may or may not be an accurate assessment of the relationship between sex and gender in tribal organizations. But it is surely not an adequate formulation for sexuality in Western industrial societies. As Foucault has pointed out, a system of sexuality has emerged out of earlier kinship forms and has acquired significant autonomy.

> Particularly from the eighteenth century onward, Western societies created and deployed a new apparatus which was superimposed on the previous one, and which, without completely supplanting the latter, helped to reduce its importance. I am speaking of the deployment of *sexuality*. . . . For the first [kinship], what is pertinent is the link between partners and definite statutes; the second [sexuality] is concerned with the sensations of the body, the quality of pleasures, and the nature of impressions.[90]

The development of this sexual system has taken place in the context of gender relations. Part of the modern ideology of sex is that lust is the province of men, purity that of women. Women have been to some extent excluded from the modern sexual system. It is no accident that pornography and the perversions have been considered part of the male domain. In the sex industry, women have been excluded from most production and consumption, and allowed to participate primarily as workers. In order to participate in the "perversions," women have had to overcome serious limitations on their social mobility, their economic resources, and their sexual freedoms. Gender affects the operation of the sexual system, and the sexual system has had gender-specific manifestations. But although sex and gender are related, they are not the same thing, and they form the basis of two distinct arenas of social practice.

In contrast to my perspective in "The Traffic in Women," I am now arguing that it is essential to separate gender and sexuality analytically to more accurately reflect their separate social existence. This goes against the grain of much contemporary feminist thought, which treats sexuality as a derivation of gender. For instance, lesbian feminist ideology has mostly analyzed the oppression of lesbians in terms of the oppression of women. However, lesbians are also oppressed as queers and perverts, by the operation of sexual, not gender, stratification. Although it pains many lesbians to think about it, the fact is that lesbians have shared many of the sociological features and suffered from many of the same social penalties as have gay men, sadomasochists, transvestites, and prostitutes.

Catherine MacKinnon has made the most explicit theoretical attempt to subsume sexuality under feminist thought. According to MacKinnon, "Sexuality is to feminism what work is to marxism . . . the molding, direction, and expression of sexuality organizes society into two sexes, women and men."[91] This analytic strategy in turn rests on a decision to "use sex and gender relatively interchangeably."[92] It is this definitional fusion that I want to challenge.

There is an instructive analogy in the history of the differentiation of contemporary feminist thought from Marxism. Marxism is probably the most supple and powerful conceptual system extant for analyzing social inequality. But attempts to make Marxism the sole explanatory system for all social inequalities have been dismal exercises. Marxism is most successful in the areas of social life for which it was originally developed – class relations under capitalism.

In the early days of the contemporary women's movement, a theoretical conflict took place over the applicability of Marxism to gender stratification. Since Marxist theory is relatively powerful, it does in fact detect important and interesting aspects of gender oppression. It works best for those issues of gender most closely related to issues of class and the organization of labor. The issues more specific to the social structure of gender were not amenable to Marxist analysis.

The relationship between feminism and a radical theory of sexual oppression is similar. Feminist conceptual tools were developed to detect and analyze gender-based hierarchies. To the extent that these overlap with erotic stratifications, feminist theory has some explanatory power. But as issues become less those of gender and more those of sexuality, feminist analysis becomes irrelevant and often misleading. Feminist thought simply lacks angles of vision which can encompass the social organization of sexuality. The criteria of relevance in feminist thought do not allow it to see or assess critical power relations in the area of sexuality.

In the long run, feminism's critique of gender hierarchy must be incorporated into a radical theory of sex, and the critique of sexual oppression should enrich feminism. But an autonomous theory and politics specific to sexuality must be developed.

It is a mistake to substitute feminism for Marxism as the last word in social theory. Feminism is no more capable than Marxism of being the ultimate and complete account of all social inequality. Nor is feminism the residual theory which can take care of everything to which Marx did not attend. These critical tools were fashioned to handle very specific areas of social activity. Other areas of social life, their forms of power, and their characteristic modes of oppression, need their own conceptual implements. In this essay, I have argued for theoretical as well as sexual pluralism.

Conclusion

. . . these pleasures which we lightly call physical . . .

Colette[93]

Like gender, sexuality is political. It is organized into systems of power, which reward and encourage some individuals and activities, while punishing and suppressing others. Like the capitalist organization of labor and its distribution of rewards and powers, the modern sexual system has been the object of political struggle since it emerged and as it has evolved. But if the disputes between labor and capital are mystified, sexual conflicts are completely camouflaged.

The legislative restructuring that took place at the end of the nineteenth century and in the early decades of the twentieth was a refracted response to the emergence of the modern erotic system. During that period, new erotic communities formed. It became possible to be a male homosexual or a lesbian in a way it had not been previously. Mass-produced erotica became available, and the possibilities for sexual commerce expanded. The first homosexual rights organizations were formed, and the first analyses of sexual oppression were articulated.[94]

The repression of the 1950s was in part a backlash to the expansion of sexual communities and possibilities which took place during World War II.[95] During the 1950s, gay rights organizations were established, the Kinsey reports were published, and lesbian literature flourished. The 1950s were a formative as well as a repressive era.

The current right-wing sexual counter-offensive is in part a reaction to the sexual liberalization of the 1960s and early 1970s. Moreover, it has brought about a unified and self-conscious coalition of sexual radicals. In one sense, what is now occurring is the emergence of a new sexual movement, aware of new issues and seeking a new theoretical basis. The sex wars out on the streets have been partly responsible for provoking a new intellectual focus on sexuality. The sexual system is shifting once again, and we are seeing many symptoms of its change.

In Western culture, sex is taken all too seriously. A person is not considered immoral, is not sent to prison, and is not expelled from her or his family, for enjoying spicy cuisine. But an individual may go through all this and more for enjoying shoe leather. Ultimately, of what possible social significance is it if a person likes to masturbate over a shoe? It may even be non-consensual, but since we do not ask permission of our shoes to wear them, it hardly seems necessary to obtain dispensation to come on them.

If sex is taken too seriously, sexual persecution is not taken seriously enough. There is systematic mistreatment of individuals and communities on the basis of erotic taste or behavior. There are serious penalties for belonging to the various sexual occupational castes. The sexuality of the young is denied, adult sexuality is often treated like a variety of nuclear waste, and the graphic representation of sex takes place in a mire of legal and social circumlocution. Specific populations bear the brunt of the current system of erotic power, but their persecution upholds a system that affects everyone.

The 1980s have already been a time of great sexual suffering. They have also been a time of ferment and new possibility. It is up to all of us to try to prevent more barbarism and to encourage erotic creativity. Those who consider themselves progressive need to examine their preconceptions, update their sexual educations, and acquaint themselves with the existence and operation of sexual hierarchy. It is time to recognize the political dimensions of erotic life.

Acknowledgments

It is always a treat to get to the point in a paper when I can thank those who contributed to its realization. Many of my ideas about the formation of sexual communities first occurred to me during a course given by Charles Tilly on "The Urbanization of Europe from 1500–1900." Few courses could ever provide as much excitement, stimulation, and conceptual richness as did that one. Daniel Tsang alerted me to the significance of the events of 1977 and taught me to pay attention to sex law. Pat Califia deepened my appreciation for human sexual variety and taught me to respect the much-maligned fields of sex research and sex education. Jeff Escoffier shared his powerful grasp of gay history and sociology, and I have especially benefited from his insights into the gay economy. Allan Bérubé's work in progress on gay history has enabled me to think with more clarity about the dynamics of sexual oppression. Conversations with Ellen Dubois, Amber Hollibaugh, Mary Ryan, Judy Stacey, Kay Trimberger, and Martha Vicinus have influenced the direction of my thinking.

I am very grateful to Cynthia Astuto for advice and research on legal matters, and to David Sachs, book-dealer extraordinaire, for pointing out the right-wing pamphlet literature on sex. I am grateful to Allan Bérubé, Ralph Bruno, Estelle Freedman, Kent Gerard, Barbara Kerr, Michael Shively, Carole Vance, Bill Walker, and Judy Walkowitz for miscellaneous references and factual information. I cannot begin to express my gratitude to those who read and commented on versions of this paper: Jeanne Bergman, Sally Binford, Lynn Eden, Laura Engelstein, Jeff Escoffier, Carole Vance and Ellen Willis. Mark Leger both edited and performed acts of secretarial heroism in preparing the manuscript. Marybeth Nelson provided emergency graphics assistance.

I owe special thanks to two friends whose care mitigated the strains of writing. E.S. kept my back operational and guided me firmly through some monumental bouts of writer's block. Cynthia Astuto's many kindnesses and unwavering support enabled me to keep working at an absurd pace for many weeks.

None of these individuals should be held responsible for my opinions, but I am grateful to them all for inspiration, information, and assistance.

A note on definitions

Throughout this essay, I use terms such as homosexual, sex worker, and pervert. I use "homosexual" to refer to both women and men. If I want to be more specific, I use terms such as "lesbian" or "gay male." "Sex worker" is intended to be more inclusive than "prostitute," in order to encompass the many jobs of the sex industry. Sex worker includes erotic dancers, strippers, porn models, nude women who will talk to a customer via telephone hook-up and can be seen but not touched, phone partners, and the various other employees of sex businesses such as receptionists, janitors, and barkers. Obviously, it also includes prostitutes, hustlers, and "male models." I use the term "pervert" as a shorthand for all the stigmatized sexual orientations. It used to cover male and female homosexuality as well but as these become less disreputable, the term has increasingly referred to the other "deviations." Terms such as "pervert" and "deviant" have, in general use, a connotation of disapproval, disgust, and dislike. I am using these terms in a denotative fashion, and do not intend them to convey any disapproval on my part.

Notes

1   Demetrius Zambaco, "Onanism and Nervous Disorders in Two Little Girls", in François Peraldi (ed.), *Polysexuality, Semiotext(e)*, vol. IV, no. 1, 1981, pp. 31, 36.
2   Linda Gordon and Ellen Dubois, "Seeking Ecstasy on the Battlefield: Danger and Pleasure in Nineteenth Century Feminist Sexual Thought", *Feminist Studies*, vol. 9, no. 1, Spring 1983; Steven Marcus, *The Other Victorians*, New York, New American Library, 1974; Mary Ryan, "The Power of Women's Networks: A Case Study of Female Moral Reform in America", *Feminist Studies*, vol. 5, no. 1, 1979; Judith R. Walkowitz, *Prostitution and Victorian Society*, Cambridge, Cambridge University Press, 1980; Judith R. Walkowitz, "Male Vice and Feminist Virtue: Feminism and the Politics of Prostitution in Nineteenth-Century Britain", *History Workshop Journal*, no. 13, Spring 1982; Jeffrey Weeks, *Sex, Politics and Society: The Regulation of Sexuality Since 1800*, New York, Longman, 1981.
3   G.J. Barker-Benfield, *The Horrors of the Half-Known Life*, New York, Harper Colophon, 1976; Marcus, op. cit.; Weeks, op. cit., especially pages 48–52; Zambaco, op. cit.
4   Sarah Senefield Beserra, Sterling G. Franklin, and Norma Clevenger (eds), *Sex Code of California*, Sacramento, Planned Parenthood Affiliates of California, 1977, p. 113.
5   Ibid., pp. 113–17.
6   Walkowitz, "Male Vice and Feminist Virtue", op. cit., p. 83. Walkowitz's entire discussion of the *Maiden Tribute of Modern Babylon* and its aftermath (pp. 83–5) is illuminating.
7   Walkowitz, "Male Vice and Feminist Virtue", op. cit., p. 85.
8   Beserra et al., op. cit., pp. 106–7.
9   Commonwealth of Massachusetts, *Preliminary Report of the Special Commission Investigating the Prevalence of Sex Crimes*, 1947; State of New Hampshire. *Report of the Interim Commission of the State of New Hampshire to Study the Cause and Prevention of Serious Sex Crimes*, 1949; City of New York, *Report of the Mayor's Committee for the Study of Sex Offences*, 1939; State of New York, *Report to the Governor on a Study of 102 Sex Offenders at Sing Sing Prison*, 1950; Samuel Hartwell, *A Citizen's Handbook of Sexual Abnormalities and the Mental Hygiene Approach to Their Prevention*, State of Michigan, 1950; State of Michigan, *Report of the Governor's Study Commission on the Deviated Criminal Sex Offender*, 1951. This is merely a sampler.
10   Estelle B. Freedman, " 'Uncontrolled Desire': The Threat of the Sexual Psychopath in America, 1935–1960", paper presented at the Annual Meeting of the American Historical Association, San Francisco, December 1983.
11   Allan Bérubé, "Behind the Spectre of San Francisco", *Body Politic*, April 1981; Allan

Bérubé, "Marching to a Different Drummer", *Advocate*, October 15, 1981; John D'Emilio, *Sexual Politics, Sexual Communities: The Making of the Homosexual Minority in the United States, 1940–1970*, Chicago, University of Chicago Press, 1983; Jonathan Katz, *Gay American History*, New York, Thomas Y. Crowell, 1976.

12   D'Emilio, op. cit., pp. 46–7; Allan Bérubé, personal communication.

13   John Gerassi, *The Boys of Boise*, New York, Collier, 1968, p. 14. I am indebted to Allan Bérubé for calling my attention to this incident.

14   Allan Bérubé, personal communication; D'Emilio, op. cit.; John D'Emilio, "Gay Politics, Gay Community: San Francisco's Experience", *Socialist Review*, no. 55, January–February 1981.

15   The following examples suggest avenues for additional research. A local crackdown at the University of Michigan is documented in Daniel Tsang, "Gay Ann Arbor Purges", *Midwest Gay Academic Journal*, vol. 1, no. 1, 1977; and Daniel Tsang, "Ann Arbor Gay Purges", part 2, *Midwest Gay Academic Journal*, vol. 1, no. 2, 1977. At the University of Michigan, the number of faculty dismissed for alleged homosexuality appears to rival the number fired for alleged communist tendencies. It would be interesting to have figures comparing the number of professors who lost their positions during this period due to sexual and political offenses. On regulatory reform, many states passed laws during this period prohibiting the sale of alcoholic beverages to "known sex perverts" or providing that bars which catered to "sex perverts" be closed. Such a law was passed in California in 1955, and declared unconstitutional by the state Supreme Court in 1959 (Allan Bérubé, personal communication). It would be of great interest to know exactly which states passed such statutes, the dates of their enactment, the discussion that preceded them, and how many are still on the books. On the persecution of other erotic populations, evidence indicates that John Willie and Irving Klaw, the two premier producers and distributors of bondage erotica in the United States from the late 1940s through the early 1960s, encountered frequent police harassment and that Klaw, at least, was affected by a congressional investigation conducted by the Kefauver Committee. I am indebted to personal communication from J.B. Rund for information on the careers of Willie and Klaw. Published sources are scarce, but see John Willie, *The Adventures of Sweet Gwendoline*, New York, Belier Press, 1974; J.B. Rund, "Preface", *Bizarre Comix*, vol. 8, New York, Belier Press, 1977; J.B. Rund, "Preface", *Bizarre Fotos*, vol. 1, New York, Belier Press, 1978; and J.B. Rund, "Preface", *Bizarre Katalogs*, vol. 1, New York, Belier Press, 1979. It would be useful to have more systematic information on legal shifts and police activity affecting non-gay erotic dissidence.

16   "Chicago is Center of National Child Porno Ring: The Child Predators", "Child Sex: Square in New Town Tells it All", "U.S. Orders Hearings On Child Pornography: Rodino Calls Sex Racket an 'Outrage' ", "Hunt Six Men, Twenty Boys in Crackdown", *Chicago Tribune*, May 16, 1977; "Dentist Seized in Child Sex Raid: Carey to Open Probe", "How Ruses Lure Victims to Child Pornographers", *Chicago Tribune*, May 17, 1977; "Child Pornographers Thrive on Legal Confusion", "U.S. Raids Hit Porn Sellers", *Chicago Tribune*, May 18, 1977.

17   For more information on the "kiddie porn panic" see Pat Califia, "The Great Kiddy Porn Scare of '77 and Its Aftermath", *Advocate*, October 16, 1980; Pat Califia, "A Thorny Issue Splits a Movement", *Advocate*, October 30, 1980; Mitzel, *The Boston Sex Scandal*, Boston, Glad Day Books, 1980; Gayle Rubin, "Sexual Politics, the New Right, and the Sexual Fringe", in Daniel Tsang (ed.), *The Age Taboo*, Boston, Alyson Publications, 1981; on the issue of cross-generational relationships, see also Roger Moody, *Indecent Assault*, London, Word Is Out Press, 1980; Tom O'Carroll, *Paedophilia: The Radical Case*, London, Peter Owen, 1980; Tsang, *The Age Taboo*, op. cit., and Paul Wilson, *The Man They Called A Monster*, New South Wales, Cassell Australia, 1981.

18   "House Passes Tough Bill on Child Porn", *San Francisco Chronicle*, November 15, 1983, p. 14.

19   George Stambolian, "Creating the New Man: A Conversation with Jacqueline Livingston", *Christopher Street*, May 1980; "Jacqueline Livingston", *Clothed With the Sun*, vol. 3, no. 1, May 1983.

20   Paul H. Gebhard, "The Institute", in Martin S. Weinberg (ed.), *Sex Research: Studies from the Kinsey Institute*, New York, Oxford University Press, 1976.

21   Phoebe Courtney, *The Sex Education Racket: Pornography in the Schools (An Exposé)*, New Orleans, Free Men Speak, 1969; Dr Gordon V. Drake, *SIECUS: Corrupter of Youth*, Tulsa, Oklahoma, Christian Crusade Publications, 1969.

22   *Pavlov's Children (They May Be Yours)*, Impact Publishers, Los Angeles, California, 1969.

23   Norman Podhoretz, "The Culture of Appeasement", *Harper's*, October 1977.

24   Alan Wolfe and Jerry Sanders, "Resurgent Cold War Ideology: The Case of the Committee on the Present Danger", in Richard Fagen (ed.), *Capitalism and the State in U.S.-Latin American Relations*, Stanford, Stanford University Press, 1979.

25   Jimmy Breslin, "The Moral Majority in Your Motel Room", *San Francisco Chronicle*, January 22, 1981, p. 41; Linda Gordon and Allen Hunter, "Sex, Family, and the New Right", *Radical America*, winter 1977–8; Sasha Gregory-Lewis, "The Neo-Right Political Apparatus", *Advocate*, February 8, 1977; Sasha Gregory-Lewis, "Right Wing Finds New Organizing Tactic", *Advocate*, June 23, 1977; Sasha Gregory-Lewis, "Unravelling the Anti-Gay Network", *Advocate*, September 7, 1977; Andrew Kopkind, "America's New Right", *New Times*, September 30, 1977; Rosalind Pollack Petchesky, "Anti-abortion, Anti-feminism, and the Rise of the New Right", *Feminist Studies*, vol. 7, no. 2, summer 1981.

26   Rhonda Brown, "Blueprint for a Moral America", *Nation*, May 23, 1981.

27   James Barr, *Quatrefoil*, New York, Greenberg, 1950, p. 310.

28   This insight was first articulated by Mary McIntosh, "The Homosexual Role", *Social Problems*, vol. 16, no. 2, fall 1968; the idea has been developed in Jeffrey Weeks, *Coming Out: Homosexual Politics in Britain from the Nineteenth Century to the Present*, New York, Quartet, 1977, and in Weeks, *Sex, Politics and Society*, op. cit.; see also D'Emilio, *Sexual Politics, Sexual Communities*, op. cit.; and Gayle Rubin, "Introduction" to Renée Vivien, *A Woman Appeared to Me*, Weatherby Lake, Mo., Naiad Press, 1979.

29   Bert Hansen, "The Historical Construction of Homosexuality", *Radical History Review*, no. 20, Spring/Summer 1979.

30   Walkowitz, *Prostitution and Victorian Society*, op. cit.; and Walkowitz, "Male Vice and Female Virtue", op. cit.

31   Michel Foucault, *The History of Sexuality*, New York, Pantheon, 1978.

32   A very useful discussion of these issues can be found in Robert Padgug, "Sexual Matters: On Conceptualizing Sexuality in History", *Radical History Review*, no. 20, spring/summer 1979.

33   Claude Lévi-Strauss, "A Confrontation", *New Left Review*, no. 62, July–August 1970. In this conversation, Lévi-Strauss calls his position "a Kantianism without a transcendental subject."

34   Foucault, op. cit., p. 11.

35   See the discussion in Weeks, *Sex, Politics and Society*, op. cit., p. 9.

36   See Weeks, *Sex, Politics and Society*, op. cit., p. 22.

37   See, for example, "Pope Praises Couples for Self-Control", *San Francisco Chronicle*, October 13, 1980, p. 5; "Pope Says Sexual Arousal Isn't a Sin If It's Ethical", *San Francisco Chronicle*, November 6, 1980, p. 33; "Pope Condemns 'Carnal Lust' As Abuse of Human Freedom", *San Francisco Chronicle*, January 15, 1981, p. 2; "Pope Again Hits Abortion, Birth Control", *San Francisco Chronicle*, January 16, 1981, p. 13; and "Sexuality, Not Sex in Heaven", *San Francisco Chronicle*, December 3, 1981, p. 50. See also footnote 62 below.

38   Susan Sontag, *Styles of Radical Will*, New York, Farrar, Strauss, & Giroux, 1969, p. 46.

39   See Foucault, op. cit., pp. 106–7.

40   American Psychiatric Association, *Diagnostic and Statistical Manual of Mental and Physical Disorders*, 3rd edn, Washington, DC, American Psychiatric Association.

41   Alfred Kinsey, Wardell Pomeroy, and Clyde Martin, *Sexual Behavior in the Human Male*, Philadelphia, W.B. Saunders, 1948; Alfred Kinsey, Wardell Pomeroy, Clyde Martin, and Paul Gebhard, *Sexual Behavior in the Human Female*, Philadelphia, W.B. Saunders, 1953.

42   John Gagnon and William Simon, *Sexual Deviance*, New York, Harper & Row, 1967; John Gagnon and William Simon, *The Sexual Scene*, Chicago, Transaction Books, Aldine, 1970; John Gagnon, *Human Sexualities*, Glenview, Illinois, Scott, Foresman, 1977.

43   Havelock Ellis, *Studies in the Psychology of Sex* (two volumes), New York, Random House, 1936.

44   Foucault, op. cit., p. 43.

45   Gilbert Herdt, *Guardians of the Flutes*, New York, McGraw-Hill, 1981; Raymond Kelly, "Witchcraft and Sexual Relations", in Paula Brown and Georgeda Buchbinder (eds), *Man and Woman in the New Guinea Highlands*, Washington, DC, American Anthropological Association, 1976; Gayle Rubin, "Coconuts: Aspects of Male/Female Relationships in New Guinea", unpublished ms., 1974; Gayle Rubin, review of *Guardians of the Flutes, Advocate*, December 23, 1982; J. Van Baal, *Dema*, The Hague, Nijhoff, 1966; F.E. Williams, *Papuans of the Trans-Fly*, Oxford, Clarendon, 1936.

46   Caroline Bingham, "Seventeenth-Century Attitudes Toward Deviant Sex", *Journal of Interdisciplinary History*, spring 1971, p. 465.

47   Stephen O. Murray, "The Institutional Elaboration of a Quasi-Ethnic Community", *International Review of Modern Sociology*, July–December 1979.

48   For further elaboration of these processes, see: Bérubé, "Behind the Spectre of San Francisco", op. cit.; Bérubé, "Marching to a Different Drummer", op. cit.; D'Emilio, "Gay Politics, Gay Community", op. cit.; D'Emilio, *Sexual Politics, Sexual Communities*, op. cit.; Foucault, op. cit.; Hansen, op. cit.; Katz, op. cit.; Weeks, *Coming Out*, op. cit.; and Weeks, *Sex, Politics and Society*, op. cit.

49   Walkowitz, *Prostitution and Victorian Society*, op. cit.

50   Vice cops also harass all sex businesses, be these gay bars, gay baths, adult book stores, the producers and distributors of commercial erotica, or swing clubs.

51   Foucault, op. cit., p. 40.

52   Karl Marx, in David McLellan (ed.), *The Grundrisse*, New York, Harper & Row, 1971, p. 94.

53   Clark Norton, "Sex in America", *Inquiry*, October 5, 1981. This article is a superb summary of much current sex law and should be required reading for anyone interested in sex.

54   Bessera et al., *op. cit.*, pp. 165–7.

55   Sarah Senefeld Beserra, Nancy M. Jewel, Melody West Matthews, and Elizabeth R. Gatov (eds.), *Sex Code of California*, Public Education and Research Committee of California, 1973, pp. 163–8. This earlier edition of the *Sex Code of California* preceeded the 1976 consenting adults statute and consequently gives a better overview of sodomy laws.

56   Esther Newton, *Mother Camp: Female Impersonators in America*, Englewood Cliffs, New Jersey, Prentice-Hall, 1973, p. 21, emphasis in the original.

57   D'Emilio, *Sexual Politics, Sexual Communities*, op. cit., pp. 40–53, has an excellent discussion of gay oppression in the 1950s which covers many of the areas I have mentioned. The dynamics he describes, however, are operative in modified forms for other erotic populations, and in other periods. The specific model of gay oppression needs to be generalized to apply, with appropriate modifications, to other sexual groups.

58   Weeks, *Sex, Politics and Society*, op. cit., p. 14.

59   Lysander Spooner, *Vices Are Not Crimes: A Vindication of Moral Liberty*, Cupertino, CA, Tanstaafl Press, 1977.

60   I have adopted this terminology from the very useful discussion in Weeks, *Sex, Politics and Society*, op. cit., pp. 14–15.

61   See Spooner, op. cit., pp. 25–9. Feminist anti-porn discourse fits right into the tradition of justifying attempts at moral control by claiming that such action will protect women and children from violence.

62   "Pope's Talk on Sexual Spontaneity", *San Francisco Chronicle*. November 13, 1980, p. 8; see also footnote 37 above. Julia Penelope argues that "we do not need anything that labels itself purely sexual" and that "fantasy, as an aspect of sexuality, may be a

phallocentric 'need' from which we are not yet free." in "And Now For the Really Hard Questions", *Sinister Wisdom*, no. 15, fall 1980, p. 103.

63 See especially Walkowitz, *Prostitution and Victorian Society*, op. cit., and Weeks, *Sex, Politics and Society*, op. cit.

64 *Moral Majority Report*, July 1983. I am indebted to Allan Bérubé for calling my attention to this image.

65 Cited in Larry Bush, "Capitol Report", *Advocate*, December 8, 1983, p. 60.

66 Cited in H. Montgomery Hyde, *A History of Pornography*, New York, Dell, 1965, p. 31.

67 See for example Laura Lederer (ed.), *Take Back the Night*, New York, William Morrow, 1980; Andrea Dworkin, *Pornography*, New York, Perigee, 1981. The *Newspage* of San Francisco's Women Against Violence in Pornography and Media and the *Newsreport* of New York Women Against Pornography are excellent sources.

68 Kathleen Barry, *Female Sexual Slavery*, Englewood Cliffs, New Jersey, Prentice-Hall, 1979; Janice Raymond, *The Transsexual Empire*, Boston, Beacon, 1979; Kathleen Barry, "Sadomasochism: The New Backlash to Feminism", *Trivia*, no. 1, fall 1982; Robin Ruth Linden, Darlene R. Pagano, Diana E. H. Russell, and Susan Leigh Starr (eds), *Against Sadomasochism*, East Palo Alto, CA, Frog in the Well, 1982; and Florence Rush, *The Best Kept Secret*, New York, McGraw-Hill, 1980.

69 Sally Gearhart, "An Open Letter to the Voters in District 5 and San Francisco's Gay Community", 1979; Adrienne Rich, *On Lies, Secrets, and Silence*, New York, W.W. Norton, 1979, p. 225. ("On the other hand, there is homosexual patriarchal culture, a culture created by homosexual men, reflecting such male stereotypes as dominance and submission as modes of relationship, and the separation of sex from emotional involvement – a culture tainted by profound hatred for women. The male 'gay' culture has offered lesbians the imitation role-stereotypes of 'butch' and 'femme', 'active' and 'passive,' cruising, sado-masochism, and the violent, self-destructive world of 'gay' bars."); Judith Pasternak, "The Strangest Bedfellows: Lesbian Feminism and the Sexual Revolution", *WomanNews*, October 1983; Adrienne Rich, "Compulsory Heterosexuality and Lesbian Existence", in Ann Snitow, Christine Stansell, and Sharon Thompson (eds), *Powers of Desire: The Politics of Sexuality*, New York, Monthly Review Press, 1983.

70 Julia Penlope, op. cit.

71 Sheila Jeffreys, "The Spinster and Her Enemies: Sexuality and the Last Wave of Feminism", *Scarlet Woman*, no. 13; part 2, July 1981, p. 26; a further elaboration of this tendency can be found in Judith Pasternak, op. cit.

72 Pat Califia, "Feminism vs. Sex: A New Conservative Wave", *Advocate*, February 21, 1980; Pat Califia, "Among Us, Against Us – The New Puritans", *Advocate*, April 17, 1980; Califia, "The Great Kiddy Porn Scare of 77 and Its Aftermath", op. cit.; Califia, "A Thorny Issue Splits a Movement", op. cit.; Pat Califia, *Sapphistry*, Tallahassee, Florida, Naiad, 1980; Pat Califia, "What Is Gay Liberation", *Advocate*, June 25, 1981; Pat Califia, "Feminism and Sadomasochism", *Co-Evolution Quarterly*, no. 33, spring 1981; Pat Califia, "Response to Dorchen Leidholdt", *New Women's Times*, October 1982; Pat Califia, "Public Sex", *Advocate*, September 30, 1982; Pat Califia, "Doing It Together: Gay Men, Lesbians, and Sex", *Advocate*, July 7, 1983; Pat Califia, "Gender-Bending", *Advocate*, September 15, 1983; Pat Califia, "The Sex Industry", *Advocate*, October 13, 1983; Deirdre English, Amber Hollibaugh, and Gayle Rubin, "Talking Sex", *Socialist Review*, July–August 1981; "Sex Issue", *Heresies*, no. 12, 1981; Amber Hollibaugh, "The Erotophobic Voice of Women: Building a Movement for the Nineteenth Century", *New York Native*, September 26–October 9, 1983; Maxine Holz, "Porn: Turn On or Put Down, Some Thoughts on Sexuality", *Processed World*, no. 7, spring 1983; Barbara O'Dair, "Sex, Love, and Desire: Feminists Struggle Over the Portrayal of Sex", *Alternative Media*, spring 1983; Lisa Orlando, "Bad Girls and 'Good' Politics", *Village Voice*, Literary Supplement, December 1982; Joanna Russ, "Being Against Pornography", *Thirteenth Moon*, vol. VI, nos 1 and 2, 1982; Samois, *What Color Is Your Handkerchief*, Berkeley, Samois, 1979; Samois, *Coming to Power*, Boston, Alyson, 1982; Deborah Sundahl,

"Stripping For a Living", *Advocate*, October 13, 1983; Nancy Wechsler, "Interview with Pat Califia and Gayle Rubin", part I, *Gay Community News*, Book Review, July 18, 1981, and part II, *Gay Community News*, August 15, 1981; Ellen Willis, *Beginning to See the Light*, New York, Knopf, 1981; for an excellent overview of the history of the ideological shifts in feminism which have affected the sex debates, see Alice Echols, "Cultural Feminism: Feminist Capitalism and the Anti-Pornography Movement", *Social Text*, no. 7, spring and summer 1983.

73   Lisa Orlando, "Lust at Last! Spandex Invades the Academy", *Gay Community News*, May 15, 1982; Ellen Willis, "Who Is a Feminist? An Open Letter to Robin Morgan", *Village Voice*, Literary Supplement, December 1982.

74   Ellen Willis, *Beginning to See the Light*, op. cit., p. 146. I am indebted to Jeanne Bergman for calling my attention to this quote.

75   See, for example, Jessica Benjamin, "Master and Slave: The Fantasy of Erotic Domination", in Snitow et al., op. cit., p. 297; and B. Ruby Rich, review of *Powers of Desire, In These Times*, November 16–22, 1983.

76   B. Ruby Rich, op. cit., p. 76.

77   Samois, *What Color Is Your Handkerchief*, op. cit.; Samois, *Coming To Power*, op. cit.; Pat Califia, "Feminism and Sadomasochism", op. cit.; Pat Califia, *Sapphistry*, op. cit.

78   Lisa Orlando, "Power Plays: Coming To Terms With Lesbian S/M", *Village Voice*, July 26, 1983; Elizabeth Wilson, "*The Context of 'Between Pleasure and Danger': The Barnard Conference on Sexuality*", *Feminist Review*, no. 13, spring 1983, especially pp. 35–41.

79   *Taylor v. State*, 214 Md. 156, 165, 133 A. 2d 414, 418. This quote is from a dissenting opinion, but it is a statement of prevailing law.

80   Bessera, Jewel, Matthews, and Gatov, op. cit., pp. 163–5. See note 55 above.

81   "Marine and Mom Guilty of Incest", *San Francisco Chronicle*, November 16, 1979, p. 16.

82   Norton, op. cit., p. 18.

83   *People* v. *Samuels*, 250 Cal. App. 2d 501, 513, 58 Cal. Rptr. 439, 447 (1967).

84   *People* v. *Samuels*, 250 Cal. App. 2d. at 513–514, 58 Cal. Rptr. at 447.

85   Mariana Valverde, "Feminism Meets Fist-Fucking: Getting Lost in Lesbian S & M", *Body Politic*, February 1980; Wilson, op. cit., p. 38.

86   Benjamin, op. cit. p. 292, but see also pp. 286, 291–7.

87   Barbara Ehrenreich, "What Is This Thing Called Sex", *Nation*, September 24, 1983, p. 247.

88   Gayle Rubin, "The Traffic in Women", in Rayna R. Reiter (ed.), *Toward an Anthropology of Women*, New York, Monthly Review Press, 1975, p. 159.

89   Rubin, "The Traffic in Women", op. cit., p. 166.

90   Foucault, op. cit., p. 106.

91   Catherine MacKinnon, "Feminism, Marxism, Method and the State: An Agenda for Theory", *Signs*, vol. 7, no. 3, spring 1982, pp. 515–16.

92   Catherine MacKinnon, "Feminism, Marxism, Method, and the State: Toward Feminist Jurisprudence", *Signs*, vol. 8, no. 4, summer 1983, p. 635.

93   Colette, *The Ripening Seed*, translated and cited in Hannah Alderfer, Beth Jaker, and Marybeth Nelson, *Diary of a Conference on Sexuality*, New York, Faculty Press, 1982, p. 72.

94   John Lauritsen and David Thorstad, *The Early Homosexual Rights Movement in Germany*, New York, Times Change Press, 1974.

95   D'Emilio, *Sexual Politics, Sexual Communities*, op. cit.; Bérubé "Behind the Spectre of San Francisco", op. cit.; Bérubé, "Marching to a Different Drummer", op. cit.

Suggestions for further reading

Foucault, Michel, *The History of Sexuality: Volume 1: An Introduction*, trans. Robert Hurley, Harmondsworth: Penguin, 1990.

Freud, Sigmund, *On Sexuality: Three Essays on the Theory of Sexuality and Other Works*, ed. Angela Richards, trans. James Strachey, Harmondsworth: Pelican, 1977.

Weeks, Jeffrey, *Sexuality and its Discontents: Meaning, Myths and Modern Sexualities*, London: Routledge and Kegan Paul, 1985.

Chapter 23

Donna J. Haraway

'A MANIFESTO FOR CYBORGS: SCIENCE, TECHNOLOGY, AND SOCIALIST FEMINISM IN THE 1980s', 1985

An ironic dream of a common language for women in the integrated circuit

THIS ESSAY IS AN effort to build an ironic political myth faithful to feminism, socialism, and materialism. Perhaps more faithful as blasphemy is faithful, than as reverent worship and identification. Blasphemy has always seemed to require taking things very seriously. I know no better stance to adopt from within the secular-religious, evangelical traditions of United States politics, including the politics of socialist-feminism. Blasphemy protects one from the moral majority within, while still insisting on the need for community. Blasphemy is not apostasy. Irony is about contradictions that do not resolve into larger wholes, even dialectically, about the tension of holding incompatible things together because both or all are necessary and true. Irony is about humor and serious play. It is also a rhetorical strategy and a political method, one I would like to see more honored within socialist feminism. At the center of my ironic faith, my blasphemy, is the image of the cyborg.

A cyborg is a cybernetic organism, a hybrid of machine and organism, a creature of social reality as well as a creature of fiction. Social reality is lived social relations, our most important political construction, a world-changing fiction. The international women's movements have constructed "women's experience," as well as uncovered or discovered this crucial collective object. This experience is a fiction and fact of the most crucial, political kind. Liberation rests on the construction of the consciousness, the imaginative apprehension, of oppression, and so of possibility. The cyborg is a matter of fiction and lived experience that changes what counts as women's experience in the late twentieth century. This is a struggle over life and death, but the boundary between science fiction and social reality is an optical illusion.

Contemporary science fiction is full of cyborgs—creatures simultaneously animal and machine, who populate worlds ambiguously natural and crafted. Modern medicine is also full of cyborgs, of couplings between organism and machine, each conceived as coded devices, in an intimacy and with a power that was not generated in the history of sexuality. Cyborg "sex" restores some of the lovely replicative baroque of ferns and invertebrates (such nice organic prophylactics against hetero-sexism). Cyborg replication is uncoupled from organic reproduction. Modern production seems like a dream of cyborg colonization of work, a dream that makes the nightmare of Taylorism seem idyllic. And modern war is a cyborg orgy, coded by c^3i, command-control-communication-intelligence, an $84 billion item in 1984's u.s. defense budget. I am making an argument for the cyborg as a fiction mapping our social and bodily reality and as an imaginative resource suggesting some very fruitful couplings. Foucault's biopolitics is a flaccid premonition of cyborg politics, a very open field.

BY THE LATE twentieth century, our time, a mythic time, we are all chimeras, theorized and fabricated hybrids of machine and organism; in short, we are cyborgs. The cyborg is our ontology; it gives us our politics. The cyborg is a condensed image of both imagination and material reality, the two joined centers structuring any possibility of historical transformation. In the traditions of "Western" science and politics—the tradition of racist, male-dominant capitalism; the tradition of progress; the tradition of the appropriation of nature as resource for the produc-tions of culture; the tradition of reproduction of the self from the reflections of the other—the relation between organism and machine has been a border war. The stakes in the border war have been the territories of production, reproduc-tion, and imagination. This essay is an argument for *pleasure* in the confusion of boundaries and for *responsibility* in their construction. It is also an effort to contrib-ute to socialist-feminist culture and theory in a post-modernist, non-naturalist mode and in the utopian tradition of imagining a world without gender, which is perhaps a world without genesis, but maybe also a world without end. The cyborg incarnation is outside salvation history.

The cyborg is a creature in a post-gender world; it has no truck with bisexuality, pre-Oedipal symbiosis, unalienated labor, or other seductions to organic whole-ness through a final appropriation of all the powers of the parts into a higher unity. In a sense, the cyborg has no origin story in the Western sense; a "final" irony since the cyborg is also the awful apocalyptic *telos* of the "West's" escalating dominations of abstract individuation, an ultimate self untied at last from all dependency, a man in space. An origin story in the "Western," humanist sense depends on the myth of original unity, fullness, bliss and terror, represented by the phallic mother from whom all humans must separate, the task of individual development and of history, the twin potent myths inscribed most powerfully for us in psychoanalysis and Marxism. Hilary Klein has argued that both Marxism and psychoanalysis, in their concepts of labor and of individuation and gender formation, depend on the plot of original unity out of which difference must be produced and enlisted in a drama of escalating domination of woman/nature. The cyborg skips the step of original unity, of identification with nature in the Western sense. This is its illegitimate promise that might lead to subversion of its teleology as star wars.

The cyborg is resolutely committed to partiality, irony, intimacy, and perversity. It is oppositional, utopian, and completely without innocence. No longer structured by the polarity of public and private, the cyborg defines a technological polis based partly on a revolution of social relations in the *oikos*, the household. Nature and culture are reworked; the one can no longer be the resource for appropriation or incorporation by the other. The relationships for forming wholes from parts, including those of polarity and hierarchical domination, are at issue in the cyborg world. Unlike the hopes of Frankenstein's monster, the cyborg does not expect its father to save it through a restoration of the garden; i.e., through the fabrication of a heterosexual mate, through its completion in a finished whole, a city and cosmos. The cyborg does not dream of community on the model of the organic family, this time without the Oedipal project. The cyborg would not recognize the Garden of Eden; it is not made of mud and cannot dream of returning to dust. Perhaps that is why I want to see if cyborgs can subvert the apocalypse of returning to nuclear dust in the manic compulsion to name the Enemy. Cyborgs are not reverent; they do not re-member the cosmos. They are wary of holism, but needy for connection—they seem to have a natural feel for united front politics, but without the vanguard party. The main trouble with cyborgs, of course, is that they are the illegitimate offspring of militarism and patriarchal capitalism, not to mention state socialism. But illegitimate offspring are often exceedingly unfaithful to their origins. Their fathers, after all, are inessential.

I WILL RETURN to the science fiction of cyborgs at the end of this essay, but now I want to signal three crucial boundary breakdowns that make the following political fictional (political scientific) analysis possible. By the late twentieth century in United States scientific culture, the boundary between human and animal is thoroughly breached. The last beachheads of uniqueness have been polluted if not turned into amusement parks—language, tool use, social behavior, mental events, nothing really convincingly settles the separation of human and animal. And many people no longer feel the need of such a separation; indeed, many branches of feminist culture affirm the pleasure of connection of human and other living creatures. Movements for animal rights are not irrational denials of human uniqueness; they are clear-sighted recognition of connection across the discredited breach of nature and culture. Biology and evolutionary theory over the last two centuries have simultaneously produced modern organisms as objects of knowledge and reduced the line between humans and animals to a faint trace re-etched in ideological struggle or professional disputes between life and social sciences. Within this framework, teaching modern Christian creationism should be fought as a form of child abuse.

Biological-determinist ideology is only one position opened up in scientific culture for arguing the meanings of human animality. There is much room for radical political people to contest for the meanings of the breached boundary.[1] The cyborg appears in myth precisely where the boundary between human and animal is transgressed. Far from signaling a walling off of people from other living beings, cyborgs signal disturbingly and pleasurably tight coupling. Bestiality has a new status in this cycle of marriage exchange.

The second leaky distinction is between animal-human (organism) and machine. Pre-cybernetic machines could be haunted; there was always the specter of the ghost in the machine. This dualism structured the dialogue between material-ism and idealism that was settled by a dialectical progeny, called spirit or history, according to taste. But basically machines were not self-moving, self-designing, autonomous. They could not achieve man's dream, only mock it. They were not man, an author to himself, but only a caricature of that masculinist reproductive dream. To think they were otherwise was paranoid. Now we are not so sure. Late-twentieth-century machines have made thoroughly ambiguous the difference between natural and artificial, mind and body, self-developing and externally-designed, and many other distinctions that used to apply to organisms and machines. Our machines are disturbingly lively, and we ourselves frighteningly inert.

Technological determinism is only one ideological space opened up by the reconceptions of machine and organism as coded texts through which we engage in the play of writing and reading the world.[2] "Textualization" of everything in post-structuralist, post-modernist theory has been damned by Marxists and social-ist feminists for its utopian disregard for lived relations of domination that ground the "play" of arbitrary reading.[3] It is certainly true that post-modernist strategies, like my cyborg myth, subvert myriad organic wholes (e.g., the poem, the primitive culture, the biological organism). In short, the certainty of what counts as nature—a source of insight and a promise of innocence—is undermined, probably fatally. The transcendent authorization of interpretation is lost, and with it the ontology grounding "Western" epistemology. But the alternative is not cynicism or faithlessness, i.e., some version of abstract existence, like the accounts of technological determinism destroying "man" by the "machine" or "meaningful political action" by the "text." Who cyborgs will be is a radical question; the answers are a matter of survival. Both chimpanzees and artifacts have politics, so why shouldn't we?[4]

The third distinction is a subset of the second: the boundary between physical and non-physical is very imprecise for us. Pop physics books on the consequences of quantum theory and the indeterminacy principle are a kind of popular scientific equivalent to the Harlequin romances as a marker of radical change in American white heterosexuality: they get it wrong, but they are on the right subject. Modern machines are quintessentially microelectronic devices: they are everywhere and they are invisible. Modern machinery is an irreverent upstart god, mocking the Father's ubiquity and spirituality. The silicon chip is a surface for writing; it is etched in molecular scales disturbed only by atomic noise, the ultimate interfer-ence for nuclear scores. Writing, power, and technology are old partners in Western stories of the origin of civilization, but miniaturization has changed our experience of mechanism. Miniaturization has turned out to be about power; small is not so much beautiful as pre-eminently dangerous, as in cruise missiles. Contrast the TV sets of the 1950s or the news cameras of the 1970s with the TV wrist bands or hand-sized video cameras now advertised. Our best machines are made of sunshine; they are all light and clean because they are nothing but signals, electro-magnetic waves, a section of a spectrum. And these machines are eminently portable, mobile—a matter of immense human pain in Detroit and Singapore. People are nowhere near so fluid, being both material and opaque. Cyborgs are either, quintessence.

The ubiquity and invisibility of cyborgs is precisely why these sunshine-belt machines are so deadly. They are as hard to see politically as materially. They are about consciousness—or its simulation.[5] They are floating signifiers moving in pickup trucks across Europe, blocked more effectively by the witch-weavings of the displaced and so unnatural Greenham women, who read the cyborg webs of power very well, than by the militant labor of older masculinist politics, whose natural constituency needs defense jobs. Ultimately the "hardest" science is about the realm of greatest boundary confusion, the realm of pure number, pure spirit, c^3I, cryptography, and the preservation of potent secrets. The new machines are so clean and light. Their engineers are sun-worshipers mediating a new scientific revolution associated with the night dream of post-industrial society. The diseases evoked by these clean machines are "no more" than the miniscule coding changes of an antigen in the immune system, "no more" than the experience of stress. The nimble little fingers of "Oriental" women, the old fascination of little Anglo-Saxon Victorian girls with doll houses, women's enforced attention to the small take on quite new dimensions in this world. There might be a cyborg Alice taking account of these new dimensions. Ironically, it might be the unnatural cyborg women making chips in Asia and spiral dancing in Santa Rita whose constructed unities will guide effective oppositional strategies.

So my cyborg myth is about transgressed boundaries, potent fusions, and dangerous possibilities which progressive people might explore as one part of needed political work. One of my premises is that most American socialists and feminists see deepened dualisms of mind and body, animal and machine, idealism and materialism in the social practices, symbolic formulations, and physical arti-facts associated with "high technology" and scientific culture. From *One-Dimensional Man* to *The Death of Nature*,[6] the analytic resources developed by progressives have insisted on the necessary domination of technics and recalled us to an imagined organic body to integrate our resistance. Another of my premises is that the need for unity of people trying to resist worldwide intensification of domination has never been more acute. But a slightly perverse shift of perspective might better enable us to contest for meanings, as well as for other forms of power and pleasure in technologically-mediated societies.

FROM ONE PERSPECTIVE, a cyborg world is about the final imposition of a grid of control on the planet, about the final abstraction embodied in a Star War apoca-lypse waged in the name of defense, about the final appropriation of women's bodies in a masculinist orgy of war.[7] From another perspective, a cyborg world might be about lived social and bodily realities in which people are not afraid of their joint kinship with animals and machines, not afraid of permanently partial identities and contradictory standpoints. The political struggle is to see from both perspectives at once because each reveals both dominations and possibilities unimaginable from the other vantage point. Single vision produces worse illusions than double vision or many-headed monsters. Cyborg unities are monstrous and illegitimate; in our present political circumstances, we could hardly hope for more potent myths for resistance and recoupling. I like to imagine LAG, the Livermore Action Group, as a kind of cyborg society, dedicated to realistically converting the laboratories that most fiercely embody and spew out the tools of technological apocalypse, and committed to building a political form that actually manages to hold together witches, engineers, elders, perverts, Christians, mothers, and Leninists long enough to disarm the state. Fission Impossible is the name of the affinity group in my town. (Affinity: related not by blood but by choice, the appeal of one chemical nuclear group for another, avidity.)

Fractured identities

IT HAS BECOME DIFFICULT to name one's feminism by a single adjective—or even to insist in every circumstance upon the noun. Consciousness of exclusion through naming is acute. Identities seem contradictory, partial, and strategic. With the hard-won recognition of their social and historical constitution, gender, race, and class cannot provide the basis for belief in "essential" unity. There is nothing about being "female" that naturally binds women. There is not even such a state as "being" female, itself a highly complex category constructed in contested sexual scientific discourses and other social practices. Gender, race, or class consciousness is an achievement forced on us by the terrible historical experience of the contradictory social realities of patriarchy, colonialism, and capitalism. And who counts as "us" in my own rhetoric? Which identities are available to ground such a potent political myth called "us," and what could motivate enlistment in this collectivity? Painful fragmentation among feminists (not to mention among women) along every possible fault line has made the concept of *woman* elusive, an excuse for the matrix of women's dominations of each other. For me—and for many who share a similar historical location in white, professional middle class, female, radical, North American, mid-adult bodies—the sources of a crisis in political identity are legion. The recent history for much of the u.s. left and u.s. feminism has been a response to this kind of crisis by endless splitting and searches for a new essential unity. But there has also been a growing recognition of another response through coalition—affinity, not identity.[8]

Chela Sandoval, from a consideration of specific historical moments in the formation of the new political voice called women of color, has theorized a hopeful model of political identity called "oppositional consciousness," born of the skills for reading webs of power by those refused stable membership in the social categories of race, sex, or class.[9] "Women of color," a name contested at its origins by those whom it would incorporate, as well as a historical consciousness marking systematic breakdown of all the signs of Man in "Western" traditions, constructs a kind of post-modernist identity out of otherness and difference. This post-modernist identity is fully political, whatever might be said about other possible post-modernisms.

Sandoval emphasizes the lack of any essential criterion for identifying who is a woman of color. She notes that the definition of the group has been by conscious appropriation of negation. For example, a Chicana or u.s. black woman has not been able to speak as a woman or as a black person or as a Chicano. Thus, she was at the bottom of a cascade of negative identities, left out of even the privileged oppressed authorial categories called "women and blacks," who claimed to make the important revolutions. The category "woman" negated all non-white women;

"black" negated all non-black people, as well as all black women. But there was also no "she," no singularity, but a sea of differences among u.s. women who have affirmed their historical identity as u.s. women of color. This identity marks out a self-consciously constructed space that cannot affirm the capacity to act on the basis of natural identification, but only on the basis of conscious coalition, of affinity, of political kinship.[10] Unlike the "woman" of some streams of the white women's movement in the United States, there is no naturalization of the matrix, or at least this is what Sandoval argues is uniquely available through the power of oppositional consciousness.

Sandoval's argument has to be seen as one potent formulation for feminists out of the worldwide development of anti-colonialist discourse, i.e., discourse dissolving the "West" and its highest product—the one who is not animal, barbarian, or woman; i.e., man, the author of a cosmos called history. As orientalism is deconstructed politically and semiotically, the identities of the occident destabilize, including those of feminists.[11] Sandoval argues that "women of color" have a chance to build an effective unity that does not replicate the imperializing, totalizing revolutionary subjects of previous Marxisms and feminisms which had not faced the consequences of the disorderly polyphony emerging from decolonization.

Katie King has emphasized the limits of identification and the political/poetic mechanics of identification built into reading "the poem," that generative core of cultural feminism. King criticizes the persistent tendency among contemporary feminists from different "moments" or "conversations" in feminist practice to taxonomize the women's movement to make one's own political tendencies appear to be the *telos* of the whole. These taxonomies tend to remake feminist history to appear to be an ideological struggle among coherent types persisting over time, especially those typical units called radical, liberal, and socialist feminism. Literally, all other feminisms are either incorporated or marginalized, usually by building an explicit ontology and epistemology.[12] Taxonomies of feminism produce epistemologies to police deviation from official women's experience. And of course, "women's culture," like women of color, is consciously created by mechanisms inducing affinity. The rituals of poetry, music, and certain forms of academic practice have been pre-eminent. The politics of race and culture in the u.s. women's movements are intimately interwoven. The common achievement of King and Sandoval is learning how to craft a poetic/political unity without relying on a logic of appropriation, incorporation, and taxonomic identification.

THE THEORETICAL AND PRACTICAL struggle against unity-through-domination or unity-through-incorporation ironically not only undermines the justifications for patriarchy, colonialism, humanism, positivism, essentialism, scientism, and other unlamented -isms, but *all* claims for an organic or natural standpoint. I think that radical and socialist/Marxist feminisms have also undermined their/our own epistemological strategies and that this is a crucially valuable step in imagining possible unities. It remains to be seen whether all "epistemologies" as Western political people have known them fail us in the task to build effective affinities.

It is important to note that the effort to construct revolutionary standpoints, epistemologies as achievements of people committed to changing the world, has been part of the process showing the limits of identification. The acid tools of post-modernist theory and the constructive tools of ontological discourse about revolutionary subjects might be seen as ironic allies in dissolving Western selves in the interests of survival. We are excruciatingly conscious of what it means to have a historically constituted body. But with the loss of innocence in our origin, there is no explusion from the Garden either. Our politics lose the indulgence of guilt with the naïveté of innocence. But what would another political myth for socialist feminism look like? What kind of politics could embrace partial, contradictory, permanently unclosed constructions of personal and collective selves and still be faithful, effective—and, ironically, socialist feminist?

I do not know of any other time in history when there was greater need for political unity to confront effectively the dominations of "race," "gender," "sexuality," and "class." I also do not know of any other time when the kind of unity we might help build could have been possible. None of "us" have any longer the symbolic or material capability of dictating the shape of reality to any of "them." Or at least "we" cannot claim innocence from practicing such dominations. White women, including socialist feminists, discovered (i.e., were forced kicking and screaming to notice) the non-innocence of the category "woman." That consciousness changes the geography of all previous categories; it denatures them as heat denatures a fragile protein. Cyborg feminists have to argue that "we" do not want any more natural matrix of unity and that no construction is whole. Innocence, and the corollary insistence on victimhood as the only ground for insight, has done enough damage. But the constructed revolutionary subject must give late-twentieth-century people pause as well. In the fraying of identities and in the reflexive strategies for constructing them, the possibility opens up for weaving something other than a shroud for the day after the apocalypse that so prophetically ends salvation history.

Both Marxist/socialist feminisms and radical feminisms have simultaneously naturalized and denatured the category "woman" and consciousness of the social lives of "women." Perhaps a schematic caricature can highlight both kinds of moves. Marxian socialism is rooted in an analysis of wage labor which reveals class structure. The consequence of the wage relationship is systematic alienation, as the worker is dissociated from his (sic) product. Abstraction and illusion rule in knowledge, domination rules in practice. Labor is the pre-eminently privileged category enabling the Marxist to overcome illusion and find that point of view which is necessary for changing the world. Labor is the humanizing activity that makes man; labor is an ontological category permitting the knowledge of a subject, and so the knowledge of subjugation and alienation.

In faithful filiation, socialist feminism advanced by allying itself with the basic analytic strategies of Marxism. The main achievement of both Marxist feminists and socialist feminists was to expand the category of labor to accommodate what (some) women did, even when the wage relation was subordinated to a more comprehensive view of labor under capitalist patriarchy. In particular, women's labor in the household and women's activity as mothers generally, i.e., reproduction in the socialist feminist sense, entered theory on the authority of analogy to the Marxian concept of labor. The unity of women here rests on an epistemology based on the ontological structure of "labor." Marxist/socialist feminism does not "naturalize" unity; it is a possible achievement based on a possible standpoint rooted in social relations. The essentializing move is in the ontological structure of labor or of its analogue, women's activity.[13] The inheritance of Marxian human-ism, with its pre-eminently Western self, is the difficulty for me. The contribution from these formulations has been the emphasis on the daily responsibility of real women to build unities, rather than to naturalize them.

CATHERINE MACKINNON's version of radical feminism is itself a caricature of the appropriating, incorporating, totalizing tendencies of Western theories of identity grounding action.[14] It is factually and politically wrong to assimilate all of the diverse "moments" or "conversations" in recent women's politics named radical feminism to MacKinnon's version. But the teleological logic of her theory shows how an epistemology and ontology—including their negations—erase or police difference. Only one of the effects of MacKinnon's theory is the rewriting of the history of the polymorphous field called radical feminism. The major effect is the production of a theory of experience, of women's identity, that is a kind of apocalypse for all revolutionary standpoints. That is, the totalization built into this tale of radical feminism achieves its end—the unity of women—by enforcing the experience of and testimony to radical non-being. As for the Marxist/socialist feminist, consciousness is an achievement, not a natural fact. And MacKinnon's theory eliminates some of the difficulties built into humanist revolutionary subjects, but at the cost of radical reductionism.

MacKinnon argues that radical feminism necessarily adopted a different ana-lytical strategy from Marxism, looking first not at the structure of class, but at the structure of sex/gender and its generative relationship, men's constitution and appropriation of women sexually. Ironically, MacKinnon's "ontology" constructs a non-subject, a non-being. Another's desire, not the self's labor, is the origin of "woman." She therefore develops a theory of consciousness that enforces what can count as "women's" experience—anything that names sexual violation, indeed, sex itself as far as "women" can be concerned. Feminist practice is the construction of this form of consciousness; i.e., the self-knowledge of a self-who-is-not.

Perversely, sexual appropriation in this radical feminism still has the epistemo-logical status of labor, i.e., the point from which analysis able to contribute to changing the world must flow. But sexual objectification, not alienation, is the consequence of the structure of sex/gender. In the realm of knowledge, the result of sexual objectification is illusion and abstraction. However, a woman is not simply alienated from her product, but in a deep sense does not exist as a subject, or even potential subject, since she owes her existence as a woman to sexual appropriation. To be constituted by another's desire is not the same thing as to be alienated in the violent separation of the laborer from his product.

MacKinnon's radical theory of experience is totalizing in the extreme; it does not so much marginalize as obliterate the authority of any other women's political speech and action. It is a totalization producing what Western patriarchy itself never succeeded in doing—feminists' consciousness of the non-existence of women, except as products of men's desire. I think MacKinnon correctly argues that no Marxian version of identity can firmly ground women's unity. But in solving the problem of the contradictions of any Western revolutionary subject for feminist purposes, she develops an even more authoritarian doctrine of experience. If my complaint about socialist/Marxian standpoints is their unintended erasure of polyvocal, unassimilable, radical difference made visible in anti-colonial discourse and practice, MacKinnon's intentional erasure of all difference through the device of the "essential" non-existence of women is not reassuring.

In my taxonomy, which like any other taxonomy is a reinscription of history, radical feminism can accommodate all the activities of women named by socialist feminists as forms of labor only if the activity can somehow be sexualized. Reproduction had different tones of meanings for the two tendencies, one rooted in labor, one in sex, both calling the consequences of domination and ignorance of social and personal reality "false consciousness."

Beyond either the difficulties or the contributions in the argument of any one author, neither Marxist nor radical feminist points of view have tended to embrace the status of a partial explanation; both were regularly constituted as totalities. Western explanation has demanded as much; how else could the "Western" author incorporate its others? Each tried to annex other forms of domination by expanding its basic categories through analogy, simple listing, or addition. Embarrassed silence about race among white radical and socialist feminists was one major, devastating political consequence. History and polyvocality disappear into political taxonomies that try to establish genealogies. There was no structural room for race (or for much else) in theory claiming to reveal the construction of the category woman and social group women as a unified or totalizable whole. The structure of my caricature looks like this:

Socialist Feminism—
structure of class//wage labor//alienation
labor, by analogy reproduction, by extension sex, by addition race
Radical Feminism—
structure of gender//sexual appropriation//objectification
sex, by analogy labor, by extension reproduction, by addition race

In another context, the French theorist Julia Kristeva claimed women appeared as a historical group after World War II, along with groups like youth. Her dates are doubtful; but we are now accustomed to remembering that as objects of knowledge and as historical actors, "race" did not always exist, "class" has a historical genesis, and "homosexuals" are quite junior. It is no accident that the symbolic system of the family of man—and so the essence of woman—breaks up at the same moment that networks of connection among people on the planet are unprecedentedly multiple, pregnant, and complex. "Advanced capitalism" is inadequate to convey the structure of this historical moment. In the "Western" sense, the end of man is at stake. It is no accident that woman disintegrates into women in our time. Perhaps socialist feminists were not substantially guilty of producing essentialist theory that suppressed women's particularity and contradictory interests. I think we have been, at least through unreflective participation in the logics, languages, and practices of white humanism and through searching for a single ground of domination to secure our revolutionary voice. Now we have less excuse. But in the consciousness of our failures, we risk lapsing into boundless difference and giving up on the confusing task of making partial, real connection.

Some differences are playful; some are poles of world historical systems of domination. "Epistemology" is about knowing the difference.

The informatics of domination

IN THIS ATTEMPT at an epistemological and political position, I would like to sketch
a picture of possible unity, a picture indebted to socialist and feminist principles
of design. The frame for my sketch is set by the extent and importance of
rearrangements in worldwide social relations tied to science and technology.
I argue for a politics rooted in claims about fundamental changes in the nature of
class, race, and gender in an emerging system of world order analogous in its
novelty and scope to that created by industrial capitalism; we are living through a
movement from an organic, industrial society to a polymorphous, information
system—from all work to all play, a deadly game. Simultaneously material and
ideological, the dichotomies may be expressed in the following chart of transitions
from the comfortable old hierarchical dominations to the scary new networks
I have called the informatics of domination:

Representation	Simulation
Bourgeois novel, realism	Science fiction, post-modernism
Organism	Biotic component
Depth, integrity	Surface, boundary
Heat	Noise
Biology as clinical practice	Biology as inscription
Physiology	Communications engineering
Small group	Subsystem
Perfection	Optimization
Eugenics	Population control
Decadence, *Magic Mountain*	Obsolescence, *Future Shock*
Hygiene	Stress Management
Microbiology, tuberculosis	Immunology, AIDS
Organic division of labor	Ergonomics/cybernetics of labor
Functional specialization	Modular construction
Reproduction	Replication
Organic sex role specialization	Optimal genetic strategies
Biological determinism	Evolutionary inertia, constraints
Community ecology	Ecosystem
Racial chain of being	Neo-imperialism, United Nations humanism
Scientific management in home/factory	Global factory/Electronic cottage
Family/Market/Factory	Women in the Integrated Circuit
Family wage	Comparable worth
Public/Private	Cyborg citizenship
Nature/Culture	Fields of difference
Cooperation	Communications enhancement

Freud	Lacan
Sex	Genetic engineering
Labor	Robotics
Mind	Artificial Intelligence
World War II	Star Wars
White Capitalist Patriarchy	Informatics of Domination

This list suggests several interesting things.[15] First, the objects on the right-hand side cannot be coded as "natural," a realization that subverts naturalistic coding for the left-hand side as well. We cannot go back ideologically or materially. It's not just that "god" is dead; so is the "goddess." In relation to objects like biotic components, one must think not in terms of essential properties, but in terms of strategies of design, boundary constraints, rates of flows, systems logics, costs of lowering constraints. Sexual reproduction is one kind of reproductive strategy among many, with costs and benefits as a function of the system environment. Ideologies of sexual reproduction can no longer reasonably call on the notions of sex and sex role as organic aspects in natural objects like organisms and families. Such reasoning will be unmasked as irrational, and ironically corporate executives reading *Playboy* and anti-porn radical feminists will make strange bedfellows in jointly unmasking the irrationalism.

Likewise for race, ideologies about human diversity have to be formulated in terms of frequencies of parameters, like blood groups or intelligence scores. It is "irrational" to invoke concepts like primitive and civilized. For liberals and radicals, the search for integrated social systems gives way to a new practice called "experimental ethnography" in which an organic object dissipates in attention to the play of writing. At the level of ideology, we see translations of racism and colonialism into languages of development and underdevelopment, rates and constraints of modernization. Any objects or persons can be reasonably thought of in terms of disassembly and reassembly; no "natural" architectures constrain system design. The financial districts in all the world's cities, as well as the export-processing and free-trade zones, proclaim this elementary fact of "late capitalism." The entire universe of objects that can be known scientifically must be formulated as problems in communications engineering (for the managers) or theories of the text (for those who would resist). Both are cyborg semiologies.

One should expect control strategies to concentrate on boundary conditions and interfaces, on rates of flow across boundaries — and not on the integrity of natural objects. "Integrity" or "sincerity" of the Western self gives way to decision procedures and expert systems. For example, control strategies applied to women's capacities to give birth to new human beings will be developed in the languages of population control and maximization of goal achievement for individual decision-makers. Control strategies will be formulated in terms of rates, costs of constraints, degrees of freedom. Human beings, like any other component or subsystem, must be localized in a system architecture whose basic modes of operation are probabilistic, statistical. No objects, spaces, or bodies are sacred in themselves; any component can be interfaced with any other if the proper standard, the proper code, can be constructed for processing signals in a common language. Exchange in this world transcends the universal translation effected by capitalist markets that Marx analyzed so well. The privileged pathology affecting all kinds of components in this universe is stress—communications breakdown.[16] The cyborg is not subject to Foucault's biopolitics; the cyborg simulates politics, a much more potent field of operations.

THIS KIND OF ANALYSIS of scientific and cultural objects of knowledge which have appeared historically since World War II prepares us to notice some important inadequacies in feminist analysis which has proceeded as if the organic, hierarchical dualisms ordering discourse in "the West" since Aristotle still ruled. They have been cannibalized, or as Zoe Sofia (Sofoulis) might put it, they have been "techno-digested." The dichotomies between mind and body, animal and human, organism and machine, public and private, nature and culture, men and women, primitive and civilized are all in question ideologically. The actual situation of women is their integration/exploitation into a world system of production/reproduction and communication called the informatics of domination. The home, workplace, market, public arena, the body itself—all can be dispersed and interfaced in nearly infinite, polymorphous ways, with large consequences for women and others— consequences that themselves are very different for different people and which make potent oppositional international movements difficult to imagine and essential for survival. One important route for reconstructing socialist-feminist politics is through theory and practice addressed to the social relations of science and technology, including crucially the systems of myth and meanings structuring our imaginations. The cyborg is a kind of disassembled and reassembled, post-modern collective and personal self. This is the self feminists must code.

Communications technologies and biotechnologies are the crucial tools recrafting our bodies. These tools embody and enforce new social relations for women worldwide. Technologies and scientific discourses can be partially understood as formalizations, i.e., as frozen moments, of the fluid social interactions constituting them, but they should also be viewed as instruments for enforcing meanings. The boundary is permeable between tool and myth, instrument and concept, historical systems of social relations and historical anatomies of possible bodies, including objects of knowledge. Indeed, myth and tool mutually constitute each other.

Furthermore, communications sciences and modern biologies are constructed by a common move — *the translation of the world into a problem of coding*, a search for a common language in which all resistance to instrumental control disappears and all heterogeneity can be submitted to disassembly, reassembly, investment, and exchange.

In communications sciences, the translation of the world into a problem in coding can be illustrated by looking at cybernetic (feedback controlled) systems theories applied to telephone technology, computer design, weapons deployment, or data base construction and maintenance. In each case, solution to the key questions rests on a theory of language and control; the key operation is determining the rates, directions, and probabilities of flow of a quantity called information. The world is subdivided by boundaries differentially permeable to information. Information is just that kind of quantifiable element (unit, basis of unity) which allows universal translation, and so unhindered instrumental power (called effective communication). The biggest threat to such power is interruption of communication. Any system breakdown is a function of stress. The fundamentals of this technology can be condensed into the metaphor C^3I, command-control-communication-intelligence, the military's symbol for its operations theory.

In modern biologies, the translation of the world into a problem in coding can be illustrated by molecular genetics, ecology, sociobiological evolutionary theory, and immunobiology. The organism has been translated into problems of genetic coding and read-out. Biotechnology, a writing technology, informs research broadly.[17] In a sense, organisms have ceased to exist as objects of knowledge, giving way to biotic components, i.e., special kinds of information processing devices. The analogous moves in ecology could be examined by probing the history and utility of the concept of the ecosystem. Immunobiology and associated medical practices are rich exemplars of the privilege of coding and recognition systems as objects of knowledge, as constructions of bodily reality for us. Biology is here a kind of cryptography. Research is necessarily a kind of intelligence activity. Ironies abound. A stressed system goes awry; its communication processes break down; it fails to recognize the difference between self and other. Human babies with baboon hearts evoke national ethical perplexity — for animal-rights activists at least as much as for guardians of human purity. Gay men, Haitian immigrants, and intravenous drug users are the "privileged" victims of an awful immune-system disease that marks (inscribes on the body) confusion of boundaries and moral pollution.

But these excursions into communications sciences and biology have been at a rarefied level; there is a mundane, largely economic reality to support my claim that these sciences and technologies indicate fundamental transformations in the structure of the world for us. Communications technologies depend on electronics. Modern states, multinational corporations, military power, welfare-state apparatuses, satellite systems, political processes, fabrication of our imaginations, labor-control systems, medical constructions of our bodies, commercial pornography, the international division of labor, and religious evangelism depend intimately upon electronics. Microelectronics is the technical basis of simulacra, i.e., of copies without originals.

Microelectronics mediates the translations of *labor* into robotics and word processing; *sex* into genetic engineering and reproductive technologies; and *mind* into artificial intelligence and decision procedures. The new biotechnologies concern more than human reproduction. Biology as a powerful engineering science for redesigning materials and processes has revolutionary implications for industry, perhaps most obvious today in areas of fermentation, agriculture, and energy. Communications sciences and biology are constructions of natural-technical objects of knowledge in which the difference between machine and organism is thoroughly blurred; mind, body, and tool are on very intimate terms. The "multinational" material organization of the production and reproduction of daily life and the symbolic organization of the production and reproduction of culture and imagination seem equally implicated. The boundary-maintaining images of base and superstructure, public and private, or material and ideal never seemed more feeble.

I have used Rachel Grossman's image of women in the integrated circuit to name the situation of women in a world so intimately restructured through the social relations of science and technology.[18] I use the odd circumlocution, "the social relations of science and technology," to indicate that we are not dealing with a technological determinism, but with a historical system depending upon structured relations among people. But the phrase should also indicate that science and technology provide fresh sources of power, that we need fresh sources of analysis and political action.[19] Some of the rearrangements of race, sex, and class rooted in high-tech-facilitated social relations can make socialist feminism more relevant to effective progressive politics.

The homework economy

THE "NEW INDUSTRIAL REVOLUTION" is producing a new worldwide working class. The extreme mobility of capital and the emerging international division of labor are intertwined with the emergence of new collectivities, and the weakening of familiar groupings. These developments are neither gender- nor race-neutral. White men in advanced industrial societies have become newly vulnerable to permanent job loss, and women are not disappearing from the job rolls at the same rates as men. It is not simply that women in third-world countries are the preferred labor force for the science-based multinationals in the export-processing sectors, particularly in electronics. The picture is more systematic and involves reproduction, sexuality, culture, consumption, and production. In the prototypical Silicon Valley, many women's lives have been structured around employment in electronics-dependent jobs, and their intimate realities include serial heterosexual monogamy, negotiating childcare, distance from extended kin or most other forms of traditional community, a high likelihood of loneliness and extreme economic vulnerability as they age. The ethnic and racial diversity of women in Silicon Valley structures a microcosm of conflicting differences in culture, family, religion, education, language.

Richard Gordon has called this new situation the homework economy.[20] Although he includes the phenomenon of literal homework emerging in connection with electronics assembly, Gordon intends "homework economy" to name a restructuring of work that broadly has the characteristics formerly ascribed to female jobs, jobs literally done only by women. Work is being redefined as both literally female and feminized, whether performed by men or women. To be feminized means to be made extremely vulnerable; able to be disassembled, reassembled, exploited as a reserve labor force; seen less as workers than as servers; subjected to time arrangements on and off the paid job that make a mockery of a limited work day; leading an existence that always borders on being obscene, out of place, and reducible to sex. Deskilling is an old strategy newly applicable to formerly privileged workers. However, the homework economy does not refer only to large-scale deskilling, nor does it deny that new areas of high skill are emerging, even for women and men previously excluded from skilled employment. Rather, the concept indicates that factory, home, and market are integrated on a new scale and that the places of women are crucial—and need to be analyzed for differences among women and for meanings for relations between men and women in various situations.

The homework economy as a world capitalist organizational structure is made possible by (not caused by) the new technologies. The success of the attack on relatively privileged, mostly white, men's unionized jobs is tied to the power of the new communications technologies to integrate and control labor despite extensive dispersion and decentralization. The consequences of the new technologies are felt by women both in the loss of the family (male) wage (if they ever had access to this white privilege) and in the character of their own jobs, which are becoming capital-intensive, e.g., office work and nursing.

The new economic and technological arrangements are also related to the collapsing welfare state and the ensuing intensification of demands on women to sustain daily life for themselves as well as for men, children, and old people. The feminization of poverty—generated by dismantling the welfare state, by the homework economy where stable jobs become the exception, and sustained by the expectation that women's wage will not be matched by a male income for the support of children—has become an urgent focus. The causes of various women-headed households are a function of race, class, or sexuality; but their increasing generality is a ground for coalitions of women on many issues. That women regularly sustain daily life partly as a function of their enforced status as mothers is hardly new; the kind of integration with the overall capitalist and progressively war-based economy is new. The particular pressure, for example, on u.s. black women, who have achieved an escape from (barely) paid domestic service and who now hold clerical and similar jobs in large numbers, has large implications for continued enforced black poverty *with* employment. Teenage women in industrializing areas of the third world increasingly find themselves the sole or major source of a cash wage for their families, while access to land is ever more problematic. These developments must have major consequences in the psychodynamics and politics of gender and race.

Within the framework of three major stages of capitalism (commercial/early industrial, monopoly, multinational)—tied to nationalism, imperialism, and multinationalism, and related to Jameson's three dominant aesthetic periods of realism, modernism, and postmodernism—I would argue that specific forms of families dialectically relate to forms of capital and to its political and cultural concomitants. Although lived problematically and unequally, ideal forms of these families might be schematized as (1) the patriarchal nuclear family, structured by the dichotomy between public and private and accompanied by the white bourgeois ideology of separate spheres and nineteenth-century Anglo-American bourgeois feminism; (2) the modern family mediated (or enforced) by the welfare state and institutions like the family wage, with a flowering of a-feminist heterosexual ideologies, including their radical versions represented in Greenwich Village around World War I; and (3) the "family" of the homework economy with its oxymoronic structure of women-headed households and its explosion of feminisms and the paradoxical intensification and erosion of gender itself.

This is the context in which the projections for worldwide structural unemployment stemming from the new technologies are part of the picture of the homework economy. As robotics and related technologies put men out of work in "developed" countries and exacerbate failure to generate male jobs in third-world "development," and as the automated office becomes the rule even in labor-surplus countries, the feminization of work intensifies. Black women in the United States have long known what it looks like to face the structural underemployment ("feminization") of black men, as well as their own highly vulnerable position in the wage economy. It is no longer a secret that sexuality, reproduction, family, and community life are interwoven with this economic structure in myriad ways which have also differentiated the situations of white and black women. Many more women and men will contend with similar situations, which will make cross-gender and race alliances on issues of basic life support (with or without jobs) necessary, not just nice.

THE NEW TECHNOLOGIES also have a profound effect on hunger and on food production for subsistence worldwide. Rae Lessor Blumberg estimates that women produce about fifty per cent of the world's subsistence food.[21] Women are excluded generally from benefiting from the increased high-tech commodification of food and energy crops, their days are made more arduous because their responsibilities to provide food do not diminish, and their reproductive situations are made more complex. Green Revolution technologies interact with other high-tech industrial production to alter gender divisions of labor and differential gender migration patterns.

The new technologies seem deeply involved in the forms of "privatization" that Ros Petchesky has analyzed, in which militarization, right-wing family ideologies and policies, and intensified definitions of corporate property as private synergistically interact.[22] The new communications technologies are fundamental to the eradication of "public life" for everyone. This facilitates the mushrooming of a permanent high-tech military establishment at the cultural and economic expense of most people, but especially of women. Technologies like video games and highly miniaturized television seem crucial to production of modern forms of "private life." The culture of video games is heavily oriented to individual competition and extraterrestrial warfare. High-tech, gendered imaginations are produced here, imaginations that can contemplate destruction of the planet and a sci-fi escape from its consequences. More than our imaginations is militarized; and the other realities of electronic and nuclear warfare are inescapable.

The new technologies affect the social relations of both sexuality and of reproduction, and not always in the same ways. The close ties of sexuality and instrumentality, of views of the body as a kind of private satisfaction- and utility-maximizing machine, are described nicely in sociobiological origin stories that stress a genetic calculus and explain the inevitable dialectic of domination of male and female gender roles.[23] These sociobiological stories depend on a high-tech view of the body as a biotic component or cybernetic communications system. Among the many transformations of reproductive situations is the medical one, where women's bodies have boundaries newly permeable to both "visualization" and "intervention." Of course, who controls the interpretation of bodily boundaries in medical hermeneutics is a major feminist issue. The speculum served as an icon of women's claiming their bodies in the 1970s; that hand-craft tool is inadequate to express our needed body politics in the negotiation of reality in the practices of cyborg reproduction. Self-help is not enough. The technologies of visualization recall the important cultural practice of hunting with the camera and the deeply predatory nature of a photographic consciousness.[24] Sex, sexuality, and reproduction are central actors in high-tech myth systems structuring our imaginations of personal and social possibility.

Another critical aspect of the social relations of the new technologies is the reformulation of expectations, culture, work, and reproduction for the large scientific and technical work force. A major social and political danger is the formation of a strongly bimodal social structure, with the masses of women and men of all ethnic groups, but especially people of color, confined to a homework economy, illiteracy of several varieties, and general redundancy and impotence, controlled by high-tech repressive apparatuses ranging from entertainment to surveillance and disappearance. An adequate socialist-feminist politics should address women in the privileged occupational categories, and particularly in the production of science and technology that constructs scientific-technical discourses, processes, and objects.[25]

This issue is only one aspect of inquiry into the possibility of a feminist science, but it is important. What kind of constitutive role in the production of knowledge, imagination, and practice can new groups doing science have? How can these groups be allied with progressive social and political movements? What kind of political accountability can be constructed to tie women together across the scientific-technical hierarchies separating us? Might there be ways of developing feminist science/technology politics in alliance with anti-military science facility conversion action groups? Many scientific and technical workers in Silicon Valley, the hightech cowboys included, do not want to work on military science.[26] Can these personal preferences and cultural tendencies be welded into progressive politics among this professional middle class in which women, including women of color, are coming to be fairly numerous?

Women in the integrated circuit

LET ME SUMMARIZE the picture of women's historical locations in advanced industrial societies, as these positions have been restructured partly through the social relations of science and technology. If it was ever possible ideologically to characterize women's lives by the distinction of public and private domains—suggested by images of the division of working-class life into factory and home, of bourgeois life into market and home, and of gender existence into personal and political realms—it is now a totally misleading ideology, even to show how both terms of these dichotomies construct each other in practice and in theory. I prefer a network ideological image, suggesting the profusion of spaces and identities and the permeability of boundaries in the personal body and in the body politic. "Networking" is both a feminist practice and a multinational corporate strategy — weaving is for oppositional cyborgs.

The only way to characterize the informatics of domination is as a massive intensification of insecurity and cultural impoverishment, with common failure of subsistence networks for the most vulnerable. Since much of this picture interweaves with the social relations of science and technology, the urgency of a socialist-feminist politics addressed to science and technology is plain. There is much now being done, and the grounds for political work are rich. For example, the efforts to develop forms of collective struggle for women in paid work, like SEIU's District 925, should be a high priority for all of us. These efforts are profoundly tied to technical restructuring of labor processes and reformations of working classes. These efforts also are providing understanding of a more comprehensive kind of labor organization, involving community, sexuality, and family issues never privileged in the largely white male industrial unions.

The structural rearrangements related to the social relations of science and technology evoke strong ambivalence. But it is not necessary to be ultimately depressed by the implications of late-twentieth-century women's relation to all aspects of work, culture, production of knowledge, sexuality, and reproduction. For excellent reasons, most Marxisms see domination best and have trouble understanding what can only look like false consciousness and people's complicity in their own domination in late capitalism. It is crucial to remember that what is lost, perhaps especially from women's points of view, is often virulent forms of oppression, nostalgically naturalized in the face of current violation. Ambivalence toward the disrupted unities mediated by high-tech culture requires not sorting consciousness into categories of "clear-sighted critique grounding a solid political epistemology" versus "manipulated false consciousness," but subtle understanding of emerging pleasures, experiences, and powers with serious potential for changing the rules of the game.

There are grounds for hope in the emerging bases for new kinds of unity across race, gender, and class, as these elementary units of socialist-feminist analysis themselves suffer protean transformations. Intensifications of hardship experienced worldwide in connection with the social relations of science and technology are severe. But what people are experiencing is not transparently clear, and we lack sufficiently subtle connections for collectively building effective theories of experience. Present efforts — Marxist, psychoanalytic, feminist, anthropological — to clarify even "our" experience are rudimentary.

I am conscious of the odd perspective provided by my historical position — a Ph.D. in biology for an Irish Catholic girl was made possible by Sputnik's impact on U.S. national science-education policy. I have a body and mind as much constructed by the post-World War II arms race and cold war as by the women's movements. There are more grounds for hope by focusing on the contradictory effects of politics designed to produce loyal American technocrats, which as well produced large numbers of dissidents, rather than by focusing on the present defeats.

The permanent partiality of feminist points of view has consequences for our expectations of forms of political organization and participation. We do not need a totality in order to work well. The feminist dream of a common language, like all dreams for a perfectly true language, of perfectly faithful naming of experience, is a totalizing and imperialist one. In that sense, dialectics too is a dream language, longing to resolve contradiction. Perhaps, ironically, we can learn from our fusions with animals and machines how not to be Man, the embodiment of Western logos. From the point of view of pleasure in these potent and taboo fusions, made inevitable by the social relations of science and technology, there might indeed be a feminist science.

Cyborgs: a myth of political identity

I WANT TO CONCLUDE with a myth about identity and boundaries which might inform late-twentieth-century political imaginations. I am indebted in this story to writers like Joanna Russ, Samuel Delaney, John Varley, James Tiptree, Jr., Octavia Butler, Monique Wittig, and Vonda McIntyre.[27] These are our storytellers exploring what it means to be embodied in high-tech worlds. They are theorists for cyborgs. Exploring conceptions of bodily boundaries and social order, the anthropologist Mary Douglas should be credited with helping us to consciousness about how fundamental body imagery is to world view, and so to political language.[28] French feminists like Luce Irigaray and Monique Wittig, for all their differences, know how to write the body, how to weave eroticism, cosmology, and politics from imagery of embodiment, and especially for Wittig, from imagery of fragmentation and reconstitution of bodies.[29]

American radical feminists like Susan Griffin, Audre Lorde, and Adrienne Rich have profoundly affected our political imaginations — and perhaps restricted too much what we allow as a friendly body and political language.[30] They insist on the organic, opposing it to the technological. But their symbolic systems and the related positions of ecofeminism and feminist paganism, replete with organicisms, can only be understood in Sandoval's terms as oppositional ideologies fitting the late twentieth century. They would simply bewilder anyone not preoccupied with the machines and consciousness of late capitalism. In that sense they are part of the cyborg world. But there are also great riches for feminists in explicitly embracing the possibilities inherent in the breakdown of clean distinctions between organism and machine and similar distinctions structuring the Western self. It is the simultaneity of breakdowns that cracks the matrices of domination and opens geometric possibilities. What might be learned from personal and political "technological" pollution? I will look briefly at two overlapping groups of texts for their insight into the construction of a potentially helpful cyborg myth: constructions of women of color and monstrous selves in feminist science fiction.

Earlier I suggested that "women of color" might be understood as a cyborg identity, a potent subjectivity synthesized from fusions of outsider identities. There are material and cultural grids mapping this potential. Audre Lorde captures the tone in the title of her *Sister Outsider*. In my political myth, Sister Outsider is the offshore woman, whom u.s. workers, female and feminized, are supposed to regard as the enemy preventing their solidarity, threatening their security. Onshore, inside the boundary of the United States, Sister Outsider is a potential amidst the races and ethnic identities of women manipulated for division, competition, and exploitation in the same industries. "Women of color" are the preferred labor force for the science-based industries, the real women for whom the worldwide sexual market, labor market, and politics of reproduction kaleidoscope into daily life. Young Korean women hired in the sex industry and in electronics assembly are recruited from high schools, educated for the integrated circuit. Literacy, especially in English, distinguishes the "cheap" female labor so attractive to the multinationals.

Contrary to orientalist stereotypes of the "oral primitive," literacy is a special mark of women of color, acquired by u.s. black women as well as men through a history of risking death to learn and to teach reading and writing. Writing has a special significance for all colonized groups. Writing has been crucial to the Western myth of the distinction of oral and written cultures, primitive and civilized mentalities, and more recently to the erosion of that distinction in "post-modernist" theories attacking the phallogocentrism of the West, with its worship of the monotheistic, phallic, authoritative, and singular word, the unique and perfect name.[31] Contests for the meanings of writing are a major form of contemporary political struggle. Releasing the play of writing is deadly serious. The poetry and stories of u.s. women of color are repeatedly about writing, about access to the power to signify; but this time that power must be neither phallic nor innocent. Cyborg writing must not be about the Fall, the imagination of a once-upon-a-time wholeness before language, before writing, before Man. Cyborg writing is about the power to survive, not on the basis of original innocence, but on the basis of seizing the tools to mark the world that marked them as other.

The tools are often stories, retold stories, versions that reverse and displace the hierarchical dualisms of naturalized identities. In retelling origin stories, cyborg authors subvert the central myths of origin of Western culture. We have all been colonized by those origin myths, with their longing for fulfillment in apocalypse. The phallogocentric origin stories most crucial for feminist cyborgs are built into the literal technologies — technologies that write the world, bio-technology and microelectronics — that have recently textualized our bodies as code problems on the grid of c^3i. Feminist cyborg stories have the task of recoding communication and intelligence to subvert command and control.

Figuratively and literally, language politics pervade the struggles of women of color; and stories about language have a special power in the rich contemporary writing by u.s. women of color. For example, retellings of the story of the indigenous woman Malinche, mother of the mestizo "bastard" race of the new world, master of languages, and mistress of Cortés, carry special meaning for Chicana constructions of identity. Cherrie Moraga in *Loving in the War Years* explores the themes of identity when one never possessed the original language, never told the original story, never resided in the harmony of legitimate hetero-sexuality in the garden of culture, and so cannot base identity on a myth or a fall from innocence and right to natural names, mother's or father's.[32] Moraga's writing, her superb literacy, is presented in her poetry as the same kind of violation as Malinche's mastery of the conquerer's language — a violation, an illegitimate production, that allows survival. Moraga's language is not "whole"; it is self-consciously spliced, a chimera of English and Spanish, both conqueror's languages. But it is this chimeric monster, without claim to an original language before violation, that crafts the erotic, competent, potent identities of women of color. Sister Outsider hints at the possibility of world survival not because of her innocence, but because of her ability to live on the boundaries, to write without the founding myth of original wholeness, with its inescapable apocalypse of final return to a deathly oneness that Man has imagined to be the innocent and all-powerful Mother, freed at the End from another spiral of appropriation by her son. Writing marks Moraga's body, affirms it as the body of a woman of color, against the possibility of passing into the unmarked category of the Anglo father or into the orientalist myth of "original illiteracy" of a mother that never was. Malinche was mother here, not Eve before eating the forbidden fruit. Writing affirms Sister Outsider, not the Woman-before-the-Fall-into-Writing needed by the phallogocentric Family of Man.

WRITING IS PRE-EMINENTLY the technology of cyborgs, etched surfaces of the late twentieth century. Cyborg politics is the struggle for language and the struggle against perfect communication, against the one code that translates all meaning perfectly, the central dogma of phallogocentrism. That is why cyborg politics insist on noise and advocate pollution, rejoicing in the illegitimate fusions of animal and machine. These are the couplings which make Man and Woman so problematic, subverting the structure of desire, the force imagined to generate language and gender, and so subverting the structure and modes of reproduction of "Western" identity, of nature and culture, of mirror and eye, slave and master, body and mind. "We" did not originally choose to be cyborgs, but choice grounds a liberal politics and epistemology that imagines the reproduction of individuals before the wider replications of "texts."

From the perspective of cyborgs, freed of the need to ground politics in "our" privileged position of the oppression that incorporates all other dominations, the innocence of the merely violated, the ground of those closer to nature, we can see powerful possibilities. Feminisms and Marxisms have run aground on Western epistemological imperatives to construct a revolutionary subject from the perspective of a hierarchy of oppressions and/or a latent position of moral superiority, innocence, and greater closeness to nature. With no available original dream of a common language or original symbiosis promising protection from hostile "masculine" separation, but written into the play of a text that has no finally privileged reading or salvation history, to recognize "oneself" as fully implicated in the world, frees us of the need to root politics in identification, vanguard parties, purity, and mothering. Stripped of identity, the bastard race teaches about the power of the margins and the importance of a mother like Malinche. Women of color have transformed her from the evil mother of masculinist fear into the originally literate mother who teaches survival.

This is not just literary deconstruction, but liminal transformation. Every story that begins with original innocence and privileges the return to wholeness imagines the drama of life to be individuation, separation, the birth of the self, the tragedy of autonomy, the fall into writing, alienation; i.e., war, tempered by imaginary respite in the bosom of the Other. These plots are ruled by a reproductive politics — rebirth without flaw, perfection, abstraction. In this plot women are imagined either better or worse off, but all agree they have less selfhood, weaker individuation, more fusion to the oral, to Mother, less at stake in masculine autonomy. But there is another route to having less at stake in masculine autonomy, a route that does not pass through Woman, Primitive, Zero, the Mirror Stage and its imaginary. It passes through women and other present-tense, illegitimate cyborgs, not of Woman born, who refuse the ideological resources of victimization so as to have a real life. These cyborgs are the people who refuse to disappear on cue, no matter how many times a "Western" commentator remarks on the sad passing of another primitive, another organic group done in by "Western" technology, by writing.[33] These real-life cyborgs, e.g., the Southeast

Asian village women workers in Japanese and u.s. electronics firms described by Aiwa Ong, are actively rewriting the texts of their bodies and societies. Survival is the stakes in this play of readings.

To RECAPITULATE, certain dualisms have been persistent in Western traditions; they have all been systemic to the logics and practices of domination of women, people of color, nature, workers, animals — in short, domination of all constituted as *others*, whose task is to mirror the self. Chief among these troubling dualisms are self/other, mind/body, culture/nature, male/female, civilized/primitive, reality/ appearance, whole/part, agent/resource, maker/made, active/passive, right/ wrong, truth/illusion, total/partial, God/man. The self is the One who is not dominated, who knows that by the service of the other; the other is the one who holds the future, who knows that by the experience of domination, which gives the lie to the autonomy of the self. To be One is to be autonomous, to be powerful, to be God; but to be One is to be an illusion, and so to be involved in a dialectic of apocalypse with the other. Yet to be other is to be multiple, without clear boundary, frayed, insubstantial. One is too few, but two are too many.

High-tech culture challenges these dualisms in intriguing ways. It is not clear who makes and who is made in the relation between human and machine. It is not clear what is mind and what body in machines that resolve into coding practices. Insofar as we know ourselves in both formal discourse (e.g., biology) and in daily practice (e.g., the homework economy in the integrated circuit), we find ourselves to be cyborgs, hybrids, mosaics, chimeras. Biological organisms have become biotic systems, communications devices like others. There is no fundamental, ontological separation in our formal knowledge of machine and organism, of technical and organic.

One consequence is that our sense of connection to our tools is heightened. The trance state experienced by many computer users has become a staple of science-fiction film and cultural jokes. Perhaps paraplegics and other severely handicapped people can (and sometimes do) have the most intense experiences of complex hybridization with other communication devices. Anne McCaffrey's *The Ship Who Sang* explored the consciousness of a cyborg, hybrid of girl's brain and complex machinery, formed after the birth of a severely handicapped child. Gender, sexuality, embodiment, skill: all were reconstituted in the story. Why should our bodies end at the skin, or include at best other beings encapsulated by skin? From the seventeenth century till now, machines could be animated — given ghostly souls to make them speak or move or to account for their orderly devel- opment and mental capacities. Or organisms could be mechanized — reduced to body understood as resource of mind. These machine/organism relationships are obsolete, unnecessary. For us, in imagination and in other practice, machines can be prosthetic devices, intimate components, friendly selves. We don't need organic holism to give impermeable wholeness, the total woman and her feminist variants (mutants?). Let me conclude this point by a very partial reading of the logic of the cyborg monsters of my second group of texts, feminist science fiction.

THE CYBORGS populating feminist science fiction make very problematic the sta- tuses of man or woman, human, artifact, member of a race, individual identity, or body. Katie King clarifies how pleasure in reading these fictions is not largely based on identification. Students facing Joanna Russ for the first time, students who have learned to take modernist writers like James Joyce or Virginia Woolf without flinching, do not know what to make of *The Adventures of Alyx* or *The Female Man*, where characters refuse the reader's search for innocent wholeness while granting the wish for heroic quests, exuberant eroticism, and serious politics. *The Female Man* is the story of four versions of one genotype, all of whom meet, but even taken together do not make a whole, resolve the dilemmas of violent moral action, nor remove the growing scandal of gender. The feminist science fiction of Samuel Delany, especially *Tales of Neveryon*, mocks stories of origin by redoing the neolithic revolution, replaying the founding moves of Western civilization to subvert their plausibility. James Tiptree, Jr., an author whose fiction was regarded as particularly manly until her "true" gender was revealed, tells tales of reproduction based on non-mammalian technologies like alternation of generations or male brood pouches and male nurturing. John Varley constructs a supreme cyborg in his arch-feminist exploration of Gaea, a mad goddess-planet-trickster-old woman-technological device on whose surface an extraordinary array of post-cyborg symbioses are spawned. Octavia Butler writes of an African sorceress pitting her powers of transformation against the genetic manipulations of her rival (*Wild Seed*), of time warps that bring a modern u.s. black woman into slavery where her actions in relation to her white master-ancestor determine the possibility of her own birth (*Kindred*), and of the illegitimate insights into identity and community of an adopted cross-species child who came to know the enemy as self (*Survivor*).

Because it is particularly rich in boundary transgressions, Vonda McIntyre's *Superluminal* can close this truncated catalogue of promising monsters who help redefine the pleasures and politics of embodiment and feminist writing. In a fiction where no character is "simply" human, human status is highly problematic. Orca, a genetically altered diver, can speak with killer whales and survive deep ocean conditions, but she longs to explore space as a pilot, necessitating bionic implants jeopardizing her kinship with the divers and cetaceans. Transformations are effected by virus vectors carrying a new developmental code, by transplant surgery, by implants of microelectronic devices, by analogue doubles, and other means. Laenea becomes a pilot by accepting a heart implant and a host of other alterations allowing survival in transit at speeds exceeding that of light. Radu Dracul survives a virus-caused plague on his outerworld planet to find himself with a time sense that changes the boundaries of spatial perception for the whole species. All the characters explore the limits of language, the dream of communicating experience, and the necessity of limitation, partiality, and intimacy even in this world of protean transformation and connection.

MONSTERS HAVE ALWAYS defined the limits of community in Western imaginations. The Centaurs and Amazons of ancient Greece established the limits of the centered polis of the Greek male human by their disruption of marriage and boundary pollutions of the warrior with animality and woman. Unseparated twins and hermaphrodites were the confused human material in early modern France who grounded discourse on the natural and supernatural, medical and legal, portents and diseases — all crucial to establishing modern identity.[34] The evolutionary and behavioral sciences of monkeys and apes have marked the multiple boundaries of late-twentieth-century industrial identities. Cyborg monsters in feminist science fiction define quite different political possibilities and limits from those proposed by the mundane fiction of Man and Woman.

There are several consequences to taking seriously the imagery of cyborgs as other than our enemies. Our bodies, ourselves; bodies are maps of power and identity. Cyborgs are no exceptions. A cyborg body is not innocent; it was not born in a garden; it does not seek unitary identity and so generate antagonistic dualisms without end (or until the world ends); it takes irony for granted. One is too few, and two is only one possibility. Intense pleasure in skill, machine skill, ceases to be a sin, but an aspect of embodiment. The machine is not an *it* to be animated, worshiped and dominated. The machine is us, our processes, an aspect of our embodiment. We can be responsible for machines; *they* do not dominate or threaten us. We are responsible for boundaries; we are they. Up till now (once upon a time), female embodiment seemed to be given, organic, necessary; and female embodiment seemed to mean skill in mothering and its metaphoric extensions. Only by being out of place could we take intense pleasure in machines, and then with excuses that this was organic activity after all, appropriate to females. Cyborgs might consider more seriously the partial, fluid, sometimes aspect of sex and sexual embodiment. Gender might not be global identity after all.

The ideologically charged question of what counts as daily activity, as experience, can be approached by exploiting the cyborg image. Feminists have recently claimed that women are given to dailiness, that women more than men somehow sustain daily life, and so have a privileged epistemological position potentially. There is a compelling aspect to this claim, one that makes visible unvalued female activity and names it as the ground of life. But *the* ground of life? What about all the ignorance of women, all the exclusions and failures of knowledge and skill? What about men's access to daily competence, to knowing how to build things, to take them apart, to play? What about other embodiments? Cyborg gender is a local possibility taking a global vengeance. Race, gender, and capital require a cyborg theory of wholes and parts. There is no drive in cyborgs to produce total theory, but there is an intimate experience of boundaries, their construction and deconstruction. There is a myth system waiting to become a political language to ground one way of looking at science and technology and challenging the informatics of domination.

One last image: organisms and organismic, holistic politics depend on metaphors of rebirth and invariably call on the resources of reproductive sex. I would suggest that cyborgs have more to do with regeneration and are suspicious of the reproductive matrix and of most birthing. For salamanders, regeneration after injury, such as the loss of a limb, involves regrowth of structure and restoration of function with the constant possibility of twinning or other odd topographical productions at the site of former injury. The regrown limb can be monstrous, duplicated, potent. We have all been injured, profoundly. We require regeneration, not rebirth, and the possibilities for our reconstitution include the utopian dream of the hope for a monstrous world without gender.

Cyborg imagery can help express two crucial arguments in this essay: (1) the production of universal, totalizing theory is a major mistake that misses most of reality, probably always, but certainly now; (2) taking responsibility for the social relations of science and technology means refusing an anti-science metaphysics, a demonology of technology, and so means embracing the skillful task of reconstructing the boundaries of daily life, in partial connection with others, in communication with all of our parts. It is not just that science and technology are possible means of great human satisfaction, as well as a matrix of complex dominations. Cyborg imagery can suggest a way out of the maze of dualisms in which we have explained our bodies and our tools to ourselves. This is a dream not of a common language, but of a powerful infidel heteroglossia. It is an imagination of a feminist speaking in tongues to strike fear into the circuits of the super-savers of the new right. It means both building and destroying machines, identities, categories, relationships, spaces, stories. Though both are bound in the spiral dance, I would rather be a cyborg than a goddess.

Acknowledgments

Research was funded by an Academic Senate Faculty Research Grant from the University of California, Santa Cruz. An earlier version of the paper on genetic engineering appeared as "Lieber Kyborg als Gottin: Für eine sozialistisch-feministische Unterwanderung der Gentechnologie," in Bernd-Peter Lange and Anna Marie Stuby, eds., *1984* (Berlin: Argument-Sonderband 105, 1984), pp. 66–84. The cyborg manifesto grew from "New Machines, New Bodies, New Communities: Political Dilemmas of a Cyborg Feminist," *The Scholar and the Feminist x: The Question of Technology*, Conference, April 1983.

The people associated with the History of Consciousness Board of ucsc have had an enormous influence on this paper, so that it feels collectively authored more than most, although those I cite may not recognize their ideas. In particular, members of graduate and undergraduate feminist theory, science and politics, and theory and methods courses have contributed to the cyborg manifesto. Particular debts here are due Hilary Klein ("Marxism, Psychoanalysis, and Mother Nature"); Paul Edwards ("Border Wars: The Science and Politics of Artificial Intelligence"); Lisa Lowe ("Julia Kristeva's *Des Chinoises*: Representing Cultural and Sexual Others"); Jim Clifford, "On Ethnographic Allegory: Essays," forthcoming.

Parts of the paper were my contribution to a collectively developed session, Poetic Tools and Political Bodies: Feminist Approaches to High Technology Culture, 1984 California American Studies Association, with History of Consciousness graduate students Zoe Sofoulis, "Jupiter Space"; Katie King, "The Pleasures of Repetition and the Limits of Identification in Feminist Science Fiction: Reimaginations of the Body after the Cyborg"; and Chela Sandoval, "The Construction of Subjectivity and Oppositional Consciousness in Feminist Film and Video." Sandoval's theory of oppositional consciousness was published as "Women Respond to Racism: A Report on the National Women's Studies Association Conference," Center for Third World Organizing, Oakland, California, n.d. For Sofoulis's semiotic-psychoanalytic readings of nuclear culture, see Z. Sofia, "Exterminating Fetuses: Abortion, Disarmament and the Sexo-Semiotics of Extraterrestrialism," Nuclear Criticism issue, *Diacritics*, vol. 14, no. 2 (1984), pp. 47–59.

King's manuscripts ("Questioning Tradition: Canon Formation and the Veiling of Power"; "Gender and Genre: Reading the Science Fiction of Joanna Russ"; "Varley's *Titan* and *Wizard*: Feminist Parodies of Nature, Culture, and Hardware") deeply inform the cyborg manifesto.

Barbara Epstein, Jeff Escoffier, Rusten Hogness, and Jaye Miller gave extensive discussion and editorial help. Members of the Silicon Valley Research Project of UCSC and participants in SVRP conferences and workshops have been very important, especially Rick Gordon, Linda Kimball, Nancy Snyder, Langdon Winner, Judith Stacey, Linda Lim, Patricia Fernandez-Kelly, and Judith Gregory. Finally, I want to thank Nancy Hartsock for years of friendship and discussion on feminist theory and feminist science fiction.

References

1   Useful references to left and/or feminist radical science movements and theory and to biological/biotechnological issues include: Ruth Bleier, *Science and Gender: A Critique of Biology and Its Themes on Women* (New York: Pergamon, 1984); Elizabeth Fee, "Critiques of Modern Science: The Relationship of Feminist and Other Radical Epistemologies," and Evelyn Hammonds, "Women of Color, Feminism and Science," papers for Symposium on Feminist Perspectives on Science, University of Wisconsin, 11–12 April, 1985 (proceedings to be published by Pergamon); Stephen J. Gould, *Mismeasure of Man* (New York: Norton, 1981); Ruth Hubbard, Mary Sue Henifin, Barbara Fried, eds., *Biological Woman, the Convenient Myth* (Cambridge, Mass.: Schenkman, 1982); Evelyn Fox Keller, *Reflections on Gender and Science* (New Haven: Yale University Press, 1985); R. C. Lewontin, Steve Rose, and Leon Kamin, *Not in Our Genes* (New York: Pantheon, 1984): *Radical Science Journal*, 26 Freegrove Road, London N7 9RQ; *Science for the People*, 897 Main St., Cambridge, MA 02139.

2   Starting points for left and/or feminist approaches to technology and politics include: Ruth Schwartz Cowan, *More Work for Mother: The Ironies of Household Technology from the Open Hearth to the Microwave* (New York: Basic Books, 1983); Joan Rothschild, *Machina ex Dea: Feminist Perspectives on Technology* (New York: Pergamon, 1983); Sharon Traweek, "Uptime, Downtime, Spacetime, and Power: An Ethnography of U.S. and Japanese Particle Physics," Ph.D. thesis, UC Santa Cruz, History of Consciousness, 1982; R. M. Young and Les Levidov, eds., *Science, Technology, and the Labour Process*, vols. 1–3 (London: CSE Books); Joseph Weizenbaum, *Computer Power and Human Reason* (San Francisco: Freeman, 1976); Langdon Winner, *Autonomous Technology: Technics Out of Control as a Theme in Political Thought* (Cambridge, Mass.: MIT Press, 1977): Langdon Winner, "Paths in Technopolis," esp. "Mythinformation in the High Tech Era" (in ms., forthcoming); Jan Zimmerman, ed., *The Technological Woman: Interfacing with Tomorrow* (New York: Praegel, 1983); *Global Electronics Newsletter*, 867 West Dana St., #204, Mountain View, CA 94041; *Processed World*, 55 Sutter St., San Francisco, CA 94104; ISIS, Women's International Information and Communication Service, P.O. Box 50 (Cornavin), 1211 Geneva 2, Switzerland, and Via Santa Maria dell'Anima 30, 00186 Rome, Italy. Fundamental approaches to modern social studies of science that do not continue the liberal mystification that it all started with Thomas Kuhn, include: Karin Knorr-Cetina, *The Manufacture of Knowledge* (Oxford: Pergamon, 1981); K. D. Knorr-Cetina and Michael Mulkay, eds., *Science Observed: Perspectives on the Social Study of Science* (Beverly Hills, Calif.: Sage, 1983); Bruno Latour and Steve Woolgar, *Laboratory Life: The Social Construction of Scientific Facts* (Beverly Hills, Calif.: Sage, 1979); Robert M. Young, "Interpreting the Production of Science," *New Scientist*, vol. 29 (March 1979),

pp. 1026–1028. More is claimed than is known about room for contesting productions of science in the mythic/material space of "the laboratory"; the 1984 Directory of the Network for the Ethnographic Study of Science, Technology, and Organizations lists a wide range of people and projects crucial to better radical analysis; available from NESSTO, P. O. Box 11442, Stanford, CA 94305.

3   Frederic Jameson, "Post Modernism, or the Cultural Logic of Late Capitalism," *New Left Review*, July/August 1984, pp. 53–94. See Marjorie Perloff, " 'Dirty' Language and Scramble Systems," *Sulfur* 11 (1984), pp. 178–183; Kathleen Fraser, *Something (Even Human Voices) in the Foreground, a Lake* (Berkeley, Calif.: Kelsey St. Press, 1984).

A provocative, comprehensive argument about the politics and theories of "post-modernism" is made by Fredric Jameson, who argues that post-modernism is not an option, a style among others, but a cultural dominant requiring radical reinvention of left politics from within; there is no longer any place from without that gives meaning to the comforting fiction of critical distance. Jameson also makes clear why one cannot be for or against post-modernism, an essentially moralist move. My position is that feminists (and others) need continuous cultural reinvention, post-modernist critique, and historical materialism; only a cyborg would have a chance. The old dominations of white capitalist patriarchy seem nostalgically innocent now: they normalized heterogeneity, e.g., into man and woman, white and black. "Advanced capitalism" and post-modernism release heterogeneity without a norm, and we are flattened, without subjectivity, which requires depth, even unfriendly and drowning depths. It is time to write *The Death of the Clinic*. The clinic's methods required bodies and works; we have texts and surfaces. Our dominations don't work by medicalization and normalization anymore; they work by networking, communications redesign, stress management. Normalization gives way to automation, utter redundancy. Michel Foucault's *Birth of the Clinic, History of Sexuality*, and *Discipline and Punish* name a form of power at its moment of implosion. The discourse of biopolitics gives way to technobabble, the language of the spliced substantive; no noun is left whole by the multinationals. These are their names, listed from one issue of *Science*: Tech-Knowledge, Genentech, Allergen, Hybritech, Compupro, Genen-cor, Syntex, Allelix, Agrigenetics Corp., Syntro, Codon, Repligen, Micro-Angelo from Scion Corp., Per-com Data, Inter Systems, Cyborg Corp., Statcom Corp., Intertec. If we are imprisoned by language, then escape from that prison house requires language poets, a kind of cultural restriction enzyme to cut the code; cyborg heteroglossia is one form of radical culture politics.

4   Frans de Waal, *Chimpanzee Politics: Power and Sex among the Apes* (New York: Harper & Row, 1982); Langdon Winner, "Do artifacts have politics?" *Daedalus*, Winter 1980.

5   Jean Baudrillard, *Simulations*, trans. P. Foss, P. Patton, P. Beitchman (New York: Semiotext(e), 1983). Jameson ("Post modernism," p. 66) points out that Plato's definition of the simulacrum is the copy for which there is no original, i.e., the world of advanced capitalism; of pure exchange.

6   Herbert Marcuse, *One-Dimensional Man* (Boston: Beacon, 1964); Carolyn Merchant, *Death of Nature* (San Francisco: Harper & Row, 1980).

7   Zoe Sofia, "Exterminating Fetuses," *Diacritics*, vol. 14, no. 2 (Summer 1984), pp. 47–59, and "Jupiter Space" (Pomona, Calif: American Studies Association, 1984).

8   Powerful developments of coalition politics emerge from "third world" speakers, speaking from nowhere, the displaced center of the universe, earth: "We live on the third planet from the sun"—*Sun Poem* by Jamaican writer Edward Kamau Braithwaite, review by Nathaniel Mackey, *Sulfur*, II (1984), pp. 200–205. *Home Girls*, ed. Barbara Smith (New York: Kitchen Table, Women of Color Press, 1983), ironically subverts naturalized identities precisely while constructing a place from which to speak called home. See esp. Bernice Reagan, "Coalition Politics, Turning the Century," pp. 356–368.

9   Chela Sandoval, "Dis-Illusionment and the Poetry of the Future: The Making of Oppos-
     itional Consciousness," Ph.D. qualifying essay, ucsc, 1984.
10   Bell Hooks, *Ain't I a Woman?* (Boston: South End Press, 1981); Gloria Hull, Patricia
     Bell Scott, and Barbara Smith, eds., *All the Women Are White, All the Men Are Black,
     But Some of Us Are Brave: Black Women's Studies* (Old Westbury, Conn.: Feminist Press,
     1982). Toni Cade Bambara, in *The Salt Eaters* (New York: Vintage/Random House,
     1981), writes an extraordinary post-modernist novel, in which the women of color
     theater group, The Seven Sisters, explores a form of unity. Thanks to Elliott Evans's
     readings of Bambara, Ph.D. qualifying essay, ucsc, 1984.
11   On orientalism in feminist works and elsewhere, see Lisa Lowe, "Orientation: Repre-
     sentations of Cultural and Sexual 'Others,' " Ph.D. thesis, ucsc; Edward Said, *Orientalism*
     (New York: Pantheon, 1978).
12   Katie King has developed a theoretically sensitive treatment of the workings of
     feminist taxonomies as genealogies of power in feminist ideology and polemic: "Pro-
     spectus," *Gender and Genre: Academic Practice and the Making of Criticism* (Santa Cruz,
     Calif.: University of California, 1984). King examines an intelligent, problematic
     example of taxonomizing feminisms to make a little machine producing the desired
     final position: Alison Jaggar, *Feminist Politics and Human Nature* (Totowa, N.J.: Rowman
     & Allanheld, 1983). My caricature here of socialist and radical feminism is also an
     example.
13   The feminist standpoint argument is being developed by: Jane Flax, "Political Phil-
     osophy and the Patriarchal Unconsciousness," in Sandra Harding and Merill Hintikka,
     eds., *Discovering Reality* (Dordrecht: Reidel, 1983); Sandra Harding, "The Contradic-
     tions and Ambivalence of a Feminist Science," ms.; Harding and Hintikka, *Discovering
     Reality*; Nancy Hartsock, *Money, Sex, and Power* (New York: Longman, 1983) and "The
     Feminist Standpoint: Developing the Ground for a Specifically Feminist Historical
     Materialism," in Harding and Hintikka, *Discovering Reality*; Mary O'Brien, *The Politics
     of Reproduction* (New York: Routledge & Kegan Paul, 1981); Hilary Rose, "Hand,
     Brain, and Heart: A Feminist Epistemology for the Natural Sciences," *Signs*, vol. 9,
     no. 1 (1983), pp. 73–90; Dorothy Smith, "Women's Perspective as a Radical Critique
     of Sociology," *Sociological Inquiry* 44 (1974), and "A Sociology of Women," in J.
     Sherman and E. T. Beck, ed., *The Prism of Sex* (Madison: University of Wisconsin
     Press, 1979).

     The central role of object-relations versions of psychoanalysis and related strong univer-
     salizing moves in discussing reproduction, caring work, and mothering in many
     approaches to epistemology underline their authors' resistance to what I am calling
     post-modernism. For me, both the universalizing moves and the versions of psycho-
     analysis make analysis of "women's place in the integrated circuit" difficult and lead to
     systematic difficulties in accounting for or even seeing major aspects of the construction
     of gender and gendered social life.
14   Catherine Mackinnon, "Feminism, Marxism, Method, and the State: An Agenda for
     Theory," *Signs*, vol. 7, no. 3 (Spring 1982), pp. 515–544. A critique indebted to
     MacKinnon, but without the reductionism and with an elegant feminist account of
     Foucault's paradoxical conservatism on sexual violence (rape), is Teresa de Lauretis,
     "Violence Engendered," forthcoming in *Semiotica*, special issue on "The Rhetoric of
     Violence," ed. Nancy Armstrong, 1985. A theoretically elegant feminist social-
     historical examination of family violence, that insists on women's, men's, children's
     complex agency without losing sight of the material structures of male domination,
     race, and class, is Linda Gordon, *Cruelty, Love, and Dependence: Family Violence and Social
     Control, Boston 1880–1960*, forthcoming with Pantheon.
15   My previous efforts to understand biology as a cybernetic command-control discourse
     and organisms as "natural-technical objects of knowledge" are: "The High Cost of

Information in Post-World War II Evolutionary Biology," *Philosophical Forum*, vol. 13, nos. 2–3 (1979), pp. 206–237; "Signs of Dominance: From a Physiology to a Cybernetics of Primate Society," *Studies in History of Biology* 6 (1983), pp. 129–219; "Class, Race, Sex, Scientific Objects of Knowledge: A Socialist-Feminist Perspective on the Social Construction of Productive Knowledge and Some Political Consequences," in Violet Haas and Carolyn Perucci, eds., *Women in Scientific and Engineering Professions* (Ann Arbor: University of Michigan Press, 1984), pp. 212–229.

16   E. Rusten Hogness, "Why Stress? A Look at the Making of Stress, 1936–56," available from the author, 4437 Mill Creek Rd., Healdsburg, CA 95448.

17   A left entry to the biotechnology debate: *GeneWatch*, a Bulletin of the Committee for Responsible Genetics, 5 Doane St., 4th floor, Boston, MA 02109; Susan Wright, forthcoming book and "Recombinant DNA: The Status of Hazards and Controls," *Environment*, July/August 1982; Edward Yoxen, *The Gene Business* (New York: Harper & Row, 1983).

18   Starting references for "women in the integrated circuit": Pamela D'Onofrio-Flores and Sheila M. Pfafflin, eds., *Scientific-Technological Change and the Role of Women in Development* (Boulder, Colo.: Westview Press, 1982); Maria Patricia Fernandez-Kelly, *For We Are Sold, I and My People* (Albany, N.Y.: SUNY Press, 1983); Annette Fuentes and Barbara Ehrenreich, *Women in the Global Factory* (Boston: South End Press, 1983), with an especially useful list of resources and organizations; Rachael Grossman, "Women's Place in the Integrated Circuit," *Radical America*, vol. 14, no. 1 (1980), pp. 29–50; June Nash and M. P. Fernandez-Kelly, eds., *Women and Men and the International Division of Labor* (Albany, N.Y.: SUNY Press, 1983); Aiwa Ong, "Japanese Factories, Malay Workers: Industrialization and the Cultural Construction of Gender in West Malaysia," in Shelley Errington and Jane Atkinson, eds., *The Construction of Gender*, forthcoming; Science Policy Research Unity, *Microelectronics and Women's Employment in Britain* (University of Sussex, 1982).

19   The best example is Bruno Latour, *Les Microbes: Guerre et Paix, suivi de Irreductions* (Paris: Metailie, 1984).

20   For the homework economy and some supporting arguments: Richard Gordon, "The Computerization of Daily Life, the Sexual Division of Labor, and the Homework Economy," in R. Gordon, ed., *Microelectronics in Transition* (Norwood, N.J.: Ablex, 1985); Patricia Hill Collins, "Third World Women in America," and Sara G. Burr, "Women and Work," in Barbara K. Haber, ed., *The Women's Annual, 1981* (Boston: G. K. Hall, 1982); Judith Gregory and Karen Nussbaum, "Race against Time: Automation of the Office," *Office: Technology and People* 1 (1982), pp. 197–236; Frances Fox Piven and Richard Cloward, *The New Class War: Reagan's Attack on the Welfare State and Its Consequences* (New York: Pantheon, 1982); Microelectronics Group, *Microelectronics: Capitalist Technology and the Working Class* (London: CSE, 1980); Karin Stallard, Barbara Ehrenreich, and Holly Sklar, *Poverty in the American Dream* (Boston: South End Press, 1983), including a useful organization and resource list.

21   Rae Lessor Blumberg, "A General Theory of Sex Stratification and Its Application to the Position of Women in Today's World Economy," paper delivered to Sociology Board, UCSC, February 1983. Also Blumberg, *Stratification: Socioeconomic and Sexual Inequality* (Boston: Brown, 1981). See also Sally Hacker, "Doing It the Hard Way: Ethnographic Studies in the Agribusiness and Engineering Classroom," California American Studies Association, Pomona, 1984, forthcoming in *Humanity and Society*; S. Hacker and Lisa Bovit, "Agriculture to Agribusiness: Technical Imperatives and Changing Roles," *Proceedings* of the Society for the History of Technology, Milwaukee, 1981; Lawrence Busch and William Lacy, *Science, Agriculture, and the Politics of Research* (Boulder, Colo.: Westview Press, 1983); Denis Wilfred, "Capital and Agriculture, a Review of Marxian Problematics," *Studies in Political Economy*, no. 7 (1982), pp. 127–154; Carolyn Sachs, *The Invisible Farmers: Women in Agricultural Production* (Totowa, N.J.:

Rowman & Allanheld, 1983). Thanks to Elizabeth Bird, "Green Revolution Imperialism," I & II, ms. ucsc, 1984.

The conjunction of the Green Revolution's social relations with biotechnologies like plant genetic engineering makes the pressures on land in the third world increasingly intense. AID's estimates (*New York Times*, 14 October 1984) used at the 1984 World Food Day are that in Africa, women produce about 90 per cent of rural food supplies, about 60–80 per cent in Asia, and provide 40 per cent of agricultural labor in the Near East and Latin America. Blumberg charges that world organizations' agricultural politics, as well as those of multinationals and national governments in the third world, generally ignore fundamental issues in the sexual division of labor. The present tragedy of famine in Africa might owe as much to male supremacy as to capitalism, colonialism, and rain patterns. More accurately, capitalism and racism are usually structurally male dominant.

22   Cynthia Enloe, "Women Textile Workers in the Militarization of Southeast Asia," in Nash and Fernandez-Kelly, *Women and Men*; Rosalind Petchesky, "Abortion, Anti-Feminism, and the Rise of the New Right," *Feminist Studies*, vol. 7, no. 2 (1981).

23   For a feminist version of this logic, see Sarah Blaffer Hrdy, *The Woman That Never Evolved* (Cambridge, Mass.: Harvard University Press, 1981). For an analysis of scientific women's story-telling practices, especially in relation to sociobiology, in evolutionary debates around child abuse and infanticide, see Donna Haraway, "The Contest for Primate Nature: Daughters of Man the Hunter in the Field, 1960–80," in Mark Kann, ed., *The Future of American Democracy* (Philadelphia: Temple University Press, 1983), pp. 175–208.

24   For the moment of transition of hunting with guns to hunting with cameras in the construction of popular meanings of nature for an American urban immigrant public, see Donna Haraway, "Teddy Bear Patriarchy," *Social Text*, forthcoming, 1985; Roderick Nash, "The Exporting and Importing of Nature: Nature-Appreciation as a Commodity, 1850–1980," *Perspectives in American History*, vol. 3 (1979), pp. 517–560; Susan Sontag, *On Photography* (New York: Dell, 1977); and Douglas Preston, "Shooting in Paradise," *Natural History*, vol. 93, no. 12 (December 1984), pp. 14–19.

25   For crucial guidance for thinking about the political/cultural implications of the history of women doing science in the United States, see: Violet Haas and Carolyn Perucci, eds., *Women in Scientific and Engineering Professions* (Ann Arbor: University of Michigan Press, 1984); Sally Hacker, "The Culture of Engineering: Women, Workplace, and Machine," *Women's Studies International Quarterly*, vol. 4, no. 3 (1981), pp. 341–53; Evelyn Fox Keller, *A Feeling for the Organism* (San Francisco: Freeman, 1983); National Science Foundation, *Women and Minorities in Science and Engineering* (Washington, D.C.: NSF, 1982); Margaret Rossiter, *Women Scientists in America* (Baltimore: Johns Hopkins University Press, 1982).

26   John Markoff and Lenny Siegel, "Military Micros," ucsc Silicon Valley Research Project conference, 1983, forthcoming in *Microelectronics and Industrial Transformation*. High Technology Professionals for Peace and Computer Professionals for Social Responsibility are promising organizations.

27   Katie King, "The Pleasure of Repetition and the Limits of Identification in Feminist Science Fiction: Reimaginations of the Body after the Cyborg," California American Studies Association, Pomona, 1984. An abbreviated list of feminist science fiction underlying themes of this essay: Octavia Butler, *Wild Seed, Mind of My Mind, Kindred, Survivor*; Suzy McKee Charnas, *Motherliness*; Samuel Delany, *Tales of Neveryon*; Anne McCaffery, *The Ship Who Sang, Dinosaur Planet*; Vonda McIntyre, *Superluminal, Dreamsnake*; Joanna Russ, *Adventures of Alix, The Female Man*; James Tiptree, Jr., *Star Songs of an Old Primate, Up the Walls of the World*; John Varley, *Titan, Wizard, Demon*.

28   Mary Douglas, *Purity and Danger* (London: Routledge & Kegan Paul, 1966), *Natural Symbols* (London: Cresset Press, 1970).

29   French feminisms contribute to cyborg heteroglossia. Carolyn Burke, "Irigaray through the Looking Glass," *Feminist Studies*, vol. 7, no. 2 (Summer 1981), pp. 288–306; Luce Irigaray, *Ce sexe qui n'en est pas un* (Paris: Minuit, 1977); L. Irigaray, *Et l'une ne bouge pas sans l'autre* (Paris: Minuit, 1979); Elaine Marks and Isabelle de Courtivron, ed., *New French Feminisms* (Amherst: University of Massachusetts Press, 1980); *Signs*, vol. 7, no. 1 (Autumn, 1981), special issue on French feminism; Monique Wittig, *The Lesbian Body*, trans. David LeVay (New York: Avon, 1975; *Le corps lesbien*, 1973).

30   But all these poets are very complex, not least in treatment of themes of lying and erotic, decentered collective and personal identities. Susan Griffin, *Women and Nature: The Roaring Inside Her* (New York: Harper & Row, 1978); Audre Lorde, *Sister Outsider* (New York: Crossing Press, 1984); Adrienne Rich, *The Dream of a Common Language* (New York: Norton, 1978).

31   Jacques Derrida, *Of Grammatology*, trans. and introd. G. C. Spivak (Baltimore: Johns Hopkins University Press, 1976), esp. part II, "Nature, Culture, Writing"; Claude Lévi-Strauss, *Tristes Tropiques*, trans. John Russell (New York, 1961), esp. "The Writing Lesson."

32   Cherrie Moraga, *Loving in the War Years* (Boston: South End Press, 1983). The sharp relation of women of color to writing as theme and politics can be approached through: "The Black Woman and the Diaspora: Hidden Connections and Extended Acknowledgments," An International Literary Conference, Michigan State University, October 1985; Mari Evans, ed., *Black Women Writers: A Critical Evaluation* (Garden City, N.Y.: Doubleday/Anchor, 1984); Dexter Fisher, ed., *The Third Woman: Minority Women Writers of the United States* (Boston: Houghton Mifflin, 1980); several issues of *Frontiers*, esp. vol. 5 (1980), "Chicanas en el Ambiente Nacional" and vol. 7 (1983), "Feminisms in the Non-Western World"; Maxine Hong Kingston, *China Men* (New York: Knopf, 1977); Gerda Lerner, ed., *Black Women in White America: A Documentary History* (New York: Vintage, 1973); Cherrie Moraga and Gloria Anzaldúa, eds., *This Bridge Called My Back: Writings by Radical Women of Color* (Watertown, Mass.: Persephone, 1981); Robin Morgan, ed., *Sisterhood Is Global* (Garden City, N.Y.: Anchor/Doubleday, 1984). The writing of white women has had similar meanings: Sandra Gilbert and Susan Gubar, *The Madwoman in the Attic* (New Haven: Yale University Press, 1979); Joanna Russ, *How to Suppress Women's Writing* (Austin: University of Texas Press, 1983).

33   James Clifford argues persuasively for recognition of continuous cultural reinvention, the stubborn non-disappearance of those "marked" by Western imperializing practices; see "On Ethnographic Allegory: Essays," forthcoming 1985, and "On Ethnographic Authority," *Representations*, vol. 1, no. 2 (1983), pp. 118–146.

34   Page DuBois, *Centaurs and Amazons* (Ann Arbor: University of Michigan Press, 1982); Lorraine Daston and Katharine Park, "Hermaphrodites in Renaissance France," ms., n.d.; Katharine Park and Lorraine Daston, "Unnatural Conceptions: The Study of Monsters in 16th and 17th Century France and England," *Past and Present*, no. 92 (August 1981), pp. 20–54.

Suggestions for further reading

Gray, Chris Hables, Figueroa-Sarreira, Heidi J., and Mentor, Steven (eds.), *The Cyborg Handbook*, New York and London: Routledge, 1995.

Haraway, Donna J., *The Companion Species Manifesto: Dogs, People, and Significant Otherness*, Chicago: Prickly Paradigm Press, 2003.

Hayles, N. Katherine, *How We Became Posthuman: Virtual Bodies in Cybernetics, Literature, and Informatics*, Chicago and London: University of Chicago Press, 1999.

_____

Chapter 24

Gloria Anzaldúa

'HOW TO TAME A WILD TONGUE', 1987

"**W**E'RE GOING TO have to control your tongue," the dentist says, pulling out all the metal from my mouth. Silver bits plop and tinkle into the basin. My mouth is a motherlode.

The dentist is cleaning out my roots. I get a whiff of the stench when I gasp. "I can't cap that tooth yet, you're still draining," he says.

"We're going to have to do something about your tongue," I hear the anger rising in his voice. My tongue keeps pushing out the wads of cotton, pushing back the drills, the long thin needles. "I've never seen anything as strong or as stubborn," he says. And I think, how do you tame a wild tongue, train it to be quiet, how do you bridle and saddle it? How do you make it lie down?

> "Who is to say that robbing a people of its language is less violent than war?"
>
> —Ray Gwyn Smith[1]

I remember being caught speaking Spanish at recess—that was good for three licks on the knuckles with a sharp ruler. I remember being sent to the corner of the classroom for "talking back" to the Anglo teacher when all I was trying to do was tell her how to pronounce my name. "If you want to be American, speak 'American.' If you don't like it, go back to Mexico where you belong."

"I want you to speak English. _Pa'hallar buen trabajo tienes que saber hablar el inglés bien. Qué vale toda tu educación si todavía hablas inglés con un_ 'accent,' " my mother would say, mortified that I spoke English like a Mexican. At Pan American University, I, and all Chicano students were required to take two speech classes. Their purpose: to get rid of our accents.

Attacks on one's form of expression with the intent to censor are a violation

of the First Amendment. *El Anglo con cara de inocente nos arrancó la lengua*. Wild
tongues can't be tamed, they can only be cut out.

Overcoming the tradition of silence

Ahogadas, escupimos el oscuro.
Peleando con nuestra propia sombra
el silencio nos sepulta.

En boca cerrada no entran moscas. "Flies don't enter a closed mouth" is a saying
I kept hearing when I was a child. *Ser habladora* was to be a gossip and a liar, to talk
too much. *Muchachitas bien criadas*, well-bred girls don't answer back. *Es una falta
de respeto* to talk back to one's mother or father. I remember one of the sins I'd
recite to the priest in the confession box the few times I went to confession:
talking back to my mother, *hablar pa' 'trás, repelar. Hocicona, repelona, chismosa*,
having a big mouth, questioning, carrying tales are all signs of being *mal criada*. In
my culture they are all words that are derogatory if applied to women—I've never
heard them applied to men.

The first time I heard two women, a Puerto Rican and a Cuban, say the word
"*nosotras*," I was shocked. I had not known the word existed. Chicanas use *nosotros*
whether we're male or female. We are robbed of our female being by the masculine plural. Language is a male discourse.

And our tongues have become
dry   the wilderness has
dried out our tongues   and
we have forgotten speech.
                    —Irena Klepfisz[2]

Even our own people, other Spanish speakers *nos quieren poner candados en
la boca*. They would hold us back with their bag of *reglas de academia*.

Oyé como ladra: el lenguaje de la frontera

Quien tiene boca se equivoca.
                                        —Mexican saying

"*Pocho*, cultural traitor, you're speaking the oppressor's language by speaking
English, you're ruining the Spanish language," I have been accused by various
Latinos and Latinas. Chicano Spanish is considered by the purist and by most
Latinos deficient, a mutilation of Spanish.

But Chicano Spanish is a border tongue which developed naturally. Change,
evolución, enriquecimiento de palabras nuevas por invención o adopción have created
variants of Chicano Spanish, *un nuevo lenguaje. Un lenguaje que corresponde a un modo
de vivir*. Chicano Spanish is not incorrect, it is a living language.

For a people who are neither Spanish nor live in a country in which Spanish is the first language; for a people who live in a country in which English is the reigning tongue but who are not Anglo; for a people who cannot entirely identify with either standard (formal, Castillian) Spanish nor standard English, what recourse is left to them but to create their own language? A language which they can connect their identity to, one capable of communicating the realities and values true to themselves—a language with terms that are neither *español ni inglés*, but both. We speak a patois, a forked tongue, a variation of two languages.

Chicano Spanish sprang out of the Chicanos' need to identify ourselves as a distinct people. We needed a language with which we could communicate with ourselves, a secret language. For some of us, language is a homeland closer than the Southwest—for many Chicanos today live in the Midwest and the East. And because we are a complex, heterogeneous people, we speak many languages. Some of the languages we speak are:

1   Standard English
2   Working class and slang English
3   Standard Spanish
4   Standard Mexican Spanish
5   North Mexican Spanish dialect
6   Chicano Spanish (Texas, New Mexico, Arizona and California have regional variations)
7   Tex-Mex
8   *Pachuco* (called *caló*)

My "home" tongues are the languages I speak with my sister and brothers, with my friends. They are the last five listed, with 6 and 7 being closest to my heart. From school, the media and job situations, I've picked up standard and working class English. From Mamagrande Locha and from reading Spanish and Mexican literature, I've picked up Standard Spanish and Standard Mexican Spanish. From *los recién llegados*, Mexican immigrants, and *braceros*, I learned the North Mexican dialect. With Mexicans I'll try to speak either Standard Mexican Spanish or the North Mexican dialect. From my parents and Chicanos living in the Valley, I picked up Chicano Texas Spanish, and I speak it with my mom, younger brother (who married a Mexican and who rarely mixes Spanish with English), aunts and older relatives.

With Chicanas from *Nuevo México* or *Arizona* I will speak Chicano Spanish a little, but often they don't understand what I'm saying. With most California Chicanas I speak entirely in English (unless I forget). When I first moved to San Francisco, I'd rattle off something in Spanish, unintentionally embarrassing them. Often it is only with another Chicana *tejana* that I can talk freely.

Words distorted by English are known as anglicisms or *pochismos*. The *pocho* is an anglicized Mexican or American of Mexican origin who speaks Spanish with an accent characteristic of North Americans and who distorts and reconstructs the language according to the influence of English.[3] Tex-Mex, or Spanglish, comes most naturally to me. I may switch back and forth from English to Spanish in the same sentence or in the same word. With my sister and my brother Nune and with Chicano *tejano* contemporaries I speak in Tex-Mex.

From kids and people my own age I picked up *Pachuco. Pachuco* (the language of the zoot suiters) is a language of rebellion, both against Standard Spanish and Standard English. It is a secret language. Adults of the culture and outsiders cannot understand it. It is made up of slang words from both English and Spanish. *Ruca* means girl or woman, *vato* means guy or dude, *chale* means no, *simón* means yes, *churo* is sure, talk is *periquiar, pigionear* means petting, *que gacho* means how nerdy, *ponte águila* means watch out, death is called *la pelona*. Through lack of practice and not having others who can speak it, I've lost most of the *Pachuco* tongue.

Chicano Spanish

Chicanos, after 250 years of Spanish/Anglo colonization have developed significant differences in the Spanish we speak. We collapse two adjacent vowels into a single syllable and sometimes shift the stress in certain words such as *maíz/maiz, cohete/cuete*. We leave out certain consonants when they appear between vowels: *lado/lao, mojado/mojao*. Chicanos from South Texas pronounced *f* as *j* as in *jue (fue)*. Chicanos use "archaisms," words that are no longer in the Spanish language, words that have been evolved out. We say *semos, truje, haiga, ansina*, and *naiden*. We retain the "archaic" *j*, as in *jalar*, that derives from an earlier *h*, (the French *halar* or the Germanic *halon* which was lost to standard Spanish in the 16th century), but which is still found in several regional dialects such as the one spoken in South Texas. (Due to geography, Chicanos from the Valley of South Texas were cut off linguistically from other Spanish speakers. We tend to use words that the Spaniards brought over from Medieval Spain. The majority of the Spanish colonizers in Mexico and the Southwest came from Extremadura—Hernán Cortés was one of them—and Andalucía. Andalucians pronounce *ll* like a *y*, and their *d*'s tend to be absorbed by adjacent vowels: *tirado* becomes *tirao*. They brought *el lenguaje popular, dialectos y regionalismos.*[4])

Chicanos and other Spanish speakers also shift *ll* to *y* and *z* to *s*.[5] We leave out initial syllables, saying *tar* for *estar, toy* for *estoy, hora* for *ahora* (*cubanos* and *puertorriqueños* also leave out initial letters of some words.) We also leave out the final syllable such as *pa* for *para*. The intervocalic *y*, the *ll* as in *tortilla, ella, hotella*, gets replaced by *tortia* or *tortiya, ea, botea*. We add an additional syllable at the beginning of certain words: *atocar* for *tocar, agastar* for *gastar*. Sometimes we'll say *lavaste las vacijas*, other times *lavates* (substituting the *ates* verb endings for the *aste*).

We use anglicisms, words borrowed from English: *bola* from ball, *carpeta* from carpet, *máchina de lavar* (instead of *lavadora*) from washing machine. Tex-Mex argot, created by adding a Spanish sound at the beginning or end of an English word such as *cookiar* for cook, *watchar* for watch, *parkiar* for park, and *rapiar* for rape, is the result of the pressure on Spanish speakers to adapt to English.

We don't use the word *vosotros/as* or its accompanying verb form. We don't say *claro* (to mean yes), *imagínate*, or *me emociona*, unless we picked up Spanish from Latinas, out of a book, or in a classroom. Other Spanish-speaking groups are going through the same, or similar, development in their Spanish.

Linguistic terrorism

Deslenguadas. Somos los del español deficiente. We are your linguistic nightmare, your linguistic aberration, your linguistic *mestizaje*, the subject of your *burla*. Because we speak with tongues of fire we are culturally crucified. Racially, culturally and linguistically *somos huérfanos*—we speak an orphan tongue.

Chicanas who grew up speaking Chicano Spanish have internalized the belief that we speak poor Spanish. It is illegitimate, a bastard language. And because we internalize how our language has been used against us by the dominant culture, we use our language differences against each other.

Chicana feminists often skirt around each other with suspicion and hesitation. For the longest time I couldn't figure it out. Then it dawned on me. To be close to another Chicana is like looking into the mirror. We are afraid of what we'll see there. *Pena.* Shame. Low estimation of self. In childhood we are told that our language is wrong. Repeated attacks on our native tongue diminish our sense of self. The attacks continue throughout our lives.

Chicanas feel uncomfortable talking in Spanish to Latinas, afraid of their censure. Their language was not outlawed in their countries. They had a whole lifetime of being immersed in their native tongue; generations, centuries in which Spanish was a first language, taught in school, heard on radio and TV, and read in the newspaper.

If a person, Chicana or Latina, has a low estimation of my native tongue, she also has a low estimation of me. Often with *mexicanas y latinas* we'll speak English as a neutral language. Even among Chicanas we tend to speak English at parties or conferences. Yet, at the same time, we're afraid the other will think we're *agringadas* because we don't speak Chicano Spanish. We oppress each other trying to out-Chicano each other, vying to be the "real" Chicanas, to speak like Chicanos. There is no one Chicano language just as there is no one Chicano experience. A monolingual Chicana whose first language is English or Spanish is just as much a Chicana as one who speaks several variants of Spanish. A Chicana from Michigan or Chicago or Detroit is just as much a Chicana as one from the Southwest. Chicano Spanish is as diverse linguistically as it is regionally.

By the end of this century, Spanish speakers will comprise the biggest minority group in the U.S., a country where students in high schools and colleges are encouraged to take French classes because French is considered more "cultured." But for a language to remain alive it must be used.[6] By the end of this century English, and not Spanish, will be the mother tongue of most Chicanos and Latinos.

So, if you want to really hurt me, talk badly about my language. Ethnic identity is twin skin to linguistic identity—I am my language. Until I can take pride in my language, I cannot take pride in myself. Until I can accept as legitimate Chicano Texas Spanish, Tex-Mex and all the other languages I speak, I cannot accept the legitimacy of myself. Until I am free to write bilingually and to switch codes without having always to translate, while I still have to speak English or Spanish when I would rather speak Spanglish, and as long as I have to accommodate the

English speakers rather than having them accommodate me, my tongue will be illegitimate.

I will no longer be made to feel ashamed of existing. I will have my voice: Indian, Spanish, white. I will have my serpent's tongue—my woman's voice, my sexual voice, my poet's voice. I will overcome the tradition of silence.

> My fingers
> move sly against your palm
> Like women everywhere, we speak in code. . . .
> —Melanie Kaye/Kantrowitz[7]

"*Vistas*," *corridos, y comida:* my native tongue

In the 1960s, I read my first Chicano novel. It was *City of Night* by John Rechy, a gay Texan, son of a Scottish father and a Mexican mother. For days I walked around in stunned amazement that a Chicano could write and could get published. When I read *I Am Joaquín*[8] I was surprised to see a bilingual book by a Chicano in print. When I saw poetry written in Tex-Mex for the first time, a feeling of pure joy flashed through me. I felt like we really existed as a people. In 1971, when I started teaching High School English to Chicano students, I tried to supplement the required texts with works by Chicanos, only to be reprimanded and forbidden to do so by the principal. He claimed that I was supposed to teach "American" and English literature. At the risk of being fired, I swore my students to secrecy and slipped in Chicano short stories, poems, a play. In graduate school, while working toward a Ph.D., I had to "argue" with one advisor after the other, semester after semester, before I was allowed to make Chicano literature an area of focus.

Even before I read books by Chicanos or Mexicans, it was the Mexican movies I saw at the drive-in—the Thursday night special of $1.00 a carload—that gave me a sense of belonging. "*Vámonos a las vistas*," my mother would call out and we'd all—grandmother, brothers, sister and cousins—squeeze into the car. We'd wolf down cheese and bologna white bread sandwiches while watching Pedro Infante in melodramatic tear-jerkers like *Nosotros los pobres*, the first "real" Mexican movie (that was not an imitation of European movies). I remember seeing *Cuando los hijos se van* and surmising that all Mexican movies played up the love a mother has for her children and what ungrateful sons and daughters suffer when they are not devoted to their mothers. I remember the singing-type "westerns" of Jorge Negrete and Miguel Aceves Mejía. When watching Mexican movies, I felt a sense of homecoming as well as alienation. People who were to amount to something didn't go to Mexican movies, or *bailes* or tune their radios to *bolero, rancherita*, and *corrido* music.

The whole time I was growing up, there was *norteño* music sometimes called North Mexican border music, or Tex-Mex music, or Chicano music, or *cantina* (bar) music. I grew up listening to *conjuntos*, three- or four-piece bands made up of folk musicians playing guitar, *bajo sexto*, drums and button accordion, which Chicanos had borrowed from the German immigrants who had come to Central Texas and Mexico to farm and build breweries. In the Rio Grande Valley, Steve Jordan and Little Joe Hernández were popular, and Flaco Jiménez was the accordion king. The rhythms of Tex-Mex music are those of the polka, also adapted from the Germans, who in turn had borrowed the polka from the Czechs and Bohemians.

I remember the hot, sultry evenings when *corridos*—songs of love and death on the Texas-Mexican borderlands—reverberated out of cheap amplifiers from the local *cantinas* and wafted in through my bedroom window.

Corridos first became widely used along the South Texas/Mexican border during the early conflict between Chicanos and Anglos. The *corridos* are usually about Mexican heroes who do valiant deeds against the Anglo oppressors. Pancho Villa's song, "*La cucaracha*," is the most famous one. *Corridos* of John F. Kennedy and his death are still very popular in the Valley. Older Chicanos remember Lydia Mendoza, one of the great border *corrido* singers who was called *la Gloria de Tejas*. Her "*El tango negro*," sung during the Great Depression, made her a singer of the people. The everpresent *corridos* narrated one hundred years of border history, bringing news of events as well as entertaining. These folk musicians and folk songs are our chief cultural mythmakers, and they made our hard lives seem bearable.

I grew up feeling ambivalent about our music. Country-western and rock-and-roll had more status. In the 50s and 60s, for the slightly educated and *agringado* Chicanos, there existed a sense of shame at being caught listening to our music. Yet I couldn't stop my feet from thumping to the music, could not stop humming the words, nor hide from myself the exhilaration I felt when I heard it.

There are more subtle ways that we internalize identification, especially in the forms of images and emotions. For me food and certain smells are tied to my identity, to my homeland. Woodsmoke curling up to an immense blue sky; wood-smoke perfuming my grandmother's clothes, her skin. The stench of cow manure and the yellow patches on the ground; the crack of a .22 rifle and the reek of cordite. Homemade white cheese sizzling in a pan, melting inside a folded *tortilla*. My sister Hilda's hot, spicy *menudo, chile colorado* making it deep red, pieces of *panza* and hominy floating on top. My brother Carito barbecuing *fajitas* in the backyard. Even now and 3,000 miles away, I can see my mother spicing the ground beef, pork and venison with *chile*. My mouth salivates at the thought of the hot steaming *tamales* I would be eating if I were home.

Si le preguntas a mi mamá, "¿Qué eres?"

> "Identity is the essential core of who we are as individuals, the conscious experience of the self inside."
>
> —Kaufman[9]

Nosotros los Chicanos straddle the borderlands. On one side of us, we are constantly exposed to the Spanish of the Mexicans, on the other side we hear the Anglos' incessant clamoring so that we forget our language. Among ourselves we don't say *nosotros los americanos, o nosotros los españoles, o nosotros los hispanos*. We say *nosotros los mexicanos* (by *mexicanos* we do not mean citizens of Mexico; we do not mean a national identity, but a racial one). We distinguish between *mexicanos del otro lado* and *mexicanos de este lado*. Deep in our hearts we believe that being Mexican has nothing to do with which country one lives in. Being Mexican is a state of soul—not one of mind, not one of citizenship. Neither eagle nor serpent, but both. And like the ocean, neither animal respects borders.

> *Dime con quien andas y te diré quien eres.*
> (Tell me who your friends are and I'll tell you who you are.)
> —Mexican saying

Si le preguntas a mi mamá, "¿Qué eres?" te dirá, "Soy mexicana." My brothers and sister say the same. I sometimes will answer *"soy mexicana"* and at others will say *"soy Chicana"* or *"soy tejana."* But I identified as *"Raza"* before I ever identified as *"mexicana"* or "Chicana."

As a culture, we call ourselves Spanish when referring to ourselves as a linguistic group and when copping out. It is then that we forget our predominant Indian genes. We are 70 to 80% Indian.[10] We call ourselves Hispanic[11] or Spanish-American or Latin American or Latin when linking ourselves to other Spanish-speaking peoples of the Western hemisphere and when copping out. We call ourselves Mexican-American[12] to signify we are neither Mexican nor American, but more the noun "American" than the adjective "Mexican" (and when copping out).

Chicanos and other people of color suffer economically for not acculturating. This voluntary (yet forced) alienation makes for psychological conflict, a kind of dual identity—we don't identify with the Anglo-American cultural values and we don't totally identify with the Mexican cultural values. We are a synergy of two cultures with various degrees of Mexicanness or Angloness. I have so internalized the borderland conflict that sometimes I feel like one cancels out the other and we are zero, nothing, no one. *A veces no soy nada ni nadie. Pero hasta cuando no lo soy, lo soy.*

When not copping out, when we know we are more than nothing, we call ourselves Mexican, referring to race and ancestry; *mestizo* when affirming both our Indian and Spanish (but we hardly ever own our Black ancestry); Chicano when referring to a politically aware people born and/or raised in the U.S.; *Raza* when referring to Chicanos; *tejanos* when we are Chicanos from Texas.

Chicanos did not know we were a people until 1965 when Cesar Chavez and the farmworkers united and *I Am Joaquín* was published and *la Raza Unida* party was formed in Texas. With that recognition, we became a distinct people. Something momentous happened to the Chicano soul—we became aware of our reality and acquired a name and a language (Chicano Spanish) that reflected that reality. Now that we had a name, some of the fragmented pieces began to fall together— who we were, what we were, how we had evolved. We began to get glimpses of what we might eventually become.

Yet the struggle of identities continues, the struggle of borders is our reality still. One day the inner struggle will cease and a true integration take place. In the meantime, *tenemos que haceria lucha. ¿Quién está protegiendo los ranchos de mí gente? Quién está tratando de cerrar la fisura entre la india y el blanco en nuestra sangre? El Chicano, sí, el Chicano que anda como un ladrón en su propia casa.*

Los Chicanos, how patient we seem, how very patient. There is the quiet of the Indian about us.[13] We know how to survive. When other races have given up their tongue, we've kept ours. We know what it is to live under the hammer blow of the dominant *norteamericano* culture. But more than we count the blows, we count the days the weeks the years the centuries the eons until the white laws and commerce and customs will rot in the deserts they've created, lie bleached. *Humildes* yet proud, *quietos* yet wild, *nosotros los mexicanos*-Chicanos will walk by the crumbling ashes as we go about our business. Stubborn, persevering, impenetrable as stone, yet possessing a malleability that renders us unbreakable, we, the *mestizas* and *mestizos*, will remain.

Notes

1 Ray Gwyn Smith, *Moorland is Cold Country*, unpublished book.
2 Irena Klepfisz, "*Di rayze aheym*/The Journey Home," in *The Tribe of Dina: A Jewish Women's Anthology*, Melanie Kay/Kantrowitz and Irena Klepfisz, eds. (Montpelier, VT: Sinister Wisdom Books, 1986), 49.
3 R.C. Ortega, *Dialectología Del Barrio*, trans. Hortencia S. Alwan (Los Angeles, CA: R.C. Ortega Publisher & Bookseller, 1977), 132.
4 Eduardo Hernandéz-Chávez, Andrew D. Cohen, and Anthony F. Beltramo, *El Lenguaje de los Chicanos: Regional and Social Characteristics of Language Used By Mexican Americans* (Arlington, VA: Center for Applied Linguistics, 1975), 39.
5 Hernandéz-Chávez, xvii.
6 Irena Klepfisz, "Secular Jewish Identity: Yidishkayt in America," in *The Tribe of Dina* Kaye/Kantrowitz and Klepfisz, eds., 43.
7 Melanie Kaye/Kantrowitz, "Sign," in *We Speak In Code: Poems and Other Writings* (Pittsburgh, PA: Motheroot Publications, Inc., 1980), 85.
8 Rodolfo Gonzales, *I Am Joaquín/Yo Soy Joaquín* (New York, NY: Bantam Books, 1972). It was first published in 1967.
9 Gershen Kaufman, *Shame: The Power of Caring* (Cambridge, MA: Schenkman Books, Inc. 1980), 68.
10 John R. Chávez, *The Lost Land: The Chicano Images of the Southwest* (Albuquerque, NM: University of New Mexico Press, 1984), 88–90.
11 "Hispanic" is derived from *Hispanis* (*España*, a name given to the Iberian Peninsula in ancient times when it was a part of the Roman Empire) and is a term designated by the U.S. government to make it easier to handle us on paper.
12 The Treaty of Guadalupe Hidalgo created the Mexican-American in 1848.
13 Anglos, in order to alleviate their guilt for dispossessing the Chicano, stressed the Spanish part of us and perpetrated the myth of the Spanish Southwest. We have accepted the fiction that we are Hispanic, that is Spanish, in order to accommodate ourselves to the dominant culture and its abhorrence of Indians. Chávez, 88–91.

Suggestions for further reading

Bhabha, Homi K., *The Location of Culture*, London and New York: Routledge, 1994.
Chabram-Dernersesian, Angie (ed.), *The Chicano/a Studies Reader,* New York and London: Routledge, 2006.
Young, Robert, *Colonial Desire: Hybridity in Theory, Culture, and Race*, London and New York: Routledge, 1995.

Chapter 25

Judith Butler

'IMITATION AND GENDER INSUBORDINATION',[1] 1991

So what is this divided being introduced into language through gender? It is an impossible being, it is a being that does not exist, an ontological joke.

Monique Wittig [2]

Beyond physical repetition and the psychical or metaphysical repetition, is there an *ontological* repetition? . . . This ultimate repetition, this ultimate theatre, gathers everything in a certain way; and in another way, it destroys everything; and in yet another way, it selects from everything.

Gilles Deleuze [3]

To theorize as a lesbian?

AT FIRST I considered writing a different sort of essay, one with a philosophical tone: the "being" of being homosexual. The prospect of *being* anything, even for pay, has always produced in me a certain anxiety, for "to be" gay, "to be" lesbian seems to be more than a simple injunction to become who or what I already am. And in no way does it settle the anxiety for me to say that this is "part" of what I am. To write or speak *as a lesbian* appears a paradoxical appearance of this "I," one which feels neither true nor false. For it is a production, usually in response to a request, to come out or write in the name of an identity which, once produced, sometimes functions as a politically efficacious phantasm. I'm not at ease with "lesbian theories, gay theories," for as I've argued elsewhere,[4] identity categories tend to be instruments of regulatory regimes, whether as the normalizing categories of oppressive structures or as the rallying points for a liberatory contestation of that very oppression. This is not to say that I will not appear at political occasions under the sign of lesbian, but that I would like to have it permanently unclear what precisely that sign signifies. So it is unclear how it is that I can contribute to this book and appear under its title, for it announces a set of terms that I propose to contest. One risk I take is to be recolonized by the sign under which I write, and so it is this risk that I seek to thematize. To propose that the invocation of identity is always a risk does not imply that resistance to it is always or only symptomatic of a self-inflicted homophobia. Indeed, a Foucaultian perspective might argue that the affirmation of "homosexuality" is itself an extension of a homophobic discourse. And yet "discourse," he writes on the same page, "can be both an instrument and an effect of power, but also a hindrance, a stumbling-block, a point of resistance and a starting point for an opposing strategy."[5]

So I am skeptical about how the "I" is determined as it operates under the title of the lesbian sign, and I am no more comfortable with its homophobic determination than with those normative definitions offered by other members of the "gay or lesbian community." I'm permanently troubled by identity categories, consider them to be invariable stumbling-blocks, and understand them, even promote them, as sites of necessary trouble. In fact, if the category were to offer no trouble, it would cease to be interesting to me: it is precisely the *pleasure* produced by the instability of those categories which sustains the various erotic practices that make me a candidate for the category to begin with. To install myself within the terms of an identity category would be to turn against the sexuality that the category purports to describe; and this might be true for any identity category which seeks to control the very eroticism that it claims to describe and authorize, much less "liberate."

And what's worse, I do not understand the notion of "theory," and am hardly interested in being cast as its defender, much less in being signified as part of an elite gay/lesbian theory crowd that seeks to establish the legitimacy and domestication of gay/lesbian studies within the academy. Is there a pregiven distinction between theory, politics, culture, media? How do those divisions operate to quell a certain intertextual writing that might well generate wholly different epistemic maps? But I am writing here now: is it too late? Can this writing, can any writing, refuse the terms by which it is appropriated even as, to some extent, that very colonizing discourse enables or produces this stumbling block, this resistance? How do I relate the paradoxical situation of this dependency and refusal?

If the political task is to show that theory is never merely *theoria*, in the sense of disengaged contemplation, and to insist that it is fully political (*phronesis* or even *praxis*), then why not simply call this operation *politics*, or some necessary permutation of it?

I have begun with confessions of trepidation and a series of disclaimers, but perhaps it will become clear that *disclaiming*, which is no simple activity, will be what I have to offer as a form of affirmative resistance to a certain regulatory operation of homophobia. The discourse of "coming out" has clearly served its purposes, but what are its risks? And here I am not speaking of unemployment or public attack or violence, which are quite clearly and widely on the increase against those who are perceived as "out" whether or not of their own design. Is the "subject" who is "out" free of its subjection and finally in the clear? Or could it be that the subjection that subjectivates the gay or lesbian subject in some ways continues to oppress, or oppresses most insidiously, once "outness" is claimed? What or who is it that is "out," made manifest and fully disclosed, when and if I reveal myself as lesbian? What is it that is now known, anything? What remains permanently concealed by the very linguistic act that offers up the promise of a transparent revelation of sexuality? Can sexuality even remain sexuality once it submits to a criterion of transparency and disclosure, or does it perhaps cease to be sexuality precisely when the semblance of full explicitness is achieved?[6] Is sexuality of any kind even possible without that opacity designated by the unconscious, which means simply that the conscious "I" who would reveal its sexuality is perhaps the last to know the meaning of what it says?

To claim that this is what I *am* is to suggest a provisional totalization of this "I." But if the I can so determine itself, then that which it excludes in order to make that determination remains constitutive of the determination itself. In other words, such a statement presupposes that the "I" exceeds its determination, and even produces that very excess in and by the act which seeks to exhaust the semantic field of that "I." In the act which would disclose the true and full content of that "I," a certain radical *concealment* is thereby produced. For it is always finally unclear what is meant by invoking the lesbian-signifier, since its signification is always to some degree out of one's control, but also because its *specificity* can only be demarcated by exclusions that return to disrupt its claim to coherence. What, if anything, can lesbians be said to share? And who will decide this question, and in the name of whom? If I claim to be a lesbian, I "come out" only to produce a new and different "closet." The "you" to whom I come out now has access to a different region of opacity. Indeed, the locus of opacity has simply shifted: before, you did not know whether I "am," but now you do not know what that means, which is to say that the copula is empty, that it cannot be substituted for with a set of descriptions.[7] And perhaps that is a situation to be valued. Conventionally, one comes out *of* the closet (and yet, how often is it the case that we are "outted" when we are young and without resources?); so we are out of the closet, but into what? what new unbounded spatiality? the room, the den, the attic, the basement, the house, the bar, the university, some new enclosure whose door, like Kafka's door, produces the expectation of a fresh air and a light of illumination that never arrives? Curiously, it is the figure of the closet that produces this expectation, and which guarantees its dissatisfaction. For being "out" always depends to some extent on being "in"; it gains its meaning only within that polarity. Hence, being "out" must produce the closet again and again in order to maintain itself as "out." In this sense, *outness* can only produce a new opacity; and *the closet* produces the promise of a disclosure that can, by definition, never come. Is this infinite postponement of the disclosure of "gayness," produced by the very act of "coming out," to be lamented? Or is this very deferral of the signified *to be valued*, a site for the production of values, precisely because the term now takes on a life that cannot be, can never be, permanently controlled?

It is possible to argue that whereas no transparent or full revelation is afforded by "lesbian" and "gay," there remains a political imperative to use these necessary errors or category mistakes, as it were (what Gayatri Spivak might call "catachrestic" operations: to use a proper name improperly[8]), to rally and represent an oppressed political constituency. Clearly, I am not legislating against the use of the term. My question is simply: which use will be legislated, and what play will there be between legislation and use such that the instrumental uses of "identity" do not become regulatory imperatives? If it is already true that "lesbians" and "gay men" have been traditionally designated as impossible identities, errors of classification, unnatural disasters within juridico-medical discourses, or, what perhaps amounts to the same, the very paradigm of what calls to be classified, regulated, and controlled, then perhaps these sites of disruption, error, confusion, and trouble can be the very rallying points for a certain resistance to classification and to identity as such.

The question is not one of *avowing* or *disavowing* the category of lesbian or gay, but, rather, why it is that the category becomes the site of this "ethical" choice? What does it mean to *avow* a category that can only maintain its specificity and coherence by performing a prior set of *disavowals?* Does this make "coming out" into the avowal of disavowal, that is, a return to the closet under the guise of an escape? And it is not something like heterosexuality or bisexuality that is disavowed by the category, but a set of identificatory and practical crossings between these categories that renders the discreteness of each equally suspect. Is it not possible to maintain and pursue heterosexual identifications and aims within homosexual practice, and homosexual identifications and aims within heterosexual practices? If a sexuality is to be disclosed, what will be taken as the true determinant of its meaning: the phantasy structure, the act, the orifice, the gender, the anatomy? And if the practice engages a complex interplay of all of those, which one of these erotic dimensions will come to stand for the sexuality that requires them all? Is it the *specificity* of a lesbian experience or lesbian desire or lesbian sexuality that lesbian theory needs to elucidate? Those efforts have only and always produced a set of contests and refusals which should by now make it clear that there is no necessarily common element among lesbians, except perhaps that we all know something about how homophobia works against women—although, even then, the language and the analysis we use will differ.

To argue that there might be a *specificity* to lesbian sexuality has seemed a necessary counterpoint to the claim that lesbian sexuality is just heterosexuality once removed, or that it is derived, or that it does not exist. But perhaps the claim of specificity, on the one hand, and the claim of derivativeness or non-existence, on the other, are not as contradictory as they seem. Is it not possible that lesbian sexuality is a process that reinscribes the power domains that it resists, that it is constituted in part from the very heterosexual matrix that it seeks to displace, and that its specificity is to be established, not *outside* or *beyond* that reinscription or reiteration, but in the very modality and effects of that reinscription? In other words, the negative constructions of lesbianism as a fake or a bad copy can be occupied and reworked to call into question the claims of heterosexual priority. In a sense I hope to make clear in what follows, lesbian sexuality can be understood to redeploy its 'derivativeness' in the service of displacing hegemonic heterosexual norms. Understood in this way, the political problem is not to establish the specificity of lesbian sexuality over and against its derivativeness, but to turn the homophobic construction of the bad copy against the framework that privileges heterosexuality as origin, and so 'derive' the former from the latter. This description requires a reconsideration of imitation, drag, and other forms of sexual crossing that affirm the internal complexity of a lesbian sexuality constituted in part within the very matrix of power that it is compelled both to reiterate and to oppose.

On the being of gayness as necessary drag

The professionalization of gayness requires a certain performance and production of a "self" which is the *constituted effect* of a discourse that nevertheless claims to "represent" that self as a prior truth. When I spoke at the conference on homosexuality in 1989,[9] I found myself telling my friends beforehand that I was off to Yale to be a lesbian, which of course didn't mean that I wasn't one before, but that somehow then, as I spoke in that context, I *was* one in some more thorough and totalizing way, at least for the time being. So I *am* one, and my qualifications are even fairly unambiguous. Since I was sixteen, being a lesbian is what I've been. So what's the anxiety, the discomfort? Well, it has something to do with that redoubling, the way I can say, I'm going to Yale to be a lesbian; a lesbian is what I've been being for so long. How is it that I can both "be" one, and yet endeavor to be one at the same time? When and where does my being a lesbian come into play, when and where does this playing a lesbian constitute something like what I am? To say that I "play" at being one is not to say that I am not one "really"; rather, how and where I play at being one is the way in which that "being" gets established, instituted, circulated, and confirmed. This is not a performance from which I can take radical distance, for this is deep-seated play, psychically entrenched play, *and this "I" does not play its lesbianism as a role*. Rather, it is through the repeated play of this sexuality that the "I" is insistently reconstituted as a lesbian "I"; paradoxically, it is precisely the *repetition* of that play that establishes as well the *instability* of the very category that it constitutes. For if the "I" is a site of repetition, that is, if the "I" only achieves the semblance of identity through a certain repetition of itself, then the I is always displaced by the very repetition that sustains it. In other words, does or can the "I" ever repeat itself, cite itself, faithfully, or is there always a displacement from its former moment that establishes the permanently non-self-identical status of that "I" or its "being lesbian"? What "performs" does not exhaust the "I"; it does not lay out in visible terms the comprehensive content of that "I," for if the performance is "repeated," there is always the question of what differentiates from each other the moments of identity that are repeated. And if the "I" is the effect of a certain repetition, one which produces the semblance of a continuity or coherence, then there is no "I" that precedes the gender that it is said to perform; the repetition, and the failure to repeat, produce a string of performances that constitute and contest the coherence of that "I."

But *politically*, we might argue, isn't it quite crucial to insist on lesbian and gay identities precisely because they are being threatened with erasure and obliteration from homophobic quarters? Isn't the above theory *complicitous* with those political forces that would obliterate the possibility of gay and lesbian identity? Isn't it "no accident" that such theoretical contestations of identity emerge within a political climate that is performing a set of similar obliterations of homosexual identities through legal and political means?

The question I want to raise in return is this: ought such threats of obliteration dictate the terms of the political resistance to them, and if they do, do such homophobic efforts to that extent win the battle from the start? There is no question that gays and lesbians are threatened by the violence of public erasure, but the decision to counter that violence must be careful not to reinstall another in its place. Which version of lesbian or gay ought to be rendered visible, and which internal exclusions will that rendering visible institute? Can the visibility of identity *suffice* as a political strategy, or can it only be the starting point for a strategic intervention which calls for a transformation of policy? Is it not a sign of despair over public politics when identity becomes its own policy, bringing with it those who would 'police' it from various sides? And this is not a call to return to silence or invisibility, but, rather, to make use of a category that can be called into question, made to account for what it excludes. That any consolidation of identity requires some set of differentiations and exclusions seems clear. But which ones ought to be valorized? That the identity-sign I use now has its purposes seems right, but there is no way to predict or control the political uses to which that sign will be put in the future. And perhaps this is a kind of openness, regardless of its risks, that ought to be safeguarded for political reasons. If the rendering visible of lesbian/gay identity now presupposes a set of exclusions, then perhaps part of what is necessarily excluded is *the future uses of the sign*. There is a political necessity to use some sign now, and we do, but how to use it in such a way that its futural significations are not *foreclosed*? How to use the sign and avow its temporal contingency at once?

In avowing the sign's strategic provisionality (rather than its strategic essentialism), that identity can become a site of contest and revision, indeed, take on a future set of significations that those of us who use it now may not be able to foresee. It is in the safeguarding of the future of the political signifiers—preserving the signifier as a site of rearticulation—that Laclau and Mouffe discern its democratic promise.

Within contemporary U.S. politics, there are a vast number of ways in which lesbianism in particular is understood as precisely that which cannot or dare not *be*. In a sense, Jesse Helms's attack on the NEA for sanctioning representations of "homoeroticism" focuses various homophobic fantasies of what gay men are and do on the work of Robert Mapplethorpe.[10] In a sense, for Helms, gay men exist as objects of prohibition; they are, in his twisted fantasy, sadomasochistic exploiters of children, the paradigmatic exemplars of "obscenity"; in a sense, the lesbian is not even produced within this discourse as a prohibited object. Here it becomes important to recognize that oppression works not merely through acts of overt prohibition, but covertly, through the constitution of viable subjects and through the corollary constitution of a domain of unviable (un)subjects—abjects, we might call them—who are neither named nor prohibited within the economy of the law. Here oppression works through the production of a domain of unthinkability and unnameability. Lesbianism is not explicitly prohibited in part because it has not even made its way into the thinkable, the imaginable, that grid of cultural intelligibility that regulates the real and the nameable. How, then, to "be" a lesbian in a political context in which the lesbian does not exist? That is, in a political discourse that wages its violence against lesbianism in part by excluding lesbianism from discourse itself? To be prohibited explicitly is to occupy a discursive site from which something like a reverse-discourse can be articulated; to be implicitly proscribed is not even to qualify as an object of prohibition.[11] And though homo-sexualities of all kinds in this present climate are being erased, reduced, and (then) reconstituted as sites of radical homophobic fantasy, it is important to retrace the different routes by which the unthinkability of homosexuality is being constituted time and again.

It is one thing to be erased from discourse, and yet another to be present within discourse as an abiding falsehood. Hence, there is a political imperative to render lesbianism visible, but how is that to be done outside or through existing regulatory regimes? Can the exclusion from ontology itself become a rallying point for resistance?

Here is something like a confession which is meant merely to thematize the impossibility of confession: As a young person, I suffered for a long time, and I suspect many people have, from being told, explicitly or implicitly, that what I "am" is a copy, an imitation, a derivative example, a shadow of the real. Compul-sory heterosexuality sets itself up as the original, the true, the authentic; the norm that determines the real implies that "being" lesbian is always a kind of miming, a vain effort to participate in the phantasmatic plenitude of naturalized heterosexual-ity which will always and only fail.[12] And yet, I remember quite distinctly when I first read in Esther Newton's *Mother Camp: Female Impersonators in America*[13] that drag is not an imitation or a copy of some prior and true gender; according to Newton, drag enacts the very structure of impersonation by which *any gender* is assumed. Drag is not the putting on of a gender that belongs properly to some other group, i.e. an act of *expropriation* or *appropriation* that assumes that gender is the rightful property of sex, that "masculine" belongs to "male" and "feminine" belongs to "female." There is no "proper" gender, a gender proper to one sex rather than another, which is in some sense that sex's cultural property. Where that notion of the "proper" operates, it is always and only *improperly* installed as the effect of a compulsory system. Drag constitutes the mundane way in which gen-ders are appropriated, theatricalized, worn, and done; it implies that all gendering is a kind of impersonation and approximation. If this is true, it seems, there is no original or primary gender that drag imitates, but *gender is a kind of imitation for which there is no original;* in fact, it is a kind of imitation that produces the very notion of the original as an *effect* and consequence of the imitation itself. In other words, the naturalistic effects of heterosexualized genders are produced through imitative strategies; what they imitate is a phantasmatic ideal of heterosexual identity, one that is produced by the imitation as its effect. In this sense, the "reality" of heterosexual identities is performatively constituted through an imita-tion that sets itself up as the origin and the ground of all imitations. In other words, heterosexuality is always in the process of imitating and approximating its own phantasmatic idealization of itself—*and failing*. Precisely because it is bound to fail, and yet endeavors to succeed, the project of heterosexual identity is propelled into an endless repetition of itself. Indeed, in its efforts to naturalize itself as the original, heterosexuality must be understood as a compulsive and compulsory repetition that can only produce the *effect* of its own originality; in other words, compulsory heterosexual identities, those ontologically consolidated phantasms of "man" and "woman," are theatrically produced effects that posture as grounds, origins, the normative measure of the real.[14]

Reconsider then the homophobic charge that queens and butches and femmes are imitations of the heterosexual real. Here "imitation" carries the meaning of "derivative" or "secondary," a copy of an origin which is itself the ground of all copies, but which is itself a copy of nothing. Logically, this notion of an "origin" is suspect, for how can something operate as an origin if there are no secondary consequences which retrospectively confirm the originality of that origin? The origin requires its derivations in order to affirm itself as an origin, for origins only make sense to the extent that they are differentiated from that which they produce as derivatives. Hence, if it were not for the notion of the homosexual *as* copy, there would be no construct of heterosexuality *as* origin. Heterosexuality here presupposes homosexuality. And if the homosexual *as* copy *precedes* the heterosexual as *origin*, then it seems only fair to concede that the copy comes before the origin, and that homosexuality is thus the origin, and heterosexuality the copy.

But simple inversions are not really possible. For it is only *as* a copy that homosexuality can be argued to *precede* heterosexuality as the origin. In other words, the entire framework of copy and origin proves radically unstable as each position inverts into the other and confounds the possibility of any stable way to locate the temporal or logical priority of either term.

But let us then consider this problematic inversion from a psychic/political perspective. If the structure of gender imitation is such that the imitat*ed* is to some degree produced—or, rather, *re*produced—by imitation (see again Derrida's inversion and displacement of mimesis in "The Double Session"), then to claim that gay and lesbian identities are implicated in heterosexual norms or in hegemonic culture generally is not to *derive* gayness from straightness. On the contrary, *imitation* does not copy that which is prior, but produces and *inverts* the very terms of priority and derivativeness. Hence, if gay identities are implicated in heterosexuality, that is not the same as claiming that they are determined or derived from heterosexuality, and it is not the same as claiming that that heterosexuality is the only cultural network in which they are implicated. These are, quite literally, *inverted* imitations, ones which invert the order of imitated and imitation, and which, in the process, expose the fundamental dependency of "the origin" on that which it claims to produce as its secondary effect.

What follows if we concede from the start that gay identities as derivative inversions are in part defined in terms of the very heterosexual identities from which they are differentiated? If heterosexuality is an impossible imitation of itself, an imitation that performatively constitutes itself as the original, then the imitative parody of "heterosexuality"—when and where it exists in gay cultures—is always and only an imitation of an imitation, a copy of a copy, for which there is no original. Put in yet a different way, the parodic or imitative effect of gay identities works neither to copy nor to emulate heterosexuality, but rather, to expose heterosexuality as an incessant and *panicked* imitation of its own naturalized idealization. That heterosexuality is always in the act of elaborating itself is evidence that it is perpetually at risk, that is, that it "knows" its own possibility of becoming undone: hence, its compulsion to repeat which is at once a foreclosure of that which threatens its coherence. That it can never eradicate that risk attests to its profound dependency upon the homosexuality that it seeks fully to eradicate and never can or that it seeks to make second, but which is always already there as a prior possibility.[15] Although this failure of naturalized heterosexuality might constitute a source of pathos for heterosexuality itself—what its theorists often refer to as its constitutive malaise—it can become an occasion for a subversive and proliferating parody of gender norms in which the very claim to originality and to the real is shown to be the effect of a certain kind of naturalized gender mime.

It is important to recognize the ways in which heterosexual norms reappear within gay identities, to affirm that gay and lesbian identities are not only structured in part by dominant heterosexual frames, but that they are *not* for that reason *determined* by them. They are running commentaries on those naturalized positions as well, parodic replays and resignifications of precisely those heterosexual structures that would consign gay life to discursive domains of unreality and unthinkability. But to be constituted or structured in part by the very heterosexual norms by which gay people are oppressed is not, I repeat, to be claimed or determined by those structures. And it is not necessary to think of such heterosexual constructs as the pernicious intrusion of "the straight mind," one that must be rooted out in its entirety. In a way, the presence of heterosexual constructs and positionalities in whatever form in gay and lesbian identities presupposes that there is a gay and lesbian repetition of straightness, a recapitulation of straightness—which is itself a repetition and recapitulation of its own ideality—within its own terms, a site in which all sorts of resignifying and parodic repetitions become possible. The parodic replication and resignification of heterosexual constructs within non-heterosexual frames brings into relief the utterly constructed status of the so-called original, but it shows that heterosexuality only constitutes itself as the original through a convincing act of repetition. The more that "act" is expropriated, the more the heterosexual claim to originality is exposed as illusory.

Although I have concentrated in the above on the reality-effects of gender practices, performances, repetitions, and mimes, I do not mean to suggest that drag is a "role" that can be taken on or taken off at will. There is no volitional subject behind the mime who decides, as it were, which gender it will be today. On the contrary, the very possibility of becoming a viable subject requires that a certain gender mime be already underway. The "being" of the subject is no more self-identical than the "being" of any gender; in fact, coherent gender, achieved through an apparent repetition of the same, produces as its *effect* the illusion of a prior and volitional subject. In this sense, gender is not a performance that a prior subject elects to do, but gender is *performative* in the sense that it constitutes as an effect the very subject it appears to express. It is a *compulsory* performance in the sense that acting out of line with heterosexual norms brings with it ostracism, punishment, and violence, not to mention the transgressive pleasures produced by those very prohibitions.

To claim that there is no performer prior to the performed, that the performance is performative, that the performance constitutes the appearance of a "subject" as its effect is difficult to accept. This difficulty is the result of a predisposition to think of sexuality and gender as "expressing" in some indirect or direct way a psychic reality that precedes it. The denial of the *priority* of the subject, however, is not the denial of the subject; in fact, the refusal to conflate the subject with the psyche marks the psychic as that which exceeds the domain of the conscious subject. This psychic excess is precisely what is being systematically denied by the notion of a volitional "subject" who elects at will which gender and/or sexuality to be at any given time and place. It is this excess which erupts within the intervals of those repeated gestures and acts that construct the apparent uniformity of heterosexual positionalities, indeed which compels the repetition itself, and which guarantees its perpetual failure. In this sense, it is this excess which, within the heterosexual economy, implicitly includes homosexuality, that perpetual threat of a disruption which is quelled through a reenforced repetition of the same. And yet, if repetition is the way in which power works to construct the illusion of a seamless hetero-sexual identity, if heterosexuality is compelled to *repeat itself* in order to establish the illusion of its own uniformity and identity, then this is an identity permanently at risk, for what if it fails to repeat, or if the very exercise of repetition is redeployed for a very different performative purpose? If there is, as it were, always a compulsion to repeat, repetition never fully accomplishes identity. That there is a need for a repetition at all is a sign that identity is not self-identical. It requires to be instituted again and again, which is to say that it runs the risk of becoming *de*-instituted at every interval.

So what is this psychic excess, and what will constitute a subversive or *de*-instituting repetition? First, it is necessary to consider that sexuality always exceeds any given performance, presentation, or narrative which is why it is not possible to derive or read off a sexuality from any given gender presentation. And sexuality may be said to exceed any definitive narrativization. Sexuality is never fully "expressed" in a performance or practice; there will be passive and butchy femmes, femmy and aggressive butches, and both of those, and more, will turn out to describe more or less anatomically stable "males" and "females." There are no direct expressive or causal lines between sex, gender, gender presentation, sexual practice, fantasy and sexuality. None of those terms captures or determines the rest. Part of what constitutes sexuality is precisely that which does not appear and that which, to some degree, can never appear. This is perhaps the most funda-mental reason why sexuality is to some degree always closeted, especially to the one who would express it through acts of self-disclosure. That which is excluded for a given gender presentation to "succeed" may be precisely what is played out sexually, that is, an "inverted" relation, as it were, between gender and gender presentation, and gender presentation and sexuality. On the other hand, both gender presentation and sexual practices may corollate such that it appears that the former "expresses" the latter, and yet both are jointly constituted by the very sexual possibilities that they exclude.

This logic of inversion gets played out interestingly in versions of lesbian butch and femme gender stylization. For a butch can present herself as capable, forceful, and all-providing, and a stone butch may well seek to constitute her lover as the exclusive site of erotic attention and pleasure. And yet, this "providing" butch who seems *at first* to replicate a certain husband-like role, can find herself caught in a logic of inversion whereby that "providingness" turns to a self-sacrifice, which implicates her in the most ancient trap of feminine self-abnegation. She may well find herself in a situation of radical need, which is precisely what she sought to locate, find, and fulfill in her femme lover. In effect, the butch inverts into the femme or remains caught up in the specter of that inversion, or takes pleasure in it. On the other hand, the femme who, as Amber Hollibaugh has argued, "orches-trates" sexual exchange,[16] may well eroticize a certain dependency only to learn that the very power to orchestrate that dependency exposes her own incontrovert-ible power, at which point she inverts into a butch or becomes caught up in the specter of that inversion, or perhaps delights in it.

Psychic mimesis

What stylizes or forms an erotic style and/or a gender presentation—and that which makes such categories inherently unstable—is a set of *psychic identifications* that are not simple to describe. Some psychoanalytic theories tend to construe identification and desire as two mutually exclusive relations to love objects that have been lost through prohibition and/or separation. Any intense emotional attachment thus divides into either wanting to have someone or wanting to be that someone, but never both at once. It is important to consider that identification and desire can coexist, and that their formulation in terms of mutually exclusive opposi-tions serves a heterosexual matrix. But I would like to focus attention on yet a different construal of that scenario, namely, that "wanting to be" and "wanting to have" can operate to differentiate mutually exclusive positionalities internal to lesbian erotic exchange. Consider that identifications are always made in response to loss of some kind, and that they involve a certain *mimetic practice* that seeks to incorporate the lost love within the very "identity" of the one who remains. This was Freud's thesis in "Mourning and Melancholia" in 1917 and continues to inform contemporary psychoanalytic discussions of identification.[17]

For psychoanalytic theorists Mikkel Borch-Jacobsen and Ruth Leys, however, identification and, in particular, identificatory mimetism, *precedes* "identity" and constitutes identity as that which is fundamentally "other to itself." The notion of this Other *in* the self, as it were, implies that the self/Other distinction is *not* primarily external (a powerful critique of ego psychology follows from this); the self is from the start radically implicated in the "Other." This theory of primary mimetism differs from Freud's account of melancholic incorporation. In Freud's view, which I continue to find useful, incorporation—a kind of psychic miming—is a response to, and refusal of, *loss*. Gender as the site of such psychic mimes is thus constituted by the variously gendered Others who have been loved and lost, where the loss is suspended through a melancholic and imaginary incorpor-ation (and preservation) of those Others into the psyche. Over and against this account of psychic mimesis by way of incorporation and melancholy, the theory of primary mimetism argues an even stronger position in favor of the non-self-identity of the psychic subject. Mimetism is not motivated by a drama of loss and wishful recovery, but appears to precede and constitute desire (and motivation) itself; in this sense, mimetism would be prior to the possibility of loss and the disappointments of love.

Whether loss or mimetism is primary (perhaps an undecidable problem), the psychic subject is nevertheless constituted internally by differentially gendered Others and is, therefore, never, as a gender, self-identical.

In my view, the self only becomes a self on the condition that it has suffered a separation (grammar fails us here, for the "it" only becomes differentiated through that separation), a loss which is suspended and provisionally resolved through a melancholic incorporation of some "Other." That "Other" installed in the self thus establishes the permanent incapacity of that "self" to achieve self-identity; it is as it were always already disrupted by that Other; the disruption of the Other at the heart of the self is the very condition of that self's possibility.[18]

Such a consideration of psychic identification would vitiate the possibility of any stable set of typologies that explain or describe something like gay or lesbian identities. And any effort to supply one—as evidenced in Kaja Silverman's recent inquiries into male homosexuality—suffers from simplification, and conforms, with alarming ease, to the regulatory requirements of diagnostic epistemic regimes. If incorporation in Freud's sense in 1914 is an effort to *preserve* a lost and loved object and to refuse or postpone the recognition of loss and, hence, of grief, then to become *like* one's mother or father or sibling or other early "lovers" may be an act of love and/or a hateful effort to replace or displace. How would we "typologize" the ambivalence at the heart of mimetic incorporations such as these?[19]

How does this consideration of psychic identification return us to the question, what constitutes a subversive repetition? How are troublesome identifications apparent in cultural practices? Well, consider the way in which heterosexuality naturalizes itself through setting up certain illusions of continuity between sex, gender, and desire. When Aretha Franklin sings, "you make me feel like a natural woman," she seems at first to suggest that some natural potential of her biological sex is actualized by her participation in the cultural position of "woman" as object of heterosexual recognition. Something in her "sex" is thus expressed by her "gender" which is then fully known and consecrated within the heterosexual scene. There is no breakage, no discontinuity between "sex" as biological facticity and essence, or between gender and sexuality. Although Aretha appears to be all too glad to have her naturalness confirmed, she also seems fully and paradoxically mindful that that confirmation is never guaranteed, that the effect of naturalness is only achieved as a consequence of that moment of heterosexual recognition. After all, Aretha sings, you make me feel *like* a natural woman, suggesting that this is a kind of metaphorical substitution, an act of imposture, a kind of sublime and momentary participation in an ontological illusion produced by the mundane operation of heterosexual drag.

But what if Aretha were singing to me? Or what if she were singing to a drag queen whose performance somehow confirmed her own?

How do we take account of these kinds of identifications? It's not that there is some kind of *sex* that exists in hazy biological form that is somehow *expressed* in the gait, the posture, the gesture; and that some sexuality then expresses both that apparent gender or that more or less magical sex. If gender is drag, and if it is an imitation that regularly produces the ideal it attempts to approximate, then gender is a performance that *produces* the illusion of an inner sex or essence or psychic gender core; it *produces* on the skin, through the gesture, the move, the gait (that array of corporeal theatrics understood as gender presentation), the illusion of an inner depth. In effect, one way that gender gets naturalized is through being constructed as an inner psychic or physical *necessity*. And yet, it is always a surface sign, a signification on and with the public body that produces this illusion of an inner depth, necessity or essence that is somehow magically, causally expressed.

To dispute the psyche as *inner depth*, however, is not to refuse the psyche altogether. On the contrary, the psyche calls to be rethought precisely as a compulsive repetition, as that which conditions and disables the repetitive performance of identity. If every performance repeats itself to institute the effect of identity, then every repetition requires an interval between the acts, as it were, in which risk and excess threaten to disrupt the identity being constituted. The unconscious is this excess that enables and contests every performance, and which never fully appears within the performance itself. The psyche is not "in" the body, but in the very signifying process through which that body comes to appear; it is the lapse in repetition as well as its compulsion, precisely what the performance seeks to deny, and that which compels it from the start.

To locate the psyche within this signifying chain as the instability of all iterability is not the same as claiming that it is inner core that is awaiting its full and liberatory expression. On the contrary, the psyche is the permanent failure of expression, a failure that has its values, for it impels repetition and so reinstates the possibility of disruption. What then does it mean to pursue disruptive repetition within compulsory heterosexuality?

Although compulsory heterosexuality often presumes that there is first a sex that is expressed through a gender and then through a sexuality, it may now be necessary fully to invert and displace that operation of thought. If a regime of sexuality mandates a compulsory performance of sex, then it may be only through that performance that the binary system of gender and the binary system of sex come to have intelligibility at all. It may be that the very categories of sex, of sexual identity, of gender are produced or maintained in the *effects* of this compulsory performance, effects which are disingenuously renamed as causes, origins, disingenuously lined up within a causal or expressive sequence that the heterosexual norm produces to legitimate itself as the origin of all sex. How then to expose the causal lines as retrospectively and performatively produced fabrications, and to engage gender itself as an inevitable fabrication, to fabricate gender in terms which reveal every claim to the origin, the inner, the true, and the real as nothing other than the effects of *drag*, whose subversive possibilities ought to be played and replayed to make the "sex" of gender into a site of insistent political play? Perhaps this will be a matter of working sexuality *against* identity, even against gender, and of letting that which cannot fully appear in any performance persist in its disruptive promise.

Notes

1   Parts of this essay were given as a presentation at the Conference on Homosexuality at Yale University in October, 1989.

2   "The Mark of Gender," *Feminist Issues* 5 no. 2 (1985): 6.

3   *Différence et répétition* (Paris: PUF, 1968), 374; my translation.

4   *Gender Trouble: Feminism and the Subversion of Identity* (New York and London: Routledge, 1990).

5   Michel Foucault, *The History of Sexuality, Vol. 1*, trans. Robert Hurley (New York: Random House, 1980), 101.

6   Here I would doubtless differ from the very fine analysis of Hitchcock's *Rope* offered by D. A. Miller in this volume. [See original text.]

7   For an example of "coming out" that is strictly unconfessional and which, finally, offers no content for the category of lesbian, see Barbara Johnson's deftly constructed "Sula Passing: No Passing" presentation at UCLA, May 1990.

8   Gayatri Chakravorty Spivak, "Displacement and the Discourse of Woman," in *Displacement: Derrida and After*, ed. Mark Krupnick (Bloomington: Indiana University Press, 1983).

9   Let me take this occasion to apologize to the social worker at that conference who asked a question about how to deal with those clients with AIDS who turned to Bernie Segal and others for the purposes of psychic healing. At the time, I understood this questioner to be suggesting that such clients were full of self-hatred because they were trying to find the causes of AIDS in their own selves. The questioner and I appear to agree that any effort to locate the responsibility for AIDS in those who suffer from it is politically and ethically wrong. I thought the questioner, however, was prepared to tell his clients that they were self-hating, and I reacted strongly (too strongly) to the paternalistic prospect that this person was going to pass judgment on someone who was clearly not only suffering, but already passing judgment on him or herself. To call another person self-hating is itself an act of power that calls for some kind of scrutiny, and I think in response to someone who is already dealing with AIDS, that is perhaps the last thing one needs to hear. I also happened to have a friend who sought out advice from Bernie Segal, not with the belief that there is an exclusive or even primary psychic cause or solution for AIDS, but that there might be a psychic contribution to be made to surviving with AIDS. Unfortunately, I reacted quickly to this questioner, and with some anger. And I regret now that I didn't have my wits about me to discuss the distinctions with him that I have just laid out.

     Curiously, this incident was invoked at a CLAGS (Center for Lesbian and Gay Studies) meeting at CUNY sometime in December of 1989 and, according to those who told me about it, my angry denunciation of the social worker was taken to be symptomatic of the political insensitivity of a "theorist" in dealing with someone who is actively engaged in AIDS work. That attribution implies that I do not do AIDS work, that I am not politically engaged, and that the social worker in question does not read theory. Needless to say, I was reacting angrily on behalf of an absent friend with AIDS who sought out Bernie Segal and company. So as I offer this apology to the social worker, I wait expectantly that the CLAGS member who misunderstood me will offer me one in turn.

10   See my "The Force of Fantasy: Feminism, Mapplethorpe, and Discursive Excess," *differences* 2, no. 2 (Summer 1990). Since the writing of this essay, lesbian artists and representations have also come under attack.

11   It is this particular ruse of erasure which Foucault for the most part fails to take account of in his analysis of power. He almost always presumes that power takes place through discourse as its instrument, and that oppression is linked with subjection and subjectivation, that is, that it is installed as the formative principle of the identity of subjects.

12   Although miming suggests that there is a prior model which is being copied, it can have the effect of exposing that prior model as purely phantasmatic. In Jacques Derrida's "The Double Session" in *Dissemination*, trans. Barbara Johnson (Chicago: University of Chicago Press, 1981), he considers the textual effect of the mime in Mallarmé's "Mimique." There Derrida argues that the mime does not imitate or copy some prior phenomenon, idea, or figure, but constitutes—some might say *performatively*—the phantasm of the original in and through the mime:

He represents nothing, imitates nothing, does not have to conform to any prior referent with the aim of achieving adequation or verisimilitude. One can here foresee an objection: since the mime imitates nothing, reproduces nothing, opens up in its origin the very thing he is tracing out, presenting, or producing, he must be the very movement of truth. Not, of course, truth in the form of adequation between the representation and the present of the thing itself, or between the imitator and the imitated, but truth as the present unveiling of the present. . . . But this is not the case. . . . We are faced then with mimicry imitating nothing: faced, so to speak, with a double that couples no simple, a double that nothing anticipates, nothing at least that is not itself already double. There is no simple reference. . . . This speculum reflects no reality: it produces mere "reality-effects". . . . In this speculum with no reality, in this mirror of a mirror, a difference or dyad does exist, since there are mimes and phantoms. But it is a difference without reference, or rather reference without a referent, without any first or last unit, a ghost that is the phantom of no flesh . . . (206)

13   Esther Newton, *Mother Camp: Female Impersonators in America* (Chicago: University of Chicago Press, 1972).

14   In a sense, one might offer a redescription of the above in Lacanian terms. The sexual "positions" of heterosexually differentiated "man" and "woman" are part of the *Symbolic*, that is, an ideal embodiment of the Law of sexual difference which constitutes the object of imaginary pursuits, but which is always thwarted by the "real." These symbolic positions for Lacan are by definition impossible to occupy even as they are impossible to resist as the structuring telos of desire. I accept the former point, and reject the latter one. The imputation of universal necessity to such positions simply encodes compulsory heterosexuality at the level of the Symbolic, and the "failure" to achieve it is implicitly lamented as a source of heterosexual pathos.

15   Of course, it is Eve Kosofsky Sedgwick's *Epistemology of the Closet* (Berkeley: University of California Press, 1990) which traces the subleties of this kind of panic in Western heterosexual epistemes.

16   Amber Hollibaugh and Cherríe Moraga, "What We're Rollin Around in Bed With: Sexual Silences in Feminism," in *Powers of Desire: The Politics of Sexuality*, ed. Ann Snitow, Christine Stansell, and Sharon Thompson (New York: Monthly Review Press, 1983), 394–405.

17   Mikkel Borch-Jacobsen, *The Freudian Subject* (Stanford: Stanford University Press, 1988); for citations of Ruth Leys's work, see the following two endnotes.

18   For a very fine analysis of primary mimetism with direct implications for gender formation, see Ruth Leys, "The Real Miss Beauchamp: The History and Sexual Politics of the Multiple Personality Concept," in *Feminists Theorize the Political*, eds. Judith Butler and Joan W. Scott (New York and London: Routledge, forthcoming 1991). For Leys, a primary mimetism or suggestibility requires that the "self" from the start is constituted by its incorporations; the effort to differentiate oneself from that by which one is constituted is, of course, impossible, but it does entail a certain "incorporative violence," to use her term. The violence of identification is in this way in the service of an effort at differentiation, to take the place of the Other who is, as it were, installed at the foundation of the self. That this replacement, which seeks to be a displacement, fails, and must repeat itself endlessly, becomes the trajectory of one's psychic career.

19   Here again, I think it is the work of Ruth Leys which will clarify some of the complex questions of gender constitution that emerge from a close psychoanalytic consideration of imitation and identification. Her forthcoming book manuscript will doubtless galvanize this field: *The Subject of Imitation*.

380   JUDITH BUTLER

Suggestions for further reading

Butler, Judith, *Gender Trouble: Feminism and the Subversion of Identity*, New York and London: Routledge, 1990.

Foucault, Michel, *The History of Sexuality: Volume 1: An Introduction*, trans. Robert Hurley, Harmondsworth: Penguin, 1990.

Osborne, Peter and Segal, Lynne, 'Gender as Performance: An Interview with Judith Butler', *Radical Philosophy*, 1994, vol. 67, 32–9.

Chapter 26

Chandra Talpade Mohanty

'UNDER WESTERN EYES: FEMINIST SCHOLARSHIP AND COLONIAL DISCOURSES'[1], 1991

A NY DISCUSSION OF the intellectual and political construction of "third world feminisms" must address itself to two simultaneous projects: the internal critique of hegemonic "Western" feminisms, and the formulation of autonomous, geographically, historically, and culturally grounded feminist concerns and strategies. The first project is one of deconstructing and dismantling; the second, one of building and constructing. While these projects appear to be contradictory, the one working negatively and the other positively, unless these two tasks are addressed simultaneously, "third world" feminisms run the risk of marginalization or ghettoization from both mainstream (right and left) and Western feminist discourses.

It is to the first project that I address myself. What I wish to analyze is specifically the production of the "third world woman" as a singular monolithic subject in some recent (Western) feminist texts. The definition of colonization I wish to invoke here is a predominantly *discursive* one, focusing on a certain mode of appropriation and codification of "scholarship" and "knowledge" about women in the third world by particular analytic categories employed in specific writings on the subject which take as their referent feminist interests as they have been articulated in the U.S. and Western Europe. If one of the tasks of formulating and understanding the locus of "third world feminisms" is delineating the way in which it resists and *works against* what I am referring to as "Western feminist discourse," an analysis of the discursive construction of "third world women" in Western feminism is an important first step.

Clearly Western feminist discourse and political practice is neither singular nor homogeneous in its goals, interests, or analyses. However, it is possible to trace a coherence of *effects* resulting from the implicit assumption of "the West" (in all its complexities and contradictions) as the primary referent in theory and praxis. My reference to "Western feminism" is by no means intended to imply that it is a monolith. Rather, I am attempting to draw attention to the similar effects of various textual strategies used by writers which codify Others as non-Western and hence themselves as (implicitly) Western. It is in this sense that I use the term *Western feminist*. Similar arguments can be made in terms of middle-class urban African or Asian scholars producing scholarship on or about their rural or working-class sisters which assumes their own middle-class cultures as the norm, and codifies working-class histories and cultures as Other. Thus, while this essay focuses specifically on what I refer to as "Western feminist" discourse on women in the third world, the critiques I offer also pertain to third world scholars writing about their own cultures, which employ identical analytic strategies.

It ought to be of some political significance, at least, that the term *colonization* has come to denote a variety of phenomena in recent feminist and left writings in general. From its analytic value as a category of exploitative economic exchange in both traditional and contemporary Marxisms (cf. particularly contemporary theorists such as Baran 1962, Amin 1977, and Gunder-Frank 1967) to its use by feminist women of color in the U.S. to describe the appropriation of their experiences and struggles by hegemonic white women's movements (cf. especially Moraga and Anzaldúa 1983, Smith 1983, Joseph and Lewis 1981, and Moraga 1984), colonization has been used to characterize everything from the most evident economic and political hierarchies to the production of a particular cultural discourse about what is called the "third world."[2] However sophisticated or problematical its use as an explanatory construct, colonization almost invariably implies a relation of structural domination, and a suppression—often violent—of the heterogeneity of the subject(s) in question.

My concern about such writings derives from my own implication and investment in contemporary debates in feminist theory, and the urgent political necessity (especially in the age of Reagan/Bush) of forming strategic coalitions across class, race, and national boundaries. The analytic principles discussed below serve to distort Western feminist political practices, and limit the possibility of coalitions among (usually white) Western feminists and working-class feminists and feminists of color around the world. These limitations are evident in the construction of the (implicitly consensual) priority of issues around which apparently *all* women are expected to organize. The necessary and integral connection between feminist scholarship and feminist political practice and organizing determines the significance and status of Western feminist writings on women in the third world, for feminist scholarship, like most other kinds of scholarship, is not the mere production of knowledge about a certain subject. It is a directly political and discursive *practice* in that it is purposeful and ideological. It is best seen as a mode of intervention into particular hegemonic discourses (for example, traditional anthropology, sociology, literary criticism, etc.); it is a political praxis which counters and resists the totalizing imperative of age-old "legitimate" and "scientific" bodies of knowledge. Thus, feminist scholarly practices (whether reading, writing, critical, or textual) are inscribed in relations of power—relations which they counter, resist, or even perhaps implicitly support. There can, of course, be no apolitical scholarship.

The relationship between "Woman"—a cultural and ideological composite Other constructed through diverse representational discourses (scientific, literary, juridical, linguistic, cinematic, etc.)—and "women"—real, material subjects of their collective histories—is one of the central questions the practice of feminist scholarship seeks to address. This connection between women as historical sub-jects and the re-presentation of Woman produced by hegemonic discourses is not a relation of direct identity, or a relation of correspondence or simple implication.[3] It is an arbitrary relation set up by particular cultures. I would like to suggest that the feminist writings I analyze here discursively colonize the material and histor-ical heterogeneities of the lives of women in the third world, thereby producing/re-presenting a composite, singular "third world woman"—an image which appears arbitrarily constructed, but nevertheless carries with it the authorizing signature of Western humanist discourse.[4]

I argue that assumptions of privilege and ethnocentric universality, on the one hand, and inadequate self-consciousness about the effect of Western scholarship on the "third world" in the context of a world system dominated by the West, on the other, characterize a sizable extent of Western feminist work on women in the third world. An analysis of "sexual difference" in the form of a cross-culturally singular, monolithic notion of patriarchy or male dominance leads to the construc-tion of a similarly reductive and homogeneous notion of what I call the "third world difference"—that stable, ahistorical something that apparently oppresses most if not all the women in these countries. And it is in the production of this "third world difference" that Western feminisms appropriate and "colonize" the constitutive complexities which characterize the lives of women in these countries. It is in this process of discursive homogenization and systematization of the oppres-sion of women in the third world that power is exercised in much of recent Western feminist discourse, and this power needs to be defined and named.

In the context of the West's hegemonic position today, of what Anouar Abdel-Malek (1981) calls a struggle for "control over the orientation, regulation and decision of the process of world development on the basis of the advanced sector's monopoly of scientific knowledge and ideal creativity," Western feminist scholar-ship on the third world must be seen and examined precisely in terms of its inscription in these particular relations of power and struggle. There is, it should be evident, no universal patriarchal framework which this scholarship attempts to counter and resist—unless one posits an international male conspiracy or a mono-lithic, ahistorical power structure. There is, however, a particular world balance of power within which any analysis of culture, ideology, and socioeconomic condi-tions necessarily has to be situated. Abdel-Malek is useful here, again, in reminding us about the inherence of politics in the discourses of "culture":

> Contemporary imperialism is, in a real sense, a hegemonic imperial-ism, exercising to a maximum degree a rationalized violence taken to a higher level than ever before—through fire and sword, but also through the attempt to control hearts and minds. For its content is defined by the combined action of the military-industrial complex and the hegemonic cultural centers of the West, all of them founded on the advanced levels of development attained by monopoly and finance cap-ital, and supported by the benefits of both the scientific and techno-logical revolution and the second industrial revolution itself. (145–46)

Western feminist scholarship cannot avoid the challenge of situating itself and examining its role in such a global economic and political framework. To do any less would be to ignore the complex interconnections between first and third world economies and the profound effect of this on the lives of women in all countries. I do not question the descriptive and informative value of most Western feminist writings on women in the third world. I also do not question the existence of excellent work which does not fall into the analytic traps with which I am concerned. In fact I deal with an example of such work later on. In the context of an overwhelming silence about the experiences of women in these countries, as well as the need to forge international links between women's political struggles, such work is both pathbreaking and absolutely essential. However, it is both to the *explanatory potential* of particular analytic strategies employed by such writing, and to their *political effect* in the context of the hegemony of Western scholarship that I want to draw attention here. While feminist writing in the U.S. is still marginalized (except from the point of view of women of color addressing privileged white women), Western feminist writing on women in the third world must be considered in the context of the global hegemony of Western scholarship—i.e., the production, publication, distribution, and consumption of information and ideas. Marginal or not, this writing has political effects and implications beyond the immediate feminist or disciplinary audience. One such significant effect of the dominant "representations" of Western feminism is its conflation with imperialism in the eyes of particular third world women.[5] Hence the urgent need to examine the *political* implications of our *analytic* strategies and principles.

My critique is directed at three basic analytic principles which are present in (Western) feminist discourse on women in the third world. Since I focus primarily on the Zed Press Women in the Third World series, my comments on Western feminist discourse are circumscribed by my analysis of the texts in this series.[6] This is a way of focusing my critique. However, even though I am dealing with feminists who identify themselves as culturally or geographically from the "West," as mentioned earlier, what I say about these presuppositions or implicit principles holds for anyone who uses these methods, whether third world women in the West, or third world women in the third world writing on these issues and publishing in the West. Thus, I am not making a culturalist argument about ethnocentrism; rather, I am trying to uncover how ethnocentric universalism is produced in certain analyses. As a matter of fact, my argument holds for any discourse that sets up its own authorial subjects as the implicit referent, i.e., the yardstick by which to encode and represent cultural Others. It is in this move that power is exercised in discourse.

The first analytic presupposition I focus on is involved in the strategic location of the category "women" vis-à-vis the context of analysis. The assumption of women as an already constituted, coherent group with identical interests and desires, regardless of class, ethnic or racial location, or contradictions, implies a notion of gender or sexual difference or even patriarchy which can be applied universally and cross-culturally. (The context of analysis can be anything from kinship structures and the organization of labor to media representations.) The second analytical presupposition is evident on the methodological level, in the uncritical way "proof" of universality and cross-cultural validity are provided. The third is a more specifically political presupposition underlying the methodologies and the analytic strategies, i.e., the model of power and struggle they imply and suggest. I argue that as a result of the two modes—or, rather, frames—of analysis described above, a homogeneous notion of the oppression of women as a group is assumed, which, in turn, produces the image of an "average third world woman." This average third world woman leads an essentially truncated life based on her feminine gender (read: sexually constrained) and her being "third world" (read: ignorant, poor, uneducated, tradition-bound, domestic, family-oriented, victimized, etc.). This, I suggest, is in contrast to the (implicit) self-representation of Western women as educated, as modern, as having control over their own bodies and sexualities, and the freedom to make their own decisions.

The distinction between Western feminist re-presentation of women in the third world and Western feminist self-presentation is a distinction of the same order as that made by some Marxists between the "maintenance" function of the housewife and the real "productive" role of wage labor, or the characterization by developmentalists of the third world as being engaged in the lesser production of "raw materials" in contrast to the "real" productive activity of the first world. These distinctions are made on the basis of the privileging of a particular group as the norm or referent. Men involved in wage labor, first world producers, and, I suggest, Western feminists who sometimes cast third world women in terms of "ourselves undressed" (Michelle Rosaldo's [1980] term), all construct themselves as the normative referent in such a binary analytic.

"Women" as category of analysis, or: we are all sisters in struggle

By women as a category of analysis, I am referring to the crucial assumption that all of us of the same gender, across classes and cultures, are somehow socially constituted as a homogeneous group identified prior to the process of analysis. This is an assumption which characterizes much feminist discourse. The homogeneity of women as a group is produced not on the basis of biological essentials but rather on the basis of secondary sociological and anthropological universals. Thus, for instance, in any given piece of feminist analysis, women are characterized as a singular group on the basis of a shared oppression. What binds women together is a sociological notion of the "sameness" of their oppression. It is at this point that an elision takes place between "women" as a discursively constructed group and "women" as material subjects of their own history.[7] Thus, the discursively consensual homogeneity of "women" as a group is mistaken for the historically specific material reality of groups of women. This results in an assumption of women as an always already constituted group, one which has been labeled "powerless," "exploited," "sexually harassed," etc., by feminist scientific, economic, legal, and sociological discourses. (Notice that this is quite similar to sexist discourse labeling women weak, emotional, having math anxiety, etc.) This focus is not on uncovering the material and ideological specificities that constitute a particular group of women as "powerless" in a particular context. It is, rather, on finding a variety of cases of "powerless" groups of women to prove the general point that women as a group are powerless.

In this section I focus on five specific ways in which "women" as a category of analysis is used in Western feminist discourse on women in the third world. Each of these examples illustrates the construction of "third world women" as a homogeneous "powerless" group often located as implicit *victims* of particular socioeconomic systems. I have chosen to deal with a variety of writers—from Fran Hosken, who writes primarily about female genital mutilation, to writers from the Women in International Development school, who write about the effect of development policies on third world women for both Western and third world audiences. The similarity of assumptions about "third world women" in all these texts forms the basis of my discussion. This is not to equate all the texts that I analyze, nor is it to equalize their strengths and weaknesses. The authors I deal with write with varying degrees of care and complexity; however, the *effect* of their representation of third world women is a coherent one. In these texts women are defined as victims of male violence (Fran Hosken); victims of the colonial process (Maria Cutrufelli); victims of the Arab familial system (Juliette Minces); victims of the economic development process (Beverley Lindsay and the [liberal] WID School); and finally, victims of *the* Islamic code (Patricia Jeffery). This mode of defining women primarily in terms of their *object status* (the way in which they are affected or not affected by certain institutions and systems) is what characterizes this particular form of the use of "women" as a category of analysis. In the context of Western women writing/studying women in the third world, such objectification (however benevolently motivated) needs to be both named and challenged. As Valerie Amos and Pratibha Parmar argue quite eloquently, "Feminist theories which examine our cultural practices as 'feudal residues' or label us 'traditional,' also portray us as politically immature women who need to be versed and schooled in the ethos of Western feminism. They need to be continually challenged . . ." (1984, 7).

Women as victims of male violence

Fran Hosken, in writing about the relationship between human rights and female genital mutilation in Africa and the Middle East, bases her whole discussion/condemnation of genital mutilation on one privileged premise: that the goal of this practice is "to mutilate the sexual pleasure and satisfaction of woman" (1981, 11). This, in turn, leads her to claim that woman's sexuality is controlled, as is her reproductive potential. According to Hosken, "male sexual politics" in Africa and around the world "share the same political goal: to assure female dependence and subservience by any and all means" (14). Physical violence against women (rape, sexual assault, excision, infibulation, etc.) is thus carried out "with an astonishing consensus among men in the world" (14). Here, women are defined consistently as the *victims* of male control—the "sexually oppressed."[8] Although it is true that the potential of male violence against women circumscribes and elucidates their social position to a certain extent, defining women as archetypal victims freezes them into "objects-who-defend-themselves," men into "subjects-who-perpetrate-violence," and (every) society into powerless (read: women) and powerful (read: men) groups of people. Male violence must be theorized and interpreted *within* specific societies, in order both to understand it better and to effectively organize to change it.[9] Sisterhood cannot be assumed on the basis of gender; it must be forged in concrete historical and political practice and analysis.

Women as universal dependents

Beverly Lindsay's conclusion to the book *Comparative Perspectives of Third World Women: The Impact of Race, Sex and Class* (1983, 298, 306) states: "dependency relationships, based upon race, sex and class, are being perpetuated through social, educational, and economic institutions. These are the linkages among Third World Women." Here, as in other places, Lindsay implies that third world women constitute an identifiable group purely on the basis of shared dependencies. If shared dependencies were all that was needed to bind us together as a group, third world women would always be seen as an apolitical group with no subject status. Instead, if anything, it is the *common context* of political struggle against class, race, gender, and imperialist hierarchies that may constitute third world women as a strategic group at this historical juncture. Lindsay also states that linguistic and cultural differences exist between Vietnamese and black American women, but "both groups are victims of race, sex, and class." Again black and Vietnamese women are characterized by their victim status.

Similarly, examine statements such as "My analysis will start by stating that all African women are politically and economically dependent" (Cutrufelli 1983, 13), "Nevertheless, either overtly or covertly, prostitution is still the main if not the only source of work for African women" (Cutrufelli 1983, 33). *All* African women are dependent. Prostitution is the only work option for African women as a *group*. Both statements are illustrative of generalizations sprinkled liberally through a recent Zed Press publication, *Women of Africa: Roots of Oppression*, by Maria Rosa Cutrufelli, who is described on the cover as an Italian writer, sociologist, Marxist, and feminist. In the 1980s, is it possible to imagine writing a book entitled *Women of Europe: Roots of Oppression?* I am not objecting to the use of universal groupings for descriptive purposes. Women from the continent of Africa can be descriptively characterized as "women of Africa." It is when "women of Africa" becomes a homogeneous sociological grouping characterized by common dependencies or powerlessness (or even strengths) that problems arise—we say too little and too much at the same time.

This is because descriptive gender differences are transformed into the division between men and women. Women are constituted as a group via dependency relationship vis-à-vis men, who are implicitly held responsible for these relationships. When "women of Africa" as a group (versus "men of Africa" as a group?) are seen as a group precisely because they are generally dependent and oppressed, the analysis of specific historical differences becomes impossible, because reality is always apparently structured by divisions—two mutually exclusive and jointly exhaustive groups, the victims and the oppressors. Here the sociological is substituted for the biological, in order, however, to create the same—a unity of women. Thus, it is not the descriptive potential of gender difference but the privileged positioning and explanatory potential of gender difference as the *origin* of oppression that I question. In using "women of Africa" (as an already constituted group of oppressed peoples) as a category of analysis, Cutrufelli denies any historical specificity to the location of women as subordinate, powerful, marginal, central, or otherwise, vis-à-vis particular social and power networks. Women are taken as a unified "powerless" group prior to the analysis in question Thus, it is then merely a matter of specifying the context *after the fact*. "Women" are now placed in the context of the family, or in the workplace, or within religious networks, almost as if these systems existed outside the relations of women with other women, and women with men.

The problem with this analytic strategy, let me repeat, is that it assumes men and women are already constituted as sexual-political subjects prior to their entry into the arena of social relations. Only if we subscribe to this assumption is it possible to undertake analysis which looks at the "effects" of kinship structures, colonialism, organization of labor, etc., on women, who are defined in advance as a group. The crucial point that is forgotten is that women are produced through these very relations as well as being implicated in forming these relations. As Michelle Rosaldo argues, "woman's place in human social life is not in any direct sense a product of the things she does (or even less, a function of what, biologically, she is) but the meaning her activities acquire through concrete social interactions" (1980, 400). That women mother in a variety of societies is not as significant as the value attached to mothering in these societies. The distinction between the act of mothering and the status attached to it is a very important one—one that needs to be stated and analyzed contextually.

Married women as victims of the colonial process

In Lévi-Strauss's theory of kinship structure as a system of the exchange of women, what is significant is that exchange itself is not constitutive of the subordination of women; women are not subordinate because of the *fact* of exchange, but because of the *modes* of exchange instituted, and the values attached to these modes. However, in discussing the marriage ritual of the Bemba, a Zambian matrilocal, matrilineal people, Cutrufelli in *Women of Africa* focuses on the fact of the marital exchange of women before and after Western colonization, rather than the value attached to this exchange in this particular context. This leads to her definition of Bemba women as a coherent group affected in a particular way by colonization. Here again, Bemba women are constituted rather unilaterally as victims of the effects of Western colonization.

Cutrufelli cites the marriage ritual of the Bemba as a multistage event "whereby a young man becomes incorporated into his wife's family group as he takes up residence with them and gives his services in return for food and maintenance" (43). This ritual extends over many years, and the sexual relationship varies according to the degree of the girl's physical maturity. It is only after she undergoes an initiation ceremony at puberty that intercourse is sanctioned, and the man acquires legal rights over her. This initiation ceremony is the more important act of the consecration of women's reproductive power, so that the abduction of an uninitiated girl is of no consequence, while heavy penalty is levied for the seduction of an initiated girl. Cutrufelli asserts that the effect of European colonization has changed the whole marriage system. Now the young man is entitled to take his wife away from her people in return for money. The implication is that Bemba women have now lost the protection of tribal laws. However, while it is possible to see how the structure of the traditional marriage contract (versus the postcolonial marriage contract) offered women a certain amount of control over their marital relations, only an analysis of the political significance of the actual practice which privileges an initiated girl over an uninitiated one, indicating a shift in female power relations as a result of this ceremony, can provide an accurate account of whether Bemba women were indeed protected by tribal laws *at all times*.

However, it is not possible to talk about Bemba women as a homogeneous group within the traditional marriage structure. Bemba women *before* the initiation are constituted within a different set of social relations compared to Bemba women *after* the initiation. To treat them as a unified group characterized by the fact of their "exchange" between male kin is to deny the sociohistorical and cultural specificities of their existence, and the differential *value* attached to their exchange before and after their initiation. It is to treat the initiation ceremony as a ritual with no political implications or effects. It is also to assume that in merely describing the *structure* of the marriage contract, the situation of women is exposed. Women as a group are positioned within a given structure, but there is no attempt made to trace the effect of the marriage practice in constituting women within an obviously changing network of power relations. Thus, women are assumed to be sexual-political subjects prior to entry into kinship structures.

Women and familial systems

Elizabeth Cowie (1978), in another context, points out the implications of this sort of analysis when she emphasizes the specifically political nature of kinship structures which must be analyzed as ideological practices which designate men and women as father, husband, wife, mother, sister, etc. Thus, Cowie suggests, women as women are not *located* within the family. Rather, it is *in* the family, as an effect of kinship structures, that women as women are *constructed*, defined within and by the group. Thus, for instance, when Juliette Minces (1980) cites *the* patriarchal family as the basis for "an almost identical vision of women" that Arab and Muslim societies have, she falls into this very trap (see especially p. 23). Not only is it problematical to speak of a vision of women shared by Arab and Muslim societies (i.e., over twenty different countries) without addressing the particular historical, material, and ideological power structures that construct such images, but to speak of the patriarchal family or the tribal kinship structure as the origin of the socioeconomic status of women is to again assume that women are sexual-political subjects prior to their entry into the family. So while on the one hand women attain value or status within the family, the assumption of a singular patriarchal kinship system (common to all Arab and Muslim societies) is what apparently structures women as an oppressed group in these societies! This singular, coherent kinship system presumably influences another separate and given entity, "women."

Thus, all women, regardless of class and cultural differences, are affected by this system. Not only are *all* Arab and Muslim women seen to constitute a homogeneous oppressed group, but there is no discussion of the specific *practices* within the family which constitute women as mothers, wives, sisters, etc. Arabs and Muslims, it appears, don't change at all. Their patriarchal family is carried over from the times of the prophet Mohammed. They exist, as it were, outside history.

Women and religious ideologies

A further example of the use of "women" as a category of analysis is found in cross-cultural analyses which subscribe to a certain economic reductionism in describing the relationship between the economy and factors such as politics and ideology. Here, in reducing the level of comparison to the economic relations between "developed and developing" countries, any specificity to the question of women is denied. Mina Modares (1981), in a careful analysis of women and Shi'ism in Iran, focuses on this very problem when she criticizes feminist writings which treat Islam as an ideology separate from and outside social relations and practices, rather than a discourse which includes rules for economic, social, and power relations within society. Patricia Jeffery's (1979) otherwise informative work on Pirzada women in purdah considers Islamic ideology a partial explanation for the status of women in that it provides a justification for the purdah. Here, Islamic ideology is reduced to a set of ideas whose internalization by Pirzada women contributes to the stability of the system. However, the primary explanation for purdah is located in the control that Pirzada men have over economic resources, and the personal security purdah gives to Pirzada women.

By taking a specific version of Islam as *the* Islam, Jeffery attributes a singularity and coherence to it. Modares notes, "'Islamic Theology' then becomes imposed on a separate and given entity called 'women.' A further unification is reached: Women (meaning *all women*), regardless of their differing positions within societies, come to be affected or not affected by Islam. These conceptions provide the right ingredients for an unproblematic possibility of a cross-cultural study of women" (63). Marnia Lazreg makes a similar argument when she addresses the reductionism inherent in scholarship on women in the Middle East and North Africa:

> A ritual is established whereby the writer appeals to religion as *the* cause of gender inequality just as it is made the source of underdevelopment in much of modernization theory. In an uncanny way, feminist discourse on women from the Middle East and North Africa mirrors that of theologians' own interpretation of women in Islam. . . .
>
> The overall effect of this paradigm is to deprive women of self-presence, of being. Because women are subsumed under religion presented in fundamental terms, they are inevitably seen as evolving in nonhistorical time. They virtually have no history. Any analysis of change is therefore foreclosed. (1988, 87)

While Jeffery's analysis does not quite succumb to this kind of unitary notion of religion (Islam), it does collapse all ideological specificities into economic relations, and universalizes on the basis of this comparison.

Women and the development process

The best examples of universalization on the basis of economic reductionism can be found in the liberal "Women in Development" literature. Proponents of this school seek to examine the effect of development on third world women, sometimes from self-designated feminist perspectives. At the very least, there is an evident interest in and commitment to improving the lives of women in "developing" countries. Scholars such as Irene Tinker and Michelle Bo Bramsen (1972), Ester Boserup (1970), and Perdita Huston (1979) have all written about the effect of development policies on women in the third world.[10] All three women assume "development" is synonymous with "economic development" or "economic progress." As in the case of Minces's patriarchal family, Hosken's male sexual control, and Cutrufelli's Western colonization, development here becomes the all-time equalizer. Women are affected positively or negatively by economic development policies, and this is the basis for cross-cultural comparison.

For instance, Perdita Huston (1979) states that the purpose of her study is to describe the effect of the development process on the "family unit and its individual members" in Egypt, Kenya, Sudan, Tunisia, Sri Lanka, and Mexico. She states that the "problems" and "needs" expressed by rural and urban women in these countries all center around education and training, work and wages, access to health and other services, political participation, and legal rights. Huston relates all these "needs" to the lack of sensitive development policies which exclude women as a group or category. For her, the solution is simple: implement improved development policies which emphasize training for women fieldworkers, use women trainees, and women rural development officers, encourage women's cooperatives, etc. Here again, women are assumed to be a coherent group or category prior to their entry into "the development process." Huston assumes that all third world women have similar problems and needs. Thus, they must have similar interests and goals. However, the interests of urban, middle-class, educated Egyptian housewives, to take only one instance, could surely not be seen as being the same as those of their uneducated, poor maids. Development policies do not affect both groups of women in the same way. Practices which characterize women's status and roles vary according to class. Women are constituted as women through the complex interaction between class, culture, religion, and other ideological institutions and frameworks. They are not "women"—a coherent group—solely on the basis of a particular economic system or policy. Such reductive cross-cultural comparisons result in the colonization of the specifics of daily existence and the complexities of political interests which women of different social classes and cultures represent and mobilize.

Thus, it is revealing that for Perdita Huston, women in the third world countries she writes about have "needs" and "problems," but few if any have "choices" or the freedom to act. This is an interesting representation of women in the third world, one which is significant in suggesting a latent self-presentation of Western women which bears looking at. She writes, "What surprised and moved me most as I listened to women in such very different cultural settings was the striking commonality—whether they were educated or illiterate, urban or rural—of their most basic values: the importance they assign to family, dignity, and service to others" (1979, 115). Would Huston consider such values unusual for women in the West?

What is problematical about this kind of use of "women" as a group, as a stable category of analysis, is that it assumes an ahistorical, universal unity between women based on a generalized notion of their subordination. Instead of analytically *demonstrating* the production of women as socioeconomic political groups within particular local contexts, this analytical move limits the definition of the female subject to gender identity, completely bypassing social class and ethnic identities. What characterizes women as a group is their gender (sociologically, not necessarily biologically, defined) over and above everything else, indicating a monolithic notion of sexual difference. Because women are thus constituted as a coherent group, sexual difference becomes coterminous with female subordination, and power is automatically defined in binary terms: people who have it (read: men), and people who do not (read: women). Men exploit, women are exploited. Such simplistic formulations are historically reductive; they are also ineffectual in designing strategies to combat oppressions. All they do is reinforce binary divisions between men and women.

What would an analysis which did not do this look like? Maria Mies's work illustrates the strength of Western feminist work on women in the third world which does not fall into the traps discussed above. Mies's study of the lace makers of Narsapur, India (1982), attempts to carefully analyze a substantial household industry in which "housewives" produce lace doilies for consumption in the world market. Through a detailed analysis of the structure of the lace industry, production and reproduction relations, the sexual division of labor, profits and exploitation, and the overall consequences of defining women as "non-working housewives" and their work as "leisure-time activity," Mies demonstrates the levels of exploitation in this industry and the impact of this production system on the work and living conditions of the women involved in it. In addition, she is able to analyze the "ideology of the housewife," the notion of a woman sitting in the house, as providing the necessary subjective and sociocultural element for the creation and maintenance of a production system that contributes to the increasing pauperization of women, and keeps them totally atomized and disorganized as workers. Mies's analysis shows the effect of a certain historically and culturally specific mode of patriarchal organization, an organization constructed on the basis of the definition of the lace makers as "non-working housewives" at familial, local, regional, statewide, and international levels. The intricacies and the effects of particular power networks not only are emphasized, but they form the basis of Mies's analysis of how this particular group of women is situated at the center of a hegemonic, exploitative world market.

This is a good example of what careful, politically focused, local analyses can accomplish. It illustrates how the category of women is constructed in a variety of political contexts that often exist simultaneously and overlaid on top of one another. There is no easy generalization in the direction of "women" in India, or "women in the third world"; nor is there a reduction of the political construction of the exploitation of the lace makers to cultural explanations about the passivity or obedience that might characterize these women and their situation. Finally, this mode of local, political analysis which generates theoretical categories from within the situation and context being analyzed, also suggests corresponding effective strategies for organizing against the exploitation faced by the lace makers. Narsapur women are not mere victims of the production process, because they resist, challenge, and subvert the process at various junctures. Here is one instance of how Mies delineates the connections between the housewife ideology, the self-consciousness of the lace makers, and their interrelationships as contributing to the latent resistances she perceives among the women:

> The persistence of the housewife ideology, the self-perception of the lace makers as petty commodity producers rather than as workers, is not only upheld by the structure of the industry as such but also by the deliberate propagation and reinforcement of reactionary patri-archal norms and institutions. Thus, most of the lace makers voiced the same opinion about the rules of *purdah* and seclusion in their communities which were also propagated by the lace exporters. In particular, the *Kapu* women said that they had never gone out of their houses, that women of their community could not do any other work than housework and lace work etc. but in spite of the fact that most of them still subscribed fully to the patriarchal norms of the *gosha* women, there were also contradictory elements in their consciousness. Thus, although they looked down with contempt upon women who were able to work outside the house—like the untouchable *Mala* and *Madiga* women or women of other lower castes, they could not ignore the fact that these women were earning more money precisely because they were *not* respectable housewives but workers. At one discussion, they even admitted that it would be better if they could also go out and do coolie work. And when they were asked whether they would be ready to come out of their houses and work in one place in some sort of a factory, they said they would do that. This shows that the *purdah* and housewife ideology, although still fully internalized, already had some cracks, because it has been confronted with several contradictory realities. (157)

It is only by understanding the *contradictions* inherent in women's location within various structures that effective political action and challenges can be devised. Mies's study goes a long way toward offering such analysis. While there are now an increasing number of Western feminist writings in this tradition,[11] there is also, unfortunately, a large block of writing which succumbs to the cultural reductionism discussed earlier.

Methodological universalisms, or: women's oppression is a global phenomenon

Western feminist writings on women in the third world subscribe to a variety of methodologies to demonstrate the universal cross-cultural operation of male dominance and female exploitation. I summarize and critique three such methods below, moving from the simplest to the most complex.

First, proof of universalism is provided through the use of an arithmetic method. The argument goes like this: the greater the number of women who wear the veil, the more universal is the sexual segregation and control of women (Deardon 1975, 4–5). Similarly, a large number of different, fragmented examples from a variety of countries also apparently add up to a universal fact. For instance, Muslim women in Saudi Arabia, Iran, Pakistan, India, and Egypt all wear some sort of a veil. Hence, this indicates that the sexual control of women is a universal fact in those countries in which the women are veiled (Deardon 1975, 7, 10). Fran Hosken writes, "Rape, forced prostitution, polygamy, genital mutilation, pornography, the beating of girls and women, purdah (segregation of women) are all violations of basic human rights" (1981, 15). By equating purdah with rape, domestic violence, and forced prostitution, Hosken asserts its "sexual control" function as the primary explanation for purdah, whatever the context. Institutions of purdah are thus denied any cultural and historical specificity, and contradictions and potentially subversive aspects are totally ruled out.

In both these examples, the problem is not in asserting that the practice of wearing a veil is widespread. This assertion can be made on the basis of numbers. It is a descriptive generalization. However, it is the analytic leap from the practice of veiling to an assertion of its general significance in controlling women that must be questioned. While there may be a physical similarity in the veils worn by women in Saudi Arabia and Iran, the specific meaning attached to this practice varies according to the cultural and ideological context. In addition, the symbolic space occupied by the practice of purdah may be similar in certain contexts, but this does not automatically indicate that the practices themselves have identical significance in the social realm. For example, as is well known, Iranian middle-class women veiled themselves during the 1979 revolution to indicate solidarity with their veiled working-class sisters, while in contemporary Iran, mandatory Islamic laws dictate that all Iranian women wear veils. While in both these instances, similar reasons might be offered for the veil (opposition to the Shah and Western cultural colonization in the first case, and the true Islamicization of Iran in the second), the concrete *meanings* attached to Iranian women wearing the veil are clearly different in both historical contexts. In the first case, wearing the veil is both an oppositional and a revolutionary gesture on the part of Iranian middle-class women; in the second case, it is a coercive, institutional mandate (see Tabari 1980 for detailed discussion). It is on the basis of such context-specific differentiated analysis that effective political strategies can be generated. To assume that the mere practice of veiling women in a number of Muslim countries indicates the universal oppression of women through sexual segregation not only is analytically reductive, but also proves quite useless when it comes to the elaboration of oppositional political strategy.

Second, concepts such as reproduction, the sexual division of labor, the family, marriage, household, patriarchy, etc., are often used without their specification in local cultural and historical contexts. Feminists use these concepts in providing explanations for women's subordination, apparently assuming their universal applicability. For instance, how is it possible to refer to "the" sexual division of labor when the *content* of this division changes radically from one environment to the next, and from one historical juncture to another? At its most abstract level, it is the fact of the differential assignation of tasks according to sex that is signifi-cant; however, this is quite different from the *meaning* or *value* that the content of this sexual division of labor assumes in different contexts. In most cases the assigning of tasks on the basis of sex has an ideological origin. There is no question that a claim such as "women are concentrated in service-oriented occupations in a large number of countries around the world" is descriptively valid. Descriptively, then, perhaps the existence of a similar sexual division of labor (where women work in service occupations such as nursing, social work, etc., and men in other kinds of occupations) in a variety of different countries can be asserted. However, the concept of the "sexual division of labor" is more than just a descriptive cate-gory. It indicates the differential *value* placed on "men's work" versus "women's work."

Often the mere existence of a sexual division of labor is taken to be proof of the oppression of women in various societies. This results from a confusion between and collapsing together of the descriptive and explanatory potential of the concept of the sexual division of labor. Superficially similar situations may have radically different, historically specific explanations, and cannot be treated as identical. For instance, the rise of female-headed households in middle-class America might be construed as a sign of great independence and feminist progress, whereby women are considered to have *chosen* to be single parents, there are increasing numbers of lesbian mothers, etc. However, the recent increase in female-headed households in Latin America,[12] where women might be seen to have more decision-making power, is concentrated among the poorest strata, where life choices are the most constrained economically. A similar argument can be made for the rise of female-headed families among black and Chicana women in the U.S. The positive correlation between this and the level of poverty among women of color and white working-class women in the U.S. has now even acquired a name: the feminization of poverty. Thus, while it is possible to state that there is a rise in female-headed households in the U.S. and in Latin America, this rise cannot be discussed as a universal indicator of women's independence, nor can it be discussed as a universal indicator of women's impoverishment. The *meaning* of and *explanation* for the rise obviously vary according to the sociohistorical context.

Similarly, the existence of a sexual division of labor in most contexts cannot be sufficient explanation for the universal subjugation of women in the work force. That the sexual division of labor does indicate a devaluation of women's work must be shown through analysis of particular local contexts. In addition, devalu-ation of *women* must also be shown through careful analysis. In other words, the "sexual division of labor" and "women" are not commensurate analytical categor-ies. Concepts such as the sexual division of labor can be useful only if they are generated through local, contextual analyses (see Eldhom, Harris, and Young 1977). If such concepts are assumed to be universally applicable, the resultant homogenization of class, race, religious, and daily material practices of women in the third world can create a false sense of the commonality of oppressions, interests, and struggles between and among women globally. Beyond sisterhood there are still racism, colonialism, and imperialism!

Finally, some writers confuse the use of gender as a superordinate category of organizing analysis with the universalistic proof and instantiation of this category. In other words, empirical studies of gender differences are confused with the analytical organization of cross-cultural work. Beverly Brown's (1983) review of the book *Nature, Culture and Gender* (Strathern and McCormack 1980) best illustrates this point. Brown suggests that nature:culture and female:male are superordinate categories which organize and locate lesser categories (such as wild/domestic and biology/technology) within their logic. These categories are universal in the sense that they organize the universe of a system of representations. This relation is totally independent of the universal substantiation of any particular category. Her critique hinges on the fact that rather than clarify the generalizability of nature:culture // female:male as subordinate organization categories, *Nature, Culture and Gender* construes the universality of this equation to lie at the level of empirical truth, which can be investigated through fieldwork. Thus, the usefulness of the nature:culture // female:male paradigm as a universal mode of the organization of representation within any particular sociohistorical system is lost. Here, methodological universalism is assumed on the basis of the reduction of the nature:culture // female:male analytic categories to a demand for empirical proof of its existence in different cultures. Discourses of representation are confused with material realities, and the distinction made earlier between "Woman" and "women" is lost. Feminist work which blurs this distinction (which is, interestingly enough, often present in certain Western feminists' self-representation) eventually ends up constructing monolithic images of "third world women" by ignoring the complex and mobile relationships between their historical materiality on the level of specific oppressions and political choices, on the one hand, and their general discursive representations, on the other.

To summarize: I have discussed three methodological moves identifiable in feminist (and other academic) cross-cultural work which seeks to uncover a universality in women's subordinate position in society. The next and final section pulls together the previous sections, attempting to outline the political effects of the analytical strategies in the context of Western feminist writing on women in the third world. These arguments are not against generalization as much as they are for careful, historically specific generalizations responsive to complex realities. Nor do these arguments deny the necessity of forming strategic political identities and affinities. Thus, while Indian women of different religions, castes, and classes might forge a political unity on the basis of organizing against police brutality toward women (see Kishwar and Vanita 1984), an *analysis* of police brutality must be contextual. Strategic coalitions which construct oppositional political identities for themselves are based on generalization and provisional unities, but the analysis of these group identities cannot be based on universalistic, ahistorical categories.

The subject(s) of power

This last section returns to an earlier point about the inherently political nature of feminist scholarship, and attempts to clarify my point about the possibility of detecting a colonialist move in the case of a hegemonic first-third world connection in scholarship. The nine texts in the Zed Press Women in the Third World series that I have discussed[13] focused on the following common areas in examining women's "status" within various societies: religion, family/kinship structures, the legal system, the sexual division of labor, education, and finally, political resistance. A large number of Western feminist writings on women in the third world focus on these themes. Of course the Zed texts have varying emphases. For instance, two of the studies, *Women of Palestine* (Downing 1982) and *Indian Women in Struggle* (Omvedt 1980), focus explicitly on female militance and political involvement, while *Women in Arab Society* (Minces 1980) deals with Arab women's legal, religious, and familial status. In addition, each text evidences a variety of methodologies and degrees of care in making generalizations. Interestingly enough, however, almost all the texts assume "women" as a category of analysis in the manner designated above.

Clearly this is an analytical strategy which is neither limited to these Zed Press publications nor symptomatic of Zed Press publications in general. However, each of the particular texts in question assumes "women" have a coherent group identity within the different cultures discussed, prior to their entry into social relations. Thus, Omvedt can talk about "Indian women" while referring to a particular group of women in the State of Maharashtra, Cutrufelli about "women of Africa," and Minces about "Arab women" as if these groups of women have some sort of obvious cultural coherence, distinct from men in these societies. The "status" or "position" of women is assumed to be self-evident, because women as an already constituted group are *placed* within religious, economic, familial, and legal structures. However, this focus whereby women are seen as a coherent group across contexts, regardless of class or ethnicity, structures the world in ultimately binary, dichotomous terms, where women are always seen in opposition to men, patriarchy is always necessarily male dominance, and the religious, legal, economic, and familial systems are implicitly assumed to be constructed by men. Thus, both men and women are always apparently constituted whole populations, and relations of dominance and exploitation are also posited in terms of whole peoples—wholes coming into exploitative relations. It is only when men and women are seen as different categories or groups possessing different *already constituted* categories of experience, cognition, and interests as *groups* that such a simplistic dichotomy is possible.

What does this imply about the structure and functioning of power relations? The setting up of the commonality of third world women's struggles across classes and cultures against a general notion of oppression (primarily the group in power—i.e., men) necessitates the assumption of what Michel Foucault (1980, 135–45) calls the "juridico-discursive" model of power, the principal features of which are "a negative relation" (limit and lack), an "insistence on the rule" (which forms a binary system), a "cycle of prohibition," the "logic of censorship," and a "uniformity" of the apparatus functioning at different levels. Feminist discourse on the third world which assumes a homogeneous category—or group—called women necessarily operates through the setting up of originary power divisions. Power relations are structured in terms of a unilateral and undifferentiated source of power and a cumulative reaction to power. Opposition is a generalized phenomenon created as a response to power—which, in turn, is possessed by certain groups of people.

The major problem with such a definition of power is that it locks all revolutionary struggles into binary structures—possessing power versus being powerless. Women are powerless, unified groups. If the struggle for a just society is seen in terms of the move from powerless to powerful for women as a *group*, and this is the implication in feminist discourse which structures sexual difference in terms of the division between the sexes, then the new society would be structurally identical to the existing organization of power relations, constituting itself as a simple *inversion* of what exists. If relations of domination and exploitation are defined in terms of binary divisions—groups which dominate and groups which are dominated—surely the implication is that the accession to power of women as a group is sufficient to dismantle the existing organization of relations? But women as a group are not in some sense essentially superior or infallible. The crux of the problem lies in that initial assumption of women as a homogeneous group or category ("the oppressed"), a familiar assumption in Western radical and liberal feminisms.[14]

What happens when this assumption of "women as an oppressed group" is situated in the context of Western feminist writing about third world women? It is here that I locate the colonialist move. By contrasting the representation of women in the third world with what I referred to earlier as Western feminisms' self-presentation in the same context, we see how Western feminists alone become the true "subjects" of this counterhistory. Third world women, on the other hand, never rise above the debilitating generality of their "object" status.

While radical and liberal feminist assumptions of women as a sex class might elucidate (however inadequately) the autonomy of particular women's struggles in the West, the application of the notion of women as a homogeneous category to women in the third world colonizes and appropriates the pluralities of the simultaneous location of different groups of women in social class and ethnic frameworks; in doing so it ultimately robs them of their historical and political *agency*. Similarly, many Zed Press authors who ground themselves in the basic analytic strategies of traditional Marxism also implicitly create a "unity" of women by substituting "women's activity" for "labor" as the primary theoretical determinant of women's situation. Here again, women are constituted as a coherent group not on the basis of "natural" qualities or needs but on the basis of the sociological "unity" of their role in domestic production and wage labor (see Haraway 1985, esp. p. 76). In other words, Western feminist discourse, by assuming women as a coherent, already constituted group which is placed in kinship, legal, and other structures, defines third world women as subjects *outside* social relations, instead of looking at the way women are constituted *through* these very structures.

Legal, economic, religious, and familial structures are treated as phenomena to be judged by Western standards. It is here that ethnocentric universality comes into play. When these structures are defined as "underdeveloped" or "developing" and women are placed within them, an implicit image of the "average third world woman" is produced. This is the transformation of the (implicitly Western) "oppressed woman" into the "oppressed third world woman." While the category of "oppressed woman" is generated through an exclusive focus on gender differ- ence, "the oppressed third world woman" category has an additional attribute— the "third world difference!" The "third world difference" includes a paternalistic attitude toward women in the third world.[15] Since discussions of the various themes I identified earlier (kinship, education, religion, etc.) are conducted in the context of the relative "underdevelopment" of the third world (which is nothing less than unjustifiably confusing development with the separate path taken by the West in its development, as well as ignoring the directionality of the first-third world power relationship), third world women as a group or category are automatically and necessarily defined as religious (read "not progressive"), family-oriented (read "traditional"), legal minors (read "they-are-still-not-conscious-of-their-rights"), illiterate (read "ignorant"), domestic (read "backward"), and sometimes revo- lutionary (read "their-country-is-in-a-state-of-war; they-must-fight!") This is how the "third world difference" is produced.

When the category of "sexually oppressed women" is located within particular systems in the third world which are defined on a scale which is normed through Eurocentric assumptions, not only are third world women defined in a particular way prior to their entry into social relations, but since no connections are made between first and third world power shifts, the assumption is reinforced that the third world just has not evolved to the extent that the West has. This mode of feminist analysis, by homogenizing and systematizing the experiences of different groups of women in these countries, erases all marginal and resistant modes and experiences.[16] It is significant that none of the texts I reviewed in the Zed Press series focuses on lesbian politics or the politics of ethnic and religious marginal organizations in third world women's groups. Resistance can thus be defined only as cumulatively reactive, not as something inherent in the operation of power. If power, as Michel Foucault has argued recently, can really be understood only in the context of resistance,[17] this misconceptualization is both analytically and strategic- ally problematical. It limits theoretical analysis as well as reinforces Western cultural imperialism. For in the context of a first/third world balance of power, feminist analyses which perpetrate and sustain the hegemony of the idea of the superiority of the West produce a corresponding set of universal images of the "third world woman," images such as the veiled woman, the powerful mother, the chaste virgin, the obedient wife, etc. These images exist in universal, ahistorical splendor, setting in motion a colonialist discourse which exercises a very specific power in defining, coding, and maintaining existing first/third world connections.

To conclude, then, let me suggest some disconcerting similarities between the typically authorizing signature of such Western feminist writings on women in the third world, and the authorizing signature of the project of humanism in general— humanism as a Western ideological and political project which involves the neces- sary recuperation of the "East" and "Woman" as Others. Many contemporary thinkers, including Foucault (1978, 1980), Derrida (1974), Kristeva (1980), Deleuze and Guattari (1977), and Said (1978), have written at length about the underlying anthropomorphism and ethnocentrism which constitute a hegemonic humanistic problematic that repeatedly confirms and legitimates (Western) Man's centrality. Feminist theorists such as Luce Irigaray (1981), Sarah Kofman (see Berg 1982), and Hélène Cixous (1981) have also written about the recuperation and absence of woman/women within Western humanism. The focus of the work of all these thinkers can be stated simply as an uncovering of the political *interests* that underlie the binary logic of humanistic discourse and ideology whereby, as a valuable recent essay puts it, "the first (majority) term (Identity, Universality, Culture, Disinterestedness, Truth, Sanity, Justice, etc.), which is, in fact, second-ary and derivative (a construction), is privileged over and colonizes the second (minority) term (difference, temporality, anarchy, error, interestedness, insanity, deviance, etc.), which is in fact, primary and originative" (Spanos 1984). In other words, it is only insofar as "Woman/Women" and "the East" are defined as *Others*, or as peripheral, that (Western) Man/Humanism can represent him/itself as the center. It is not the center that determines the periphery, but the periphery that, in its boundedness, determines the center. Just as feminists such as Kristeva and Cixous deconstruct the latent anthropomorphism in Western discourse, I have suggested a parallel strategy in this essay in uncovering a latent ethnocentrism in particular feminist writings on women in the third world.[18]

As discussed earlier, a comparison between Western feminist self-presentation and Western feminist re-presentation of women in the third world yields signifi-cant results. Universal images of "the third world woman" (the veiled woman, chaste virgin, etc.), images constructed from adding the "third world difference" to "sexual difference," are predicated upon (and hence obviously bring into sharper focus) assumptions about Western women as secular, liberated, and having control over their own lives. This is not to suggest that Western women *are* secu-lar, liberated, and in control of their own lives. I am referring to a *discursive* self-presentation, not necessarily to material reality. If this were a material reality, there would be no need for political movements in the West. Similarly, only from the vantage point of the West is it possible to define the "third world" as under-developed and economically dependent. Without the overdetermined discourse that creates the *third* world, there would be no (singular and privileged) first world. Without the "third world woman," the particular self-presentation of Western women mentioned above would be problematical. I am suggesting, then, that the one enables and sustains the other. This is not to say that the signature of Western feminist writings on the third world has the same authority as the project of Western humanism. However, in the context of the hegemony of the Western scholarly establishment in the production and dissemination of texts, and in the context of the legitimating imperative of humanistic and scientific discourse, the definition of "the third world woman" as a monolith might well tie into the larger economic and ideological praxis of "disinterested" scientific inquiry and pluralism which are the surface manifestations of a latent economic and cultural colonization of the "non-Western" world. It is time to move beyond the Marx who found it possible to say: They cannot represent themselves; they must be represented.

Notes

This essay would not have been possible without S. P. Mohanty's challenging and careful reading. I would also like to thank Biddy Martin for our numerous discussions about

feminist theory and politics. They both helped me think through some of the arguments
herein.

1   This is an updated and modified version of an essay published in *Boundary 2* 12, no. 3/13,
no. 1 (Spring/Fall 1984), and reprinted in *Feminist Review*, no. 30 (Autumn 1988).

2   Terms such as *third* and *first world* are very problematical both in suggesting oversimpli-
fied similarities between and among countries labeled thus, and in implicitly reinforcing
existing economic, cultural, and ideological hierarchies which are conjured up in using
such terminology. I use the term "*third world*" with full awareness of its problems, only
because this is the terminology available to us at the moment. The use of quotation
marks is meant to suggest a continuous questioning of the designation. Even when I do
not use quotation marks, I mean to use the term critically.

3   I am indebted to Teresa de Lauretis for this particular formulation of the project of
feminist theorizing. See especially her introduction in de Lauretis, *Alice Doesn't: Feminism,
Semiotics, Cinema* (Bloomington: Indiana University Press, 1984); see also Sylvia Wynter,
"The Politics of Domination," unpublished manuscript.

4   This argument is similar to Homi Bhabha's definition of colonial discourse as strategically creating a space for a subject people through the production of knowledges and
the exercise of power. The full quote reads: "[colonial discourse is] an apparatus of
power. . . . an apparatus that turns on the recognition and disavowal of racial/cultural/
historical differences. Its predominant strategic function is the creation of a space for a
subject people through the production of knowledges in terms of which surveillance
is exercised and a complex form of pleasure/unpleasure is incited. It (i.e. colonial
discourse) seeks authorization for its strategies by the production of knowledges by
coloniser and colonised which are stereotypical but antithetically evaluated" (1983, 23).

5   A number of documents and reports on the UN International Conferences on Women,
Mexico City, 1975, and Copenhagen, 1980, as well as the 1976 Wellesley Conference
on Women and Development, attest to this. Nawal el Saadawi, Fatima Mernissi, and
Mallica Vajarathon (1978) characterize this conference as "American-planned and organized," situating third world participants as passive audiences. They focus especially on
the lack of self-consciousness of Western women's implication in the effects of imperialism and racism in their assumption of an "international sisterhood." A recent essay by
Valerie Amos and Pratibha Parmar (1984) characterizes as "imperial" Euro-American
feminism which seeks to establish itself as the only legitimate feminism.

6   The Zed Press Women in the Third World series is unique in its conception. I choose to
focus on it because it is the only contemporary series I have found which assumes that
"women in the third world" are a legitimate and separate subject of study and research.
Since 1985, when this essay was first written, numerous new titles have appeared in the
Women in the Third World series. Thus, I suspect that Zed has come to occupy a rather
privileged position in the dissemination and construction of discourses by and about
third world women. A number of the books in this series are excellent, especially those
which deal directly with women's resistance struggles. In addition, Zed Press consistently publishes progressive feminist, antiracist, and antiimperialist texts. However, a
number of the texts written by feminist sociologists, anthropologists, and journalists are
symptomatic of the kind of Western feminist work on women in the third world that
concerns me. Thus, an analysis of a few of these particular works in this series can serve
as a representative point of entry into the discourse I am attempting to locate and define.
My focus on these texts is therefore an attempt at an internal critique: I simply expect
and demand more from this series. Needless to say, progressive publishing houses also
carry their own authorizing signatures.

7   Elsewhere I have discussed this particular point in detail in a critique of Robin Morgan's
construction of "women's herstory" in her introduction to *Sisterhood Is Global: The
International Women's Movement Anthology* (New York: Anchor Press/Doubleday, 1984).
See my "Feminist Encounters: Locating the Politics of Experience," *Copyright* 1, "Fin de
Siecle 2000," 30–44, especially 35–37.

8   Another example of this kind of analysis is Mary Daly's (1978) *Gyn/Ecology*. Daly's

assumption in this text, that women as a group are sexually victimized, leads to her very problematic comparison between the attitudes toward women witches and healers in the West, Chinese footbinding, and the genital mutilation of women in Africa. According to Daly, women in Europe, China, and Africa constitute a homogeneous group as victims of male power. Not only does this label (sexual victims) eradicate the specific historical and material realities and contradictions which lead to and perpetuate practices such as witch hunting and genital mutilation, but it also obliterates the differences, complexities, and heterogeneities of the lives of, for example, women of different classes, religions, and nations in Africa. As Audre Lorde (1983) pointed out, women in Africa share a long tradition of healers and goddesses that perhaps binds them together more appropriately than their victim status. However, both Daly and Lorde fall prey to universalistic assumptions about "African women" (both negative and positive). What matters is the complex, historical range of power differences, commonalities, and resistances that exist among women in Africa which construct African women as "subjects" of their own politics.

9   See Eldhom, Harris, and Young (1977) for a good discussion of the necessity to theorize male violence within specific societal frameworks, rather than assume it as a universal fact.

10   These views can also be found in differing degrees in collections such as Wellesley Editorial Committee, ed., *Women and National Development: The Complexities of Change* (Chicago: University of Chicago Press, 1977), and *Signs*, Special Issue, "Development and the Sexual Division of Labor," 7, no. 2 (Winter 1981). For an excellent introduction of WID issues, see ISIS, *Women in Development: A Resource Guide for Organization and Action* (Philadelphia: New Society Publishers, 1984). For a politically focused discussion of feminism and development and the stakes for poor third world women, see Gita Sen and Caren Grown, *Development Crises and Alternative Visions: Third World Women's Perspectives* (New York: Monthly Review Press, 1987).

11   See essays by Vanessa Maher, Diane Elson and Ruth Pearson, and Maila Stevens in Kate Young, Carol Walkowitz, and Roslyn McCullagh, eds., *Of Marriage and the Market: Women's Subordination in International Perspective* (London: CSE Books, 1981); and essays by Vivian Mota and Michelle Mattelart in June Nash and Helen I. Safa, eds., *Sex and Class in Latin America: Women's Perspectives on Politics, Economics and the Family in the Third World* (South Hadley, Mass.: Bergin and Garvey, 1980). For examples of excellent, self-conscious work by feminists writing about women in their own historical and geographical locations, see Marnia Lazreg (1988) on Algerian women, Gayatri Chakravorty Spivak's "A Literary Representation of the Subaltern: A Woman's Text from the Third World," in her *In Other Worlds: Essays in Cultural Politics* (New York: Methuen, 1987), 241–68, and Lata Mani's essay "Contentious Traditions: The Debate on SATI in Colonial India," *Cultural Critique* 7 (Fall 1987), 119–56.

12   Olivia Harris, "Latin American Women—An Overview," in Harris, ed., *Latin American Women* (London: Minority Rights Group Report no. 57, 1983), 4–7. Other MRG Reports include Ann Deardon (1975) and Rounaq Jahan (1980).

13   List of Zed Press publications: Patricia Jeffery, *Frogs in a Well: Indian Women in Purdah* (1979); Latin American and Caribbean Women's Collective, *Slaves of Slaves: The Challenge of Latin American Women* (1980); Gail Omvedt, *We Shall Smash This Prison: Indian Women in Struggle* (1980); Juliette Minces, *The House of Obedience: Women in Arab Society* (1980); Bobby Siu, *Women of China: Imperialism and Women's Resistance, 1900–1949* (1981); Ingela Bendt and James Downing, *We Shall Return: Women in Palestine* (1982); Maria Rosa Cutrufelli, *Women of Africa: Roots of Oppression* (1983); Maria Mies, *The Lace Makers of Narsapur: Indian Housewives Produce for the World Market* (1982); Miranda Davis, ed., *Third World/Second Sex: Women's Struggles and National Liberation* (1983).

14   For succinct discussions of Western radical and liberal feminisms, see Hester Eisenstein, *Contemporary Feminist Thought* (Boston: G. K. Hall & Co., 1983), and Zillah Eisenstein, *The Radical Future of Liberal Feminism* (New York: Longman, 1981).

15   Amos and Parmar describe the cultural stereotypes present in Euro-American feminist

thought: "The image is of the passive Asian woman subject to oppressive practices within the Asian family with an emphasis on wanting to 'help' Asian women liberate themselves from their role. Or there is the strong, dominant Afro-Caribbean woman, who despite her 'strength' is exploited by the 'sexism' which is seen as being a strong feature in relationships between Afro-Caribbean men and women" (9). These images illustrate the extent to which *paternalism* is an essential element of feminist thinking which incorporates the above stereotypes, a paternalism which can lead to the definition of priorities for women of color by Euro-American feminists.

16   I discuss the question of theorizing experience in my "Feminist Encounters" (1987) and in an essay coauthored with Biddy Martin, "Feminist Politics: What's Home Got to Do with It?" in Teresa de Lauretis, ed., *Feminist Studies/Critical Studies* (Bloomington: Indiana University Press, 1986), 191–212.

17   This is one of M. Foucault's (1978, 1980) central points in his reconceptualization of the strategies and workings of power networks.

18   For an argument which demands a *new* conception of humanism in work on third world women, see Marnia Lazreg (1988). While Lazreg's position might appear to be diametrically opposed to mine, I see it as a provocative and potentially positive extension of some of the implications that follow from my arguments. In criticizing the feminist rejection of humanism in the name of "essential Man," Lazreg points to what she calls an "essentialism of difference" within these very feminist projects. She asks: "To what extent can Western feminism dispense with an ethics of responsibility when writing about different women? The point is neither to subsume other women under one's own experience nor to uphold a separate truth for them. Rather, it is to allow them to *be* while recognizing that what they are is just as meaningful, valid, and comprehensible as what we are. . . . Indeed, when feminists essentially deny other women the humanity they claim for themselves, they dispense with any ethical constraint. They engage in the act of splitting the social universe into us and them, subject and objects" (99–100).

    This essay by Lazreg and an essay by S. P. Mohanty (1989) entitled "Us and Them: On the Philosophical Bases of Political Criticism" suggest positive directions for self-conscious cross-cultural analyses, analyses which move beyond the deconstructive to a fundamentally productive mode in designating overlapping areas for cross-cultural comparison. The latter essay calls not for a "humanism" but for a reconsideration of the question of the "human" in a posthumanist context. It argues that (1) there is no necessary "incompatibility between the deconstruction of Western humanism" and such "a positive elaboration" of the human, and moreover that (2) such an elaboration is essential if contemporary political-critical discourse is to avoid the incoherences and weaknesses of a relativist position.

References list

Abdel-Malek, Anouar. 1981. *Social Dialectics: Nation and Revolution.* Albany: State University of New York Press.

Amin, Samir. 1977. *Imperialism and Unequal Development.* New York: Monthly Review Press.

Amos, Valerie, and Pratibha Parmar. 1984. "Challenging Imperial Feminism." *Feminist Review* 17:3–19.

Baran, Paul A. 1962. *The Political Economy of Growth.* New York: Monthly Review Press.

Berg, Elizabeth. 1982. "The Third Woman." *Diacritics* (Summer):11–20.

Bhabha, Homi. 1983. "The Other Question—The Stereotype and Colonial Discourse." *Screen* 24, no. 6:23.

Boserup, Ester. 1970. *Women's Role in Economic Development.* New York: St. Martin's Press; London: Allen and Unwin.

Brown, Beverly. 1983. "Displacing the Difference—Review, *Nature, Culture and Gender.*" *m/f* 8:79–89.

Cixous, Hélène. 1981. "The Laugh of the Medusa." In Marks and De Courtivron (1981).
Cowie, Elizabeth, 1978. "Woman as Sign." m/f 1:49–63.
Cutrufelli, Maria Rosa. 1983. Women of Africa: Roots of Oppression. London: Zed Press.
Daly, Mary. 1978. Gyn/Ecology: The Metaethics of Radical Feminism. Boston: Beacon Press.
Deardon, Ann, ed. 1975. Arab Women. London: Minority Rights Group Report no. 27.
de Lauretis, Teresa. 1984. Alice Doesn't: Feminism, Semiotics, Cinema. Bloomington: Indiana
      University Press.
——— . 1986. Feminist Studies/Critical Studies. Bloomington: Indiana University Press.
Deleuze, Giles, and Felix Guattari. 1977. Anti-Oedipus: Capitalism and Schizophrenia. New York:
      Viking.
Derrida, Jacques. 1974. Of Grammatology. Baltimore. Johns Hopkins University Press.
Eisenstein, Hester. 1983. Contemporary Feminist Thought. Boston: G. K. Hall and Co.
Eisenstein, Zillah. 1981. The Radical Future of Liberal Feminism. New York: Longman.
Eldhom, Felicity, Olivia Harris, and Kate Young. 1977. "Conceptualising Women." Critique of
      Anthropology "Women's Issue", no. 3.
el Saadawi, Nawal, Fatima Mernissi, and Mallica Vajarathon. 1978. "A Critical Look at the
      Wellesley Conference." Quest 4, no. 2 (Winter):101–107.
Foucault, Michel. 1978. History of Sexuality: Volume One. New York: Random House.
——— . 1980. Power/Knowledge. New York: Pantheon.
Gunder-Frank, Audre. 1967. Capitalism and Underdevelopment in Latin America. New York:
      Monthly Review Press.
Haraway, Donna. 1985. "A Manifesto for Cyborgs: Science, Technology and Socialist Feminism
      in the 1980s." Socialist Review 80 (March/April):65–108.
Harris, Olivia. 1983a. "Latin American Women—An Overview." In Harris (1983b).
——— . 1983b. Latin American Women. London: Minority Rights Group Report no. 57.
Hosken, Fran. 1981. "Female Genital Mutilation and Human Rights." Feminist Issues 1, no. 3.
Huston, Perdita. 1979. Third World Women Speak Out. New York: Praeger.
Irigaray, Luce. 1981. "This Sex Which Is Not One" and "When the Goods Get Together."
      In Marks and De Courtivron (1981).
Jahan, Rounaq, ed. 1980. Women in Asia. London: Minority Rights Group Report no. 45.
Jeffery, Patricia. 1979. Frogs in a Well: Indian Women in Purdah. London: Zed Press.
Joseph, Gloria, and Jill Lewis. 1981. Common Differences: Conflicts in Black and White Feminist
      Perspectives. Boston: Beacon Press.
Kishwar, Madhu, and Ruth Vanita. 1984. In Search of Answers: Indian Women's Voices from
      Manushi. London: Zed Press.
Kristeva, Julia. 1980. Desire in Language. New York: Columbia University Press.
Lazreg, Marnia. 1988. "Feminism and Difference: The Perils of Writing as a Woman on
      Women in Algeria." Feminist Issues 14, no. 1 (Spring):81–107.
Lindsay, Beverley, ed. 1983. Comparative Perspectives of Third World Women: The Impact of Race,
      Sex and Class. New York: Praeger.
Lorde, Audre. 1983. "An Open Letter to Mary Daly." In Moraga and Anzaldúa (1983), 94–97.
Marks, Elaine, and Isabel De Courtivron. 1981. New French Feminisms. New York: Schocken
      Books.
Mies, Maria. 1982. The Lace Makers of Narsapur: Indian Housewives Produce for the World Market.
      London: Zed Press.
Minces, Juliette. 1980. The House of Obedience: Women in Arab Society. London: Zed Press.
Modares, Mina. 1981. "Women and Shi'ism in Iran." m/f 5 and 6:61–82.
Mohanty, Chandra Talpade. 1987. "Feminist Encounters: Locating the Politics of Experience."
      Copyright 1, "Fin de Siecle 2000," 30–44.
Mohanty, Chandra Talpade, and Biddy Martin. 1986. "Feminist Politics: What's Home Got to
      Do with It?" In de Lauretis (1986).
Mohanty, S. P. 1989. "Us and Them: On the Philosophical Bases of Political Criticism." Yale
      Journal of Criticism 2 (March):1–31.

Moraga, Cherríe. 1984. *Loving in the War Years*. Boston: South End Press.

Moraga, Cherríe, and Gloria Anzaldúa, eds. 1983. *This Bridge Called My Back: Writings by Radical Women of Color*. New York: Kitchen Table Press.

Morgan, Robin, ed. 1984. *Sisterhood Is Global: The International Women's Movement Anthology*. New York: Anchor Press/Doubleday; Harmondsworth: Penguin.

Nash, June, and Helen I. Safa, eds. 1980. *Sex and Class in Latin America: Women's Perspectives on Politics, Economics and the Family in the Third World*. South Hadley, Mass.: Bergin and Garvey.

Rosaldo, M. A. 1980. "The Use and Abuse of Anthropology: Reflections on Feminism and Cross-Cultural Understanding." *Signs* 53:389–417.

Said, Edward. 1978. *Orientalism*. New York: Random House.

Sen, Gita, and Caren Grown. 1987. *Development Crises and Alternative Visions: Third World Women's Perspectives*. New York: Monthly Review Press.

Smith, Barbara, ed. 1983. *Home Girls: A Black Feminist Anthology*. New York: Kitchen Table Press.

Spanos, William V. 1984. "Boundary 2 and the Polity of Interest: Humanism, the 'Center Elsewhere' and Power." *Boundary 2* 12, no. 3/13, no. 1 (Spring/Fall).

Spivak, Gayatri Chakravorty. 1987. *In Other Worlds: Essays in Cultural Politics*. London and New York: Methuen.

Strathern, Marilyn, and Carol McCormack, eds. 1980. *Nature, Culture and Gender*. Cambridge: Cambridge University Press.

Tabari, Azar. 1980. "The Enigma of the Veiled Iranian Women." *Feminist Review* 5:19–32.

Tinker, Irene, and Michelle Bo Bramsen, eds. 1972. *Women and World Development*. Washington, D.C.: Overseas Development Council.

Young, Kate, Carol Walkowitz, and Roslyn McCullagh, eds. 1981. *Of Marriage and the Market: Women's Subordination in International Perspective*. London: CSE Books.

Suggestions for further reading

Narayan, Uma, *Dislocating Cultures: Identities, Traditions and Third World Feminism*, New York and London: Routledge, 1997.

Spivak, Gayatri Chakravorty, 'Can the Subaltern Speak?', in Cary Nelson and Lawrence Grossberg (eds.) *Marxism and the Interpretation of Culture*, London: Macmillan, 1988, pp. 271–313.

Weedon, Chris, *Feminism, Theory and the Politics of Difference*, Oxford: Blackwell, 1999.

_____

Chapter 27

Giorgio Agamben

INTRODUCTION TO *HOMO SACER: SOVEREIGN POWER AND BARE LIFE*, 1995

T HE GREEKS HAD no single term to express what we mean by the word "life." They used two terms that, although traceable to a common etymological root, are semantically and morphologically distinct: *zoē*, which expressed the simple fact of living common to all living beings (animals, men, or gods), and *bios*, which indicated the form or way of living proper to an individual or a group. When Plato mentions three kinds of life in the *Philebus*, and when Aristotle distinguishes the contemplative life of the philosopher (*bios theōrētikos*) from the life of pleasure (*bios apolaustikos*) and the political life (*bios politikos*) in the *Nichomachean Ethics*, neither philosopher would ever have used the term *zoē* (which in Greek, significantly enough, lacks a plural). This follows from the simple fact that what was at issue for both thinkers was not at all simple natural life but rather a qualified life, a particular way of life. Concerning God, Aristole can certainly speak of a *zoē aristē kai aidios*, a more noble and eternal life (*Metaphysics*, 1072b, 28), but only insofar as he means to underline the significant truth that even God is a living being (similarly, Aristotle uses the term *zoē* in the same context—and in a way that is just as meaningful—to define the act of thinking). But to speak of a *zoē politikē* of the citizens of Athens would have made no sense. Not that the classical world had no familiarity with the idea that natural life, simple *zoē* as such, could be a good in itself. In a passage of the *Politics*, after noting that the end of the city is life according to the good, Aristotle expresses his awareness of that idea with the most perfect lucidity:

> This [life according to the good] is the greatest end both in common for all men and for each man separately. But men also come together and maintain the political community in view of simple living, because there is probably some kind of good in the mere fact of living itself [*kata to zēn auto monon*]. If there is no great difficulty as to the way of life

[*kata ton bion*], clearly most men will tolerate much suffering and hold on to life [*zoē*] as if it were a kind of serenity [*euēmeria*, beautiful day] and a natural sweetness.

(1278b, 23–31)

In the classical world, however, simple natural life is excluded from the *polis* in the strict sense, and remains confined—as merely reproductive life—to the sphere of the *oikos*, "home" (*Politics*, 1252a, 26–35). At the beginning of the *Politics*, Aristotle takes the greatest care to distinguish the *oikonomos* (the head of an estate) and the *despotēs* (the head of the family), both of whom are concerned with the reproduction and the subsistence of life, from the politician, and he scorns those who think the difference between the two is one of quantity and not of kind. And when Aristotle defined the end of the perfect community in a passage that was to become canonical for the political tradition of the West (1252b, 30), he did so precisely by opposing the simple fact of living (*to zēn*) to politically qualified life (*to eu zēn*): *ginomenē men oun tou zēn heneken, ousa de tou eu zēn*, "born with regard to life, but existing essentially with regard to the good life" (in the Latin translation of William of Moerbeke, which both Aquinas and Marsilius of Padua had before them: *facta quidem igitur vivendi gratia, existens autem gratia bene vivendi*).

It is true that in a famous passage of the same work, Aristotle defines man as a *politikon zōon* (*Politics*, 1253a, 4). But here (aside from the fact that in Attic Greek the verb *bionai* is practically never used in the present tense), "political" is not an attribute of the living being as such, but rather a specific difference that determines the genus *zōon*. (Only a little later, after all, human politics is distinguished from that of other living beings in that it is founded, through a supplement of politicity [*policità*] tied to language, on a community not simply of the pleasant and the painful but of the good and the evil and of the just and the unjust.)

Michel Foucault refers to this very definition when, at the end of the first volume of *The History of Sexuality*, he summarizes the process by which, at the threshold of the modern era, natural life begins to be included in the mechanisms and calculations of State power, and politics turns into *biopolitics*. "For millennia," he writes, "man remained what he was for Aristotle: a living animal with the additional capacity for political existence; modern man is an animal whose politics calls his existence as a living being into question" (*La volonté*, p. 188).

According to Foucault, a society's "threshold of biological modernity" is situated at the point at which the species and the individual as a simple living body become what is at stake in a society's political strategies. After 1977, the courses at the Collège de France start to focus on the passage from the "territorial State" to the "State of population" and on the resulting increase in importance of the nation's health and biological life as a problem of sovereign power, which is then gradually transformed into a "government of men" (*Dits et écrits*, 3: 719). "What follows is a kind of bestialization of man achieved through the most sophisticated political techniques. For the first time in history, the possibilities of the social sciences are made known, and at once it becomes possible both to protect life and to authorize a holocaust." In particular, the development and triumph of capitalism would not have been possible, from this perspective, without the disciplinary control achieved by the new bio-power, which, through a series of appropriate technologies, so to speak created the "docile bodies" that it needed.

Almost twenty years before *The History of Sexuality*, Hannah Arendt had already analyzed the process that brings *homo laborans*—and, with it, biological life as such—gradually to occupy the very center of the political scene of modernity. In *The Human Condition*, Arendt attributes the transformation and decadence of the political realm in modern societies to this very primacy of natural life over political action. That Foucault was able to begin his study of biopolitics with no reference to Arendt's work (which remains, even today, practically without continuation) bears witness to the difficulties and resistances that thinking had to encounter in this area. And it is most likely these very difficulties that account for the curious fact that Arendt establishes no connection between her research in *The Human Condition* and the penetrating analyses she had previously devoted to totalitarian power (in which a biopolitical perspective is altogether lacking), and that Foucault, in just as striking a fashion, never dwelt on the exemplary places of modern biopolitics: the concentration camp and the structure of the great totalitarian states of the twentieth century.

Foucault's death kept him from showing how he would have developed the concept and study of biopolitics. In any case, however, the entry of *zoē* into the sphere of the *polis*—the politicization of bare life as such—constitutes the decisive event of modernity and signals a radical transformation of the political-philosophical categories of classical thought. It is even likely that if politics today seems to be passing through a lasting eclipse, this is because politics has failed to reckon with this foundational event of modernity. The "enigmas" (Furet, *L'Allemagne nazi*, p. 7) that our century has proposed to historical reason and that remain with us (Nazism is only the most disquieting among them) will be solved only on the terrain—biopolitics—on which they were formed. Only within a biopolitical horizon will it be possible to decide whether the categories whose opposition founded modern politics (right/left, private/public, absolutism/democracy, etc.)—and which have been steadily dissolving, to the point of entering today into a real zone of indistinction—will have to be abandoned or will, instead, eventually regain the meaning they lost in that very horizon. And only a reflection that, taking up Foucault's and Benjamin's suggestion, thematically interrogates the link between bare life and politics, a link that secretly governs the modern ideologies seemingly most distant from one another, will be able to bring the political out of its concealment and, at the same time, return thought to its practical calling.

One of the most persistent features of Foucault's work is its decisive abandonment of the traditional approach to the problem of power, which is based on juridico-institutional models (the definition of sovereignty, the theory of the State), in favor of an unprejudiced analysis of the concrete ways in which power penetrates subjects' very bodies and forms of life. As shown by a seminar held in 1982 at the University of Vermont, in his final years Foucault seemed to orient this analysis according to two distinct directives for research: on the one hand, the study of the *political techniques* (such as the science of the police) with which the State assumes and integrates the care of the natural life of individuals into its very center; on the other hand, the examination of the *technologies of the self* by which processes of

subjectivization bring the individual to bind himself to his own identity and consciousness and, at the same time, to an external power. Clearly these two lines
(which carry on two tendencies present in Foucault's work from the very beginning) intersect in many points and refer back to a common center. In one of
his last writings, Foucault argues that the modern Western state has integrated
techniques of subjective individualization with procedures of objective totalization
to an unprecedented degree, and he speaks of a real "political 'double bind,'
constituted by individualization and the simultaneous totalization of structures of
modern power" (*Dits et écrits*, 4: 229–32).

Yet the point at which these two faces of power converge remains strangely
unclear in Foucault's work, so much so that it has even been claimed that Foucault
would have consistently refused to elaborate a unitary theory of power. If Foucault
contests the traditional approach to the problem of power, which is exclusively
based on juridical models ("What legitimates power?") or on institutional models
("What is the State?"), and if he calls for a "liberation from the theoretical privilege
of sovereignty" in order to construct an analytic of power that would not take law
as its model and code, then where, in the body of power, is the zone of indistinction (or, at least, the point of intersection) at which techniques of individualization
and totalizing procedures converge? And, more generally, is there a unitary
center in which the political "double bind" finds its *raison d'être*? That there is a
subjective aspect in the genesis of power was already implicit in the concept of
servitude volontaire in Étienne de La Boétie. But what is the point at which the
voluntary servitude of individuals comes into contact with objective power? Can
one be content, in such a delicate area, with psychological explanations such as
the suggestive notion of a parallelism between external and internal neuroses?
Confronted with phenomena such as the power of the society of the spectacle
that is everywhere transforming the political realm today, is it legitimate or even
possible to hold subjective technologies and political techniques apart?

Although the existence of such a line of thinking seems to be logically implicit
in Foucault's work, it remains a blind spot to the eye of the researcher, or rather
something like a vanishing point that the different perspectival lines of Foucault's
inquiry (and, more generally, of the entire Western reflection on power) converge
toward without reaching.

The present inquiry concerns precisely this hidden point of intersection
between the juridico-institutional and the biopolitical models of power. What this
work has had to record among its likely conclusions is precisely that the two
analyses cannot be separated, and that the inclusion of bare life in the political
realm constitutes the original—if concealed—nucleus of sovereign power. *It can
even be said that the production of a biopolitical body is the original activity of sovereign
power.* In this sense, biopolitics is at least as old as the sovereign exception. Placing
biological life at the center of its calculations, the modern State therefore does
nothing other than bring to light the secret tie uniting power and bare life, thereby
reaffirming the bond (derived from a tenacious correspondence between the modern and the archaic which one encounters in the most diverse spheres) between
modern power and the most immemorial of the *arcana imperii*.

If this is true, it will be necessary to reconsider the sense of the Aristotelian
definition of the *polis* as the opposition between life (*zēn*) and good life (*eu zēn*).

The opposition is, in fact, at the same time an implication of the first in the second, of bare life in politically qualified life. What remains to be interrogated in the Aristotelian definition is not merely—as has been assumed until now—the sense, the modes, and the possible articulations of the "good life" as the *telos* of the political. We must instead ask why Western politics first constitutes itself through an exclusion (which is simultaneously an inclusion) of bare life. What is the relation between politics and life, if life presents itself as what is included by means of an exclusion?

The structure of the exception delineated in the first part of this book appears from this perspective to be consubstantial with Western politics. In Foucault's statement according to which man was, for Aristotle, a "living animal with the additional capacity for political existence," it is therefore precisely the meaning of this "additional capacity" that must be understood as problematic. The peculiar phrase "born with regard to life, but existing essentially with regard to the good life" can be read not only as an implication of being born (*ginomenē*) in being (*ousa*), but also as an inclusive exclusion (an *exceptio*) of zoē in the *polis*, almost as if politics were the place in which life had to transform itself into good life and in which what had to be politicized were always already bare life. In Western politics, bare life has the peculiar privilege of being that whose exclusion founds the city of men.

It is not by chance, then, that a passage of the *Politics* situates the proper place of the *polis* in the transition from voice to language. The link between bare life and politics is the same link that the metaphysical definition of man as "the living being who has language" seeks in the relation between *phonē* and *logos*:

> Among living beings, only man has language. The voice is the sign of pain and pleasure, and this is why it belongs to other living beings (since their nature has developed to the point of having the sensations of pain and pleasure and of signifying the two). But language is for manifesting the fitting and the unfitting and the just and the unjust. To have the sensation of the good and the bad and of the just and the unjust is what is proper to men as opposed to other living beings, and the community of these things makes dwelling and the city.
> (1253a, 10–18)

The question "In what way does the living being have language?" corresponds exactly to the question "In what way does bare life dwell in the *polis*?" The living being has *logos* by taking away and conserving its own voice in it, even as it dwells in the *polis* by letting its own bare life be excluded, as an exception, within it. Politics therefore appears as the truly fundamental structure of Western metaphysics insofar as it occupies the threshold on which the relation between the living being and the *logos* is realized. In the "politicization" of bare life—the metaphysical task *par excellence*—the humanity of living man is decided. In assuming this task, modernity does nothing other than declare its own faithfulness to the essential structure of the metaphysical tradition. The fundamental categorial pair of Western politics is not that of friend/enemy but that of bare life/political existence, zoē/bios, exclusion/inclusion. There is politics because man is the living being who, in language, separates and opposes himself to his own bare life and, at the same time, maintains himself in relation to that bare life in an inclusive exclusion.

The protagonist of this book is bare life, that is, the life of *homo sacer* (sacred man), who *may be killed and yet not sacrificed*, and whose essential function in modern politics we intend to assert. An obscure figure of archaic Roman law, in which human life is included in the juridical order [*ordinamento*][1] solely in the form of its exclusion (that is, of its capacity to be killed), has thus offered the key by which not only the sacred texts of sovereignty but also the very codes of political power will unveil their mysteries. At the same time, however, this ancient meaning of the term *sacer* presents us with the enigma of a figure of the sacred that, before or beyond the religious, constitutes the first paradigm of the political realm of the West. The Foucauldian thesis will then have to be corrected or, at least, completed, in the sense that what characterizes modern politics is not so much the inclusion of *zoē* in the *polis*—which is, in itself, absolutely ancient—nor simply the fact that life as such becomes a principal object of the projections and calculations of State power. Instead the decisive fact is that, together with the process by which the exception everywhere becomes the rule, the realm of bare life—which is originally situated at the margins of the political order—gradually begins to coincide with the political realm, and exclusion and inclusion, outside and inside, *bios* and *zoē*, right and fact, enter into a zone of irreducible indistinction. At once excluding bare life from and capturing it within the political order, the state of exception actually constituted, in its very separateness, the hidden foundation on which the entire political system rested. When its borders begin to be blurred, the bare life that dwelt there frees itself in the city and becomes both subject and object of the conflicts of the political order, the one place for both the organization of State power and emancipation from it. Everything happens as if, along with the disciplinary process by which State power makes man as a living being into its own specific object, another process is set in motion that in large measure corresponds to the birth of modern democracy, in which man as a living being presents himself no longer as an *object* but as the *subject* of political power. These processes—which in many ways oppose and (at least apparently) bitterly conflict with each other—nevertheless converge insofar as both concern the bare life of the citizen, the new biopolitical body of humanity.

If anything characterizes modern democracy as opposed to classical democracy, then, it is that modern democracy presents itself from the beginning as a vindication and liberation of *zoē*, and that it is constantly trying to transform its own bare life into a way of life and to find, so to speak, the *bios* of *zoē*. Hence, too, modern democracy's specific aporia: it wants to put the freedom and happiness of men into play in the very place—"bare life"—that marked their subjection. Behind the long, strife-ridden process that leads to the recognition of rights and formal liberties stands once again the body of the sacred man with his double sovereign, his life that cannot be sacrificed yet may, nevertheless, be killed. To become conscious of this aporia is not to belittle the conquests and accomplishments of democracy. It is, rather, to try to understand once and for all why democracy, at the very moment in which it seemed to have finally triumphed over its adversaries and reached its greatest height, proved itself incapable of saving *zoē*, to whose happiness it had dedicated all its efforts, from unprecedented ruin. Modern democracy's decadence and gradual convergence with totalitarian states in post-democratic spectacular societies (which begins to become evident with Alexis de Tocqueville and finds its final sanction in the analyses of Guy Debord) may well be rooted in this aporia, which marks the beginning of modern democracy and forces it into complicity with its most implacable enemy. Today politics knows no value (and, consequently, no nonvalue) other than life, and until the contradictions that this fact implies are dissolved, Nazism and fascism—which transformed the decision on bare life into the supreme political principle—will remain stubbornly with us. According to the testimony of Robert Antelme, in fact, what the camps taught those who lived there was precisely that "calling into question the quality of man provokes an almost biological assertion of belonging to the human race" (*L'éspèce humaine*, p. 11).

The idea of an inner solidarity between democracy and totalitarianism (which here we must, with every caution, advance) is obviously not (like Leo Strauss's thesis concerning the secret convergence of the final goals of liberalism and communism) a historiographical claim, which would authorize the liquidation and leveling of the enormous differences that characterize their history and their rivalry. Yet this idea must nevertheless be strongly maintained on a historico-philosophical level, since it alone will allow us to orient ourselves in relation to the new realities and unforeseen convergences of the end of the millennium. This idea alone will make it possible to clear the way for the new politics, which remains largely to be invented.

In contrasting the "beautiful day" (*euēmeria*) of simple life with the "great difficulty" of political *bios* in the passage cited above, Aristotle may well have given the most beautiful formulation to the aporia that lies at the foundation of Western politics. The 24 centuries that have since gone by have brought only provisional and ineffective solutions. In carrying out the metaphysical task that has led it more and more to assume the form of a biopolitics, Western politics has not succeeded in constructing the link between *zoē* and *bios*, between voice and language, that would have healed the fracture. Bare life remains included in politics in the form of the exception, that is, as something that is included solely through an exclusion. How is it possible to "politicize" the "natural sweetness" of *zoē*? And first of all, does *zoē* really need to be politicized, or is politics not already contained in *zoē* as its most precious center? The biopolitics of both modern totalitarianism and the society of mass hedonism and consumerism certainly constitute answers to these questions. Nevertheless, until a completely new politics—that is, a politics no longer founded on the *exceptio* of bare life—is at hand, every theory and every praxis will remain imprisoned and immobile, and the "beautiful day" of life will be given citizenship only either through blood and death or in the perfect senselessness to which the society of the spectacle condemns it.

Carl Schmitt's definition of sovereignty ("Sovereign is he who decides on the state of exception") became a commonplace even before there was any understanding that what was at issue in it was nothing less than the limit concept of the doctrine of law and the State, in which sovereignty borders (since every limit concept is always the limit between two concepts) on the sphere of life and becomes

indistinguishable from it. As long as the form of the State constituted the fundamental horizon of all communal life and the political, religious, juridical, and
economic doctrines that sustained this form were still strong, this "most extreme
sphere" could not truly come to light. The problem of sovereignty was reduced to
the question of who within the political order was invested with certain powers,
and the very threshold of the political order itself was never called into question.
Today, now that the great State structures have entered into a process of dissolution and the emergency has, as Walter Benjamin foresaw, become the rule, the
time is ripe to place the problem of the originary structure and limits of the form
of the State in a new perspective. The weakness of anarchist and Marxian critiques
of the State was precisely to have not caught sight of this structure and thus to have
quickly left the *arcanum imperii* aside, as if it had no substance outside of the
simulacra and the ideologies invoked to justify it. But one ends up identifying with
an enemy whose structure one does not understand, and the theory of the State
(and in particular of the state of exception, which is to say, of the dictatorship of
the proletariat as the transitional phase leading to the stateless society) is the reef
on which the revolutions of our century have been shipwrecked.

   This book, which was originally conceived as a response to the bloody mystification of a new planetary order, therefore had to reckon with problems—first of
all that of the sacredness of life—which the author had not, in the beginning,
foreseen. In the course of the undertaking, however, it became clear that one
cannot, in such an area, accept as a guarantee any of the notions that the social
sciences (from jurisprudence to anthropology) thought they had defined or pre-
supposed as evident, and that many of these notions demanded—in the urgency of
catastrophe—to be revised without reserve.

Note

1   "Order" renders the Italian *ordinamento*, which carries the sense not only of order
    but of political and juridical rule, regulation, and system. The word *ordinamento* is
    also the Italian translation of Carl Schmitt's *Ordnung*. Where the author refers to
    ordinamento as *Ordnung*, the English word used is the one chosen by Schmitt's translators,
    "ordering."—Trans.

Bibliography

Antelme, Robert. *L'espèce humaine*. Paris: Gallimard, 1994. (*The Human Race*. Trans. Jeffrey
       Haight and Annie Mahler. Malboro, Vt.: Malboro Press, 1992.)
Foucault, Michel. *Dits et écrits*. Vols. 3–4. Paris: Gallimard, 1994.
——— . *La volonté de savoir*. Paris: Gallimard, 1976. (*History of Sexuality, Volume I: An Introduc-
       tion*. Trans. Robert Hurley. New York: Random House, 1978.)
Furet, François, ed. *L'Allemagne nazi et le génocide juif*. Paris: Seuil, 1985. (*Unanswered Ques-
       tions: Nazi Germany and the Genocide of the Jews*. New York: Schocken, 1989.)
Schmitt, Carl. "Führertum als Grundbegriff des nationalsozialistischen Rechts." *Europäische
       Revue*, 9 (1933).
——— . *Das Nomos von der Erde*. Berlin: Duncker & Humbolt, 1974.
——— . *Politische Theologie, Vier Kapitel zur Lehre von der Souveränität*. Munich-Leipzig: Duncker

& Humbolt, 1922. (*Political Theology: Four Chapters on the Concept of Sovereignty*. Trans. George Schwab. Cambridge, Mass.: MIT Press, 1985.)

——— . "Staat, Bewegung, Volk." In Carl Schmitt, *Die Dreigliederung der politischen Einheit*. Hamburg: Hanseatische Verlagsanstalt, 1933.

——— . *Theorie des Partisanen, Zwischenbemerkung zum Begriff des Politischen*. Berlin: Duncker & Humbolt, 1963.

——— . *Über Schuld und Schuldarten, Eine terminologische Untersuchung*. Breslau: Schletter, 1910.

——— . *Verfassungslehre*. Munich-Leipzig: Duncker & Humbolt, 1928.

Suggestions for further reading

Agamben, Giorgio, *State of Exception,* trans. Kevin Attell, Chicago and London: University of Chicago Press, 2005.

Foucault, Michel, '*Society Must Be Defended': Lectures at the Collège de France, 1975– 76,* ed. Mauro Bertani and Alessandro Fontana, trans. David Macey, London: Allen Lane, 2003.

Hardt, Michael and Negri, Antonio, *Multitude: War and Democracy in the Age of Empire,* New York: Penguin, 2004.

Chapter 28

Lauren Berlant and Michael Warner

'WHAT DOES QUEER THEORY TEACH US ABOUT X?', 1995

WORD OF NEW intellectual developments tends to travel indirectly, like gossip. Soon, more and more people feel the need to know what the real story is: they want manifestos, bibliographies, explanations. When a journal does a special issue or commissions an editorial comment, it is often responding to this need.

We have been invited to pin the queer theory tail on the donkey. But here we cannot but stay and make a pause, and stand half amazed at this poor donkey's present condition. Queer theory has already incited a vast labor of metacommentary, a virtual industry: special issues, sections of journals, omnibus reviews, anthologies, and dictionary entries. Yet the term itself is less than five years old. Why do people feel the need to introduce, anatomize, and theorize something that can barely be said yet to exist?

The critical mass of queer work is more a matter of perception than of volume. Queer is hot. This perception arises partly from the distortions of the star system, which allows a small number of names to stand in for an evolving culture. Most practitioners of the new queer commentary are not faculty members but graduate students. The association with the star system and with graduate students makes this work the object of envy, resentment, and suspicion. As often happens, what makes some people queasy others call sexy.

In our view, it is not useful to consider queer theory a thing, especially one dignified by capital letters. We wonder whether *queer commentary* might not more accurately describe the things linked by the rubric, most of which are not theory. The metadiscourse of "queer theory" intends an academic object, but queer commentary has vital precedents and collaborations in aesthetic genres and journalism. It cannot be assimilated to a single discourse, let alone a propositional program. Certainly, recent years have seen much queer criticism that tried to think through theoretical problems rigorously, often by way of psychoanalysis. But the notion that this work belonged to "queer theory" arose after 1990, when AIDS and queer activism provoked intellectuals to see themselves as bringing a queerer world into being. Narrating the emergence of queer theory was a way to legitimate many experiments, relatively few of which still looked like theory in the sense of rigorous, abstract, metadisciplinary debate.

We do not wish to use this editorial to define, purify, puncture, sanitize, or otherwise entail the emerging queer commentary. Nor are we looking to fix our seal of approval or disapproval on anybody's claim to queerness. We would like to cultivate a rigorous and intellectually generous critical culture without narrowing its field. We want to prevent the reduction of queer theory to a specialty or a metatheory.

We also want to frustrate the already audible assertions that queer theory has only academic—which is to say, dead—politics. Beginnings take a long time, and uneven developments are often experienced as premature deaths, a subject on which queer work is sadly expert. Because almost everything that can be called queer theory has been radically anticipatory, trying to bring a world into being, any effort to summarize it now will be violently partial.

Is this editorial comment, then, queer theory? After all, *PMLA* is not a queer space in any sense. We are not proposing to queer *PMLA*, and we could not perform such a change by willing it. Nor can we act as native informants, telling a presumptively straight assembly of colleagues something about what queers are, do, and think.

What follows is a kind of anti-encyclopedia entry: queer theory is not the theory *of* anything in particular, and has no precise bibliographic shape.

We *can* say that queer commentary has been animated by a sense of belonging to a discourse world that only partly exists yet. This work aspires to create publics, publics that can afford sex and intimacy in sustained, unchastening ways; publics that can comprehend their own differences of privilege and struggle; publics whose abstract spaces can also be lived in, remembered, hoped for. By *publics* we do not mean populations of self-identified queers. Nor is the name *queer* an umbrella for gays, lesbians, bi-sexuals, and the transgendered. Queer publics make available different understandings of membership at different times, and membership in them is more a matter of aspiration than it is the expression of an identity or a history. Through a wide range of mongrelized genres and media, queer commentary allows a lot of unpredictability in the culture it brings into being.

Queer commentary takes on varied shapes, risks, ambitions, and ambivalences in various contexts. The word *queer* itself can be a precious source of titillation at a conference; part of ordinary, bland patter in a nightclub; unintelligible noise in the official policy public; a crashing faux pas at a dinner party; or a reminder of half-deadened optimism at a rally. The danger of the label *queer theory* is that its makes its queer and nonqueer audiences forget these differences and imagine a context (theory) in which *queer* has a stable referential content and pragmatic force. The panicky defensiveness that many queer and non-queer-identified humanists express has to do with the multiple localities of queer theory and practice. Separately, these localities often seem parochial, or simply local—like little ornaments appliquéd over real politics or real intellectual work. They carry the odor of the luxuriant. And one corpus of work (often Eve Sedgwick's or Judith Butler's) is commonly made a metonym for queer theory or queer culture building itself, exemplary either for good or for bad. But no particular project is metonymic of queer commentary. Part of the point of using the word *queer* in the first place was the wrenching sense of recontextualization it gave, and queer commentary has tried hard to sustain awareness of diverse context boundaries.

For example, queer critics have incited a broad rethinking in cultural studies of the relation between the official policy public and the media public sphere. It is no accident that queer commentary—on mass media, on texts of all kinds, on discourse environments from science to camp—has emerged at a time when United States culture increasingly fetishizes the normal. A fantasized mainstream has been invested with normative force by leaders of both major political parties. The national lesbian and gay organizations have decided to float with the current, arguing that lesbians and gays should be seen just as people next door, well within a mainstream whose highest aspirations are marriage, military patriotism, and protected domesticity. At both national and local levels, lesbians and gays can sometimes enter visibility in the official public sphere. But the idea that queerness can be anything other than a pathology or an evil, let alone a good, cannot even be entertained yet in most public contexts.

AIDS activism forced the issue of translating queerness into the national scene. AIDS made those of us who confronted it realize the deadly stakes of discourse; it made us realize the public and private unvoiceability of so much that mattered, about anger, mourning, and desire; it made us realize that different frames of reference—science, news, religion, ordinary homophobia—compete and that their disjunction is lethal. AIDS also taught us not to assume a social environment of community and of support for legitimate politics. Far from preexisting as sources of activism and critical commentary, communities of support had to be created by a public labor. AIDS also showed that rhetorics of expertise limit the circulation of knowledge, ultimately authorizing the technocratic administration of peoples' lives. Finally, in a way that directly affects critics of polite letters, AIDS taught us the need to be disconcertingly explicit about such things as money and sexual practices, for as long as euphemism and indirection produce harm and privilege.

The labor of bringing sexual practices and desires to articulacy has tended to go along with a labor of ambiguating categories of identity. Just as AIDS activists were defined more by a concern for practice and for risk than by identity, so queer commentary has refused to draw boundaries around its constituency. And without forgetting the importance of the hetero-homo distinction of object choice in modern culture, queer work wants to address the full range of power-ridden normativities of sex. This endeavor has animated a rethinking of both the perverse and the normal: the romantic couple, sex for money, reproduction, the genres of life narrative. Queer commentary in this sense is not necessarily superior to or more inclusive than conventional lesbian and gay studies; the two have overlapping but different aims and therefore potentially different publics.

There are, of course, many intermediate contexts between the *Congressional Record* and queer studies conferences or "zine" culture. There are even components of the national mass media, such as *Details* and MTV, that have cultivated a language of queerness in their highly capitalized forums. Mostly in youth culture, these forums allow people to be and to talk queer without assimilating queerness to a familiar minority identity like gay. They are reminders that the publics in which queerness becomes articulate are not just made up of queers; most of these publics, in their internal principles and material conditions, are oriented to other ends. In mass youth culture, for example, the process of making queerness imaginable exhibits the ordinary contradictions of capital: the need to acquire one's individuality from a genericizing exchange and to produce one's individuality through acts of consumption that are only indirectly conceived as social.

Given such conditions, the rhetoric of queering identity in mass youth culture can seem like a luxury. There are those who dismiss the rhetoric as consumerist and then trivialize all queer issues as matters of "lifestyle." But even if that perception were true, is lifestyle really unconnected to violence and world transformation? Politics so often turns on competing standards of seriousness that any narrow understanding of violence, need, and interest should be resisted. Queer culture comes into being unevenly, in obliquely cross-referencing publics, and no one scene of importance accounts for its politics—neither hyperabstracted contexts, like "the Symbolic," nor hyperconcrete ones, like civil disobedience.

When we talk about queer theory in *PMLA*, we mean to keep in mind the special character of this discourse context. Academic citation creates its own virtual world. In the 1990s, that world has allowed queer talk to be taken seriously. But it would be wrong to take this provisional seriousness for a fully inhabitable world or to suppose that queer theory has become dominant in any general sphere of endeavor.

It is not unusual for citation to create virtual worlds. Members of Congress routinely refer to the telegrams in their offices as "the American people." The official and mass-media publics produce, by citation, virtual worlds of great potency. Like the academic public, these are spaces that nobody lives in. The burden of translating oneself from one of them into another falls unequally, often violently, on different people; while this burden might produce political rage, the incommensurability of these publics is usually experienced as cognitive dissonance or amnesia—which is to say, hardly experienced except as nameless unhappiness.

No wonder we hear the worry that queer studies promotes both dangerous and silly objects of analysis. Much queer commentary has been on the political environments of sexuality; it sees intimate sex practices and affects as related not just to family, romance, or friendship but also to the public world governing both policy and everyday life. While to many these spheres are separate, in queer thinking they are one subject. Queer commentary has tried to challenge some major conditions of privacy, so that shame and the closet would be understood no longer as isolation chambers but as the architecture of common culture, so that vernacular performances would no longer stammer with the ineloquence of tacit codes, barely self-acknowledged, and so that questions of propriety and explicitness would no longer be burdened by the invisible normativity of heterosexual culture. Amalgamating politics and feeling in a way that requires constant syncretic gestures and movements, queer commentary has tried to drive into visibility both the cultural production of sexuality and the social context of feeling.

We acknowledge that a lot of work in queer studies has no explicit interest in making publics. Many critics equate the erotic and the political, arguing that power is absorbed into the subject through the Symbolic order. Queerness becomes a question of identification. Much work in queer studies equates cultural politics with politics itself, bracketing or deferring the question of how oppressions and sublimations around sex and sexuality meet up with other kinds of violence and oppression—with exploitation, racial formation, the production of feminine subjectivity or of national culture. We suggest that what brings these different kinds of criticism together as queer theory is a desire to create new contexts, and not just professional ones in which cool work can be performed. Criticism need not have a certain kind of political content to share the aim of making the world queerer. Making these linkages theoretically and politically is difficult. And many of the projects that are driven by queer aspirations may look partial; seen collectively, they are part of a broader and longer-term set of transformations.

If queer commentary were expected either to master or to adjudicate "the politics" of a developing critical culture, it would be condemned to the failure of mere theory or to the resentfulness of a critique that could not usefully be heard. One of the stresses on queer intellectuals in the academy is that there are few queer intellectual publics outside it. Like the mainstream straight press, the organs of the national gay press—in particular, the *Advocate, Out, Deneuve, Ten Percent*—have been either oblivious or hostile to queer theory. (Exceptions to this trend are *On Our Backs* and *Girlfriends*.) And even inside the academy, questions about queer theory's political utility are occasionally not in the best faith. Sometimes they serve to ward off theory from a model of gay studies that has a more affirmative relation to its imagined constituency. In this context, queer commentary provides exactly what some fear it will: perspectives and archives to challenge the comforts of privilege and unself-consciousness.

Sometimes, though, the questions of political utility arise from a real sense of political need. We have been asked, for example, "What does queer theory teach us about twelve-step programs?" "the power of new markets?" "spirituality?"

What does queer theory teach us about *x*?

When a new thing emerges, people want to know how it is going to solve problems. When it is called theory, it is expected to produce a program, and when the theory addresses the broad issue of queerness, the program is expected to explain queer life. But queer theory has not yet undertaken the kind of general description of the world that would allow it to produce practical solutions. People want to know what costs, risks, and tactics are involved in getting from this order of things to a better one. Asked for these reasons, the question of *x* is both a challenge and a hope. And it is a hard question.

The question of *x* might be more ordinary in disciplines that have long histories of affiliation with the state. Sociology, psychology, anthropology, and political science, for example, have earned much of their funding and expert authority by encouraging questions of utility. Queer theory has flourished in the disciplines where expert service to the state has been least familiar and where theory has consequently meant unsettlement rather than systematization. This failure to systematize the world in queer theory does not mean a commitment to irrelevance; it means resistance to being an apparatus for falsely translating systematic and random violences into normal states, administrative problems, or minor constituencies.

Sometimes the question of what queer theory teaches us about *x* is not about politics in the usual sense but about personal survival. Like feminist, African American, Latina/Latino, and other minority projects, queer work strikes its readers as knowledge central to living. This demand puts tremendous pressure on emerging work, pressure that makes the work simultaneously conventional and unprecedented in the humanities and social sciences—traditional insofar as pedagogy has long involved the formation of identities and subjectivities, radical in the aspiration to live another way now, here.

What does queer theory teach us about *x*? As difficult as it would be to spell out programmatic content for an answer, this simple question still has the power to wrench frames.

What does queer commentary teach us about literature or about the *L* in *PMLA*? How do literary engagements participate in queer world building? This question is not frequently posed, for fear that the answer would be, Nothing.

Queer commentary has involved a certain amount of experimenting, of prancing and squatting on the academic stage. This is partly to remind people that there *is* an academic stage and that its protocols and proprieties have maintained an invisible heteronormativity, one that infiltrates our profession, our knowledge, and this editorial. This does not mean we embrace, or disavow, the indecorous per se. Indecorum can be a way of bringing some dignity to the abject. But it is also a way of changing the public for academic work, of keeping the door ajar.

In our view, the question of culture building should be the baseline issue for humanists. On this point we might agree with traditionalists who believe that the humanities should not be limited by the present. Historical consciousness and a resistance to presentism can be indispensable to a critical culture. But unlike some varieties of traditionalism, queer commentary refuses to subordinate emergent cultures to whatever happens to pass for common culture. We want to promote the building not of culture in general but of a culture whose marginal history makes it inevitably controverted, even when it involves authors and themes of the greatest canonical prestige. Many of the critics of queer theory would like to dismiss it as merely particular, the infection of general culture by narrow interest. But the relation between the general and the particular is exactly what is at issue. Queer commentary shows that much of what passes for general culture is riddled with heteronormativity. Conversely, many of the issues of queerness have more general relevance than one is normally encouraged to think.

This is true not only of explicitly general notions of subjectivity—such as the unconscious, abjection, embodiment, knowledge, and performativity—and not only of the prestigious authors who have been so brilliantly queered but also of a range of specifically literary issues. Queer commentary has produced rich analyses of these areas: cultures of reception; the relation of the explicit and the implicit, or the acknowledged and the disavowed; the use and abuse of biography for life; the costs of closure and the pleasure of unruly subplots; vernacular idioms and private knowledge; voicing strategies; gossip; elision and euphemism; jokes; identification and other readerly relations to texts and discourse. Queer commentary has also distinguished itself through experiments in critical voice and in the genre of the critical essay. Along with queer experiments in pedagogy and classroom practice, it marks a transformation of both the object and the practice of criticism.

Of course, we have deferred asking the crucial question: what does queer theory teach us about sex?

Suggestions for further reading

Dollimore, Jonathan, *Sexual Dissidence: Augustine to Wilde, Freud to Foucault*, Oxford: Clarendon Press, 1991.

Foucault, Michel, *The History of Sexuality: Volume 1: An Introduction*, trans. Robert Hurley, Harmondsworth: Penguin, 1990.

Sedgwick, Eve Kosofsky, *Epistemology of the Closet*, Berkeley and Los Angeles: University of California Press, 1990.

Chapter 29

Marjorie Garber

'WHO OWNS "HUMAN NATURE"?', 2003

The proper study of mankind is man.

—Alexander Pope, "Essay on Man"

In the wake of the events of September 11, 2001, people around the world struggled to understand what the terrorist attacks on the World Trade Center and the Pentagon could possibly tell us about "human nature." The *London Guardian* suggested that "we are struggling to adapt our perception of the world, our safety in it, and our understanding of human nature—to incorporate a new dimension of evil."[1] A letter to *Newsday* remarked that the actions taken by rescue workers at the World Trade Center showed that "when it is required of people to disregard basic human nature, which is greed and selfishness, and put the needs of a civilization first, it can be done."[2] (The author of this sober assessment was a high school senior.) The *Los Angeles Times* observed that the job of a firefighter seemed "almost antithetical to human nature: When everyone else flees from danger, they run toward it."[3] And an obituary notice for one of the thousands of victims lost in the World Trade Center attack began with a poignant observation: "It is a quirk of human nature that the person who does an act of kindness may forget it, but the recipient does not."[4] What is "human nature"? And what kind of measure can define and assess it?

"It's just human nature," people often say with a shrug about cultural, social, political, and moral actions from greed to optimism to studied indifference. It is human nature to think we can win the lottery; it is human nature not to want to "get involved" in reporting a crime; it is human nature to believe that our current affair of the heart is true love. (Thus Samuel Johnson defined a second marriage as "the triumph of hope over experience.") The shameful silence of the thirty-eight witnesses to the rape and murder of Kitty Genovese on a quiet street in Kew Gardens, New York, in 1964 (none of whom called the police until after she was dead) was attributed to human nature, but so is kindness to animals, and a passion for team sports. The "dark side of human nature" turns up in many journalistic accounts of mayhem, trickery, and violence. And it is not just "life," but art, that is periodically called to witness. A production of *The Nutcracker* ballet is said by a critic to plumb the "tragic side of human nature." Reality television is said to cast a "bleakly pessimistic light . . . on human nature."[5]

"Human nature" is praised, or blamed, for the good behavior of Samaritans and the bad behavior of politicians. Journalists use it all the time. A reporter writing during the Monica Lewinsky scandal announced that "human nature being what it is" in the case of male politicians and female interns, we have a long way to go before attaining equality between the sexes.[6] The idea that Americans could quickly forget the irregularities of the presidential election "contradicts whatever we might have observed about human nature,"[7] wrote Francine Prose. It was simply "a matter of human nature" that political contributors wanted to go to Senator Hillary Clinton's new house for a fund-raiser, observed Democratic strategist James Carville.[8] The national debate about stem cell research suggested to conservative columnist George Will that "the parties represent different sensibilities—different stances toward nature, including human nature."[9]

What in the world is "human nature"? Few phrases are used so confidently and promiscuously, by parents and children, religious figures and laity, optimists and pessimists, humanists and scientists. And few phrases have been responsible for so much disinformation, or so much attitudinizing. John Keats thought it finer than scenery. William Wordsworth exulted that it had been born again in the early years of the French Revolution. Karl Marx called it an "aesthetic delusion."[10] Journalist turned fiction writer Anna Quindlen, disclaiming any right to be considered an ethicist or a philosopher, announced, with mock modesty, "I'm a novelist. My work is human nature. Real life is really all I know."[11]

But where writers from the sixteenth to the mid-twentieth centuries—from William Shakespeare to David Hume to Virginia Woolf—felt both the necessity and the right to offer opinions on this key phrase and its ramifications, studies of human nature in the latter years have focused, symptomatically, on science: evolutionary biology and psychology, gene theory, behaviorism, and cultural evolution. It is a suggestive fact about human nature that it was once the intellectual property of poets, philosophers, and political theorists and is now largely the domain of scientists.

"Genome Project Can't Explain Human Nature," declared the caption of a *Boston Globe* letter to the editor responding to the mapping of the human genome by two scientific teams. The letter writer, voicing an opinion shared by many commentators after the reports disclosed that humans had fewer genes than formerly believed, observes that it is absurd to expect "that the answers science provides can explain the unique nature of humanity."[12] The news that human beings had only 30,000 genes, not many more than go into the making of a roundworm, a fruit fly, or a plant, and that only about 300 of those genes are different from the genome of a mouse, raised what the media persistently called "humbling" questions about how to explain "human complexity" and what it means to be human.[13] And yet this is just what is so ardently desired, at least in some quarters—an answer to the question, an answer that science alone is thought, these days, to provide.

In a book entitled *Our Posthuman Future* (2002), political scientist Francis Fukuyama warns against recent developments in biotechnology—from cloning to Prozac, from plastic surgery to genetic engineering—that threaten to modify human nature. At stake was the view, strongly championed by Fukuyama, that an essential and unchanging theory of human nature is "fundamental to our notions of justice, morality, and the good life," and that tampering with the genome may cause us "to lose our humanity."[14]

Is human nature fixed or mutable? Something that science helps us to understand, or something that science itself has the capacity to change? Something that was once powerfully described by literature and philosophy, but that has now become the realm of science? How did "human nature," once deemed the proper study of mankind, get to be the privileged territory of geneticists and biologists?

II

The term "human nature" can be inflected on the first word (*human* nature, as contrasted with that of animals, angels, or God) or the second (human *nature*, what is intrinsic rather than eccentric or acculturated for human beings). The first of these modes suggests a difference *between* humankind and other beings and thus implicitly asserts the commonality of *human* experience in contrast with that of others. (The paradoxical phrase "the human nature of Christ," common in many works of Christian theology, points up the issue, as does the section of Jared Diamond's evolutionary study *The Third Chimpanzee*, which focuses on a quartet of activities he calls "uniquely human": language, art, agriculture, and substance addiction.) That which is particular to humans in this concept of human nature is, ordinarily, what differentiates them from beasts or gods. In Western thought this has been associated with the so-called Great Chain of Being, derived from Hellenic philosophy and adapted for Christian and neo-Platonic use in the medieval and early modern periods the *ur*-text here may be the eighth Psalm: "What is man, that thou art mindful of him. And the son of man, that thou visitest him? For thou hast made him a little lower than the angels" (8:4–5), or its passionate adaptation in Hamlet's famous speech of existential despair:

> What a piece of work is a man! How noble in reason! How infinite in faculty! In form and moving how express and admirable, in action, how like an angel, in apprehension, how like a god; . . . And yet, to me, what is this quintessence of dust?
>
> (*Hamlet* 2.2.303–08)

If we change the inflection to stress the second term rather than the first ("human *nature*"), we alter the field of interpretation considerably, since what is now emphasized is what could be called a difference *within*. What is "natural" to humans and what is "learned," "cultural," "adapted," or even "unnatural"? Both of these senses are operative in the history of the phrase, and both have had telling effects on how the various disciplines of the humanities have understood their relation to the age-old question, "What is man?" Yet in fact it is a question not frequently posed, these days, within the humanities. This is the conundrum that has provoked my inquiry.

Humanists have, by and large, abandoned their claims to an interest in this most interesting of problems, tending in recent years to regard the phrase *human nature* as a reductive mode of fuzzy thinking. This skepticism is frequently justified, for all too often human nature turns up (on student papers, for example, or in journalistic opinion pieces) as an *answer*, a solution or explanation for a quirk or a kink of character. If the explanation for human action, or human behavior, whether in literature or in life, is simply "human nature," then analysis and interpretation have been replaced by tautology. In addition, for twentieth- and twenty-first-century humanists, the word *human* itself often seems like a version of what has been called "essentializing"—that is, a refusal to acknowledge both cultural differ-ence and the formative influence of history, economics, regionalism, personal biography, and other social and political elements that go into the "construction" of a person in the world. Feminists and other cultural theorists have also called into question the troublesome word *man*, which seemed to some to erase *woman* in a gesture toward the universal subject. Before we conclude that this gesture is a peculiarity of ideologues and latter-day separatists, we might recall that Hamlet himself parses the word in a similar fashion at the end of that same famous speech—a speech that, though it often misremembered as a soliloquy, is in fact addressed to his mischievous schoolfellows, Rosencrantz and Guildenstern. "Man delights not me—nor woman neither, though by your smiling you seem to say so," he tells them, making the artful shift (no one does this better than Shakespeare) from the general to the particular, and thus exposing the intrinsic ambiguities and doubleness implicit in the grandest of ideas (*Hamlet* 2.2.309–10). Is *man* a term that transcends mere gender, or is it a name that produces gender trouble? In any case, *man* has fallen out of favor in literary and cultural studies, together with universal pronouns like *we* and *us*, leaving the field of "human nature" open to other disciplines. Thus anthropologist Clifford Geertz could refer parenthetically, in his groundbreaking 1973 book *The Interpretation of Cultures*, to "(what used, in a simpler day, to be called 'human nature')."[15]

But this shift in the disciplinary custody of "human nature" has serious consequences for the value of that amorphous enterprise called "the humanities." For if the place to investigate "human nature" is not "the humanities," what is the use of the humanistic disciplines? What else gives them cultural authority? And, equally to the point, what is the use of funding, supporting, studying, and teaching them?

"Human nature" is an artifact of culture and language, of fantasy and projec-tion. In other words, the very idea of human nature as a normative, identifiable essence is both a political and a psychological wish, with important side effects. What is most fascinating to me about the concept of human nature is the way the quest for it has become a self-fulfilling dream, a lure of full self-knowledge, a ruse of research paradigms and protocols from the theological to the anthropo-logical, from behaviorism to genomics. In the Enlightenment it was political phil-osophers; in the nineteenth century it was religious believers, psychologists, and anthropologists; today it is scientists working at the level of the gene.

III

The migration of "human nature" across disciplines in the last several hundred years, from moral philosophy to religion, psychology, Freud and Freudianism, and the new Darwinists, is a fascinating history, represented in literally hundreds of works like *Human Nature and Railroads* (1915); *Human Nature in Business* (1920); *Human Nature and Management* (1929); *Human Nature and Christian Marriage* (1958); *Human Nature in Politics* (1977); *Human Nature and Predictability* (1981); *The Human Nature of Birds* (1993); *Human Nature at the Millennium* (1997), and so on. Starting as early as Thomas Boston's resoundingly titled *Human Nature in Its Four Fold State of Primitive Integrity, Entire Depravity, Begun Recovery and Consummate Happiness or Misery* (1744), phrases like "human nature and . . ." or "human nature in . . ." or "the human nature of . . ." became the watchwords of a certain kind of cultural advice, analysis, and wisdom. "Suffering," "the gospel," "the nature of evil," "the peace problem," "world disorder," and "selling goods"—all have been linked with "human nature" in the titles of books in the last century. The books on business and management, and indeed some of the books on Christianity, are boosterist in spirit: "America" as well as "Christianity" seems to be a consequence of, or a fulfillment of, the best in "human nature."

Eighteenth-century political theorists like David Hume had speculated on the nature of "human nature" in quest of a theory of the individual, of reason, and of human agency. But later accounts by thinkers from Sigmund Freud to Charles Darwin, radically altered the question of control and mastery. Who or what controlled human nature? Was man indeed a rational animal, or rather a creature dominated by the unconscious or by heredity and evolution? Karl Marx's skepticism about the development of human nature as an ideology by political theorists is still a cogent argument today: "The prophets of the eighteenth century," Marx contended, "saw this individual not as an historical result, but as the starting-point of history; not as something evolving in the course of history, but posited by nature, because for them this individual was in conformity with nature, in keeping with their idea of human nature. This delusion has been characteristic of every new epoch hitherto."[16] Whether delusory or not, the relationship of the individual to human nature came to dominate a whole range of social, cultural, political and religious writings concerned with human betterment.[17]

In some cases medical science seemed to offer specific answers, as if human nature were a pathological symptom. It was the nerves, or the glands, that held the key, in scientific studies like *The Mysteries of Human Nature Explained by a New System of Nervous Physiology* (1857), by J. Stanley Grimes, a professor of medical jurisprudence, or *The Glands Regulating Personality: A Study of the Glands of Internal Secretion in Relation to the Types of Human Nature* (1921) by Louis Berman, a doctor of medicine.[18] "The future," thought Berman, "belongs to the biochemist" since the glands are really in charge: "In short, they control human nature, and whoever controls them, controls human nature." Thus "the answer to the question: 'What is Man?' is 'Man is regulated by his Glands of Internal Secretion.'" The upshot was a theory of glandular social betterment: "The raising of the general level of intelligence by the judicious use of endocrine extracts will mean a good deal to the sincere statesmen" and may thus help to prevent war.[19]

This focus on the operation of a particular internal body part, the glands, to explain everything about human nature, runs counter to the lofty and seemingly timeless generalizations of philosophy. But the borderline between the timeless and the local or situational is constantly being crossed. A good example is offered by the surprising itinerary of John Dewey's *Human Nature and Conduct*, an influential work of social psychology written in 1918, at the end of World War I, and published in 1922. Addressing issues like "habit" and the "alterability of human nature," Dewey, a philosopher and educational reformer, pointed out that modern warfare operates on quite a different basis from that of the *Iliad*, the "classic expression of war's traditional psychology as well as the source of the literary tradition regarding its motives and glories." Idealized figures like Helen, Hector, and Achilles were long gone, he noted. "The activities that evoke and incorporate a war are no longer personal love, love of glory, or the soldier's love of his own privately amassed booty, but are of a collective, prosaic political and economic nature." This, indeed, was the very reason why literature is invoked to glorify the "mass movements of soldiery" deployed by "a depersonalized general staff":

> The more horrible a depersonalized scientific mass war becomes, the more necessary it is to find universal ideal motives to justify it. Love of Helen of Troy has become a burning love for all humanity, and hatred of the foe symbolizes a hatred of all the unrighteousness and injustice and oppression which he embodies. The more prosaic the actual causes, the more necessary it is to find glowingly sublime motives.

"Such considerations," Dewey continues, "destroy that argument for [war's] necessary continuance which is based on the immutability of specified forces in original human nature."[20] He wrote this dark account of the "alterability of human nature," at the end of World War I. But his sentiments would be invoked by the U.S. government in 1944, when *Human Nature and Conduct* was reprinted by the War Department as *War Department Education Manual EM 618*, "an aid in instruction in certain educational activities of the armed forces." Thus, by the end of the Second World War, John Dewey's ironic and trenchant account of human nature in ancient and modern warfare had become part of the standard curriculum of the United States Armed Forces Institute setting out a program for the manipulation of public perception. Seldom has the timeless been more directly placed in the service of the times. To a twenty-first-century reader, Dewey's resounding phrases about "depersonalized scientific mass war" and the instrumental rhetoric of "unrighteousness," "injustice," and "oppression" will carry yet another set of local meanings.

As Dewey's instrumental reading of Homer will suggest, poetry and literature have not been completely shut out in the gradual move of human nature toward the social and the scientific. Following the emergence of the phrase in eighteenth-century philosophy, the romantic poets adopted the term with enthusiasm, and by the beginning of the twentieth century "human nature" had become both ubiquitous and commonplace in literary language, appearing regularly in the writings of belletrists of all kinds. Virginia Woolf—a writer with a distinctly unromantic sensibility—seems to have employed it as a matter of course. Reviewing an edition

428   MARJORIE GARBER

of Montaigne's *Essays*, Woolf observes that he "never ceases to pour scorn upon the misery, the weakness, the vanity of human nature." She congratulates Defoe for dealing with it ("He belongs . . . to the school of the great plain writers, whose work is founded upon what is most persistent, though not most seductive, in human nature") and suggests that Jane Austen was the doyenne of the field: "Her gaze passes straight to the mark, and we know precisely where, upon the map of human nature, that mark is." As for George Eliot, "she gathers in her large grasp a great bunch of the main elements of human nature and groups them together with a tolerant and wholesome understanding."[21] To illuminate human nature is, in all of these cases, something to be sought, and praised.

Woolf is a novelist as well as an essayist, and it may be imagined that she found some authorial utility in the concept of human nature as it plays into the business of creating characters and social dramas. But in the works of her contemporary and fellow essayist T. S. Eliot—a very different kind of writer—the term also surfaces with surprising regularity. Likewise, Eliot speaks easily of "that dolorous aspect of human nature which in comedy is best portrayed by Molière" and of William Blake's "capacity for considerable understanding of human nature." By building "an attitude of self-dramatization" into some of his heroes, Eliot thought, Shakespeare was "illustrating, consciously or unconsciously, human nature."[22] Plainly in the 1920s and 1930s, when these pieces were written, "human nature" as a general category was itself alive and well in the minds of major writers of fiction, essays, poetry, and drama. Yet the appearance of the concept today in literary discourse is something of an anomaly and a throwback.[23] The term itself is suspect. In a multicultural world, how could there be *one* "human nature"?

Literary critic Harold Bloom's insistence on Shakespeare as the inventor of "the human," while hardly a new claim for Shakespeare studies, was startling in its assumption of a single "human" point of view, as embodied in Bloom's free-wheeling use of the word *we* to mean *I*: "Can we conceive of ourselves without Shakespeare?" he asked rhetorically. And, "Our ideas as to what makes the self authentically human owe more to Shakespeare than ought to be possible."[24] It is this magisterial and unquestioning *we* that marks the problem for some modern theorists—and made Bloom's approach so comforting for some readers. This *we* is as important to the book's success as its effusive lionization of Shakespeare—a return to an older fashion of speaking.

What do we mean when we say *we* or *I*? or, for that matter, *you* or *they*? Who is speaking when I say *I*? What is "the human" in this sense? And how is it counter-poised to more theoretical notions of the "inhuman" and the "posthuman" with technology, as well as with what philosophers in the last century called "the human condition"? Hannah Arendt contrasts "the problem of human nature" with the "conditions of human existence—life itself, natality and mortality, worldliness, plurality, and the earth," which "can never 'explain' what we are or answer the question of who we are for the simple reason that they never condition us abso-lutely."[25] Jean-François Lyotard asks, "[W]hat if human beings, in humanisms's sense, were in the process of, constrained into, becoming inhuman," and "what if what is 'proper' to humankind were to be inhabited by the inhuman?"—a question increasingly asked, as well, by cybertheorists and students of modern technology and communication.[26] Are we "electrical," as has been claimed in a book called *The*

Post-Human Condition?[27] Or are we in fact relentlessly and deterministically "biological," as has been asserted, with authority, by sociobiologist E. O. Wilson?

IV

I want now to turn directly to an examination of the term "human nature" as it has appeared in the writings of late-twentieth- and twenty-first-century scientists, and principally in the work of E. O. Wilson and his followers. The influence of these books and their claims has been very great, and the implications for the (apparently diminished) role of the humanities in a modern world are far reaching. It is now commonplace for human nature—the term, the concept, and the book title—to appear in conjunction with arguments concerning genetics, evolutionary psychology, the biological mating strategies of the human animal. Yet, as will become clear, the articulation of these arguments depends, both explicitly and implicitly, upon a use of categories, texts, and questions that have been inherited from the long history of the humanities.

E. O. Wilson begins his Pulitzer Prize-winning book *On Human Nature* (1978) with an epigraph from Hume's *Inquiry Concerning Human Understanding* (1748), one of the grandest achievements of eighteenth-century philosophy:

> What though these reasonings concerning human nature seem abstract and of difficult comprehension, this affords no presumption of their falsehood. On the contrary, it seems impossible that what has hitherto escaped so many wise and profound philosophers can be very obvious and easy. And whatever pains these researches may cost us, we may think ourselves sufficiently rewarded, not only in point of profit but of pleasure, if, by that means, we can make any addition to our stock of knowledge in subjects of such unspeakable importance.

Wilson's own ruminations begin by taking up this quotation, and paraphrasing the questions that, he tells us, "the great philosopher David Hume said are of unspeakable importance: How does the mind work, and beyond that why does it work in such a way and not another, and from these two considerations together, what is man's ultimate nature?" For Wilson the last century of scientific inquiry, since Darwin, has altered expectations for any answers to these questions: "We are biological," he asserts. An acknowledgment of natural selection is "the essential first hypothesis for any serious consideration of the human condition":

> Without it the humanities and social sciences are the limited descriptors of surface phenomena, like astronomy without physics, biology without chemistry, and mathematics without algebra. With it, human nature can be laid open as an object of fully empirical research, biology can be put to the service of liberal education, and our self-conception can be enormously and truthfully enriched.[28]

The chapters of Wilson's book address in turn a series of topics that for him make up a map of human nature: Heredity, Development, Emergence, Aggression, Sex, Altruism, Religion, and Hope. Here is a characteristically brilliant crescendo of generalization that displays Wilson comfortably astride his sociobiological hobbyhorse in a chapter on "Altruism":

> Can the cultural evolution of higher ethical values gain a direction and momentum of its own and completely replace genetic evolution? I think not. The genes hold culture on a leash. The leash is very long, but inevitably values will be constrained in accordance with their effects on the human gene pool. The brain is a product of evolution. Human behavior—like the deepest capacities for emotional response which drive and guide it—is the circuitous technique by which human genetic material has been and will be kept intact. Morality has no other demonstrable ultimate function.[29]

Ethics and morality are by-products of biological development, essentially defense mechanisms for keeping "human genetic material" intact. "Morality has no other demonstrable ultimate function." Philosophy is thus something like an optical illusion, as are poetry, fable, and aphorism. What we think are our "highest" functions are fully indebted to our "lowest"—to the body, to its self-preservation and circulation.

The glossary of terms appended to Wilson's book, which runs from A for *adaptation* to Z for *zoology*, pauses at the letter H (between *homozygous*, "when the genes located at a given site on [a] chromosome pair are identical to each other," and *hymenoptera*, "the insect order that contains all bees, wasps, and ants") to define *human nature* in a single pithy sentence:

> *Human nature.* In the broader sense, the full set of innate behavioral predispositions that characterize the human species; and in the narrower sense, those predispositions that affect social behavior.[30]

The key words here are *innate, behavioral, social,* and *predisposition*. A human being can act against his predisposition—biology is not destiny in a completely deterministic sense—but social, moral, and ethical practices have their underlying basis in the "nature" side of human nature. In a section called "Hope," Wilson calls for the development of what he terms a "biology of ethics," which will enable "the selection of a more deeply understood and enduring code of moral values." If dinosaurs had grasped the concept of "nobility," he suggests, "they might have survived. They might have been us."[31]

This is eloquent, and it is also troubling. What is the place of things like art, music, and poetry in Wilson's concept of human nature? Simply put, they are ornamental figures, illustrative metaphors deployed by a writer who has had a broad liberal education. "The processes of sexual pairbonding vary greatly among cultures, but they are everywhere steeped in emotional feeling." he writes. "In cultures with a romantic tradition, the attachment can be rapid and profound, creating love beyond sex which, once experienced, permanently alters the adolescent mind. Description of this part of human ethology is the refined specialty of poets, as we see in the remarkable expression by James Joyce." At this point in his text Wilson quotes a long passage from Joyce's *Portrait of the Artist As a Young Man*, in which Stephen Daedalus sees a girl standing in the water who looks like a "strange and beautiful seabird." It is not surprising that the naturalist's eye is caught by a figure of speech that invokes, and uses as its point of reference, an image from the natural world. The purely decorative role Wilson assigns to literature is clear in the fact that he does not footnote this passage, although he is careful to provide notes to all his scientific references, however glancing. (The notes are genteelly banished to the back of the book, signifying that *On Human Nature* is a piece of "philosophical" writing for the mainstream reader, not an insider text for scientists.)

Sometimes quoting literature out of context has inadvertent effects. Here is a telling example, from a discussion of "Group Selection and Altruism" in Wilson's 1980 classic, *Sociobiology*:

> Selection will discriminate against the individual if cheating has later adverse effects on his life and reproduction that outweigh the momentary advantage gained. Iago stated the essence in *Othello*: "Good name in man and woman, dear my lord, is the immediate jewel of their souls."[32]

There is no mention here of Iago's position as the most arrant hypocrite in all of Shakespeare, nor of his own contempt for "good name" as compared to more material and vengeful rewards. Arguably "cheating" by Iago himself has later adverse effects on his life, since once his machinations are discovered he is led off in chains to be tortured at the play's close, but this does not seem to be the intent of the citation, which rather appears to aim at an endorsement of the sentiment expressed, despite the bad faith with which it is offered, in context, to the credulous Othello.

The literary references in *On Human Nature* tend to be less startling, but also more frequent. William Butler Yeats is invoked to support the belief, ascribed to "the reflective person," that "his life is in some incomprehensible manner guided through a biological ontogeny. . . . He senses that with all the drive, wit, love, pride, anger, hope, and anxiety that characterize the species he will in the end be sure only of helping to perpetuate the same cycle. Poets have defined this truth as tragedy. Yeats called it the coming of wisdom. Here Wilson inserts a four-line poem from Yeats, "The Coming of Wisdom with Time," in this case footnoted, but not commented upon within the text. The poetry is there to reinforce the cultural generalization. Again, and not surprisingly, the metaphors are drawn from the physical world, as if "truth" were a botanical effect:

> Though leaves are many, the root is one;
> Through all the lying days of my youth
> I swayed my leaves and flowers in the sun;
> Now I may wither into the truth.

Yeats makes another brief appearance in Wilson's text ("what Yeats called the artifice of eternity"), as does *Pilgrim's Progress* and a poem by Sappho, the latter again introduced with a now-familiar formula: "Poets have noted it well, as in the calm phrasing of Mary Barnard's [translation of] Sappho." The poem is then quoted.[33] I want here to call attention to the repetition of this move

- "Description of this part of human ethology is the refined specialty of poets . . ."
- "Poets have defined this truth as tragedy."
- "Poets have noted it well . . ."

not only because of the supporting or cameo role in which it casts imaginative literature in its relationship to the quest for "human nature," but also because of the gauntlet that Wilson throws down toward the end of *On Human Nature*, in a passage in which he decries the *absence* of modern science and modern scientists from distinguished cultural conversations. Of all the assertions in his book, published in 1978, this peroration is perhaps the most surprising to modern-day readers, since—in large part due to Wilson's own successes, and those of his students and disciplines—it is precisely science and scientists that now, a quarter-century later, dominate the public conversation about human nature. Here is Wilson's long, passionate, and beautifully written conclusion:

> In the United States intellectuals are virtually defined as those who work in the prevailing mode of the social sciences and humanities. Their reflections are devoid of the idioms of chemistry and biology, as though humankind were still in some sense a numinous spectator of physical reality. In the pages of *The New York Review of Books, Commentary, The New Republic, Daedalus, National Review, Saturday Review*, and other literary journals articles dominate that read as if most of basic science had halted during the nineteenth century. Their content consists largely of historical anecdotes, diachronic collating of outdated, verbalized theories of human behavior, and judgements of current events according to personal ideology—all enlivened by the pleasant but frustrating techniques of effervescence. Modern science is still regarded as a problem-solving activity and a set of technical marvels, the importance of which is to be evaluated in an ethos extraneous to science. It is true that many "humanistic" scientists step outside scientific materialism to participate in the culture, sometimes as expert witnesses and sometimes as aspiring authors, but they almost never close the gap between the two worlds of discourse. With rare exceptions they are the tame scientists, the token emissaries of what must be viewed by their hosts as a barbaric culture still ungraced by a written language. They are degraded by the label they accept too readily: popularizers. Very few of the great writers, the ones who can trouble and move the deeper reaches of the mind, ever address real science on its own terms. Do they know the nature of the challenge?[34]

This is appropriately fierce, even though Wilson himself may at the end be looking sideways in the mirror; he, after all, is both a "great writer" and a "popularizer," as the success and esteem of this book and its author attest. In a later and equally ambitious attempt at synthesis, a book entitled *Consilience* (literally, "jumping together," or "concurrence," a term from the history of science[35]), he will say explicitly, "The search for human nature can be viewed as the archaeology of the epigenetic rules." In other words, fields that appear to be distinct from one another, like economics and aesthetics, will be unified under this umbrella of genetic understanding. Science will explain the humanities.

Many subsequent accounts of "human nature" have followed Wilson's lead, filling the gap he lamented. In the years since Wilson's announcement of "socio-biology" in the 1970s dozens of books and hundreds of articles have tried to account for, or to rebut, the claim that human nature can be described, if not explained, by science. Consider the title *Man, Beast and Zombie: What Science Can and Cannot Tell Us about Human Nature*, by Kenan Malik.[36] One of the most successful new books on this topic, Paul Ehrlich's *Human Natures: Genes, Cultures, and the Human Prospect*, stresses what Ehrlich, an evolutionary biologist, calls "cultural evolution." His book begins by asking "What is human nature?" and he then goes on to explain why the term needs to be put in the plural. "'Human nature' as a singular concept embodies the erroneous notion that people possess a common set of rigid, genetically specified behavioral predilections that are unlikely to be altered by circumstances." But the study of human evolution in recent decades has taken account of behavioral flexibility and diversity in areas "as different as sexual preferences and political systems." Thus he resolves, "in light of this scientific progress," to "highlight human *natures*: the diverse and evolving behaviors, beliefs, and attitudes of *Homo sapiens*."[37]

Ehrlich writes as a scientist, but he writes against "the extreme hereditary determinism that infests much of the current discussion of human behavior," and in favor of the idea that biology has to be considered in the context of culture, and that "our culture is changing through an evolutionary process that is generally thought of as history."[38] Yet his book's references to philosophers (Immanuel Kant, Jürgen Habermas, Martin Heidegger, Charles Sanders Peirce, Richard Rorty) and poets (Samuel Taylor Coleridge, Percy Bysshe Shelley, J. W. von Goethe) appear almost exclusively in the footnotes, not in the text: humanities, literature, and the arts may underpin scientific observations but they are clearly secondary to his argument.[39] Erhlich's notion of "cultural evolution," however politically progressive, still strongly emphasizes a theory of natural selection. (Characteristically, this softening of a brilliant and powerful paradigm, the shift from Wilson's uncompromising singular *nature* to Ehrlich's more affable plural, *natures*, robs the original insight of some of its force, even as it renders the evolutionary claims of sociobiology more acceptable to critical audiences.)

Of the host of other recent books by biologists on some aspect of human nature, most address questions of genetics, heredity, and evolution—and many bear enthusiastic blurbs by E. O. Wilson. Designed to cross over into the mainstream, these books have deliberately catchy titles. "*Mean Genes* is brilliant," Wilson writes of a book by Terry Burnham and Jay Phelan subtitled *From Sex to Money to Food: Taming Our Primal Instincts*. Burnham and Phelan, who have become talk-show favorites, take on such eye-catching topics as Debt, Fat, Drugs, Risk, Greed, Gender, Beauty, Infidelity, Family, and Friends and Foes. "*Mean Genes* seeks to foster a deep understanding of human existence," they announce in the introduction. "The foundation of the book is evolutionary biology."[40] In *Are We Hardwired?* authors William R. Clark and Michael Grunstein address "the role of genes in human behavior," following in the controversial path of Richard Dawkins's *The Selfish Gene*.[41] Jared Diamond's *The Third Chimpanzee: The Evolution and Future of the Human Animal*, another Pulitzer Prize-winning study, asks, "What were those few key ingredients that made us human?" "*The Third Chimpanzee* will endure," the voice of Wilson asserts on the jacket flap, adding an evolutionary happy ending to the literary enterprise. In fact, though, Diamond's book is both a history and a warning, as is clear from the concluding section, entitled "Reversing Our Progress Overnight."

I might note that Diamond, like Wilson, occasionally uses a literary text to point a moral. Thus Shelley's "Ozymandias," a poem about a once-omnipotent king whose statue lies dismantled—a "colossal wreck"—in a desert wasteland, is quoted at the end of a chapter on golden ages. The inscription on the ruin's pedestal offers an inadvertently ironic commentary, since it too promises to "endure": "My name is Ozymandias, king of kings: Look on my works, ye mighty, and despair!"

These are the books that E. O. Wilson wants to promote in the place of those by "tame scientists." All are clearly aimed at a general readership, and many have become best-sellers. What is most striking to me, as I have already noted, is how completely the dominance in this discussion of human nature has swung around from the humanities to the sciences.

V

"Books," Jean-Paul Sartre wrote, "do serve some purpose. Culture doesn't save anything or anyone, it doesn't justify. But it's a product of man: he projects himself into it, he recognizes himself in it; that critical image alone offers him his image."[42] It seems to be human nature to *believe* in human nature, whatever those terms are taken to mean.

In point of fact, it is literature and the history of the imaginative arts that have *produced* "human nature." In the intellectual parlor game of "Man is the animal that . . ." (e.g., Carlyle's "man is a tool-using animal"; Spinoza's "man is a social animal"; Thomas Jefferson's "man is the only animal which devours his own kind") it is arguable that "man is the animal that speculates endlessly upon human nature," and that the history of that speculation, as much as any forensic tracing of cause and effect, is what constitutes the nature of human nature for our time.

Let me, then, return to my fundamental question: Why is "human nature" now, as it seems, firmly in the custody of biologists and evolutionary psychologists, on the one hand, and journalists, on the other? Why do so many of these books on "human nature" take as their subject politics, or social theory, or psychology, whether of the hard, soft, or pop variety? How can we account for the strong drift away from such questions by literary scholars and theorists, and by humanistic cultural critics?

The answers are not too far to seek, and they are reasonable enough: multiculturalism, diversity, a respect for cultural difference, a suspicion of the politics

are increasing. So many interdisciplinary dissertations are being written—and interdisciplinary courses being taught—that it is sometimes difficult to guess which department is the host of a course in, for example, Fraud and Intellectual Property (History of Science); Eighteenth-Century Ethical Dilemmas (Romance Languages and Literatures); Culture, Politics, and Media (Anthropology); or Literature, Science, and Technology in the Nineteenth Century (English). These are all courses taught at Harvard College today. Fraud, ethics, media, science, and technology: this is a pretty fair glossary of terms for "human nature." And these are just courses randomly picked from one college course catalog, where dozens of other course catalogs might tell the same story.

Of course, by this time "interdisciplinarity" is not news. It has its proponents and its skeptics, and the latter include many people who believe that a professional training, or even a degree, is a necessary passport for anyone seeking to embark upon research in a field. We may note that the absence of such a degree in, say, literature, philosophy, or the history of art has not deterred physicists and biologists from saying wise things about poetry en passant. This lack of equity between the sciences and the humanities—the idea that we can all speak about literature, and that, in fact, a professional discourse about literary studies renders the work in that field arcane and obstructive—is part of the problem about the current custody of "human nature"; for the very existence and prominence of interdisciplinary studies in the narrative fields suggests that an interest in human nature has survived, and returned, in those fields. It has, of course, staged its comeback stealthily, as was necessary, lest it be laughed off the platform. But this is human nature with a difference—human nature approached, as it were, from within and from below, rather than magisterially from above.

Interdisciplinarity, we could say—borrowing one term from E. O. Wilson and another from contemporary political philosophy—is *consilience* without *hegemony*. Or, to speak more plainly, it is mutually respectful collaborative work among the disciplines (largely but not exclusively the discursive and narrative disciplines, the humanities and the less-quantitative branches of science and social science). Interdisciplinarity, in short, is the space, or the mode of collective inquiry, in which questions about "human nature" are *now*, at present, being investigated. And this makes perfect sense. It explains, in part, the dissatisfaction with the boundaries of the present-day disciplines, for breaching boundaries—itself arguably a natural human desire—is not in itself sufficient to explain this explosion of integrated interests. The old-fashioned questions about human nature, about ethics and morality, idealization and expression, humankind reaching close to the angels and the beasts, are accommodated in new places and new guises by interdisciplinary inquiry. Often the impetus moves from the apparently popular to the apparently learned or specialized. Thus, for example, the release of a new film version of *Planet of the Apes* (2001) provoked a discussion of the relationship of humans and chimpanzees, orangutans, gorillas, and bonobos, and led to an interesting exchange of views among animal behaviorists, theoretical biologists, anthropologists, and lawyers on the question of rights for apes.[44]

But the humanities have a single, easy-to-forget point to repeat over and over in these intellectual investigations. Language is not a secondary but a primary constituent of human nature, whatever may turn out to be the case in other spheres. Language is not transparent, though fantasies of its transparency, its merely denotative role, have always attracted and misled some of its users, both writers and readers. Language is not only a window but also a door, a barrier as well as a portal, requiring a handle, some unlocking, and a key.

It is precisely because no one kind of inquiry holds the key to "human nature" that interdisciplinary groupings form and re-form. The humanities sometimes play an ironic role in this by appearing to pose a set of framing illusions that science can demystify. But this is true only from the perspective of the humanities themselves. Scientists often take pleasure in demonstrating that William Shakespeare was right about human nature, even though he had no access to modern scientific information. They are frequently impatient, or uncomprehending, about the work of humanists who question the sources, the sincerity, and the consistency of a "Shakespeare" who is to a certain extent the creation of editors, poets, and critics who lived long after his time. Far from demystifying categories like truth and beauty, scientists often write as if the humanities could still be relied upon to be the quaint but lovable guardians of such notions. In this sense many scientists retain a nineteenth-century notion of the humanities, even as they suggest that humanists cling to a nineteenth-century notion of science.

When a leading scientist like E. O. Wilson could aver some years ago that "[m]odern science is still regarded as a problem-solving activity and a set of technical marvels, the importance of which is to be valuated in an ethos extraneous to science," it is well worth asking him to consider the obverse of this proposition: that modern humanistic study is all too often regarded as a style-enhancing activity and a set of linguistic tricks, the importance of which is to be evaluated in an ethos extraneous to the humanities.

As the popularity of programs in the history of science and technology suggests, science itself has a history, and, in the very nature of such things, it is a history of falsehoods in pursuit of truth. The philosopher Miguel de Unamuno put it clearly when he wrote, "Science is a cemetery of dead ideas, even though life may issue from them," and, "True science teaches, above all, to doubt and to be ignorant."[45] From the Ptolemaic universe (the sun rotates around the earth) to phlogiston (the hypothetical substance supposed to be the "matter of fire," whose existence was affirmed through much of the eighteenth century, only to be rejected and abandoned by 1800) science has proceeded by hypothesis, by theory, and by inspired accident and guess. The "beautiful theories" of the past have become either facts or follies. Will today's answers be any more ahistorical, transcendent, and permanent than all those that have gone before?

It is striking that the term "science wars" has been coined to describe the efforts on the part of some nonscience scholars to understand how scientists construct their notions of truth. The term itself has been highly contestatory, producing heated exchanges and a good deal of willful misunderstanding on all sides. What I have been describing here might perhaps have been called "humanities wars," save for the fact that the humanities are regarded not as specialized knowledge or even as a research field, but rather as the ground of our common knowledge and common inheritance, accessible to scientists, social scientists, and humanists alike. Instead of "humanities wars," then, we have the far more aversive "culture wars," as if the progress of scholarship in the humanities was itself a "war" against, as well as for custody of, certain cultural values and touchstones that are thought to be enshrined in literature and art. I share with Ian Hacking a dislike of the facile use of "war" to describe these intellectual debates. As he says, terms like "culture wars," "science wars," and "Freud wars" suggest gladiatorial contests, in which the pleasure—and the "war" terminology—belongs to "the bemused spectators."[46] But somewhat obscured by the inflammatory rhetoric, fanned by the flames of cultural journalists, is a fundamental dissymmetry in the way "scientific know-ledge" and "humanistic knowledge" are weighed, valued, and assessed.

Is it really necessary to ban all scientific experimentation in order to preserve human nature as a constant and unchanging essence? Francis Fukuyama's concern that contemporary biotechnology will "alter human nature and thereby move us into a 'posthuman' stage of history," with "possibly malign consequences for liberal democracy and the nature of politics,"[47] is one that has in fact been contemplated, sans alarm, by many thoughtful scholars in various branches of the humanities, where "posthuman" is not a scare word but an interesting field for philosophical, ethical, and aesthetic speculation. Perhaps we need the humanities more than ever precisely because it is so obvious that scientific progress cannot be stopped. Here is where humanists can do themselves, and the world, a favor by stressing the ways in which all knowledge is an aspect of rhetoric as well as an aspect of logic. Increas-ingly, scientists speak in metaphors and in linguistic coinages in order to explain their work. *Relativity; quark; revolution; game theory; prisoner's dilemma:* these appro-priations of language, analogy, and neologism enrich understanding by becoming figural, by pointing out that the reality of the world itself is a voiced reality, a reality of figure. Humanists might reasonably point out the rhetorical and "poetic" nature of these terms, the impossibility of science without image and figure. But at the same time these humanists also might return the serve, and the favor, by laying claim once again to the most underrated and overliteralized of these figures: the metaphor of human nature.

So, to restate the question with which we have been wrestling: Why is it that today's scientists write about human nature, while today's humanists do not? My answer, at least in part, is that humanists *do* write about this question, constantly, but that neither they nor many of their readers—not to mention their critics—have been willing to acknowledge that that is what they are doing. Somewhere along the way, the concept of human nature became both stale and saccharine: a set of bromides or truisms, often inflected with religion, and frequently invoked as a "so there" pseudo-explanation ("it's just human nature . . .") rather than explored as a conundrum or a puzzlement.

I am eager, here—or, to be franker about it, I am anxious—not to be heard as deploring the present moment in humanistic writing and research, and harking back, wistfully, to a time when men were men, women were women, and human-ists cared about human nature. My point is really close to the opposite of this nostalgic, and retrogressive, thought: what I have been contending is that today's humanists are asking "human nature" questions all the time, when they talk about psychic violence, or material culture, or epistemic breaks, or the history of the book, or the counterintuitive. Many of the theoretical explorations and innov-ations of the last fifty years of humanistic scholarship have been aimed at demystify-ing a unitary and positivistic sense of "human nature." But to aim to demystify something is tacitly to acknowledge its mystified status, and not only for others; also for oneself. Avoiding the topic of "human nature" is a mistake, one that has political as well as intellectual ramifications—a mistake based on underestimating what and how we read and write today. "Human nature," as a term and as a field of inquiry, need not be solely the concern of social conservatives or of scientists, however well-meaning and however well-placed. In debunking all the illusions fostered under this ubiquitous term, contemporary humanistic scholars have sometimes failed to see in what ways we are working within it.

When I suggest that to discard a big and baggy idea like human nature is a political mistake, what I mean is that it has given aid and comfort to unthinking critics of the humanities. If we are willing to reflect seriously and critically, we will readily be able to demonstrate that fields like cultural anthropology, structural linguistics, women's studies, cybertheory, and posthumanism are indeed addressing the Big Questions: the Who Am I questions, the What Am I Doing Here questions, the What Lies in the Future questions that all attach themselves to the heritage of "human nature." These questions have never been more pressing—nor more "human"—than they are today. And you can quote me on that.

Notes

1   Madeleine Bunting, "The Morning After," *Guardian* (London), September 12, 2001, 14.
2   Joelle Sumner (John F. Kennedy High School, Bellmore, N.Y.), "Student Briefing Page on the News," *Newsday* (Long Island, N.Y.), October 4, 2001, A24.
3   Mimi Avins, Cara Mia DiMassa, "Amid Disaster, Heroes Ran toward Danger, Not from It," *Los Angeles Times*, September 21, 2001, sec. 5, 1.
4   Nicholas M. Christian, Glenn Collins, Jim Dwyer, Joseph P. Fried, Jan Hoffman, Mireya Navarro, Maria Newman, Mirta Ojito, Barbara Stewart, and Joyce Wadler, "A Nation Challenged: The Missing," *New York Times*, October 2, 2001, B9.
5   Madeleine Bunting, "The Launch of a TV Game That Trades on Our Dark Side," *Guardian* (London), May 21, 2001, 20.
6   Joyce Purnick, "Intern's Role Appears to Be Same Sad Tale," *New York Times*, July 12, 2001, B1.
7   Francine Prose, "The Big Surprise? Our Surprise," *Washington Post*, February 18, 2001, B1.
8   James Carville, quoted in Ellen Gamerman, "Hillary Clinton, Fund-Raiser," *Baltimore Sun*, April 25, 2001, 1A.
9   George F. Will, "A Principled Solution to Stem Cell Dilemma," *Baltimore Sun*, April 16, 2001, 19A.
10 Karl Marx, "Introduction to a Critique of Political Economy," in Karl Marx and Friedrich Engels, *The German Ideology*, ed. C. J. Arthur (New York: International Publishers, 1974), 124.
11 Anna Quindlen, *A Short Guide to a Happy Life* (New York: Random House, 2000), 1.
12 Ken Karnofsky, "Genome Project Can't Explain Human Nature" (letter to the editor), *Boston Globe*, February 16, 2001, A18.
13 "Mysteries of the Genes" (editorial), *New York Times*, February 17, 2001, A30.
14 Francis Fukuyama, *Our Posthuman Future* (New York: Farrar, Straus and Giroux, 2002), 83.
15 Clifford Geertz, *The Interpretation of Cultures* (New York: Basic Books, 1973), 67.
16 Karl Marx, "Introduction to a Critique of Political Economy," 124.
17 For example, from *Human Nature and the Social Order* (1902) to *Human Nature and Railroads* (1915); to *Human Nature and Management* (1929) to *Human Nature and Christian Marriage* (1958); from *Human Nature in Its Fourfold State, Of Primitive Interiority, Entire*

Deprivation, Begun Recovery and Consummate Happiness or Misery in The Parents of Mankind in Paradise, The Unregenerate, The Regenerate, All Mankind in the Future State (1729) to *Human Nature in Business: How to Capitalize Your Everyday Habits and Characteristics* (New York: G. P. Putnam's Sons 1920); *The Human Nature of Birds* (1993); *The Human Nature of Christ* (1965); *The Human Nature of a University* (1969).

18   J. Stanley Grimes, *The Mysteries of Human Nature Explained by a New System of Nervous Physiology, To Which Is Added, a Review of the Errors of Spiritualism, and Instructions for Developing or Refining the Influence by Which Subjects and Mediums Are Made* (Buffalo: R. M. Wanzer, 1857); Louis Berman, *The Glands Regulating Personality: A Study of the Glands of Internal Secretion in Relation to the Types of Human Nature* (New York: Macmillan, 1921), viii.

19   Berman, *The Glands Regulating Personality*, 21, 23, 26, 329.

20   John Dewey, *Human Nature and Conduct* (Madison, Wisc.: Henry Holt, 1944), 113–14.

21   Virginia Woolf, *The Common Reader* (1925; reprint, New York: Harcourt Brace and Company, 1984), 63, 93, 137, 167; emphasis added.

22   T. S. Eliot, *Selected Essays 1917–1932* (New York: Harcourt, Brace and Company, 1932), 111, 158, 279.

23   A few critical works using the phrase have continued to appear from time to time, though they are in a great minority: e.g., Ruth Caplan, *Human Nature in Richardson's Clarissa* (Ph.D diss. 1974) and David Green, *Human Nature in the Drawing Room: The Aristocratic World of George Meredith* (Ph.D diss. 1944).

24   Harold Bloom, *Shakespeare: The Invention of the Human* (New York: Riverhead Books, 1998), 1, 17.

25   Hannah Arendt, *The Human Condition*, 2d ed. (Chicago: University of Chicago Press, 1998), 11.

26   Jean-François Lyotard, *The Inhuman: Reflections on Time*, trans. Geoffrey Bennington and Rachel Bowlby (Cambridge: Polity Press, 1991), 2.

27   Robert Pepperell, *The Post-Human Condition* (Oxford: Intellect, 1995), i.

28   E. O. Wilson, *On Human Nature* (Cambridge, Mass.: Harvard University Press, 1978), 2.

29   Ibid., 167.

30   Ibid., 281.

31   Ibid., 196; 197.

32   E. O. Wilson, *Sociobiology* (Cambridge, Mass.: Belknap Press of Harvard University Press, 1980), 58.

33   Wilson, *On Human Nature*, 200.

34   Ibid., 203.

35   William Whewell, *Philosophical Inductions of Science* (1840, part 2, vol. 6, ed. G. Buchdahl and L. L. Sauden (London: Frank Cass and Co., Ltd. 1967) 65.): "[T]he cases in which inductions from classes of facts altogether or different have thus *jumped together*, belong only to the best established theories which the history of science contains. . . . [I] will term it the *Consilience of Inductions*."

36   Kenan Malik, *Man, Beast and Zombie: What Science Can and Cannot Tell Us about Human Nature* (New York: Weidenfeld, 2000).

37   Paul Ehrlich, *Human Natures* (Washington, D.C.: Island Press, 2000), ix.

38   Ibid., x. Even these footnotes are of the most perfunctory and summary kind (a "romantic response" to Enlightenment science, representing "a preference for feeling, intuition, imagination, and self-expression over rational analysis and intellect," is said to be "associated with such writers and thinkers as German philosopher Friedrich von Schelling and Johann von Goethe, John von Schiller, Samuel Taylor Coleridge, and Percy Bysshe Shelley." This is the sort of thing one finds in readers' encyclopedias and school texts; a generalization this unnuanced from a literary critic speaking about science would surely evoke protests from scientific theorists and practitioners.

39   Ibid., 426, n. 73.

40   Terry Burnham and Jay Phelan, *Mean Genes* (Cambridge, Mass.: Perseus, 2000), 8.

41   William R. Clark and Michael Grunstein, *Are We Hardwired?* (New York: Oxford University Press, 2000).

42   Jean-Paul Sartre, *Les Mots (The Words)*, trans. Bernard Frechtman (New York: G. Braziller, 1964), 254.

43   Lyotard, *The Inhuman*, 3.

44   Rowan Taylor of the Great Ape Project, quoted in Seth Mydans, "He's Not Hairy, He's My Brother," *New York Times*, August 12, 2001, sec. 4, 5.

45   Miguel de Unamuno, *Tragic Sense of Life*, trans. J. E. Crawford Fitch (New York: Dover, 1954), 90, 93.

46   Ian Hacking, *The Social Construction of What?* (Cambridge, Mass.: Harvard University Press, 1999), 4.

47   Francis Fukuyama, *Our Posthuman Future* (New York: Farrar, Straus & Giroux, 2002), 7.

Suggestions for further reading

Badmington, Neil, 'Cultural Studies and the Posthumanities', in Gary Hall and Clare Birchall (eds.), *New Cultural Studies: Adventures in Theory*, Edinburgh: Edinburgh University Press, 2006, pp. 260–72.

Haraway, Donna J., *When Species Meet*, Minneapolis and London: University of Minnesota Press, 2008.

Soper, Kate, *Humanism and Anti-Humanism*, London: Hutchinson, 1986.

Glossary

biopolitics   A theme developed in the later work of Michel Foucault (notably 'Society Must Be Defended': Lectures at the Collège de France, 1975–76) and more recently taken up by Giorgio Agamben. Biopolitics emerges when human life itself becomes subjected to governmental intervention, regulation, manipulation, and rationalization.

castration complex   According to Sigmund Freud, this takes place when the child discovers the anatomical difference between the sexes. The boy assumes that the female's penis has been cut off and, because of this threat of castration, renounces his desire for the mother. For the girl, the discovery leads to resentment of the mother, whom she blames for castration, and the redirection of her desires to the father. See Oedipus complex.

cogito   Devised by the philosopher, René Descartes, the cogito is the formulation, 'I think, therefore I am', which encapsulates conventional Western ways of thinking about the subject. It implies a subject who is defined by consciousness and is therefore unified, autonomous, and in control of its meanings and actions. This has been challenged by psychoanalysis, poststructuralism and Marxism, where the subject is produced by, and an effect of, the unconscious, language, and the social order.

diachronic   The analysis of the historical development of language. See synchronic.

ego, id, superego   The three parts of the human psyche, as described in Freud's later work. The id is the unconscious realm of drives and desires. (While Freud's earlier texts refer to the unconscious, the more mature texts regularly discuss the id.) The ego, which never quite manages to separate itself from the id, is the realm of reason that seeks to regulate and censor the unruly demands of the id with the acceptable conventions of society. In addition to wrestling with the id, the ego must also reckon with the pressures of the superego (the agency of conscience and moral imperatives which constantly makes demands about how the human *subject* ought to behave).

empiricism   The belief that human knowledge derives from experience.

epistemology   The theory of knowledge, of what it is possible to know.

fetish   Usually associated with Sigmund Freud, for whom the fetish originates with the male child's horror of female castration (see *castration complex*), where he represses this lack and substitutes an object, which is unsuited to serve the normal sexual aim, for the missing penis. Karl Marx sees objects of everyday life, or commodities, as fetish objects that seem to possess powers beyond that which they actually have.

hegemony   A ruling group can be said to enjoy a position of hegemony when its authority has become so all-pervasive that those in a position of subordination have come to see their domination as natural and inevitable, which means that they give their consent to being ruled.

hyperreal   Term associated with the work of Umberto Eco and Jean Baudrillard. A reproduction is hyperreal when it is so perfect and accurate that it is indistinguishable from – or perhaps even better than – the real thing.

id   See *ego, id, superego.*

idealism   While everyday English often uses 'idealism' to refer to overly ambitious or utopian thinking, in critical theory it more specifically names the belief that ideas are prior to culture, language, and history. In Marx's terms, idealism is the outmoded claim that human consciousness precedes social existence.

ideology   The system of thoughts and beliefs that determine the *subject*'s action and behaviour. According to Karl Marx, ideologies stem from the economic base and are internalized by the individual.

imaginary   This is the realm of images and identification described by Jacques Lacan. According to Lacan, images play a part in constituting the *subject*, but do so in an illusory and deceptive way (thus the meaning of 'imaginary' as 'fictional' or 'delusive') because they give a false impression of the subject's mastery, autonomy and plenitude (see *méconnaissance*).

jouissance   A sexual/orgasmic pleasure that also involves pain. The term was used by Jacques Lacan but was developed by feminist critics including Julia Kristeva.

language games   Concept introduced by Ludwig Wittgenstein and developed by Jean-François Lyotard. Language games are the rules that inform a particular discourse and that make the pragmatic functioning of that discourse possible. Different discourses have different rules of operation, and these may seem wholly natural and just within the context of each discourse. In Lyotard's account, any attempt to overrule different language games with a single judgement, or from an apparently elevated position, leads to injustice.

materialism   Although everyday English commonly uses 'materialism' to refer to the excessive love of material belongings, in Marx's work materialism replaces *idealism* by giving precedence to everyday material existence. In the materialist model, (material) social existence determines consciousness.

méconnaissance   A French word used by Jacques Lacan to describe how the *subject* 'misrecognises' itself as unified, autonomous and self-constituting.

metaphysics   In the work of Jacques Derrida, who takes some of his understanding of the term from the work of Martin Heidegger, metaphysics is truth-seeking philosophy.

mise-en-scène   In the language of film theory, the mise-en-scène is everything that can be seen upon the screen at a given moment (actors, props, background, and so on).

objet a   A term used by Jacques Lacan to designate the lost object in the *real*, which is the cause of desire.

Oedipus complex   For Sigmund Freud, this is a formative stage in development where the child (usually the male) desires the parent of the opposite sex and is hostile towards the parent of the same sex. See *castration complex*.

ontology   The theory of being, of what exists.

panopticon   A building of correction, devised by the English philosopher, Jeremy Bentham, in which prisoners were controlled by being watched (or thinking they were being watched) from a central tower. Michel Foucault employs the idea of the panopticon to describe how knowledge and power can be gained through visual relations.

phallocentrism/phallogocentrism   Terms developed by feminist theorists to criticise the privileging of the male (phallus) and the logos (the system of reason, order and intelligibility) in Western literature and thought.

phoneme   A basic unit or 'building block' of speech that cannot be broken down into smaller parts.

positivism   The method by which careful human observation brings to light the truth about the universe (in the form of general, unchanging laws).

posthuman   The figure that emerges when 'the human' has either been superseded or undermined to such an extent that it no longer seems credible, no longer goes without saying. Haraway's cyborg could, for this reason, be described as an example of the posthuman.

poststructuralism   Poststructuralist criticism employs structuralist ideas (most specifically Saussurean linguistics), but works to develop and challenge them. Jacques Derrida, for example, stresses that meanings are not as fixed as structuralism seems to imply. He uses the term 'differance' (spelt with an 'a' to distinguish it from 'difference') to describe the play of language, in which meanings are not only defined according to their negative difference from everything else in the system (which Derrida adapts from Saussure), but are also constantly deferred or postponed, referring to other absent meanings in a way that makes closure or full intelligibility an impossibility. See *trace*.

rationalism   The belief that human reason is the source of knowledge.

real   Part of the triad of the real, the *imaginary* and the *symbolic* defined by Jacques Lacan. The real refers to a world of full and present things that precede the *subject* but to which it has no access because the subject is already part of a system of language which names these things and, in so doing, takes their place.

referent   The object in the world that the *signifier* points to.

semiology   Also called semiotics. The science of *signs*, largely developed by Roland Barthes, which analyses how signs function at all levels of human experience.

signifier, signified, sign   The basic components of language as defined by Ferdinand de Saussure. The signifier is the 'sound-image': the sound of the word or its visual appearance. A signified is the concept or meaning attached to the signifier. These two components come together to form the sign. Jacques Derrida complicates these definitions, using the term 'signifier' rather than 'sign' to indicate that there is no simple meaning attached to a word. The meaning, or possibility of a full and secure meaning, is constantly deferred in an endless play of language.

simulacrum   A copy of a copy. A copy for which no original exists. (NB: The plural of 'simulacrum' is 'simulacra'.)

speech act   An utterance whose purpose is to make the intentions of its speaker happen in the world. 'I declare this building open' is a speech act, then, because its utterance has the performative effect of opening the building to which it refers.

subject   *Poststructuralism* challenges the idea of subjectivity formulated in the Cartesian *cogito* to suggest that the subject is an effect of language, a being that speaks and says 'I'. As part of a linguistic system over which it has no control, the subject is never autonomous or fully present to itself but is unfixed and in process.

superego   See *ego, id, superego*.

symbolic order   A term used by Jacques Lacan to describe the system of language and law that constitutes the *subject*.

synchronic   The analysis of language at a given point in time. Ferdinand de Saussure approached language synchronically, viewing it as a system or structure frozen in time. See *diachronic*.

Taylorism   The attempt, based upon the management theories of Frederick Winslow Taylor, scientifically to subject every part of the working process (on, say, the production line in a factory) to principles of efficiency, time-saving, and maximized productivity.

trace   In Jacques Derrida's radicalisation of Saussure's theory of meaning, every *signifier* is marked by the trace of the other signifiers from which it is different. The trace is the trace of otherness, therefore, without which meaning would not be possible.

uncanny   In the work of Freud, the uncanny names the moment at which the human *subject* is unsettled by the familiar suddenly seeming unfamiliar, or the unfamiliar suddenly seeming familiar.

unconscious   According to Freudian psychoanalysis, the unconscious is the location of repressed desires and wishes, to which the *subject* has no access. It thus undermines the Cartesian *cogito* and the idea that the subject is unified, fixed, or in control of its actions and meanings.

Index